Inside
Smalltalk

Inside Smalltalk

Volume II

Wilf R. LaLonde

School of Computer Science
Carleton University

John R. Pugh

School of Computer Science
Carleton University

PRENTICE HALL
Englewood Cliffs, New Jersey 07632

Library of Congress Cataloging-in-Publication Data

```
(Revised for vol. 2)
LaLonde, Wilf R.
   Inside Smalltalk.

   1. Smalltalk (Computer program language)
2. Object-oriented programming.  3. Smalltalk-80
(Computer system)  I. Pugh, John R.
II. Title.
QA76.73.S59L35 1991    005.13'3    90-6785
ISBN 0-13-468414-1 (v. 1)
ISBN 0-13-465964-3 (v. 2)
```

Editorial/production supervision: Christina Burghard
Cover design: Wanda Lubelska
Manufacturing buyer: Lori Bulwin

Printed in the United States of America
10 9 8 7 6 5 4 3 2 1

ISBN 0-13-465964-3

Prentice-Hall International (UK) Limited, *London*
Prentice-Hall of Australia Pty. Limited, *Sydney*
Prentice-Hall Canada Inc., *Toronto*
Prentice-Hall Hispanoamericana, S.A., *Mexico*
Prentice-Hall of India Private Limited, *New Delhi*
Prentice-Hall of Japan, Inc., *Tokyo*
Simon & Schuster Asia Pte. Ltd., *Singapore*
Editora Prentice-Hall do Brasil, Ltda., *Rio de Janeiro*

Table of Contents

Table of Contents

Preface

INTRODUCTION

In the seventies, structured programming revolutionized the way programmers constructed software systems. Today, many are predicting that the object-oriented programming paradigm will be the second major revolution in software engineering and that object-oriented systems will become the predominant programming tools of the nineties. In the two volumes of **Inside Smalltalk**, we take an in-depth look at the Smalltalk-80 environment — the programming system that most consistently adheres to the object-oriented paradigm and that has served both as a model for object-oriented extensions to existing languages and as the basis for a new generation of languages supporting inheritance. It can be argued that Smalltalk has had more impact on software development in the last decade than any other programming language. Smalltalk fosters the notions of *programming in the large* and *programming by extension* rather than by *re-invention*. Smalltalk provided the foundation for window-based graphical user interfaces, for the development of truly reusable class libraries, and for the introduction of on-line tools such as code browsers. Our objective in **Inside Smalltalk** is to provide a comprehensive survey of the Smalltalk environment, the language, and the library. A secondary goal is to show how interactive graphical applications can be constructed using object-oriented programming techniques and the unique Smalltalk programming environment. Moreover, we show how Smalltalk's underlying philosophy of reusing and extending existing code permits the development of such applications with high productivity.

Programming in Smalltalk is different from programming in other languages such as Pascal, C, or Ada because of the major influence played by the object-oriented programming paradigm, the large class library, and the interactive programming environment. Developing programs in Smalltalk requires familiarity with all three of these components and the learning curve for programmers is therefore longer than for more traditional languages. Although there is no substitute for programming with the Smalltalk system itself, our objective is to reduce this learning curve by providing a comprehensive description of the Smalltalk language, the class library and programming environment and by illustrating the use of object-oriented programming techniques to develop interactive graphical applications. The need for a Smalltalk guru to be close at hand when learning the system will then be minimized. In addition, **Inside Smalltalk** will be a valuable reference to accomplished Smalltalk programmers whenever they venture into uncharted territory in the class library.

Be forewarned that it will take you considerably longer to become an accomplished Smalltalk programmer than an accomplished Pascal programmer. However, the return on your investment will be an ability to develop interactive graphical applications with all the features of modern user interfaces; e.g., windows, menus, mouse interaction. Indeed, a major emphasis of the second volume is to describe the Smalltalk features that make this possible; namely, the model-view-controller paradigm for constructing user interfaces and the graphical and window classes in the library. At the time of this writing, and despite the fact that it is this material that gives Smalltalk much of its appeal, no in-depth presentation of the graphical and user interface classes was available in any other text.

Although the Smalltalk language is itself quite small, the Smalltalk system is large. Initially this limited its use to expensive, powerful workstations. However, efficient implementations of Smalltalk are now readily accessible to large numbers of users on the current generation of personal computers bringing the power of Smalltalk to the classroom and a mass audience.

ORGANIZATION OF THE BOOK

Inside Smalltalk consists of two volumes with the first volume divided into 4 major sections. In this, the second volume we concentrate on the window and user interface classes and describe how Smalltalk may be used to develop applications involving WIMP-based (Windows, Icons, Menu, and Pointer) user interfaces.

VOLUME ONE

The first section of Volume One introduces the fundamentals of object-oriented programming and Smalltalk, the second describes the Smalltalk programming environment, and the final two sections divide the class library into basic classes (objects, magnitudes, and collections), and graphical classes. A common thread throughout the latter two sections is to describe a set of related classes from the class library, to explain some of the rationale behind design decisions taken by the designers, and then to show how new classes may be added to extend the existing classes in some useful way. In addition, Chapter 10 is devoted entirely to extended case studies describing the implementation of graphics-based applications. Problem sets are included at the end of each chapter; these range from simple exercises, to extensions of examples presented in the text, and finally to major projects.

Fundamentals

In this section, we introduce the reader to the fundamental concepts of object-oriented programming. Using a language independent approach, Chapter 1 characterizes object-oriented programming as programming with objects, programming by simulation, computation via message passing and programming in the presence of polymorphism, inheritance, and a large class library.

Chapter 2 describes how these fundamental notions manifest themselves in Smalltalk. Smalltalk is a language somewhat smaller in size than Pascal and based on a surprisingly small set of concepts; namely objects, messages, classes, subclassing, and inheritance. Our approach is to introduce these new concepts by relating them to their counterparts in traditional programming paradigms and programming languages. In particular, programming in Smalltalk is introduced by contrasting Smalltalk code with its Pascal equivalent.

The Programming Environment

Developing Smalltalk programs is characterized by a total integration of tools and an absence of modes. Editors, file managers, compilers, debuggers, and print utilities are all included within the Smalltalk environment. Chapters 3, 4, and 5 provide an introduction to the integrated collection of powerful and sophisticated tools that together form the Smalltalk programming environment. Chapter 3 provides an introduction to basic features of the user interface, in particular, windows and menu interaction and how to enter, edit, and evaluate Smalltalk code. Chapter 4 describes the central role played by browsers in the programming process both for navigating the class library and for editing and compiling additions to this library. Chapter 5 describes the use of inspectors to investigate the internal state of objects and the use of notifiers and debuggers to view and modify the state of a suspended computations.

Basic Classes

In this section, we describe the basic classes — those classes that form the core of the class library. Chapter 6 introduces the default behavior for operations such as copying, printing and comparing that are supported by class Object — the ultimate superclass of all classes. Chapter 7 describes the Magnitude classes including the numeric, character, date and time classes. Chapter 8 describes the Collection and Stream classes that are as fundamental to Smalltalk as lists are to Lisp. To provide a better understanding of the numerous and closely related collection classes, we consider the classes from a logical perspective partitioning them into four major logical groups.

Graphics

In this section, the classes supporting the interactive creation and manipulation of graphical images are surveyed and their use illustrated through three case studies. Chapter 9 explains the use of forms and the bitblt operations that serve as a base for the Smalltalk graphical model. Interaction with the mouse and keyboard is addressed together with a description of simple graphical interaction techniques. The chapter concludes with a review of the path or trajectory classes (arcs, circles, curves, lines, linear fits, and splines) and the use of pens.

Chapter 10 presents three extended graphical examples: film loops, a magnifying glass, and a simple video game. Film loops are never ending movies and show how simple animation sequences can be developed. Techniques for obtaining flicker-free displays and for storage of graphical forms on disk are also introduced. The latter facility illustrates the use of object mutation — the ability for one object to mutate into another. The magnifying glass application allows a user to move a magnifier over the display while magnifying the image under the magnifying glass. This application illustrates advanced graphical programming techniques and, in particular, describes how circular rather than rectangular forms may be manipulated. Finally, the video game illustrates the evolutionary approach that characterizes the design and development of Smalltalk applications. The design decisions that took place during the development of the game are described in detail along with the use of notions such as reusability, specialization, and generalization that differentiate object-oriented design from traditional design methodologies.

VOLUME TWO

In Volume Two, we describe the Smalltalk classes that provide the familiar overlapping windows, pop-up menus, and mouse interaction facility that characterize the Smalltalk user interface. This includes details of the model-view-controller framework for the construction of user interfaces, the protocol of the existing classes, examples that use the existing classes, examples that extend them, and finally, examples that create new classes of windows.

Window Preliminaries

Chapter 1 provides an introduction to the small number of windows that can be constructed easily by novices, and includes an in-depth discussion of the model-view-controller paradigm and dependency maintenance, the distinction between process management and window management, and the window transformation protocol.

Windows: An Overview and Basics

Chapter 2 provides an overview of the existing window classes and provides a detailed description of the basic views and controllers that support the window classes described in subsequent chapters. In particular, classes Model, View, and Controller are described in detail along with other important classes like NoController, MouseMenuController, StandardSystemController, StandardSystemView, ScreenController, and ScrollController. Extensive examples are provided to show how views and controllers can be created and used.

Permanently Visible Windows

Chapters 3 through 6 describe text, menu, switch, and form (graphics) windows respectively. Each of these chapters describes the detailed protocol of the relevant classes and the differences between the standard classes and pluggable classes. In particular, each chapter shows how users can (1) use the existing classes, (2) modify the classes to provide extensions, and (3) create new classes based on the existing ones for special applications.

Text windows are created from instances of TextHolder, StringHolder, or TextCollection and associated controllers and views; i.e., StringHolderView and StringHolderController. Pluggable text windows are created from arbitrary models and instances of TextController and

TextView. To illustrate extensions to these classes, we design and implement symbolic manipulation windows and note pads (windows that also play the role of streams).

Menu windows are created from instances of TextList, ListController, LockedListController, and ListView. Pluggable menu windows are created from arbitrary models and instances of SelectionInListController and SelectionInListView. To illustrate extensions, we design and implement an electronic phone book.

Switch windows are created from instances of Switch, Button, OneOnSwitch, SwitchView, SwitchController, IndicatorOnSwitchController, and LockedSwitchController. Pluggable switch windows are created from arbitrary models, instances of BooleanView, and one of the above switch controllers. For illustration, we design and implement a pizza query window.

Form windows are created from instance of Form (actually any displayable object), FormView, FormHolderView, and NoController. A simple example that displays a magnified picture is used to illustrate form windows.

Pop-up Windows

Chapter 7 is concerned exclusively with pop-up windows. Pop-up menus are provided by instances of PopUpMenu or ActionMenu (the latter instances are used exclusively by pluggable windows and should be used in new designs). These instances simultaneously play the role of model, view, and controller. Other pop-up windows that request textual responses (as opposed to choice selection of menu items) are constructed from instances of FillInTheBlank, FillInTheBlankController, CRFillInTheBlankController, and FillInTheBlankView. Pop-up windows requiring a simple yes/no answer are constructed from instances of BinaryChoice, BinaryChoiceController, and BinaryChoiceView. They are illustrated with small simple examples. Additionally, a new kind of pop-up window (a pie-menu window) is designed to illustrate how the system can be extended.

A Window Application

Finally, Chapter 8 provides an extended example to illustrate the construction of a large-scale window application. It deals with the design of a window maker — an editor that helps users create user interfaces. In the process, a design for a library of switch forms and a library editor is developed. The existing window classes are extended to support the window maker application and more than a dozen subwindows are designed to support the window maker editor. This chapter will be of interest to those who are interested in designing better interfaces or designing special purpose windows since many of the problems involved will have been identified and solved.

WHO SHOULD READ THIS BOOK?

Smalltalk provides a new programming paradigm and the two volumes are therefore aimed at readers who are receptive to new ways of thinking about problem solving and new programming language concepts. We expect that most readers will have some programming experience in a procedural language. Programmers familiar with Pascal, C, Ada, or Fortran will find the language easy to learn and will be pleasantly surprised at the extensive set of support tools in the environment.

To gain full benefit from the book, readers should have access to a Smalltalk system and be prepared to adopt an exploratory hands-on approach to programming and problem solving. **Inside Smalltalk** is for the professional programmer and serious student who wish to use the Smalltalk system as a powerful, efficient prototyping and development environment. The book can be effectively used in undergraduate and graduate courses in object-oriented programming or software engineering where Smalltalk will be a language of instruction. The book will be particularly valuable for students carrying out extensive thesis and project work in Smalltalk.

SMALLTALK DIALECTS

Two releases of Smalltalk-80 have been licensed by the Xerox Corporation. These are known as Smalltalk-80 Version 1 and Smalltalk-80 Version 2 respectively. Version 2 includes several features, notably support for multiple inheritance, not supported by Version 1. ParcPlace Systems[1] now has exclusive worldwide ownership of the Smalltalk-80 system. The Smalltalk language[2] is available under royalty-free license from ParcPlace. Smalltalk-80 Version 2 is now accepted as the standard Smalltalk-80 system and it is this dialect of Smalltalk that is described in this book. Indeed, whenever we use the term Smalltalk in this text we are referring to Smalltalk-80. Smalltalk-80 for Sun, Macintosh, Apollo, DEC, Hewlett Packard, and 80386 MS-DOS systems is available from ParcPlace Systems. Smalltalk-80 code is almost entirely portable across different host platforms. The Smalltalk-80 system is now marketed by ParcPlace Systems under the name Objectworks for Smalltalk-80.

Digitalk[3] markets Smalltalk/V, a dialect of Smalltalk for Macintosh and IBM PC computers. Excluding the user interface classes, there is a great deal of commonality between the Smalltalk/V and Smalltalk-80 class libraries. Similarly, the range of programming tools is similar, although there are distinct differences in the structure and functionality of specific tools such as the browser, in the method of interaction with the environment, and in the degree of integration with the specific platform

ACKNOWLEDGMENTS

First and foremost, we would like to acknowledge the great contribution made to the software community by the group of researchers at the Xerox Palo Alto Research Center (PARC) who were responsible for the development of the Smalltalk system. In particular, we single out Alan Kay, Adele Goldberg, and Dan Ingalls, who in 1987 received formal recognition of their work with the 1987 ACM Software Systems Award. In recognition for

---

[1]ParcPlace Systems, 1550 Plymouth Street, Mountain View, CA 94043.

[2]Goldberg, A. and Robson, D., *Smalltalk-80: The Language and its Implementation* (Reading, Mass.: Addison-Wesley, 1983).

[3]Digitalk, Inc., 9841 Airport Road Blvd., Los Angeles, CA 90045.

the development of a software system that has had a lasting influence, has reflected contributions to new and still evolving concepts, and has resulted in commercial acceptance, the Xerox PARC group received the award for seminal contributions to object-oriented programming languages and related programming techniques. Smalltalk was cited as having provided the foundation for explorations in new software methodologies, graphical user interface designs, and forms of on-line assistance to the software development process. Our thanks also to ParcPlace Systems for continuing to develop and market the Smalltalk-80 system.

We also thank Dave Thomas who, many years ago, foresaw the potential of object-oriented programming and motivated us to become involved in research in the area. To the many students at Carleton University in Ottawa and to others who attended our object-oriented programming and Smalltalk workshops, our sincere thanks for being such willing guinea pigs for much of the material that now appears in this book. Our thanks also to the reviewers and, in particular, Richard Bernat of the University of Texas at Austin and Bharot Jayaraman of the University of North Carolina at Chapel Hill, for their helpful comments. To Marcia Horton, Christina Burghard, and their colleagues at Prentice Hall, for their support and patience in the development of the book. Finally, on a more personal note, we thank our respective wives, Marla Doughty and Christine Pugh, for their support and understanding, and our children, Brannon, Robin, Chloé, and Gareth, who have yet to understand why their "daddies" were too often unavailable.

Inside
Smalltalk

1

Window Preliminaries

1.1 INTRODUCTION

Smalltalk does not have a class of objects called **windows**, but it does have a comprehensive family of classes concerned with window management. By the term **window**, we will mean either a class or set of classes that have been purposely designed to provide an interactive graphical interface.

Windows as interfaces are not mere passive objects; i.e., they play a significant active role in controlling both the keyboard activity and mouse interactions. Different kinds of windows are designed with different uses in mind. Consequently, there is a great deal of variability between the different varieties. Additionally, windows can themselves consist of many subwindows, each with its own characteristics. With many windows potentially active at the same time, a scheduling scheme is required for coordinating their respective actions.

Effective use of windows requires knowledge about (1) the overall philosophy underlying the window paradigm, (2) process management and window management (a special case), (3) dependency maintenance and how it can be used to relate windows to the objects they are displaying, and (4) window transformations. This basic knowledge serves as a preliminary for more detailed discussions on the specifics of the window classes, how they relate to each other, their detailed protocol, and how they may be used in complex applications. This chapter is concerned with these preliminaries.

1.2 WINDOWS AND WINDOW SUPPORT FOR THE NOVICE

Windows can be created in three ways: (1) via menu commands while browsing, debugging, or inspecting, (2) by explicit code that relinquishes control to it never to return, and (3) by explicit code that relinquishes control to it with the expectation that it will return to continue execution.

The first method is well known. The second and third are of more interest to the reader. Unfortunately, the range of possibilities is very limited at this stage. Complex windows for specific user applications cannot be created and manipulated without substantial effort.

Nevertheless, browsers and inspectors are easy to create. They were designed to execute as separate processes and fall into the second category; i.e., they can be initiated with explicit code, but control does not automatically return to the initiator. On the other hand, pop-up windows and confirmers fall into the third category; they are easily used for arbitrary purposes since they return with useful information.

This section serves as a repository of useful odds and ends for novice users of the system. It summarizes selected protocol for mouse interactions, keyboard interactions, cursor manipulations, and simple built-in windowing facilities. This protocol and the protocol associated with the graphical classes are a sufficient basis for understanding the details to be considered later in this chapter.

1.2.1 Creating Inspectors and Browsers

Inspectors (see Fig. 1.1) and browsers (see Fig. 1.2) are easy to produce with explicit code; control does not automatically return to the initiator.

creating inspectors

- anObject **inspect**

    Constructs an inspector permitting the detailed contents of the object to be viewed and modified. Control does not return.

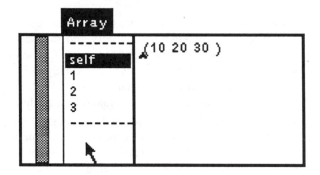

Figure 1.1 Inspecting an array.

creating browsers

- BrowserView
    openListBrowserOn:
        (SortedCollection **with:** 'Float class pi' **with:** 'Integer factorial')
    label: 'A list browser on two methods'.

    Constructs a browser with title 'A list browser on two methods' and containing two menu entries: 'Float class pi' and 'Integer factorial'. Each entry is a class name; e.g., 'Float class' or 'Integer' followed by a method name; e.g., 'pi' or 'factorial'. Selecting a menu entry displays the associated method and permits the usual browsing activities. Control does not return.

- Smalltalk **browseAllCallsOn:** aMethodName
- Smalltalk **browseAllCallsOn:** aMethodName **and:** anotherMethodName
- Smalltalk **browseAllImplementorsOf:** aMethodName
- Smalltalk **browseAllSelect:** aBlockThatReturnsTrueForSelectedMethodNames
- Smalltalk **browseChangedMessages**
- Smalltalk **showMenuThenBrowse:** aCollectionOfMethodNames
- Browser **newOnClass:** aClassName

Each creates a browser that permits one or more methods (menu selectable) to be viewed and modified. The browseChangedMessages method permits browsing all methods changed since the last execution of 'Smalltalk noChanges'; Smalltalk has a sophisticated change management system for tracking modifications. The showMenuThenBrowse method permits browsing the implementors of a selected method. Control does not return.

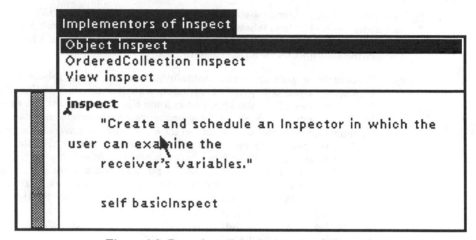

Figure 1.2 Browsing all implementors of 'inspect'.

1.2.2 Creating Notifiers, Pop-up Menus, Confirmers, and Text Query Windows

More interesting is the construction of windows (see Figs. 1.3 to 1.6) with features that can be customized by the user for specific applications. These return to the message sender.

creating notifiers and debuggers

- self **halt**
- self **halt:** 'Break point right here'.

Creates a notifier window (the second version is titled) that permits the user to optionally invoke the debugger. The yellow button menu provides two choices: proceed and debug. If the user chooses proceed, the notifier window disappears and the computation continues from where it left off. If the user chooses debug, the notifier window again disappears and a debugger window is created in its place (the user specifies where the debugger window is placed). After browsing the execution state in the debugger window, the user can choose to proceed or close (among other possibilities). In either case, the debugger window disappears. Execution continues for proceed and terminates for close.

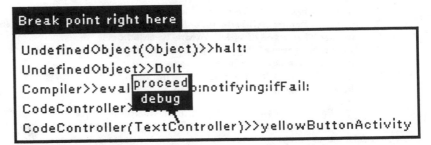

Figure 1.3 A notifier window for invoking a debugger.

creating pop-up menus

- anInteger ← (PopUpMenu **labels:** 'pig\cow\horse\hen' **withCRs**) **startUp**
- anInteger ← (PopUpMenu **labels:** 'pig\cow\horse\hen' **withCRs lines:** #(1 3)) **startUp**
- anInteger ← (PopUpMenu **labels:** '...' **withCRs lines:** #(1 3)) **startUp:** aButton
  withHeading: 'Choose an animal' **withCRs**

  Constructs a pop-up menu containing the specified labels vertically
  displayed as menu items. The variation with lines: will additionally add
  horizontal lines after the specified entries; e.g., after pig and horse above.
  Note that each item is an arbitrary sequence of characters; the items must
  be separated by a carriage return (withCRs is used to convert backslashes to
  carriage returns). Once the menu pops up, the user can either select one of
  the entries with the mouse (any mouse button) or select outside the pop-up
  menu. Selecting an entry will cause the position of the entry; e.g., 1, 2, 3, or
  4 in this example, to be returned; selecting outside causes 0 (zero) to be
  returned. In either case, once the mouse button is released, the pop-up
  menu disappears. The startUp:withHeading: variation permits a multi-lined
  title to be provided; aButton is typically #anyButton but can also be
  #yellowButton, #redButton, or #blueButton.

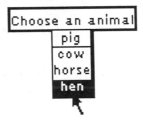

Figure 1.4 A pop-up menu window.

creating confirmers

- aBoolean ← self **confirm:** 'Did the chicken come before the egg?\Well!' **withCRs**.

  Constructs a confirmer; i.e., a window with the specified confirmation
  message (multi-lined if carriage returns are contained) with both a yes box
  and a no box. The user is forced to choose one or the other. If yes is chosen,
  true is returned; otherwise, false. Attempts to ignore the confirmer by
  trying to activate other windows result in the screen flashing. Once a choice
  is made, the window disappears. The confirm: message can be sent to any
  object but the receiver is ignored.

Inside Smalltalk

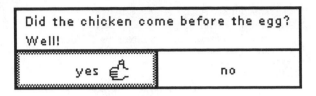

Figure 1.5 A confirmer window.

- aString ← FillInTheBlank **request**: 'What is your name?'
- aString ← FillInTheBlank **request**: 'Do you wish to continue?' **initialAnswer**: 'yes'

> Constructs a text-query window with the specified request message (multi-lined if carriage returns are contained) as the title. The user is forced to type a textual response in a text window below the title; editing is permitted. The response is terminated either by a carriage return or by choosing accept in the yellow button pop-up menu. At that point, the window disappears. Attempts to ignore the request by trying to make other windows active are signaled by flashing. The typed response is returned to the sender as a string. The initial answer, if provided, is returned by immediately typing a carriage return or accepting the text. It can be edited to provide a different answer.

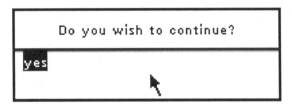

Figure 1.6 A text-query window.

1.2.3 Screen, Transcript, Cursor, Keyboard, and Mouse Protocol

Other miscellaneous activities that might prove useful include restoring the screen to its original state (after an experiment), displaying information on the transcript, changing the cursor, and so on.

restoring the display

- ScheduledControllers **restore**

> Clears the screen to gray and then displays the windows of the scheduled controllers in the reverse of the scheduling order; e.g., the active window is displayed last.

transcript manipulation

- Transcript **clear**
- Transcript **show**: 'any string'
- Transcript **print**: anObject
- Transcript **store**: anObject

- Transcript **cr**
- Transcript **crtab**
- Transcript **crtab**: aSpecifiedNumberOfTabs
- Transcript **space**
- Transcript **tab**

> The system transcript (unless explicitly closed by the user) is always available for displaying information. It is used, for example, during file-in operations while methods are being compiled or for indicating that a browser will not be created on an empty list of candidate methods. It is also used for displaying debugging information. Most of the operations are typical stream operations. However, characters sent to the transcript are not made visible until a subsequent show: operation is executed; show: is equivalent to the nextPutAll: operation for streams with the additional side effect of making all changes visible. Method clear removes all text from the window and also makes the change visible.

cursor manipulation

- Cursor **blank**   "A cursor: white; i.e., invisible"
- Cursor **corner**   "A cursor: the bottom right corner of a rectangle"
- Cursor **crossHair**   "A cursor: a cross"
- Cursor **down**   "A cursor: a down arrow"
- Cursor **execute**   "A cursor: a starred arrow pointing left and up"
- Cursor **marker**   "A cursor: a right arrow"
- Cursor **normal**   "A cursor: an arrow pointing left and up"
- Cursor **origin**   "A cursor: top left corner of a rectangle"
- Cursor **read**   "A cursor: eyeglasses"
- Cursor **square**   "A cursor: a small black square"
- Cursor **up**   "A cursor: an up arrow"
- Cursor **wait**   "A cursor: an hourglass"
- Cursor **write**   "A cursor: a pen writing"
- *Sensor* **currentCursor**   "Obtaining the current cursor"
- *Sensor* **currentCursor**: aNewCursor   "Changing the current cursor"
- aCursor **show**   "A better way of changing the current cursor"
- aNewCursor **showWhile**: aBlock

> Different cursors can be obtained from class Cursor via messages like corner, crossHair, write, and so on. The current cursor can be obtained and changed via messages currentCursor and currentCursor: to Sensor (it can also be changed with cursor message show). Sensor is a global variable containing an instance of class InputSensor that provides an interface to the user-input devices for mouse, keyboard, and cursor interactions. It is shown in italic to indicate that it is not a class name. The receiver of showWhile: is the new cursor to be used during execution of the block; once the block terminates, the old cursor is restored. Note: The cursor is restored only if the block terminates normally; i.e., if there is no explicit return within the block.

keyboard manipulation

- *Sensor* **keyboardPressed**
- *Sensor* **keyboardPeek**

- *Sensor* **keyboard**
- *Sensor* **flushKeyboard**

> As mentioned above, Sensor is a global variable containing an instance of class InputSensor. Message keyboard returns the next character (if more characters are typed, they are queued) and removes it from the queue; keyboardPeek returns the next character without dequeuing it. Neither message should be sent if keyboardPressed returns false. Message flushKeyboard removes and discards all remaining queued characters.

mouse manipulation

- *Sensor* **waitButton**   "Wait for any button down"
- *Sensor* **waitNoButton**   "Wait for any button up"
- *Sensor* **waitClickButton**   "Wait for any button down and up"
                                   "Return the current mouse coordinates"

- *Sensor* **redButtonPressed**
- *Sensor* **blueButtonPressed**
- *Sensor* **yellowButtonPressed**   "Return a boolean result"
- *Sensor* **anyButtonPressed**
- *Sensor* **noButtonPressed**

- *Sensor* **mousePoint**   "The current mouse coordinates"
- *Sensor* **cursorPoint**   "The mouse point displaced by the cursor offset; i.e., the cursor hot spot"

> Messages waitButton and waitNoButton should be interpreted as *wait for button down* and *wait for button up* respectively. Message waitClickButton waits for a combined *down followed by up* action. All three are independent of the specific mouse button used; they return the current mouse coordinates. The ...ButtonPressed messages selectively check for specific mouse buttons. Messages wait... and mousePoint return the screen coordinates of the top left corner of the cursor; cursorPoint returns the coordinates of the cursor hot spot; e.g., the cursor point of the cross would be at the intersection of the two lines rather than at the top. Note: Changing the cursor when the mouse is fixed may have the effect of changing the cursor point but not the mouse point.

1.3 THE MODEL-VIEW-CONTROLLER PARADIGM

Every application generally requires special windows for information display and user interaction. If we are lucky, we might be able to use an existing class of windows. Usually, though, the available windows are not quite right and new ones must be devised either by specializing existing ones, assembling smaller window components into larger units, or devising entirely new variations. In an effort to simplify the task, Smalltalk subscribes to partitioning its windows into three components:

- a **model**: the object to be looked at and/or modified.

- a **view**: the object that determines the precise manner in which the model is to be displayed.

- a **controller**: an object that handles the keyboard and mouse interactions for this window.

The **model** can be any object without restriction. For an inspector window, it is typically any user object. For a debugger window, it is typically the current context along with any information attached to it. A context is a stack frame that represents the execution state of a program. For a source code window in a browser, it is typically a string of characters comprising a method. A window created for the purpose of manipulating a model is short-lived by comparison with the model; i.e., once the window itself is no longer needed, it can be closed and purged from the system, but the model remains.

The **view** is responsible for providing a visual representation of the object. For example (see Fig. 1.7), a view designed for displaying binary trees might display the tree graphically. Alternatively, it might display the tree textually with indentation conventions to indicate the hierarchical relationships. A third approach might be to partition the display into several **subviews**, each designed to display the model in a different way or to display a different aspect of the same model.

The **controller** is responsible for interfacing between the user and the model/view. It interprets keyboard characters along with mouse movements and clicking. It either handles the interactions locally, passes the information directly to the view for processing, or performs some local preprocessing before passing it along. It is also concerned with activating and deactivating itself so that many windows can be manipulated independently by a user. In a browser, for example, a user might first select a method in a menu window and then edit the method in the source code window. The menu window controller that has control initially must be deactivated in order for the controller for the source code window to be activated. If a view has subviews, as in this example, each has a corresponding controller for handling its own interface interactions.

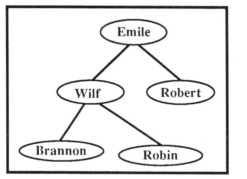

Figure 1.7 Two views of a tree.

1.3.1 Advantages of the Model-View-Controller Philosophy

There are several advantages to windows designed as a **model-view-controller** triad (**MVC** for short).

- It permits **multiple views** of the same object and, more generally, **multiple windows** on the same model.

- It permits views to be used as parts for assembly into larger units; **new** kinds of **views** can be constructed using existing views as **subviews**.

- It permits **controllers** to be **interchanged**, allowing different user-interaction modes; e.g., expert versus nonexpert mode.

- It **separates input** processing (controllers) **from output** processing (view displaying).

1.3.2 Explicit Connections Between Members of the MVC Triad

As indicated in Fig. 1.8, an MVC triad is intimately connected. In particular, the view knows explicitly about the model and the controller. The controller knows explicitly about the model and the view. However, *there is no explicit connection from the model to the other two.*

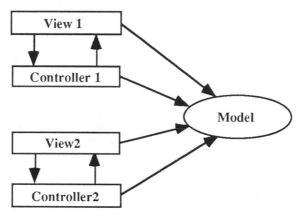

Window1: View1, Controller1, Model
Window2: View2, Controller2, Model

Figure 1.8 Explicit connections between models, views, and controllers.

1.3.3 Explicit Connections Between Views and Subviews

When a complex view consists of several subviews, each in turn potentially containing additional subviews (to arbitrary depth), the individual views in the hierarchy are explicitly connected, as in Fig. 1.9, but not the controllers. If view A is above B in this hierarchy, B is called a **subview** of A while A is a **superview** of B. The highest view in the hierarchy is the **top-level** view. Views are provided with operations for extracting subviews and the superview. On the other hand, although we can invent a terminology for referring to the corresponding controllers as **subcontrollers** and the **supercontroller** respectively, there are no corresponding controller methods. To obtain the subcontrollers, one typically obtains the associated view from a controller, then obtains the subviews, and finally obtains their controllers.

1.3.4 Implicit Connections Between Models and Their Views

So far there is nothing that connects a model to a view or a controller. Yet, they must be connected if a change to the model is to be reflected in all views. If an arbitrary computation

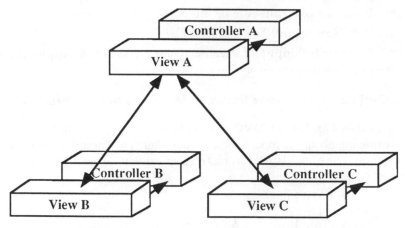

Only views (not controllers) are connected.

Figure 1.9 A hierarchy of views and subviews.

modifies the model, there is no magic technique that will automatically notify the views about the change to the model. The only solution is for the model itself to explicitly signal the views. The difficulty is that a model is an arbitrary object. Because the majority of objects never get used as models, it seems unreasonable to add a field in each object for keeping track of related views. On the other hand, this solution is viable when objects are specially designed to serve as models for special-purpose views and controllers.

Assuming that the total number of active models in the system is reasonably small (there is a limit to the number of open windows), the most general solution is to keep all objects playing the role of models in an identity dictionary as shown in Fig. 1.10. Each model serves as a key in the dictionary and the associated value is a collection of views on that model. A special protocol is provided whereby a model can signal its views of a change. More specifically, the model sends itself a **changed** message; each view receives an **update** message. We will consider this protocol and its usage in detail later.

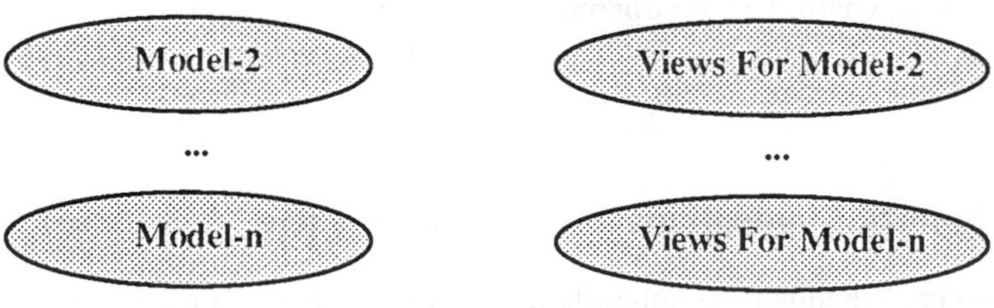

**A Global Identity Dictionary
for Keeping Track of Dependencies**

Keys	Values
Model-1	Views For Model-1
Model-2	Views For Model-2
...	...
Model-n	Views For Model-n

Figure 1.10 Implicit connections between models and views.

The mechanism mentioned above is very general; it can be used for arbitrary **dependency maintenance**. Keeping track of views as **dependents** of models is a particular application to window management. Both aspects will be investigated. To summarize so far:

- Views have exactly one controller and one model that they keep track of explicitly. They can also have subviews and a superview that they explicitly maintain.

- Controllers have exactly one view and one model that they keep track of explicitly.

- Models can have many views associated with them that they keep track of implicitly. In particular, they are maintained as dependents; i.e., there exists a unique identity dictionary in which the model is the key and the collection of views is the value.

1.3.5 Window Management Versus Process Management

During an interactive session, users generally manipulate many windows. They may interact with one window for a while, then switch to another for a short time, and finally switch back. A window may pop up as a consequence of some user-initiated action and wait for a specific response. Once provided, the window may disappear and the previous window regains control. The interesting thing about this scenario is that there is only one **active** window at a time; i.e., only one window actually executing. The others, the **inactive** windows, are held in abeyance waiting for a turn at becoming the active window. To be more precise, there is only **one active controller**.

The window manager, an instance of class **ControlManager** kept in global variable **ScheduledControllers**, is responsible for coordinating the activation and deactivation of the window controllers. The controllers themselves are designed to cooperate with the scheduling scheme provided. In order for a controller to be active, a **process** must be created for executing that controller and scheduled for execution.

The process manager, an instance of class **ProcessScheduler** kept in global variable **Processor**, is responsible for coordinating the activation and deactivation of processes. For example, there are processes for monitoring keyboard and mouse events (they simply queue information for later use by controllers), for determining if space is low, for monitoring the system clock, and for controlling a window. Processes are provided with different priority levels for scheduling purposes. For example, mouse and keyboard monitoring is done at a higher priority than the other processes to ensure that characters are immediately available to controllers.

The process manager is responsible for all processes in the system; the window manager is responsible for one of them, the process corresponding to the active window controller. Detailed understanding of the working of controllers, therefore, requires an understanding of window management, which in turn requires an understanding of process management. We will discuss process management and window management further in a later section.

1.3.6 Customizing Windows

The next challenge is understanding the complexities of windows with many subviews (or **panes**). The best example of such a window is the browser. The class and method panes, to pick just two for illustration, are concerned with displaying a list of class names and a list of method names respectively. The entries are menu items that can be selected by the user with the mouse. The important point is that both panes consist of the same kind of windows, but they are used for different purposes. Systems with inheritance generally provide two ways for users to produce customizations that can be used for different purposes:

- Create specializations of the window; e.g., classNameWindow and methodName-Window as specializations of the more general menu selectable window (the **specialization** approach).

- Use two different instances of the same class of menu selectable windows but embed the different data needed for the different applications in the instances (the **pluggable views** approach).

Earlier versions of Smalltalk were based entirely on the specialization approach, but the pluggable views approach is becoming more popular. The browser, for example, is constructed using the pluggable views methodology. The reason the two approaches coexist is that windows designed for *plugging-in* must be considerably more general than the former. Smalltalk was originally designed for execution in a sophisticated multi-window environment. However, the window classes were designed specifically for the Smalltalk programming environment. It was not until such environments became more commonplace that the need for user-customizable application windows became apparent.

1.3.7 Relaxing the MVC Paradigm

The MVC metaphor is a powerful organizing paradigm for constructing window classes but it is often relaxed in several ways:

- When a window is relatively simple, it may be convenient to merge the view with the controller; e.g., this is done with **PopUpMenu**.

- When a model is distributed or lacking in functionality, it may be convenient to create a **virtual** model that contains the actual model; e.g., the model for a browser view is an instance of **Browser**, the model for an inspector view is an instance of **Inspector**, which itself contains the actual model (the object being inspected).

1.4 DEPENDENCY MAINTENANCE

The Smalltalk **dependency maintenance** mechanism is concerned with providing a simplified notification facility for participants that have agreed to abide by the communication rules. Participants (or **sponsors**) are allowed to communicate (indirectly) only with those other objects denoted **dependents**. Sponsors can add and remove dependents dynamically. The implied relationship that results is called a **dependency graph**. As we explained above, the mechanism is used to associate views (dependents) with a model (the sponsor).

To use the dependency mechanism, a sponsor does not have to know (nor does it care to know) how many dependents are associated with it at any one time. A sponsor simply notifies itself of an event worthy of notification and the dependency maintenance mechanism informs all dependents. More specifically, a sponsor sends itself a **changed** message and the dependents are informed via an **update:** message.

The dependency mechanism is provided as part of the protocol for class **Object** and duplicated for windows in a class called **Model**. The dependency graph for **Object** is maintained in a global identity dictionary called **DependentsFields**; each sponsor is a key in the dictionary; and the corresponding value is an ordered collection of dependents. The dependency graph for **Model** is maintained by the model instances; each instance is a sponsor locally maintaining the dependents in an ordered collection managed by an instance variable called **dependents**. These details, however, need not be remembered since neither the global dictionary nor the instance variable **dependents** is ever manipulated directly by a user.

The dependency maintenance mechanism can be used to advantage when designing objects with specialized views. For example, binary trees could be designed with two distinct display views: one graphical and the other textual. If the same tree were being simultaneously viewed with a graphical view and a textual view (we could even have several of each kind of view), it would be nice if the different views were consistent with each other and with the tree as an object. In particular, if one of the objects were modified through interaction with one view, the other views should be made aware of the change. Alternatively, if a separate process unknown to the views actually changed the tree, that too should cause the views to be notified. Although such an example is too complex for this section because it requires detailed understanding of views and controllers, it would be an interesting exercise for a later section.

The power of the dependency handling mechanism comes from the fact that

- Dependents can be associated dynamically with any object (the sponsor).

- Sponsors can **broadcast** messages to all dependents. In particular, sending a **changed** message to a sponsor causes all dependents to be sent an **update:** message.

Four methods are provided for adding, removing, and obtaining dependents. Sponsors and dependents can be arbitrary objects.

dependency graph operations

- aSponsor **addDependent**: aDependent
  Makes aDependent be a dependent of aSponsor and returns aDependent.
- aSponsor **removeDependent**: aDependent
  Ensures that aDependent is no longer a dependent of aSponsor and returns aDependent. No error results if aDependent was not already a dependent.
- aSponsor **release**
  Removes all dependents of aSponsor and returns aSponsor.
- aSponsor **dependents**
  Returns all dependents of aSponsor in an ordered collection.

Sponsors can communicate with their dependents in three ways: (1) by broadcasting a zero- or one-parameter message, (2) by indicating that they have changed, or (3) by requesting that they be allowed to make a change. Dependents, on the other hand, react either to an update command or to a query by a sponsor asking for permission to modify itself. More details follow.

messages received by objects and relayed to dependents

- aSponsor **broadcast**: aUnaryMessage
  Sends aUnaryMessage to all dependents of aSponsor and returns aSponsor.
- aSponsor **broadcast**: aOneParameterMessage **with**: aParameter
  Sends aOneParameterMessage with aParameter to all dependents of aSponsor and returns aSponsor.

- aSponsor **changed**
  Usually sent by a sponsor to itself to indicate that it has *changed*. Causes all dependents to be sent an 'update: nil with: nil from: self' message, which defaults to the simpler 'update: nil' message if the method is inherited from Object. Returns aSponsor.
- aSponsor **changed**: aParameter
  Usually sent by a sponsor to itself to indicate that it has *changed*. Causes all dependents to be sent an 'update: aParameter with: nil from: self' message, which defaults to the simpler 'update: aParameter' message if the method is inherited from Object. Returns aSponsor.
- aSponsor **changed**: aParameter **with**: anotherParameter
  Usually sent by a sponsor to itself to indicate that it has *changed*. Causes all dependents to be sent an 'update: aParameter with: anotherParameter from: self' message. Returns aSponsor. Not currently used.

- aSponsor **changeRequest**
  Usually sent by a sponsor to itself to indicate that it *desires to change itself*. Causes all dependents to be sent an 'updateRequest' message. Returns true if all dependents return true; otherwise, returns false.
- aSponsor **changeRequest**: aParameter
  Usually sent by a sponsor to itself to indicate that it *desires to change itself*. Causes all dependents to be sent an 'updateRequest: aParameter' message. Returns true if all dependents return true; otherwise, returns false. Not currently used.
- aSponsor **changeRequestFrom**: aDependent
  Usually sent by a dependent of aSponsor to indicate that it wishes to *change the object*. Behaves like changeRequest except for the fact that aDependent is not informed.

messages received by dependents

- aDependent **update**: aParameter
  The sponsor has changed. The dependent should *readjust* itself taking aParameter into account.
- aDependent **update**: aParameter **with**: anotherParameter
  The sponsor has changed. The dependent should *readjust* itself taking both parameters into account. Not currently used in the system. The default in Object is to discard the second parameter and send a 'self update: aParameter' message. Subclasses can override the method in new applications. Not currently overriden.
- aDependent **update**: aParameter **with**: anotherParameter **from**: aSender
  The sponsor has changed. The dependent should *readjust* itself taking both parameters and the sender into account. Not currently used in the system. The default in Object is to discard the sender and send a 'self update: aParameter with: anotherParameter' message. Subclasses can override the method in new applications. Not currently overriden.

Inside Smalltalk

- aDependent **updateRequest**

  Returns true if the sponsor should be allowed to update itself; otherwise, returns false. For example, the dependent may refuse the request (return false) if it has cached important information that it thinks should be incorporated into the object first.

- aDependent **updateRequest**: aParameter

  Returns true if the sponsor, taking the parameter into account, should be allowed to update itself; otherwise, returns false. For example, the dependent may refuse the request (return false) if it has cached important information that it thinks should be incorporated into the object first. Not currently used in the system. The default in Object is to discard the parameter and send a 'self updateRequest' message. Subclasses can override the method in new applications. Not currently overriden.

Once a dependency graph has been established, there are several ways the above methods can be used for maintaining consistency:

- A sponsor modifies itself and consequently sends itself a **changed** or **changed:** message; the dependents all receive an **update:** message and adjust themselves accordingly. If desired, an additional parameter can be passed along from the sponsor to the dependents to help them decide how to update themselves.

- A sponsor is about to modify itself; hence, it requests clearance from its dependents by sending a **changeRequest** message to itself. Each dependent gets an **updateRequest** message to which it replies **true** if it is agreeable to the change. An additional parameter can be transmitted if desired.

In both protocols, **change in any context** is associated with an arbitrary sponsor; **update** is associated only with dependents. The protocol "**changed:** (sponsor) ⇒ **update:** (dependent)" is widely used in managing windows with multiple subviews. The protocol "**changeRequest** (sponsor) ⇒ **updateRequest** (dependent)" is used, for example, by the browser. Whenever an entry is selected in a subwindow or an operation such as closing the window is initiated, a **changeRequest** message is sent to the browser view. When the code view (a dependent subview) gets an **updateRequest** message, it immediately grants the request if no modifications have been made to the code; otherwise, it explicitly prompts the user and asks whether the modifications should be discarded. If the user agrees, it grants the request and otherwise denies it. A denied request cancels the original user operation.

1.4.1 The Duck Imprinting Example

For our immediate purposes, we will consider a toy problem that does not require windows. In particular, consider a contrived **duck imprinting problem**: We envisage a mother duck displaying herself on the screen along with a brood of ducklings (see Fig. 1.11). Although only two possibilities are shown, we provide four distinct forms created with the bit editor. The mother and each duckling in her brood are displayed with the same form; the mother duck is larger than the others. Additionally, the mother is attached to the mouse and is visible only when the mouse button is depressed; moving the mouse causes the mother to move. The ducklings head toward the mother only when the mother is visible. Since there are three mouse buttons, we will associate one mother duck with each button.

Figure 1.11 A mother duck and her brood (a second brood is also visible).

A duckling maintains (1) its position on the screen, and (2) an icon, a form, for displaying itself. Moving is simplistically achieved by whitening the area occupied by the icon on the screen and then displaying the icon at the new position. This will work well in most cases, although there will be interactions when distinct ducks overlap. A mother duck subclass is created primarily to distinguish mothers from their ducklings; i.e., only one class is really needed. The class is also relatively impoverished, since its main aim is to illustrate the usage of the dependency mechanism.

The primary method is **example** in class **MotherDuck**. It creates three mother ducks and then proceeds to have them track the movements of the respective mouse buttons; i.e., depressing a mouse button causes the corresponding mother duck to follow it. When a mother duck is created, the user is also asked to create an associated brood of ducklings at random points on the screen. Each duckling is made a dependent of the mother.

As long as a mouse button is depressed, the corresponding mother will quack. The quack method actually displays the mother and executes 'self **change:** self'. This causes each dependent to execute the duckling method 'aDuckling **update:** aMother' which moves the duckling one tenth of the way toward the mother. Hence all ducklings head toward the mother. Although method **quack** was intended to convey an auditory expression, there is no facility to explicitly create sound. We must imagine that the mother is quacking as she moves on the screen.

The example illustrates keyboard interactions, mouse tracking, and user interaction.

Class Duckling

```
class name                Duckling
superclass                Object
instance variable names   position icon
comment                   I am a small duck with the ability to move and display
                          myself on the screen.

instance methods

access

icon
     ↑icon
```

position
      ↑position

modification

icon: anIcon
      icon ← anIcon

position: aPoint
      position ← aPoint

displaying

display
      "I display myself by displaying my icon at the current position."
      icon **displayAt:** position

erase
      "I erase myself by whitening the area occupied by my icon."
      Display **white:** (position **extent:** icon **extent**).

responding to mother

update: mother
      "Move a tenth of the way toward mom and update the display to show the
      movement."
      self **erase.** "whiten old location"
      position ← (position + ((mother **position** - position) * 0.10)) **rounded**.
      self **display** "display at new location"

Class MotherDuck

class name   MotherDuck
superclass   Duckling
instance variable names   "no additional ones"
class variable names   DuckIconMenuNames DuckIcons
comment   I am a more mature duck. I can move and display myself a
                                    little bigger than ducklings. When I quack, my ducklings
                                    follow me.

class methods

class initialization

initialize
      "MotherDuck initialize"

      "Older implementation definitions."
      DuckIcons ← (1 **to:** 7) **collect:** [:index |
          Cursor
              perform: (#(origin corner crossHair up down read write)
              at: index)].
      DuckIconMenuNames ← ('left corner\right corner\cross hair\up arrow\',
          'down arrow\eyeglass\pen writing') **withCRs.**

"Newer implementation definitions."
DuckIcons ← Array
    with: (Form
        extent: 50@50
        fromArray: #(0 0 0 0 0 0 0 0 0 0 0 0 0 0 0 0 0 0 0 0 0 0 0 0 0 0 0 0 0 0 0 0 0
            0 0 0 0 0 1536 0 0 0 768 0 15 57344 896 0 31 61440 390 0 56 6144 204
            0 48 3072 220 0 97 33792 112 0 103 58880 240 0 480 512 176 0 1008
            768 432 0 3888 480 864 0 16368 496 544 0 7984 26 608 0 2032 15
            1568 0 510 5 33888 0 127 35840 60512 0 3 50688 14528 0 0 59136
            4544 0 0 29568 384 0 0 12672 384 0 0 12480 12672 0 0 6368 29056 0
            0 7291 50048 0 0 3135 33536 0 0 1567 1792 0 0 1792 1536 0 0 768
            3072 0 0 896 7168 0 0 449 61440 0 0 255 57344 0 0 63 0 0 60 0 0 6
            0 0 0 6 0 0 0 6 0 0 0 6 0 0 0 15 0 0 0 31 32768 0 0 58 49152 0 0 50
            24576 0 0 34 24576 0)
        offset: 0@0)
    with: (Form
        extent: 50@50
        fromArray: #(0 0 0 0 0 511 0 0 0 2047 49152 0 0 7681 61440 0 0 30720
            61440 0 1 49152 30720 0 3 32768 7168 0 7 0 3584 0 6 0 1536 0 6 0
            768 0 12 15360 768 0 24 65024 62336 0 25 50947 63872 0 57 37639
            7360 0 49 14726 20160 0 49 64900 59072 0 113 65415 63072 0 96
            1793 65120 0 96 0 3680 0 224 248 32 0 224 49151 32 0 199 63503
            57376 0 511 1 63536 0 504 0 15408 0 448 0 3888 0 384 0 944 0 128 0
            992 0 128 0 224 0 192 0 192 0 64 0 384 0 96 0 768 0 33 0 1536 0 49
            57408 3072 0 17 61560 6144 0 24 124 12288 0 24 0 24576 0 12 0
            49152 0 14 1 32768 0 6 3 0 0 7 6 0 0 3 12 0 0 1 32792 0 0 1 32824 0 0
            3 49276 0 0 3 49368 0 0 6 24972 0 0 6 26380 0 0 12 15372 0 0 12
            14348 0 0 12 4100 0 0)
        offset: 0@0)
    with: (Form
        extent: 50@50
        fromArray: #(0 0 0 0 0 0 0 0 0 0 0 0 0 0 0 0 0 0 0 0 0 0 0 12 0 0 0 28 0 0 0 60
            0 0 0 120 0 0 0 240 0 0 0 480 0 0 0 960 0 0 0 960 0 0 0 3840 0 0 0 7936
            0 3 65408 32256 0 7 65408 60416 0 14 225 55296 0 28 99 47104 0 56
            118 28672 0 112 28732 57344 0 96 63544 49664 0 96 65329 34304 0
            96 65059 7168 0 96 61446 6144 0 97 49166 28672 0 113 32783 57344
            0 56 7 49152 0 56 3 32768 0 56 0 49152 0 56 0 24576 0 24 14 14336 0
            12 63 36352 0 12 51 63360 0 14 112 32192 0 6 192 4080 0 6 448 1016
            0 14 2944 508 0 14 15104 126 0 28 15104 31 0 56 29184 7 0 112
            26112 0 0 224 60928 0 0 225 52224 0 0 451 39936 0 0 899 38912 0 0
            1799 12288 0 0 3598 28672 0 0 7196 24576 0 0 6200 49152 0 0)
        offset: 0@0)
    with: (Form
        extent: 50@50
        fromArray: #(0 0 0 0 0 0 0 0 0 0 0 0 0 0 0 0 224 0 0 0 2032 0 0 0 7984 0 0 0
            31768 0 0 0 52632 0 0 0 60444 0 0 0 31772 0 0 0 16380 0 0 0 4092 0 6
            0 510 0 6 0 30 0 15 32768 14 0 15 32768 14 0 28 0 14 0 2040 0 14 0
            32752 0 30 3 65136 0 28 7 61552 0 28 31 49264 0 28 127 224 0 28 992
            8416 0 30 1984 25024 0 14 3968 25536 0 15 7680 50048 0 7 64513
            50944 0 7 63619 36352 0 3 63687 7168 0 1 63742 14336 0 0 61564
            61440 0 0 30723 63488 0 0 14343 63488 0 0 7903 39936 0 0 4095
            35840 0 0 2041 52736 0 0 0 50944 0 0 0 50048 0 0 0 49600 0 0 0
            49344 0 0 0 49600 0 0 3 50048 0 0 15 1792 0 0 28 3840 0 0 56 3584 0
            0 112 7168 0 0 224 14336 0 0 480 12288 0 0 448 28672 0)
        offset: 0@0).

DuckIconMenuNames ←
    'left looking duck\front looking duck\right looking duck\ostrich' **withCRs**.

newMother: aName
    | mother aPopUpMenu ducklingIconChoice ducklingIcon characterTyped duckling |

    "First, ask the user which icon he/she wants to use for this duck and its ducklings"
    aPopUpMenu ← PopUpMenu **labels**: DuckIconMenuNames.
    ducklingIconChoice ← aPopUpMenu **startUp**: #anyButton **withHeading**: (
        'For the ', aName, ' mother duck,\',
        'choose one of the following duck icons.\',
        'Afterward, start clicking all over the screen.\',
        'Each click will create a new duckling for this mother duck.\',
        'When you have enough of them, type any character\',
        'at the keyboard to stop the process.') **withCRs**.
    ducklingIconChoice = 0 **ifTrue**: [self **error**: 'You did not follow instructions, did you?'].
    ducklingIcon ← DuckIcons **at**: ducklingIconChoice.

    "Next, create a mother duck with a bigger icon."
    mother ← self **new**. mother **icon**: (ducklingIcon **magnifyBy**: 2@2).

    "Finally, create the ducklings and have them stay on the screen. Note that we can't
    simply wait for a mouse button click because it will never come after the keyboard
    is pressed."
    Sensor flushKeyboard. characterTyped ← false.
    [characterTyped]
        whileFalse: [
            [(characterTyped ← Sensor **keyboardPressed**) **or**:[Sensor **anyButtonPressed**]]
                whileFalse: [].
            characterTyped
                ifFalse: [
                    duckling ← Duckling **new**
                        position: Sensor **mousePoint** - (ducklingIcon **extent** // 2);
                        icon: ducklingIcon.
                    duckling **display**.
                    mother **addDependent**: duckling.
            Sensor **waitNoButton** "wait for release; otherwise, the loop will repeat
                and create a second duckling, then a third, then a fourth, ..."]].
    Sensor **flushKeyboard**.

    ↑mother

example
    | redMother blueMother yellowMother savedCursor |
    Display **white**.
    self **confirm**: ('For the imprinting game, we will create 3 mother ducks:\',
        'a yellow duck, a red duck, and a blue duck\each with it''s own brood of ducklings.\',
        'Each will be controlled by a different mouse button.\',
        'Holding a mouse button down will cause the ducklings\to move toward the mother.\',
        'More instructions will indicate how to construct the broods.\',
        'Are you ready to proceed?') **withCRs**. "ignore answer"

    yellowMother ← MotherDuck **newMother**: 'yellow'.
    redMother ← MotherDuck **newMother**: 'red'.
    blueMother ← MotherDuck **newMother**: 'blue'.

```
self confirm: ('To start, hold down any mouse key.\',
        'To stop, type any character on the keyboard.\',
        'Are you ready?') withCRs. "ignore answer"

"We want the mother ducks to play the role of cursors"
[true]
    whileTrue: [
        Sensor redButtonPressed
            ifTrue: [Cursor blank showWhile: [redMother quack]].
        Sensor blueButtonPressed
            ifTrue: [Cursor blank showWhile: [blueMother quack]].
        Sensor yellowButtonPressed
            ifTrue: [Cursor blank showWhile: [yellowMother quack]].
        Sensor keyboardPressed ifTrue: [
            (self confirm: 'Did you really want to quit?')
                ifTrue: [
                    redMother release. blueMother release. yellowMother release.
                    Sensor flushKeyboard. "discard extra characters if any"
                    ScheduledControllers restore. "redraw the display as it was before
                    ↑nil]
                ifFalse: [Sensor flushKeyboard "discard extra characters if any"]]].

    "MotherDuck example"

instance methods

mother quacking

quack
    "Mother keeps quacking as long as mouse is depressed."
    | iconOffset newPosition |

    "Make myself visible at the current mouse position."
    iconOffset ← self icon extent // 2.
    self position: Sensor mousePoint - iconOffset. self display.

    "As long as the mouse is depressed, I keep displaying myself."
    [Sensor anyButtonPressed]
        whileTrue: [
            "If I moved, I erase myself at the old location and redisplay myself at the
            new location."
            newPosition ← Sensor mousePoint - iconOffset.
            (newPosition = self position)
                ifFalse: [self erase. self position: newPosition. self display].
            "Simulate a quack to cause the brood to head toward me."
            self changed: self "Notify all the ducklings."].
    "Hide myself."
    self erase
```

1.4.2 Switch: A Class that Uses the Dependency Mechanism

Smalltalk already has the dependency handling protocol imbedded within a specialized **Switch** class. A **switch** is a class of object that can either be **on** or **off**. Additionally, both an **on action** and an **off action** can be associated with the switch by providing it with corresponding blocks; the default is **nil** (no action). When a switch is turned on (or off), it modifies its local state appropriately, sends itself a *self changed* message, and then executes the corresponding action (if nonnil). The switch protocol is the following:

creating new switch and button instances

- Switch **newOn**
  Returns a new switch with the on and off actions set to **nil** (no action) and the state set to **on**.
- Switch **newOff**
  Returns a new switch with the on and off actions set to **nil** (no action) and the state set to **off**.
- Switch **new**
  A more traditional alternative to **newOff**.

testing the switch state

- aSwitch **isOn**
  Returns **true** if the switch is on; **false** otherwise.
- aSwitch **isOff**
  Returns **true** if the switch is off; **false** otherwise.

changing the switch state without executing the actions

- aSwitch **set**
  Set the switch to **on**. If it was previously **off**, *self changed* is sent. The receiver's on action is **not** executed.
- aSwitch **clear**
  Set the switch to **off**. If it was previously **on**, *self changed* is sent. The receiver's on action is **not** executed.

changing the switch state with automatic action execution

- aSwitch **turnOn**
  Set the switch to **on**. If it was previously **off**, *self changed* is sent and the receiver's on action is executed.
- aSwitch **turnOff**
  Set the switch to **off**. If it was previously **on**, *self changed* is sent and the receiver's off action is executed.
- aSwitch **switch**
  Performs a **turnOn** if it was originally off; otherwise, a **turnOff**.

setting the actions

- aSwitch **offAction**: anAction
  Sets the off action of the receiver to anAction, either a block or **nil**.
- aSwitch **onAction**: anAction
  Sets the on action of the receiver to anAction, either a block or **nil**.

modifications to the standard dependents processing protocol

- aSwitch **removeDependent**: aDependent
  In addition to the standard dependency processing, sets the on and off actions to **nil** if the last dependent is removed.
- aSwitch **release**
  In addition to the standard dependency processing, sets the on and off actions to **nil**.

It is the on and off actions that provide switches with generality since these can be tailored to any application. We can demonstrate switches with an example similar to the duckling imprinting problem; i.e., the **coordinated lights problem**. The problem is a variation of the **traffic light problem** discussed in *Smalltalk-80: The Language and Its Implementation* by Goldberg and Robson (Addison-Wesley, Reading, Mass., 1983).

1.4.3 The Coordinated Lights Example

For this example, we construct a demonstration subclass of Switch (DemonstrationLight) with one class method called **example** for coordinating the demonstration and three instance methods: two initialization methods for associating the current mouse position with the light and for displaying it either in state on (the crosshair in reverse video) or off (the normal crosshair) and an **update:** method for reacting to **changed:** messages.

The **example** method supervises the construction of ten demonstration lights (one on and nine off), as shown in Fig. 1.12. Each light is made a dependent of the other nine. The user types a character between 0 and 9, which causes the associated light to turn on. The dependency mechanism takes care of turning off all other lights.

Figure 1.12 A snapshot of coordinated lights.

More specifically, the **example** method sends a **turnOn** message. The **update:** method sends a **turnOff** message. In each case, the corresponding **action** reverses the icon bits and redisplays the icon at its old position. Both the **turnOn** and **turnOff** methods send **changed** messages that result in **update:** messages to dependents. To properly coordinate the lights, it is not sufficient for the **update:** method to simply send a **turnOff** message to itself.

To see why, suppose light B was already on and we wanted to turn light A on by sending it a **turnOn** message.

```
A would be turned on
    ⇒  a changed message is sent to A (to itself)
        ⇒  an update: message is sent to B (and all other dependents; A, in particular,
           is not a dependent of itself)
        ⇒  B is turned off
            ⇒  a changed message is sent to B (to itself)
                ⇒  an update: message is sent to A and all other dependents of B
                    ⇒  A is turned off (this causes another changed message to
                       be sent with another round of updates: messages; this
                       time all lights are off, so turning it off has no effect).
```

Inside Smalltalk

Although we want the act of turning on A to cause B to turn off, we don't want the act of turning off B to cause A in turn to be turned off. The solution is to turn off the dependent lights only when the sponsor was just turned on. The fact that a sponsor has just turned off is not of interest to a dependent and should therefore be ignored.

Class DemonstrationLight

class name	DemonstrationLight
superclass	Switch
instance variable names	position
class variable names	LightBulb

instance methods

private initialization

privateInitializeOff
    position ← Sensor **mousePoint**.
    LightBulb **displayAt**: position.
    self **onAction**: [Display **reverse**: (position **extent**: LightBulb **extent**)].
    self **offAction**: [Display **reverse**: (position **extent**: LightBulb **extent**)].

privateInitializeOn
    self **privateInitializeOff**.
    Display **reverse**: (position **extent**: LightBulb **extent**).

dependency management

changed
    "Make it clear that the sponsor must be sent as a parameter."
    self **changed**: self

update: aSponsor
    "Only listen to sponsors that are already on (in which case we should turn off)."
    aSponsor **isOn ifTrue**: [self **turnOff**].

class methods

class initialization

initialize
    "DemonstrationLight initialize"

    "Set up the Light cursor icon."
    LightBulb ← (Form
        extent: 20@32
        fromArray: #(0 0 0 240 0 780 0 1542 0 3171 0 6241 32768 4192 32768 8288
            16384 8288 16384 8288 16384 8288 16384 8192 16384 4096 32768 2145 0
            1026 0 516 0 264 0 144 0 144 0 144 0 144 0 144 0 408 0 504 0 264 0
            504 0 264 0 504 0 144 0 0 0)
        offset: 0@0).

example
```
    | lights character |
    "DemonstrationLight example"

    "First, create ten special lights on the screen"
    lights ← Array new: 10.
    Display white.
    self confirm: (
        'For the coordinated lights game, you will need to create ten\',
        'lights by clicking ten times anywhere on the screen.\',
        'These lights will be numbered 0, 1, 2, ..., 9.\',
        'If you click too many times, we will just ignore the extra clicks.\',
        'More instructions will be forthcoming.\',
        'Are you ready to proceed?') withCRs. "ignore result"

    Cursor crossHair showWhile: [
        1 to: 10 do: [:whichLight |
            Sensor waitButton. "Button down"
            lights at: whichLight put:
                (whichLight = 1
                    ifTrue: ["The first one is to be on" self newOn privateInitializeOn]
                    ifFalse: ["The others are to be off" self newOff privateInitializeOff]).
            Sensor waitNoButton "Button up"]].

    "Next, set up the light dependencies and provide final instructions"
    1 to: 10 do: [:aLight |
        1 to: 10 do: [:aLightDependent |
            aLight = aLightDependent
                ifFalse: [(lights at: aLight) addDependent: (lights at: aLightDependent)]]].

    self confirm: (
        'Now hit any of the numeric keys 0, 1, ..., 9\',
        'to turn the corresponding light on.\',
        'Hit any other key to end the game.\',
        'Are you ready to proceed?') withCRs. "ignore result"

    "Now play the game"
    Sensor flushKeyboard. "A precaution in case some key was accidently hit."
    [true]
        whileTrue: [
            character ← Sensor keyboard digitValue + 1.
            (character between: 1 and: 10)
                ifTrue: [
                    (lights at: character) turnOn]
                ifFalse: [
                    (self confirm: 'Did you really want to quit?')
                        ifTrue: [
                            1 to: 10 do: [:whichLight | whichLight release].
                            Sensor flushKeyboard. "discard remaining characters"
                            ScheduledControllers restore. "redraw display"
                            ↑nil]]]
```

1.5 PROCESS MANAGEMENT

The **process manager**, an instance of class **ProcessScheduler** kept in global variable **Processor**, is responsible for coordinating the activation and deactivation of processes. There are processes for monitoring keyboard and mouse events (they simply queue information for later use by controllers), for determining if space is low, for monitoring the system clock, and for controlling a window. There are also **shared queues** and **semaphores** for coordinating communication between processes; e.g., between a window and the processes concerned with monitoring the keyboard and the mouse. A segment of code selected for execution by a user in a browser or workspace is executed as part of the process for the controlling window.

The set of processes is partitioned into a number of priority levels with the processes within a level organized in a queue. Thus, the process manager schedules the first process ready to execute in the highest priority queue. The manager can suspend execution of a process when a higher priority process becomes available, it can reorder the processes within a queue, it can change process priorities, and it can create new processes and terminate existing ones.

Warning: In following discussion of the process scheduling protocol, we deviate from our standard practice of specifying the message receiver as aProcessScheduler for instance methods. The reason is simple: There is only one process scheduler and this instance is in global variable Processor. This global variable is difficult enough to remember on its own without it being referenced indirectly as aProcessScheduler. We will italicize it to highlight the fact that it is a deviance from our normal practice.

1.5.1 The Existing Priority Structure

The existing priority levels are listed below from highest to lowest priority. The priority of a window process, **user scheduling priority**, is midway between the lowest, **system background priority**, and the highest, **timing priority**, for monitoring the clock. Immediately above and below user scheduling priority are **user interrupt priority** and **user background priority**. The former is used for execution interruption (typing control-c or control-., depending on the system) or special emergency evaluators (typing control-shift-c on some systems). The background process is intended for processes that can execute whenever window activities are dormant. However, since there is always one active window and it only relinquishes control to another window, there is never an opportunity for background processes to execute. Future extensions to the system will likely remove this deficiency.

process priorities

- *Processor* **timingPriority**
  Priority for the timing process that monitors the system clock. This process is set up by class Delay. Existing processes can be delayed either by a fixed amount or until a specified time is reached via special messages to Delay.
- *Processor* **highIOPriority**
  Priority for the process that monitors the local network communication device (if there is one).

- *Processor* **lowIOPriority**

  Priority for the input device monitoring process that handles the keyboard and mouse hardware interrupts and performs packet distribution from the local network (should there be one). The process is set up by class InputState; it queues keyboard events for subsequent access by other processes.

- *Processor* **userInterruptPriority**

  Priority for any process created by a window that should be executed immediately. Examples include the process that responds to user-interrupts and processes that spy on the active user process (see class MessageTally).

- *Processor* **userSchedulingPriority**

  Priority for the window process that enables the user to perform editing, viewing, programming, and debugging. This process is set up by class ScheduledControllers.

- *Processor* **userBackgroundPriority**

  Priority for any process intended to be executed whenever the window processes are doing nothing.

- *Processor* **systemBackgroundPriority**

  Priority for any process intended to be executed whenever nothing is happening; e.g., incremental garbage collectors or processes that determine space usage.

1.5.2 Process Creation, Suspension, Resumption, and Destruction

At any one time, there is exactly one process executing, the **active** process. All other processes are either not available for execution (**suspended**) or awaiting execution. Suspended processes and new processes can be made available for execution by sending them a **resume** message or by executing a **signal** on a semaphore that causes them to be suspended (see semaphores in Sect. 1.5.5). A process that is active or awaiting execution can be made unavailable by sending it a **suspend** message, by requesting that it be delayed (see delays in Sect. 1.5.3), or by performing a **wait** on a semaphore.

Processes are created by sending special messages **fork**, **forkAt:**, **newProcess**, and **newProcessWith:** to blocks. The first two messages both create and schedule the block for execution; the latter two only create the processes (they can be specifically scheduled via a **resume** message). A process that has already been scheduled can be unscheduled temporarily with a **suspend** message and permanently with a **terminate** message. An active process can be rescheduled at the end of the queue of waiting processes (there is a separate queue for each priority) by sending a **yield** message to **Processor** (the scheduler). The scheduler can be queried about the active process and the priority of the active process, and it can also be asked to terminate the active process.

creating and scheduling processes

- aBlock **fork**

  Creates and schedules a process executing aBlock. The process is created with the same priority as the currently executing process; it terminates itself upon completion. The result returned by the fork is the block (the receiver).

- aBlock **forkAt:** aPriority

  Creates and schedules a process executing aBlock. The process is created with the indicated priority; it terminates itself upon completion. The result returned by the fork is the block (the receiver).

creating processes without scheduling them

- aBlock **newProcess**

  Creates and returns (without scheduling) a process executing aBlock. The process is created with the same priority as the currently executing process. Once scheduled, it will terminate itself upon completion.

- aBlock **newProcessWith**: anArrayOfParametersToTheBlock

  Creates and returns (without scheduling) a process executing aBlock. The process is created with the same priority as the currently executing process. Once scheduled, it will terminate itself upon completion.

- aProcess **priority**

  Returns the priority of the process.

- aProcess **priority**: aPriority

  Can be used to set the priority of a process if the existing default is not desired.

scheduling, suspending, and terminating processes

- aProcess **resume**

  Schedules the process for execution at the end of the queue of processes awaiting execution (the queue for the specified priority). Returns the process. It is an error to attempt to schedule a process that is already in the queue.

- aProcess **suspend**

  Removes the process from the queue of processes awaiting execution. If it was already active, its execution is stopped. The process can be restarted later at the point it left off by executing a resume.

- aProcess **terminate**

  Permanently removes the process from the queue of processes awaiting execution. If it was already active, its execution is stopped.

- *Processor* **yield**

  Suspends and resumes the active process. Has the effect of placing it at the end of the queue of processes waiting execution at the same priority, thereby allowing other processes a turn at execution.

interrogating and changing the processor state

- *Processor* **activeProcess**

  Returns the process that is currently executing.

- *Processor* **activePriority**

  Returns the priority of the active process; i.e., the process that is currently executing.

- *Processor* **terminateActive**

  Permanently removes the active process from execution.

Relevant examples are provided in the next section dealing with window management. For the moment, we consider only simple toy examples.

Example

Consider the problem of computing the **factorial** of an integer using processes. Of course, we will add the new method to class Integer. For the moment, we will assume the answer is to be printed in the system transcript rather than returned.

```
factorialPrint
    "Create a process and schedule it."
    [
        Transcript show: self factorial printString; cr
    ] fork.
    "Return the receiver; the answer will be printed in the transcript."
    ↑self
```

If '50 factorialPrint' is selected for execution in a workspace and option **print it** is specified, we will find that 50 is returned and printed before the answer is printed on the transcript. This is because the new process is scheduled for execution at the end of the queue for this priority. It will not become the active process until the current process yields (this will occur immediately after returning if no other work is pending in the workspace window).

We could change this order by forking the process at a higher priority.

```
factorialPrint
    "Create a process and schedule it at a higher priority than the active process."
    [
        Transcript show: self factorial printString; cr
    ] forkAt: (Processor activePriority + 1).
    "Return the receiver; the answer will be printed in the transcript."
    ↑self
```

When we discuss semaphores, we will consider a proper solution that returns the factorial result instead of printing it. On the other hand, such a solution can be devised without semaphores if we make certain assumptions about the processes in the system. One approach is the following:

```
factorialViaProcesses
    | answer myProcess |
    "Obtain and save the active process."
    myProcess ← Processor activeProcess.
    "Create a new process and schedule it."
    [
        "This process will start after the active process is suspended."
        answer ← self factorial.
        "Now that it has computed the answer, it can restart the former active process."
        myProcess resume
    ] fork.
    "Relinquish control"
    myProcess suspend.
    "Return the answer (assume its been computed by the forked process)."
    ↑answer
```

This solution makes the reasonable assumption that the forked process will not preempt the active process. Such preemption could occur, for example, if a higher priority process were to suddenly get control. This would cause the active **factorial** process to be placed at the end of its queue. The forked process would then start executing before 'myProcess **suspend**' was executed. Since myProcess is already in the queue, it is an error for the forked process to attempt to **resume** it. Clearly, this solution is not adequate. Another approach is the following:

factorialViaProcesses
> | answer |
>   "Create a new process and schedule it."
>   [
>   "This process will start before the factorial process can return the answer."
>   answer ← self **factorial**.
>   ] **forkAt:** (Processor **activePriority** + 1).
>   "Return the answer (assume it's been computed by the forked process)."
>   ↑answer

This solution assumes that no other processes will change the priority of the factorial and fork processes.

In the previous example, all processes were created using parameterless blocks (as required by **fork** and **forkAt:**). Corresponding versions with parameters could be designed and added to class BlockContext. The additions illustrate the use of **newProcessWith:**.

>   **forkWith:** anArrayOfParameters
>   "The receiver is a block with parameters"
>   ↑(self **newProcessWith:** anArrayOfParameters) **resume**

After creating the process, it is scheduled for execution using **resume**. The corresponding **forkAt:** method would be implemented as follows:

>   **forkAt:** aPriority **with:** anArrayOfParameters
>   "The receiver is a block with parameters"
>   ↑(self **newProcessWith:** anArrayOfParameters) **priority:** aPriority; **resume**

By analogy, it should be clear that **fork** could have been implemented as follows:

>   **fork**
>   ↑self **newProcess resume**

1.5.3 Associating Processes with the System Clock (Delays)

A **delay** is an object that can be used to suspend an active process. It also encodes either a **duration** (a length of time during which the process must remain suspended) or a **wakeup time** (the time at which the process must be resumed). An active process is delayed by sending a **wait** message to the delay object. When a delay object is no longer needed, it should be sent a **disable** message.

The timer process is responsible for keeping track of all delayed processes and restarting them (via a **resume** message) at the appropriate time. A process delayed via a duration delay can, after it has resumed, be delayed again with the same delay object, since durations are relative to the current time. Of course, it makes little sense to delay a process for a second time if a wakeup time delay was used, since that time has already passed.

Duration delays are constructed by specifying a time either in seconds or milliseconds. Wakeup time delays are specified with a time from the **millisecond time clock**. A special protocol (Delay **millisecondClockValue**) is provided for obtaining the current millisecond time. Although the normal clock and the millisecond time clock are intimately related, the two are rarely equivalent. Hence, users must not substitute them; i.e.,

>   Time **now asSeconds** * 1000 *is not equivalent to* Delay **millisecondClockValue**

The value returned by the millisecond time clock is not a time object but an integer object. Consequently, all of the integer operations are available for manipulating the times. A convenient conversion routine (an instance method) can be added to Time as follows:

```
asMillisecondTime
    "Assumes the millisecond time clock and normal clock differ by a constant factor"
    | millisecondTimeNow normalTimeNow constantFactor |
    millisecondTimeNow ← Delay millisecondClockValue.
    normalTimeNow ← Time now.
    constantFactor ← millisecondTimeNow - (normalTimeNow asSeconds * 1000).
    ↑self asSeconds * 1000 + constantFactor
    "(Time readFrom: (ReadStream on: '7:30 am')) asMillisecondTime"
```

The delay protocol is quite small by comparison with other classes.

delayed and repetitive execution

- Delay **forMilliseconds**: milliseconds
- Delay **forSeconds**: seconds
  Returns a delay object that **will** delay the active process by the specified amount once it is sent a **wait** message. Once reactivated, a subsequent **wait** will repeat the delay.
- Delay **untilMilliseconds**: millisecondTimeClockInteger
  Returns a delay object that **will** delay the active process until the specified time once it is sent a **wait** message. Parameter millisecondTimeClockInteger is **not** a time but an integer that must be computed relative to the current millisecond time clock value.
- Delay **millisecondClockValue**
  Returns an integer denoting the current millisecond clock time in milliseconds.
- aDelay **resumptionTime**
  Returns an integer denoting the millisecond time clock value at which the associated process will resume.
- aDelay **wait**
  Suspends the active process for the amount of time specified by the delay.
- aDelay **disable**
  Ensures that the delay can no longer be enabled.

Example

Suppose that we want to work for one hour and we would like a reminder at the end of that time period. Additionally, suppose it is early morning and we need to be reminded of lunch at noon. The two reminders can be produced as follows:

```
| theOneHourReminderBlock theLunchHourReminderBlock |
theOneHourReminderBlock ←
    [
        "First create a duration delay object."
        (Delay forSeconds: (60 "minutes" * 60 "seconds") "i.e., 1 hour")
            "Now send it a wait message to delay the process in which this block is
            executing."
            wait.
        "When execution resumes, we will execute the following:"
        10 timesRepeat: [Transcript show: 'One hour is up!!!'; cr]
    ]
```

"Now create the process and schedule it for execution at a higher priority."
theOneHourReminderBlock **forkAt**: (Processor **activePriority** + 1).

theLunchHourReminderBlock ←
    [
        "First create a wakeup delay object."
        (Delay **untilMilliseconds**:
            (Time **readFrom**: (ReadStream **on**: '12:00 am')) **asMillisecondTime**)
                "Now send it a wait message to delay the process in which this block
                is executing."
                wait.
        "When execution resumes, we will execute the following:"
        10 **timesRepeat**: [Transcript **show**: 'It''s time for lunch!!!'; **cr**]
    ].

"Now create the process and schedule it for execution at a higher priority."
theLunchHourReminderBlock **forkAt**: (Processor **activePriority** + 1).

1.5.4 Obtaining Execution Profiles

Although we will not go into it in detail, Smalltalk provides a class MessageTally that provides a simple run-time execution profile of an executing block. The two principal class methods are

obtaining a run-time execution profile

*   MessageTally **spyOn**: aBlock
    Executes the block and presents the user with a new workspace
    summarizing the run-time execution profile of the block.
*   MessageTally **spyOn**: aBlock **to**: aFile
    As above, except that it summarizes the result in a file.

The two methods suggest trying the following examples:

MessageTally **spyOn**: [Pen **example**]

    or

MessageTally **spyOn**: [Smalltalk **asSortedCollection**] **to**: 'spy.results'.
(FileStream **oldFileNamed**: 'spy.results') **edit**.

The basic technique is to create a higher priority process that periodically starts up (using a duration delay) and inspects the context of the suspended process. A **context** is the Smalltalk terminology for the stack frame associated with an executing method. The essence of the spy strategy consists of the following:

sampleSpyOn: blockToBeSpiedOn
    | observedProcess howOftenToSpy spyDelay spying spyProcessBlock result |

    "First, set up initial information"
    observedProcess ← Processor **activeProcess**. "To obtain the current process"
    howOftenToSpy ← 20. "Every 20 milliseconds"
    spyDelay ← Delay **forMilliseconds**: howOftenToSpy.
    spying ← true.

"Second, create a block for spying (**suspendedContext** extracts the required context)."
spyProcessBlock ←
        [
            spyDelay **wait**.
            [spying] **whileTrue:** [
                self **tally:** observedProcess **suspendedContext**. spyDelay **wait**]
        ]

"Third, start up the spy process at a higher priority."
spyProcessBlock **forkAt:** Processor **userInterruptPriority**.

"Fourth, execute the block to be spied on (note that we are spying on this particular process)."
result ← blockToBeSpiedOn **value**.

"Fifth, deactivate the spy process."
spying ← false.

"Sixth and last, return the result (the profile information was stored by **tally:** above)."
↑result

1.5.5 Semaphores and Process Coordination

Semaphores provide the only safe mode of communication between processes. They are used to synchronize processes; e.g., a process requiring a value computed by another process can use semaphores to ensure that it accesses the value only after the other process has actually finished computing it.

Two messages are sufficient for communication: **signal** and **wait**. Both messages can be sent to a semaphore in an arbitrary order. However, a **wait** message sent to a semaphore will return only **after** the corresponding number of **signals** have been sent. When the return is delayed, the process sending the **wait** is suspended and placed in a queue associated with the semaphore. This suspended process is removed from the queue and rescheduled via **resume** only after the required number of **signals** is received. Thus if three processes send a **signal** and two **waits** respectively on the same semaphore, the last process sending a **wait** is suspended until the next **signal** is sent.

Synchronization is achieved in two ways: (1) by having distinct processes cooperate by matching **signal** and **wait** messages, or (2) by permitting only one process at a time to have access to common information. The first protocol is the following:

- A process computes a value and sends a **signal** when the value is available (a **producer process**).

- A process requires a value and sends a **wait** to ensure that it is available (a **consumer process**). Both processes communicate via the same semaphore which initially has been sent no messages.

The second protocol requires a semaphore that is initially sent one **signal** message. All processes requiring access to the common information adhere to the following convention:

Inside Smalltalk

- Send a **wait** message to the semaphore (the **access request**).

- Access the shared information.

- Send a **signal** message to the semaphore (the **access release**).

This latter technique is the **mutual exclusion** protocol. It is useful enough to be provided as the special message **critical:**; e.g.,

- aSemaphore **critical:** aBlockAccessingTheSharedInformation

As indicated above, this semaphore must be initialized differently. The semaphore protocol includes the linked list protocol, since Semaphore is a specialization of LinkedList (the waiting processes are kept in this list). Directly manipulating this list is not recommended.

creating semaphores

- Semaphore **new**
     Returns a new semaphore without any signals (or waits).
- Semaphore **forMutualExclusion**
     Returns a new semaphore with one signal outstanding.

using semaphores

- aSemaphore **initSignals**
     Zeros the semaphore signal (and wait) count and returns the semaphore. Should not be used unless the semaphore queue is empty.
- aSemaphore **signal**
     Increments the semaphore signal count and permits a previously waiting process (if extra waits were previously done) to resume execution and return from a wait. Returns the semaphore.
- aSemaphore **wait**
     Increments the semaphore wait count and causes the sender to be suspended if fewer signals were previously performed. Returns the semaphore.
- aSemaphore **critical:** aBlock
     Permits the block to be executed only if no other critical block controlled by the same semaphore is executing; otherwise, causes the active process to suspend until the block can be executed. Technically, waits on the semaphore, executes the block, and then signals the semaphore. This semaphore should have been created using forMutualExclusion. Returns the result of the block.

useful protocol inherited from LinkedList

- aSemaphore **size**
     Returns the number of processes waiting on the semaphore.
- aSemaphore **isEmpty**
     Returns true if no process is waiting on the semaphore; false otherwise.

Example

For the first example, it is instructive to consider the implementation of method **yield** sent to Processor. Message **yield** is sent in order to permit another process to have a turn executing at the current priority level. The method is implemented as follows:

```
yield
    "Give other processes at the current priority a chance to run"
    | aSemaphore |
    aSemaphore ← Semaphore new.
    [aSemaphore signal] fork.
    aSemaphore wait
```

The **fork** creates a new process that is scheduled at the same priority as the current process. Because of the scheduling algorithm, this new process goes at the end of the queue. The current process continues executing and immediately sends a **wait**. Since no signals or waits have been previously sent, the current process is suspended. The scheduling algorithm will then select another process for execution. Ultimately, the new process will execute. It sends a **signal** that causes the suspended process to be resumed. Since there is nothing else to execute after the **signal**, the new process terminates and another process is selected for execution.

Note that it is not sufficient to simply suspend the process because some other process would have to resume it. Additionally, if a higher priority process were to be activated between the fork and the wait (an almost impossible situation), everything would still work. In that case, the current active process would be rescheduled at the end of its process queue without having had time to send the wait message. The next process in the queue (if any) would have a chance at execution. Ultimately, the forked process will execute, send a signal, and terminate. Finally, the original process would resume execution, send a wait (canceling the signal without being suspended), and continue.

Example

Getting back to our factorial problem using processes, we can now provide a solution without assumptions. A semaphore is used to ensure that the value is available when desired.

```
factorialViaProcesses
    | answer  aSemaphore |
    "Create a semaphore for synchronization purposes (producer/consumer strategy)."
    aSemaphore ← Semaphore new.
    "Create a new process and schedule it."
    [
        answer ← self factorial.
        "Indicate that the answer is ready."
        aSemaphore signal
    ] fork.
    "Wait until the answer becomes available and return it."
    aSemaphore wait.
    ↑answer
```

We are actually in a position to derive a version with a large number of processes. Presumably, this would be advantageous on a multiprocessor with fine-grained parallelism.

```
factorialViaProcesses
    | answer  aSemaphore |
    self < 0 ifTrue: [self error: 'factorial needs a nonnegative number].
    ↑1 productUpTo: self
```

```
productUpTo: aLimit
    | midPoint leftSolution rightSolution aSemaphore |
    "Handle the trivial cases simply"
    self > aLimit ifTrue: [↑1].
    self = aLimit ifTrue: [↑self].
    "Handle the more complex case by splitting the problem into two."
    midPoint ← (self + aLimit) // 2.
    "Create a semaphore for synchronization purposes (producer/consumer strategy)."
    aSemaphore ← Semaphore new.
    "Create two new processes and schedule them."
    [
        leftSolution ← self productUpTo: midPoint.
        "Indicate that the answer is ready."
        aSemaphore signal
    ] fork.
    [
        rightSolution ← midPoint + 1 productUpTo: aLimit.
        "Indicate that the answer is ready."
        aSemaphore signal
    ] fork.
    "Wait until both answers become available and return their product."
    aSemaphore wait. aSemaphore wait.
    ↑leftSolution * rightSolution
```

The mutual exclusion protocol is illustrated in the next section.

1.5.6 Classes for Shared Access Between Processes

When distinct processes access shared objects, the access must be controlled to ensure consistency. For example, suppose distinct processes were manipulating the same stack. It is easy to visualize one process in the midst of executing a push action suddenly being preempted by another at a higher priority that attempts to perform a pop on the same stack. Since the push was never completed, the stack could very well be in a partially modified state.

At the moment, Smalltalk provides only one class of objects that is safe to use by cooperating processes: **shared queues**. Elements are placed in a shared queue using message **nextPut:** and removed using **next** (or **peek**). If no elements are available, the process performing a **next** (or **peek**) is suspended until a corresponding **nextPut:** that makes an element available. The protocol consists of the following:

creating shared queues

- SharedQueue **new**
- SharedQueue **new**: anInitialSize
    Returns a new shared queue.

using shared queues

- aSharedQueue **isEmpty**
    Returns true if the shared queue has no elements; otherwise false.
- aSharedQueue **size**
    Returns the number of elements in the shared queue.

- aSharedQueue **next**

    Returns and removes the first element from the shared queue if there is one; otherwise, suspends the sending process until an element is available.
- aSharedQueue **peek**

    Returns but does not remove the first element from the shared queue if there is one; otherwise, suspends the sending process until an element is available.
- aSharedQueue **nextPut**: anElement

    Inserts the new element at the end of the queue and returns anElement. It will allow a process that was previously waiting for an element to proceed.

Shared queues are used by the input process for recording keyboard events. They are implemented with two semaphores: one semaphore for coordinating user access and another for mutual exclusion while executing critical code. For example, the **nextPut:** and **next** methods are modelled after the following:

nextPut: anElement
    mutualExclusionSemaphore critical: [*add anElement to the shared queue*].
    readingSynchronizationSemaphore signal. "Indicate that a value is now available."
    ↑anElement

next
    | anElement |
    readingSynchronizationSemaphore wait. "Wait for a value to become available."
    mutualExclusionSemaphore critical: [*remove anElement from head of shared queue*].
    ↑anElement

This solution permits the number of elements added to run arbitrarily far ahead of the number removed; i.e., the queue is not bounded.

In general, creating new shared classes is relatively easy. A specialization of the original class is created with two new instance variables to play the role of the two semaphores described above. Then, all operations with side effects are revised following the above template. If the method being revised is called **aMethod**, the critical section code is simply a variation of 'super **aMethod**' (the result is either saved or discarded depending on the situation).

1.6 WINDOW MANAGEMENT

The process manager is responsible for all processes in the system; the window manager is responsible for one of them — the process corresponding to the active window controller. More specifically, the window manager, an instance of class **ControlManager** kept in global variable **ScheduledControllers**, is responsible for coordinating the activation and deactivation of the window controllers. The controllers themselves are designed to cooperate with the scheduling scheme provided. In order for a controller to become active, the window manager creates a **process** for it and schedules it. It will not permit a second controller to be made active while the first is still executing.

To repeat, the window manager maintains a list of scheduled controllers and chooses one for activation. A process is constructed corresponding to this chosen controller and the process is scheduled for execution. When the process completes, another controller is chosen and the algorithm is repeated. Thus, at any one time, there is exactly one window process and many scheduled controllers.

Two additional facts should be stressed: (1) not all controllers need to be scheduled controllers and (2) both the process manager and the window manager are special objects, but neither are processes. A **scheduled** controller is a controller that has been given to the window manager for potential activation; it corresponds to a top-level window on the screen. Controllers associated with subordinate windows in a multi-level window are **unscheduled** controllers. When running, such unscheduled controllers execute as part of the process associated with the top-level scheduled controller.

The fact that the process manager and window manager are not processes is not surprising. If they were, communicating with them would be slow; they couldn't respond until they themselves were activated. More important, who would be managing them? The alternative means that any code can communicate with the managers instantaneously. In the case of the process manager, any code in any executing process can have it create and schedule new processes. The same is true with the window manager. Any code can ask it to create and schedule new window controllers.

If the window manager is entrusted to create a process for only one of the scheduled controllers and the process is activated, who sends a message to the window manager to create a replacement process when the latter terminates? The answer is simple: The window manager adds the code at the end of the activated process. So each activated scheduled controller automatically ensures that a successor controller is located (in the list of scheduled controllers) and activated. What if the controller terminates abnormally or fails in some way to reach the code at the end? If that happens, error code or code associated with a debugger explicitly requests the window manager to make it the active controller. This causes the current active controller to be placed at the end of the queue, the associated process to be deactivated, and a process for the new controller to be created and activated. This new process also has code at the end to choose a successor controller. How does all this relate to the screen when a user successively clicks on different windows to activate them in succession? In this case, clicking on an inactive window causes the currently active window to notice that the mouse has been clicked outside its boundary. It responds by terminating normally, which causes the code at the end to choose a new window to activate; in this case, the one over which the mouse was depressed. What about clicking outside all windows? This is really not any different because it is viewed as a special window managed by the **screen controller**, an instance of ScreenController. This controller handles all interactions underneath the windows.

Window managers are created whenever a new project is constructed. Switching projects involves switching window managers; i.e., deactivating the current manager and activating a new one. Only one window manager is active at any one time. When the Smalltalk system was bootstrapped, a **main project** was created with the first window manager. The active window manager is kept as global variable ScheduledControllers.

We now consider window management in more detail. A window process is created and activated by sending the window manager the message **searchForActiveController**. This has two consequences: (1) one of the scheduled controllers is selected, a process is created for it, and it is scheduled at the userscheduling priority, and (2) the process sending the activation message is **terminated**. Consequently, when starting up Smalltalk as part of the initialization code or when switching projects, the **searchForActiveController** message is the last one sent. Now consider the details of the actual window manager method.

```
searchForActiveController
    "Find a controller that is available for execution. Call it aController."
    ... code not shown ...
    "Make it become the active controller; i.e. create a process and schedule it"
    self "the window manager" activeController: aController
    "Relinquish control to the new process by terminating this process"
    Processor terminateActive

activeController: aController
    activeController ← aController.
    "Move activeController to the head of the list of scheduled controllers."
    ... code not shown ...
    "Fork a new process for the active controller."
    activeControllerProcess ← [activeController startUp. self searchForActiveController].
    activeControllerProcess forkAt: (Processor userSchedulingPriority)
```

There are two important points to notice. First, as indicated above, the last line of the **searchForActiveController** method terminates the process that sent the message. Second, the process associated with the controller to be activated both starts up the chosen controller and then, after it terminates, chooses a new controller for subsequent activation.

To repeat, the **active controller** is simply a controller object. The **active controller process** is a process that executes the start-up code for the active controller, schedules a new active process, and terminates itself. This design eliminates the need for the window manager to be a process. Window managing is in fact performed at the end, and as part of, each active controller process. This also explains why the window manager really only manages one window process, a process that always creates a successor process before terminating.

1.6.1 Scheduling New Controllers

Although it is not yet clear how new controllers are actually created, it is still possible to interact with the window manager to restore the display, to obtain the existing list of scheduled controllers, to change the order, and to add new ones (included for completeness). The fact that the scheduled controllers are ordered is very evident. For example, choosing the menu entry **restore display** while in Smalltalk causes all windows to be displayed in the reverse scheduling order. Each window displayed is represented by one of the scheduled controllers.

At any one time, one controller in the list of scheduled controllers is active. When the active controller process is created, the controller is always promoted to the beginning of the list. Subsequently, however, the list may be reordered. When a new active controller is needed, the list is scanned in the specified order for the first controller that wants control. Precisely how a controller decides whether or not it wants control will be discussed in detail when dealing with controllers. Some controllers, for example, want control when the mouse is currently positioned inside their window; others want control only if the mouse has been clicked inside their window.

Warning: For discussing the window manager protocol, it is convenient to adopt a convention that was used for discussing the process manager protocol. More specifically, we deviate from our standard practice of specifying the message receiver as aControlManager for control manager instance methods. The reason here, too, is simple. All communication with instances of control managers is done through global variable ScheduledControllers. This global variable is difficult enough to remember on its own without it being referenced indirectly as aControlManager. We will italicize it to highlight the fact that it is a deviance from our normal practice. The window manager protocol is the following:

restoring the display

- *ScheduledControllers* **restore**
  Clears the screen to gray and then displays the windows of the scheduled controllers in the reverse of the scheduling order; e.g., the active window is displayed last.

querying the active controller and process

- *ScheduledControllers* **activeController**
  Returns the active scheduled controller.

- *ScheduledControllers* **activeControllerProcess**
  Returns the process for the active scheduled controller.

- *ScheduledControllers* **inActiveControllerProcess**
  Returns true if the executing process is the active controller process; false otherwise. A user-created process (perhaps delayed) would be an example of a process that is not the active controller process while it executes. Only processes associated with scheduled window controllers can be active controller processes.

querying, ordering, and removing scheduled controllers

- *ScheduledControllers* **scheduledControllers**
  Returns the scheduled controllers as a new ordered collection.

- *ScheduledControllers* **promote**: aScheduledController
  Moves aScheduledController to the front of the list of scheduled controllers.

- *ScheduledControllers* **pullBottomToTop**
  Searches the list of scheduled controllers in the reverse order for a controller that wants control and places it at the beginning of the list (if there is one). Used for scheduling windows that are underneath other windows.

- *ScheduledControllers* **activeController**: aScheduledController
  Adds aScheduledController to the beginning of the list of scheduled controllers, creates a process for it, and makes its activation pending termination of the sending process (it is the responsibility of the sending process to terminate itself).

- *ScheduledControllers* **unschedule**: aScheduledController
  Removes aScheduledController from the list of scheduled controllers but does not terminate it. Hence, it can keep executing until it loses control; at that point, it will no longer reappear.

scheduling new controllers

- *ScheduledControllers* **schedulePassive**: anUnscheduledController
  Adds anUnscheduledController to the beginning of the list of scheduled controllers. The current active controller remains active.

- *ScheduledControllers* **scheduleActive**: anUnscheduledController
  Adds anUnscheduledController to the beginning of the list of scheduled controllers, creates a process for it, makes it active, and terminates the sending process.

- *ScheduledControllers* **scheduleActiveNoTerminate**: anUnscheduledController
  Adds anUnscheduledController to the beginning of the list of scheduled controllers, creates a process for it, and makes its activation pending termination of the sending process (it is the responsibility of the sending process to terminate itself).

- *ScheduledControllers* **scheduleOnBottom**: anUnscheduledController
  Adds anUnscheduledController to the end of the list of scheduled controllers.

creating and switching window managers (used by projects)

- ControlManager **new**
  Creates and returns a new window manager with the screen controller as its only scheduled controller.

- ControlManager **scheduleActive**: anOldWindowManager
  Deactivates the existing window manager and replaces it with anOldWindowManager, which is then activated.

We are now in a position to provide a more detailed view of the **searchForActive-Controller** method. As mentioned previously, the exact manner that controllers respond to message **isControlWanted** depends on the class of controllers. Note also that the window manager keeps track of the screen controller explicitly via an instance variable.

```
searchForActiveController
    "Finds a scheduled controller to activate and deactivates the current active
    controller."
    | aController |
    activeController ← nil.
    activeControllerProcess ← Processor activeProcess. "not used"
    "Find a willing controller and call it aController (its initially nil by default)"
    "If none is found, keep repeating the search until one is found"
    ["Beginning of search loop"
        Processor yield. "Allow other processes a turn (this could be a long loop)."
        "Look for a willing controller, choosing the screen controller as a last choice."
        aController ←
            scheduledControllers
                detect: [:candidate |
                    candidate isControlWanted and: [candidate ~~ screenController]]
                ifNone: [
                    screenController isControlWanted
                        ifTrue: [screenController]
                        ifFalse: [nil]].
        aController isNil
    ] whileTrue.
    "Make it become the active controller; i.e. create a process and schedule it"
    self activeController: aController "Sets activeController and activeControllerProcess."
    "Relinquish control to the new process by terminating this process"
    Processor terminateActive
```

1.6.2 How Controllers Behave and Interact with the Window Manager

Controllers have access to the view they are associated with, the model, the keyboard, and the primary sensor they interact with. Usually, this is the mouse; however, with additional hardware, it could be a paddle or a joystick, for example. To properly interface with the window manager, the controllers must be able to indicate when they want control, they must have a compatible strategy for relinquishing control, and they must interact with the view and model to which they are intimately connected. Additionally, scheduled controllers must also interact with lower-level unscheduled controllers in a multi-pane window.

So far, we have seen that all controllers must be able to respond to **isControl-Wanted** and **startUp**. The response to the first message is a function of the class of controllers actually used. To provide a feel for this, consider a few examples.

for class Controller (all other controller classes are specializations)

isControlWanted
    ↑self **viewHasCursor**

for class NoController

isControlWanted
    ↑false

for class ScreenController (ultimately inherits from Controller)

isControlWanted
    "Requires both that the view contain the cursor and the yellow button be depressed."
    "super **isControlWanted** is really self **viewHasCursor** (always **true** for screens)."
    ↑super **isControlWanted and:** [sensor **yellowButtonPressed**]

Once the window manager has determined that a particular controller wants control, it creates a process that starts the controller executing. When the controller returns, a new controller is selected, a process for it is created and scheduled, and the previous process is terminated. The interesting question is how long does the controller retain control and what is the protocol used to maintain this control? This can best be answered by looking at the **startUp** methods used by controllers. Almost all controller classes inherit the **startUp** method from Controller (an exception is class PopUpMenu, which uses its own specialized protocol).

for class Controller (the standard protocol)

startUp
    self **controlInitialize.**
    self **controlLoop.**
    self **controlTerminate**

where

controlLoop
    [self **isControlActive**] **whileTrue:** [Processor **yield.** self **controlActivity**]

for class NoController

startUp
    "Does nothing"
    ↑self

The standard protocol is to perform special initialization, then loop executing **controlActivity** as long as control is active, and finally to perform special termination code. Note that **yield** is a process manager message and not a window manager message; i.e., it permits other processes at the same priority to be given control, but it doesn't change the active window controller. Currently, no existing class redefines the control loop. However, many classes redefine **controlInitialize**, **isControlActive**, **controlActivity**, and **controlTerminate**. Method **controlActivity**, in particular, must be different for each class of controllers. The next most interesting method is **isControlActive** for retaining control.

for class Controller (not the usual default)

isControlActive
    ↑self **viewHasCursor** & sensor **blueButtonPressed not**

for class NoController

isControlActive
    ↑false

for class ScreenController (inherits from MouseMenuController)

isControlActive
    "Requires that both the view contain the cursor and the yellow button be depressed."
    "super **isControlActive** is really self **viewHasCursor** (redundantly **true** for screens)"
    ↑super **isControlActive and**: [sensor **yellowButtonPressed**]

for class MouseMenuController (the more usual default)

isControlActive
    ↑self **viewHasCursor**

for class StandardSystemController (old version without icons)

isControlActive
    "Remains active as long as no button is pressed outside the view."
    ↑status == #active **and**: [
        sensor **anyButtonPressed ifTrue**: [self **viewHasCursor**] **ifFalse**: [true]]

for class StandardSystemController (new version with icons)

isControlActive
    "Same as above but asks the icon controller (a subview) when the view is collapsed and a button is pressed."
    ↑status == #active **and**: [
        sensor **anyButtonPressed**
            ifTrue: [
                (view **containsPoint**: sensor **cursorPoint**)
                    ifTrue: [
                        view **isCollapsed**
                            ifTrue: [view **subViewWantingControl** ~~ nil]
                            ifFalse: [true]]
                    ifFalse: [false]]
            ifFalse: [true]]

for class BinaryChoiceController (inherits from Controller)

isControlActive
>"super **isControlActive** is really self **viewHasCursor**"
>model **actionTaken ifTrue:** [↑false].
>[super **isControlActive**] **whileFalse:** [view **flash**].
>↑true

Although we have not yet discussed the controller hierarchy, it is worthwhile knowing that most controllers are either instances of StandardSystemController or inherit from MouseMenuController. The few remaining controllers do not provide the usual blue button facilities that permit window resizing, framing, closing, and so on. Hence, they relinquish control whenever the blue button is depressed. Although this protocol should have been provided in the few classes that require it, it was placed in class Controller to avoid duplication.

Consider the other controllers. Screen controllers, for instance, retain control only as long as the yellow button is depressed. The more usual multi-paned window controllers, standard system controllers, retain control no matter where the mouse is as long as it isn't depressed outside the view. Most unscheduled controllers (a topic for later discussion) inherit from MouseMenuController. They retain control only while the mouse is currently in their view. That's why simply moving the mouse around to the different panes of a browser without clicking causes menu bars to pop up wherever the mouse is. Binary choice controllers insist that users select either **yes** or **no**. Moving the mouse outside the selection area causes the view to flash. Control is relinquished only after a choice is made by the user.

There is an important distinction between obtaining control (**isControlWanted**) and keeping it (**isControlActive**). For screen controllers, the two are the same: i.e., it is obtained and kept by keeping the yellow button depressed. For a standard system controller, control is obtained by simply having the mouse in the controller's view. To lose control, the user must explicitly click outside the view. This is evident when Smalltalk starts up. The window that becomes active is not the window you click on but the window that happens to be underneath the mouse. Similarly, if you click outside the windows, the current window loses control. The next window that gets control need not be clicked (touching it with the mouse is sufficient).

Now consider the default initialization (**controlInitialize**), main activity (**control-Activity**), and termination (**controlTerminate**) messages provided by class **Controller**.

controlInitialize
>"Do nothing"
>↑self

controlActivity
>"Startup an unscheduled subview controller (if there is one) that wants control."
>self **controlToNextLevel**

controlTerminate
>"Do nothing"
>↑self

where

controlToNextLevel
>| aSubView |
>aSubView ← view **subViewWantingControl**.
>aSubView ~~ nil **ifTrue:** [aSubView **controller startUp**]

The default initialization and termination is to do nothing. The main activity is simply to delegate control lower down the view hierarchy (if subviews are provided). If there are no subviews, the default is to do nothing. Note that a subview controller when started up is not scheduled through the window manager. It is simply started as part of the current process. When the subcontroller returns, execution continues without involving the process or window manager. Had it been scheduled as the active window process (via **schedule-Active:**), control would not have returned. The current window would have been deactivated and control could only be given to it again through the normal window manager search loop (it would start over at the beginning).

By contrast with Controller, the StandardSystemController provides initialization that **emphasizes** the title tab of the view by darkening it while termination **deemphasizes** it. Control activity is inherited from MouseMenuController; it is more complex since all mouse buttons are considered.

in StandardSystemController (old version without icons)

controlInitialize
    "The new version is more complex; handles caching for fast redrawing."
    view **displayEmphasized**.
    status ← #active

in MouseMenuController (inherited by StandardSystemController)

controlActivity
    "Handle the mouse buttons individually and then use the method in Controller for handing direct control to lower level unscheduled controllers."
    | insideView |
    insideView ← self **viewHasCursor**.
    sensor **redButtonPressed** & insideView **ifTrue**: [↑self **redButtonActivity**].
    sensor **yellowButtonPressed** & insideView **ifTrue**: [↑self **yellowButtonActivity**].
    sensor **blueButtonPressed** & insideView **ifTrue**: [↑self **blueButtonActivity**].
    super **controlActivity**

in StandardSystemController

controlTerminate
    "Handle specific statuses specially and make the view look inactive."
    status == #closed **ifTrue**: [*... releases the view, unschedules itself, and quits ...*].
    status == #inactive **ifTrue**: [*... cache display bits ...*].
    view **deEmphasize**
    ... additional caching code not shown ...

1.6.3 The Difference Between *startUp* and *open*

A controller can be given autonomous control by scheduling it explicitly using, for example,

        ScheduledControllers **scheduleActive**: anUnscheduledController

The more standard approach to achieving the same goal is to **open** the controller using

        anUnscheduledController **open**

Neither approach returns control to the sender. The sender regains control only by becoming the active window (again). Consequently, it will start executing at the beginning as it reacts to the normal **startUp** message.

On the other hand, sending a **startUp** message to a controller starts it executing in the current process. When it relinquishes control, a normal return is executed. Hence **open** is intended to start a new process with the sender losing control, and **startUp** is intended to execute the controller in the current process with the sender regaining control. Consequently, testing a new controller is best done by sending it a **startUp** message.

In practice, the **open** message has not been standardized across all controllers. It is understood by StandardSystemController (the controller for multi-paned windows) and its specializations. Variations of the messages include **open:**, **openBrowser**, **openOn:**, and **open:label:**. Additionally, many windows open the view instead of the controller. Examples include

```
StandardSystemController open
BrowserView openOn: SystemOrganization
ScreenController openBrowser
ProjectView open
ProjectView open: aProject
ProjectBrowser open
ChangeListView open
StringHolderView open
StringHolderView open: aStringHolder
TextCollectorView open
StringHolderView open: aStringHolder label: aString
TextCollectorView open: aTextCollector label: aString
```

Our discussion so far provides an intuitive feel for the workings of controllers. We have also seen examples of the methods used for providing this behavior. Some of the methods have been using messages that intuitively make sense but have never been discussed in detail. Consequently, we should understand enough to realize that designing new controllers requires methods (either explicitly written or inherited) called **isControlWanted**, **isControlActive**, **controlInitialize**, **controlActivity**, and **controlTerminate**. We may also need methods **redButtonActivity**, **yellowButtonActivity**, and **blueButtonActivity**. On the other hand, we don't have enough information about the specifics of controllers and views to actually go about designing a new window or even using existing windows for a specific application. That is the subject of the next chapter.

1.7 THE WINDOW TRANSFORMATION PROTOCOL

Windowing transformations are used to transform objects such as points and rectangles from one coordinate system (the **source coordinate system**) to another (the **destination coordinate system**). The transformation takes into account both a **scale** (a stretch or shrink factor applied to the coordinates) and a **translation** (an absolute displacement similarly applied). Scaling is relative to the origin of the source coordinate system; e.g., if a line from -10@0 to 10@0 is stretched by a factor of two, the left end stretches to -20@0, the center 0@0 is unchanged, and the right end stretches to 20@0. The further away from the origin, the more the points are displaced; e.g. 0@0 is displaced by 0 units, 5@0 by 5, and 10@0 by 10. Since the transformations are linear, a transformed multi-point object retains the same overall shape, although squares (see Fig. 1.13) can turn into rectangles and circles into elipses if the x- and y-scaling are different.

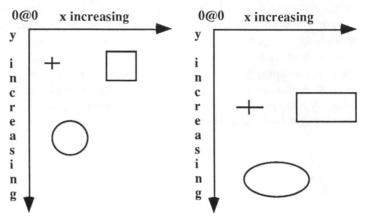

Figure 1.13 Scaling and translating points, rectangles, and circles.

In applying a windowing transformation to an object (see Fig. 1.14), *the object is first scaled* around the origin of the source coordinate system *and then translated*. If the translation were applied first, the scaling would be in terms of the destination coordinates instead of the source coordinates. This way, both scaling and translation are in terms of source coordinates.

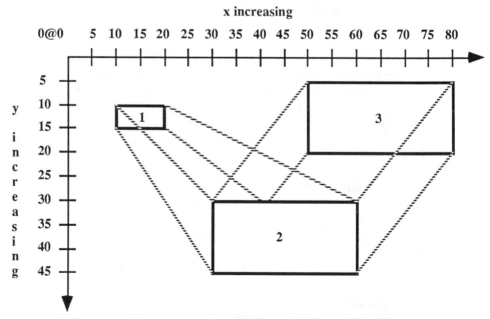

Figure 1.14 Scaling object 1 by 3, translating object 2 by 20@-25.

Windowing transformations can be applied to any object that responds to **scaleBy:** and **translateBy:** messages; e.g., display objects such as forms, display text, paths, arcs, curves, lines, and splines; along with points, rectangles, quadrangles, views, and windowing transformations themselves. It is also possible to apply a series of transformations (one after the other) to some object to successively transform it to a final shape and location. Such a series of transformations can easily be combined into a single transformation that achieves the same result.

Scaling and translation amounts can be specified with an integer, a float, or a point comprised of an integer or float; an **identity scale** (no stretching or shrinking) can also be specified as **nil**. A single integer or float indicates that both the x and y coordinates are to be transformed by the same amount. A point indicates that the x and y coordinates are transformed independently. For example, the identity scale can be specified either as **nil**, 1, 1.0, 1@1, 1.0@1.0, 1@1.0, or 1.0@1. Similarly, a **null translation** (no displacement) is indicated as 0, 0.0, 0@0, 0.0@0.0, 0@0.0, or 0.0@0 (in this case, **nil** is not allowed). An **identity transformation** can be specified as 'WindowingTransformation **scale:** nil **translation:** 0@0'.

Windowing transformations can be created with a default identity scale and translation, with a specified scale and translation, or with a scale and translation computed from a window (a rectangle in the source coordinate system) and a viewport (a rectangle in the destination coordinate system). The distinction between windows and viewports is considered in detail in the section on views. For this section, it is sufficient to think of the viewport simply as the window seen from the perspective of a destination coordinate system. In general, the windowing transformation protocol is required only in exceptional circumstances because it is superseded and managed more directly by views. Nevertheless, it is important to have a general understanding of the notions.

creating new windowing transformations

- WindowingTransformation **identity**
  Returns a windowing transformation with no scaling (nil) and no translation (0@0).

- View **identityTransformation**
  As above, returns an identity windowing transformation. Typically invoked automatically during view instantiation.

- WindowingTransformation **scale:** aScale **translation:** aTranslation
  Returns a windowing transformation with a scale factor of aScale and a translation of aTranslation. When the transformation is applied, the scale is applied first, followed by the translation.

- WindowingTransformation **window:** sourceRectangle **viewport:** destinationRectangle
  Returns a windowing transformation with a scale and translation computed from sourceRectangle and destinationRectangle. The scale and translation are computed such that sourceRectangle is transformed to destinationRectangle. This method might have been better named source:destination:.

querying the scale and translation

- aWindowingTransformation **scale**
  Returns a copy of the transformation's scale as a point.

- aWindowingTransformation **noScale**
  Returns **true** if the scaling is an identity scale and **false** otherwise.
- aWindowingTransformation **translation**
  Returns a copy of the transformation's translation as a point.

printing and storing

- aWindowingTransformation **printOn**: aStream
- aWindowingTransformation **storeOn**: aStream

Example

Although transformations are easily created explicitly via **identity** or **scale:translation:**, the more usual approach is to create them implicitly. For instance,

WindowingTransformation
    window: (0@0 **corner**: 10@10) **viewport**: (100@200 **corner**: 200@300)

creates a transformation that provides a scale of 10 and a translation of 100@200. Of course, we could have just as easily created the transformation using

WindowingTransformation **scale**: 10 **translation**: 100@200

On the other hand, it is a little more difficult to determine the transformation for the following:

WindowingTransformation
    window: (-10@-10 **corner**: 10@10) **viewport**: (200@200 **corner**: 500@500)

The answer is that the scale is 15 and the displacement is 350, not exactly intuitive. To see that it is right, consider the x coordinate of the top left corner; i.e. -10. When scaled by a factor of 15, it becomes -150, which when displaced by 350 becomes 200. Similarly, the x coordinate of the bottom right corner, i.e., 10, when scaled becomes 150, which when displaced by 350 becomes 500. The reflex approach to determining a transformation is to first consider the displacement, since it is so much easier than the scale, but this is wrong because translation is applied after scaling. Scaling must be determined first; e.g., by taking the length of the left side of the window (20 units) and determining the scale that gives the length of the left side of the viewport (300 units) ⇒ the scale is 300/20 or 15. Actually, this only gives us the scaling for the x coordinate; the same must be done for the y coordinate (it's the same by chance). After scaling -10@-10 to -150@-150, it is now relatively easy to determine the translation (350@350) that must be added to give the new top left corner 200@200.

    Once a transformation is constructed, it is sometimes necessary to modify or adjust it. For example, a temporary zoom effect could be achieved by scaling the transformation itself by 2. It can then be restored by scaling it by 0.5. Alternatively, a displacement could be added to change the destination coordinates. Sometimes this displacement is specified in source coordinates; at other times, it is specified in destination coordinates. **Scrolling** is the term used to refer to a displacement in source coordinates; method **scrollBy:** uses source coordinates for the displacement amount, and **translateBy:** uses destination coordinates.

- aWindowingTransformation **scaleOfOne**
  Changes the scale of the windowing transformation to the identity scale.
- aWindowingTransformation **scaleBy**: aScale
  Returns a new windowing transformation obtained by scaling both the original scale and translation.

adjusting the translation

- aWindowingTransformation **translateBy**: aDestinationAmountAsAPoint
  Returns a new windowing transformation displaced by the specified amount (given in destination coordinates).
- aWindowingTransformation **scrollBy**: aSourceAmountAsAPoint
  Returns a new windowing transformation displaced by 'aSourceAmountAs-APoint scaled by the current scale' (the amount is given in source coordinates); i.e., positive amounts move down (or right) and negative amounts up (or left).

adjusting the transformation

- aWindowingTransformation **align**: anOldDestinationPoint **with**: aNewDestinationPoint
  Returns a new windowing transformation displaced by an amount that transforms anOldDestinationPoint to aNewDestinationPoint.

Example

Suppose we had a large form, much too large for the screen, that contained a map to be displayed. We will ignore the actual details of the displaying protocol since they are not relevant to this discussion. More specifically, suppose that the map was 500 by 500 in size and that our window on the map was 100 by 100. Suppose this was to be displayed at an arbitrary scale and location determined by aDisplayRectangle. We could begin by creating a transformation that properly manages the change in viewpoint as follows:

```
| aWindow aTransformation |
aWindow ← 0@0 corner: 100@100.
aTransformation ← WindowingTransformation
      window: aWindow viewpoint: aDisplayRectangle
```

There are two things we might want to do in an application such as this: (1) move the display rectangle so that the same information is displayed at a different spot, or (2) move the window on the map so that different information is displayed in the display rectangle. Presumably, the amount by which to move the window would be in source coordinates, and the amount by which to move the display rectangle would be in destination coordinates. For later reference, suppose

aWindowAmount = aWindowXAmount@aWindowYAmount
aDisplayAmount = aDisplayXAmount@aDisplayYAmount

To move the location of the display rectangle by aDisplayAmount, it is sufficient to change the windowing transformation as follows:

```
aTransformation ← aTransformation translateBy: aDisplayAmount
```

Note that it is crucial for the display amount to be in destination coordinates. To move the window on the map without changing the display rectangle, two steps are needed. First, we move the window by changing the coordinates of the rectangle (no transformation is involved at this stage).

    aWindow **translateBy**: aWindowAmount

Note the need to have the window amount be in source coordinates. If the information underneath the window were displayed with the existing transformation, the display rectangle would display in a new location (we haven't changed the transformation). We can fix this by modifying the transformation so as to move the display rectangle back to its original location.

    aNegatedWindowAmount ← aWindowXAmount **negated** @ aWindowYAmount **negated**
    aTransformation ← aTransformation **scrollBy**: aNegatedWindowAmount

As required by the scrolling method, the scroll amount must be in source coordinates. Being able to transform the window and the windowing transformation in terms of source coordinates was handy. Had we used **translateBy:** instead of **scrollBy:**, we would have been forced to convert aNegatedWindowAmount into destination coordinates.

Let's try it just for fun. For a more concrete value to work with, suppose aNegatedWindowAmount were -10@-10 for simplicity. If we interpret these as lengths (ignoring signs), it should be clear that such lengths would be scaled to the new length '10 * aTransformation **scale**'. Displacing the window by 10 units in source coordinates must be equivalent to displacing the display rectangle by '10 * aTransformation **scale**' in destination coordinates. This should justify the following computation:

    aDisplayXAmount ← aWindowXAmount * aTransformation **scale**
    aDisplayYAmount ← aWindowYAmount * aTransformation **scale**
    aNegatedDisplayAmount ← aDisplayXAmount **negated** @ aDisplayYAmount **negated**
    aTransformation ← aTransformation **translateBy**: aNegatedDisplayAmount

The more general protocol for applying transformations and their inverses, along with the protocol for composing a series of transformations, are considered next.

applying and composing transformations

- aWindowingTransformation **applyTo**: anObject
  Applies the transformation to anObject and returns the result. Used to map an object in source coordinates to one in destination coordinates.

- aWindowingTransformation **applyInverseTo**: anObject
  Applies the inverse of the transformation to anObject and returns the result. Used to map an object in destination coordinates to one in source coordinates.

- aWindowingTransformation **compose**: aTransformation
  Returns a new windowing transformation that combines the receiver and aTransformation into one; i.e., the new transformation applied to an object gives the same result as first applying the receiver to the object and then applying aTransformation to its result.

Example

The following provides a simple illustration of the above protocol:

```
| aTransformation |
aTransformation ← WindowingTransformation scale: 10 translation: 50.
aTransformation applyTo: 0@1 ⇒ 50@60
aTransformation applyInverseTo: 50@60 ⇒ 0@1

anotherTransformation ← aTransformation compose: aTransformation
        ⇒ WindowingTransformation scale: 100 translation: 550
aTransformation applyTo: 50@60 ⇒ 550@650
anotherTransformation applyTo: 0@1 ⇒ 550@650
```

1.7.1 Relationships with Other Classes

We mentioned previously that some of the transformation operations can be applied to several graphical classes. We will document them here for completeness. More important is the notion that display operations can be provided with a transformation to control the final visual result. The more important operation, from the point of view of users, is **displayOn:transformation:clippingBox:**. However, it is not defined for all displayable objects (it should be). In that case, it is usually possible to use the more general operation **displayOn:transformation:clippingBox:rule:mask:** instead.

adjusting the scaling

- aGraphicalObject **scaleBy**: aScale$^{\$\$}$
    Returns a new graphical object obtained by scaling the original. For forms and their variations, only the offset is scaled (not the form itself).

adjusting the translation

- aGraphicalObject **translateBy**: anAmountAsAPoint$^{\$\$}$
    Returns a new graphical object displaced by the specified amount.
- aGraphicalObject **moveBy**: anAmountAsAPoint[*]
    Same as above but restricted to rectangles and quadrangles.
- aGraphicalObject **moveTo**: aPoint[*]
    Returns a new graphical object whose origin is moved to the specified point. Restricted to rectangles and quadrangles.
- aGraphicalObject **align**: anOldPoint **with**: aNewPoint$^{\$}$
    Returns a new graphical object displaced by an amount that moves anOldPoint to aNewPoint.

displaying

For the following methods, "..." denotes
        displayOn: aDisplayMedium
        transformation: aTransformation
        clippingBox: aRectangle

- aGraphicalObject ...[***]
- aGraphicalObject ... **rule**: aRuleNumber **mask**: aForm[**]
- aGraphicalObject ... **align**: anOldPoint **with**: aNewPoint[**]

- aGraphicalObject ...**align**:anOldPoint **with**:aNewPoint **rule**:aRuleNumber **mask**: aForm[**]
  Displays the graphical object on the display medium taking into account the transformation and clipping area. When omitted, assumes the rule 'Form over' and the mask 'Form black'. When provided, alignment points are in destination coordinates. See Appendix A for a more thorough discussion.

Exceptions
$$: Applicable to display objects (forms, cursors, display text, paths, ...), points, rectangles, quadrangles, views, and transformations.

$: Applicable to display objects, rectangles, quadrangles, views, and transformations (points excluded).

***: Applicable to display objects and quadrangles.

**: Applicable to display objects.

*: Applicable to rectangles and quadrangles only.

Example

To illustrate the display messages using transformations, we construct six special paths in two rows of three squares, as shown in Fig. 1.15.

Figure 1.15 Displaying objects via display transformations.

More specifically, we display a line, a circle, a curve followed by a path, a linear fit, and a spline (these last three consist of the same five points).

```
| aDot aLine aCircle aCurve aPath aLinearFit aSpline aTransformation aBox d t |
aDot ← (Form extent: 4@4) black.

"Create display objects intended for display on a 10 by 10 area."
aLine ← Line from: 2@2 to: 8@8 withForm: aDot.
aCircle ← Circle new form: aDot; radius: 4; center: 5@5; yourself.
aCurve ← Curve new
       form: aDot; firstPoint: 2@8; secondPoint: 5@2; thirdPoint: 8@8; yourself.
aPath ← Path new
       form: aDot; add: 2@8; add: 2@2; add: 5@8; add: 8@2; add: 8@8; yourself.
aLinearFit ← LinearFit new
       form: aDot; add: 2@8; add: 2@2; add: 5@8; add: 8@2; add: 8@8; yourself.
aSpline ← Spline new
       form: aDot; add: 2@8; add: 2@2; add: 5@8; add: 8@2; add: 8@8; yourself.
aSpline computeCurve. "Otherwise, the spline cannot be displayed"

"Display them in two rows of three squares each 113 by 113 units (just to pick an odd size)."
aTransformation ← WindowingTransformation
       window: (0@0 corner: 10@10) viewport: (0@0 corner: 113@113).
aBox ← Display boundingBox. "The rectangle for the entire display"
```

Display **white**. "Start with a nice display"

d ← Display. t ← aTransformation. "Just to fit subsequent statements into one line."
aLine **displayOn**: d **transformation**: t **clippingBox**: aBox **align**: 0@0 **with**: 100@100.
aCircle **displayOn**: d **transformation**: t **clippingBox**: aBox **align**: 0@0 **with**: 213@100.
aCurve **displayOn**: d **transformation**: t **clippingBox**: aBox **align**: 0@0 **with**: 326@100.
aPath **displayOn**: d **transformation**: t **clippingBox**: aBox **align**: 0@0 **with**: 100@213.
aLinearFit **displayOn**: d **transformation**: t **clippingBox**: aBox **align**: 0@0 **with**: 213@213.
aSpline **displayOn**: d **transformation**: t **clippingBox**: aBox **align**: 0@0 **with**: 326@213.

"By aligning 0@0 with 213@100, for example, we are causing the display to shift right
by 213 pixels. Clearly, 213 must be in destination coordinates. If it were in source
coordinates, the actual amount shifted would be 't applyTo: 213'; to get exactly 213, we
would have to actually supply 't applyInverseTo: 213' (the display method would then
transform it to cancel out the inverse operation; i.e., 't applyTo: (t applyInverseTo: 213)'
is 213."

ScheduledControllers **restore**. "To place the display into its previous state"

1.8 SUMMARY

This chapter has provided a first introduction to Smalltalk windows and the supporting
classes. In particular, we have discussed the following notions:

- Window creation for the novice.

- The overall philosophy underlying the model-view-controller (MVC) paradigm.

- Process management and window management (a special case).

- Dependency maintenance and how it can be used to relate windows to the objects
  they are displaying.

- Window transformations.

1.9 EXERCISES

*The following exercises may require some original thought, rereading some of the material,
and/or browsing through the system.*

1. Design an example method that
   prompts a user for his name and
   whether or not he is a novice.

2. Design an example method that
   provides a menu of all possible
   cursors for the user to choose from.
   If a choice is made, change the
   current cursor to the selected cursor.

3. Revise the solution to the **duck
   imprinting** problem to use opaque
   forms instead of the standard forms
   used in the original.

4. Change the implementation of ducks
   so that they keep track of a master
   form on which to draw. When a
   mother quacks, she can clear the
   master form, have all the ducklings
   display themselves on the form using
   'Form **under**', for example, and then
   display the master form on the
   display.

5. Change the implementation of class DemonstrationLight to avoid using the dependency mechanism. Hint: Keep a collection of all lights accessible by the on block.

6. Change the implementation of class DemonstrationLight so that all lights blink while the mouse button is depressed (like a Xmas tree).

7. Use the **factorialViaProcesses** method as a guideline for designing another operation that uses multiple processes for its solution; e.g., fibonacci, sort, and interactive querying, as in Question 1.

8. Test the Delay class by writing a code fragment that clears the screen and, ten seconds later, restores the display.

9. Write a code fragment that pops up a form for one second at ten-second intervals. Is there any way to disable this code if no previous precautions were taken?

10. Explain why it is not possible to implement a version of **collect:**, say for arrays, that logically computes the elements in parallel using processes. Hint: Consider the semantics of blocks.

11. Describe how the shared queue methods **next** and **nextPut:** would have to be modified for a specialization called BoundedSharedQueue.

12. Choose one of the collection classes like Array or Set and design a corresponding shared specialization.

13. Construct a quadrangle with a non-zero width border. Use windowing transformations to display it along a circle. Additionally, have the quadrangle grow as it traces the circle.

1.10 GLOSSARY AND IMPORTANT FACTS

classes

ControlManager A class with one instance called the window manager, kept in global variable **ScheduledControllers**, that is responsible for coordinating the activation and deactivation of the window controllers.

Delay A class of objects used to suspend an active process either for a particular **duration** or until a specified **wakeup time** occurs.

InputSensor A class with one instance in global variable **Sensor** that is responsible for keeping track of the keyboard and mouse events.

MessageTally A class that can provide a simple run-time execution profile of an executing block. The two principal class methods are 'MessageTally **spyOn:** aBlock' and 'MessageTally **spyOn:** aBlock **to:** aFile'.

ProcessScheduler A class with one instance called the **process manager**, kept in global variable **Processor**, which is responsible for coordinating the activation and deactivation of processes.

Semaphore A class of objects used for synchronizing parallel communicating processes.

SharedQueue A class of queues designed for use by parallel processes.

Switch A class of objects that can either be **on** or **off**. Additionally, both **on** and **off action** blocks (default **nil**) can be associated with the switch for execution when it is **turned on** or **off** respectively.

WindowingTransformation A class of objects used to transform geometric objects such as points and rectangles from one coordinate system to another.

controller The object that handles the keyboard and mouse interactions.

dependent An arbitrary object that is affected by changes to a sponsor.

destination coordinate system The coordinate system to which a windowing transformation is intended to transform.

model The object being displayed and/or modified by a window's view or controller.

process A block that is independently scheduled for execution in parallel with other processes.

process manager Responsible for managing all processes in the system; uses a number of process queues, each handling a different priority. The process manager is kept in global variable **Processor**, an instance of class **ProcessScheduler**.

scale A stretch or shrink factor maintained by a windowing transformation.

source coordinate system The coordinate system being transformed by a windowing transformation.

sponsor An arbitrary object whose modification can affect other objects called dependents.

translation An absolute displacement maintained by a windowing transformation.

view The object that determines the precise manner in which the model is to be displayed.

window Colloquially used to mean either a class or set of classes designed to present a purposeful graphical interface (a more technical definition is discussed in the next chapter).

window manager Responsible for managing one process, the process that keeps track of the scheduled window controllers. The window manager is kept in global variable **ScheduledControllers**, an instance of class **ControlManager**.

important facts

dependency maintenance A mechanism concerned with providing a simplified notification facility between **sponsors** (objects whose changes may affect others) and **dependents** (objects affected). A sponsor simply notifies itself of an event worthy of notification, and the dependency maintenance mechanism informs all dependents.

MVC triad A model-view-controller triple that distinguishes input processing (the **controller**) from output processing (the **view**) and the object being processed (the **model**).

pluggable views General views designed for *plugging-in* information specific to an application. Browsers are an example using the methodology. The alternative is to create application specific classes by specialization.

process control At any one time, there is exactly one process executing — the **active** process. All other processes are either **suspended** or awaiting execution. Suspended processes and new processes can be made available for execution by sending them a **resume** message or by executing a **signal** on a semaphore. A process that is active or awaiting execution can be made unavailable by sending it a **suspend** message, by requesting that it be delayed, or by performing a **wait** on a semaphore. Processes are created by sending special messages **fork**, **forkAt:**, **newProcess**, and **newProcessWith:** to blocks. A process that has already been scheduled can be unscheduled temporarily with a **suspend** message and permanently with a **terminate** message. An active process can be rescheduled at the end of the queue of waiting processes (there is a separate queue for each priority) by sending a **yield** message.

testing controllers Send it a **startUp** message instead of an **open** message. The **startUp** message permits control to be returned to the sender of the message; the **open** message does not (it makes the new controller active, which causes the current scheduled controller to become inactive — when later reactivated, it restarts at the beginning instead of continuing where it left off).

time delays A **delay** is an object that can be used to suspend an active process. It also encodes either a **duration** (a length of time during which the process must remain suspended) or a **wakeup time** (the time at which the process must be resumed). An active process is delayed by sending a **wait** message to the delay.

2

Windows: An Overview and Basics

2.1 INTRODUCTION

As we will see later when we discuss viewports and display boxes, the term window has a precise technical meaning in Smalltalk. Nevertheless, window is also used in another entirely different but more intuitive sense. It is used to denote a portion of a graphical interface that is designed to interact in a particular way with its users. By the term **window**, we mean the class or set of classes that collectively provide this interface component. Hence, we consider the screen to consist of many windows and subwindows, with some partially or totally occluded by others.

A **window** is defined by the model-view-controller (MVC) triple that implements it. For some classes of windows, the model, view, and controller are integrated into one class. For others, the model is required to satisfy particular requirements; e.g., that it be a string. Sometimes, the model can be provided by users of the window. At other times, it is already provided as part of the window. In that case, the user's model (if any) is imbedded within the window model; i.e., a model for the model.

2.1.1 A Logical Characterization

Windows (see Fig. 2.1) can be partitioned into two classes: **permanently visible windows** and **pop-up windows**; i.e., windows that appear suddenly when an interaction request is required and then immediately disappear after an appropriate reply.

The pop-up windows exist in two varieties: **pop-up menu windows** and **pop-up text-query windows**. Pop-up menu windows provide users with a choice of menu entries to select from. It is also possible to make no choice. Pop-up text-query windows are used to request a textual response to some query; **pop-up binary text-query windows** are a special case in which the response is either **yes** or **no**.

The permanently visible windows are either **scrollable** or **nonscrollable**. Scrollable windows typically provide access to information that is too voluminous to be displayed in its entirety on the screen. Consequently, only a small part is visible at a time. Other parts can be made visible either by **scrolling up** or **scrolling down**. Nonscrollable windows, on the other hand, are designed to display smaller amounts of information that can be completely displayed on the screen. Hence, scrolling is not provided.

The scrollable windows include **text windows** and **menu windows**. The text windows provide facilities for creating and editing textual information. The menu windows permit scrolling over collections of strings. Selecting one causes the associated model to be notified and modified in some way. Although it is not noticeable from the logical viewpoint, the number of specialized text windows far exceeds the other classes of windows in number and complexity.

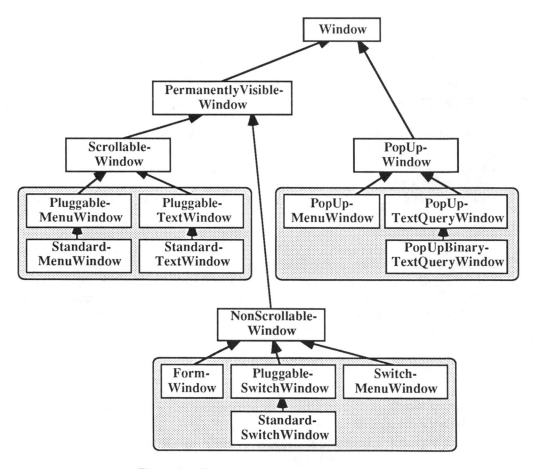

Figure 2.1 The window hierarchy: A logical view.

Varieties of text and menu windows are also provided that permits more customization than the **standard** windows. These are termed **pluggable windows**; in particular, **pluggable text windows** and **pluggable menu windows**. Pluggable windows are designed to display some user-specifiable aspect of an arbitrary model. The **standard windows** on the other hand do not permit such flexibility. Pluggable text windows permit some arbitrary textual aspect of a model to be displayed and modified. Pluggable menu windows permit the menu aspect of a model to be displayed in a permanent scrollable window. Selecting a menu item can have side effects on the model.

The nonscrollable windows include **form windows, switch windows,** and **switch-menu windows.** Form windows permit pictorial or graphical information to be displayed. Switch windows permit switches, buttons, and one-on switches to be graphically displayed and manipulated. Switch-menu windows are used for building editors that require menus of buttons. For example, they could be used for designing a graphical editor that uses buttons to specify whether the current object to be drawn is a circle, a square, or a line.

Standard switch windows can be used for typical applications, since they are provided with most of the capability of **pluggable switch windows.** However, the latter does conform to the same convention that the other pluggable windows adhere to. Typically, standard switch windows are used for switch models, even though more general models can be used. Pluggable switch windows are used to permit some aspect of an arbitrary model to be viewed and modified as if it were an on/off property of the object.

Since windows are decomposed into models, views, and controllers, there should correspondingly exist a model hierarchy, view hierarchy, and controller hierarchy. Generally speaking, classes **View** and **Controller** respectively lie at the top of the view and controller hierarchies. There is also a model hierarchy with class **Model** at the top. However, not all models are in this hierarchy; e.g., strings are models for display text views.

2.1.2 The Typical Window Models

There are a number of classes (see Fig. 2.2) privately used by text and menu window controllers for maintaining the working text and menu information; namely, **Paragraph,**

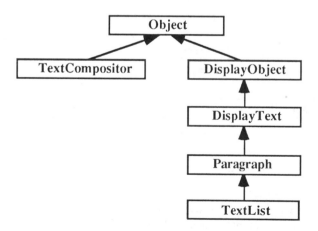

Figure 2.2 Private support classes for text window controllers.

TextCompositor, and **TextList**. Because they are intimately related to the models and because they are used pervasively by the controllers, they are sometimes confused with the models. We have explicitly differentiated them from the typical window models (see Fig. 2.3) to highlight this distinction.

There are a number of important classes (see Fig. 2.3) that serve as models for specific view/controller pairs. Class **Model** duplicates the dependency maintenance protocol provided by class Object. Its instances record dependency information locally. Hence, failure to release dependents in error situations is inconsequential. By comparison, unreleased dependencies recorded in class **Object** must ultimately be physically removed by the user. Classes **TextCollector**, **StringHolder**, and **TextHolder**, in particular, provide models for permanently visible text and pluggable text windows. There are no classes designed specifically to serve as models for permanently visible menu windows. The **Switch**, **Button**, and **OneOnSwitch** classes provide models for the switch and pluggable switch windows. The **Icon** class is the model for **collapsed** windows; i.e., windows shrunk to contain only a label tab or small form. The **FillInTheBlank** class provides models for the pop-up text-query windows. Finally, the **BinaryChoice** class provides models for pop-up binary text-query windows. There are other classes of objects that serve as models for browsers, debuggers, and inspectors. We will not be considering these models specifically, although we will be considering the basic concepts used in their implementation.

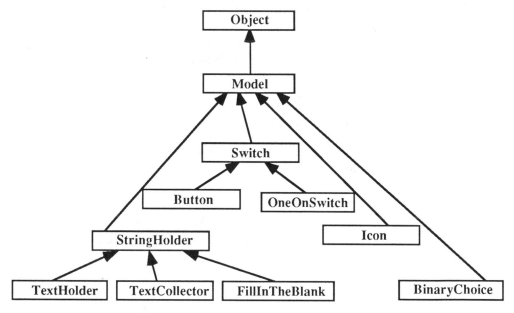

Figure 2.3 A subset of the Model hierarchy.

2.1.3 The View Hierarchy

The view hierarchy (see Fig. 2.4) is shallow by comparison with the controller hierarchy. One reason for this is the extensive generality provided by class **View**. Class **Standard-SystemView** complements **StandardSystemController**, the only controller designed specifically to be a scheduled controller. Class **IconView** supports the icon controller for

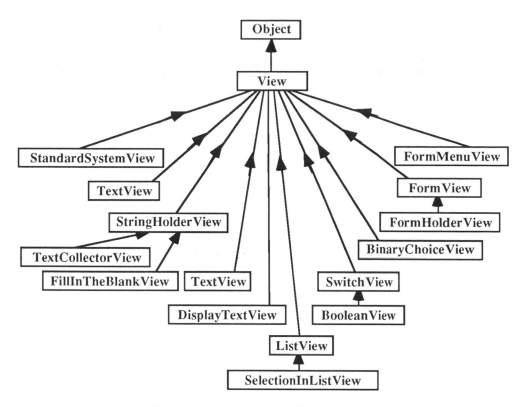

Figure 2.4 A subset of the View hierarchy.

displaying collapsed windows. **StringHolderView**, **TextCollectorView**, **TextView**, and **DisplayTextView** are part of text windows and pluggable text windows. **FillInTheBlank-View** and **BinaryChoiceView** are part of pop-up text-query windows and pop-up binary text-query windows respectively. **ListView** and **SelectionInListView** are used for menu windows and pluggable menu windows respectively; **SwitchView** and **BooleanView** for switch windows and pluggable switch windows respectively; and **FormView** and **FormHolderView** for form windows. Finally, **FormMenuView** is part of switch-menu windows.

2.1.4 The Controller Hierarchy

The controller hierarchy (see Fig. 2.5) is much deeper than the view hierarchy. Except for classes **PopUpMenu** and **ActionMenu**, which combine the model-view-controller notion into one, class **Controller** provides the basic protocol for all other controllers. Class **NoController** provides the proper interface for controllers that ignore mouse and keyboard interactions. Class **MouseMenuController** provides the basic protocol for controllers that have yellow, red, and blue button pop-up menus. **StandardSystemController** is the only class specifically designed to be a scheduled controller. Class **IconController** manages collapsed windows. **ScrollController** provides the template for subclasses that provide up and down scrolling capabilities. **ScreenController** manages the screen background. It provides a special yellow button menu. Classes **ParagraphEditor** and **TextEditor**, along with their subclasses (except for classes **FillInTheBlankController** and **CRFillInThe-BlankController**), provide the controller protocol for text and pluggable text windows. **ListController** and its subclasses similarly provide the controller protocol for menu and pluggable menu windows. **SwitchController** and its subclasses provide support for switch windows and pluggable switch windows. The **FillInTheBlankController** class and its subclass support pop-up text-query windows, and the **BinaryChoiceController** class supports pop-up binary text-query windows. **FormMenuController** supports switch-menu windows.

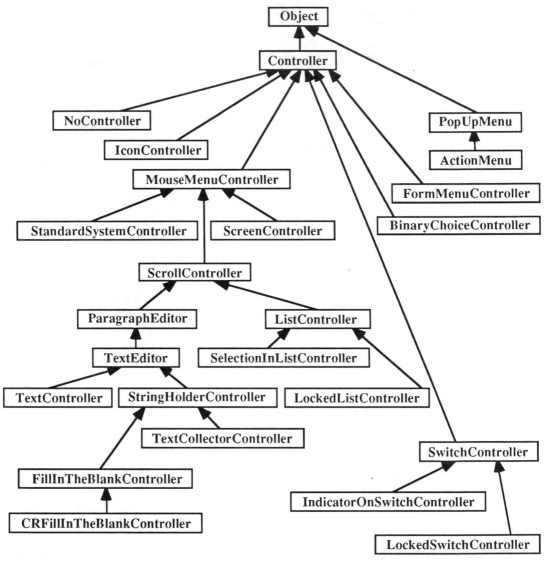

Figure 2.5 A subset of the Controller hierarchy.

2.1.5 Windows versus MVCs

The model-view-controller (MVC) paradigm permits some mix and match between different models, views, and controllers. However, arbitrary mixing is not possible. It makes little sense to try to match a menu controller with a switch view, for example. In this section, we summarize the combinations that were explicitly designed for in the system. With care, other combinations might also be created.

Windows
  Pop-Up Windows
    Pop-Up Menu Windows
      PopUpMenu (a combined model-view-controller)
      ActionMenu (a combined model-view-controller)
    Pop-Up Text-Query Windows
      FillInTheBlank-FillInTheBlankView-FillInTheBlankController
      FillInTheBlank-FillInTheBlankView-CRFillInTheBlankController
    Pop-Up Binary Text-Query Windows
      BinaryChoice-BinaryChoiceView-BinaryChoiceController
  Permanently Visible Windows
    Scrollable Windows
    Text Windows
      Pluggable Text Windows
        AnyObjectWithATextLikeAspect-TextView-TextController
      Standard Text Windows
        StringHolder-StringHolderView-StringHolderController
        TextHolder-StringHolderView-StringHolderController
        TextCollector-TextCollectorView-TextCollectorController
        Paragraph-DisplayTextView-NoController
    Menu Windows
      Pluggable Menu Windows
        AnyObjectWithAMenuLikeAspect-SelectionInListView-
            SelectionInListController
      Standard Menu Windows
        TextList-ListView-ListController
        TextList-ListView-LockedListController
    Nonscrollable Windows
    Form Windows
      Form-FormView-FormEditor
      Form-FormHolderView-FormEditor
      Form-FormView-NoController
      Form-FormHolderView-NoController
    Switch Windows
      Pluggable Switch Windows
        AnyObjectWithASwitchLikeAspect-BooleanView-SwitchController
      Standard Switch Windows
        SwitchOrButtonOrOneOnSwitch-SwitchView-SwitchController
        SwitchOrButtonOrOneOnSwitch-SwitchView-IndicatorOnSwitchController
        SwitchOrButtonOrOneOnSwitch-SwitchView-LockedSwitchController
    Switch-Menu Windows
      ACollectionOfSwitches-FormMenuView-FormMenuController
      (model not explicitly used)

2.1.6 The Basic Models, Controllers, and Views

Models, controllers, and **views** are the three components in the model-view-controller (MVC) triad that serve to represent and implement windows. The **model** provides the details to be displayed in the window. The **controller**'s responsibility is to interface with the window manager and dispatch keyboard and mouse events to the other components of the triad, the model, and the view. The **view**'s responsibility is to display the model and provide visual feedback for controller interactions, to manage hierarchies of interrelated views, and to provide both an automatic resizing and repositioning facility and a coordinate transformation facility.

There is an extremely large number of models, controllers, and views in the system. Most are highly specialized. Nevertheless, they are based on one basic model class, four basic controller classes, and two basic view classes. The basic model class is Model (see Fig. 2.6). The basic controllers (see Fig. 2.7) include Controller, MouseMenuController, StandardSystemController, and NoController. The basic views (see Fig. 2.8) include View and StandardSystemView.

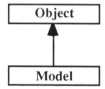

Figure 2.6 A portion of the Model hierarchy.

Model serves as the base for constructing special window models. It duplicates the dependency maintenance mechanism provided by class Object, but differs in storing this information locally rather than globally. If the model is no longer referenced, the dependency information is also no longer accessible. By constrast, this will not happen if the dependency mechanism in Object is used.

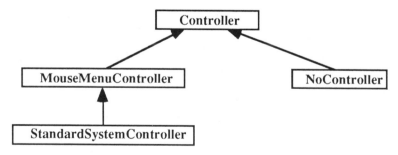

Figure 2.7 A portion of the Controller hierarchy.

Controller provides the basic protocol for interfacing with the window manager. Its control activity merely hands over control to subordinate unscheduled controllers (if there are any). **NoController** interfaces by doing nothing in all cases. **MouseMenuController** refines the basic control activity protocol by distinguishing between the three mouse buttons and activating specific menu responses. **StandardSystemController** is designed specifically to play the role of a scheduled controller; it directly supports subordinate unscheduled controllers.

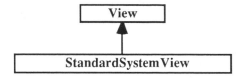

Figure 2.8 A portion of the View hierarchy.

The view hierarchy (see Fig. 2.8) is much simpler. On the other hand, class **View** itself is much more complex than the corresponding **Controller** class. It provides almost all the required display functionality, including the management of hierarchies of views. **StandardSystemView** elaborates the view protocol by providing a view that can be distinguished as belonging to a scheduled controller. In particular, it provides a label box that serves to identify the view.

In the sections that follow, we will consider classes **Controller** and **View** separately in great detail. We start with class **Controller** because it is simpler. Then we will consider the remaining controllers and views. Finally, we consider more complex specializations.

2.2 THE MODEL CLASS

Class **Model** duplicates exactly the dependency maintenance mechanism provided by class **Object**. Unlike class **Object**, which stores the dependency information in a global dictionary, class **Model** stores it locally in each instance. For a detailed explanation of the dependency mechanism and the associated protocol, see Sect. 1.4, *Dependency Maintenance*. Since the protocol is exactly the same, there is no point in duplicating it here. However, it is important to consider the advantages of the new class.

When a window is opened, the model is associated with the view. This causes the view to become a dependent of the model. When the window is closed, the controller releases the view, which in turn removes itself from the model's collection of dependents. If the actual model used inherits from **Model**, the dependency information is kept locally in the model; otherwise, it is recorded in a global dictionary. Two advantages result from local storage.

1. Finding the dependents is faster. Hence, the change/update protocol used by the MVC triad is speeded up.

2. Failure to release the view because of an unrecoverable error — usually while the window is undergoing testing — can be safely ignored.

The last point is important and needs further explanation. Suppose a new class of windows is being developed. Assume the model does not inherit from **Model**. Several things can go wrong. The close facility might be improperly implemented so that it is not possible to close the window. The controller might refuse to accept control after it has relinquished it so that it is impossible to close it. The view might encounter an error every time it attempts to display the model. So every time the designer attempts to activate the window, an error notifier pops up before it can be closed. If an error notifier appears or it is possible to interrupt it, the designer can eliminate the problem window by explicitly unscheduling it from the window manager. For example, if any controller or view associated with the window can be found in the debugger, the following will remove the window from the window manager:

```
self "assuming a controller" view topView release.
ScheduledControllers
        unschedule: self "assuming a controller" view topView controller
```

Typically, the designer will forget to release the view. If this occurs often — as may be the case when a complex new window is being developed — the system will progressively have less and less space available. The reason is that the model (typically a new one each time the window is tested) and the view are permanently recorded in the global dependency dictionary. Inspecting the global DependentsFields dictionary, as shown in the following, will allow the designer to see all the old models and their views.

```
DependentsFields inspect
```

He can then explicitly remove them while in the inspector. This will both speed up the system and free up unused space. If the new window being designed makes use of a standard system view as the top view (not all of them do), the window can be removed in a simpler way.

```
self "assuming a controller" view topView closeAndUnschedule
```

In that case, the top view is properly released and no problems will occur. An alternative to this scenario is to have the new model inherit from **Model**. If an error results in that case, unscheduling the controller using either of the above techniques will work without having to worry about releasing the view. The reason is simple. By unscheduling the controller, no external references to the MVC triad will exist. Although a cycle of mutual references exists in the triad, the triad will ultimately be garbage collected away. This couldn't happen when the dependency information was stored globally. The conclusion is simple — "where possible, it is advantageous to inherit from **Model**".

2.3 THE CONTROLLER CLASS

Class **Controller** provides the basic interface between windows and the window manager. Its primary role is to furnish the protocol for obtaining, maintaining, and relinquishing control. This protocol is concerned entirely with mouse interactions. Keyboard interactions and more sophisticated mouse interactions are provided through specializations of the **Controller** class. The **Controller** class also serves as an interface for the corresponding model and view.

2.3.1 Creating Controllers (a Preview)

As we will see later, controllers are typically created automatically by their associated views when they are needed. Users create the view; the view creates the controller. On the other hand, the controller that is created is the default controller for the view. Sometimes, users wish to use nonstandard controllers; e.g., switch views can be used with three classes of controllers. Creating a nonstandard controller is as simple as creating an arbitrary object.

aControllerClass **new**

The newly created controller is fully initialized. Applications developers making use of the existing facilities have no need to understand the more detailed controller protocol. Of course, those who need to create specializations will need to understand controllers in more detail.

2.3.2 The Controller Protocol

The controller protocol consists of approximately twenty methods. A cursory knowledge of processes and window management is required to understand the protocol in detail.

creating new controllers

- Controller **new**
  Returns an initialized controller. Thus, subclasses need only provide instance method **initialize** when providing specializations.

initializing and releasing controllers

- aController **initialize**
  Initializes the controller by associating the default sensor with it (usually, the mouse). Subclasses should include 'super initialize' when redefining this message to ensure proper initialization.
- aController **release**
  Breaks the cycle between the controller and its view; i.e., sets the view's controller to **nil** (if the view was non**nil**) and also the controller's view to **nil**. In an MVC triad, the standard convention is to release only the view; it in turn automatically sends a release message to the associated controller.

access to the model, view, and sensor

- aController **model**
  Returns the controller's model.
- aController **model**: aModel
  Changes the receiver's model.

- aController **view**
  Returns the controller's view.
- aController **view**: aView
  Changes the controller's view.

- aController **sensor**
  Returns the controller's sensor.
- aController **sensor**: aSensor
  Changes the controller's sensor. Subclasses may use other objects that are not instances of Sensor or its subclasses if more general kinds of input/output functions are required.

testing for control

- aController **isControlWanted**

    This message is normally sent to determine whether or not *control is desired by a controller that does not yet have control*. In the protocol of class **Controller, true** is returned if the associated view contains the mouse cursor. This method is often redefined in specializations.

- aController **isControlActive**

    This message is normally sent to determine whether or not *control is to be retained by a controller that already has control*. In the protocol of class **Controller, true** is returned if the cursor is inside the view and the blue button is not pressed. Consequently, pressing the blue button normally causes control to be relinquished to a higher level controller that usually responds with the standard reframe/close pop-up menu. This method is often redefined in specializations.

providing control

- aController **startUp**

    Gives control to the controller via the standard control sequence shown below.

    > self **controlInitialize**.
    > self **controlLoop**.
    > self **controlTerminate**

    Afterward, control is returned to the sender of the **startUp** message. This control sequence is used to coordinate the interactions with its view and model. In general, it consists of polling the sensor for user input, testing the input with respect to the current display of the view, and updating the model to reflect intended changes.

- aController **controlInitialize**

    Sent by **startUp** as part of the standard control sequence. It provides a place in the standard control sequence for initializing the controller (taking into account the current state of its model and view). In the protocol of class **Controller**, it does *nothing*. This method is often redefined in specializations to perform some specific action.

- aController **controlLoop**

    Sent by **startUp** as part of the standard control sequence. It provides a place in the standard control sequence for maintaining control. In the protocol of class **Controller**, the following code is executed. Note the use of **yield** to ensure that control is not maintained for an indefinitely long period of time. It causes the window manager to be rescheduled at the end of the queue without changing its priority. This does not cause other windows to become active, since there is only one active window managed by the window manager. However, it will permit other nonwindow tasks at the same priority to begin execution; e.g., tasks initiated by the window process (see processes and the window manager for more details).

    > [self **isControlActive**] **whileTrue**: [Processor **yield**. self **controlActivity**]

    In specializations, **isControlActive** and **controlActivity** are often redefined.

- aController **controlTerminate**

  Sent by **startUp** as part of the standard control sequence. It provides a place in the standard control sequence for terminating the controller (taking into account the current state of its model and view). In the protocol of class **Controller**, it does *nothing*. This method is often redefined in specializations to perform some specific action.

- aController **controlActivity**

  Sent as part of the standard control loop. It provides a place in the standard control sequence for controlling the MVC triad. In the protocol of class **Controller**, control is simply passed down to a lower level controller, if there is one, by executing the following code:

  > self **controlToNextLevel**

  This method is *almost always* redefined in specializations to perform some specific action.

- aController **controlToNextLevel**

  Passes control to a subcontroller if one exists that wants control. In the protocol of class **Controller**, the view actually interrogates the controllers of the associated subviews. Hence, the controller must have a corresponding view associated with it. In particular, the following code is executed:

  > | aView |
  > aView ← view **subViewWantingControl**.
  > aView ~~ nil **ifTrue**: [aView **controller startUp**]

  Note that the subcontroller (if one exists) is given control without scheduling it. Hence, it executes in the process of the current controller and also returns when it relinquishes control. This method is *never redefined* (so far) in specializations.

cursor interrogations

- aController **centerCursorInView**

  Positions the sensor's mousePoint (which is assumed to be connected to the cursor) at the center of the associated view's inset display box (see **insetDisplayBox** in **View**). Some Smalltalk implementations insist that the users have complete control of the mouse; hence, this method is a no-op. Other implementations move the mouse to the designated point independent of where it used to be.

- aController **viewHasCursor**

  Returns **true** if the cursor point of the receiver's sensor lies within the inset display box of the receiver's view (see **insetDisplayBox** in **View**) and **false** otherwise.

2.3.3 Using the Controller Protocol: The ESP Game

As an aid to understanding the protocol provided, we consider an application with a simplified view that we will construct ourselves. Our goal will be to create a version of the Extra Sensory Perception (ESP) game; i.e., a game that permits players to guess which of a number of possible pictures (maximum 9) the system will choose next. Three classes are defined: ESPGame, ESPController, and ESPView.

Class ESPGame provides a simple but complete protocol for playing the game independent of whether or not there is an associated controller or view. However, in anticipation of the fact that it will serve as a model for a special view, we could have it inherit from **Model** instead of **Object**. Either way, the basic functionality is unchanged. However, in this simple implementation, we avoid using the dependency mechanism. Hence, the choice is inconsequential. Method **example1** demonstrates how the game can be played via confirmers and fill-in-the-blank requests.

An ESPGame keeps track of a number generator, statistics like the number of correct guesses and incorrect guesses made, how many values one is allowed to guess from (any positive value, but typically between 1 and 9), whether or not the last guess was correct, and the correct answer for the last guess. The game is played via the message 'aGame **guess:** aNumber'. Whether or not the guess was correct, what the correct answer is, and statistics about the game are obtained *after* the guess is made.

To play the game, a new ESP game is created via 'ESPGame **new:** guessPossibilities' followed by successive guesses as indicated above. GuessPossibilities can be any positive number. The most important statistic to be gathered is the guess **average**. An average of more than 50 per cent for two possibilities, 33.3 per cent for three possibilities, 25 per cent for four, and so on indicates the presence of ESP (so it is claimed). A new game can be played by creating another game or reinitializing the old one.

Class ESPGame

class name	ESPGame
superclass	Model
instance variable names	aNumberGenerator correctGuessesMade
	incorrectGuessesMade possibilitiesToGuessFrom
	lastGuessWasCorrect lastCorrectAnswer

class methods

instance creation

new
    "Creates an ESP game with three possible guesses."
    ↑self **new:** 3

new: guessPossibilities
    "Creates an ESP game with a user-determined number of possible guesses."
    ↑super **new initialize:** guessPossibilities

open
    "Creates and schedules an ESP game with the default number of possible guesses."
    self **open:** 3

open: numberOfPictures
    "Creates and schedules an ESP game with a user-determined number of possible guesses. Constructs a new view that both creates and initializes the corresponding model and controller. The new controller is scheduled (note that there is no return from the scheduling)."
    ScheduledControllers
        scheduleActive: (ESPView **new:** numberOfPictures) **controller**.
    "ESPGame open: 9"

examples

example1
>"Play the game directly (no controllers or views are involved). The interface is simplistic."
>I aGame response responseStream aGuess lastCorrectAnswer I
>aGame ← ESPGame **new:** 5. lastCorrectAnswer ← nil.
>[true] **whileTrue:** [
>>response ← FillInTheBlank **request:**
>>>('Your guessing average so far is ', aGame **average printString**,
>>>'.\Successful guesses: ', aGame **correctGuesses printString**,
>>>'   Unsuccessful guesses: ', aGame **incorrectGuesses printString**,
>>>(lastCorrectAnswer **isNil**
>>>>**ifTrue:** [''] "the first time through"
>>>>**ifFalse:** ["all other times"
>>>>>'.\Last correct answer was ', lastCorrectAnswer **printString**,
>>>>>'. You guessed ', aGuess **printString**]),
>>>'.\To make a guess, provide a number between 1 and ',
>>>>aGame **possibilitiesToGuessFrom printString**,
>>>'.\To terminate the guessing game, hit return.') **withCRs**.
>>responseStream ← ReadStream **on:** response. responseStream **skipSeparators**.
>>responseStream **atEnd ifTrue:** [↑self "quit the game"].
>>aGuess ← Integer **readFrom:** responseStream.
>>aGame **guess:** aGuess.
>>lastCorrectAnswer ← aGame **lastCorrectAnswer**].

>"ESPGame example1"

example2
>"Play the game using a specially designed fully autonomous scheduled controller and view."
>self **open:** 5
>"ESPGame example2"

instance methods

instance initialization

initialize: guessPossibilities
>aNumberGenerator ← Random **new**.
>correctGuessesMade ← 0. incorrectGuessesMade ← 0.
>lastGuessWasCorrect ← true.
>possibilitiesToGuessFrom ← guessPossibilities.

reInitialize
>correctGuessesMade ← 0. incorrectGuessesMade ← 0.
>lastGuessWasCorrect ← true.

querying about the state of the game

average
>I total I
>(total ← self **guesses**) = 0 **ifTrue:** [↑0.0].
>↑(correctGuessesMade / total) * 100

correctGuesses
>↑correctGuessesMade

incorrectGuesses
   ↑incorrectGuessesMade

guesses
   ↑correctGuessesMade + incorrectGuessesMade

lastGuessWasCorrect
   ↑lastGuessWasCorrect

possibilitiesToGuessFrom
   ↑possibilitiesToGuessFrom

lastCorrectAnswer
   ↑lastCorrectAnswer

playing the game

guess: aGuess
   "Determines if the guess matches a randomly generated value. Updates the relevant statistics. The methodology is to convert a random float number between 0 (inclusive) and 1 (exclusive) to a number between 0 (inclusive) and possibilitiesTo-GuessFrom (exclusive). By truncating, the result is between 0 and possibilitiesTo-GuessFrom - 1 (inclusive). By adding 1, the result is between 1 and possibilitiesTo-GuessFrom (inclusive)."
   lastCorrectAnswer ← (aNumberGenerator **next** * possibilitiesToGuessFrom)
       truncated+1.
   (lastGuessWasCorrect ← aGuess = lastCorrectAnswer)
       ifTrue: [correctGuessesMade ← correctGuessesMade + 1]
       ifFalse: [incorrectGuessesMade ← incorrectGuessesMade + 1]

A more visually interesting version of the game is demonstrated in method **example2**. This variation creates an ESP view along with its corresponding ESP controller and schedules the controller for immediate activation. Fig. 2.9 provides a snapshot of the ESP game in progress. Although the ESP game permits any number of values to be guessed, the interactive version using views and controllers is limited to a maximum of 9. This limitation can be removed by creating more pictures for selection by the player.

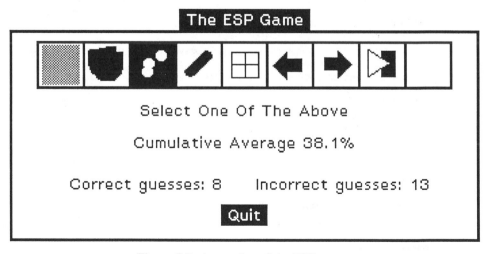

Figure 2.9 A snapshot of the ESP game.

The ESP controller is defined as a specialization of Controller. In keeping with conventions that we have yet to consider, the view (see **open:** in the ESP game above) is created first; it obtains a new ESP game and a new ESP controller and combines them into an MVC triad. The controller is then scheduled for execution.

The controller is designed to retain control (see **isControlActive**) if the mouse is inside the view or if it is outside but no mouse button has been pressed. To lose control, a player must deliberately press a mouse button outside the view. Since this differs from the default behavior of **Controller** (it loses control if the mouse is outside the view or if the blue button is depressed), a new method is provided to override it. Control is also lost if the view suddenly becomes **nil**. This happens when the controller is unscheduled as a consequence of the controller being sent a **close** message. Method **controlInitialize** (previously a no-op) was also overridden to display the view.

The heart of the controller is provided by **controlActivity**. Its main task is to keep track of the mouse. As long as the red mouse button is not depressed, it is ignored. Once it is depressed, it is considered only when depressed inside the view. Once these two prerequisites are met, the mouse is tracked in **redButtonActivity**. The view considers the game area to be divided into inactive areas and active rectangles. It can be queried via message **whereIs:** to determine if the mouse is in an active area. If it is, a rectangle is returned; otherwise **nil**. When in an active area, the controller highlights the rectangle by reversing the form, taking care to dehighlight the previously highlighted rectangle (if any). This is repeated as long as the mouse button is depressed. If released in an active area, the area is dehighlighted and the view is sent a **processSelection:** message to perform a task specific to the particular active area. There are two such classes of areas: One is a picture rectangle (the view interprets this as the players next guess and plays the game), and the other is a quit rectangle (the view sends the controller the **close** message).

Class ESPController

class name	ESPController
superclass	Controller
instance variable names	"none"

instance methods

controlling activities

isControlActive
> "To lose control, the user must have pressed a button while outside the view or released the view."
> ↑view ~~ nil **and:**
> > [self **viewHasCursor or:** [sensor **anyButtonPressed not**]]

controlInitialize
> "Simply displays the view."
> view **displayView**

controlActivity
> "Handle attempts to play the game."
> sensor **redButtonPressed**
> > **ifTrue:** [self **viewHasCursor ifTrue:** [↑self **redButtonActivity**]]

redButtonActivity

"Determine which selection was made (if any) and update the information."
| newHighlightedRectangle lastHighlightedRectangle |
"To reach this method, the red button has to have been depressed. As long as the red button is depressed, track the mouse highlighting the active rectangle (if any) underneath it."
lastHighlightedRectangle ← nil.
[sensor **redButtonPressed**]
    whileTrue: [
        "Determine which square (if any) the mouse is on."
        newHighlightedRectangle ← view **whereIs:** sensor **mousePoint**.
        newHighlightedRectangle == lastHighlightedRectangle **ifFalse:** [
            "Only changes are registered."
            lastHighlightedRectangle **isNil**
                ifFalse: [Display **reverse:** lastHighlightedRectangle].
            newHighlightedRectangle **isNil**
                ifFalse: [Display **reverse:** newHighlightedRectangle].
            lastHighlightedRectangle ← newHighlightedRectangle]].
"Now the button has been released."
lastHighlightedRectangle **isNil**
    ifFalse: [
        "Make sure the last rectangle highlighted is not left highlighted."
        Display **reverse:** lastHighlightedRectangle.
        "Since the player let go the mouse while on an active rectangle, make the appropriate play."
        view **processSelection:** lastHighlightedRectangle].
"Do nothing if no active rectangle was selected."

handling future menu messages

close

"Confirm whether or not the player wishes to terminate or restart"
(self **confirm:** 'Do you really wish to close?')
    ifTrue: [view **release**. "Makes the view nil"
            ScheduledControllers **unschedule:** self]
    ifFalse: [
        (self **confirm:** 'Do you wish to restart?')
            ifTrue: [view **reInitialize**. view **displayView**]]

Since we have not considered views in detail yet, we develop an ESP view without making use of the more advanced facilities of the existing view classes. For simplicity, we relinquish the ability to resize or move the ESP view (something we could get for free had we not designed our own).

The view is designed to display its model (an ESP game) and interact with its controller (an ESP controller). It keeps two forms: one for the game title and one for the game playing area. The playing area (see Fig. 2.9) is divided into active and inactive areas. The active areas are rectangular in shape and consist of the picture rectangles (an array with one rectangle per picture) and a quit rectangle. For simplicity, we designed the game form to be fixed-sized. Since the number of pictures used in a game is user specifiable, different games will have slightly different game forms. These variations are obtained by overlaying the required number of pictures over a copy of GameForm (a predefined class variable). The picture and quit rectangles respectively are computed from class variables Pictures (containing the forms for the pictures) and QuitRectangle (specifying the relative location of the quit box in GameForm). Since the average and number of correct and incorrect guesses change over the course of a game, updating these values requires information about their placement. Offsets relative to the origin of GameForm are provided in class variables AverageOffset, CorrectGuessesOffset, and IncorrectGuessesOffset. Forms HappyFace and SadFace are also provided as success/failure cues for the reader.

Class method **initialize** sets up BorderSize, HorizontalWhiteSpace, and VerticalWhiteSpace for use in formatting the forms and makes use of method **initializePicturesHappyFaceAndSadFace** to initialize the picture and face forms and method **initializeGameFormInformation** to initialize the remaining class variables. The pictures and two faces were created with the bit editor and then inserted into the first method using **storeString**. *The form data was not created by hand.* Detailed instructions are provided in the method. Instance method **initialize:** sets up the model (a new ESP game) and the controller (a new ESP controller) and then creates the required forms and rectangles. The initialization methods are particularly lengthy, but extensive comments are provided in an attempt to make them more understandable. On a first reading, it might be better for the reader to ignore the detail.

Although the initialization methods form the bulk of the view code, it is the other methods that are important. The view contains (1) the typical operations for manipulating models and controllers, (2) display method **displayView**, (3) querying operation **whereIs:**, (4) the game playing operation **processSelection:**, and (5) operation **release**.

Method **displayView** simply displays the title and game forms and then invokes **displayDynamicPortionOfView** to display the average and the number of successful and unsuccessful guesses on top. Methods **whereIs:** and **processSelection:** were specifically designed to work in conjunction with the ESP controller. The former determines which of the picture rectangles or the quit rectangle (if any) contains the supplied point, and the latter either stops the game by sending a **close** message to the controller (if the quit rectangle was selected) or extracts guess i from the fact that the ith picture was selected. It then sends the guess to the ESP game (the model). If successful, it displays a happy face over the picture; otherwise, it displays a sad face and then later flashes the happy face on top of the correct choice. Finally, **release** is sent by the **close** method in the ESP controller. It simply sets the controller's view to **nil**. This task could have been more easily done by the controller. However, as we will see later, it is the view's responsibility to release the model, itself, and its controller. Note that we have not made the view a dependent of the model in this case; hence, there was no need to remove the dependency.

Our initial design assumed these methods were sufficient for integrating with the ESP controller. However, additional methods had to be added due to interactions with the window manager and existing methods in class **Controller**. For example, **containsPoint:** is sent to the view to determine if it wants control. The window manager also makes use of **deEmphasize** when switching to another scheduled controller and also sends **display**, **displayBox**, and **insetDisplayBox** messages.

Most of the time, it is easy to determine what methods need to be added. Simply run the prototype until a debugging window comes up. However, tricky bugs can spring up. For example, the controller might refuse to relinquish control so that you cannot get rid of it. It might refuse to accept control after it relinquished it once. In our case, an even nastier bug showed up. Running the game with any bug in it on a version 1 system simply caused the system to run away until memory was exhausted and a fatal error occurred. Attempts to add debugging output to the transcript didn't help. We found the problem by running the game on a version 2 system. In this version, the problem wasn't fatal. As it turned out, we were missing the **deEmphasize** method (it seemed so innocuous). The method is used to indicate visually that the view is no longer active; e.g., by graying some portion of the view. Since our view lacked the method, a debugging window was created (but not yet displayed). Since the active controller was to change, a **deEmphasize** message was indirectly sent to the active controller's view (the result was infinite recursion until space was exhausted; more important, there were no outward signs that this was occurring). Sending information to the transcript caused the same problem since it, too, sent a **deEmphasize** message to the active controller's view.

In the code that follows, two long methods are explicitly truncated. They are shown at the end of the section so as not to detract from the presentation.

Class ESPView

class name	ESPView
superclass	Object
instance variable names	model controller titleForm titleRectangle gameForm gameRectangle pictureRectangles quitRectangle
class variable names	Pictures HappyFace SadFace BorderSize HorizontalWhiteSpace VerticalWhiteSpace GameForm QuitRectangle AverageOffset CorrectGuessesOffset IncorrectGuessesOffset

class methods

class initialization

initialize
>   BorderSize ← 2.
>   HorizontalWhiteSpace ← 20 "pixels". "Spacing to the sides of the pictures."
>   VerticalWhiteSpace ← 15 "pixels". "Spacing between the different text lines."
>   self **initializePicturesHappyFaceAndSadFace**.
>   self **initializeGameFormInformation**
>
>   "ESPView initialize"

initializePicturesHappyFaceAndSadFace
>   "Sets up the Pictures forms, the HappyFace form, and the SadFace form."
>   ... *code shown later* ...

initializeGameFormInformation
>   "Sets up the game form (without the pictures), computes the offsets for numeric data that can change, and determines the rectangle for the quit box."
>   ... *code shown later* ...

instance creation

new
>   "Creates an ESP view with three possible guesses."
>   ↑self **new:** 3

new: numberOfPictures
>"Creates an ESP view with a user determined number of possible guesses."
>↑super **new initialize**: numberOfPictures

class querying

borderedPicturesSize: numberOfPictures
>"Computes the size of the pictures with borders. All pictures are the same size. A border is to be provided for each picture but adjacent borders are overlapped; i.e., the right border of a picture is overlapped with the left border of the neighbor; except for the rightmost picture, only the left borders are counted."
>| pictureSize |
>pictureSize ← (Pictures **at**: 1) **extent**.
>↑((pictureSize **x** + BorderSize) * numberOfPictures + BorderSize)
>>@ (pictureSize **y** + (2 * BorderSize))

instance methods

instance initialization

initialize: numberOfPictures
>"Sets up the model-view-controller triad, creates the title and game forms, and the rectangles for the title, game, pictures, and quit areas."
>| titleOrigin sizeForOnePicture borderForOnePicture borderedPictureOrigin unborderedPictureOrigin sizeForAllPictures xOriginForAllPictures yOriginForAllPictures |
>
>"Is the number of pictures to choose from acceptable?"
>numberOfPictures <= Pictures **size ifFalse**: [
>>self **error**: 'Can''t guess from ', numberOfPictures **printString**,
>>>' possibilities (too many)'].
>
>"Set the model and controller for the view."
>self **model**: (ESPGame **new**: numberOfPictures). self **controller**: ESPController **new**.
>"Set the model and view for this controller."
>controller **model**: model; **view**: self.
>
>"Create the game form and game rectangle (centered)."
>gameForm ← GameForm **deepCopy**.
>gameRectangle ← (Display **extent** - gameForm **extent**) // 2
>>**extent**: gameForm **extent**.
>
>"Create the title form and title rectangle (centered just above the game form)."
>titleForm ← ' The ESP Game '
>>**asDisplayText form reverse** "You can't reverse display text".
>titleOrigin ← (Display **extent x** - titleForm **extent x**) // 2
>>@ (gameRectangle **origin y** - titleForm **extent y**).
>titleRectangle ← titleOrigin **extent**: titleForm **extent**.
>
>"Draw the pictures (with borders) onto the game form and construct the picture rectangles (without borders). The pictures are all the same size and the borders separating adjacent horizontal pictures overlap. Note that the pictures are being drawn onto the gameForm but the rectangles must be specified in terms of the ultimate location of the gameForm (in absolute coordinates)."
>sizeForAllPictures ← ESPView **borderedPicturesSize**: numberOfPictures.
>xOriginForAllPictures ← (gameForm **extent x** - sizeForAllPictures **x**) // 2.
>yOriginForAllPictures ← VerticalWhiteSpace "Extra white space at the top".

```
sizeForOnePicture ← (Pictures at: 1) extent.
borderForOnePicture ← Quadrangle new
    region: (0@0 extent: sizeForOnePicture + (2 * BorderSize));
    borderWidth: BorderSize;
    yourself.

pictureRectangles ← Array new: numberOfPictures.
(1 to: numberOfPictures) inject: xOriginForAllPictures into: [:xOrigin :pictureIndex |
    borderedPictureOrigin ← xOrigin @ yOriginForAllPictures.
    unborderedPictureOrigin ← borderedPictureOrigin + BorderSize.
    borderForOnePicture moveTo: borderedPictureOrigin.
    borderForOnePicture displayOn: gameForm. "the border"
    (Pictures at: pictureIndex)
        displayOn: gameForm at: unborderedPictureOrigin. "the picture"
    pictureRectangles
        at: pictureIndex
        put: (gameRectangle origin+unborderedPictureOrigin
            extent: sizeForOnePicture).
    xOrigin + BorderSize + sizeForOnePicture x "next xOrigin"].

"Finally, compute the quit rectangle (QuitRectangle assumes the game form is at
0@0)."
quitRectangle←gameRectangle origin+QuitRectangle origin
    extent: QuitRectangle extent
```

reInitialize
> model reInitialize.

model and controller access

controller
> ↑controller

controller: aController
> controller ← aController

model
> ↑model

model: aModel
> model ← aModel

querying

whereIs: aPoint
> "Returns the active rectangle containing the point if there is one; **nil** otherwise."
> (quitRectangle **containsPoint**: aPoint) **ifTrue**: [↑quitRectangle].
> pictureRectangles **do**: [:aPictureRectangle |
>   (aPictureRectangle **containsPoint**: aPoint) **ifTrue**: [↑aPictureRectangle]].
> ↑nil

displaying

displayView
> "Display the complete view. All information is static except for the average and
> guess counts."
> titleForm **displayAt**: titleRectangle **origin**.
> gameForm displayAt: gameRectangle **origin**.
> self **displayDynamicPortionOfView**

displayDynamicPortionOfView
"Display the part of the view that can change."
| average |

"For the average, use 3 digits; e.g., '25.0' where possible. The exception is 100.0.
Follow it by '%' and enough spaces to handle a prior printing with 4 digits."
average ← (model **average roundTo:** 0.1) **asFloat printString**.
    "asFloat ensures 0 is in form 0.0"
average size < 4
    ifTrue: [average ← ('0000' **copyFrom:** 1 **to:** 4 - average **size**), average].
(average, '% ') **displayAt:** gameRectangle **origin** + AverageOffset.

"For the number of guesses, the values are always increasing. Hence additional
spaces are not needed."
model **correctGuesses printString**
    displayAt: gameRectangle **origin** + CorrectGuessesOffset.
model **incorrectGuesses printString**
    displayAt: gameRectangle **origin** + IncorrectGuessesOffset

processing selection

processSelection: aRectangle
"If the quit rectangle was selected, stop the game by closing the controller (it makes
sure you really want to). If the ith picture was selected, guess the value i. If
successful, display a happy face over the picture; otherwise, display a sad face and
then later flash the happy face on the correct choice."

| correctRectangle |
aRectangle == quitRectangle **ifTrue:** [controller **close**].
1 **to:** pictureRectangles **size do:** [:i |
    aRectangle == (pictureRectangles **at:** i) **ifTrue:** [
        model **guess:** i.
        model **lastGuessWasCorrect**
            ifTrue: [HappyFace **displayAt:** aRectangle **origin**]
            ifFalse: [SadFace **displayAt:** aRectangle **origin**].
        (Delay **forSeconds:** 3) **wait**.
        (Pictures **at:** i) **displayAt:** aRectangle **origin**.
        model **lastGuessWasCorrect ifFalse:** [
            correctRectangle ← pictureRectangles **at:** model **lastCorrectAnswer**.
            HappyFace **displayAt:** correctRectangle **origin**.
            3 **timesRepeat:** [Display **flash:** correctRectangle].
            (Pictures **at:** model **lastCorrectAnswer**)
                displayAt: correctRectangle **origin**].
        self **displayDynamicPortionOfView**]].

releasing control

release
    controller **view:** nil

methods that had to be added to work

containsPoint: aPoint
    ↑gameRectangle **containsPoint:** aPoint

display
    self **displayView**

displayBox
　　↑gameRectangle

insetDisplayBox
　　↑gameRectangle **insetBy:** BorderSize

deEmphasize
　　"When this method was omitted, attempts to debug by writing on the system
　　transcript failed because this message was sent to the currently active controller's
　　view. Since it lacked the method, a debugging window was created (but not yet
　　displayed). The first thing it did was send a deEmphasize message to the active
　　controller's view (the result was infinite recursion until space was exhausted; more
　　important, there were no outward signs that this was occurring)."
　　Display **gray:** titleRectangle

The Two Lengthy ESPView Class Methods

For completeness, we include the details omitted from the two previous class methods. This
section may be skipped easily without penalty. We present the **initializeGameForm-
Information** method before the **initializePicturesHappyFaceAndSadFace** method
because it is more interesting.

initializeGameFormInformation
　　"Sets up the game form (without the pictures), computes the offsets for numeric
　　data that can change, and determines the rectangle for the quit box."
　　| picturesSize textHeight gameFormXSize gameFormYSize gameBorder forms
　　offsets aForm xOrigin |

　　"Make the form big enough to contain everything."

　　picturesSize ← self **borderedPicturesSize:** Pictures **size.**
　　textHeight ← 'H' **asDisplayText form extent** y. "a sample character"
　　gameFormXSize ← picturesSize **x** + (2*HorizontalWhiteSpace "each side").
　　gameFormYSize ← picturesSize **y** + (6*VerticalWhiteSpace "separation") +
　　　　(4*textHeight "4 lines of text").
　　GameForm ← Form **extent:** gameFormXSize @ gameFormYSize.

　　"Draw the undersurface and border and prepare to draw all other forms on top."

　　gameBorder ← Quadrangle **new**
　　　　region: GameForm **boundingBox; borderWidth:** BorderSize; **yourself.**
　　gameBorder **displayOn:** GameForm. "The white undersurface and the border"

　　"Separately create the text forms to be displayed on top so that we can easily
　　center them."

　　forms ← (Array **new:** 4)
　　　　at: 1 **put:** ' Select One Of The Above ' **asDisplayText form;**
　　　　at: 2 **put:** ' Cumulative Average 00.0% ' **asDisplayText form**
　　　　　　"A case that will change";
　　　　at: 3 **put:** ' Correct guesses: 0   Incorrect guesses: 0 ' **asDisplayText form**
　　　　　　"Another one";
　　　　at: 4 **put:** ' Quit ' **asDisplayText form reverse;** "You can't reverse display text"
　　　　yourself.

"Determine the origin of the centered text forms."

```
offsets ← Array new: forms size.
(1 to: forms size)
    inject: picturesSize y + (2 * VerticalWhiteSpace)
    into: [:yOrigin :formIndex |
        aForm ← forms at: formIndex.
        xOrigin ← (GameForm extent x - aForm extent x) // 2.
        offsets at: formIndex put: xOrigin @ yOrigin.
        yOrigin + aForm extent y + VerticalWhiteSpace].
```

"Draw the centered text forms onto the game form."

```
1 to: forms size do: [:i |
    (forms at: i) displayOn: GameForm at: (offsets at: i)].
```

"Compute the offsets of the three numbers that can continually change."

```
AverageOffset ← (offsets at: 2) +
    (' Cumulative Average ' asDisplayText form extent x @ 0).
CorrectGuessesOffset ← (offsets at: 3) +
    (' Correct guesses: ' asDisplayText form extent x @ 0).
IncorrectGuessesOffset ← (offsets at: 3) +
    (' Correct guesses: 0    Incorrect guesses: ' asDisplayText form extent x @ 0).
```

"Compute the rectangle for the quit box."
```
QuitRectangle ← (offsets at: 4) extent: (forms at: 4) extent.
```

initializePicturesHappyFaceAndSadFace

"The code body below was created by starting with an initialize method without code and executing 'self **halt**. ESPView **initializePicturesHappyFaceAndSadFace**'. After initializing Pictures, HappyFace, and SadFace as shown below,

```
Pictures ← (1 to: 9) collect: [:i | Form extent: 32@32].
HappyFace ← Form extent: 32@32.
SadFace ← Form extent: 32@32.
```

the following was executed one statement at a time while in the debugger. Note that we could not execute the whole sequence of statements at once because the bit editor does not return control. Hence, only the first statement would be executed.

```
(Pictures at: 1) bitEdit.
(Pictures at: 2) bitEdit.
(Pictures at: 3) bitEdit.
(Pictures at: 4) bitEdit.
(Pictures at: 5) bitEdit.
(Pictures at: 6) bitEdit.
(Pictures at: 7) bitEdit.
(Pictures at: 8) bitEdit.
(Pictures at: 9) bitEdit.

HappyFace bitEdit.
SadFace bitEdit.
```

Finally, 'Pictures **storeString**', 'HappyFace **storeString**', and 'SadFace **storeString**' were printed into the method and reformatted into the following."

Pictures ← (Array **new:** 9)
    at: 1 **put:** (Form
        extent: 32@32
        fromArray: #(0 0 5461 21844 10922 43688 5461 21844 10922 43688 5461
            21844 10922 43688 5461 21844 10922 43688 5461 21844 10922
            43688 5461 21844 10922 43688 5461 21844 10922 43688 5461 21844
            10922 43688 5461 21844 10922 43688 5461 21844 10922 43688 5461
            21844 10922 43688 5461 21844 10922 43688 5461 21844 10922
            43688 5461 21844 10922 43688 5461 21844 10922 43688 0 0)
        offset: 0@0);
    at: 2 **put:** (Form
        extent: 32@32
        fromArray: #(0 0 0 0 1 65024 63 65024 8191 65024 16383 65024 16383
            65520 16383 65520 16383 65520 16383 65520 16383 65520 16383
            65520 16383 65520 16383 65520 16383 65520 16383 65520 16383
            65520 8191 65520 8191 65520 8191 65520 4095 65504 4095 65504
            2047 65504 511 65472 255 65408 255 65280 127 65024 31 64512 0 0
            0 0 0 0 0 0)
        offset: 0@0);
    at: 3 **put:** (Form
        extent: 32@32
        fromArray: #(65535 65535 65535 65535 65535 65535 65535 65535 65535
            65535 65535 61695 65535 57471 65535 49215 65535 49215 65535
            49215 65535 49215 65505 57471 65472 61695 65408 32767 65408
            32767 65408 32767 65408 32767 65472 65535 65409 65535 65280
            65535 65280 65535 65280 65535 65280 65535 65409 65535 65475
            65535 65535 65535 65535 65535 65535 65535 65535 65535 65535
            65535 65535 65535 65535)
        offset: 0@0);
    at: 4 **put:** (Form
        extent: 32@32
        fromArray: #(0 0 0 0 0 0 0 0 0 0 3584 0 8064 0 16256 0 32704 0 65472 1
            65472 3 65408 7 65280 15 65024 31 64512 63 63488 127 61440 255
            57344 511 49152 1023 32768 2047 0 2046 0 1020 0 1016 0 224 0 0 0 0
            0 0 0 0 0 0 0 0 0 0)
        offset: 0@0);
    at: 5 **put:** (Form
        extent: 32@32
        fromArray: #(0 0 0 0 0 0 0 0 0 0 0 0 1023 65504 512 32800 512 32800 512
            32800 512 32800 512 32800 512 32800 512 32800 512 32800 1023
            65504 512 32800 512 32800 512 32800 512 32800 512 32800 512
            32800 512 32800 512 32800 512 32800 1023 65504 0 0 0 0 0 0 0 0 0
            0 0)
        offset: 0@0);
    at: 6 **put:** (Form
        extent: 32@32
        fromArray: #(0 0 0 0 0 0 0 0 0 0 0 0 4 0 12 0 28 0 60 0 124 0 252 0 511
            65408 1023 65408 2047 65408 4095 65408 8191 65408 4095 65408
            2047 65408 1023 65408 511 65408 252 0 124 0 60 0 28 0 12 0 4 0 0 0
            0 0 0 0 0 0 0 0)
        offset: 0@0);

at: 7 **put**: (Form
    extent: 32@32
    fromArray: #(0 0 0 0 0 0 0 0 0 0 0 0 0 16384 0 24576 0 28672 0 30720 0
        31744 0 32256 511 65280 511 65408 511 65472 511 65504 511 65520
        511 65504 511 65472 511 65408 511 65280 0 32256 0 31744 0 30720
        0 28672 0 24576 0 16384 0 0 0 0 0 0 0 0 0 0)
    offset: 0@0);
at: 8 **put**: (Form
    extent: 32@32
    fromArray: #(0 0 0 0 0 0 0 0 0 1793 65472 1409 65472 1249 65472 1073
        65472 1053 65472 1031 65472 1027 65472 1024 65472 1024 16320
        1024 8128 1024 1984 1024 8128 1024 16320 1024 65472 1027 65472
        1031 65472 1053 65472 1073 65472 1249 65472 1409 65472 1793
        65472 0 0 0 0 0 0 0 0 0 0)
    offset: 0@0);
at: 9 **put**: (Form
    extent: 32@32
    fromArray: #(0 0 0 0 0 0 0 0 0 0 0 0 0 0 0 0 0 0 0 0 0 0 0 0 0 0 0 0 0 0 0
        0 0 0 0 0 0 0 0 0 0 0 0 0 0 0 0 0 0 0 0 0 0 0 0 0 0 0 0 0 0 0 0 0)
    offset: 0@0);
yourself.
HappyFace ← (Form
    extent: 32@32
    fromArray: #(0 0 0 0 0 15 63488 112 3840 224 896 1344 448 2688 224 3072
        16 2048 16 4096 16 4096 8 480 15364 9008 26124 8720 16900 8192 4
        8200 32770 17413 98 9986 196 8960 388 8640 1804 4592 7684 2172
        64516 1087 61448 15 49168 256 32 224 64 30 29952 1 32768 0 0 0 0 0)
    offset: 0@0).
SadFace ← (Form
    extent: 32@32
    fromArray: #(0 0 0 0 0 15 63488 125 20224 224 10112 1344 448 1664 224
        1024 16 2048 24 4592 15896 4880 8972 8696 32260 8600 26126 8432
        15366 28676 8198 8203 49154 24581 49154 8192 4 12291 59398 2079
        65036 5144 780 2672 396 1584 136 256 48 320 160 232 192 30 64768 1
        59392 0 0 0 0 0)
    offset: 0@0)

2.4 THE VIEW CLASS

A **view** is one of the components in the model-view-controller (MVC) triad that implements a window. Its primary responsibilities are to display the model and provide visual feedback for controller interactions, to manage hierarchies of interrelated views, to provide an automatic resizing and repositioning facility that is transparent to users of the view, and to provide coordinate transformations between views that contain it (**superviews**) and views that it contains (**subviews**). The use of views greatly simplifies the development of user applications.

Class **View** provides the basic display protocol for activities that involve both the controller and the model. It is intended as a building block for the construction of more complex views. Unlike class **Controller**, which is intended to interact primarily with one view, class **View**, on the other hand, is intended to interact with a hierarchy of views (and their associated controllers). A view that is subordinate to an existing view is called a subview; the converse is a **superview**. The relationship between views is hierarchical; i.e., a view can have any number of subviews but only one superview (if any). A view that has no superview is a **topview**. A view that has no subviews is a **bottomview**.

2.4.1 Creating Views (a Preview)

Views have default controllers associated with them. Creating a view will indirectly cause a default controller to be constructed if and when it is needed; i.e., a default controller is created if no other controller has been explicitly provided and one is now needed, for example, because it is to be started up. As with controllers, creating a view is as simple as creating an arbitrary object.

aViewClass **new**

The newly created view is fully initialized, but the default border size (zero) and inside color (transparent) are not typically what users want. Views are more usually created via

aViewClass **new borderWidth**: 1; **insideColor**: Form **white**

or if a nonstandard controller is used

aViewClass **new**
       borderWidth: 1; **insideColor**: Form **white**; **controller**: aNonStandardController

Note that modification messages such as **borderWidth:**, **insideColor:**, and **controller:** typically return the receiver. Hence, it is not necessary to append '; **yourself**' to the above messages in order to get the newly created (and modified) view.

2.4.2 Windows, Viewports, and Display Boxes

Applications can be made independent of a view's screen location or size by referencing all points in the view's **local coordinate system**. These points can be mapped easily to and from the **screen coordinate system** via a special transformation called the **display transformation**. For example, the display transformation could be used to map a point at coordinate (10,10) in the view's local coordinate system to a location that happens to be at, say, (50,100) in screen coordinates. Conversely, a mouse point at screen coordinate (50,100) can be mapped to the view's local coordinate system using the inverse of the display transformation.

Although the above transformation is sufficient for many applications, the management of views with arbitrarily nested subviews requires the use of two transformations: a **local transformation** that maps objects in the coordinate system of the view to objects in the coordinate system of its superview and a **display transformation** that maps objects in the coordinate system of the view to objects in the screen coordinate system. The display transformation is in fact composed from the successive local transformations between a view and its topview (there can be a series of intervening views).

Intuitively, a window is that portion of the view that is displayed on the screen. However, the term has a much more technical meaning. More precisely, a **window** is a rectangle in the local coordinate system of the view. When transformed to the coordinate system of the superview, the window is called a **viewport**. When transformed to the coordinate system of the screen, the window is called a **display box**. Alternatively, a viewport is a window as seen from the superview; a display box is a window as seen from the screen. Fig. 2.10 provides an illustration.

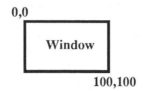

As Seen Locally: The Window = 0@0 **corner:** 100@100
A Window Is A Rectangle In VIEW Coordinates

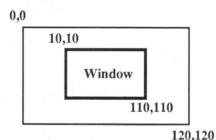

As Seen By The Superview: The Window is called A Viewport
ViewPort = 10@10 **corner:** 110@110
A ViewPort Is A Window In SUPERVIEW Coordinates

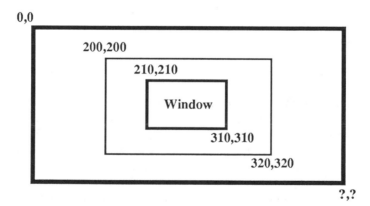

As Seen By The Display Screen: A Window is called A DisplayBox
DisplayBox = 210@210 **corner:** 310@310
A DisplayBox Is A Window In DISPLAY SCREEN Coordinates

Figure 2.10 Relationship between window, viewport, and display box.

For another perspective, consider Fig. 2.11. Each view manipulates its own window using its unique local coordinate system. A window, as long as it is not the screen, can be repositioned anywhere inside its superview's window. Actually, it can be repositioned anywhere, but if it lies outside the superview's window, it will be clipped; the clipped portions are not seen. In Fig. 2.11, a relatively wide window is transformed into one that looks more like a square and is positioned in the lower right quadrant of the superview's window. The superview's window is itself shrunk and positioned in the top left quadrant of the display screen. Each transformation can either magnify or shrink the x and y sizes independently and also reposition the origin. In this example, an application would work in the local coordinates of the specified window. Information to be displayed would be mapped via the display transformation to the small display box visible on the screen. Conversely, the mouse point could be mapped using the inverse display transformation to the local coordinates of the window.

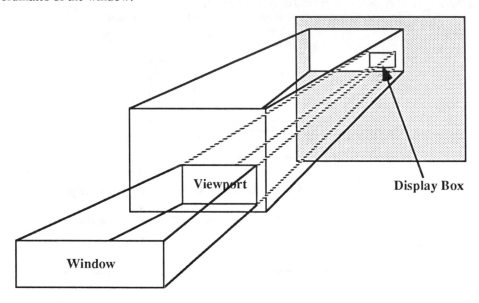

Figure 2.11 Windows, viewports, and display boxes again.

In general, a window includes a **border** of arbitrary width in pixels with an arbitrary **border color** (a form or **nil**). The size of the **left, right, top,** and **bottom** borders can be independently controlled. A border width of 0 is permitted along with a transparent border color (**nil**). The part of the window, viewport, or display box without the border is the **inset window, inset viewport,** and **inset display box** respectively. Inset windows and display boxes are widely used; inset viewports are not. Fig. 2.12 provides an illustration of the relationship between windows and inset windows. Similar diagrams hold for display boxes and inset display boxes. The color of the inset window is referred to as the **inside color** (it, too, may be transparent).

2.4.3 View Creation, Model and Controller Interfacing

Views have the same basic protocol as controllers for their creation and for accessing other members of the MVC triad. The default usage is to create an appropriate view, use it for display purposes until it is no longer required, and then release it. The corresponding

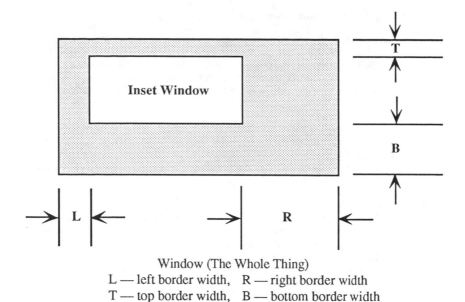

Window (The Whole Thing)
L — left border width,   R — right border width
T — top border width,   B — bottom border width

Figure 2.12 Window versus inset window.

controller is created automatically and is also released automatically. Thus, an MVC triad is manufactured primarily through the view. Explicit reference to controllers will be needed only when associating nonstandard controllers with the view.

As long as no controller is needed by the view, the controller can remain unspecified; i.e., **nil**. When needed (e.g., as a result of an explicit query for the controller or as a consequence of starting up the MVC triad), a default controller is created and integrated with the model and view. Changes to the view's model or controller automatically integrate the new information with all members of the MVC triad. For example, changing the view's model automatically changes it for the controller too. It also makes the view a dependent of the model (see Sect. 1.4 on dependency maintenance). Changing the view's controller automatically updates the controller's model to that of the view.

The default view obtained via **new** is transparent. When creating hierarchies of views, this is convenient because only bottom views are meant to be visible. A bottom view can be made visible by providing a white form for the inside color; a border can be provided by changing the border width (it is already black and of width 0 by default).

creating new views

- View **new**
    Returns an initialized view that is transparent and ready for sizing (the default is the screen size); i.e., the view has no subviews, the transformation is an identity transformation, the border width is 0, the border color is black, and the inside color is transparent. The fact that the view is transparent makes it convenient for creating views that contain other visible views. On the other hand, the inside color must be explicitly changed to make it visible.

initializing and releasing views

- aView **initialize**

  Initializes the view so that it has no subviews, the transformation is an identity transformation, the border width is 0, the border color is black, and the inside color is transparent. Subclasses should include 'super **initialize**' when redefining this message to ensure proper initialization.

- aView **release**

  Removes the view from its model's list of dependents (if the model exists), releases the associated controller, and releases all of its subviews and controllers. This message should be sent to a topview when the view is no longer needed. Subclasses should include 'super **release**' when redefining release.

- aView **releaseSubViews**

  Performs a portion of the above operation. Supplied to complete the implementation of the above and should not be needed under normal conditions.

- aView **releaseSubView**: aSubview

  Removes aSubview from the view's list of subviews and individually releases it. Supplied to complete the implementation of the above and should not be needed under normal conditions.

access to the model and controller

- aView **model**

  Returns the view's model.

- aView **model**: aModel

  Changes both the view and controller's model and adds the view to aModel's list of dependents; i.e., *integrates the new information with all members of the MVC triad.*

- aView **controller**

  If the view's controller is **nil** (the default case), a default controller (see **defaultController**) is *integrated with all members of the MVC triad.* Returns the view's controller.

- aView **controller**: aController

  Changes the view's controller to aController and updates the controller's model to the view's model; i.e., *integrates the new information with all members of the MVC triad.* An instance of NoController can be specified to indicate that the view will not have a controller. **nil** can be used to indicate that a default controller (see **defaultController**) is to be manufactured when required.

- aView **model**: aModel **controller**: aController

  Changes both the view and controller's model to aModel, adds the view to aModel's list of dependents, and sets the view's controller to aController; i.e., *integrates the new information with all members of the MVC triad.* An instance of NoController can be specified to indicate that the view will not have a controller; **nil** can be used to indicate that a default controller (see **defaultController**) is to be manufactured when required.

- aView **defaultController**

  Returns an initialized instance of the view's default controller class; equivalent to 'self **defaultControllerClass new**'. Subclasses should redefine this message only if the default controller instances need to be initialized in a nonstandard way.

Inside Smalltalk

- aView **defaultControllerClass**

    Returns the class of the default controller for the view; equivalent to 'Controller'. Subclasses should redefine this message to obtain other controller classes.

debugging and inspecting

- aView **inspect**

    Builds an inspector on the model, view, and controller triad.

basic control testing

- aView **containsPoint**: aPointInScreenCoordinates

    Returns **true** if aPointInScreenCoordinates is within the view's display box and **false** otherwise.

- aView **subViewContaining**: aPointInScreenCoordinates

    Returns the first subview that contains aPointInScreenCoordinates within its display box and **nil** otherwise.

- aView **subViewWantingControl**

    Returns the first subview with a controller that responds **true** to message **isControlWanted**.

dependency maintenance

- aView **update**

    Normally sent by the view's model in order to notify it of a change in the model's state. The code body expands to 'self **update**: self'. Subclasses implement this message to do a particular update action.

- aView **update**: aParameter

    Normally sent by the view's model to notify it of a change in the model's state. *Currently does nothing.* Subclasses implement this message to do a particular update action. A typical action that might be required is to redisplay the view.

2.4.4 Coloring and Sizing Windows and Borders

Typically, windows are transparent (**nil**) or colored white (Form **white**) while borders are colored gray, light gray, or black (Form **gray**, Form **lightGray**, or Form **black**). The default window color is transparent; for borders it is black. The four sides of a border can be sized independently by providing a **sizing rectangle** of the form 'LeftWidth@TopWidth **corner**: RightWidth@BottomWidth'. A border is specified either with a sizing rectangle or an integer that indicates equal widths all around. Widths are specified in pixels; the typical width is 2 pixels.

The simplest way to indicate the size of a window is to provide two rectangles: one for the window (in local coordinates) and one for the viewport (in superview coordinates). For a topview, the viewport is in screen coordinates. The two rectangles are used to automatically compute the local transformation. Additionally, the display transformation is computed automatically from the successive local transformations of the view and its superviews when an attempt is made to use it. This sizing (and positioning) message insulates users from the structure of transformations and from their construction. Of course, users will still have to know how to use the transformations (a subject to be considered later).

window and border coloring

- aView **borderColor**
    Returns the view's border color.
- aView **borderColor**: aColor
    Sets the view's border color to aColor.

- aView **insideColor**
    Returns the color of the inset window.
- aView **insideColor**: aColor
    Sets the color of the inset window to aColor.

border sizing

- aView **borderWidth**
    Returns either 0, indicating no border, or a rectangle indicating the four border widths as 'Left@Top **corner**: Right@Bottom'.
- aView **borderWidth**: borderValue
    Sets the four border widths of the view to an integer (all four widths the same) or to a rectangle such as 'Left@Top **corner**: Right@Bottom'.
- aView **borderWidthLeft**: leftWidth **right**: rightWidth **top**: topWidth **bottom**: bottomWidth
    Sets the border widths of the view to the rectangle 'leftWidth@topWidth **corner**: rightWidth@topWidth'.

window sizing and positioning

- aView **window**: aWindowRectangle **viewport**: aViewportRectangle
    Sets the view's window to aWindowRectangle, its viewport to aViewportRectangle, and creates a new local transformation such that aWindowRectangle, when transformed, coincides with aViewportRectangle. It is used to position a window within some specific region of its superview.

Example

We can easily construct simple views without models and display them as shown. The default size for the view is the screen size, and the associated local and display transformation are identity transformations. The view's size and position can be changed at any time.

```
| aView |
aView ← View new. aView display. "Nothing is seen since the window is transparent"
aView borderWidth: 50. aView display. "A large black band is displayed around the
    screen. But the center part of the screen was untouched; the inset window is
    transparent"
aView insideColor: Form white. aView borderColor: Form gray. aView display.
    "This time, the entire screen is changed"
aView window: (0@0 corner: 10@10) viewport: (200@200 corner: 300@300).
    "Create a 10 by 10 window but have it display as a 100 by 100 display box at
    200@200. For topviews, the viewport is the same as the display box"
aView display. "Try it"
```

2.4.5 Displaying Views

Views are typically **cleared** (i.e., painted in either the border color or inside color), **highlighted** (i.e., painted in reverse video), **flashed** (i.e., highlighted twice in succession), and simply displayed. A view is **displayed** by painting its display box and the display boxes of all subviews. A display box is painted by first displaying it in the border color, then displaying the inset display box in the inside color, and finally displaying the model specific information. Clipping occurs if displayed information lies outside the inset display box of the view or any of its superviews.

When top-level window controllers are scheduled for execution, at most one is active at any one time. The active window is generally **emphasized** and all others are **deemphasized** to provide visual feedback to users. Typically, the view is emphasized (or deemphasized) by highlighting (or graying) some part of the display box. Class **View** provides the protocol that causes a view and all subviews to be emphasized (or deemphasized). The general recursive message is **emphasize** (or **deEmphasize**); the message that applies to a specific receiving view is **emphasizeView** (or **deEmphasizeView**). The default action for these messages is to do nothing. Subclasses of **View**, such as **StandardSystemView**, provide more substantial visual effects.

clearing the display box and inset display box

- aView **clear**

    Uses the border color to paint the display box of the view. Note that this includes the border.
- aView **clear**: aColor

    Uses aColor to paint the display box of the view. Note that this includes the border.

- aView **clearInside**

    Uses the inside color to paint the inset display box of the view. Note that this excludes the border.
- aView **clearInside**: aColor

    Uses aColor to paint the inset display box of the view. Note that this excludes the border.

messages for gaining attention

- aView **highlight**

    Causes the inset display box of the view to be complemented once.
- aView **flash**

    Causes the inset display box of the view to be complemented twice in succession.

displaying the view

- aView **display**

    Paints the display boxes of the view and all subviews. A display box is painted by first displaying it in the border color, then displaying the inset display box in the inside color, and finally displaying the model specific information. Clipping occurs if displayed information lies outside the inset display box of the view or any of its superviews.

- aView **displayBorder**

    Actually a misnomer. Displays the entire display box — the border in the border color and the inset display box in the inside color.
- aView **displayView**

    Displays the information about the model in the inset display box. *The default is to do nothing.* Subclasses should redefine this method to display model specific information.
- aView **displaySubViews**

    Displays all the subviews of the view.

emphasizing and deemphasizing

- aView **emphasize**

    Modifies the emphasis of the view and its subviews to indicate that they are active.
- aView **emphasizeView**

    Modifies the emphasis of the view to indicate that it is active. *The default is to do nothing.* Subclasses should redefine this method to provide model or view specific indications.
- aView **emphasizeSubViews**

    Sends the emphasize message to each of the view's subviews.

- aView **deEmphasize**

    Modifies the emphasis of the view and its subviews to indicate that they are inactive.
- aView **deEmphasizeView**

    Modifies the emphasis of the view to indicate that it is inactive. *The default is to do nothing.* Subclasses should redefine this method to provide model or view specific indications.
- aView **deEmphasizeSubViews**

    Sends the deEmphasize message to each of the view's subviews.

Example

At this stage, we are still relegated to performing simple experiments. It is relatively easy to construct a view, color it, and display it.

```
| aView |
aView ← View new.
aView borderWidthLeft: 2 right: 6 top: 4 bottom: 8.
    "Try border sizes of 2, 4, 6, 8 clockwise"
aView insideColor: Form gray.
aView flash. "Should be noticeable"
aView clear. "Should paint the display box black"
aView clearInside. "Should paint the inset display box gray"
aView emphasize "Should not have any effect (the default is to do nothing)"
```

2.4.6 Viewing Transformations

Local transformations map window coordinates to viewport coordinates. Display transformations map window coordinates to display screen coordinates and vice versa. Local transformations are provided automatically when a view is obtained; the default is an identity local transformation along with a window and a viewport that consists of the screen. It can also be supplied indirectly by messages like **window:viewport:** (among others).

The display transformation and display box are automatically computed from the local transformations and viewports of a view and its superviews, when required. If it is computed, the view is said to be **locked**; otherwise, **unlocked**. A protocol is provided for determining if a view is locked or not and for locking or unlocking it. Locking a view, for instance, forces the display information (the display transformation and the display box) to be computed. Unlocking it causes it to forget the existing display information and leaves it in a state that will force it to be recomputed when required. The locking/unlocking protocol is provided for completeness; i.e., it is of little concern to users since it is managed automatically by the system. For example, the system automatically unlocks a view when the local transformation of a view or one of its superviews is changed.

lock access

- aView **isLocked**
    Returns whether or not the view is locked; i.e., whether or not its display transformation and display box are defined.
- aView **isUnlocked**
    Returns whether or not the view is unlocked.

- aView **lock**
    Locks the view and all of its subviews. This has the effect of computing and defining the display transformation and display box of the view and its subviews.
- aView **unlock**
    Unlocks the view and all of its subviews. This has the effect of forcing the display transformation and display box of the view and its subviews to be recomputed the next time they are needed.

Objects to be displayed are normally managed in window coordinates. If the display box is suddenly moved or resized, the change has no effect on the objects. On the other hand, the objects must be transformed for actual display to the screen. Message **displayTransform:** is used for that purpose. Conversely, when a mouse point is obtained from the screen, the coordinates of the mouse are in display screen coordinates. The inverse of the display transform is used to obtain the corresponding window coordinates. Message **inverseDisplayTransform:** is used.

It is also possible to transform the objects to viewport coordinates, but the need is rare. Although **transform:** is provided for that purpose, there is no corresponding message for the inverse.

display transformation

- aView **displayTransform:** anObject
    Applies the display transformation of the view to anObject. Transforms an object such as a rectangle or point in the view's local coordinate system to the corresponding object in display coordinates. For example, the window transforms to the display box.
- aView **inverseDisplayTransform:** anObject
    Applies the inverse of the display transformation of the view to anObject. Transforms an object such as a rectangle or point in the view's display coordinate system to the corresponding object in local coordinates. For example, the inverse transformation applied to the display box is the window. It is typically used to convert a mouse point to local coordinates.

- aView **transform**: anObject

  Applies the local transformation of the view to anObject. Transforms an object such as a rectangle or point in the view's local coordinate system to the corresponding object in viewport coordinates. For example, the window transforms to the viewport.

- aView **displayTransformation**

  Returns the view's display transformation (not a copy), computing it if necessary.

- aView **transformation**

  Returns a copy of the view's local transformation.

- aView **transformation**: aTransformation

  Sets the view's local transformation to a copy of aTransformation, unlocks the view, and sets the viewport to undefined (this forces it to be recomputed when needed).

Example

Suppose we wanted to draw a line or a circle in the window for display on the screen. Additionally, suppose we wanted to know how far the mouse was from the center of the circle. The following could be done:

```
| aLineStart aLineEnd aCenter aRadius mouseLocation mouseDistance |
aLineStart ← 10@10. aLineEnd ← 20@30.
(Line
      from: (aView displayTransform: aLineStart)
      to: (aView displayTransform: aLineEnd)
      withForm: aDot) display

aCenter ← 30@40. aRadius ← 10.
(Circle new form: aDot;
      center: (aView displayTransform: aCenter);
      radius: (aRadius * aView displayTransformation scale x);
      yourself) display

mouseLocation ← View inverseDisplayTransform: Sensor mousePoint.
mouseDistance ← (mouseLocation - aCenter) r. "r provides the polar coordinate radius"
```

More explicit control of the construction of local transformations is also provided. However, constructing transformations explicitly is not standard practice.

directly specifying and changing local transformations

- aView **scale**: aScale **translation**: aTranslation

  Creates a new local transformation for the view with a scale factor of aScale and a translation offset of aTranslation.

- aView **scaleBy**: aScale

  Scales the view by aScale, either an integer, a float, or a point. The scale is an adjustment of the current transformation of the view.

- aView **translateBy**: aPoint

  Translates the view by aPoint. The translation is an adjustment of the current transformation of the view.

2.4.7 Window, Viewport, Display Box, and Bounding Box Queries

The notion of a display box as the window transformed to display coordinates is only an approximation to its true nature. The more exact notion takes into account two complications: (1) it is tedious to position a window in the superview's window (i.e., to compute the viewport) if the superview's border must be taken into account, and (2) when a window is transformed to its display box, the borders inside the window are transformed to nonintegral thicknesses.

To illustrate the first problem, consider positioning two windows, A and B, side by side in the superview's window. It should be clear that the top left corner of A's viewport must start at a point to the right and below the superview window's top left corner (the exact amount depends on the border thicknesses). The corresponding bottom right corner's x coordinate must start at the horizontal midpoint of the superview window; the y coordinate must be positioned at the lowest window point elevated by the bottom border size. Positioning B is similarly tedious. Clearly, it is advantageous to have a technique that doesn't require knowing the border sizes. Without having to consider such sizes, it is considerably simpler to position the top left corner of A's viewport at the superview window's top left corner. The corresponding bottom right corner is positioned at the average of the superview window's bottom left and bottom right corners.

Now consider the situation when the window's borders are transformed. For example, consider a window's 2-pixel border being transformed so that the horizontal and vertical borders are 1.73 and 2.46 pixels thick respectively. Of course, it's not possible to display nonintegral thicknesses. The most convenient solution is to prevent the borders from being transformed. Of course, this causes the resulting space for the inset display box to expand or contract to take in the extra slack.

We need a more complex definition of display box and inset display box that takes into account both of the above notions. First, however, consider Fig. 2.13, which illustrates the revised definition. It contains a view and its subview both identical in size and both with 2-pixel borders. If the windows and viewports of the view and subview are defined to be identical rectangles, then both the local transformation and the display transformation must be identity transformations. Under the simplistic but incorrect definition, the subview's display box would be the window transformed to display coordinates; i.e., the same as the window. Similarly, the subview's inset display box would be the window's inset box. The result would be that the subview's borders would exactly overlap the superview's borders; we would see a final window with borders that are only 2 pixels wide.

Having defined both the subview and superview to have 2-pixel borders, we should expect the result to have a 4-pixel border. Under the revised definition, the subview's display box must map inside the topview's borders. Similarly, the subview's inset display box must map inside the combined 4-pixel border.

To provide a more exact definition of display box and inset display box that takes into account fixed size borders and the requirement to nest the borders, one or the other of the two terms must be defined operationally. Then the other term can be defined in terms of the first. For example, if display box were defined operationally, then **inset display box** would be defined as the display box inset by the border. Alternatively, if inset display box were defined operationally, then **display box** would be defined as the inset display box expanded by the border. The latter approach was adopted by the Smalltalk designers.

Chapter 2 Windows: An Overview and Basics

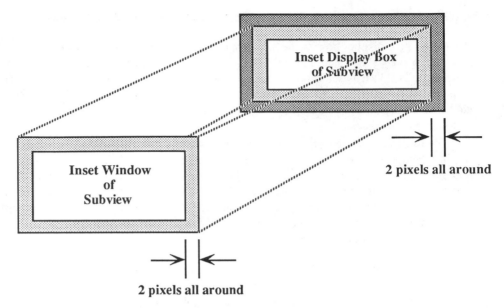

For simplicity, assume all windows and viewports are equal-sized and centered at the origin. Inset display boxes for successive views from a subview to a topview are nested inside the border.

The inset display box for the topview is 2 pixels inside the top viewport.
The inset display box for the subview is 4 pixels inside the top viewport.

The display box for the topview is the entire top viewport.
The display box for the subview is 2 pixels inside the top viewport.

Figure 2.13 Illustrating a more exact display box and inset display box terminology.

A view's **inset display box** can be defined operationally as follows: (1) if the view is a top view, the answer is the viewport inset by the border; otherwise, (2) transform the window to display coordinates and exclude those parts that lie outside the superview's inset display box (recursion is involved here); the answer is this result further inset by this view's border.

This notion of display boxes ensures that borders are additive. It ensures, for example, that mapping a subview with a 1-pixel border to a superview with a 2-pixel border doesn't get part of its inset display box overwritten by the superview's larger border. What is ultimately displayed on the screen is a window with a 3-pixel border. Additionally, a window transformed to display coordinates could overlap with the final position of the successive superviews' borders or even lie outside those borders. This would happen for example, if the viewport was defined to lie outside the superview's window. Those parts that lie outside or on the borders are not displayable; they are said to be **clipped**.

Since the window transformed to display coordinates can be larger than the display box (see Fig. 2.13), there is a need for a term that describes the former. It is called a **bounding box**. Note that the bounding box will be the same size as the display box when all borders are zero pixels wide. This will also remain true even if the bottom views are permitted to have nonzero width borders. Like display boxes, bounding boxes also exclude areas that are clipped.

Rectangles for windows, inset windows, viewports, bounding boxes, display boxes, and inset display boxes can be determined (some can be changed) with the following protocol. Since rectangles can be destructively modified, the standard protocol normally assigns and/or returns copies. A nonstandard protocol, normally intended for use by designers of subclasses, is provided that manipulates the originals; it is differentiated from the standard protocol by the prefix **get** or **set** and detailed separately.

window access

- aView **defaultWindow**

  Returns a default rectangle that encloses all subview windows (if there are any) or the entire display screen otherwise. Subclasses should redefine this method to provide an alternative default.

- aView **window**

  Returns a copy of the view's window.
- aView **window**: aWindow

  Set the view's window to a copy of aWindow.

- aView **insetWindow**

  Returns a copy of the view's inset window; i.e., the window exclusive of the border.

viewport access

- aView **viewport**

  Returns a copy of the view's viewport.

display box access

- aView **boundingBox**

  Returns the view's bounding box; i.e., its window is transformed to display coordinates taking clipping into account.

- aView **displayBox**

  Returns a copy of the view's display box. See above for a more detailed description of display boxes.

- aView **insetDisplayBox**

  Returns the view's inset display box (not a copy). See above for a more detailed description of inset display boxes.

nonstandard protocol for designers of subclasses (automatically locks and unlocks)

- aView **getController**

  Returns the view's controller if one exists and **nil** otherwise; **nil** indicates that the default controller is to be used when needed.

- aView **getWindow**

  Returns the view's window (not a copy). If no window has been specified, the default window is created, saved, and returned.

- aView **getViewport**

    Returns the view's viewport (not a copy). If no viewport has been specified, it is first computed from the window and the local transformation.

- aView **setTransformation**: aTransformation

    Sets the view's local transformation to aTransformation (not a copy) and unlocks the view.

- aView **setWindow**: aRectangle

    Sets the view's window to aRectangle and unlocks the view.

- aView **superView**: aView

    Sets the view's superview to aView and unlocks the view. Not normally needed since it is superseded by a more general protocol discussed in the next section.

2.4.8 Adding, Removing, and Querying Subviews

The protocol for constructing views is relatively simple. However, when views are to be hierarchically organized, an extra complication arises. First, the hierarchical structure must be specified; i.e., each view must specify its superview (the topview is an exception) and its subviews. Second, the window of a view must be partitioned into subwindows and integrated with the viewports of the subviews. We will call this latter requirement **viewport adjusting**.

The two tasks can be performed independently, with one protocol for querying and constructing the hierarchy and another protocol for viewport adjusting. A more general protocol is also provided for performing both tasks together. The hierarchy construction operations, in particular, eliminate the need to explicitly set superviews; i.e., associating a subview with a view automatically sets the superview of the subview. Viewport adjusting involves not only sizing a particular viewport but also positioning it to cover some small part of the superview's window. It can be specified by aligning one point with another, aligning one viewport with another, or providing proportional information that can be used for automatically sizing and positioning relative to an existing window.

superview access

- aView **isTopView**

    Returns **true** if the view is a topview; i.e., if it has no superview.

- aView **superView**

    Returns the superview of the view; **nil** for topviews.

- aView **topView**

    Returns the first view in the superview path (inclusive of itself) that is a topview.

subview access

- aView **firstSubView**

    Returns the first subview in the view's list of subviews if it is not empty, otherwise **nil**.

- aView **lastSubView**
  Returns the last subview in the view's list of subviews if it is not empty, otherwise **nil**.

- aView **subViews**
  Returns the view's collection of subviews.

subview inserting without viewport adjusting

- aView **addSubView**: aSubview
  Removes aSubview from the tree of views it is in (if any) and adds it to the rear of the list of subviews of aView. Sets the superview of aSubview to aView. An error is generated if aSubview is the same as aView, or its superview, etc.

- aView **addSubView**: aSubview **ifCyclic**: exceptionBlock
  Removes aSubview from the tree of views it is in (if any) and adds it to the rear of the list of subviews of aView. Sets the superview of aSubview to aView. The exception block is executed if aSubview is the same as aView, or its superview, and so on.

- aView **insertSubView**: aSubview **before**: anotherSubview **ifCyclic**: exceptionBlock
  Removes aSubview from the tree of views it is in (if any) and adds it before anotherSubview in the list of subviews of aView. Sets the superview of aSubview to aView. The exception block is executed if aSubview is the same as aView, or its superview, and so on. This method is not currently used.

viewport adjusting

- aView **align**: aViewportPoint **with**: aNewPositionForAViewportPoint
  Adds a displacement to the local transformation so that the point in the window coordinate system that is used to map to aViewportPoint now maps to aNewPositionForAViewportPoint.

- aView **scrollBy**: aPointSpecifyingAnAmountInWindowCoordinates
  Scrolls the view window in both the x and y directions. Positive amounts are up or left; negative amounts are down or right. Note that this is opposite to the direction in which transformations scroll. The viewport (or display box) is unchanged.

subview inserting and viewport adjusting with low-level protocol

- aView **addSubView**: aSubview **align**: aViewportPoint **with**: aNewViewportPoint
  Adds aSubview to the view's list of subviews and adds a displacement to the local transformation so that the point in the window coordinate system that used to map to aViewportPoint now maps to aNewViewportPoint.

subview inserting and viewport adjusting with high-level protocol

- aView **addSubView**: aSubview **above**: aLowerView
  Adds aSubview so that it lies above aLowerView.

- aView **addSubView**: aSubview **below**: aHigherView
  Adds aSubview so that it lies below aHigherView.

- aView **addSubView**: aSubview **toLeftOf**: aRightView
  Adds aSubview so that it lies to the left of aRightView.

- aView **addSubView**: aSubview **toRightOf**: aLeftView
  Adds aSubview so that it lies to the right of aLeftView

- aView **insertSubView**: aSubview **above**: aLowerView
  All **addSubView**: methods above insert aSubview at the end of the collection of subviews; this method inserts it before aLowerView. This can make a difference only if there is some overlap between subviews during the search for a subview to be given control. This method is not currently used.

- aView **addSubView**: aSubview **in**: aProportionalRectangle **borderWidth**: width
  Constructs a new window and viewport for aSubview that is proportional to aView's window; the border is specified as width. Each coordinate of aProportionalRectangle must be between 0 and 1 (typically a real). If the x coordinate of the origin of aRelativeRectangle is 0.5, the viewport will start at a position that is 0.5 of the original window width (half as wide). Similarly, if the x extent is 0.33, it will extend for .33 of the original window extent (one third the width). The same applies for the y direction. Both the new window and viewport are the same size but the window always starts at 0@0.

- aView **addSubView**: aSubview **viewport**: aViewport Rectangle
  Adds aSubview to aView and uses the existing subview's window and the new viewport to position it.

- aView **addSubView**: aSubview
  window: aWindowRectangle **viewport**: aViewportRectangle
  Adds aSubview to aView and uses the new window and viewport to position it.

subview removing

- aView **removeFromSuperView**
  Deletes the view from its superview's collection of subviews. Supplied to complete the implementation of **release** and should not be needed under normal conditions.

- aView **removeSubView**: aSubview
  Removes aSubview from the view's list of subviews. If the list of subviews does not contain aSubview, an error is reported. Supplied to complete the implementation of **release** and should not be needed under normal conditions.

- aView **removeSubViews**
  Removes all of the view's subviews. Supplied to complete the implementation of **release** and should not be needed under normal conditions.

Example

Consider the construction of a three-paned window as shown in Fig. 2.14. To be illustrative, we will attempt to construct it in many different ways. We construct aTopView with three subviews: leftTopView, rightTopView, and bottomView.

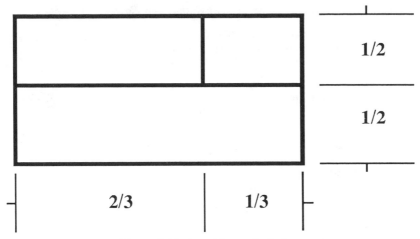

Figure 2.14 A multi-paned window.

Our goal is to have 2-pixel wide lines everywhere. The solution is to provide a 1-pixel wide boundary for aTopView and a 1-pixel wide boundary for each subview. In the final result, each line is 2 pixels wide. The alternative in which aTopView is 0 pixels wide with each subview 2 pixels wide does not work. It would cause the common boundaries, e.g., the line separating the top and bottom halves, to be 4 pixels wide.

For simplicity, we make the topview invisible (by default) and the subviews white. The topview is created with a given window and viewport. The task is to map the subview viewports to a portion of the topview window. To emphasize that the subview window size is not relevant to the exercise, we have made it abnormally large.

```
| aTopView aTopViewWindowSize leftTopView rightToView bottomView
aSubViewWindowSize |

{Common Code For Each Technique}
aTopViewWindowSize ← 0@0 extent: 100@100.
aTopView ← View new borderWidth: 1; yourself.
aTopView window: aTopViewWindowSize viewport: (100@100 corner: 300@300).

aSubViewWindowSize ← 0@0 extent: 1000@1000.
leftTopView ← View new insideColor: Form white; borderWidth: 1; yourself.
rightTopView ← View new insideColor: Form white; borderWidth: 1; yourself.
bottomView ← View new insideColor: Form white; borderWidth: 1; yourself.

{Technique 1: Using proportional sizing (the recommended technique)}

leftTopView window: aSubViewWindowSize.
rightTopView window: aSubViewWindowSize.
bottomView window: aSubViewWindowSize.

"For this approach, it was unnecessary to previously specify the border width."
aTopView addSubView: leftTopView in: (0@0 corner: 0.66@0.5) borderWidth: 1.
aTopView addSubView: rightTopView in: (0.66@0 corner: 1@0.5) borderWidth: 1.
aTopView addSubView: bottomView in: (0@0.5 corner: 1@1) borderWidth: 1.
"Note that this works independent of the actual value of aTopViewWindowSize."
```

{Technique 2: Using absolute sizing (window and viewport separated)}

leftTopView **window**: aSubViewWindowSize.
rightTopView **window**: aSubViewWindowSize.
bottomView **window**: aSubViewWindowSize.

aTopView **addSubView**: leftTopView **viewport**: (0@0 **corner**: 66@50).
aTopView **addSubView**: rightTopView **viewport**: (66@0 **corner**: 100@50).
aTopView **addSubView**: bottomView **viewport**: (0@50 **corner**: 100@100).
"The viewport sizes would have to change if aTopViewWindowSize were changed."

{Technique 3: Using absolute sizing (window and viewport together)}

aTopView **addSubView**: leftTopView
    window: aSubViewWindowSize **viewport**: (0@0 **corner**: 66@50).
aTopView **addSubView**: rightTopView
    window: aSubViewWindowSize **viewport**: (66@0 **corner**: 100@50).
aTopView **addSubView**: bottomView
    window: aSubViewWindowSize **viewport**: (0@50 **corner**: 100@100).
"A minor variation of technique 2."

{Technique 4: Using relative sizing and relative positioning}

leftTopView **window**: aSubViewWindowSize **viewport**: (0@0 **corner**: 66@50).
rightTopView **window**: aSubViewWindowSize **viewport**: (0@0 **corner**: 44@50).
bottomView **window**: aSubViewWindowSize **viewport**: (0@0 **corner**: 100@50).
"Note that the viewports all start at 0@0; i.e., positioning is done via the **addSubView**: methods."

aTopView **addSubView**: leftTopView.
aTopView **addSubView**: rightTopView **toRightOf**: leftTopView.
aTopView **addSubView**: bottomView **below**: leftTopView.
"The **addSubView**: methods reposition by adjusting the origin of the viewport rectangles."

{Technique 5: Using relative sizing and absolute positioning}

leftTopView **window**: aSubViewWindowSize **viewport**: (0@0 **corner**: 66@50).
rightTopView **window**: aSubViewWindowSize **viewport**: (0@0 **corner**: 44@50).
bottomView **window**: aSubViewWindowSize **viewport**: (0@0 **corner**: 100@50).
"Note that the viewports all start at 0@0; i.e., positioning is done via the **addSubView**: methods."

aTopView **addSubView**: leftTopView.
aTopView **addSubView**: rightTopView
    align: rightTopView **viewport topLeft with**: leftTopView **viewport topRight**.
aTopView **addSubView**: bottomView
    align: bottomView **viewport topLeft with**: leftTopView **viewport bottomLeft**.
"Positioning information is supplied by the alignment points."

{Technique 6: As above but specifying hierarchy and pane adjustments separately}

leftTopView **window**: aSubViewWindowSize **viewport**: (0@0 **corner**: 66@50).
rightTopView **window**: aSubViewWindowSize **viewport**: (0@0 **corner**: 44@50).
bottomView **window**: aSubViewWindowSize **viewport**: (0@0 **corner**: 100@50).
"Note that the viewports all start at 0@0; i.e., positioning is done via the **align**: methods."

Inside Smalltalk

```
aTopView addSubView: leftTopView.
aTopView addSubView: rightTopView.
aTopView addSubView: bottomView.

rightTopView
    align: rightTopView viewport topLeft with: leftTopView viewport topRight.
bottomView
    align: bottomView viewport topLeft with: leftTopView viewport bottomLeft.
```

It should be clear that proportional positioning is the most convenient. To see that, consider changing the size of the topview window. All viewports for the subviews have to be correspondingly adjusted.

Example

In general, it seems advisable to avoid pane adjustments with such low-level operations as **align:with:**. However, there are situations where the more convenient operations are inadequate. For instance, suppose the viewports for subview1 and subview2 were different sizes and we wished to stack them up in the superview's window so that their centers lined up. One solution is the following:

```
superviewCenter ← subview1 superview window center

newSubview1Center ← superviewCenter - (0 @ (subview1 viewport height // 2))
newSubview2Center ← superviewCenter + (0 @ (subview2 viewport height // 2))

subview1 align: subview1 viewport center with: newSubview1Center
subview2 align: subview2 viewport center with: newSubview2Center
```

2.4.9 The Tic-Tac-Toe Game

As an aid to understanding the protocol provided, we consider a version of the game tic-tac-toe. Three classes are defined: TicTacToeGame, TicTacToeController, and TicTacToeView.

Class TicTacToeGame provides a complete protocol for playing the game independent of whether or not there is an associated controller or view. Because we anticipate that it will be used as a model, we have it inherit from **Model**. Method **example1** demonstrates how the game can be played via confirmers and fill-in-the-blank requests. We discuss method **example2** later.

A TicTacToeGame keeps track of a playing board, the last player, whether or not a winner has already been determined, and the winning squares if there has been a winner. The board is a 3 by 3 array linearized to one dimension containing either #X, #O, or #Empty and responding to messages such as 'at: rowIndex and: columnIndex' and 'at: rowIndex and: columnIndex put: aValue'. The last player is either #X, #O, or #None. Rather than have the winner be a boolean, we decided to make it either **nil** (uninitialized), #X, or #O. Consequently, if it is nonnil, its values must also be the same as the last player. The sequence of winning squares is a 3-element array containing the coordinates (as points) of the winning row, column, or diagonal.

To start the game, a new tic-tac-toe game is created (**new** automatically initializes it) and the next player is set either to #X or #O. A move is made by specifying a player (either #X or #O), a rowIndex, and a columnIndex via '**play:** aPlayer **at:** rowIndex **and:** columnIndex'. An error message is generated if either an incorrect player is specified, an illegal board position is provided (one that is either outside the bounds or already occupied with #X or #O), or a winner has already been determined. The error message can be avoided by first testing if the move is legal using the boolean protocol 'isLegalFor: aPlayer toPlayAt: rowIndex and: columnIndex'. The winner is determined by sending the message **winner** to the game. When a winner has been determined or if no moves are possible, method **gameOver** returns **true**. A new game can be played by creating another game or reinitializing the old one.

Class TicTacToeGame

class name	TicTacToeGame
superclass	Model
instance variable names	board lastPlayer winner winningSquares

class methods

instance creation

new
    ↑super **new initialize**

open
    "Creates a new view that both creates and initializes the corresponding model and controller. The new controller is scheduled (note that there is no return from the scheduling)."
    ScheduledControllers **scheduleActive**: TicTacToeView **new resize controller**

examples

example1
    "Play the game directly (no controllers or views are involved)."
    | aGame nextPlayerIsX response responseStream row column |
    aGame ← TicTacToeGame **new**.
    "Use our own interface."
    aGame **nextPlayer**:
        ((self **confirm**: 'Does the X player want to start first?') **ifTrue**: [#X] **ifFalse**: [#O]).
    [aGame **gameOver**] **whileFalse**: [
        response ← FillInTheBlank **request**:
            ('Player ', (aGame **nextPlayer**),
                ', please provide the next board\coordinate as two integers', '
                separated by blanks') **withCRs**.
        responseStream ← ReadStream **on**: response.
        row ← Integer **readFrom**: responseStream.
        responseStream **skipSeparators**.
        column ← Integer **readFrom**: responseStream.
        (aGame **isLegalFor**: (aGame **nextPlayer**) **toPlayAt**: row **and**: column)
            ifTrue: [aGame **play**: (aGame **nextPlayer**) **at**: row **and**: column]
            ifFalse: [
                (self **confirm**: 'Bad move, do you want to continue?') **ifFalse**: [↑self]]].

    "The game is over"
    self **confirm**:
        ((aGame **winner** == #None
            ifTrue: ['It''s a tie']
            ifFalse: ['You win, player ', aGame **winner**]),
                '.\Acknowledge with either yes or no.') **withCRs**.
    "TicTacToeGame **example1**"

example2
"Play the game using a specially designed fully autonomous scheduled controller and view."
self **open**

"TicTacToeGame **example2**"

instance methods

instance initialization

initialize
board ← (Array **new:** 9) **atAllPut:** #Empty; **yourself**.
winner ← nil.
lastPlayer ← #None

nextPlayer: aPlayer
(lastPlayer == #None) & ((aPlayer == #X) | (aPlayer == #O))
    ifFalse: [self **error:** 'initialize with #X or #O only at the beginning'].
lastPlayer ← aPlayer == #X **ifTrue:** [#O] **ifFalse:** [#X].
↑aPlayer

testing

winningSquares
↑winningSquares

winner
"Returns either #X, #O, or #None."
| row column piece |

"Has the winner been previously computed and cached in instance variable winner?"
winner ~~ nil **ifTrue:** [↑winner].

"First, check the three rows."
1 **to:** 3 **do:** [:row |
    piece ← self **at:** row **and:** 1.
    (piece ~~ #Empty) & (piece == (self **at:** row **and:** 2)) &
        (piece == (self **at:** row **and:** 3))
        ifTrue: [
            winner ← piece.
            winningSquares ← Array **with:** row@1 **with:** row@2 **with:** row@3.
            ↑winner]].

"Second, check the three columns."
1 **to:** 3 **do:** [:column |
    piece ← self **at:** 1 **and:** column.
    (piece ~~ #Empty) &
        (piece == (self **at:** 2 **and:** column)) & (piece == (self **at:** 3 **and:** column))
        ifTrue: [
            winner ← piece.
            winningSquares ←
                Array **with:** 1@column **with:** 2@column **with:** 3@column.
            ↑winner]].

```
        "Third, check the two diagonals."
        piece ← self at: 1 and: 1.
        (piece ~~ #Empty) & (piece == (self at: 2 and: 2)) & (piece == (self at: 3 and: 3))
            ifTrue: [
                winner ← piece.
                winningSquares ← Array with: 1@1 with: 2@2 with: 3@3. ↑winner].
        piece ← self at: 1 and: 3.
        (piece ~~ #Empty) & (piece == (self at: 2 and: 2)) & (piece == (self at: 3 and: 1))
            ifTrue: [
                winner ← piece.
                winningSquares ← Array with: 1@3 with: 2@2 with: 3@1. ↑winner].
        "Fourth, there is no winner"
        ↑#None

nextPlayer
        ↑lastPlayer == #X ifTrue: [#O] ifFalse: [#X]

gameOver
        "A game is over is there is a winner or there are no more moves to make."
        self winner ~~ #None ifTrue: [↑true].
        board do: [:piece | piece == #Empty ifTrue: [↑false]
        ↑true

board manipulation

at: rowIndex and: columnIndex
        "The board subscripts are linearized to 3 * (row - 1) + column."
        ↑board at: 3 * (rowIndex - 1) + columnIndex

at: rowIndex and: columnIndex put: aValue
        "The board subscripts are linearized to 3 * (row - 1) + column."
        ↑board at: 3 * (rowIndex - 1) + columnIndex put: aValue

playing

isLegalFor: aPlayer toPlayAt: rowIndex and: columnIndex
        (rowIndex between: 1 and: 3) & (columnIndex between: 1 and: 3) ifFalse: [↑false].
        (self at: rowIndex and: columnIndex) == #Empty ifFalse: [↑false].
        self winner == #None ifFalse: [↑false].
        ↑lastPlayer ~= aPlayer

play: aPlayer at: rowIndex and: columnIndex
        (self isLegalFor: aPlayer toPlayAt: rowIndex and: columnIndex)
            ifTrue: [self at: rowIndex and: columnIndex put: aPlayer]
            ifFalse: [
                self error: 'you can''t play at ', rowIndex printString, ' and ',
                    columnIndex printString].
        lastPlayer ← aPlayer
```

A more visually interesting version of the game is demonstrated in method **example2**. This variation opens a new tic-tac-toe controller which causes it to be scheduled by the window manager. Fig. 2.15 provides two snapshots of the interactive game.

The tic-tac-toe controller is designed to retain control (see **isControlActive**) if the view has not yet been closed (view ~~ **nil**) and either the mouse is inside the view (independent of whether or not a button is depressed) or outside with no button depressed. To lose control, a player must deliberately press a mouse button outside the view. Since this differs from the default behavior of **Controller** (it loses control if the mouse is outside the view or the blue button is depressed), a new method is provided to override it. Method **controlInitialize** (previously a no-op) was also overridden to display the view.

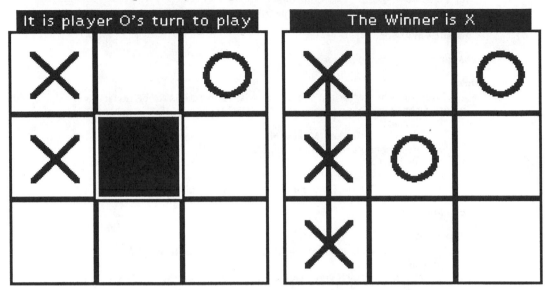

Figure 2.15 A snapshot of the tic-tac-toe game.

The heart of the controller is provided by **controlActivity**. Its main task is to keep track of the mouse. While the red mouse button is not depressed, nothing is processed. Once it is depressed, three possibilities can occur: Either the mouse is inside the title box, inside the remainder of the view, or outside. The first possibility results in an attempt to close the view (this is confirmed with the player in case it was accidental). *Hence, the game is terminated by depressing the red button in the title box.* In a later section, we will make use of the standard blue button pop-up menus for this purpose. The second possibility results in direct control of the game (see **redButtonActivity**). Nothing happens for the third possibility; presumably control is subsequently lost and some other scheduled controller is activated.

Method **redButtonActivity** is concerned with tracking the mouse and making game moves. Tracking the mouse involves highlighting the tic-tac-toe square it is over and dehighlighting it as it leaves; when off the board, nothing happens. To simplify matters, the view was designed to keep track of the last highlighted square. To highlight a new square, the view automatically dehighlights the previously highlighted square (if any). Tracking continues as long as the mouse button is depressed. Once it is released, the mouse coordinate is used to determine where it was released (via message **whereIs:**). Nothing happens if it was off the board. If it was on the board, it is interpreted as a move for the next player. If the move is legal, the move is played and the board is redisplayed. More is involved than simply leaving the new square highlighted. The header on the board indicating the next player to play must be changed. Additionally, a more global change is required if this move won the game (a line is drawn across the winning squares). After the display, a check is made to see if the game is over. If it is, the game is restarted automatically. Alternatively, if the move was illegal, the board is flashed to indicate an illegal move and nothing is changed.

Class TicTacToeController

class name	TicTacToeController
superclass	Controller
instance variable names	"none: all inherited"

instance methods

handling future menu messages

close
"Confirm whether or not the player wishes to terminate or restart"
(self **confirm**: 'Do you really wish to close?')
    ifTrue: [
        view **release**. "Makes this controller's view nil (among other things)."
        ScheduledControllers **unschedule**: self]
    ifFalse: [
        (self **confirm**: 'Do you wish to restart?')
            ifTrue: [view **reInitialize**. view **displayView**]]

scheduling control

isControlActive
"To lose control, user must have pressed a button while outside the view or released the view."
↑view ~~ nil **and**: [self **viewHasCursor or**: [sensor **anyButtonPressed not**]]

controlInitialize
"Simply displays the view."
view **displayView**

controlActivity
"Handle attempts to play the game or end it independently."
sensor **redButtonPressed** & self **viewCloseAreaHasCursor ifTrue**: [↑self **close**].
sensor **redButtonPressed** & self **viewHasCursor ifTrue**: [↑self **redButtonActivity**].

redButtonActivity
"Determine whether no move, a legal move, or an illegal move was made."
| squareLocationAsAPoint row column |
"As long as the red button is depressed, track the mouse highlighting the squares underneath it."
self **track**.

"Next, determine where it was released"
squareLocationAsAPoint ← view **whereIs**: sensor **mousePoint**.
(squareLocationAsAPoint **isKindOf**: Point)
    ifTrue: [
        "Player let go the mouse while on a square. Make the appropriate play."
        row ← squareLocationAsAPoint **x**. column ← squareLocationAsAPoint **y**.
        (model **isLegalFor**: (model **nextPlayer**) **toPlayAt**: row **and**: column)
            ifTrue: [
                model **play**: (model **nextPlayer**) **at**: row **and**: column.
                view **displaySquare**: row **and**: column.
                view **displayTitle**. view **displayWinnerLine**.
                model **gameOver ifTrue**: [view **reInitialize**]]
            ifFalse: [view **flash** "Not legal"]].
"Do nothing if the mouse is off the board."

track
>"Track the mouse, highlighting the squares it goes over."
>| squareLocationAsAPoint |
>[sensor **redButtonPressed**]
>>   **whileTrue**: [
>>>   "Determine which square (if any) the mouse is on."
>>>   squareLocationAsAPoint ← view **whereIs**: sensor **mousePoint**.
>>>   (squareLocationAsAPoint **isKindOf**: Point)
>>>>   **ifTrue**: [
>>>>   view
>>>>>   **highLight**: squareLocationAsAPoint **x**
>>>>>   **and**: squareLocationAsAPoint **y**]
>>>>   **ifFalse**: [view **deHighLight**]].
>"Now the button has been released. Make sure the last square highlighted is not left highlighted."
>view **deHighLight**

viewCloseAreaHasCursor
>   ↑view **closeAreaContainsPoint**: sensor **cursorPoint**

viewHasCursor
>   ↑(super **viewHasCursor**) **or**: [self **viewCloseAreaHasCursor**]

The tic-tac-toe view maintains one rectangle to delimit the game title and another one for the outer perimeter of the board, a dictionary of rectangles (one per square) to delimit the squares on the board, an indication of the last highlighted square, and four forms: aWhiteSquare, anX, anO, and aDot. The title rectangle is used to answer the controller's **closeAreaHasCursor** query; the board rectangle (among other things) is used for flashing when a move is illegal. The dictionary is indexed via points corresponding to the coordinates of the squares; i.e., 1@1, 1@2, 1@3, 2@1, 2@2, 2@3, 3@1, 3@2, and 3@3; it is used for determining which square (if any) the mouse is on. The forms are obviously used for drawing the squares; form aDot is used to draw a line across the winning squares.

All rectangles are positioned at absolute screen coordinates. Drawing the board consists of displaying the appropriate forms at the origin of the rectangles for the squares. Note that the three square forms all have a border of width 2. Hence, when two of them touch, the common border has width 4. This explains why the outer border of the board is thinner than the lines separating the squares.These forms are reconstructed from forms LargeX and LargeO (class variables) whenever the game board is resized.

Class initialization constructs the two large forms. Form LargeX is constructed from a white form by drawing two lines across it. Form LargeO is similarly constructed by drawing a circle across it. The resize facility mentioned above obtains a rectangle from the user (for positioning and sizing) and then constructs local versions anX and anO modelled after LargeX and LargeO. Two completely different strategies are presented out of interest. The first strategy, the one currently used, is illustrated in method **privateVERSION1Cons-tructNewBoardFrom:**. It first computes the required size of the square (in general, its shape can be rectangular if the user provided a nonsquare sizing rectangle). Then, it draws two lines appropriately directed on form anX and a circle on form anO. LargeX and LargeO are not actually used. The second strategy illustrated in **privateVERSION2ConstructNew-BoardFrom**: obtains anX by displaying LargeX on anX using a suitable transformation. The transformation is obtained by using LargeX as the window and anX as the viewport. In actuality, the details are a minor variation because anX and anO have a border, while LargeX and LargeO do not.

Instance initialization sets instance variable lastSquareHighlighted to **nil** to indicate that no square has been highlighted. It also sets the view's model and controller. Since a tic-tac-toe view inherits from class **View**, the controller's model and view are set automatically as a side effect. The viewport is then set up as the board rectangle.

The major methods are concerned with displaying the board. First, the title is displayed. One of two possible titles is constructed by converting a chosen string to display text, extracting the associated form, and reversing it to get reverse video. It is then centered above the board. Then each square is processed and displayed using one of the three preconstructed forms. Finally, a winning line is displayed across the winning squares if the game is over.

Highlighting and dehighlighting is achieved by reversing the appropriate rectangular area on the display screen. The view keeps track of the last square highlighted (if any).

Class TicTacToeView

class name	TicTacToeView
superclass	View
instance variable names	titleRectangle boardRectangle squareRectangles
	lastSquareHighlighted aWhiteSquare anX anO aDot
class variable names	LargeX LargeO

class methods

class initialization

initialize
        | aDot |

        "Create the large X and O objects of size 100 by 100."
        aDot ← (Form **extent:** 4@4) **black**.
        LargeX ← Form **extent:** 100@100. LargeO ← Form **extent:** 100@100.

        "Now, draw the X and O."
        (Line **from:** 25@25 **to:** 75@75 **withForm:** aDot) **displayOn:** LargeX.
        (Line **from:** 75@25 **to:** 25@75 **withForm:** aDot) **displayOn:** LargeX.
        (Circle **new form:** aDot; **radius:** 25; **center:** 50@50; **yourself**) **displayOn:** LargeO.

        "TicTacToeView initialize"

instance methods

instance initialization

initialize
        super **initialize**.
        lastSquareHighlighted ← nil.
        self **model:** TicTacToeGame **new controller:** TicTacToeController **new**

reInitialize
> lastSquareHighlighted ← nil.
> model **initialize**.
> controller **initialize**

resizing

resize
> "Constructs a new board rectangle from the user supplied positioning rectangle. Currently uses version1 but could be replaced by version2."
> self **privateVERSION1ConstructNewBoardFrom**: Rectangle **fromUser**.
>
> "Position the window and viewport (now the revised boardRectangle)."
> "The window position or size doesn't matter"
> self **window**: (0@0 **corner**: 100@100) **viewport**: boardRectangle.

querying

closeAreaContainsPoint: aPoint
> ↑titleRectangle **containsPoint**: aPoint

whereIs: aPoint
> "Returns the square containing the point in the form row@column if there is one; **nil** otherwise. Recall that the square rectangles are in display coordinates."
> 1 **to**: 3 **do**: [:row |
> > 1 **to**: 3 **do**: [:column |
> > > ((squareRectangles **at**: row@column) **containsPoint**: aPoint)
> > > > **ifTrue**: [↑row@column]]].
> ↑nil

highlighting

highLight: row **and**: column
> "If its already highlighted, do nothing. If another square is highlighted already, it must be dehighlighted before the new one is highlighted."
> | newSquareToHighlight |
> newSquareToHighlight ← row@column.
> lastSquareHighlighted = newSquareToHighlight **ifTrue**: [↑self].
> lastSquareHighlighted ~~ nil
> > **ifTrue**: [Display **reverse**: (squareRectangles **at**: lastSquareHighlighted)].
> Display **reverse**: (squareRectangles **at**: newSquareToHighlight).
> lastSquareHighlighted ← newSquareToHighlight

deHighLight
> "Dehighlight the highlighted square (if any exists)."
> lastSquareHighlighted ~~ nil
> > **ifTrue**: [Display **reverse**: (squareRectangles **at**: lastSquareHighlighted)].
> lastSquareHighlighted ← nil

displaying

displayView
> "Shows all squares either as an X, O, or white."
> self **displayTitle**.
> 1 **to**: 3 **do**: [:row | 1 **to**: 3 **do**: [:column | self **displaySquare**: row **and**: column]].
> self **displayWinnerLine**

displayTitle
"The title will change depending on who's turn it is to play."
| theWinner title aTitleForm titleXOrigin titleYOrigin |
"Make both titles the same size to ease overwriting."
(theWinner ← model **winner**) == #None
    ifTrue: [title ← ' It is player ', model **nextPlayer**, '''s turn to play ']
    ifFalse: [title ← '   The Winner is ', theWinner, '   '].
aTitleForm ← title **asDisplayText form reverse.** "You can't reverse display text"
titleXOrigin ← boardRectangle **origin x** +
    ((boardRectangle **width** - aTitleForm **width**)//2).
titleYOrigin ← boardRectangle **origin y** - aTitleForm **height.**
titleRectangle ← titleXOrigin @ titleYOrigin **extent:** aTitleForm **extent.**
aTitleForm **displayAt:** titleOrigin.

displaySquare: row **and:** column
| square squareForm |
"Recall: the squares are in display coordinates."
square ← model **at:** row **and:** column.
squareForm ← square = #X
    ifTrue: [anX]
    ifFalse: [square = #O **ifTrue:** [anO] **ifFalse:** [aWhiteSquare]].
squareForm **displayAt:** (squareRectangles **at:** row@column) **origin.**

displayWinnerLine
| moves firstSquare lastSquare startPoint lastPoint |
model **winner** ~~ #None
    ifTrue: [
        moves ← model **winningSquares.**
        firstSquare ← squareRectangles **at:** moves **first.**
        lastSquare ← squareRectangles **at:** moves **last.**
        startPoint ← firstSquare **origin** + (firstSquare **extent** // 2).
        lastPoint ← lastSquare **origin** + (lastSquare **extent** // 2).
        (Line **from:** startPoint **to:** lastPoint **withForm:** ADot) **displayOn:** Display]

flash
Display **flash:** boardRectangle

private

privateVERSION1ConstructNewBoardFrom: aRectangle
| desiredBoardSize squareWidth squareHeight squareSize
oneQuarterOfDesiredWidth oneHalfOfDesiredWidth threeQuartersOfDesiredWidth
oneQuarterOfDesiredHeight threeQuartersOfDesiredHeight
oneHalfOfDesiredHeight |

"Determine the desired size of the individual squares."
desiredBoardSize ← aRectangle **extent.**
squareWidth ← (desiredBoardSize **x** / 3) **truncated.**
squareHeight ← (desiredBoardSize **y** / 3) **truncated.**
squareSize ← squareWidth@squareHeight.

"Compute useful sizes."
oneQuarterOfDesiredWidth ← (squareWidth * 0.25) **truncated.**
oneHalfOfDesiredWidth ← (squareWidth * 0.5) **truncated.**
threeQuartersOfDesiredWidth ← (squareWidth * 0.75) **truncated.**
oneQuarterOfDesiredHeight ← (squareHeight * 0.25) **truncated.**
threeQuartersOfDesiredHeight ← (squareHeight * 0.75) **truncated.**
oneHalfOfDesiredHeight ← (squareHeight * 0.5) **truncated.**

"Create the dot, white square, X and O and also draw the X and O."
aWhiteSquare ← (Form **extent:** squareSize) **borderWidth:** 2.
anX ← (Form **extent:** squareSize) **borderWidth:** 2.
anO ← (Form **extent:** squareSize) **borderWidth:** 2.
aDot ← (Form **extent:** 4@4) **black**.
(Line
    from: oneQuarterOfDesiredWidth @ oneQuarterOfDesiredHeight
    to: threeQuartersOfDesiredWidth @ threeQuartersOfDesiredHeight
    withForm: aDot) **displayOn:** anX.
(Line
    from: threeQuartersOfDesiredWidth @ oneQuarterOfDesiredHeight
    to: oneQuarterOfDesiredWidth @ threeQuartersOfDesiredHeight
    withForm: aDot) **displayOn:** anX.
(Circle **new**
    form: aDot;
    radius: (oneQuarterOfDesiredWidth min: oneQuarterOfDesiredHeight);
    center: oneHalfOfDesiredWidth @ oneHalfOfDesiredHeight;
    yourself) **displayOn:** anO.

"Finish up the board computations."
self **privateAdjustBoardParametersFrom:** aRectangle **and:** squareSize.

privateVERSION2ConstructNewBoardFrom: aRectangle
    | squareSize aBox aTransformation |

"Determine the desired size of the individual squares."
squareSize ← (aRectangle **extent** / 3) **rounded**.

aWhiteSquare ← (Form **extent:** squareSize) **borderWidth:** 2.
anX ← (Form **extent:** squareSize) **borderWidth:** 2.
anO ← (Form **extent:** squareSize) **borderWidth:** 2.
aDot ← (Form **extent:** 4@4) **black**.

"Redraw the large X and O over the inset display box of the X and O"
aBox ← 2@2 **corner:** anX **extent** - (2@2). "The insetDisplayBox for the form"
aTransformation ← WindowingTransformation
    window: (LargeX **boundingBox**) **viewport:** aBox.

LargeX **displayOn:** anX **transformation:** aTransformation **clippingBox:** aBox.
LargeO **displayOn:** anO **transformation:** aTransformation **clippingBox:** aBox.

"Finish up the board computations."
self **privateAdjustBoardParametersFrom:** aRectangle **and:** squareSize.

privateAdjustBoardParametersFrom: aRectangle **and:** squareSize
    | xOffset yOffset |
"Compute the origin of each square in display coordinates"
squareRectangles ← Dictionary **new**.
1 **to:** 3 **do:** [:row |
    1 **to:** 3 **do:** [:column |
        xOffset ← (column - 1) * squareSize **x** + aRectangle **origin x**.
        yOffset ← (row - 1) * squareSize **y** + aRectangle **origin y**.
        squareRectangles
            at: row@column
            put: (xOffset@yOffset **extent:** squareSize)]].

"Finally, adjust the board as close as possible to the desired size"
boardRectangle ← aRectangle **origin extent:** squareSize * 3.
titleRectangle ← boardRectangle. "Temporary until the board is displayed"

2.5 THE SUPPORTING CONTROLLERS AND VIEWS

By a **supporting** controller or view (see Fig. 2.16), we mean one that extends the protocol already provided by classes **Controller** and **View** and that can either be **instantiated** (instances can be created) or serve as the basis for the design of more complicated specializations. The supporting controllers and views include the remaining basic controllers and views; i.e., **NoController**, **MouseMenuController**, **StandardSystemController**, and **StandardSystemView**, along with **ScreenController** and **ScrollController**. The basic controllers and views can all be instantiated. The screen controller was designed to provide the one instance that controls the screen's background; additional instances were not intended. The scroll controller was designed as an abstract class that could be refined by specializations.

We consider these classes in the order in which they were mentioned. The reader interested primarily in using existing classes of controllers and views should concentrate on the basic controllers and views. Those intending to develop their own specializations should consider the screen controller as an example of the specialization methodology; i.e., a class obtained by specializing MouseMenuController. The scroll controller is of interest for two reasons: (1) it introduces the scroll bar terminology used by the system, and (2) it provides enough detail for those wishing to develop their own specialized scroll bars.

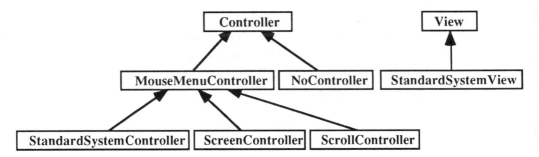

Figure 2.16 Supporting controller and view classes.

2.5.1 The NoController Class

Class **NoController** (see Fig. 2.17) provides the basic protocol for applications that are non-interactive; i.e., that never explicitly require control as a consequence of keyboard or mouse interactions. It is a subclass of controller that cannot be started and that does not want to get or keep control.

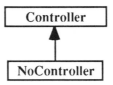

Figure 2.17 The inheritance structure for NoController.

Creating Instances of NoController (a Preview)

An instance of NoController can be created in the usual way; i.e.,

NoController **new**

The NoController Protocol

The NoController protocol refines the Controller protocol by specializing four of the existing methods. No new protocol is added.

creating new non-interactive controllers

- NoController **new**
  Returns an initialized non-interactive controller.

the revised control protocol

- aNoController **startUp**
  Does nothing.
- aNoController **isControlActive**
  Always returns **false**.
- aNoController **isControlWanted**
  Always returns **false**.

Instances of **NoController** are useful when some window displays *read-only* information. For example, the bit editor displays the form being edited twice: once in an expanded size (this is the version that can be modified by the user) and once in normal size (the read-only version; the view uses an instance of **NoController**). An instance of **NoController** is also used to prevent write-access to a displayed FillInTheBlank request. Of course, a more active controller is used for the subview into which the user is to reply.

2.5.2 The MouseMenuController Class

Class **MouseMenuController** (see Fig. 2.18) provides the basic protocol for applications that use menus. Facilities are provided to associate pop-up menus with the three mouse buttons and for selecting entries in the menus. Typically, pop-up menus are only associated with the yellow and blue buttons. The yellow button tends to be used for application specific menus; the blue button for application independent menus such as closing or resizing the window. The red button is not currently attached to pop-up menus.

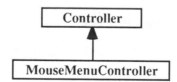

Figure 2.18 The inheritance structure for MouseMenuController.

To associate a menu with the yellow button, we must first create a pop-up menu, for example, with three entries containing 'top,' 'middle,' and 'bottom,' along with a corresponding array of symbols, say, containing #topHandler, #middleHandler, and #bottomHandler. Both the pop-up menu and the array are then associated with the yellow button with a special mouse-menu controller message. Subsequently, depressing the yellow button causes the pop-up menu to appear. Selecting the 'middle' entry causes the unary message **middleHandler** to be sent to the **menu message receiver**, which, by default, is the current mouse menu controller. Typically, each application defines a subclass of MouseMenuController and associates menu messages like **middleHandler** with the subclass.

Creating Mouse-Menu Controllers (a Preview)

Mouse-menu controllers are created in the usual way, but they must be extended with appropriate yellow, red, and blue button menus. Typically, only yellow button menus are added. No window currently uses red button menus and the blue button menu provided by the top view (usually a standard system view) need not be extended; most subviews relinquish control to the top view when the blue button is depressed. The following illustrates how a new mouse-menu controller with a yellow button menu is set up. Equivalent code for red and blue button menus can also be added.

```
aMouseMenuControllerClass
        "e.g., MouseMenuController or TextCollectorController" new
            yellowButtonMenu: UserYellowButtonMenu
            yellowButtonMessages: UserYellowButtonMessages
```

where UserYellowButtonMenu and UserYellowButtonMessages are usually class variables set up as follows:

```
UserYellowButtonMenu ←
        (PopUpMenu
            labels: 'left\right\up\down' withCRs
            lines: #(2)).
UserYellowButtonMessages ← #(left right up down).
```

Additionally, the class must have methods **left**, **right**, **up**, and **down** specified by UserYellowButtonMessages. When the yellow button is depressed, the yellow button pop-up menu appears with the four selections. Selecting 'right,' for example, causes the controller to be sent the **right** message. Note that we could use local variables instead of class variables. The existing classes that provide specialized yellow button menus all use class variables as a convention. It also means that each controller instance uses the same pop-up menu (as opposed to creating a new pop-up menu for each controller).

The MouseMenuController Protocol

The mouse-menu protocol overrides the basic controller methods to permit yellow, red, and blue button pop-up menus. Although it is permitted, there is currently no controller in the system that uses red button pop-up menus.

creating new controllers

- MouseMenuController **new**
      Returns a mouse menu controller *without* associated menus but otherwise properly initialized.

initializing and releasing controllers

- aMouseMenuController **initialize**

  Initializes the mouse menu controller but *does not modify associated menus* (if any).

- aMouseMenuController **release**

  Breaks the cycle between the controller and its view. Also releases the pop-up menus associated with the controller. In an MVC triad, the standard convention is to release only the view; it in turn automatically sends a release message to the associated controller.

- aMouseMenuController **reset**

  Eliminates references to all mouse button menus *but does not release them.* This method is not currently used.

controlling mouse menu activity

- aMouseMenuController **isControlActive**

  This message is normally sent to determine whether or not *control is to be retained by a controller that already has control.* In the protocol of class **MouseMenuController**, true is returned if the cursor is inside the view.

- aMouseMenuController **controlActivity**

  Activates the yellow, red, or blue pop-up menu (if any are provided) whenever the corresponding button is depressed inside the associated view and then defaults to the standard controller protocol for the remaining interactions; i.e., passing control down to lower-level controllers. The pop-up menus are activated by sending either the **yellowButtonActivity**, **redButtonActivity**, or **blueButtonActivity** messages.

- aMouseMenuController **yellowButtonActivity**
- aMouseMenuController **redButtonActivity**
- aMouseMenuController **blueButtonActivity**

  Determines which item in the associated pop-up menu is selected. If one is selected, sends the corresponding unary message to the menu message receiver.

setting up the menus

- aMouseMenuController
  yellowButtonMenu: aPopUpMenu
      yellowButtonMessages: anArrayOfUnaryMessages
- aMouseMenuController
  redButtonMenu: aPopUpMenu
      redButtonMessages: anArrayOfUnaryMessages
- aMouseMenuController
  blueButtonMenu: aPopUpMenu
      blueButtonMessages: anArrayOfUnaryMessages

  Associates the pop-up menu with the specified mouse button. When the mouse button is subsequently depressed in the view, the pop-up menu is activated. If an entry is selected, the corresponding unary message is sent to the menu message receiver. Can be used to permanently disassociate the mouse button from a pop-up menu by providing **nil** to both parameters.

determining the menu message receiver

- aMouseMenuController **menuMessageReceiver**

  Returns the object that should be sent the unary message associated with a selected menu item. The default is to return self. To change the menu message receiver, a subclass of MouseMenuController must be created and this method overridden.

Setting Up Mouse Menus

When an existing controller inherits a menu (say, a blue button menu) that is not appropriate for the specialization, it can be removed very simply as follows:

aController **blueButtonMenu:** nil **blueButtonMessages**: nil

This is done, for example, by the bit editor (try BitEditor **magnifyOnScreen** and focus on *a very small portion of the screen*; e.g., 1 cm square) to eliminate the standard protocol for closing the editor. In this case, the editor is closed by simply clicking outside the editor view. Creating a new blue button menu is not much more difficult. The standard system blue button menu for example could be created as follows:

```
aController "for example, aStandardSystemController"
        blueButtonMenu:
            (PopUpMenu
                    labels: 'under\move\frame\collapse\close' withCRs
                    lines: #(4))
        blueButtonMessages:
            #(under move expand collapse close)
```

Recall (see Sect.1.2, *Windows and Window Support for the Novices*) that 4 in **lines:** causes a line to be added *after* the fourth entry; i.e., after collapse. In practice, most classes with mouse menus are designed with class variables that contain the information needed to set up appropriate menus. For example, the information needed to set up the standard system blue button menu is first created and stored in class variables such as ScheduledBlueButton-Menu and ScheduledBlueButtonMessages (set up by class method **initialize**) as follows:

```
ScheduledBlueButtonMenu ←
        (PopUpMenu
            labels: 'under\move\frame\collapse\close' withCRs
            lines: #(4)).
        ScheduledBlueButtonMessages ← #(under move expand collapse close).
```

This information is then associated with a controller in the obvious way, for example,

```
aController "for example, aStandardSystemController"
        blueButtonMenu: ScheduledBlueButtonMenu
        blueButtonMessages: ScheduledBlueButtonMessages
```

Creating New Mouse Menus in Specializations

When a specialization is created, it is often the case that new menu entries need to be added. Unfortunately, there is no protocol for extending existing menus. Such a protocol would be an interesting and useful extension. The current strategy requires that the existing menu entries be first discovered, duplicated, and then extended.

For example, a specialization UserController of StandardSystemController that needs to add new entry 'fileOutView' must first discover the existing menu structure. One way might be to first determine the inheritance hierarchy and then view method **blueButton-Menu:blueButtonMessages:** in StandardSystemController using the browser. By querying for all implementors, it is a simple matter to determine the nearest superclass in the hierarchy that initializes the blue button menu. When this method is investigated, one typically discovers that the menu information is to be found in class variables as illustrated above.

Such variables are usually initialized in the **initialize** class method. This method can be found by looking at all class variable references.

Once the existing menu information is determined, it can be copied and used for setting up the modified mouse menus. For some controllers, the **initialize** instance method is often (but not always) designed to send an **initializeYellowButtonMenu** or an **initializeBlue-ButtonMenu** message. The former, for instance, is sent by controller ParagraphEditor (and its subclasses dealing with scrollable text controllers). The latter is sent by the standard system controller. The **initializeYellowButtonMenu** instance method is designed to send a **yellowButtonMenu:yellowButtonMessages:** message to itself to set up the yellow button menu. Typically, the parameters are class variables such as UserYellowButtonMenu and UserYellowButtonMessages. These class variables are set up in the **initialize** class method. In our scenario, these class variables would be set up from the copied menu information modified to include a new entry for 'fileOutView.'

```
initializeYellowButtonMenu "define this for subclasses of ParagraphEditor"
    self
            yellowButtonMenu: UserYellowButtonMenu
            yellowButtonMessages: UserYellowButtonMessages
initializeBlueButtonMenu "define this for subclasses of StandardSystemController"
    self
            blueButtonMenu: UserBlueButtonMenu
            blueButtonMessages: UserBlueButtonMessages
```

The Tic-Tac-Toe Game Revisited

We could easily extend the Tic-Tac-Toe game to make use of a restart/close menu. We start off by changing the superclass from Controller to MouseMenuController. Conventionally, an application specific operation like **restart** would be placed in a yellow button menu. An operation like **close** would be associated with the blue button. On the other hand, it seems a bit much to have two separate menus each with one entry. So we will provide only one yellow button menu with the two entries.

We need to change instance method **initialize** in class TicTacToeController to construct a menu for the yellow button. Methods for handling the menu selections are then provided. Method **controlActivity** must also be modified to handle the yellow menu. Two approaches are possible: Handle the red mouse button locally and use inheritance to handle the rest (via 'super **controlActivity**') or handle everything locally.

Class TicTacToeController

```
class name              TicTacToeController
superclass              MouseMenuController
instance variable names "none: all inherited"

instance methods

instance initialization

initialize
    super initialize. "Make sure the default initialization is done."
    self
            yellowButtonMenu: (PopUpMenu labels: 'restart\close' withCRs)
            yellowButtonMessages: #(restart close)
```

restart
    self **view initialize**. self **model initialize**. "Nothing to reinitialize in the controller"
close
    "Release the view, unschedule the controller, and restore the display."
    view **release**.
    ScheduledControllers **unschedule**: self. ScheduledControllers **restore**

controlling activities

controlActivity
    | squareLocationAsAPoint row column |
    sensor **redButtonPressed** & self **viewHasCursor**
        ifTrue: [
            "Track the mouse highlighting the squares underneath it."
            self **track**.
            squareLocationAsAPoint ← view **whereIs**: sensor **mousePoint**.
            (squareLocationAsAPoint **isKindOf**: Point)
                ifTrue: [
                    "User let go the mouse while on a square."
                    row ← squareLocationAsAPoint **x**.
                    column ← squareLocationAsAPoint **y**.
                    (model **isLegalFor**: (model **nextPlayer**) **toPlayAt**: row **and**: column)
                        ifTrue: [
                            model **play**: (model **nextPlayer**) **at**: row **and**: column.
                            view **displaySquare**: row **and**: column.
                            view **displayTitle**. view **displayWinnerLine**]
                        ifFalse: [view **flash** "Not legal"]].
            ↑self "To avoid next test (*as if it matters*)"].
    sensor **yellowButtonPressed** & self **viewHasCursor**
        ifTrue: [self **yellowButtonActivity**].
    "super **controlActivity** *is the alternative to the above statement (it would retest the*
    red button; does it matter?)"
    "TicTacToeController new startUp"

2.5.3 The StandardSystemController and StandardSystemView Classes

Class **StandardSystemController** (see Fig. 2.19) provides the basic protocol for scheduled controllers; i.e., controllers that are separately scheduled by the window manager. Such controllers are not intended to return control once opened. Additionally, the class provides a blue button menu for moving, resizing, collapsing, and closing its associated view; and it also permits views hidden underneath to be selected. Instances are not normally explicitly created. Instead, they are created automatically when instances of **StandardSystemView** are obtained. **StandardSystemController** is the default controller class for **StandardSystemView**.

Standard system controllers lose control only when a button is pressed outside the corresponding view or when an explicit blue button menu item like **close** or **under** is selected. Other useful menu items include **move**, **collapse**, and **expand**. These can also be explicitly sent as messages to the controller.

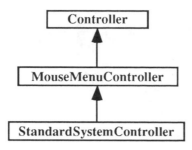

Figure 2.19 The inheritance structure for StandardSystemController.

Class **StandardSystemView** (see Fig. 2.20) provides the basic protocol for displaying views associated with scheduled controllers; i.e., those controllers intended to execute independently. Its associated controller is assumed to be an instance of **StandardSystemController** (the default) or one of its specializations. More specifically, class **StandardSystemView** extends class **View** by providing it with a special **label** tab at the top left corner of the window that can be changed, emphasized, and deemphasized for its visual effect. Additionally, it provides support for the blue button menu messages provided by its controller; i.e., messages for moving, resizing, collapsing, and closing its associated view, and the message that permits views hidden underneath to be selected.

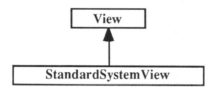

Figure 2.20 The inheritance structure for StandardSystemView.

The display box of a standard system view excludes the area for the label tab. This area is the **label display box**. A point is considered to be inside the view if it is inside either the view display box or the label display box. A view is either **expanded** or **collapsed**; if expanded, information is displayed in both the label display box and the view display box; if collapsed, only information in the label display box is visible. When the view is expanded, the label is immediately above the view and aligned with the left edge. When the view is collapsed, the label is moved down to replace the view's display box.

In more detail, when the view is collapsed, the subviews and additional information that is irrelevant to this discussion are moved to a temporary storage area — another instance variable. The subviews are then replaced by a solitary icon view — one member of an icon/icon view/icon controller triad. In the collapsed state, the corresponding icon controller gets control since the standard system controller always hands control to subviews that want it. The protocol for this triad (Fig. 2.21) is relatively simple and dedicated to moving and displaying the label tab. It also provides the capability to expand back to its original state, which is easily restored. This expansion can be initiated either by choosing **expand** in the yellow button menu or by clicking on the label tab — this latter feature is easily provided in the icon controller but it would have been quite messy to provide in the standard system controller. We leave it to the reader to investigate the icon triad protocol in detail.

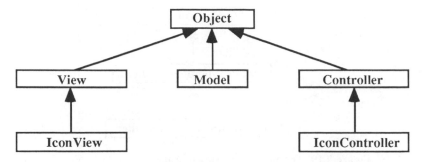

Figure 2.21 The inheritance structure for icons (collapsed views).

Special application views are usually specializations of **StandardSystemView**. Normally, the application is responsible for creating, initializing, and closing its view. The view itself automatically creates, initializes, and releases its controller; i.e., the application can assume the associated controller is properly set up and terminated when appropriate.

Creating Standard System Views (a Preview)

Standard system views and controllers are a matched pair; i.e., standard system controllers are the default controllers for standard system views. Consequently, it is sufficient to create a standard system view. If the user does not provide an alternative controller, the default standard system controller is automatically created whenever some message request requires access to the controller.

Since standard system views are designed to be scheduled as top views, they are provided with a label for the label tab. Additionally, they are provided with subviews. These subviews can be positioned within the standard system view by specifying rectangles that indicate their relative position and size with respect to the standard system view. For this purpose, the standard system view is assumed to be a rectangle with origin 0@0 and corner 1@1; i.e., a rectangle with a width and height of 1 pixel. In the example that follows, two subviews are created: view1, which is twice the size of view2, and view2, which is immediately below view1.

```
I view1 view2 aStandardSystemView I
view1 ← View new insideColor: Form white.
view2 ← View new insideColor: Form white.
aStandardSystemView ← StandardSystemView new
    label: 'A Demonstration Label';
    borderWidth: 1 "this is the standard system view border"
    addSubView: view1 in: (0@0 corner: 1@0.66) borderWidth: 1;
    addSubView: view2 in: (0@0.66 corner: 1@1) borderWidth: 1.
```

Note that view1 extends from 0 to 1 in the x direction (the width of the standard system view); and it extends from 0 to 0.66 (two thirds of the way down) in the y direction. View2 uses up the remaining one third of the area. If the resulting standard system view were inspected after its construction, we would notice that its controller was **nil**; i.e., it has not yet been constructed. As we mentioned above, the view is left without a controller until an explicit controller is provided or until it is forced to construct a default controller. A standard

Inside Smalltalk

system controller (the default) would be constructed, for example, if we attempted to open it as follows:

aStandardSystemView **controller open**

The standard system view would appear on the screen as shown in Fig. 2.22. Since both the standard system view and the subviews have a border width of 1, the combined border width all around is 2.

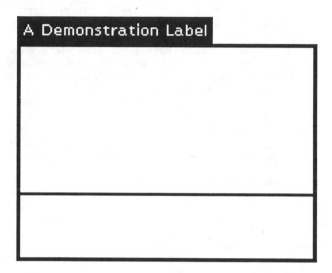

Figure 2.22 An example standard system view with two subviews.

We could have provided a nonstandard controller by adding the following after **label:** above, for example.

controller: aControllerClass **new;**

The StandardSystemController Protocol

The StandardSystemController protocol is roughly the same size as the Controller protocol. It inherits the protocol for pop-up menus from MouseMenuController.

methods redefined specially for this class

- aStandardSystemController **initialize**
- aStandardSystemController **initializeBlueButtonMenu**
- aStandardSystemController **isControlActive**
- aStandardSystemController **controlInitialize**
- aStandardSystemController **controlTerminate**

    Initialization handles the specifics for this class of controllers. Control is maintained until either a mouse button is pressed outside the view or an explicit blue button menu item like **close** or **under** is selected. Control initialization ensures that the view is emphasized. Correspondingly, control termination deemphasizes it or unschedules it if the controller has been previously closed.

methods that can be selected via the blue button menu or explicitly sent as messages

- aStandardSystemController **move**

  Causes the user to reposition the controller's view.

- aStandardSystemController **close**

  Causes all finalization activity for the controller, model, and view to be performed and then unschedules the controller. The finalization activity includes releasing the view from its sponsor (the model), releasing all its subviews, erasing the view, and changing the internal status of the controller. Note that this method has the intended effect only if the receiver is active (see **closeAndUnschedule** below).

- aStandardSystemController **collapse**

  If not already collapsed, causes the controller's view to change to a collapsed view on the screen. In a collapsed view, only the label tab is visible. The user is also asked to position the collapsed view.

- aStandardSystemController **expand**

  If not already expanded, causes the controller's collapsed view to be opened once again.The user is asked to resize and reposition the expanded view.

- aStandardSystemController **under**

  Deactivates the receiver's scheduled view and passes control to any view that might be positioned directly underneath it and the cursor.

additional methods (not in the blue button menu) to complement the above

- aStandardSystemController **open**

  Causes the controller to be scheduled as the active controller. The user is asked to resize and reposition the view.

- aStandardSystemController **openDisplayAt:** aPoint

  Causes the controller to be scheduled as the active controller and centers the existing viewport at the specified point. Automatically repositions the specified point (as much as possible) if portions are off the screen.

specialized methods for opening and closing

- aStandardSystemController **openNoTerminate**
- aStandardSystemController **openNoTerminateDisplayAt:** aPoint

  Differs from **open** and **openDisplayAt:** above by not terminating the currently active controller. Used in specialized applications like debugging.

- aStandardSystemController **closeAndUnschedule**
- aStandardSystemController **closeAndUnscheduleNoErase**

  Although method **close** above erases the view immediately, it does not perform the finalization activity until the next iteration around the control loop. These two variations cause the finalization code to be performed immediately. This is necessary, for example, to close an unscheduled controller other than your own. The reason the simpler **close** does not work in this case is subtle. To actually execute the finalization activity, the other controller must first be made active; e.g., by clicking on the associated window. However, the initialization code eliminates the pending close.

specialized class initialization methods

- StandardSystemController **initialize**
- StandardSystemController **ScheduledBlueButtonMenu**

  Returns the menu with labels 'under, move, frame, collapse, and close.'

- StandardSystemController **ScheduledBlueButtonMessages**

  Returns the message symbols for the labels (currently, the same names).

The StandardSystemView Protocol

The StandardSystemView protocol complements the corresponding StandardSystem–Controller protocol and extends the View protocol.

creating new views

- StandardSystemView **new**

    Returns an initialized standard system view with the following defaults: It has no subviews, the transformation is an identity transformation, the border width is 0, the border color is black, the inside color is light gray, the label tab is **nil** (does not display), the minimum size is 50@50, and the maximum size is the entire screen.

- StandardSystemView **model:** aModel **label:** aString **minimumSize:** aPoint

    Creates an initialized standard system view (see **new** above) with the model, label tab, and minimum size explicitly changed. The x coordinate of the point is the width; the y coordinate is the height. Also sets the border width to 1.

Generally speaking, the second method above is rarely needed since it can just as easily be accomplished via 'StandardSystemView **new model:** aModel; **label:** aString; **minimumSize:** aPoint; **yourself**'.

initializing and releasing views

- aStandardSystemView **initialize**

    Initializes the view so that it has no subviews, the transformation is an identity transformation, the border width is 0, the border color is black, the inside color is light gray, the label tab is **nil** (does not display), the minimum size is 50@50, and the maximum size is the entire screen. Subclasses should include 'super **initialize**' when redefining this method to ensure proper initialization.

- aStandardSystemView **release**

    Removes the view from its model's list of dependents (if the model exists), releases the associated controller, and releases all of its subviews and controllers. This message is normally sent by the controller when it is closed. Subclasses should include 'super **release**' when redefining **release**.

As indicated above, explicit **initialize** and **release** messages are not needed by users of standard system views since **initialize** is sent by **new** when the view is created and **release** is sent by **close** when the associated controller is closed. On the other hand, users can provide more detailed initialization information through the following methods.

more specific initialization

- aStandardSystemView **label:** aStringOrNil

    Sets the view's label to aStringOrNil. When set to **nil**, no label tab is shown. When unspecified, the default is **nil**.

- aStandardSystemView **minimumSize:** aPoint

    Sets the minimum width and height of the view to the point; the width is the x coordinate; the height is the y coordinate. When unspecified, the default is 50@50.

- aStandardSystemView **maximumSize**: aPoint
  Sets the maximum width and height of the view to the point; the width is the x coordinate; the height is the y coordinate. When unspecified, the default is the entire screen.

Although the above initialization information is minimal, one should not forget the additional initializing methods available from the superclass **View**. It provides facilities to set the border color, the inside color, and the border width, for example.

basic control testing

- aStandardSystemView **containsPoint**: aPointInScreenCoordinates
  Returns **true** if aPointInScreenCoordinates is within the view's display box or the view's label display box.

controller access

- aStandardSystemView **defaultControllerClass**
  Returns the class of the default controller for the view. For standard system views, this class is StandardSystemController. Subclasses should redefine this method to obtain other controller classes.

Asking for the view's controller automatically causes it to be set to the default controller if it is not already set. Consequently, when a standard system view is created, there is no need to explicitly create a controller and associate it with the view unless the default controller is not wanted.

interrogating the view

- aStandardSystemView **label**
  Returns the string that appears in the view's label tab.

- aStandardSystemView **labelDisplayBox**
  Returns the rectangle that borders the visible parts of the view's label on the display screen. For expanded views, this rectangle is above the view's display box and aligned with the left edge. For collapsed views, it is moved down and made coincident with the view's display box that is shrunk to the size of the label display box.

- aStandardSystemView **labelFrame**
  Returns the quadrangle for the label. It prints in the form '0@0 **corner**: anotherPoint'.

- aStandardSystemView **minimumSize**
  Returns a point representing the minimum width and height of the view.

- aStandardSystemView **maximumSize**
  Returns a point representing the maximum width and height of the view.

- aStandardSystemView **isCollapsed**
  Returns **true** if the view is collapsed and **false** if it is expanded.

displaying the view

- aStandardSystemView **displayView**
  Displays the view.

- aStandardSystemView **displayEmphasized**
  Displays the view with the label highlighted to indicate that it is active.

- aStandardSystemView **deEmphasizeView**
  Deemphasizes the view.

- aStandardSystemView **emphasizeLabel**
  Highlights the label.

- aStandardSystemView **deEmphasizeLabel**
  If the label is highlighted, reverses it.

Superclass **View** provides the **display, emphasize,** and **deEmphasize** protocol. The methods have the same basic structure.

- First, they perform some method specific computation; **display** paints the border and inside color; **emphasize and deEmphasize** do nothing.

- Second, they respectively send the messages **displayView, emphasizeView,** and **deEmphasizeView** to 'self'.

- Finally, they respectively send the messages **display, emphasize,** or **deEmphasize** recursively to all subviews.

In superclass **View**, each of the **displayView, emphasizeView,** and **deEmphasizeView** methods do nothing. Hence, one would expect each to be redefined in **StandardSystemView**. However, only the first and last are redefined. Method **displayView** is redefined to display the label tab with emphasis. The display box information gets displayed by subviews. Method **deEmphasizeView** is redefined to display the label tab in reverse video. Since **emphasizeView** is not redefined, sending an **emphasize** message to the view has no effect. On the other hand, the standard system view does provide an equivalent method **displayEmphasized**, which has the effect of emphasizing the label (in addition to displaying the view). This method is, however, used only by the standard system controller in three situations: when the control loop is initiated (**controlInitialize**), when the view is expanded, and when the view is moved. The fact that the **View** protocol is not followed by standard system views will not be noticed unless an explicit **emphasize** message is sent to the view.

support for the controller blue button messages

- aStandardSystemView **collapse**
  If the view is expanded, changes it so that only the label can be seen when displayed. If the label is **nil**, replaces it by 'No Label' so that it can be seen.

- aStandardSystemView **expand**
  If the view is collapsed, changes it so that the label and all of its subviews can be seen when displayed.

- aStandardSystemView **erase**
  Erases the label display box and view display box by displaying them in gray.

- aStandardSystemView **resize**
  Prompts the user for a rectangular area bounded by the minimum and maximum sizes allowed by the view and changes the view so that its display box is in the specified area.

- aStandardSystemView **resizeMinimumCenteredAt**: aPoint
  Changes the view so that its display box is minimum size and centered at the specified point.

- aStandardSystemView **getFrame**
  Prompts the user for a rectangular area bounded by the minimum and maximum sizes allowed by the view.

miscellaneous methods
- aStandardSystemView **clippingBox**
  Returns the label display box. Appears to be a misnomer but it has no effect since it is used only locally.

- aStandardSystemView **labelFrame**: aQuadrangle
  Sets the bounding box for the label to be aQuadrangle. Currently, this method is not used. The label bounding box is created automatically whenever the label is changed.

2.5.4 The ScreenController Class

Class **ScreenController** (see Fig. 2.23) is a scheduled controller that provides a yellow button menu for a number of activities such as restoring the display; entering and exiting projects; opening system browsers and file browsers; opening workspaces, the system transcript, and the system workspace; saving; suspending; and quitting. The view that is associated with the controller is a form view with an infinite gray form.

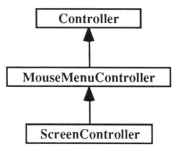

Figure 2.23 The inheritance structure for ScreenController.

The ScreenController Protocol

The ScreenController protocol is activated when the mouse button is depressed outside existing windows. The protocol is mostly concerned with supporting the yellow button menu.

methods redefined specially for this class
- ScreenController **initialize**
- aScreenController **initialize**
- aScreenController **isControlActive**
- aScreenController **isControlWanted**
  Initialization handles the specifics for this class of controllers; e.g., by initializing the blue button menu. Control is obtained when no other controller wants control and the yellow button is depressed. Control is maintained as long as the yellow button remains depressed.

yellow button menu messages (code expansion shown as a comment)

- aScreenController **restoreDisplay** "ScheduledControllers **restore**"
- aScreenController **openProjectBrowser** "ProjectBrowser **open**"
- aScreenController **exitProject** "Project **current exit**"
- aScreenController **openFileList** "FileList **open**"
- aScreenController **openBrowser** "BrowserView **openOn**: SystemOrganization"
- aScreenController **openProject** "ProjectView **open**"
- aScreenController **openWorkspace** "StringHolderView **open**"
- aScreenController **openTranscript** "TextCollectorView
  open: Transcript
  label: 'System Transcript'"
- aScreenController **openSystemWorkspace** "StringHolderView
  openSystemWorkspace"

yellow button menu messages (code not shown since lengthy and obvious in effect)

- aScreenController **quit**
- aScreenController **save**
- aScreenController **suspend**

The screen controller is initialized by performing the standard controller initialization and then initializing the yellow button menu, which is defined as follows:

initializeYellowButtonMenu
    self
        yellowButtonMenu: ScreenYellowButtonMenu
        yellowButtonMessages: ScreenYellowButtonMessages

The class variables are set up in class method **initialize** in the usual way (see MouseMenuControllers for examples).

2.5.5 The ScrollController Class

Class **ScrollController** extends the **MouseMenuController** protocol by providing a **scroll bar** and a **marker** (see Fig. 2.24) for vertically adjusting the information visible in the associated viewport. The **scroll bar** is a rectangular area that pops up whenever the scroll controller is active. The **marker** is a small gray rectangle of fixed width but varying height inside the scroll bar. The vertical **size** of the marker is indicative of the amount of information currently visible; e.g., if the marker is half the size of the window, then half of the information is visible; if it is one fifth the size of the window, then one fifth of the information is visible, and so on. The **position** of the marker indicates which part of the information is being viewed; e.g., if the marker is at the top, then the top part of the information is being viewed; if it is in the middle or bottom, then the middle or bottom parts respectively are being viewed.

When the cursor is in the scroll bar region, it is replaced by one of three different arrows, depending on the horizontal position of the cursor. In particular, a **down** arrow appears when the cursor is on the left side of the marker, a **right** arrow when it is on the marker, and an **up** arrow when it is on the right side. Clicking the red button while the cursor is a down arrow causes the view to be scrolled downward; for an up arrow, the view is scrolled upward. For a right arrow, the center of the marker is moved up or down to the cursor position and the view is correspondingly repositioned vertically. Scrolling for the down and up arrows is not smooth but rather jumps by an amount that is proportional to the distance from the top of the scroll bar. For instance, if the cursor is near the top of the scroll bar, the view is scrolled by a small amount; e.g., one line in a text view. If it is near the middle of the scroll bar, it will scroll by half of the amount visible. If it is near the bottom of the scroll bar, it will scroll by an entire window.

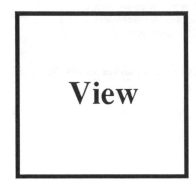

Before the Scroll Bar Pops Up

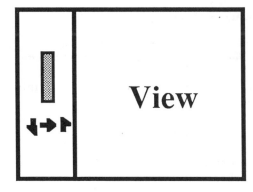

After the Scroll Bar Pops Up

Marker: Small gray rectangle inside the scroll bar.
Scroll Bar: Rectangle that appears in the "after" shot.
Arrows: one of them replaces the cursor when in the scroll bar area.

The scroll bar is partitioned horizontally into three areas.
To the Left of Marker: down arrow appears (causes view material to scroll down)
On Marker: right arrow appears (causes view material to be positioned absolutely)
To the Right of Marker: up arrow appears (causes view material to scroll up)

Figure 2.24 A scroll bar and marker.

As designed, the down and up arrows are *scrolling oriented*; i.e., the down arrow causes the view information to scroll *down* while the up arrow causes it to scroll *up*. Users, on the other hand, operate from a different perspective. They want to either move up the document or down the document. To move up a document, for example, a user will have to click on the down arrow; when a document scrolls down, new information is visible higher up. In our experience, we have found this behavior to be contrary to user expectations. Nevertheless, it doesn't take long to get used to it. Alternatively, we can easily modify the system to make it *user oriented* by switching the two cursors in the private **scrollUp** and **scrollDown** methods.

The ScrollController Protocol

The scroll bar appears on the left side of the view only when the controller is activated and is removed when it is deactivated. The controller keeps control as long as the cursor is inside the view or the scroll bar area. When the scroll bar area is about to be displayed, the area underneath is saved first. This makes it easy to restore the display to its previous state when the controller is deactivated.

creating new unscheduled controllers

- ScrollController **new**

  Returns an initialized scroll controller without associated menus (recall that a scroll controller is a mouse-menu controller).

control operations redefined specially for this class

- aScrollController **initialize**
- aScrollController **controlInitialize**
- aScrollController **controlTerminate**
- aScrollController **isControlWanted**
- aScrollController **isControlActive**
- aScrollController **controlActivity**

  Initialization handles the specifics for scroll controllers; i.e., initializes the scroll controller without associated menus but with the mouse cursor as the default sensor and with a properly set up scroll bar. When control is initialized, the form underneath the scroll area is saved and the marker is set up at the top. When it is terminated, the saved form is restored. Control is obtained by moving the mouse cursor into the view. It is maintained as long as it remains in the view or the scroll bar area. Control activity performs scrolling as long as the mouse is in the scroll bar area and performs the normal activity when in the view; i.e., activates the mouse button menus (if any are provided and the corresponding button is depressed) or passes control down to lower-level controllers.

cursor changing and interrogation

- aScrollController **changeCursor**: aCursor

  Sets the current cursor to aCursor.
- aScrollController **markerContainsCursor**

  Returns **true** if and only if the cursor is in the marker area.
- aScrollController **scrollBarContainsCursor**

  Returns **true** if and only if the cursor is in the scroll bar area.

scrolling operations that interrogate the marker position

- aScrollController **canScroll**
  Returns **true** if and only if the marker can be moved; i.e., some information is not visible.
- aScrollController **scrollView**
  Updates the view to correspond to the location of the marker.
- aScrollController **scrollView**: anInteger
  Used privately by the above method.
- aScrollController **viewDelta**
  Returns how much the view should be scrolled (positive for up and negative for down) so as to make it conform to the current marker position.

marker operations that interrogate the view

- aScrollController **moveMarker**
  Updates the location of the marker to correspond to the view.
- aScrollController **moveMarker**: anInteger
  Used privately by the above method. Displaces the marker by anInteger (usually the negative of the marker delta computed below; i.e., positive for down and negative for up) and redisplays it.
- aScrollController **markerDelta**
  Returns how much the marker should be moved (positive for up and negative for down) so as to make it conform to the current view position.
- aScrollController **computeMarkerRegion**
  Determines how large the marker should be as a function of the amount of information visible in the view and returns an appropriate rectangle.
- aScrollController **markerRegion**: aRectangle
  Adjusts the marker area to the specified rectangle and redisplays it. This rectangle is usually computed via the above method.

scrolling operations that interrogate the mouse position

- aScrollController **scroll**
  This is the method executed whenever the cursor is in the scroll bar area. It switches to either the down, right, or up arrows and scrolls the view accordingly whenever the mouse is depressed.
- aScrollController **scrollAbsolute**
- aScrollController **scrollDown**
- aScrollController **scrollUp**
- aScrollController **scrollViewDown**
- aScrollController **scrollViewUp**
  Used privately by the **scroll** method to adjust the marker and view as a function of the mouse position. The first three methods handle the switch to the appropriate cursor arrows, scroll the view accordingly, and adjust the marker to reflect the state of the view. The latter two methods are used by **scrollDown** and **scrollUp** respectively.
- aScrollController **scrollAmount**
  Returns a positive displacement in view coordinates that is proportional to the vertical distance between the mouse and the top of the scroll bar; i.e., it varies from 0 for the mouse at the top of the scroll bar to the viewport height for the mouse at the bottom of the scroll bar.

Most of the time, the scroll controller and its subclasses are manipulated directly through mouse interactions. When special application methods are needed that affect the disposition of the view, it sometimes becomes necessary to manipulate the scroll controller indirectly through messages. Two approaches are possible: (1) modify the marker via

moveMarker: messages and then have the view adjusted via a **scrollView** message, or (2) modify the view using a **scrollView:** message and then adjust the marker to correspond via a **moveMarker** message. The latter is the customary approach used. Note that manipulating the view through **scrollBy:** messages is not usually successful for views that manipulate paragraphs of text, since these must actually adjust the paragraphs.

A word of warning: The marker is designed to be moved only when the scroll controller is active. For example, if a specialization of ScrollController were designed to react to an **update:** message from another window, invoking **moveMarker** would not be appropriate. The reason is that **moveMarker:** (used privately by **moveMarker**) assumes that the marker is visible. It is not visible in this situation since the other window is the active one. The result is a whitening of an area where the marker would have been and a darkening of the area where it should be now. The method can be generalized to work in both situations by eliminating the display code (as shown) when the marker is not visible.

```
aScrollController moveMarker: yDistance
    "from moveMarker: adds a test that displays the marker only if it is visible."
    | minimumY maximumY newMarker |
    minimumY ← scrollBar inside bottom - marker bottom.
    maximumY ← scrollBar inside top - marker top.
    newMarker ← marker
        translateBy: 0 @ ((yDistance min: minimumY) max: maximumY).
    savedArea notNil ifTrue: [
        Display fill: marker mask: scrollBar insideColor.
        newMarker displayOn: Display].
    marker ← newMarker
```

Scrolling Details

Since scroll controllers are relatively simple, we will have a look at two other methods: **scroll** and **scrollAbsolute**. The first illustrates a problem that is easy to fix; the second illustrates how ghost markers are created and displayed.

```
aScrollController scroll
    This is the method executed whenever the cursor is in the scroll bar area. It
    switches to either the down, right, or up arrows and scrolls the view accordingly
    whenever the mouse is depressed.
    | savedCursor regionPercent |
    savedCursor ← sensor currentCursor.
    [self scrollBarContainsCursor] whileTrue: [
        Processor yield. "In case some other controller desires control."
        regionPercent ← 100 * (sensor cursorPoint x - scrollBar left) // scrollBar width.
        regionPercent <= 40
            ifTrue: [self scrollDown]
            ifFalse: [
                regionPercent >= 60
                    ifTrue: [self scrollUp]
                    ifFalse: [self scrollAbsolute]]].
    savedCursor show
```

On some machines, an interesting phenomenon occurs when the cursor is placed at certain special locations near the right side of the marker. The cursor oscillates wildly, between a right arrow and an up arrow. This will occur even if the cursor is perfectly still. If we look at the previous method, we can deduce that the cursor will be an up arrow if the **scrollUp** message is sent and a right arrow if the **scrollAbsolute** message is sent instead. Since the choice is controlled by *regionPercent*, we must infer that this variable keeps changing. Can you guess how that might happen if the mouse is perfectly still? Since the scroll bar is not moving, the problem must lie with **cursorPoint**. It must be returning different values even when the mouse is still. Can that be?

The cursor point is a function of both the mouse point and the cursor offset (the two are actually subtracted); i.e., not every cursor point is at the top left corner of the cursor. More specifically, the right arrow cursor (called the marker) has an x-offset of -7 whereas the up cursor has an x-offset of 0. If the x coordinate of the mouse point is, say, 36 and the current cursor is the up arrow, then the cursor point is 36-(0) = 36. If this results in a region per cent of 56, the **scrollAbsolute** method is invoked. It changes the cursor to a right arrow and does nothing else if no mouse is depressed. The loop is then repeated. In this case, the cursor point is 36-(-7) = 43, since the right arrow x-offset is now used. This will result in a region per cent of 78, causing the **scrollUp** method to be invoked and the cursor to be changed to an up arrow. We have come full circle and the process will repeat indefinitely.

Is there a simple modification that will prevent this? We could replace message **cursorPoint** above by **mousePoint**. However, the down arrow, for example, stays active even when the mouse is on the marker; also, the right arrow stays active in that part of the region that should be an up arrow. A simple solution is to change the 40 and 60 percentages to empirically determined values that work, such as 26 and 66 per cent respectively. The lesson to remember is that a mouse point is a constant if the mouse is still, but the cursor point can change if the cursor is changed.

The next example illustrates the notion of a ghost marker. To position the marker absolutely, a user depresses the red button over the marker and moves it to a new destination. The original marker position is outlined and the new position is displayed. Since both marker positions are displayed, the original outline is referred to as a **ghost marker**. The approach used to do this is interesting because it could be used in other applications.

```
aScrollController scrollAbsolute
    "Changes to a right arrow cursor, repositions the marker, and adjusts the
    corresponding view."
    | oldMarker |
    self changeCursor: Cursor marker. "The right arrow."
    self canScroll & sensor anyButtonPressed ifTrue: [
        [sensor anyButtonPressed] whileTrue: [
            oldMarker ← marker. "First save it."
            "Next move it making sure it's inside the scroll bar."
            marker ← marker translateBy:
                0 @
                    ((sensor cursorPoint y - marker center y
                    min: scrollBar inside bottom - marker bottom)
                    max: scrollBar inside top - marker top).
            "Create and display the new marker rectangle and the ghost rectangle."
            (oldMarker areasOutside: marker), (marker areasOutside: oldMarker)
                do: [:region | Display fill: region rule: Form reverse mask: Form gray].
            self scrollView].
        scrollBar display. "Whiten the entire scroll bar to eliminate the ghost."
        self moveMarker "Display the final marker"]
```

The method constructs a new marker based on the cursor point. This new marker is intersected with the old marker (via rectangle message **areasOutside**) to obtain the *new protruding part*. The old marker is also intersected with the new marker in the same way to obtain the *old portion to be deleted* (see Fig. 2.25). The resulting collections of rectangles are concatenated together to obtain regions that need to be reversed. In both cases, the regions exclude the border. When the *new protruding part* is reversed, it turns from white to gray. When the *old portion to be deleted* is reversed, it turns from gray to white. The ghost effect is caused by the fact that the first marker's original border remains. The view is then adjusted to conform to the marker and the process is repeated. The loop works because it starts off with the latest marker, which is all gray, while all other accessible areas are white (the borders are not accessible).

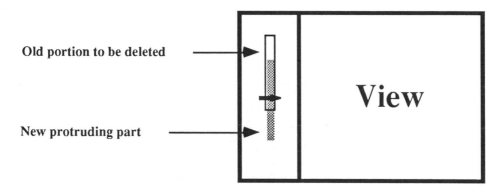

Figure 2.25 Moving the marker an absolute amount.

Creating Specializations of ScrollController

Scroll controllers are designed to permit scrolling of a small rectangle (the **visible rectangle**) over a much larger rectangle (the **total rectangle**). The marker plays the role of the visible part and the scroll bar area plays the role of the total rectangle. To provide proper visual feedback (see Fig. 2.26), the ratio of the marker height m (or offset from the top Δ_m) to the scroll bar area height M must be the same as the ratio of the visible rectangle height r (or offset from the top Δ_r) to the total rectangle height R. We will refer to

- $m/M = r/R$ as the **height equation,** and
- $\Delta_m/M = \Delta_r/R$ as the **offset equation.**

To specialize ScrollController, it is necessary to redefine those methods that maintain the height and offset equations. These include marker methods **computeMarkerRegion** and **markerDelta**, along with scrolling methods **canScroll**, **scrollView:**, **scrollAmount**, and **viewDelta**. Currently, these methods should be read with the following interpretations in mind:

- view window $\Rightarrow$ visible rectangle
- view boundingBox $\Rightarrow$ total rectangle

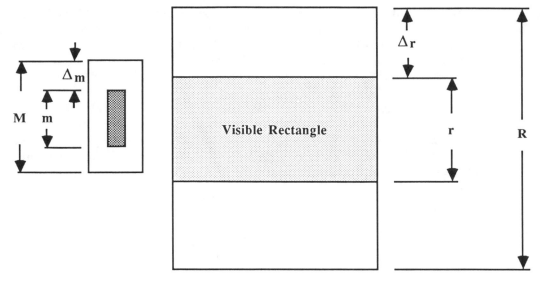

$$m/M = r/R \text{ (height equation)}$$
$$\Delta_m/M = \Delta_r/R \text{ (offset equation)}$$

Figure 2.26 Ratios maintained by scroll controllers.

Since the bounding box is roughly the viewport and there is no relationship between the window and the viewport (e.g., the viewport can be resized and moved to any point on the screen), it stands to reason that these methods were not intended to be executed. Rather, they were intended as templates for creating specialized versions in subclasses.

For example, consider method **computeMarkerRegion** with comments that relate it to the height equation.

```
aScrollController computeMarkerRegion
    "Determines how large the marker should be as a function of the amount of
    information visible in the view and returns a rectangle of the appropriate size."
    "↑0@0 extent: 10@(r / R * M)" " i.e., solve for m in the height equation"
    ↑0@0 extent: 10@
        ((view window height asFloat / view boundingBox height
            * scrollBar inside height) rounded
        min:
            scrollBar inside height)
```

Special versions of this method would be obtained by replacing 'view **window**' by code equivalent to 'self **visibleRectangle**', and 'view **boundingBox**' by code equivalent to 'self **totalRectangle**'. In general, it would be more logical for the **visibleRectangle** and **totalRectangle** messages to be sent to the views. Unfortunately, the required information is almost always maintained by the controller.

For didactic reasons, we will repeat the above and all other methods with these substitutions explicitly made. We will also include three additional substitutions.

- self **visibleRectangle** ⇒ view **window**
- self **totalRectangle** ⇒ view **boundingBox**

- self **canScrollEpsilon** ⇒ 0 (i.e., zero)   Used by **canScroll**
- self **viewDeltaRoundingAmount** ⇒ 1 (i.e., one)   Used by **viewDelta**
- self **scrollViewDirectlyBy:** anAmount ⇒ 1
  (i.e., one) Used by **scrollView:** yDistance

aScrollController **computeMarkerRegion**
"Determines how large the marker should be as a function of the amount of information visible in the view and returns a rectangle of the appropriate size."
"↑0@0 **extent:** 10@(r / R * M)" "i.e., solve for m in the height equation"
↑0@0 **extent:** 10@
    ((self **visibleRectangle height asFloat** / self **totalRectangle height**
        * scrollBar **inside height**) **rounded**
   min:
      scrollBar **inside height**)

aScrollController **markerDelta**
"Returns how much the marker should be moved (positive for up and negative for down) so as to make it conform to the current view position."

"If the visible rectangle has been moved, the current displacement Δ_m from the top of the marker to the top of the scroll bar area is no longer up-to-date. If we let x denote the amount by which the new displacement must be adjusted, this new displacement can be written (Δ_m - x). Solving for x (the delta) in offset equation (Δ_m - x)/M = Δ_r/R gives us x = Δ_m - Δ_r/R*M. Note that if the visible rectangle moves up, Δ_r decreases and so must (Δ_m - x) in which case x must increase; i.e., be positive. Since the marker must also move up, x positive implies moving up. A similar argument can be made for x negative."
↑(marker **top** - scrollBar **inside top**) "Δ_m" -
    ((self **visibleRectangle top** - self **totalRectangle top**) **asFloat** "Δ_r" /
    self **totalRectangle height asFloat** "R" *
    scrollBar **inside height asFloat** "M") **rounded**

aScrollController **canScroll**
"Returns true if the visible rectangle is smaller (by an epsilon) than the total rectangle; false otherwise."
"↑(scrollBar **inside height** - marker **region height**) > self **canScrollEpsilon** OR"
↑(self **totalRectangle height** - self **visibleRectangle height**) > self **canScrollEpsilon**

aScrollController **scrollView:** yDistance
"Scrolls the scroll controller's view by a y-distance (positive for up and negative for down)."
| maximumAmount minimumAmount actualAmount |
maximumAmount ← (self **visibleRectangle top** - self **totalRectangle top**) **max:** 0.
minimumAmount ← (self **visibleRectangle bottom** -
    self **totalRectangle bottom**) **min:** 0.
actualAmount ← (yDistance **min:** maximumAmount) **max:** minimumAmount.
actualAmount ~= 0 **ifTrue:** [self **scrollViewDirectlyBy:** anAmount]

aScrollController **scrollAmount**
"Returns a positive displacement in view coordinates that is proportional to the vertical distance between the mouse and the top of the scroll bar; i.e., it varies from 0 for the mouse at the top of the scroll bar to the viewport height for the mouse at the bottom of the scroll bar."
"↑sensor **cursorPoint y** - scrollBar **inside top** (if view and screen coordinates are the same)"
↑(view **inverseDisplayTransform:** sensor **cursorPoint**) **y** -
    (view **inverseDisplayTransform:** scrollBar **inside topCenter**) **y**

aScrollController **viewDelta**

"Returns how much the view should be scrolled (positive for up and negative for down) so as to make it conform to the current marker position."

"If the marker has been moved, the current displacement Δ_r from the top of the visible rectangle to the top of the total rectangle is no longer up-to-date. If we let x denote the amount by which the new displacement must be adjusted, this new displacement can be written $(\Delta_r - x)$. Solving for x (the delta) in offset equation $\Delta_m/M = (\Delta_r - x)/R$ gives us $x = \Delta_r - \Delta_m/M*R$. Note that if the marker moves up, Δ_m decreases and so must $(\Delta_r - x)$ in which case x must increase; i.e., be positive. Since the visible rectangle must also move up, x positive implies moving up. A similar argument can be made for x negative."

$\uparrow$((self **visibleRectangle top** - self **totalRectangle top** "Δ_r") -
   ((marker **top** - scrollBar **inside top**) **asFloat** "Δ_m" /
      scrollBar **inside height asFloat** "M" *
      self **totalRectangle height asFloat** "R")
) **roundTo:** self **viewDeltaRoundingAmount**

As you can see, the most complex method from the point of view of refinement is **scrollView:**, since it requires detailed code for scrolling and redisplaying. The others are relatively simple. To provide a feel for actual refinements used in specific specializations, we provide a list below. These classes are discussed in more detail in later sections.

In ScrollController
    self **visibleRectangle** $\Rightarrow$ view **window**
    self **totalRectangle** $\Rightarrow$ view **boundingBox**
    self **canScrollEpsilon** $\Rightarrow$ 0
    self **viewDeltaRoundingAmount** $\Rightarrow$ 1
    self **scrollViewDirectlyBy:** anAmount $\Rightarrow$
        view **scrollBy:** anAmount. view **clearInside**. view **display**.

In ParagraphEditor
    self **visibleRectangle** $\Rightarrow$ paragraph **clippingRectangle**
    self **totalRectangle** $\Rightarrow$ paragraph **compositionRectangle**
    self **canScrollEpsilon** $\Rightarrow$ "Not needed; see below"
    self **viewDeltaRoundingAmount** $\Rightarrow$ paragraph **lineGrid**
    self **scrollViewDirectlyBy:** anAmount $\Rightarrow$
        self **deselect**. self **scrollBy:** anAmount **negated**. self **select**

In ListController
    self **visibleRectangle** $\Rightarrow$ view **list clippingRectangle**
    self **totalRectangle** $\Rightarrow$ view **list compositionRectangle**
    self **canScrollEpsilon** $\Rightarrow$ view **list lineGrid** // 2
    self **viewDeltaRoundingAmount** $\Rightarrow$ view **list lineGrid**
    self **scrollViewDirectlyBy:** anAmount $\Rightarrow$
        view **deselect**. view **list scrollBy:** anAmount **negated**.
        view **isSelectionBoxClipped ifFalse:** [view **displaySelectionBox**].

In general, these substitutions and the template methods in class ScrollController permit us to derive most refinements in the other classes. However, special modifications are sometimes made. For example, **computeMarkerRegion** in ParagraphEditor handles an anomalous situation that the corresponding template above does not handle; **canScroll** also simply returns **true**.

Creating Controllers with New Scroll Bars

Consider creating a new class of controllers with scroll bars that do not switch mouse cursors. As with the old scroll bars, depressing a mouse button on the marker provides direct movement control. On the other hand, depressing it above (or below) the marker causes the view to move up (or down). We would also like to provide small variations of the scroll bars to be able to configure it, so to speak, with a range of alternative behaviors.

The obvious approach would be to modify class ScrollController and the affected subclasses. This seems too drastic a step for what might be termed an experiment. A better alternative would be to create an objectified version of the configurable scrollers. These objectified scroll bars, or **scrollers** for short, could then be added to a specialization of some existing scrollable window.

To test the notion, we will also provide a specialization of StringHolderController that we will call StringHolderControllerWithScroller. To understand this example, it is not necessary to understand string holders and their associated views and controllers. Simply interpret StringHolderController as your favorite controller class.

Because the standard ScrollController operations in StringHolderControllerWith-Scroller are replaced by the new scroller operations, most of the existing scrolling operations are rerouted to the new scrollers. The scroller objects are added to the string holder controller in a new instance variable. The class has been designed to use methods canScrollEpsilon, viewDeltaRoundingAmount, visibleRectangle, totalRectangle, and scrollViewDirectlyBy:.

Scrollers can be created and specified via two options — the appearance option or the marker option:

The Appearance Option: either #PopUp, #SlideIn, or #FadeIn.

The Marker Option: either #FixedSize or #VariableSize.

The pop-up option provides an equivalent to the existing scroll bars; the slide-in option has the scroll bars smoothly slide in and out; and the fade-in option makes it slowly materialize and dematerialize. The existing scroll bars are variable-sized. Fixed-sized scroll bars are also available. To differentiate them from the existing scroll bars, the color of the scroll bar and marker have been switched; i.e., the marker is now white instead of gray. Fig. 2.27 demonstrates an example of four string holder views with controllers that are instances of StringHolderControllerWithScroller. The fourth controller (the bottom right view), to pick one, was set up with

```
controller4 scroller:
    (Scroller on: controller4 appearanceOption: #FadeIn markerOption: #FixedSize).
```

Fig. 2.27 shows four windows with the new scrollers visible. Normally, only the active window has a scroll bar visible. To create the diagram, we modified the code to partially display the scroll bar and prevent them from disappearing after the window was deactivated. The top left view has a pop-up scroll bar with variable-sized marker; the top right view has a fixed-size marker instead. The bottom left view illustrates a scroll bar that is in the process of sliding out (only half of it is shown so far). The bottom right view shows a scroll bar that is only partially faded in.

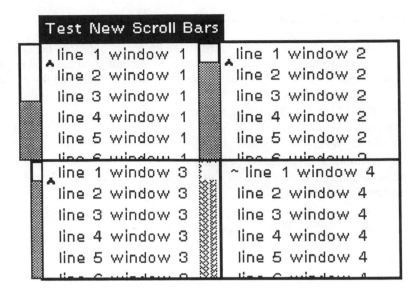

Figure 2.27 Windows with scrollers.

The design could be evolved in two directions: (1) providing more options, and (2) providing both horizontal and vertical scroll bars.

The most difficult part of the design was the development of the fade-in operation. We needed the ability to overlay an existing form over another one through a mask. The black areas of the mask specified which parts of the existing form were to pass through. Both white and black pixels had to pass through. The conventional operations mask only the black pixels. The details can be obtained from the **overlay:given:onto:mask:** operation. To get the fade-in effect, we had to overlay the original form with successively denser masks. These masks had to have a speckled look to avoid streaks and lines from showing up. For an initial version, we hand constructed the masks. The version shown uses an algorithmic approach. Better algorithms could be developed.

To parameterize the scrollers, we provided distinct methods for computing the marker region, making the scroll bar visible, and making it invisible. When the options are specified, three corresponding instance variables are initialized with the required method names. The corresponding operations are executed with a **perform**.

Class Scroller

class name	Scroller
superclass	Object
instance variable names	controller view scrollBar marker savedArea makeScrollBarInvisible makeScrollBarVisible computeMarkerRegion
class variable names	FadeInMasks
comment	An objectified version of vertical configurable scrollers.

class methods

class initialization

initialize
"Initializes the class variable FadeInMasks."
"Scroller initialize"
| maskArray result addPoint x y rowIndex columnIndex row addPoints points index |
"A form consists of a 16-element array where each element is an integer interpreted as 16 bits."
maskArray ← Array **new:** 16. maskArray **atAllPut:** 0.
result ← OrderedCollection **new**.

"Create two local functions: addPoint and addPoints."
addPoint ← [:aPoint |
    "Note that the points given are in range 1@1 to 8@8 with y going upward. The points in the form are in the range 1@1 to 16@16 with y going downward. Moreover, the points given lie in an 8 by 8 area that corresponds to the top right quarter of the form. Variables rowIndex and columnIndex provide the suitable change of coordinates."
    x ← aPoint **x**. y ← aPoint **y**. rowIndex ← 9-x. columnIndex ← 8+y.
    row ← maskArray **at:** rowIndex.

    ((1 **bitShift:** 16-columnIndex) **bitAnd:** row) = 0 **ifTrue:** [
        "This bit was previously off; turn it on. Also turn on the three corresponding points in the other quadrants."
        maskArray
            at: rowIndex
            put: ((row
                bitOr: (1 **bitShift:** 16-columnIndex)) "top right"
                bitOr: (1 **bitShift:** columnIndex-1)). "top left"
        row ← maskArray **at:** 17-rowIndex.
        maskArray
            at: 17-rowIndex
            put: ((row
                bitOr: (1 **bitShift:** 16-columnIndex)) "bottom right"
                bitOr: (1 **bitShift:** columnIndex-1)). "bottom left"
        result **add:** (Form **extent:** 16@16 **fromArray:** maskArray **offset:** 0@0)]].

addPoints ← [:radius :angleStart :angleIncrement |
    "Obtain the associated top right quadrant points: x and y coordinates in range 1 to 8."
    points ← self **pointsAtRadius:** radius **angle:** angleStart
        angleIncrement: angleIncrement.
    points **do:** [:aPoint | addPoint **value:** aPoint]].

"Add selected points."
addPoint **value:** 1@1. addPoint **value:** 4@4.
addPoint **value:** 2@6. addPoint **value:** 6@2.
addPoint **value:** 7@7.

"Systematically fill in other points from the center outward."
#(22.5 11.25 5.625 2.3125) **do:** [:anAngle |
    #(45.0 22.5 11.25 5.625) **do:** [:anAngleIncrement |
        #(2 4 6 8 10) **do:** [:aRadius |
            addPoints **value:** aRadius **value:** anAngle **value:** anAngleIncrement]].
    Transcript **nextPutAll:** 'done systematic angle '; **print:** anAngle; **nextPutAll:** ' <';
        print: result **size**; **show:** ' points recorded>'; **cr.**].

```
"Do everything else we missed."
1 to: 12.5 by: 0.5 do: [:aRadius |
    addPoints value: aRadius value: 0.0 value: 1.0.
    Transcript nextPutAll: 'done detailed radius '; print: aRadius; nextPutAll: ' <';
        print: result size; show: ' points recorded>'; cr.].
index ← maskArray findFirst: [:row | row ~= 2r1111111111111111].
index = 0 ifFalse: [
    Transcript cr; show: 'Last mask NOT ALL BLACK:'; cr.
    maskArray do: [:aRow | Transcript show: (aRow radix: 2); cr].
    self error: 'only ', result size printString, ' mask points filled in'].

FadeInMasks ← result asArray
```

```
pointsAtRadius: aRadius angle: anAngle angleIncrement: anIncrement
    "Provides the coordinates of all points in an 8 by 8 area of the top right quadrant at
    the specified radius, angle, and angle increment. Points on the x- and y-axis are not
    suitable candidates."
    | points theta x y |
    points ← OrderedCollection new.
    anAngle to: 90 by: anIncrement do: [:angleInDegrees |
        theta ← angleInDegrees degreesToRadians.
        x ← (aRadius * theta cos) rounded. y ← (aRadius * theta sin) rounded.
        (x between: 1 and: 8) & (y between: 1 and: 8) ifTrue: [points add: x@y]].
    ↑points
```

instance creation

```
on: aController appearanceOption: aSymbol markerOption: anotherSymbol
    ↑self new
            on: aController appearanceOption: aSymbol markerOption: anotherSymbol
```

instance methods

instance initialization

```
on: aController appearanceOption: appearanceOptionSymbol
markerOption: markerOptionSymbol
    "Initializes all instance variables of the scroller."

    controller ← aController. view ← controller view.

    (#(PopUp SlideIn FadeIn) includes: appearanceOptionSymbol)
        ifTrue: [
            makeScrollBarVisible ←
                'makeScrollBarVisibleVia', appearanceOptionSymbol.
            makeScrollBarInvisible ←
                'makeScrollBarInvisibleVia', appearanceOptionSymbol]
        ifFalse: [self error: 'Illegal appearance option'].

    (#(FixedSize VariableSize) includes: markerOptionSymbol)
        ifTrue:
            [computeMarkerRegion ←
                'computeMarkerRegionVia', markerOptionSymbol]
        ifFalse: [self error: 'Illegal marker option'].

    makeScrollBarVisible ← (makeScrollBarVisible, 'Option') asSymbol.
    makeScrollBarInvisible ← (makeScrollBarInvisible, 'Option') asSymbol.
    computeMarkerRegion ← (computeMarkerRegion, 'Option') asSymbol.
```

scrollBar ← Quadrangle **new**. marker ← Quadrangle **new**.
"Reverse the coloring to distinguish it from the standard scroll controller."
scrollBar **borderWidthLeft**: 1 **right**: 0 **top**: 1 **bottom**: 1; **insideColor**: Form **gray**.
marker **borderWidth**: 1; **insideColor**: Form **white**

scroll bar displaying

makeScrollBarVisible
    scrollBar **region**: self **computeScrollBarRegion**.
    marker **region**: self **computeMarkerRegion**.
    scrollBar ← scrollBar
        align: scrollBar **inside topRight**
        with: view **insetDisplayBox topLeft** - (view **borderWidth left**@0).
    marker ← marker **align**: marker **topLeft with**: scrollBar **inside topLeft**.

    self **perform**: makeScrollBarVisible "for the given appearance option"

makeScrollBarInvisible
    self **perform**: makeScrollBarInvisible "for the given appearance option"

makeScrollBarVisibleViaPopUpOption
    "Simply displays the scroll bar and marker after saving the area underneath for
    later restoring."
    savedArea ← Form **fromDisplay**: scrollBar.
    scrollBar **displayOn**: Display.
    self **moveMarker**

makeScrollBarVisibleViaSlideInOption
    "Causes the scroll bar and marker to smoothly slide out after saving the area
    underneath for later restoring."
    | form formOffset clippingBoxExtent |

    "Adjust the marker but make sure it does not display."
    savedArea ← nil. self **moveMarker**.

    "Create a form to contain the scroll bar and marker."
    form ← Form **extent**: scrollBar **extent**.
    scrollBar **displayOn**: form
        align: scrollBar **topLeft**
        with: 0@0 **clippingBox**: form **boundingBox**.
    marker **displayOn**: form
        align: marker **topLeft**
        with: (marker **origin** - scrollBar **origin**) **clippingBox**: form **boundingBox**.

    savedArea ← Form **fromDisplay**: scrollBar.

    "Display more and more of the form as its display offset is shifted left."
    formOffset ← scrollBar **topLeft** + (form **width**@0).
    clippingBoxExtent ← 0@form **height**.
    1 to: form **width do**: [:i |
        formOffset ← formOffset - (1@0).
        clippingBoxExtent ← clippingBoxExtent + (1@0).
        form **displayOn**: Display
            at: formOffset **clippingBox**: (formOffset **extent**: clippingBoxExtent)]

makeScrollBarVisibleViaFadeInOption
"Causes the scroll bar and marker to fade in after saving the area underneath for later restoring."
| form |

"Adjust the marker but make sure it does not display."
savedArea ← nil. self **moveMarker**.

"Create a form to contain the scroll bar and marker."
form ← Form **extent**: scrollBar **extent**.
scrollBar **displayOn**: form
    align: scrollBar **topLeft**
    with: 0@0 **clippingBox**: form **boundingBox**.
marker **displayOn**: form
    align: marker **topLeft**
    with: (marker **origin** - scrollBar **origin**) **clippingBox**: form **boundingBox**.
    savedArea ← Form **fromDisplay**: scrollBar. "save the old version for restoring"
self **fadeIn**: form **at**: scrollBar **topLeft** "display the scroll bar and marker"

makeScrollBarInvisibleViaPopUpOption
"Simply re-displays the saved area and indicates that it is no longer needed."
savedArea **notNil ifTrue**: [
    savedArea **displayOn**: Display **at**: scrollBar topLeft. savedArea ← nil]

makeScrollBarInvisibleViaSlideInOption
"Causes the scroll bar and marker to slide in while restoring the area underneath."
| scrollBarForm scrollBarOrigin forms newForm |

savedArea **notNil ifTrue**: [
    scrollBarForm ← Form **fromDisplay**: scrollBar.
    scrollBarOrigin ← scrollBar **topLeft**.
    "To get the same performance as the corresponding makeScrollBarVisible method, each iteration should perform at most one display operation. So precompute a little."
    forms ← (1 **to**: savedArea **width**) **collect**: [:offset |
        "Successive forms have more saved area shown and scroll bar area shift right."
        scrollBarForm **displayOn**: (newForm ← savedArea **deepCopy**)
            at: offset+1@0.
        newForm].
    forms **do**: [:aForm | aForm **displayOn**: Display **at**: scrollBarOrigin].
    savedArea ← nil]

makeScrollBarInvisibleViaFadeInOption
"Causes the area underneath the scroll bar and marker to be restored by fading in."
savedArea **notNil ifTrue**: [
    self **fadeIn**: savedArea **at**: scrollBar **topLeft**. "restore the previous background"
    savedArea ← nil]

fadeIn: sourceForm **at**: aPoint
"Causes the form to be slowly painted over the existing forms."
| sourceFormReverse destinationForm |
sourceFormReverse ← sourceForm **deepCopy reverse**.
destinationForm ← Form **fromDisplay**: (aPoint **extent**: sourceForm **extent**).
FadeInMasks **do**: [:aMask |
    self **overlay**: sourceForm
        given: sourceFormReverse **onto**: destinationForm **mask**: aMask.
    destinationForm **displayAt**: aPoint]

overlay: form1 **given**: form1Reverse **onto**: form2 **mask**: aMask
"Causes form1's masked bits (both white and black bits) to be overlaid on top of form2. This operation should be generalized and added as a form operation."

"First, overlay the white bits in two steps: (1) or the inverted bits (hence the mask will in effect mask the bits that used to be off before the inversion of form2) => result is black if one or the other of the inverted bits are black => result is black if one or the other of the bits are white, and (2) invert the result => result is white if one or the other of the bits are white (masking is used for form1)."
form1Reverse
    displayOn: form2 **at**: 0@0
    clippingBox: form2 **boundingBox**
    rule: 11 "this is really receiver (form1Reverse) bitOr: form2 inverse"
    mask: aMask.
form2 **reverse**.

"Second, overlay the black bits."
form1
    displayOn: form2 **at**: 0@0
    clippingBox: form2 **boundingBox**
    rule: Form **under**
    mask: aMask.

region construction

computeMarkerRegion
    ↑self **perform**: computeMarkerRegion "for the given marker size option"

computeMarkerRegionViaFixedSizeOption
    "Constructs a fixed size marker"
    ↑0@0 **extent**: scrollBar **inside width**@15

computeMarkerRegionViaVariableSizeOption
    "Determines how large the marker should be as a function of the amount of information visible in the view and returns a rectangle of the appropriate size. Enforces a minimum size of 15 pixels."
    "↑0@0 extent: scrollBar inside width@(r / R * M)" "i.e., solve for m in the height equation"
    | height |
    height ← (controller **visibleRectangle height asFloat** /
        controller **totalRectangle height** * scrollBar **inside height**) **rounded**.
    ↑0@0 **extent**: scrollBar **inside width**@((height **max**: 15) **min**: scrollBar **inside height**)

computeScrollBarRegion
    "Computes the size of the scroll bar area (including the border)."
    ↑0@0 **extent**: (15@view **insetDisplayBox height**) + (1@2) "for border"

cursor interrogation

cursorAboveMarker
    ↑Sensor **cursorPoint y** < marker **top**

cursorBelowMarker
    ↑Sensor **cursorPoint y** > marker **bottom**

markerContainsCursor
    ↑marker **containsPoint**: Sensor **cursorPoint**

scrollBarContainsCursor
    ↑scrollBar **inside containsPoint**: Sensor **cursorPoint**

canScroll

"Returns **true** if the visible rectangle is smaller (by an epsilon) than the total rectangle; **false** otherwise."

"↑(scrollBar inside height - marker region height) > controller canScrollEpsilon OR"
↑(controller **totalRectangle height** - controller **visibleRectangle height**) >
    controller **canScrollEpsilon**

scrollAmount

"Returns a positive displacement in view coordinates that is proportional to the vertical distance between the mouse and the top of the scroll bar; i.e., it varies from 0 for the mouse at the top of the scroll bar to the viewport height for the mouse at the bottom of the scroll bar."

"↑Sensor cursorPoint y - scrollBar inside top (if view and screen coordinates are the same)"

↑(view **inverseDisplayTransform**: Sensor **cursorPoint**) **y** -
    (view **inverseDisplayTransform**: scrollBar **inside topCenter**) **y**

viewDelta

"Returns how much the view should be scrolled (positive for up and negative for down) so as to make it conform to the current marker position."

"If the marker has been moved, the current displacement Δ_r from the top of the visible rectangle to the top of the total rectangle is no longer up-to-date. If we let x denote the amount by which the new displacement must be adjusted, this new displacement can be written (Δ_r - x). Solving for x (the delta) in offset equation $\Delta_m/M = (\Delta_r - x)/R$ gives us $x = \Delta_r - \Delta_m/M*R$. Note that if the marker moves up, Δ_m decreases and so must (Δ_r - x) in which case x must increase; i.e., be positive. Since the visible rectangle must also move up, x positive implies moving up. A similar argument can be made for x negative."

↑((controller **visibleRectangle top** - controller **totalRectangle top** "Δ_r") -
    ((marker **top** - scrollBar **inside top**) **asFloat** "Δ_m" /
        scrollBar **inside height asFloat** "M" *
        controller **totalRectangle height asFloat** "R")
) **roundTo**: controller **viewDeltaRoundingAmount**

markerDelta

"Returns how much the marker should be moved (positive for up and negative for down) so as to make it conform to the current view position."

"If the visible rectangle has been moved, the current displacement Δ_m from the top of the marker to the top of the scroll bar area is no longer up-to-date. If we let x denote the amount by which the new displacement must be adjusted, this new displacement can be written (Δ_m - x). Solving for x (the delta) in offset equation (Δ_m - x)/M = Δ_r/R gives us $x = \Delta_m - \Delta_r/R*M$. Note that if the visible rectangle moves up, Δ_r decreases and so must (Δ_m - x) in which case x must increase; i.e., be positive. Since the marker must also move up, x positive implies moving up. A similar argument can be made for x negative."

↑(marker **top** - scrollBar **inside top**) "Δ_m" -
    ((controller **visibleRectangle top** - controller **totalRectangle** top) **asFloat** "Δ_r" /
    controller **totalRectangle height asFloat** "R" *
    scrollBar **inside height asFloat** "M") **rounded**

moveMarker
> "The view window has changed. Update the marker."
> self **moveMarker:** self **markerDelta negated**

moveMarker: yDistance
> "Obtained from moveMarker: by adding a test that displays the marker only if it is visible."
> I minimumY maximumY newMarker I
> minimumY ← scrollBar **inside bottom** - marker **bottom**.
> maximumY ← scrollBar **inside top** - marker **top**.
> newMarker ← marker **translateBy:**
>   0 @ ((yDistance **min:** minimumY) **max:** maximumY).
> savedArea **notNil ifTrue:** [
>   Display **fill:** marker **mask:** scrollBar **insideColor**.
>   newMarker **displayOn:** Display].
> marker ← newMarker

scrolling operations

scroll
> "This is the method executed whenever the cursor is in the scroll bar area. Unlike the standard scroll operation, does not change cursors. Depressing a mouse button on the marker causes absolute scrolling. Depressing it above (below) the marker causes the user's viewpoint to move up (down)."

> [self **scrollBarContainsCursor**] **whileTrue:** [
>   Sensor **anyButtonPressed ifTrue:** [
>   self **markerContainsCursor ifTrue:** [self **scrollAbsolute**].
>   self **cursorAboveMarker ifTrue:** [self **scrollUp**].
>   self **cursorBelowMarker ifTrue:** [self **scrollDown**]]]

scrollAbsolute
> "Differs from the standard method by (1) not changing cursors, and (2) busy-waiting until the button is released if scrolling is not possible."
> I grabPoint cursorPoint oldMarkerI
> self **canScroll ifFalse:** [↑[Sensor **anyButtonPressed**] **whileTrue**].
> grabPoint ← Sensor **cursorPoint y**.
> [Sensor **anyButtonPressed**] **whileTrue:** [
>   self **scrollBarContainsCursor ifTrue:** [
>   (cursorPoint ← Sensor **cursorPoint y**) ~= grabPoint **ifTrue:** [
>   oldMarker ← marker. "First save it."
>   marker ← marker **translateBy:**
>   "Move it making sure it's inside the scroll bar."
>   0 @
>   ((cursorPoint - grabPoint
>   **min:** scrollBar **inside bottom** - marker **bottom**)
>   **max:** scrollBar **inside top** - marker **top**).
>   "Create and display both the new marker rectangle and the ghost rectangle."
>   (oldMarker **areasOutside:** marker),
>   (marker **areasOutside:** oldMarker) **do:** [:region I
>   Display **fill:** region **rule:** Form **reverse** mask: Form **gray**].
>   grabPoint ← cursorPoint.
>   self **scrollView**]]].
> scrollBar **display**. "Eliminate the ghost."
> self **moveMarker**. "Make the marker visible."

scrollToTop
>   self **scrollView**: controller **visibleRectangle top** - controller **totalRectangle top**

scrollUp
>   "Differs from the standard method by (1) not changing cursors, (2) busy-waiting until the button is released if scrolling is not possible, and (3) being user oriented; i.e., scrolling up from the user's perspective causes the view to scroll down from its perspective."
>   self **canScroll ifFalse**: [↑[Sensor **anyButtonPressed**] **whileTrue**].
>   [Sensor **anyButtonPressed**] **whileTrue**: [
>   self **scrollBarContainsCursor ifTrue**: [
>   self **markerContainsCursor ifTrue**: [↑self].
>   self **scrollViewDown**.
>   self **moveMarker**]]

scrollDown
>   "Differs from the standard method by (1) not changing cursors, (2) busy-waiting until the button is released if scrolling is not possible, and (3) being user oriented; i.e., scrolling up from the user's perspective causes the view to scroll down from its perspective."
>   self **canScroll ifFalse**: [↑[Sensor **anyButtonPressed**] **whileTrue**].
>   [Sensor **anyButtonPressed**] **whileTrue**: [
>   self **scrollBarContainsCursor ifTrue**: [
>   self **markerContainsCursor ifTrue**: [↑self].
>   self **scrollViewUp**.
>   self **moveMarker**]]

scrollView: yDistance
>   "Scrolls the view by a y-distance (positive for up and negative for down)."
> | maximumAmount minimumAmount actualAmount |
>   maximumAmount ← (controller **visibleRectangle top** -
>   controller **totalRectangle top**) **max**: 0.
>   minimumAmount ← (controller **visibleRectangle bottom** -
>   controller **totalRectangle bottom**) **min**: 0.
>   actualAmount ← (yDistance **min**: maximumAmount) **max**: minimumAmount.
>   actualAmount ~= 0 **ifTrue**: [controller **scrollViewDirectlyBy**: actualAmount]

copied scrolling operations

scrollView
>   "The scroll bar jump method was used so that the view should be updated to correspond to the location of the scroll bar gray area."
>   self **scrollView**: self **viewDelta**

scrollViewUp
>   "Scroll the receiver's view up the default amount."
>   self **scrollView**: self **scrollAmount negated**

scrollViewDown
>   "Scroll the receiver's view down the default amount."
>   self **scrollView**: self **scrollAmount**

StringHolderControllerWithScroller was obtained by adding one instance variable 'scroller' to StringHolderController. All of the existing ScrollController operations, except for the five special ones that subclasses should refine, were rerouted to this scroller. For the experiment to work, we also needed to revise the **controlInitialize** and **control-Terminate** operations in ScrollController. However, intervening **controlInitialize** and **controlTerminate** methods exist that perform 'super **controlInitialize**' and 'super **controlTerminate**' respectively. Our approach was to simply copy the code. However, this is not a good solution because changes to the original methods will not be reflected in the copied code.

Class StringHolderControllerWithScroller

class name	StringHolderControllerWithScroller
superclass	StringHolderController
instance variable names	scroller
comment	A string holder controller with an objectified version of vertical configurable scrollers.
class methods	

examples

example
```
| topView subView subViews subView1 controller1 subView2 controller2 subView3
controller3 subView4 controller4 sampleContents |
"StringHolderControllerWithScroller example"

topView ← StandardSystemView new label: 'Test New Scroll Bars'; borderWidth: 1.
subViews ← (1 to: 4) collect: [:viewIndex |
    sampleContents ← (1 to: 10) inject: '' into: [:string :stringIndex |
        string, ' line ', stringIndex printString,
        ' window ', viewIndex printString, (String with: Character cr)].
    subView ← StringHolderView
        container: (StringHolder new contents: sampleContents).
    subView controller: StringHolderControllerWithScroller new.
    subView].

subView1 ← subViews at: 1. controller1 ← subView1 controller.
subView2 ← subViews at: 2. controller2 ← subView2 controller.
subView3 ← subViews at: 3. controller3 ← subView3 controller.
subView4 ← subViews at: 4. controller4 ← subView4 controller.

controller1 scroller: (Scroller on: controller1
    appearanceOption: #PopUp markerOption: #VariableSize).
controller2 scroller: (Scroller on: controller2
    appearanceOption: #PopUp markerOption: #FixedSize).
controller3 scroller: (Scroller on: controller3
    appearanceOption: #SlideIn markerOption: #FixedSize).
controller4 scroller: (Scroller on: controller4
    appearanceOption: #FadeIn markerOption: #FixedSize).

topView addSubView: subView1 in: (0@0 corner: 0.5@0.5) borderWidth: 1.
topView addSubView: subView2 in: (0.5@0 corner: 1@0.5) borderWidth: 1.
topView addSubView: subView3 in: (0@0.5 corner: 0.5@1) borderWidth: 1.
topView addSubView: subView4 in: (0.5@0.5 corner: 1@1) borderWidth: 1.

topView controller open
```

instance methods

control sequence operations (revised)

controlInitialize
> "We need to override controlInitialize for ScrollController. But that is the super's super. Since we can't override a method that far up the hierarchy, just copy the code."

> "First, the scroll controller controlInitialize (everything above it in the hierarchy is a no-op)."
> scroller **makeScrollBarVisible**.

> "Second, the paragraph editor controlInitialize (everything in the hierarchy between it and this controller class is a no-op)."
> startBlock ← paragraph **characterBlockForIndex**: startBlock **stringIndex**.
> stopBlock ← paragraph **characterBlockForIndex**: stopBlock **stringIndex**.
> self **initializeSelection**.
> beginTypeInBlock ← nil.

controlTerminate
> "We need to override controlTerminate for ScrollController. But that is the super's super. Since we can't override a method that far up the hierarchy, just copy the code."

> "First, the scroll controller controlTerminate (everything above it in the hierarchy is a no-op)."
> scroller **makeScrollBarInvisible**.

> "Second, the paragraph editor controlTerminate (everything in the hierarchy between it and this controller class is a no-op)."
> self **closeTypeIn ifTrue**: [startBlock ← stopBlock **copy**].
> "so leaving and entering window won't select last type-in"

re-routed operations

canScroll
> ↑scroller **canScroll**

computeMarkerRegion
> ↑scroller **computeMarkerRegion**

markerDelta
> ↑scroller **markerDelta**

moveMarker: yDistance
> ↑scroller **moveMarker**: yDistance

scroll
> ↑scroller **scroll**

scrollAmount
> ↑scroller **scrollAmount**

scrollBarContainsCursor
> ↑scroller **scrollBarContainsCursor**
scrollToTop
> ↑scroller **scrollToTop**
scrollView: yDistance
> ↑scroller **scrollView**: yDistance

viewDelta
↑scroller **viewDelta**

operations that subclasses may override

visibleRectangle
↑paragraph **clippingRectangle**

totalRectangle
↑paragraph **compositionRectangle**

canScrollEpsilon
↑0

viewDeltaRoundingAmount
↑paragraph **lineGrid**

scrollViewDirectlyBy: anAmount
self **deselect**. self **scrollBy:** anAmount **negated**. self **display**. self **select**

scroller access

scroller
↑scroller

scroller: aScroller
scroller ← aScroller

2.6 SUMMARY

This chapter has provided a first introduction to detailed Smalltalk window classes. In particular, we have discussed the following notions:

- A logical characterization of the window classes including the model hierarchy, the view hierarchy, and the controller hierarchy.

- The basic model class called Model.

- The basic window classes Controller and View.

- View creation along with model and controller interfacing.

- An illustration of controllers (and secondarily views) using the ESP game.

- The distinction between windows, viewports, and display boxes.

- Coloring and sizing windows and borders; displaying views; viewing transformations; and adding, removing; and querying subviews.

- An illustration of views (and secondarily controllers) using the Tic-Tac-Toe game.

- The supporting controllers and views: classes NoController, MouseMenu-Controller (setting up mouse menus and creating specializations), Standard-SystemController, StandardSystemView, ScreenController, and ScrollController (creating specializations with new kinds of scroll bars).

2.7 EXERCISES

The following exercises are designed to test your knowledge of windows, models, views, controllers in general, and the basic views and controllers in particular.

1. Create and open a window that is inert; i.e., that ignores mouse and keyboard interactions. Hint: Create a standard system view with one subview that has an inert controller.

2. Create a window with a blue button menu that permits a view's border width, border color, and inside color to be respecified dynamically. Is this feature difficult to add more generally?

3. Interrupt existing windows and inspect the associated models, views, and controllers.

4. Investigate the difference between a view's inset display box and the rectangle obtained by applying the display transform to the view's window and the window indented by the border. Make sure to try out views deeply nested inside other views, where all views have borders.

5. Create a window with a large number of small subviews each arbitrarily positioned inside the topview; use **addSubView:in:borderWidth:** to position the subviews. Create some that intersect with each other.

6. Is it possible to have standard system views as subviews of some other standard system view?

7. Is it possible to use **startUp** on a standard system controller instead of **open**? Does it help to send **resize** to the corresponding view before starting up the controller?

8. Extend standard system views (and controllers) so that the minimum and maximum view size can be changed via the blue button menu.

9. Add a new facility to the screen controller; e.g., to remove models from the dependency mechanism if all dependents are views that are no longer scheduled. An easier task might be to add a **find-window** facility whereby a pop-up menu of scheduled window labels is presented; if the user selects one, it is made the active window.

10. Modify class MouseMenuController so that the menu message receiver can be changed easily. Note that if no mouse menu receiver is explicitly provided, the default should be self to be upward compatible.

11. Attempt to eliminate methods **closeAndUnschedule** and **closeAndUnscheduleNoErase** in the standard system controller by modifying **close** to perform the finalization activity immediately rather than delaying it until the next iteration of the control loop.

12. Replace method **displayEmphasized** by an equivalent method called **emphasizeView** to force the emphasis protocol for **StandardSystemView** and **View** to conform.

13. There is currently no standard way of notifying all views to **adjust** themselves when a window is moved or resized. Devise such a protocol. Should it be integrated with the **lock/unlock** mechanism?

14. Investigate the possibility of creating scroll bars that can scroll vertically and horizontally depending on a creation option.

15. Consider the design of scroll bars that are permanently visible views that can be independently manipulated.

16. Modify the ESP game to use views for the respective 'guess' pictures.

17. Modify the tic-tac-toe game to use views for the respective squares.

2.8 GLOSSARY AND IMPORTANT FACTS

classes

ActionMenu A combined model-view-controller class for pop-up menu windows; used for the yellow button menus by pluggable windows.

BinaryChoice The model class for pop-up binary text-query windows.

BinaryChoiceController The controller class for pop-up binary text-query windows.

BinaryChoiceView The view class for pop-up binary text-query windows.

BooleanView The view class for pluggable switch windows.

Button A model class for the switch and pluggable switch windows.

Controller The top of the controller hierarchy; provides the basic protocol for all other controller classes; its primary responsibility is to interface with the window manager and dispatch keyboard and mouse events to the other components of the triad, the model, and the view.

DisplayTextView A view class for non-editable text windows.

FillInTheBlank The model class for pop-up text-query windows.

FillInTheBlankController The controller class for pop-up text-query windows.

FillInTheBlankView The view class for pop-up text-query windows.

FormHolderView A view class for form windows with a special protocol for accepting and canceling a modification.

FormMenuController The controller class for switch-menu windows.

FormMenuView The view class for switch-menu windows.

FormView A view class for form windows.

Icon The model for **collapsed** windows; associated with instances of **IconController** and **IconView**.

IconController The controller for **collapsed** windows; the standard controller for **IconView**.

IconView The view for **collapsed** windows; typically a subview of the collapsed window when the corresponding controller can be activated.

ListController The basic controller class for standard menu windows; much of its protocol is inherited by pluggable menu windows.

ListView The basic view class for standard menu windows; much of its protocol is inherited by pluggable menu windows.

Model A class that duplicates the dependency maintenance protocol provided by class **Object**. Because its instances record dependency information locally, failure to release dependents in error situations is inconsequential. By comparison, unreleased dependencies recorded in class **Object** must ultimately be physically removed by the user.

MouseMenuController A controller class for windows that have yellow, red, and blue button pop-up menus.

NoController A controller class for windows ignoring mouse and keyboard interactions.

OneOnSwitch A model for switch and pluggable switch windows.

Paragraph A class privately used by text window controllers for maintaining the working text.

ParagraphEditor The basic controller class for text and pluggable text windows; provides editing capabilities.

PopUpMenu A combined model-view-controller class for pop-up menu windows.

ScreenController A controller class that manages the screen background; it provides a special yellow button menu for a number of activities such as restoring the display; entering and exiting projects; opening system browsers and file browsers; opening workspaces, the system transcript, and the system workspace; saving, suspending, and quitting. The view that is associated with the controller is a form view with an infinite gray form.

ScrollController A controller class that provides the functionality for subclasses with scrolling capabilities; specifically provides a scroll bar and a marker for vertically adjusting the information visible in the associated window.

SelectionInListController The controller class for pluggable menu windows.

SelectionInListView The view class for pluggable menu windows.

StandardSystemController A controller class designed specifically to be a scheduled controller; it directly supports subordinate unscheduled controllers.

StandardSystemView A view class that complements **StandardSystemController**; elaborates the standard view protocol by (1) providing a label box that serves to identify the view, and (2) providing support for the blue button menu messages handled by its controller; e.g., messages for moving, resizing, collapsing, and closing the view.

StringHolder A model class for text and pluggable text windows. Maintains a string instead of text (see **TextHolder**).

StringHolderController A controller class for text windows.

StringHolderView A view class for text windows.

Switch A model class for the switch and pluggable switch windows.

SwitchController The basic controller class for switch windows and pluggable switch windows.

SwitchView The basic view class for switch windows; much of its protocol is inherited by pluggable switch windows.

TextCollector The model class for text windows with write stream functionality.

TextCollectorController The controller class for text windows with write stream functionality.

TextCollectorView The view class for text windows with write stream functionality.

TextCompositor A class privately used by text window controllers for maintaining the working text. A recent addition that is an efficient substitute for **Paragraph**.

TextController The controller class for pluggable text windows.

TextHolder A model class for text and pluggable text windows. Maintains text instead of a string (see **StringHolder**).

TextList A class privately used by menu window controllers for maintaining the menu information.

TextView The view class for pluggable text windows.

View The top of the view hierarchy; provides the basic protocol for all other views. Its responsibility is to display the model and provide visual feedback for controller interactions, to manage hierarchies of interrelated views, and to provide both an automatic resizing and repositioning facility and a coordinate transformation facility.

selected terminology

border The boundary of the window, viewport, or display box.

border color A form or **nil** (denoting transparent) used to draw the border; typically, borders are colored gray, light gray, or black (Form **gray**, Form **lightGray**, or Form **black**).

bounding box The window transformed to display coordinates.

bottomview A view that has no subviews.

clipping The term used to indicate that information lying outside the inset display box of a view is not displayed.

collapsed windows The window that results when the **collapse** entry in the blue button menu is selected. The window typically consists of only the label tab of the original window.

deemphasizing Displaying a window in such a manner as to provide a visual indication that it is inactive.

dehighlighting Undoing the visual indication of acknowledgment (see highlighting).

display box A window transformed to the coordinate system of the screen; a window as seen from the screen.

display transformation A windowing transformation that maps objects in the coordinate system of the view to objects in the screen coordinate system. The display transformation is composed from the successive local transformations between a view and its topview.

emphasizing Displaying a window in such a manner as to provide a visual indication that it is active; e.g., the label tab of an active window is often displayed in reverse video.

flashing Displaying a window in reverse video twice in succession.

form window A window that permits pictorial or graphical information to be displayed.

ghost marker An outline of the marker; can be seen when the marker is moved with the mouse prior to releasing the button.

highlighting Providing a visual indication of acknowledgment; the most often used technique in the system is to use reverse video.

inset display box A display box inset by the border (approximately).

inset viewport A viewport inset by the border (approximately).

inset window A window inset by the border (approximately).

inside color A form or **nil** (denoting transparent) used to draw the inside of a display box; typically, windows are transparent (**nil**) or colored white (Form **white**).

label display box A rectangle for the label tab displayed at the top of a standard system view display box.

local transformation A windowing transformation that maps objects in the coordinate system of the view to objects in the coordinate system of its superview.

locked In the context of views, indicates that the display transformation and the display box *have been computed* from the local transformations of the view and its superviews. In the content of string holders and string holder controllers (see the chapter on text windows), indicates that a working copy is different from the string holder contents; when the controller updates the string holder, the two are unlocked.

marker A small gray rectangle of fixed width but varying height inside the scroll bar. The vertical **size** of the marker indicates how much information is visible while the **position** of the marker indicates which part of the information is being viewed.

menu window A window that permits scrolling over collections of strings. Selecting one causes the associated model to be notified and modified in some way.

permanently visible window A window that remains on the screen until explicitly removed by the user.

pluggable window A window that permits more customization than the **standard** windows.

pluggable menu window A menu window that permits some menu aspect of an arbitrary model to be displayed and selected.

pluggable text window A text window that permits some textual aspect of an arbitrary model to be displayed and modified.

pluggable switch window A window that permits some switch aspect of an arbitrary model to be displayed and selected.

pop-up window A window that appears suddenly when an interactive request is made and then immediately disappears after an appropriate reply.

pop-up menu window A window that provides users with a choice of menu entries to select from; it is also possible to make no choice.

pop-up text-query window A window used to request a textual response to some query.

pop-up binary text-query window A special case of pop-up text-query window in which the response is either **yes** or **no**.

startUp A message sent to a controller to start it executing; afterward, control is returned to the sender of the **startUp** message.

scroll bar A rectangular area that pops up whenever the scroll controller is active.

scrollable window A window that provides access to information too voluminous to be displayed in entirety on the screen. Consequently, only a small part is visible at a time. Other parts can be made visible either by **scrolling up** or **down**.

standard window A nonpluggable window.

subview A view that is subordinate to an existing view. A view can have any number of subviews.

superview A view to which this view is subordinate. A view can have at most one superview; a topview has no superview.

supporting controller An instance of class NoController, class MouseMenuController, class StandardSystemController, class ScreenController, or class ScrollController.

switch window A window that permits switches, buttons, and one-on switches to be graphically displayed and manipulated.

switch-menu window A window that is used for building editors with menus of buttons that can be invoked through the keyboard.

text window A window that provides facilities for creating and editing textual information.

topview A view that has no superview.

unlocked See locked.

viewport A window transformed to the coordinate system of the superview; a window as seen from the superview.

viewport adjusting The process of sizing a particular viewport and also positioning it to cover some small part of the superview's window. It can be specified by aligning one point with another, aligning one viewport with another, or providing proportional information that can be used for automatically sizing and positioning it.

window Intuitively, the class or set of classes that collectively provides this interface component; defined by the model-view-controller (MVC) triple that implements it. More technically, the rectangle in the local coordinate system of the view.

important facts

default controllers Controllers are typically created automatically by their associated views when they are needed and also released when they are no longer needed. Users create the view; the view creates and releases the controller.

getting control Message **isControlWanted** is sent to a controller that does not yet have control to determine whether or not control is desired. In the protocol of class **Controller**, **true** is returned if the associated view contains the mouse cursor. This method is often redefined in specializations.

keeping control Message **isControlActive** is sent to a controller that already has

control to determine whether or not control is to be retained. In the protocol of class **Controller**, **true** is returned if the cursor is inside the view and the blue button is not pressed. This method is often redefined in specializations.

locking protocol The display transformation and display box are automatically computed from the local transformations and viewports of a view and its superviews when required. If it is computed, the view is said to be **locked**; otherwise, **unlocked**.

view defaults The default view border size is zero (no border) and the inside color is transparent (**nil**).

3

Text Windows

3.1 INTRODUCTION

Permanently visible scrollable text windows (see Fig. 3.1), or simply **text windows** for short, provide the ability to manipulate textual data that may be too voluminous to fit the visible portion of the window. The invisible parts (if any) are made accessible by scrolling. Unlike their counterpart, **pop-up text windows**, which we will never abbreviate, text windows are meant to remain on the screen even after the window is no longer active.

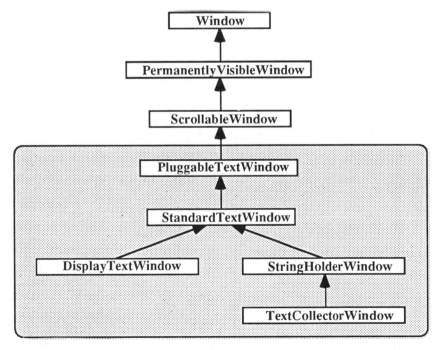

Figure 3.1 Text windows: A logical view.

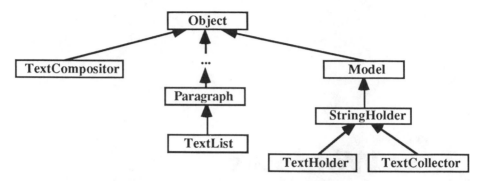

Figure 3.2 Text windows: Models and support.

There are essentially three varieties of **standard** text windows: **display-text windows,** which provide non-editable textual displays, **string (or text) holder windows,** which provide additional editing and execution capabilities, and **text collector windows,** which extend string holder windows so they can be used as write streams. **Pluggable text windows** are provided for more general applications.

Text windows are logically a small part of the window classes. However, from the implementation perspective, the volume of code in the supporting classes (see Figs. 3.2, 3.3, and 3.4) is by far the largest of any other class of windows.

All of the text windows maintain their textual data internally as an instance of class Paragraph or TextCompositor (see Fig. 3.2). Class TextCompositor is a recent addition that is more efficient than Paragraph for handling large amounts of text. Most (but not all) users of paragraphs have switched to text compositors — their protocols are almost identical. However, the Paragraph class still supports the TextList subclass used by menu windows. The paragraph and text compositor used as internal representations for the paragraph and text editors are distinct from the models being manipulated. The display-text windows use any objects that can be converted to paragraphs as their models; e.g., string, text, display-text instances, or paragraphs. String holder windows use string holders, text holder windows use text holders, text collector windows use text collectors, and pluggable text windows permit more general models that conform to special requirements.

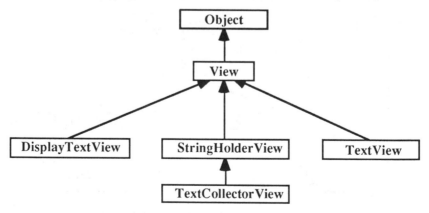

Figure 3.3 Text windows: The view hierarchy.

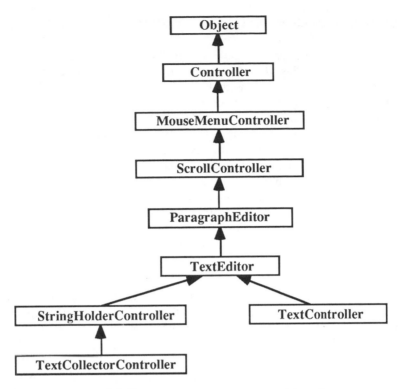

Figure 3.4 Text windows: The controller hierarchy.

The most used nonpluggable text window is a **string holder window** as implemented by string holders, string holder controllers, and string holder views. **Text holder windows** are a variation of string holder windows obtained by replacing the string holder by a text holder — the same string holder controller and view is used. **Text collector windows** are implemented by text collectors, text collector controllers, and text collector views. **Display-text windows** are made up of display-text views and are typically used with instances of NoController. The **pluggable text windows** are implemented with text views and text controllers.

The majority of the text editing protocol is provided by controller class ParagraphEditor, which in turn has recently been re-implemented more efficiently by TextEditor. Although it is possible to make use of instances of ParagraphEditor (or TextEditor), the classes were likely intended to be abstract classes for supporting the various specializations. Paragraph editors maintain the textual information internally in an instance of class Paragraph. Text editors maintain it in an instance of TextCompositor. In each case, the model is distinct from the respective paragraph or text compositor used by the controllers.

In the sections that follow, we will consider paragraph (and text) editors first. Then we will consider the text windows in the order discussed above; i.e., display-text windows, string (text) holder windows, text collector windows, and pluggable text windows.

3.2 THE PARAGRAPHEDITOR (TEXTEDITOR) PARTIAL PROTOCOL

Most of the protocol for manipulating scrollable text in windows is provided by class **ParagraphEditor**. Class **TextEditor** re-implements only those parts of the protocol that can take advantage of the increased efficiency provided by substituting text compositors for paragraphs. Paragraph editors support interactive cutting, pasting, deletion, and insertion of text. Detailed understanding of paragraph editors requires detailed knowledge of many classes that are actually **private** to paragraph editors; i.e., character blocks, character scanners, character block scanners, composition scanners, display-text, and paragraphs. Corresponding additional classes also exist for text editors; e.g., text display scanners, text alignment scanners, text character block scanners, and text compositors. Fortunately, paragraph (and text) editors were not intended for non-interactive use. Unless we need to modify the existing implementation, we can easily get by without knowing these classes and the complicated implementation details. Moreover, it is sufficient to consider the interesting aspects of **ParagraphEditor** since **TextEditor** provides little additional protocol.

Class **ParagraphEditor** extends the **ScrollController** protocol by providing support for interactively editing text in a window. The text is actually maintained as an instance of class **Paragraph**, whose protocol we need not consider. A portion of this text is always selected and called the **selection**; the selection can be an empty string. If nonempty, it can either be highlighted or not. When highlighted, characters typed or pasted replace the highlighted selection. A **caret** or insertion point character is visible when the selection is empty. Text can be highlighted by pressing the mouse at a starting point (this will insert the caret at that position), then dragging it to a destination point either ahead or behind the start, and releasing it. If necessary, the window will scroll up or down to reach the destination point. To permit text to be copied across multiple paragraph editors, a special **shared buffer** is used. Each paragraph editor also maintains a copy of the original paragraph so that it can be restored by a **cancel** operation. This copy can also be replaced by the current paragraph through an **accept** operation. Finally, the text is aligned **flush left** by default; i.e., the right margin is ragged. Other **alignment** possibilities include **flush right**, **centered**, and **justified**, which aligns both sides. One can cycle through these alignment possibilities (in the order described) with the **align** operation. The yellow button menu entries provided by the paragraph editor include the following:

- **again** — repeat last text substitution (for the entire paragraph if the left shift key is down).
- **undo** — undo the last cut or paste from information in the shared buffer.
- **copy** — make a copy of the selection and store it in the shared buffer.
- **cut** — cut out the selection and store it in the shared buffer.
- **paste** — replace the selection by the text in the shared buffer.
- **accept** — save the current paragraph for later canceling (implicitly done at start up).
- **cancel** — restore the current paragraph to the last accepted version.
- **align** — align the text according to the next alignment possibility.
- **fit** — fit the text into the available space and show the visible part (unfinished experiment).

Each of these menu entries can also be invoked directly via messages of the same name (except for **copy**, which must be specified as **copySelection**). On some systems, the copy, cut, and paste commands can also be invoked via special keyboard keys. The actual key used, however, may differ between systems. For example, some systems use **control c**, **control x**, and **control v** respectively; others permit only cut via the **delete** key. The **escape** character causes the characters previously typed to be selected; **control w** causes the previous word to be cut; **control t**, **control f**, and **control d** cause 'ifTrue:', 'ifFalse:', and the current date respectively to be typed; **control 0** through **control 9**, **control shift 1**, **control shift 2**, **control minus**, and **control shift minus** cause the current selected fonts to change. Converting a text selection to boldface is achieved by typing **control b** (**control shift b** undoes it); converting it to italics (on some systems) is done with **control i** (**control shift i** undoes it).

When text is already selected, typing **control** followed by one of the open brackets ({[<'" (the last two characters are single and double quotes respectively) causes the selected text to be surrounded by the open bracket and the corresponding close bracket, one of)}]>'"; e.g., if the selection is **hello**, typing **control {** replaces it by {hello}and **control '** replaces it by **'hello'**. Repeating the process toggles the action and removes the matched pair. Additionally, double clicking to the immediate right of an open bracket or to the immediate left of a close bracket causes the text up to the corresponding matching bracket to be selected (and highlighted).

Double clicking at the beginning or end of a paragraph causes the entire paragraph to be selected. Double clicking at the beginning or end of a line selects the line. Similarly, double clicking on a word causes the word to be selected.

The protocol that follows is only a small part of the total. It should be sufficient for use when defining specializations that are intended to adopt the basic facilities.

class initialization

- ParagraphEditor **initialize**
  Initializes the yellow button menu information, the keyboard map for special control characters, and the shared buffers for copying text across views and managing undo.

instance creation

- ParagraphEditor **new**
  Returns a new paragraph editor with an empty paragraph to be edited.
- ParagraphEditor **newParagraph**: aParagraph
  Returns a new paragraph editor with aParagraph as the text to be edited. A paragraph can be created via 'aString **asParagraph**' or 'aText **asParagraph**'. Alternatively, it can be created with 'Paragraph **withText**: aText'.

- TextEditor **new**
  Returns a new text editor with an empty text compositor to be edited.
- Text **newCompositor**: aTextCompositor
  Returns a new text editor with aTextCompositor as the text to be edited. A text compositor can be created via 'TextCompositor **withText**: aText'.

miscellaneous

- aParagraphEditor **scrollToTop**
  Scrolls so that the paragraph is at the top of the view.

- aParagraphEditor **flash**

  Causes the view of the paragraph to complement twice in succession.
- aParagraphEditor **text**

  Returns the text of the paragraph being edited (as text).

menu messages

- aParagraphEditor **again**

  Repeats the last text substitution performed. If the left shift key is down, the substitution is made throughout the entire paragraph; otherwise, only the next possible substitution is made.
- aParagraphEditor **undo**

  Resets the state of the paragraph to what is was prior to the previous cut or paste operation.
- aParagraphEditor **copySelection**

  Copies the current selection and stores it in the shared buffer.
- aParagraphEditor **cut**

  Cuts out the current selection and stores it in the shared buffer.
- aParagraphEditor **paste**

  Pastes the text from the shared buffer over the current selection.
- aParagraphEditor **accept**

  Saves the text being edited in a special location so that subsequent cancel operations can restore it. This operation was implicitly done at the beginning.
- aParagraphEditor **cancel**

  Restores the text of the paragraph to its last accepted value.
- aParagraphEditor **align**

  Aligns the text according to the next alignment possibility: cycling among flush left, flush right, centered, and justified (flush left and flush right).
- aParagraphEditor **fit**

  Makes the bounding rectangle of the paragraph contain all the text, while not changing the width of the paragraph.

text selection messages

- aParagraphEditor **selection**

  Returns the window's current highlighted selection (as a string).
- aParagraphEditor **selectionAsStream**

  Returns the window's current highlighted selection (as a stream on the string).
- aParagraphEditor **select**

  Highlights the currently selected text (if not already highlighted).
- aParagraphEditor **deselect**

  Dehighlights the currently selected text (if not already dehighlighted). Does not change the selected text.
- aParagraphEditor **reverseSelection**

  Reverses the highlighting polarity of the currently selected text. Does not change the selected text.
- aParagraphEditor **selectAt**: anInteger

  Creates an empty selection at character position anInteger; i.e., typing will cause characters to be inserted at position anInteger displacing the character already there (if any) to the right.
- aParagraphEditor **selectFrom**: aStartInteger **to**: aStopInteger

  Creates a selection from character position aStartInteger to aStopInteger inclusive. An empty selection results if aStopInteger is aStartInteger-1. Typing causes the selection to be replaced by the new characters typed.

- aParagraphEditor **selectAndScroll**

  Scrolls until the selection is in the view and then highlights it.
- aParagraphEditor **selectAndScrollFrom**: start **to**: stop

  A combined operation that both makes a selection and scrolls until it is visible.
- aParagraphEditor **replaceSelectionWith**: aText

  Replaces the currently selected text by the text provided. Note that this is an insertion if an empty selection was previously made.
- aParagraphEditor **findAndSelect**: aString

  Searches the text for the given string starting at the end of the current selection. If found, the portion of text is selected, highlighted, and made visible. Returns a boolean indicating whether or not the text was found.

Note that no protocol is provided for determining the character positions of selected text. By investigating method **selection**, however, we can easily deduce how to obtain the information. The following methods could be added to eliminate the need to know. The alternative is to access the paragraph editor's instance variables directly. Of course, this is only possible in the paragraph editor or its subclasses.

> **selectionStart**
> Returns the start of the current selection.
> ↑startBlock **stringIndex**
> **selectionEnd**
> Returns the end of the current selection.
> ↑stopBlock **stringIndex** - 1
> **afterSelection**
> Returns the index of the first character after the current selection.
> ↑stopBlock **stringIndex**

One might also guess and subsequently verify that methods such as the following would provide information about the index of the first and last available characters.

> **firstCharacter**
> Returns the index of the first available character (if any).
> ↑1
> **lastCharacter**
> Returns the index of the last available character (0 if none).
> ↑paragraph **size**

Class **TextEditor** adds no additional instance variables. The text compositor, for example, is maintained in instance variable 'paragraph'.

3.2.1 Creating Paragraph Editor Windows

Since paragraph editors have no corresponding paragraph views, instances were probably not meant to be created. ParagraphEditor was designed as an abstract class to support more refined subclasses such as workspaces and transcripts. Nevertheless, we might wish to create paragraph editor windows for two reasons: (1) in contrast to browsers, workspaces, and transcripts, for example, paragraph editors do not permit text in the window to be executed, and (2) it is important to understand where it is incomplete if we wish to design our own specializations. An attempt at creating a paragraph editor window might proceed as follows:

```
| topView subView |
topView ← StandardSystemView new label: 'Paragraph Editor'.
subView ← View new
    controller: (ParagraphEditor newParagraph: 'A test string to edit.' asParagraph);
    borderWidth: 2.
topView addSubView: subView. topView controller open.
```

There are two problems with the above. First, the view background is clear instead of white (you can see through it). This might be expected since it is the default for views. The second problem is more serious. The paragraph actually displays outside the window in the top left corner of the screen. Upon reflection, something like that might be expected. After all, why should views know how to display paragraphs!

One solution is to create an appropriate paragraph editor view. All it needs to do is change the background to white during initialization and display the paragraph properly. Fortunately, paragraph editors are already provided with a **display** method that does the displaying correctly. The paragraph editor view only needs to relay the display request to the controller. A bit more work needs to be done to ensure that the window works properly when a user moves or resizes the window. When a window is moved, for example, the viewport is changed causing the window to be unlocked. This will cause all window transformations to be recomputed when needed. However, there is no simple mechanism that will notify the controller of the change. The approach taken by the views associated with subclasses of ParagraphEditor is to place a check in **display** or **displayView** that determines whether or not the view has been moved. We have extracted the code for doing this and placed it in a method called **reframeParagraphIfNecessary** (see the following).

Class ParagraphEditorView

class name	ParagraphEditorView
superclass	View
instance variable names	"none"
comment	Completes the protocol required to use instances of paragraph editors.

instance methods

instance initialization

initialize
    super **initialize**.
    self **insideColor**: Form **white**

displaying

displayView
    controller **reframeParagraphIfNecessary**.
    controller **display**

Method **reframeParagraphIfNecessary** added to ParagraphEditor was designed by investigating StringHolderView. The test was obtained from method **display** in StringHolderView, the **recomposeIn:clippingBox:** code from method **positionDisplay-Contents**, and the rest from **recomputeSelection** (it differs by excluding the part that deselects the current selection; the deselection would cause the caret to be displayed at its old position when the window was moved).

aParagraphEditor **reframeParagraphIfNecessary**
"Recomposes the paragraph and repositions the caret. Should be executed when the paragraph editor's view is moved or resized; e.g, when the view is opened."
(view **insetDisplayBox** == paragraph **clippingRectangle**) **ifFalse**: [
    paragraph
        recomposeIn: (view **insetDisplayBox insetBy**: 6 @ 0)
        clippingBox: view **insetDisplayBox**.
    startBlock ← paragraph **characterBlockForIndex**: startBlock **stringIndex**.
    stopBlock ← paragraph **characterBlockForIndex**: stopBlock **stringIndex**.
    selectionShowing ← false]

Instead of having **displayView** reframe the paragraph, we also tried reframing the paragraph in **controlInitialize**. This did not work because it was bypassed by the move menu command, which directly requests the view to display itself at the new location (without the reframing, it caused the paragraph to be displayed at its old location). A paragraph editor window can then be created as follows:

```
| topView subView |
topView ← StandardSystemView new
    label: 'Paragraph Editor with ParagraphEditorView'.
subView ← ParagraphEditorView new
    controller: (ParagraphEditor newParagraph: 'A test string to edit.' asParagraph);
    borderWidth: 2.
topView addSubView: subView. topView controller open.
```

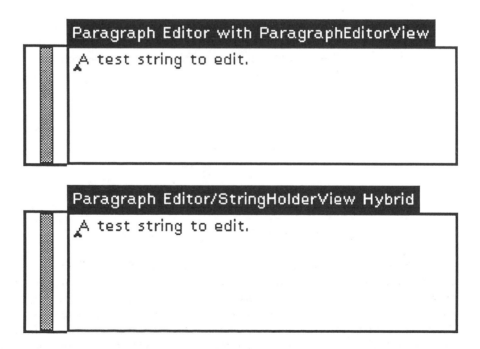

Figure 3.5 Two paragraph editor windows.

An alternative is to attempt to use a view associated with a specialization of ParagraphEditor. The following is such a solution. Note that the model is changed after the view and controller are initialized. This forces both the view and controller to be properly updated. Attempts at creating a string holder view with a pre-initialized model or a paragraph editor with a pre-initialized paragraph (or both) failed to achieve the proper updating. See the section on string holder windows for a more detailed explanation of the protocol.

```
| topView subView |
topView ← StandardSystemView new
    label: 'Paragraph Editor/StringHolderView Hybrid'.
subView ← StringHolderView container
    controller: ParagraphEditor new; borderWidth: 2.
subView model: (StringHolder new contents: 'A test string to edit.').
    "Updates the view and controller indirectly."
topView addSubView: subView. topView controller open.
```

The windows appear as shown in Fig. 3.5.

3.3 DISPLAY-TEXT WINDOWS

Display-text windows are implemented with (1) a model consisting of any object that can be converted to a paragraph; e.g., string, text, or display-text instances along with paragraphs themselves, (2) a controller that is an instance of NoController, and (3) a display-text view. The unique behavior of display-text windows is therefore manifested by the display-text view rather than the controller.

Class **DisplayTextView** (see Fig. 3.6) was probably one of the earliest classes designed in the system. It has largely been superseded by the string holder MVC. Nevertheless, it is still in use for constructing non-editable views containing small titles. For example, it could be used to display a copyright notice. The title information can be displayed either centered or not.

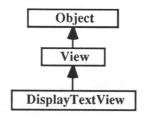

Figure 3.6 The display-text view hierarchy.

Note that display-text views are provided with a default controller that is an instance of ParagraphEditor. This controller does permit scrolling and editing of the textual data. However, there are deficiencies that have been eliminated in the more general counterpart, string holder windows. Moreover, no actual use is made of display-text views with the default paragraph editor as controller. Instead, all display-text views in use make use of an instance of NoController, as mentioned previously. In addition to losing the ability to edit the text, this also eliminates the scrolling capability. Hence, it is essential to avoid voluminous textual data. From the implementation point of view, display-text windows are therefore scrollable text windows; from the user's point of view, they are not. We have described display-text windows for their use and categorized them as scrollable windows for historical reasons.

3.3.1 Creating Display-Text Windows

To create a non-editable text window using a display-text view, three things must be done: (1) a string, text, or display-text model must be selected, (2) the default controller, which happens to be a paragraph editor, must be changed to an instance of NoController, and (3) the inside color must be changed from the default to a white form. Additionally, one can optionally specify whether or not the textual data is to be centered.

Example

A standard system view with a non-editable display-text subview could be created and scheduled as follows. Such a display-text subview would typically be used with other views that have more active controllers.

```
| topView aDisplayTextView |
aDisplayTextView ← DisplayTextView new
    model: 'Seek the highest mountain\and you shall be peaked!' withCRs;
    controller: NoController new;
    borderWidth: 1;
    insideColor: Form white;
    centered. "omit this if centering is not wanted"

topView ← StandardSystemView new
    label: 'Non-editable Text Window'; borderWidth: 1.
topView addSubView: aDisplayTextView. topView controller open
```

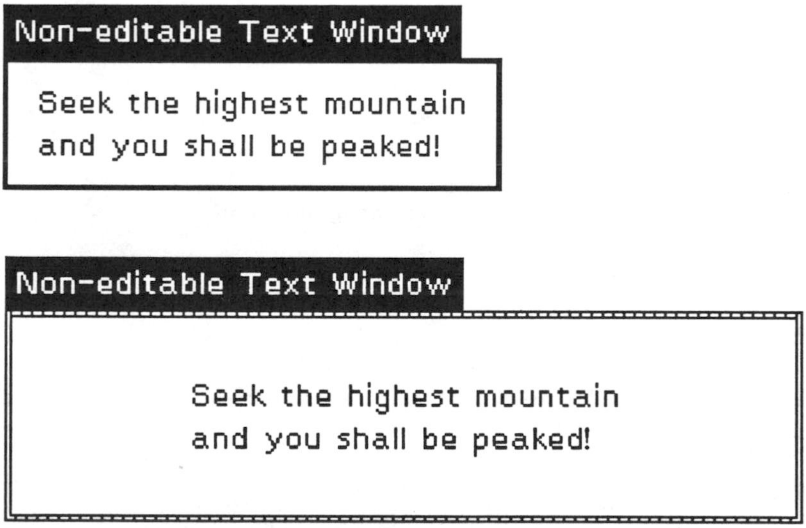

Figure 3.7 A DiplayText subwindow.

If the standard system view is opened as a small rectangle (as opposed to one that is much larger than required to contain the textual data), the first window (see Fig. 3.7) would be displayed. The second results if a large window is used.

As you can see, if the subview is too large for the text, there is a tendency for the subview border to detach itself from the superview border; i.e., one can see a ring between the two borders. The color of the ring is the inside color of the top view. This can be eliminated in more polished applications by removing the display-text view border entirely and enclosing it within a traditional view with the original's border size and inside color. The display-text view border is still inset but it is no longer visible. More specifically, the above would be revised as follows:

```
| topView aDisplayTextView |
aDisplayTextView ← DisplayTextView new
    model: 'Seek the highest mountain\and you shall be peaked!' withCRs;
    controller: NoController new;
    borderWidth: 0; "or leave it as the default"
    insideColor: Form white;
    centered. "omit this if centering is not wanted"

topView ← StandardSystemView new
    label: 'Safer Non-editable Text Window'; borderWidth: 1.
topView addSubView: (View new
    borderWidth: 1; insideColor: Form white; addSubView: aDisplayTextView).
topView controller open
```

3.3.2 The DisplayTextView Partial Protocol

Rather than provide the complete protocol, we will consider only the subset that is useful to users. This subset includes the protocol from class View in order to be complete.

instance creation

* View **new**

    When sent to class DisplayTextView, returns a new initialized view with centering turned off.

instance initialization

* aDisplayTextView **initialize**

    Initializes the view with centering turned off.

centering

* aDisplayTextView **isCentered**

    Returns **true** if centering is on.
* aDisplayTextView **centered**

    Causes the associated text to be centered; centering is turned on.

masks and rules

* aDisplayTextView **mask**

    Returns the mask used for displaying the display-text model; the default is Form **black**. The mask is a specialized instance of class Form.

- aDisplayTextView **mask**: aForm
  Changes the mask used for displaying the display-text model. Returns the view.

- aDisplayTextView **rule**
  Returns the rule used for displaying the display-text model; the default is Form **over**. The rule is an integer from 0 to 15 that indicates which of the sixteen display rules to be used when copying the model onto the display screen.
- aDisplayTextView **rule**: anInteger
  Changes the rule used for displaying the display-text model. Returns the view.

useful operations

- aDisplayTextView **model**: anObjectThatCanBeConvertedToAParagraph
  Used to set up the text to be displayed.
- aView **controller**: aController
  Typically, used to change from the default controller to an instance of NoController.
- aView **window**
  Used to determine the window size needed to display the complete text.
- aView **insideColor**: aForm
  Typically used to change the inside color to Form white.
- aView **borderWidth**: anInteger
  Used to specify the border.

3.3.3 Where Display-Text Views Are Currently Used

Display-text views are currently used as subviews in binary-choice views and fill-in-the-blank views. A binary-choice query of the form

BinaryChoice
    message: 'Do you really wish to terminate?\Depress yes or no button' **withCRs**.

results in a pop-up view with three visible subviews: a display-text view with the above message and two switch views for **yes** and **no** immediately below (actually, there are four subviews, because the switch views are themselves subviews of a standard view). An important requirement is that the switch views be the same size as the display-text view. This is achieved by setting each switch view window size to half the size of the display-text view.

aSwitchView **window**: 0@0 **extent**: (aDisplayTextView **window** width // 2)@aHeight

Similarly, a fill-in-the-blank query of the form

FillInTheBlank
    request: 'Do you really wish to terminate?\Reply with yes or no.' **withCRs**
    initialAnswer: 'no'

results in a pop-up view with two visible subviews: a display-text view with the request message and a fill-in-the-blank view (a specialization of string holder view) for the reply.

Once again, the sizes of the two views must match. This is achieved in the same manner as the switch view:

aFillInTheBlankView **window**: 0@0 **extent**: aDisplayTextView **window width**@aHeight

For the binary-choice case, the height is a function of the switch labels; for the fill-in-the-blank case, the height is simply 40.

3.4 STRING AND TEXT HOLDER WINDOWS

A **string (or text) holder window** provides a scrollable textual workspace that can be edited and modified for arbitrary purposes. It also permits selections in the text to be executed as Smalltalk code with the result inserted into the workspace. A string holder window is implemented by the model-view-controller triple consisting of classes StringHolder, StringHolderView, and StringHolderController. A text holder window replaces class StringHolder by TextHolder. The actual string (text) being edited, i.e., what you would normally expect to be the model, is kept in a special object called a **string (text) holder**. Hence, this is an example of an MVC instance that has a model for the model; i.e., it requires a special string (text) holder model for keeping what users normally think of as the model, a string (text).

String holders, string holder controllers, and string holder views (see Fig. 3.8) respectively inherit from Model, TextEditor, and View. TextHolder inherits from StringHolder. As expected, most of the protocol for manipulating text in windows is already provided by class TextEditor.

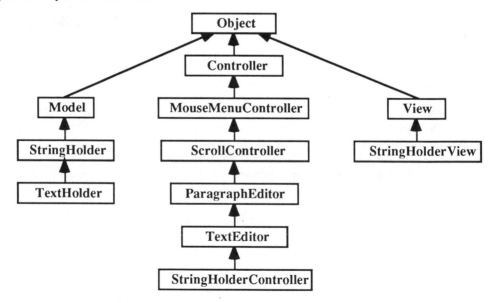

Figure 3.8 The string holder hierarchy.

The string kept in the string holder, to be called the **string holder contents**, can be extracted for external use if desired (although this is not normally done). The window permits modifications to a copy of the string holder contents that we will call the **working text**. The string holder contents can be replaced by this working text (the string part for a string holder, the entire text by a text holder) by choosing **accept** in the yellow button menu. Alternatively, the working text can be re-initialized to the string holder contents by choosing **cancel**. Attempts to close the window when the working text differs from the string holder contents result in the confirmer requesting user certification for the close action. Since text holders inherit from string holders, the same applies to text holders.

3.4.1 Creating String/Text Holder Windows (a Preview)

String holder views have the usual default string holder controllers associated with them. Hence, it is not necessary to explicitly construct the controller. On the other hand, the string holder that is to serve as a model must be constructed explicitly if a pre-initialized string is to be used. The same applies if a text holder is to be used instead of a string holder. The following provides an example of a standard system view with one string holder subview.

Note that the string holder is made a model of both the top view and the string holder view. This is needed to force a confirmer to appear when the window is closed and user modifications to the text have been made. See Sect. 3.4.7, *Ensuring That Close Confirmers Work*, for more detail. Additionally, string holder views are automatically created with a 1-pixel border.

```
| topView subView aHolder |
aHolder ← StringHolder new contents: 'A test string.'.
topView ← StandardSystemView new
        label: 'String Holder Example1'; model: aHolder; borderWidth: 1.
subView ← StringHolderView container: aHolder. "Creates a view and sets the model."
topView addSubView: subView. topView controller open.
```

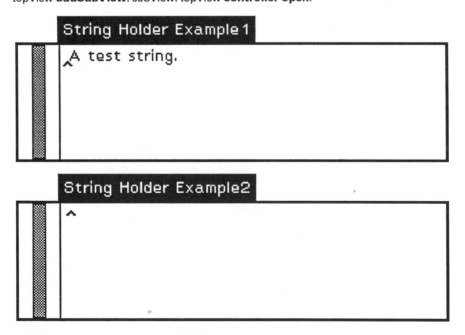

Figure 3.9 Two string holder subviews.

Fig. 3.9 provides an illustration of the view that results. A text holder window would have resulted by changing the first line above to the following:

```
aHolder ← TextHolder new contents: 'A test string.' asText.
```

If the string holder was to be empty to start with, there is no need to explicitly construct it if the string holder view is constructed as follows. Note that the top view should still be provided with the string holder model.

```
| topView subView |
subView ← StringHolderView container. "A view with an empty string holder model."
topView ← StandardSystemView new
    label: 'String Holder Example2'; model: subView model; borderWidth: 1.
topView addSubView: subView. topView controller open.
```

3.4.2 Locking String/Text Holders and Their Controllers

When the working text differs from the string/text holder contents, the string/text holder and its controller are said to be **locked**. When the window is initially opened and after choosing **accept**, the two strings (texts) are equal and the string/text holder and controller are said to be **unlocked**. The idea is that you should not be able to accidentally close a window if the string/text holder is locked because it is not up-to-date.

This terminology should not be confused with the same terms used in a totally different context with respect to views. Recall that a view is also said to be **locked** if its display transformation has been computed; otherwise, it is **unlocked**.

We are only concerned here with locking/unlocking as it applies to string holders and their controllers. Since a substantial portion of the protocol is concerned with the locking and unlocking activity, we will consider it in totality in this section and isolate it from the remainder of the protocol. The locking/unlocking protocol is not usually needed for user access.

string/test holder lock protocol

- aStringOrTextHolder **lock**
  Locks the string/text holder; i.e., notes that the working text has been modified.
- aStringOrTextHolder **unlock**
  Unlocks the string/text holder; i.e., notes that the working text matches the original string (text). Assumes the two have been made to conform prior to unlocking the string/text holder.

- aStringOrTextHolder **isLocked**
  Returns **true** if and only if the string/text holder is locked; i.e., if the working text has been modified since the last time it was unlocked.
- aStringOrTextHolder **isUnlocked**
  Returns **true** if and only if the string/text holder is unlocked.

string holder controller lock protocol

- aStringHolderController **lockModel**
  Locks the model if the controller is already locked. Does not change the lock status of the controller.

Inside Smalltalk

- aStringHolderController **unlockModel**
    Unlocks the model if the controller is already locked. Does not change the lock status of the controller.

- aStringHolderController **turnLockingOn**
    Locks the controller.
- aStringHolderController **turnLockingOff**
    Unlocks the controller.

- aStringHolderController **isLockingOn**
    Returns **true** if and only if the controller is locked.
- aStringHolderController **isLockingOff**
    Returns **true** if and only if the controller is unlocked.

Note that no facility is provided above for forcing the string/text holder contents to match the working text. The string/text holder keeps track of the string/text holder contents, while the controller keeps track of the working text. More specifically, the controller keeps track of a text compositor (previously a paragraph) that contains the working text.

3.4.3 The String Holder Protocol

Class StringHolder maintains a special class variable called **Workspace**, an instance of StringHolder, that contains the contents of the **system workspace**. If additional system workspaces are opened, they all share this one special string holder. Since string holders contain strings and not text, boldface and italic information is maintained only by the string holder controller. This information must have been added explicitly to the current system workspace via editing operations. This should explain why secondary workspaces have no boldface or italic characters.

class initialization and instance creation

- StringHolder **initialize**
    Although originally designed to create the special workspace string holder (an empty one), has been modified to act as a no-op to prevent accidental loss of this information.
- StringHolder **new**
    Creates a new initialized string holder.

obtaining the special workspace string holder

- StringHolder **workspace**
    Returns the special workspace string holder.

instance initialization

- aStringHolder **initialize**
    Unlocks the string holder and sets the string holder contents to an empty string.

retrieving and changing the string holder contents

- aStringHolder **contents**
    Returns the string holder contents.
- aStringHolder **contents**: aString
    Sets the string holder contents to aString.

- aStringHolder **doItContext**
     Returns the context in which a text selection can be evaluated. Currently returns **nil**. See the debugger for alternatives.
- aStringHolder **doItReceiver**
     Returns the object that should be informed of the result of evaluating a text selection. Currently returns **nil**. See the debugger for alternatives.

If we wish to extract the string holder contents from a string holder view or controller for some specific application, we can easily execute code such as

aViewOrController **model contents**

3.4.4 The Text Holder Protocol

Class TextHolder inherits all of its functionality from StringHolder. No new protocol or instance variables are provided. Indeed, only one method is redefined, method **contents:**.

changing the text holder contents

- aTextHolder **contents**: aText
     Sets the text holder contents to aText.

The code is shown below.

```
contents: aStringOrText
     "Change the contents of the text holder to aStringOrText ."
     contents ← aStringOrText
```

3.4.5 The StringHolderController Protocol

Each instance of StringHolderController is a text editor that permits text to be inserted, deleted, and copied. It also provides entries in the yellow button menu enabling text selection to be evaluated and the capability to move the working text (the contents of the text compositor) to and from the string/text holder. The menu entries differ from those of paragraph/text editors by eliminating the **align** and **fit** entries and adding the following:

- **doIt** — evaluates the text selection as an expression.
- **printIt** — same as doIt but inserts a printstring of the result after the selection.

Additionally, the **accept** and **cancel** entries are revised to deal with string/text holders.

- **accept** — stores the working text into the string/text holder contents.
- **cancel** — stores the string/text holder contents into the working text.

The controller also properly manages the locking and unlocking protocol with the string/text holder so that a subsequent close request on the view will prevent it from closing if the working text and string/text holder contents differ. A confirmer is used to make sure it was intentional.

instance and class initialization

- StringHolderController **initialize**
     Initializes class variables for the yellow button pop-up menu. These are used when instances are initialized.

- aStringHolderController **initialize**

  Initializes the controller by setting up the yellow button pop-up menu and unlocking the controller.

menu message handling

- aStringHolderController **accept**

  Replaces the string/text holder contents by the working text and unlocks both the string/text holder (the model) and itself.

- aStringHolderController **cancel**

  Replaces the working text by the string/text holder contents and unlocks both the string/text holder (the model) and itself.

- aStringHolderController **doIt**

  Evaluates the current text selection.

- aStringHolderController **printIt**

  Evaluates the current text selection, inserts a printstring of the result after the selection, and makes this printstring the new text selection.

text selection messages (most inherited from ParagraphEditor and TextEditor)

- aParagraphEditor **selection**

  Returns the window's current highlighted selection (as a string).

- aParagraphEditor **selectionAsStream**

  Returns the window's current highlighted selection (as a stream on the string).

- aParagraphEditor **select**

  Highlights the currently selected text (if not already highlighted).

- aParagraphEditor **deselect**

  Dehighlights the currently selected text (if not already dehighlighted). Does not change the selected text.

- aParagraphEditor **reverseSelection**

  Reverses the highlighting polarity of the currently selected text. Does not change the selected text.

- aParagraphEditor **selectAt**: anInteger

  Creates an empty selection at character position anInteger; i.e., typing will cause characters to be inserted at position anInteger, displacing the character already there (if any) to the right.

- aParagraphEditor **selectFrom**: aStartInteger **to**: aStopInteger

  Creates a selection from character position aStartInteger to aStopInteger inclusive. An empty selection results if aStopInteger is aStartInteger-1. Typing causes the selection to be replaced by the new characters typed.

- aParagraphEditor **selectAndScroll**

  Scrolls until the selection is in the view and then highlights it.

- aParagraphEditor **selectAndScrollFrom**: start **to**: stop

  A combined operation that both makes a selection and scrolls until it is visible.

- aParagraphEditor **findAndSelect**: aString

  Searches the text for the given string starting at the end of the current selection. If found, the portion of text is selected, highlighted, and made visible. Returns a boolean indicating whether or not the text was found.

- aStringHolderController **replaceSelectionWith**: aString

  Replaces the currently selected text by the string provided. Note that this is an insertion if an empty selection was previously made.

- aStringHolderController **afterSelectionInsertAndSelect**: aString

  Follows the currently selected text by a blank and the string provided and selects the string.

- aStringHolderController **insertAndSelect**: aString **at**: anInteger
  Inserts and selects the string provided at the position specified by anInteger.

methods redefined specially

- aStringHolderController **model**: aModel
- aStringHolderController **initializeYellowButtonMenu**

As indicated in the section on paragraph/text editors, it is possible to define methods for determining specific character positions in selected text; i.e., **selectionStart** (startBlock **stringIndex**), **selectionEnd** (stopBlock **stringIndex** - 1), **afterSelection** (stopBlock **stringIndex**), **firstCharacter** (1), and **lastCharacter** (paragraph **size**).

3.4.6 The StringHolderView Protocol

Class StringHolderView manages the display of the working text. Its default controller is StringHolderController.

creating unscheduled views

- StringHolderView **container**
- StringHolderView **container**: aStringOrTextHolder
  Returns a new initialized string holder view with a model that is either (1) a new string holder on an empty string, or (2) the given string/text holder. The view is provided with a 1-pixel border.

creating scheduled views

- StringHolderView **open**
- StringHolderView **open**: aStringOrTextHolder
- StringHolderView **open**: aStringOrTextHolder **label**: aString
  Creates and schedules a standard system view with a new initialized string holder view as a subview. The model for the string holder view is either a new string holder on an empty string (the first case) or the string/text holder provided (the last two cases). The label for the standard system view is respectively 'Workspace', 'StringHolder', or the supplied string. The standard system view, with its 1-pixel border combined with the 1-pixel border of the string holder view, results in a window with an effective 2-pixel border.

- StringHolderView **openSystemWorkspace**
  Creates and schedules a view of the system workspace; i.e., a standard system view with a string holder view as a subview. The model for the subview is the workspace string holder. The same workspace string holder is used in each case so that modifications accepted in one scheduled view can be reflected in other scheduled views; e.g., by canceling them.

operations redefined specially for this class

- aStringHolderView **initialize**
- aStringHolderView **display**
- aStringHolderView **displayView**
- aStringHolderView **deEmphasizeView**
- aStringHolderView **model**: aLockedModel

- aStringHolderView **update**: aSymbol
    Assumes the model has been changed. Replaces the controller's text compositor by a new one constructed from the model contents and displays it if it differs from the one that is already there.
- aStringHolderView **updateRequest**
    Returns **true** if the model is unlocked. Otherwise, prompts the user for confirmation and returns the result (the model is unlocked if the user confirms the request).

redefinition of the default controllers

- aStringHolderView **defaultController**
- aStringHolderView **defaultControllerClass**
    Respectively returns either an instance of a string holder controller or class StringHolderController.

3.4.7 Ensuring That Close Confirmers Work

Closing a window causes the following sequence of events (see Fig. 3.10). First, the standard system controller is sent a **close** message. This causes the model to be sent a **changeRequest** message — intuitively, the model is asked if it can be changed (it can if it is up-to-date). This causes all dependents of the model to be sent an **updateRequest** message — the dependents are asked to verify that updates to the model will be consistent; i.e., the most up-to-date version will be updated. If the dependent is a string holder view, it

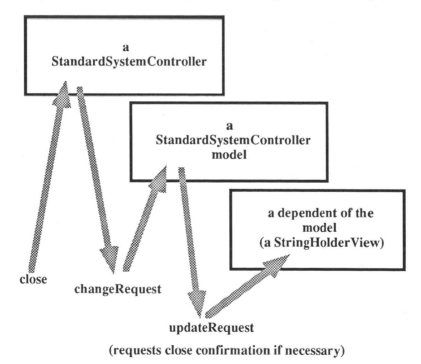

Figure 3.10 The dependency chain for closing an instance of StandardSystemController.

will reply **true** if the model is unlocked (the working text matches the string/text holder contents). Otherwise, it will prompt the user to confirm if the working text can be discarded.

To make sure that the string/text holder MVC works correctly when the superview is closed, we must ensure that the standard system view's model has the string holder view as a dependent. There are two ways to do this:

1. Make the string/text holder be a model for the standard system view in addition to being a model for the string holder view.

2. Create an arbitrary object to serve as a model for the standard system view and make the string holder view be one of its dependents.

The first approach will work if only one string holder subview is required. If more than one string holder subview is used, the second approach is required. This works because the standard system view (or controller) makes little use of its model. In fact, it doesn't matter what the model is. We illustrate the technique below.

Example That Does Not Work

A string holder window created with the following code will fail to request confirmation for the close even when changes have been made to the window.

```
| topView subView |
topView ← StandardSystemView new label: 'String Holder'.
subView ← StringHolderView container: (StringHolder new contents: 'A test string.').
topView addSubView: subView.
topView controller open.
```

Example That Works for One String Holder

If the string holder is also made a model for the standard system view, the required confirmer will now appear when the window is closed.

```
| topView subView aStringHolder |
aStringHolder ← StringHolder new contents: 'A test string.'
topView ← StandardSystemView new label: 'String Holder'; model: aStringHolder.
subView ← StringHolderView
        container: aStringHolder. "This creates a view and sets the model."
topView addSubView: subView.
topView controller open.
```

Example That Works for Several String Holders

When several string holder subviews are used, it is not possible to make them both models for the one standard system view (views only keep track of one model). Hence, an arbitrary object is created to serve as the model (avoid using a small integer or an existing object like **true**, **false**, or **nil** for the model because the model is used as the key for retrieving dependents from an identity dictionary).

```
| topView subView1 subView2 stringHolder1 stringHolder2 aVirtualModel |
stringHolder1 ← StringHolder new contents: 'A test string.'
stringHolder2 ← StringHolder new contents: 'Another test string.'
aVirtualModel ← Object new.

topView ← StandardSystemView new label: 'String Holder'; model: aVirtualModel.
subView1 ← StringHolderView
      container: stringHolder1. "This creates a view and sets the model."
subView2 ← StringHolderView
      container: stringHolder2. "This creates a view and sets the model."

aVirtualModel addDependent: subView1; addDependent: subView2.
topView addSubView: subView1; addSubView: subView2 toRightOf: subView1.

topView controller open.
```

An alternative is to generalize the **close** method in StandardSystemView so that it sends a **changeRequest** message to all subview models in addition to its own model. This would eliminate the need for special initialization code for string holder views and their subviews; e.g., text collector views.

3.4.8 Symbolic Manipulation Windows: An Application

As a simple demonstration of the use of string holder windows, consider designing a variation (see Fig. 3.11) that permits symbolic expressions to be evaluated and printed. To illustrate the idea, we create a skeletal collection of classes for demonstrating symbolic manipulation. Since symbolic manipulation per se is not the issue, these classes are quite

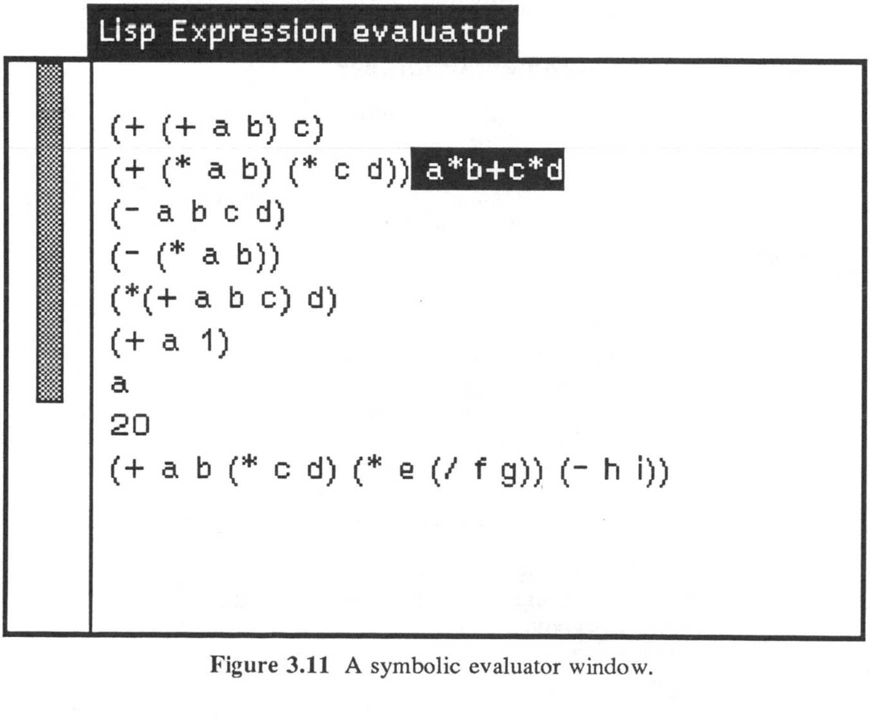

Figure 3.11 A symbolic evaluator window.

rudimentary. In particular, we can get along with two classes: SymbolicExpression and SymbolicPrimitive. The former permits expressions like '(+ a b c (* d e))' writteń in the lisp style to be converted to an internal representation and printed in a more familiar notation; i.e., 'a+b+c+d*e'. The latter handles expressions without operations; e.g., 'a' and '20'.

The important issue here is not symbolic manipulation but symbolic manipulation windows. We would like to be able to select an arbitrary symbolic expression in the window, evaluate it, and have the simplified result printed. A general facility would provide its own special parser because symbolic expressions would not likely be valid Smalltalk expressions. We will not go so far as to develop our own parser but we will assume the expression is provided in the lisp style for simplicity.

All we need to do is intercept the **printIt** and **doIt** messages that are already implemented by string holder windows or write our own. In our case, the easiest thing to do is copy the existing methods into a new class that inherits from StringHolderController. The modified methods are shown below. Since the copied methods show us how to interface with the compiler, we will take advantage of this knowledge and use a variation of the same technique to construct an array out of the selected string. In particular, if a user types 'a' or '(+ a b)', we surround the selection string with characters for an array constructor to obtain '#(a)' and '#((+ a b))' respectively. If the compiler doesn't complain, we get back an array containing the arbitrarily nested symbolic expression. Note that comments imbedded within the selection, for instance, are discarded by the compiler.

The first element of this array is our original selection. All we need to do is convert it to a symbolic expression using the class conversion operation **convert:**. The result is then printed in the window after the original selection. If the compiler detects an error, the error message is printed instead at the error point. Method **notify:at:in:**, also obtained from the string holder controller, is suitably modified and added to our new controller to perform this task. More details can be found in the actual code for **printIt** and **notify:at:in:**. Note that **doIt** was modified to do nothing. We don't expect symbolic expressions to have side effects.

Class SymbolicArithmeticController

class name	SymbolicArithmeticController
superclass	StringHolderController
instance variable names	"none"
comment	This controller revises the printIt and doIt menu messages to deal with symbolic expressions.

class methods

examples

example1
```
"SymbolicArithmeticController example"
| aStringHolder subView topView |
aStringHolder ← StringHolder new contents:
      ('\(+ (+ a b) c)\(+ (* a b) (* c d))\',
      '(- a b c d)\(- (* a b))\(*(+ a b c) d)\(+ a 1)\a\20\',
      '(+ a b (* c d) (* e (/ f g)) (- h i))') withCRs.
subView ← (StringHolderView container: aStringHolder)
      controller: SymbolicArithmeticController new.
topView ← StandardSystemView new
      label: 'Lisp Expression evaluator'; borderWidth: 1.
topView addSubView: subView.
topView controller open
```

instance methods

menu messages

doIt
>"do nothing"

printIt
>"Assumes the user has typed a Lisp-style expression. If not, the compiler will sometimes object. Wrap up the selection in an extra layer of brackets to ensure that an array is returned."
>
>"Normally, the compiler is asked to evaluate a read stream on a small part of the window text, the selected part. Hence, if it detects an error, the error point (see notify:at:in: in compiler access) is an index from the beginning of the entire text. In our case, the compiler is given a read stream on a newly constructed string. Hence, the error point index will be relative to the beginning of this collection. We use this in method notify:at:in:."
>| result |
>self **controlTerminate**. "causes the scroll bars to disappear"
>result ← model **doItReceiver class evaluatorClass new**
>>**evaluate**: (ReadStream **on**:
>>>'#(', self **selection string**, ')' "used to be self **selectionAsStream**")
>>**in**: model **doItContext**
>>**to**: model **doItReceiver**
>>**notifying**: self
>>**ifFail**: [self **controlInitialize**. ↑#failedDoit].
>self **controlInitialize**. "causes the scroll bars to reappear"
>result == #failedDoit
>>**ifFalse**: [self **afterSelectionInsertAndSelect**:
>>>(SymbolicExpression **convert**: result **first**) **printString**]

compiler access

notify: aString **at**: anIntegerIndex **in**: aStream
>"Compilation of the text failed. The syntax error is message aString. Insert it in the text at starting character position anIntegerIndex. This index is relative to the beginning of the string we asked the compiler to evaluate. This string is longer than the current selection by 3 characters, '#(' at the beginning and ')' at the end. We must compute the index relative to the beginning of the window text that contains the selection."
>| originalSelectionStart offsetFromSelectionStart selectionIndex |
>originalSelectionStart ← startBlock **stringIndex**.
>>"see new method **selectionStart** for ParagraphEditor"
>offsetFromSelectionStart ←
>>(anIntegerIndex-2 "for #(") **min**: aStream **contents size** - 3.
>selectionIndex ← (originalSelectionStart + offsetFromSelectionStart) **max**: 1.
>self **insertAndSelect**: aString **at**: selectionIndex

Class SymbolicExpression

class name	SymbolicExpression
superclass	OrderedCollection
instance variable names	"none"
comment	A symbolic expression consists of an operation and a number of operands. Currently, we support operations +, -, *, and /. Operations + and - are assumed to have 1 or more operands; e.g., (- a), (- a b), (- a b c) mean -a, a-b, and a-b-c respectively. Operations * and / are assumed to have 2 or more operands.

class methods

conversion

convert: aCollectionOrSymbolOrNumber
> "If the parameter is a collection, assumes it is of the form (operator operand1 operand2 ...). Otherwise, assumes it is a primitive. Note: The operator is kept unchanged (a symbol) and the operands are recursively converted."

> | anExpression aStream |
> (aCollectionOrSymbolOrNumber **isKindOf:** Symbol)
> > **ifTrue:** [↑SymbolicPrimitive **convert:** aCollectionOrSymbolOrNumber].
> (aCollectionOrSymbolOrNumber **isKindOf:** Collection)
> > **ifTrue:** [
> > > anExpression ← self **new**.
> > > aStream ← ReadStream **on:** aCollectionOrSymbolOrNumber.
> > > anExpression **add:** aStream next.
> > > aStream **do:** [:anOperand | anExpression **add:** (self **convert:** anOperand)].
> > > ↑anExpression **simplify**].
> > ↑SymbolicPrimitive **convert:** aCollectionOrSymbolOrNumber

instance methods

component accessing

operation
> "An expression is of the form (operation operand1 operand2 ...)."
> ↑self **first**

operands
> "An expression is of the form (operation operand1 operand2 ...)."
> ↑(self **asOrderedCollection**) **removeFirst; yourself**

simplification

priority
> "We assume priorities 10 20 30 30 for operators + - * / with two or more operands and 40 for operands like 10 or x. Unary operators + and - use the priority of their operands if it is higher."

> | operation operands index priority |
> operation ← self **operation**. operands ← self **operands**.

> "First, get the priority assuming two or more operands."
> index ← #(+ - * /) **findFirst:** [:aSymbol | aSymbol = operation].
> index = 0 **ifTrue:** [self **error:** 'illegal symbolic expression'].
> priority ← #(10 20 30 30) **at:** index.

> "Second, handle the unary operation case."
> operands **size** = 1
> > **ifTrue:** [↑priority **max:** operands **first**]
> > **ifFalse:** [↑priority]

simplify
> "Not implemented yet."

printOn: aStream

"The operation must be interspersed between the operands; e.g. (+ a b c) is a+b+c. Equal or higher priority operands are printed without surrounding brackets. Hence, (+ (+ a b) (* c d)) prints as a+b+c*d. This rule applies for operations +, *, and / but not for -. Although (+ (+ a b) (+ c d)) can print as a+b+c+d, (- (- a b) (- c d)) cannot print as a-b-c-d; it should be a-b-(c-d). Hence, the rule for - is to print without surrounding brackets only if the operands are strictly higher priority."

| priority operation operands operand printOperand printRemainingOperands |
priority ← self **priority**. operation ← self **operation**. operands ← self **operands**.

"We make use of two functions that access priority, operand, and operands non-locally."
printOperand ← [:comparison |
    (operand **priority perform**: comparison **with**: priority)
        ifTrue: [operand **printOn**: aStream]
        ifFalse:[aStream **nextPut**: $(; **print**: operand; **nextPut**: $)]].
printRemainingOperands ← [:anotherComparison |
    operands **do**: [:anOperand |
        operation **printOn**: aStream.
        operand ← anOperand. printOperand **value**: anotherComparison]].

operand ← operands **removeFirst**. "Note: has a side effect on operands."

(operation = #+) | (operation = #*) | (operation = #/) **ifTrue**: [
    printOperand **value**: #>=. printRemainingOperands **value**: #>=.
    ↑self].
operation = #- **ifTrue**: [
    operands **size** = 0 **ifTrue**: [operation **printOn**: aStream].
    printOperand **value**: #>=. printRemainingOperands **value**: #>. "note the change"
    ↑self].

self **error**: 'illegal symbolic expression'

Class SymbolicPrimitive

class name	SymbolicPrimitive
superclass	Magnitude
instance variable names	content
comment	A symbolic primitive contains either a number or a symbol.

class methods

conversion

convert: aSymbolOrNumber
"Error check and create a primitive with the data as content."
((aSymbolOrNumber **isKindOf**: Symbol) **or**: [aSymbolOrNumber **isKindOf**: Number])
    ifTrue: [↑self **new content**: aSymbolOrNumber]
    ifFalse: [↑self **error**: 'illegal symbolic expression']

instance methods

content manipulation

content
    ↑content
content: aNumberOrSymbol
    content ← aNumberOrSymbol

simplification

priority
    "Recall that expressions with operators +, -, *, and / range in priority from 10 to 30."
    ↑40
simplify
    "Not implemented yet."

printing

printOn: aStream
    content **printOn**: aStream

3.5 TEXT COLLECTOR WINDOWS

Text collector windows extend string holder windows by permitting them to be used as write streams. The model-view-controller triple that implements a text collector window consists of instances of classes **TextCollector, TextCollectorView**, and **TextCollector-Controller**. Text collectors extend string holders by permitting them to be treated as writable file streams. Since text collectors, text collector controllers, and text collector views respectively inherit from StringHolder, StringHolderController, and StringHolderView (see Fig. 3.12), it stands to reason that this triple, too, is an example of an MVC instance providing a model for the model; i.e., it requires a special text collector model for keeping what users normally think of as the model, a string.

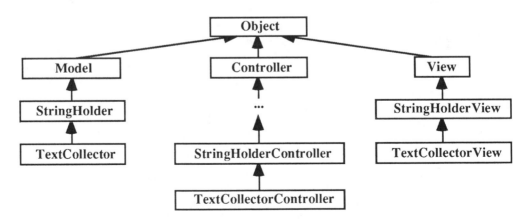

Figure 3.12 The TextCollector hierarchy.

Since text collectors provide write-only windows, they are used extensively for debugging purposes; e.g., newly prototyped code often includes output to a text collector to provide a trace of the ongoing activity.

3.5.1 Creating Text Collector Windows (a Preview)

Because text collector classes inherit from the corresponding string holder classes, an analogous protocol is used for creating text collector windows. Unlike the former protocol, text collectors must always be explicitly constructed. You may use **container:** (inherited from StringHolderView) but not **container**, because it creates a string holder model instead of a text collector model. Additionally, since modifications to the text collector view are generally not meant to be kept, there is no need to make the text collector a model of the top view. The view constructed has a 1-pixel border.

```
| topView aView |
topView ← StandardSystemView new label: 'A Text Collector Example'; borderWidth: 1.
aView ← TextCollectorView container: (TextCollector new contents: 'A test string').
topView addSubView: aView. topView controller open
```

The resulting text collector subwindow (see Fig. 3.13) has little to differentiate it from a string holder subwindow. Of course, you can output to it; e.g., by sending a message to the text collector.

```
(aView model) cr; nextPutAll: '10 factorial is '; print: 10 factorial; show: '.'; cr.
```

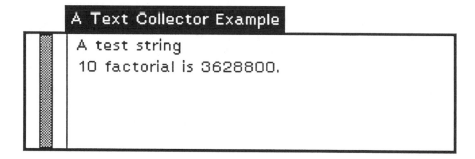

Figure 3.13 A TextCollector subwindow.

3.5.2 The TextCollector Protocol

Class TextCollector is a specialization of StringHolder that permits stream output to a window; i.e., it provides write-only windows. An example of a text collector is the **system transcript** referenced through global variable **Transcript**.

The text collector maintains a stream, to be called the **text collector stream**, for accumulating characters. Stream messages like **nextPut:**, **nextPutAll:**, **print:**, **space**, and **cr** simply store the characters in the stream. Messages like **show:** and **endEntry** cause the stream characters to be transferred to the string holder (recall that the text collector is a string holder) and displayed. Unlike string holders, however, the size of the text collector contents is bounded by a **character limit** that is fixed by the implementation. When this limit is exceeded, the text collector contents is replaced by a suffix of itself that is half the size of the character limit.

changing the system transcript

- TextCollector **newTranscript**: aTextCollector
  Changes the system transcript to aTextCollector and returns it.

examples using the system transcript

- TextCollector **example**
  Provides examples of how to output to the system transcript.

instance initialization

- aTextCollector **initialize**
  Unlocks the text collector, sets its contents to an empty string, and prepares it for subsequent stream commands.

stream output commands

- aTextCollector **space**
- aTextCollector **tab**
- aTextCollector **cr**
- aTextCollector **crtab**
- aTextCollector **crtab**: anInteger
  Appends the indicated character or characters onto the text collector stream; i.e., spaces, tabs, carriage returns — **crtab**: appends one carriage return and anInteger number of tabs. Does **not** make this information visible.

- aTextCollector **next**: anIntegerRepetitionCount **put**: aCharacter
- aTextCollector **nextPut**: aCharacter
- aTextCollector **nextPutAll**: aCollectionOfCharacters
  Appends the specified character or characters onto the text collector stream. Does **not** make this information visible.

- aTextCollector **print**: anObject
- aTextCollector **store**: anObject
  Appends a print (or store) string of anObject to the text collector stream. Does **not** make this information visible.

- aTextCollector **show**: aCollectionOfCharacters
  Appends the specified characters onto the text collector stream. Additionally, **makes this information visible**.

clearing and displaying

- aTextCollector **clear**
  Removes all characters in the text collector and makes the window visible.
- aTextCollector **refresh**
  Brings the window to the front of the screen and makes it visible.

entry control

- aTextCollector **beginEntry**
  Initializes the text collector stream for accumulating characters; makes it empty.

- aTextCollector **appendEntry**

  Appends the text collector stream characters onto the text collector (a string holder) contents and truncates it on the left if it exceeds the implementation defined character limit. Displays the window if the text collector stream is nonempty.
- aTextCollector **endEntry**

  Performs an appendEntry and displays the window.
- aTextCollector **nextEntry**

  Returns the contents of the text collector stream.

private

- aTextCollector **characterLimit**

  Returns the implementation defined character limit for the text collector (a string holder) contents. Can be recompiled to change the limit.

Most character insertion operations have no effect on the visual appearance of the text collector window. Special messages are needed to make the modifications visible. This can be done in one of two ways. The standard approach is to use **show:** on the last string of characters to be appended. Alternatively, **endEntry** can be sent to the text collector. The latter approach is typically used if the last entry cannot be provided via **show:**; e.g., if the last character inserted is a tab or carriage return. Of course, it is always possible to send the message 'show: "'. The other entry methods tend to be used privately.

Since **show:** has the side effect of displaying the window (an expensive and slow operation), it is good practice to avoid using multiple **show:** messages in a row. The alternative is to use successive **nextPutAll:** messages and to use **show:** as the last message. It is also common practice to end most textual messages with a carriage return (as opposed to starting the message with one). Since most messages end with **show:**, the last carriage return is typically displayed when the next textual message is provided.

Example

A typical sequence of outputs to a text collector is shown below. Assume that each statement was provided independently of the others.

```
Transcript
    print: aNumber; nextPutAll: ' factorial is '; print: aNumber factorial; cr; endEntry.
Transcript
    nextPutAll: 'pi/4 is '; print: (Float pi / 4); cr; endEntry.
Transcript
    show: 'Reached the problem method'; cr. "The cr will be displayed later."
```

Other examples include

```
Transcript
    show: aNumber. "not legal since aNumber is not a collection of characters"
Transcript
    show: aNumber printString "legal but less efficient than Transcript print: aNumber"
Transcript
    show: 'pi/4 is ', (Float pi / 4) printString; cr. "lazy but effective throw away code"
```

3.5.3 The TextCollectorController Protocol

Class TextCollectorController is a specialization of StringHolderController that ensures that the size of the text collector contents (a string holder) is restricted to the implementation defined character limit. It adds three methods used exclusively by the corresponding view's **update:** method.

*used privately by TextCollectorView's **update:** method*

- aTextCollectorController **appendEntry**
- aTextCollectorController **changeText:** aText
- aTextCollectorController **viewToTop**
  Used privately by the **update:** method in TextCollectorView in response to #appendEntry, #update, and #refresh requests (see dependency maintenance).

3.5.4 The TextCollectorView Protocol

Class **TextCollectorView** is a specialization of StringHolderView that ensures that the size of the string holder contents is restricted to the implementation defined character limit.

creating and scheduling text collector views

- TextCollectorView **open**
  Schedules a new empty text collector with default label 'TextCollector'.
- TextCollectorView **open:** aTextCollector **label:** aString
  Schedules an existing text collector aTextCollector with label aString.

updating

- aTextCollectorView **update:** aParameter
  Responds to #appendEntry, #update, and #refresh requests.

default controllers

- aTextCollectorView **defaultControllerClass**
  Returns class TextCollectorController.

Example

The obvious approach for creating a text collector window is to use **open** and **open:label:** as shown.

```
TextCollectorView open
TextCollectorView open: TextCollector new label: 'My TextCollector'
```

A text collector view can also be created for insertion into standard system views using **container:** (see the section on creating text collector windows). We can also use the more familiar technique shown below using **new**. In that case, the border size must be explicitly specified to avoid the zero width default.

```
| topView aView |
topView ← StandardSystemView new label: 'A Text Collector Window'.
aView ← TextCollectorView new model: TextCollector new; borderWidth: 1.
topView addSubView: aView. topView controller open
```

3.5.5 Dependency Maintenance

Three categories of changes are managed by text collectors: **#refresh**, **#update**, and **#appendEntry**. More specifically,

aTextCollector **changed**: #refresh	Causes the text collector window to be displayed.
aTextCollector **changed**: #update	Causes the text collector controller's working text to be replaced by the text collector contents (a string holder). *Does not include the text collector stream in the working text nor does it clear it.*
aTextCollector **changed**: #appendEntry	Causes the text collector stream to be inserted into both the text collector contents (a string holder) and the text collector controller's working text. Also causes the text collector window to be displayed. *Does not clear the stream.*

The above messages are sent by TextCollector methods **refresh**, **clear**, and **endEntry** respectively. Because the **changed**: messages are only partially complete, the **clear** method (in addition to clearing the text collector contents) must also explicitly clear the text collector stream by sending a **beginEntry** message to itself. The **endEntry** method must similarly send a **beginEntry** message. These methods are shown next.

```
aTextCollector clear
    "Removes all characters in the text collector and makes the window visible."
    contents ← Text new. "Clear the text collector contents."
    self beginEntry. "Clear the text collector stream."
    self changed: #update "Update the text compositor from the text collector contents
        and display it."
```

```
aTextCollector endEntry
    "Appends the text collector stream characters onto the text collector (a string
    holder) contents and truncates it on the left if it exceeds the implementation
    defined character limit. Displays the window if the text collector stream is
    nonempty."
    entryStream isEmpty ifFalse: ["Do nothing if the text collector stream is empty"
        self changed: #appendEntry. "Update the text compositor from the text
            collector contents and the text collector stream and display it."
        self beginEntry. "Clear the text collector stream."]
```

A detailed history of the change/update protocol is shown in Fig. 3.14. When a text collector is sent either a **clear**, **refresh**, or **endEntry** message, a corresponding **changed**: message is sent to self; respectively, **changed**: #update, **changed**: #refresh, and **changed**: #appendEntry. These **changed**: messages cause the text collector dependents, the text collector views, to be notified via **update**: messages. This causes corresponding messages to be sent to the text collector controller for proper handling. The text collector view could handle the **refresh** request itself but not the **update** and **appendEntry** requests, because they require changes to the associated working text that is maintained by the controller in the text compositor.

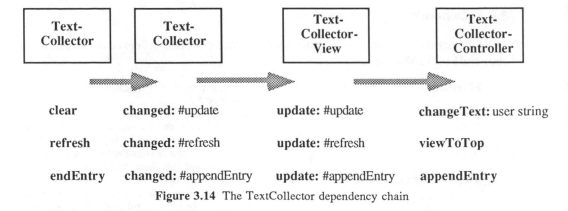

Text-Collector	Text-Collector	Text-Collector-View	Text-Collector-Controller
clear	changed: #update	update: #update	changeText: user string
refresh	changed: #refresh	update: #refresh	viewToTop
endEntry	changed: #appendEntry	update: #appendEntry	appendEntry

Figure 3.14 The TextCollector dependency chain

In more detail, the **update:** method that relays the request from the text collector view to the text collector controller is shown next:

```
aTextCollectorView update: aParameter
    self topView isCollapsed ifTrue: [model appendEntry].
    (self controller isKindOf: TextCollectorController) ifTrue: [
        aParameter == #appendEntry ifTrue: [↑controller appendEntry].
        aParameter == #update ifTrue: [↑controller changeText: model contents asText].
        aParameter == #refresh ifTrue:[↑controller viewToTop]]
```

Sending message **appendEntry** to the model causes the text collector stream to be moved to the text collector (a string holder) and cleared. Sending this message twice in a row would have no ill effects since the second such message is an effective no-op. It is interesting to observe that executing 'model **appendEntry**', whether or not the view is collapsed, eliminates the minor inadequacies noted with the **changed:** message. A more efficient solution can be obtained by slightly modifying the text collector controller methods.

When scheduled text collectors are created via **open** and **open:label:**, the associated text collector is typically made a model of both a standard system view and a text collector subview. As with string holder views, this ensures that the text collector is notified when the scheduled controller is closed. For the close to work properly, the text collector must be made a dependent of the standard system view. This is because the close protocol only notifies the dependents of the top view and not the subviews. Of course, when the text collector is sent a **changed:** message, the standard system view, in addition to the text collector view, is sent a corresponding **update:** message. For the standard system view, this is fortunately of little consequence because the **update:** method is a no-op. On the other hand, we mentioned before that text collector windows are intended more for tracing or debugging situations. In that case, there is little need to save its contents.

3.5.6 Note Pads: Unbounded Transcripts with File-Out

This section illustrates a simple way in which text collectors can be extended. Two extensions are considered: (1) eliminating the implementation imposed character limit, and (2) adding a facility to file out the window contents. To distinguish these unbounded text collectors from the standard text collectors, we will call them note pads. A typical note pad is shown in Fig. 3.15.

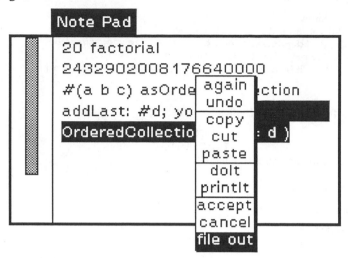

Figure 3.15 A note pad: An unbounded text collector with file-out.

The obvious way to proceed is to modify text collectors so that a length specification is optional and to add a file-out capability. A nondestructive alternative is to create a new subclass of text collectors that overrides the **characterLimit** message so that it can never be exceeded. We consider the second alternative here.

Class NotePad

class name	NotePad
superclass	TextCollector
instance variable names	"none"
comment	This text collector has no character limit and can file-out its contents.

class methods

creating and scheduling note pads

open
    NotePadView **open**: NotePad **new label**: 'Note Pad'

transcript switching

openNormalTranscript
    "NotePad openNormalTranscript. Transcript show: 'simple test'; cr"
    Transcript ← TextCollector **new**.
    TextCollectorView **open**: Transcript **label**: 'System Transcript'

openUnboundedTranscript
    "NotePad openUnboundedTranscript. Transcript show: 'simple test'; cr"
    Transcript ← NotePad **new**.
    NotePadView **open**: Transcript **label**: 'Note Pad'

instance methods

character limit support

characterLimit
        "Make it larger than the current sizes"
        ↑1 + (self **dependents inject: contents size** into: [:size :aView |
            (aView **isKindOf**: NotePadView)
                ifTrue: [size **max**: aView **controller paragraphSize**]
                ifFalse: [size]])

Class NotePadController

class name   NotePadController
superclass   TextCollectorController
instance variable names   "none"

instance methods

character limit support

paragraphSize
        ↑paragraph **text size**

menu messages

fileOut
        "Print the contents of the stream onto an external file."
        | fileName fileStream |
        self **controlTerminate**. "get rid of the scroll bars"
        fileName ← FillInTheBlank
            request: 'File name?'
            initialAnswer: (view **topView label copyWithout**: Character **blank**), '.window'.
        fileStream ← FileStream **fileNamed**: fileName.
        Cursor **write showWhile**: [
            fileStream **timeStamp**; **nextPutAll**: paragraph **string**; **shorten**; **close**].
        Transcript **cr**; **show**: fileName; **cr**.
        self **controlInitialize** "get the scroll bars back"

initializeYellowButtonMenu
        self
            yellowButtonMenu: (PopUpMenu
                labels: 'again\undo\copy\cut\paste\doIt\printIt\accept\cancel\file out' **withCRs
                lines**: #(2 5 7 9))
            yellowButtonMessages:
                #(again undo copySelection cut paste doIt printIt accept cancel fileOut)

Class NotePadView

class name   NotePadView
superclass   TextCollectorView
instance variable names   "none"

instance methods

controller access

defaultControllerClass
        ↑NotePadController

3.5.7 Symbolic Manipulation Windows: Debugging

One way to simplify debugging is to use the system transcript to record a trace of the processing activity. However, this can be inconvenient for two reasons: (1) the system transcript may be physically distant from the active window, and (2) it must continually pop up, obscuring whatever is underneath. A better alternative is to use a private transcript builtin to the development window. After providing such a transcript, it may also be convenient to keep it permanently and advertise it as a feature.

The symbolic manipulation window that we described previously was augmented with such a text collector window. We could have placed this 'debugging' window either below the 'symbolic processing' window or to its right. We opted for the latter choice as shown in Fig. 3.16.

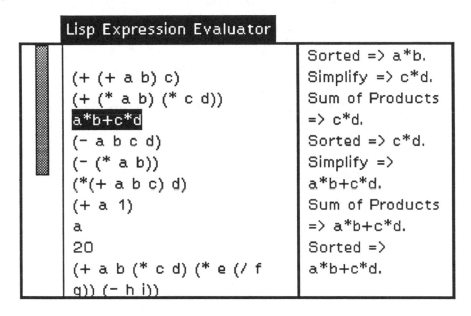

Figure 3.16 A symbolic evaluator window with a trace subwindow.

Since arbitrary methods need access to the text collector window to output trace information, it seems natural to make it a global variable[1]. In our case, we called it SymbolicProcessingTranscript to differentiate it from Transcript. However, there can be a problem because users are permitted to open several symbolic processing windows. Do all of them get updated? Since only one window can be active at a time, the solution is simple. Ensure that SymbolicProcessingTranscript always contains the text collector for the active window. The easiest way to do this is to add the proper initialization and finalization code in **controlInitialize** and **controlTerminate**. The new methods are shown below.

Note that we added some tracing code to **simplify** in class SymbolicExpression. We haven't yet actually enhanced the class with extra functionality.

---

[1] The knowledgeable reader might wish to consider alternatives that avoid the use of global variables.

Class SymbolicArithmeticController

class name	SymbolicArithmeticController
superclass	StringHolderController
instance variable names	"none"
comment	This controller revises the printIt and doIt menu messages to deal with symbolic expressions. It also integrates the use of SymbolicProcessingTranscript.

class methods

examples

example2
```
"SymbolicArithmeticController example2"
| aStringHolder subView1 subView2 topView |
aStringHolder ← StringHolder new contents:
    ('\(+ (+ a b) c)\(+ (* a b) (* c d))\',
    '(- a b c d)\(- (* a b))\(*(+ a b c) d)\(+ a 1)\a\20\',
    '(+ a b (* c d) (* e (/ f g)) (- h i))') withCRs.
subView1 ← (StringHolderView container: aStringHolder)
    controller: SymbolicArithmeticController new.
subView2 ← TextCollectorView container: TextCollector new.

topView ← StandardSystemView new
    label: 'Lisp Expression Evaluator'; borderWidth: 1.
topView
    addSubView: subView1 in: (0@0 corner: 0.6@1) borderWidth: 1;
    addSubView: subView2 in: (0.6@0 corner: 1@1) borderWidth: 1.
topView controller open
```

instance methods

controlling

controlInitialize
```
"Assume there is only one text collector view associated with the top window."
SymbolicProcessingTranscript ← self currentTextCollectorFrom: view topView.
SymbolicProcessingTranscript isNil
    ifTrue: [SymbolicProcessingTranscript ← Transcript "good old fall back"].
↑super controlInitialize
"Smalltalk at: #SymbolicProcessingTranscript put: Transcript."
```

controlTerminate
```
"Assume there is only one text collector view associated with the top window."
SymbolicProcessingTranscript ← Transcript "good old fall back".
↑super controlTerminate
"Smalltalk at: #SymbolicProcessingTranscript put: Transcript."
```

currentTextCollectorFrom: aView
```
| result |
(aView isKindOf: TextCollectorView) ifTrue: [↑aView model].
aView subViews do: [:aSubView |
    result ← self currentTextCollectorFrom: aSubView.
    result isNil ifFalse: [↑result]].
↑nil
```

Class SymbolicExpression

class name	SymbolicExpression
superclass	OrderedCollection
instance variable names	"none"

instance methods

simplification

simplify
    "Demonstrate how a text collector could be used for tracing."
    | partialResult1 partialResult2 |
    SymbolicProcessingTranscript **nextPutAll**: 'Simplify => '; **print**: self; **show**: '.'; **cr**.
    partialResult1 ← self **sumOfProducts**.
    SymbolicProcessingTranscript
        nextPutAll: 'Sum of Products => ';
        print: partialResult1; **show**: '.'; **cr**.
    partialResult2 ← partialResult1 **order**.
    SymbolicProcessingTranscript **nextPutAll**: 'Sorted => '; **print**: partialResult2; **show**: '.'; **cr**.
    "Of course, there is more for someone else to do."
    ↑partialResult2

    "Smalltalk at: #SymbolicProcessingTranscript put: Transcript."

private

order
    ↑self "And this?"
sumOfProducts
    ↑self "Is this good enough?"

3.5.8 Implementing Window Streams

Smalltalk does not provide facilities for using windows as read or read-write streams. In this section, we consider an implementation of such streams, to be called **window streams**. The design is intended to demonstrate the notion of window streams and to provide incentive for others to improve the design. We make no claims to completeness.

Window streams divide the display area into two parts: (1) a portion that has been previously read by the model (an instance of ReadWindowStream or ReadWriteWindow-Stream), and (2) a portion that is so far unread. The unread part is always highlighted.

When characters are read from the window stream, they are obtained from the unread portion of the window. As unread characters are extracted, they are dehighlighted. When all characters have been extracted and more are requested, the window stream will flash until additional characters are supplied. A user can type as many characters as he wishes. These characters will only be inserted at the end of the window characters. He can also backspace over unread characters. However, the newly typed text will not be made available until he types an escape character. Two escape characters in a row signal the end of the stream.

Writing into the stream causes the newly written text to be inserted in front of the unread text. Hence, overlapped reading and writing with a form of type-ahead are supported. Note that unlike text collectors and string holder windows, selecting text with the mouse is not permitted.

The following demonstrates how a window stream could be constructed and used. The resulting window is shown in Fig. 3.17.

```
| aStream |
aStream ← ReadWriteWindowStream
        label: 'Read Write Window Test'
        readContents: 'Portion contained initially.\' withCRs
        unreadContents: 'Portion yet to be read.\' withCRs.
aStream nextPutAll: 'Portion added with a nextPutAll:.'; cr.
```

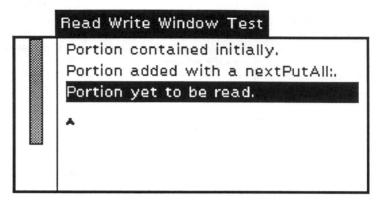

Figure 3.17 A read-write window stream.

Classes ReadWriteWindowStream and ReadWindowStream provide the text collector analogues. The latter inherits from the former but overrides the major write messages to indicate that they are illegal. Unlike text collectors, read-write window streams always update the window on each character. Thus, there is no need to send messages **show:** or **endEntry** to make the information visible. Most of the write messages are of the form 'super **messageNameAndParameters**. self **endEntry**'. The read messages were obtained from the stream classes and modified to work with the associated window.

The read-write window stream inherits the change-update protocol from the text collector. In addition, it provides two new parameters for the protocol: #promptForInput and #readEntry. The former is used when the window needs to be activated to obtain more characters, the latter when an individual character is picked up and read (the window dehighlights the character read). To manage this, the window stream keeps track of the start of the unread characters and whether or not the end of the stream has been signaled. Recall that the end of the stream is signaled by typing two escapes in a row in the window. Note that the end of the stream is reached when two conditions are satisfied: (1) atEnd is **true** (this is set when two escapes are typed), and (2) there are no more unread characters.

Class ReadWriteWindowStream

class name	ReadWriteWindowStream
superclass	TextCollector
instance variable names	startOfUnreadPortion atEnd
comment	Supports a window stream that behaves like a read/write stream.

class methods

instance creation

label: aLabelString **readContents:** string1 **unreadContents:** string2
    | topView subView container |
    topView ← StandardSystemView **new label:** aLabelString; **borderWidth:** 1.
    container←super **new**
        contents: string1, string2 **startOfUnreadPortion:** string1 size+1.
    subView ← (WindowStreamView **container:** container) **borderWidth:** 1.
    topView **addSubView:** subView; **resize; display.** "creator is prompted"
    subView **controller select.**
    ScheduledControllers **schedulePassive:** topView **controller.**
    ↑subView **model**

new
    ↑self **label:** 'A ReadWriteStream' **readContents:** '' **unreadContents:** ''

examples

example1
    "ReadWriteWindowStream example1"
    | aStream |
    aStream ← ReadWriteWindowStream
        label: 'Read Write Window Test'
        readContents: 'A test string.\' **withCRs**
        unreadContents: 'Yet to be read.\' **withCRs.**
    aStream **nextPutAll:** 'Hello there.'; **cr.**
    Transcript **show:** (aStream **upTo:** Character **cr**); **cr.**
    Transcript **show:** 'THE NEXT LINE IS'; **cr.**
    Transcript **show:** (aStream **upTo:** Character **cr**); **cr.**

instance methods

instance initialization

initialize
    super **initialize.**
    startOfUnreadPortion ← 1.
    atEnd ← false

revised entry control

appendEntry
    "Append the text contents of the receiver's WriteStream to its text."
    contents ← contents, self **nextEntry asText.**
    "Removed code that truncated the paragraph if it was longer than characterLimit."
    self **beginEntry**

access protocol

startOfUnreadPortion
    ↑startOfUnreadPortion
endOfUnreadPortion
    ↑contents **size**
getAtEnd
    ↑atEnd "not to be confused with stream **atEnd** message"
setEndOfStream
    atEnd ← true

contents: aString
    self **contents:** aString **startOfUnreadPortion:** aString **size** + 1
contents: aString **startOfUnreadPortion:** anInteger
    super **contents:** aString. startOfUnreadPortion ← anInteger

write protocol

space
    super **space**. super **endEntry**
tab
    super **tab**. super **endEntry**
cr
    super **cr**. super **endEntry**
crtab
    super **crtab**. super **endEntry**
crtab: anInteger
    super **crtab:** anInteger. super **endEntry**
next: anIntegerRepetitionCount **put:** aCharacter
    anIntegerRepetitionCount **timesRepeat:** [super **nextPut:** aCharacter].
    super **endEntry**.
    ↑aCharacter
nextPut: aCharacter
    super **nextPut:** aCharacter. super **endEntry**
nextPutAll: aCollectionOfCharacters
    aCollectionOfCharacters **do:** [:aCharacter | super **nextPut:** aCharacter].
    super **endEntry**.
    ↑aCollectionOfCharacters
print: anObject
    super **print:** anObject. super **endEntry**
store: anObject
    super **store:** anObject. super **endEntry**
show: aCollectionOfCharacters
    ↑self **nextPutAll:** aCollectionOfCharacters

read protocol

isEmpty
    ↑contents **size** = 0
atEnd
    startOfUnreadPortion <= self **endOfUnreadPortion ifTrue:** [↑false].
    atEnd **ifTrue:** [↑true]. self **changed:** #promptForInput.
    ↑self **atEnd**
next
    "Returns the next character in the Stream and also advances it."
    | aCharacter |
    self **atEnd ifTrue:** [self **error:** 'attempt to read past end of stream'].
    aCharacter ← contents **at:** startOfUnreadPortion.
    startOfUnreadPortion ← startOfUnreadPortion + 1.
    self **changed:** #readEntry.
    ↑aCharacter
next: anInteger
    "Returns the next anInteger elements of the receiver."
    | newString |
    newString ← String **new:** anInteger.
    1 **to:** anInteger **do:** [:index | newString **at:** index **put:** self **next**].
    ↑newString

peek
    "Returns the next character in the Stream."
    self **atEnd** **ifTrue**: [self **error**: 'attempt to look past end of stream'].
    ↑contents **at**: startOfUnreadPortion
peekFor: aCharacter
    "Returns whether or not the next character is equal to aCharacter. If it is, also
    advances the stream."
    aCharacter = self peek **ifTrue**: [self next. ↑true] **ifFalse**: [↑false].
skip: anInteger
    anInteger **timesRepeat**: [self **next**]
skipTo: aCharacter
    "Attempts to read past the next occurrence of aCharacter. Returns **true** if it did,
    false if end of stream was encountered first."
    [self **atEnd**] **whileFalse**: [self **next** = aCharacter **ifTrue**: [↑true]].
    ↑false
skipSeparators
    [self **atEnd** **not** and: [self **peek** **isSeparator**]] **whileTrue**: [self **next**]
upTo: aCharacter
    "Returns a string from the current character up to aCharacter; aCharacter is read
    and discarded."
    | newStream element |
    newStream ← WriteStream **on**: (String **new**: 100).
    [self **atEnd** or: [(element ← self **next**) = aCharacter]]
        whileFalse: [newStream **nextPut**: element].
    ↑newStream **contents**
reverseContents
    "Returns a copy of the receiver's contents, in the reverse order."
    | newString size |
    size ← contents **size**. newString ← String **new**: size.
    1 **to**: size **do**: [:i | newString **at**: i **put**: (contents **at**: size-i+1)].
    ↑newString
do: aBlock
    "Evaluates aBlock for each of the characters accessible by receiver."
    [self **atEnd**] **whileFalse**: [aBlock **value**: self **next**]

positioning protocol

close
    "Included for FileStream compatibility."
    self **setEndOfStream**
reopen
    atEnd ← false
reset
    ↑self **notPositionable**
position
    ↑self **notPositionable**
position: anInteger
    ↑self **notPositionable**
setToEnd
    ↑self **notPositionable**
notPositionable
    self **error**: 'window streams are not positionable'

Class ReadWindowStream

class name	ReadWindowStream
superclass	ReadWriteWindowStream
instance variable names	"none"
comment	Supports a window stream that behaves like a read stream.

class methods

instance creation

new
    ↑self **label:** 'A ReadStream' **readContents:** '' **unreadContents:** ''

examples

example1
    "ReadWindowStream example1"
    | aStream |
    aStream ← ReadWindowStream
        label: 'Read Window Test'
        readContents: 'A test string.\' **withCRs**
        unreadContents: 'Yet to be read.\' **withCRs.**
    Transcript **show:** (aStream **upTo:** Character **cr**); **cr.**
    Transcript **show:** (aStream **upTo:** Character **cr**); **cr.**

instance methods

write protocol

nextPut: aCharacter
    self **error:** 'cannot write into a read stream'
nextPutAll: aCollectionOfCharacters
    self **error:** 'cannot write into a read stream'
show: aCollectionOfCharacters
    self **error:** 'cannot write into a read stream'

The window stream controller makes use of methods that have been obtained by browsing the paragraph editor and text controller protocols in detail. The selection methods, in particular, were created by modifying existing variations.

The window stream controller endeavors to maintain the current selection point to the right of the last character; i.e., as an empty selection. Exceptions occur either to insert text newly written into the stream or to make sure a specific character is visible on the screen (using **selectAndScroll**). Any method, such as **replaceSelectionWith:**, that could change the current selection was overriden in order to reset it at the right end.

The inherited text collector protocol keeps track of whether or not text is highlighted. A **select** message will highlight the text if it is not already highlighted; otherwise, it will do nothing. Similarly, a **deselect** message will dehighlight it only if it is already highlighted. In both cases, the work is done by **reverseSelection**. The method was overriden to do something unknown to the rest of the code; i.e., it actually highlights and dehighlights the characters that have not yet been read. Additionally, the standard method to display the caret (which, by the way, actually *reverses* it rather than writes it *over* the display) was not designed to leave the caret visible when a section of text is highlighted. Unfortunately, it overlaps with the reversed text to produce an indistinct caret. The solution we used was to display the caret using a much smaller form to prevent overlapping (the caret is the same size but the form is smaller).

Preventing the user from selecting arbitrary portions of the text with the mouse was simply a matter of overriding the **redButtonActivity** message to make it do nothing. The paragraph editor already provides a method for handling the escape character, **selectCurrent-TypeIn:**, which causes the currently typed text to be selected. We changed it for its new role. Recall that escape means "I finished adding characters" while two escapes in a row mean "There will be no more characters after this".

When the window stream requests additional characters from the controller, the window is activated via the **specialStartUp** message. This will cause the window to flash as long as the mouse is outside its boundaries. Processing continues until instance variable waitingFor-Escape becomes **false**. Of course, this is set to **false** when an escape is typed.

Class WindowStreamController

class name	WindowStreamController
superclass	TextCollectorController
instance variable names	waitingForEscape

instance methods

instance initialization

changeParagraph: aParagraph
    "Install aParagraph as the one to be edited by the receiver."
    super **changeParagraph**: aParagraph.
    self **selectBottomInvisibly**

controlling

specialStartUp
    | topView |
    "First, make sure the window is visible."
    view **topView display**.

    "Next, start up the WindowStream panel."
    self **controlInitialize**.

        waitingForEscape ← true.
        [waitingForEscape] **whileTrue**: [
            [self **viewHasCursor or**: [self **scrollBarContainsCursor**]]
                whileFalse: [view flash].
            self **controlActivity**.
            Processor **yield**].
        model
            contents: paragraph **text**
            startOfUnreadPortion: model **startOfUnreadPortion**.

    self **controlTerminate**

view update support

appendEntry
"Append the text in the model's writeStream to the editable text. Obtained by modifying appendEntry in TextCollectorController"
| start newText |
view **topView isCollapsed**
    ifTrue: [
            paragraph **text**
                replaceFrom: 1
                to: paragraph **text size**
                with: model **contents asText**.
            self **selectBottomInvisibly**]
    ifFalse: [
        self **deselect**. "Removed the code that truncated the paragraph if it was
        longer than characterLimit."
            self **selectInvisiblyAt:** (start←model **startOfUnreadPortion**)."for next replace"
            self **replaceSelectionWith:** (newText ← model **nextEntry asText**).
            model
                contents: paragraph **text**
                startOfUnreadPortion: (start ← start + newText **size**).
            self **selectBottomInvisibly**]

changeText: aText
"The paragraph to be edited is changed to aText. Obtained by modifying change-
Text: in TextCollectorController."

paragraph **text:** aText. self **resetState**.
self **selectInvisiblyAt:** model **startOfUnreadPortion**. "to see start of unread portion"
self **selectAndScroll**.
self **selectBottomInvisibly**. "for subsequent keyboard insertions"
paragraph **displayOn:** Display

readEntry
"A portion of the unread text was read."
| start stop |
view **topView isCollapsed ifFalse:** [
    selectionShowing
            ifTrue: [
                "Reverse only the first character."
                start ← model **startOfUnreadPortion**-1. stop ← start.
                paragraph
                    reverseFrom: (paragraph **characterBlockForIndex:** start)
                    to: (paragraph **characterBlockForIndex:** stop+1)]
            ifFalse: [self **reverseSelection**].
    "Make sure the next unread character is visible."
    self **selectInvisiblyAt:** model **startOfUnreadPortion**. "next unread character"
    self **selectAndScroll**. "make it visible"].
"Position selection at the end to get new keyboard characters."
self **selectBottomInvisibly**

mouse and keyboard operations

processRedButton
"Deactivate red button processing (return self; no code)."

readKeyboard
    model **getAtEnd**
        ifTrue: [
            (self **confirm**: ('End of stream already signaled.\',
                'Do you wish to reopen the stream?') **withCRs**)
                ifTrue: [model **reopen**. ↑self **readKeyboard**]
                ifFalse: [sensor **flushKeyboard**]]
        ifFalse: [↑super **readKeyboard**]

selectCurrentTypeIn: characterStream
    "A modification of the equivalent method in ParagraphEditor."
    | escapeCharacter |
    escapeCharacter ← sensor **keyboard**. "flush character"
    sensor **keyboardPressed ifTrue**: [
        sensor **keyboardPeek** = escapeCharacter
            ifTrue: [sensor **flushKeyboard**. model **setEndOfStream**]].
    waitingForEscape ← false.
    ↑false "further process characterStream"

selection operations

replaceSelectionWith: aText
    "Handle attempts to backspace beyond the unread portion."
    self **deselect**.
    self **selectInvisiblyFrom**: (self **selectionStart max**: model **startOfUnreadPortion**)
        to: self **selectionEnd**.
    super **replaceSelectionWith**: aText.
    self **selectBottomInvisibly**. "position at the end"

reverseSelection
    "A modification of reverseSelection in ParagraphEditor that reverses the current
    selection highlight. Note that as far as the super is concerned, there can be no
    selection. However, we keep the unread portion of the text highlighted."

    | start stop localStartBlock localStopBlock caretPoint caret |
    selectionShowing ← selectionShowing **not**.
    start ← model **startOfUnreadPortion**. stop ← paragraph **text size**.
    localStartBlock ← paragraph **characterBlockForIndex**: start.
    localStopBlock ← paragraph **characterBlockForIndex**: stop+1.
    start <= stop **ifTrue**: [paragraph **reverseFrom**: localStartBlock **to**: localStopBlock].

    "The standard paragraph displayCaret overlaps with the reversed text. So handle it
    specially."
    caretPoint ← localStopBlock **topLeft** + (0 @ paragraph **textStyle baseline**).
    caret ← selectionShowing
        ifTrue: [Form
            extent: 6@5
            fromArray: #(
                2r0011000000000000
                2r0011000000000000
                2r0111100000000000
                2r1111110000000000
                2r1100110000000000)
            offset: 0@0]
        ifFalse: [(Form **extent**: 6@5) **white**].
    caret **displayOn**: Display **at**: caretPoint **clippingBox**: paragraph **clippingRectangle**

selectInvisiblyAt: characterIndex
"Like selectAt: but avoids deselection, reselection, and scrolling."
startBlock ← paragraph **characterBlockForIndex**: characterIndex.
stopBlock ← startBlock **copy**.

selectInvisiblyFrom: start **to**: stop
"Like selectFrom:to: but avoids deselection, reselection, and scrolling."
startBlock ← paragraph **characterBlockForIndex**: start.
stopBlock ← paragraph **characterBlockForIndex**: stop + 1

selectBottomInvisibly
self **selectInvisiblyAt**: paragraph **size** + 1

menu messages

fileOut
"Print the contents of the stream onto an external file."
| fileName fileStream |
self **controlTerminate**. "get rid of the scroll bars"
fileName ← FillInTheBlank
    request: 'File name?'
    initialAnswer: (view **topView label copyWithout**: Character **space**), '.window'.
fileStream ← FileStream **fileNamed**: fileName.
Cursor write **showWhile**: [
    fileStream **timeStamp; nextPutAll**: paragraph **string; shorten; close**].
Transcript **cr; show**: fileName; **cr**.
self **controlInitialize** "get the scroll bars back"

initializeYellowButtonMenu
self
    yellowButtonMenu:(PopUpMenu **labels**: 'undo\paste\file out' **withCRs lines**: #(2))
    yellowButtonMessages: #(undo paste fileOut)

new selection protocol

selectionStart
    ↑startBlock **stringIndex**
selectionEnd
    ↑stopBlock **stringIndex** - 1

The primary role of the window stream view is to handle the **update**: message sent by the window stream. It relays the two new requests to the controller and handles the rest through inheritance.

Class WindowStreamView

class name   WindowStreamView
superclass   TextCollectorView
instance variable names   "none"

instance methods

controller access

defaultControllerClass
    ↑WindowStreamController

updating

update: aSymbol
    aSymbol == #promptForInput **ifTrue**: [↑controller **specialStartUp**].
    aSymbol == #readEntry **ifTrue**: [↑controller **readEntry**].
    super **update**: aSymbol

resize support

isCollapsed
    ↑self **topView isCollapsed**

3.6 PLUGGABLE WINDOWS: THE PHILOSOPHY

Pluggable windows are an attempt to eliminate the explosion of view and controller specializations that result when application specific windows are required. For example, each application specific window that was designed so far has required either a special purpose controller to override a menu message or a specialized view that needed to do something an existing view didn't do.

Take the existing browser as a better illustration. The first version of the browser needed a special controller and view for each pane (2 classes times 5 panes) in addition to a browser model, a browser view, and a browser controller. This requirement for 13 browser classes made the design appear to be overly complex. The second generation design attempted to use the same model (called a browser instead of a browser model) for all panes, along with instances of more general controllers and views. These were designed to be instantiated with parameters that tailored them to their specific application. How well the designers succeeded can be judged by looking at the existing browser.

A **pluggable window** consists of a **pluggable view** and a special controller that supports the parameterization that has been designed into the view. Of course, the parameterization is designed with a specific functionality in mind; i.e., it is not possible

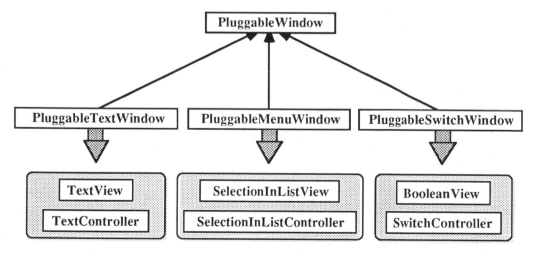

Figure 3.18 The pluggable windows.

to design a window that can be used for totally arbitrary purposes. That is why there are currently three classes of pluggable views (see Fig. 3.18): for text (TextView and TextController), menus (SelectionInListView and SelectionInListController), and switches (BooleanView and SwitchController). SwitchController is anomalous because it is the standard controller used with nonpluggable switch views. New application domains will undoubtedly require the design of new pluggable windows.

The notion of pluggable views as a category of views that permit application specific behaviors to be added without having to construct specializations is relatively new to Smalltalk since it did not exist in the version 1 image. The idea is to provide a view that can be **plugged onto** any object, rather than having to define a new subclass specific to every kind of object that needs to be viewed. Each pluggable view is designed to interface with a fairly arbitrary model and to react to one **aspect** or feature of the model; e.g., its size, color, value, and so on.

The aspect is specified to the pluggable view via three message selectors: an **aspect selector**, a **changed aspect selector**, and a **yellow menu selector**. Depending on the kind of pluggable view, additional parameters might also be required. These specific parameters respectively specify how to get a value for the chosen aspect, how to change its value, and how to get a pop-up menu for the yellow button.

For example, if a train schedule text window were to be created and we had already designed a train station that contains such information, we would parameterize the pluggable text view with three selectors: #trainSchedule, #trainSchedule:, and #trainScheduleYellow-Menu. The pluggable view could obtain the train schedule by executing 'model **perform**: *aspectSelector*', change it by executing 'model **perform**: *changedAspectSelector* **with**: *newText*', and obtain the yellow menu selector with 'model **perform**: *yellowMenu-Selector*'.

If the model is externally changed so that the aspect being viewed is no longer up-to-date, the model has the responsibility to notify its dependents of the change. In the previous example, the model would execute 'self **changed**: #trainSchedule', which causes the corresponding '**update**: #trainSchedule' message to be sent to the view. The view is designed to react only if the update parameter matches the aspect selector, as it would in this case. If, for example, the train station personnel had been changed instead and a 'self **changed**: #personnel' message was sent by the model, the view would ignore the change. In general, each class of pluggable views is designed to react in a manner tailored to its application. For example, the SectionInListView obtains a new menu list from the model and redisplays it. The TextView obtains new text from the model and displays it. The BooleanView obtains a boolean result from the model and displays it normally or complemented, depending on the result.

Recall that the blue button menu is primarily window independent since it is concerned with such details as closing the window, reframing it, moving it, and so on. The yellow button menu, however, is specialized to the application. For our train schedule example, it is clear that the yellow button menu should have entries dealing with operations that can be done on the train schedule. For example, one entry could be 'highlight trains about to leave'. Assuming this were done, a second use of the yellow button menu might find the entry changed to 'dehighlight trains about to leave'. To be able to do this, the view must ask the model for the yellow button menu each time the yellow button is depressed. It is not sufficient to provide one that is used once and for all. Hence, the parameter is a yellow menu selector that can be used to obtain a pop-up menu rather than the pop-up menu itself. Once the pop-up menu is obtained, the associated menu message (if an entry was chosen) is sent to the model. Note, however, that pop-up menus are inadequate since they contain only the menu items, not the menu messages. Fortunately, a specialization called **action menus** was designed to carry both pieces of information. More details can be found in the section on pop-up windows. Examples to follow will illustrate their use without having to look it up. Keep in mind that all pluggable windows use action menus instead of regular pop-up menus.

3.7 PLUGGABLE TEXT WINDOWS

Pluggable text windows provide a text editing window on some aspect of an object that can be manipulated as text. Specializations **TextView** and **TextController** (see Fig. 3.19) of View and TextEditor respectively provide the implementation for **pluggable text views** and **pluggable text controllers**. Pluggable text views behave like string holder views. If a pluggable text view is a dependent of the model associated with a standard system view, attempts to close the view result in a change request that is satisfied only if the pluggable view is unlocked. Hence, partial modifications are not forgotten if the standard system view is closed.

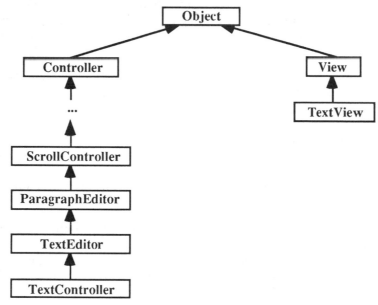

Figure 3.19 The pluggable text hierarchy.

Pluggable text views are used in several different contexts: in browsers, debuggers, file lists, file models, inspectors, projects, and syntax-error processing. In each case, the model is either a browser, a debugger, a syntax-error object, an inspector, a file model, or a file list. The aspect selector is usually #text and the change selector is #acceptText:from:. Thus, each model is specially designed to respond to the **text** and **acceptText:from:** messages.

3.7.1 Creating Pluggable Text Windows

To create a pluggable text window, two things must be done: (1) a suitably parameterized pluggable text view must be created, and (2) the model must be checked to make sure it adheres to the requirements of the view.

Obtaining a Pluggable Text View

Pluggable text views can be created by specifying a model along with three message selectors that the model must respond to.

- TextView
    on: aModel
    aspect: aspectSelector **change**: changeSelector **menu**: yellowMenuSelector

These selectors (actually symbols) must be designed to perform the following tasks:

- **aspectSelector** (no parameters) should return the value of the model's aspect as text. This symbol *must* be used as the model's **changed**: parameter for the view to react to the change.

- **changeSelector** (one or two parameters) must update the model in response to a user modification in the view. The first parameter is the revised text for the model's aspect. The second (supplied only if the selector takes two parameters) is the controller associated with the change. The model has the option to accept or refuse to accept the change. If it accepts, the method should return **true**; otherwise, **false**.

- **yellowMenuSelector** (no parameters) must return an action menu, a special kind of pop-up menu, that can react to yellow button requests. The pop-up menu selectors themselves are divided into two groups: editor selectors and non-editor selectors. The former messages are sent to the controller. The latter are sent to the model. Additionally, those sent to the model can either be zero-parameter or two-parameter selectors. The two-parameter selectors are provided with the currently accepted text and the active controller. The editing labels should include a subset of {again, undo, copy, cut, paste, accept, cancel} with corresponding selectors {again, undo, copySelection, cut, paste, accept, cancel}.

Permitting selectors with controllers as parameters is useful if the controller needs be interrogated. For example, selecting a piece of application specific text and choosing **explain** in the yellow button menu cannot be accommodated by the model unless the controller is provided. From the controller, we can get the current selection, deselect it, and insert a response. It is also possible to get the view; e.g., to cause it to flash.

It is also possible to set the above selectors to **nil** to indicate that the corresponding actions are not to be executed. For example, when the change selector is **nil**, modifications are not allowed. When the yellow menu selector is **nil**, using the yellow button is disallowed. In general, yellow button menu selections that have to do with the standard paragraph/text editor operations (cut, paste, copy, again, undo, cancel, and accept) are handled by the superclass TextEditor. Hence, these menu items must be supplied in the action menu if these features are not to be deactivated. When other menu items are specified, they are relayed to the model.

Ensuring That The Model Accommodates The View

To accommodate the view, the model must be provided with the methods that were specified in the view through parameterization, with the proper change/update protocol, and with additional methods that support the view protocol. More specifically, the model must satisfy the following requirements:

- It should have an **aspectSelector** that returns **text** (*returning a string is not sufficient*).

- It should have a **changeSelector** that accepts **text** (and a controller if there is a second parameter) and also returns a **boolean** (*returning any other value is unacceptable*). The boolean indicates whether or not the change request was accepted and made; i.e., **true** means the change was made, **false** means it was not.

- It should have a **yellowMenuSelector** that returns an **action menu**.

- It should have methods for the **non-text editing menu messages**; i.e., messages other than those in the set {again, undo, copySelection, cut, paste, accept, cancel}. These methods normally take no parameters; however, they could optionally take two: the current text and the controller.

- External changes to the model that affect the aspect being viewed should send a 'self **changed**: *aspectSelected*' message. Note that the change selector could do this. There is no possibility that an infinite loop will occur because the view updates itself only if the model's aspect is different from its own version.

- The model must have a method called '**changeRequestFrom**: aView' that returns a boolean indicating whether or not the view is allowed to change the model's aspect.

A detailed example is considered in the next section.

3.7.2 Example: Pluggable Text Windows

This section illustrates how pluggable text windows can be created. Because of the requirements enumerated in the previous section, creating text windows on classes of objects that already exist is not likely to work. One normally creates such windows for use in new browsers. The browsers then serve as the models for the pluggable text view requests. Alternatively, new classes of objects can be designed with the expectation that specific aspects will be viewed through pluggable text windows. This is the approach we consider in this section.

In our case, we will design a class called Person that contains a small subset of the information in a personnel file. In particular, we will focus on two distinct aspects of a person: background and extra-curricular activities. Our goal is to properly design these two aspects so that we can create pluggable text views on each of them independently. To illustrate the notion, we provide an operation called **edit** that creates a two-paned window with text subwindows on the two different aspects. The result is shown in Fig. 3.20. In a more general design (not considered), we would provide a personnel browser that additionally has a pluggable menu window for choosing the distinct people to be viewed. The information shown in Fig. 3.20 would be only a small part of the displayed information.

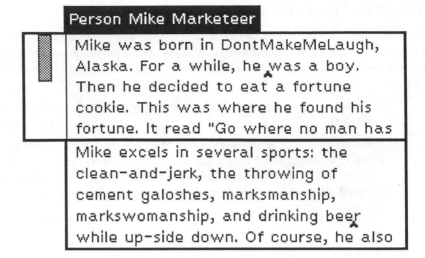

Figure 3.20 Two pluggable text subwindows.

As defined, an instance of Person contains only three components: name, background, and extraActivities. We provide the usual operations for accessing and modifying these fields. For example, the background is obtained and modified via **background** and **background:**. Note that the latter sends a **changed** message to notify its dependents. Note also that we provided a variation called **viewBackground:** to be used as the pluggable view's change selector. The normal **background:** message is inadequate since it does not return a boolean.

We could have optimized the **viewBackground:** method by eliminating the **changed** message. Clearly, if the view changes the model, there is no need for the view to be asked to update itself to correspond to the revised model. As we said before, the view is smart enough to notice that the revised model's aspect is the same as its own version and therefore avoid making another change (this could have led to an infinite loop if the view was less careful). The inefficiency, however, must be tolerated if distinct windows are allowed to manipulate the same aspect of the same model. For example, two personnel browsers on the same person would work with this design. If one browser's view changed the background, both would be notified and updated with this approach.

Notice that **changeRequestFrom:** was needed to satisfy the view's change/update protocol. In our case, we always return **true**. This would be upgraded if we added special yellow menu items for making changes to the person in stages; e.g., through menu messages corresponding to stage1, stage2, and so on. Presumably, the **changeRequest-From:** method would return **false** while in the intermediate stages.

The yellow menu message returns an action menu that contains only the standard editing items. Hence, no new menu messages were added.

Class Person

class name	Person
superclass	Object
instance variable names	name background extraActivities

instance methods

name manipulation

name
    ↑name
name: aString
    name ← aString

background manipulation

background
    ↑background
background: aText
    background ← aText
    self **changed**: #background
viewBackground: aText
    self **background**: aText.
    ↑true "yes, I actually did accept your request to perform the update"

extra activities manipulation

extraActivities
    ↑extraActivities
extraActivities: aText
    extraActivities ← aText
    self **changed**: #extraActivities
viewExtraActivities: aText
    self **extraActivities**: aText.
    ↑true "yes, I actually did accept your request to perform the update"

conforming to the view's change/update protocol

changeRequestFrom: aView
    ↑true

menu handling

getYellowMenu
    ↑ActionMenu
        labels: 'again\undo\copy\cut\paste\do it\print it\accept\cancel' **withCRs**
        lines: #(2 5 7)
        selectors: #(again undo copySelection cut paste doIt printIt accept cancel)

editing

edit
    "(Person new name: 'Mike Marketeer') edit"
    | topView subView1 subView2 virtualObject |

    "Create the views."
    topView ← StandardSystemView **new label**: 'Person ', self **name**; **borderWidth**: 1.
    subView1 ← TextView **on**: self
        aspect: #background **change**: #viewBackground: **menu**: #getYellowMenu.
    subView2 ← TextView **on**: self
        aspect: #extraActivities **change**: #viewExtraActivities: **menu**: #getYellowMenu.

"Position the subviews within the top view."
topView **addSubView**: subView1 **in**: (0@0 **corner**: 1@0.5) **borderWidth**: 1.
topView **addSubView**: subView2 **in**: (0@0.5 **corner**: 1@1) **borderWidth**: 1.

"Make sure that the subviews request close confirmation if changes have been made."
virtualObject ← Object **new**.
topView **model**: virtualObject.
virtualObject **addDependent**: subView1; **addDependent**: subView2.

"Finally, try it out."
topView **controller open**

3.7.3 Implementation: The TextController Protocol

Specialization **TextController** of TextEditor basically overrides the accept and yellow button activity messages. The **accept** method differs from the version higher up in the hierarchy by explicitly sending a **changeRequestFrom:** message to the model before sending it the changeSelector message. The **yellowButtonActivity** method uses the menu selector associated with the chosen menu item as the message to be sent to the model (for all the non-editor operations).

control operations redefined specially for this class

- aTextController **accept**
- aTextController **yellowButtonActivity**
    Minor modifications to ensure that the model is invoked through the proper selector protocols.

additional minor operations redefined specially for this class

- aTextController **insertAndSelect**: aString **at**: anInteger
- aTextController **wrappingBox**: wrapRectangle **clippingBox**: clipRectangle

new minor operations

- aTextController **paragraph**
- aTextController **textHasChanged**
- aTextController **localMenuItem**: selector
    Method **paragraph** provides access that should have been provided by ParagraphEditor; **textHasChanged** returns a boolean indicating whether or not the contained text differs from the previously accepted text; **localMenuItem**: determines whether or not the selector provided is one of the editor operations handled locally by the paragraph/text editor.

Two example methods are shown for interest's sake.

aTextController **localMenuItem**: selector
    "Note that selectors align and fit are omitted from the paragraph/text editor menu ."
    ↑#(cut paste copySelection again undo cancel accept) **includes**: selector

```
aTextController yellowButtonActivity
    | index menu selector |
    menu ← view yellowButtonMenu. "get it from the model"
    menu == nil
        ifTrue: [view flash. super controlActivity] "none provided"
        ifFalse: [
            index ← menu startUpYellowButton. "activate it"
            index ~= 0 ifTrue: [
                selector ← menu selectorAt: index. "editing to self, rest to model"
                (self localMenuItem: selector)
                    ifTrue: [self perform: selector] "it was an editor operation"
                    ifFalse: ["it was a model operation"
                        self controlTerminate. "hide the scroll bars"
                        selector numArgs = 2
                            ifTrue: [model perform: selector with: self text with: self]
                            ifFalse: [model perform: selector].
                        self controlInitialize "bring the scroll bars back"]]]
```

3.7.4 Implementation: The TextView Protocol

Specialization **TextView** of View provides the majority of the methods for pluggable text views. However, most of the methods are redefinitions of those that exist in class View.

instance creation and initialization

- TextView
    on: anObject
    aspect: aspectSelector **change**: changeSelector **menu**: yellowMenuSelector
- aTextView
    on: anObject
    aspect: aspectSelector **change**: changeSelector **menu**: yellowMenuSelector

view operations redefined specially for this class

- aTextView **initialize**
- aTextView **display**
- aTextView **displayView**
- aTextView **emphasizeView**
- aTextView **deEmphasizeView**
- aTextView **update**: aSymbol
- aTextView **updateRequest**
- aTextView **defaultControllerClass**

    The **initialize** method performs the default initialization and changes the inside color from clear to white. The display and emphasis methods properly interface with the controller (recall that paragraph/text editors, from which text controllers inherit, manage their own working text and also perform selection and deselection). The **update**: method obtains new text from the model only if the update parameter is the same as the aspect selector. The **updateRequest** method replies **true** in response to a **changeRequest** (for example, arising from a close operation) if no change to the text has been made in the view. If a change has been made, the user is prompted to determine whether or not the changes can be discarded. The **default-ControllerClass** method returns TextController.

operations dealing with the message selectors

- aTextView **getText**
- aTextView **newText**: aText
- aTextView **accept**: aText **from**: aController
- aTextView **yellowButtonMenu**

> The first, third, and fourth methods send corresponding aspectSelector, changeSelector, and yellowMenuSelector messages to the model. The changeSelector message requires one parameter (the text) or two, in which case the controller is also provided. This may be useful if the model must send special instructions to the controller. Similarly, the non-editor menu selectors for the yellow menu are either zero-parameter selectors or two-parameter selectors provided with the currently accepted text and the active controller when invoked. The second method, **newText**:, is used privately by **display** and **update**: to change the text in the controller without notifying the model.

The following are some of the more interesting methods.

```
aTextView update: aSymbol
    | text |
    "partMsg is the aspect selector"
    aSymbol == partMsg ifTrue:[
        text ← self getText. "from the model"
        self controller text ~= text ifTrue: [self newText: text. self displayView]]
```

```
aTextView updateRequest
    | cancel |
    self controller textHasChanged ifFalse: [↑true].
    self superView isCollapsed ifFalse:[
        Display reverse: insetDisplayBox mask: Form gray.
        Display reverse: (insetDisplayBox insetBy: 4) mask: Form gray].
    cancel ← self confirm: 'The text showing has been altered.\',
        'Do you wish to discard those changes?' withCRs.
    self superView isCollapsed ifFalse: [
        Display reverse: insetDisplayBox mask: Form gray.
        Display reverse: (insetDisplayBox insetBy: 4) mask: Form gray].
    ↑cancel
```

```
aTextView getText
    | text |
    partMsg == nil ifTrue: [↑Text new]. "partMsg is the aspect selector"
    text ← model perform: partMsg.
    text == nil ifTrue: [↑Text new].
    ↑text
```

```
aTextView accept: aText from: aController
    "acceptMsg is the change selector"
    acceptMsg == nil ifTrue: [self flash. ↑false].
    ↑acceptMsg numArgs = 1
        ifTrue: "one parameter selectors get text only"
            [model perform: acceptMsg with: aText]
        ifFalse: "two parameter selectors get text and controller as well"
            [model perform: acceptMsg with: aText with: aController]
```

```
aTextView yellowButtonMenu
    "menuMsg is the yellowButton selector"
    menuMsg == nil ifTrue: [↑nil].
    ↑model perform: menuMsg
```

3.8 SUMMARY

This chapter has provided the details of **text windows**, which provide the ability to manipulate scrollable textual data. In particular, we have discussed the following notions:

- The model, view, and controller hierarchies associated with text windows.

- The most important protocol for classes ParagraphEditor and TextEditor.

- The protocol for display-text windows — non-editable text windows.

- The protocol for string/text holders, string holder controllers, and string holder views — the major text windows used in browsers.

- The locking and unlocking protocol of string/text holder windows.

- An example that illustrates the use of application specific string holder subclasses for a symbolic manipulation system.

- The protocol for text collectors, text collector controllers, and text collector views — the major workspace windows in the system.

- An example that illustrates specializations of text collectors — the design of note pads as unbounded text collectors with a file-out capability.

- An example that illustrates the use of text collectors as error message or debugging information windows.

- An example implementing window streams, i.e., windows that can also be used externally by some object as a stream.

- The basic pluggable windows philosophy.

- Pluggable text windows, including the detailed protocol for classes TextController and TextView.

- An example illustrating the use of pluggable text windows for displaying a subset of a personnel data base.

3.9 EXERCISES

The following exercises are intended to provide some additional insight into text windows and their applications.

1. Investigate changes to Paragraph-Editor and/or TextEditor that permit the addition of user-specifiable character macros.

2. Create a special kind of non-editable display-text window that vaporizes itself when a mouse click occurs inside. Make a window with a string holder view and a self vaporizing view that provides a welcome message for new users.

3. Investigate the changes required to View to ensure that computing new window transformations is done by sending itself a **lock** message. This would enable the views for subclasses of paragraph/text editors to provide their own version of **lock** that recomposes the paragraph/text compositor in addition to executing 'super **lock**'.

4. One reason that special attention is required to ensure that close confirmation works properly for string holder windows is that no close protocol is provided for views and controllers in general. Consider adding a **close** method either to View and StandardSystemView or to Controller and StandardSystemController (which is most appropriate?). Assuming the former, the View default might be to close all subviews; the StandardSystemView default might be to use 'super **close**' followed by the existing code. The StringHolderView **close** could now invoke the confirmers explicitly.

5. Redesign StringHolderView so that it does not maintain a shared version of the controller's text compositor (the working text); i.e., have it ask the controller for the text compositor when it needs it.

6. Are string holder windows and text collector windows interchangeable if you never use the window as a stream?

7. Simplify string holder controllers by eliminating the lock protocol; instead have senders directly access its model for lock manipulation.

8. Modify string holders to contain text instead of strings.

9. See what happens if you attempt to print #failedDoit in a text window. Explain it.

10. Send successive **changed:** #appendEntry, **changed:** #update, and **changed:** #refresh messages to the Transcript. Verify that the #appendEntry variation fails to empty the text collector stream. How can this be remedied? Hint: TextCollector method **endEntry** sends a **beginEntry** message after the **changed:** message. Perhaps the **beginEntry** message should be sent by the controller when it reacts to the corresponding **update:** message.

11. Redesign window streams using multiple-inheritance.

12. Extend the binary tree class to support a pluggable text window on a tree. The window would be designed to display the tree labels using indentation to indicate the structure. It would be nice if changes to the tree were reflected in the window. What about the converse?

3.10 GLOSSARY AND IMPORTANT FACTS

classes

ActionMenu A class of pop-up menus for plugging into pluggable windows; typically used for yellow button menus.

BooleanView The view class for pluggable switch windows; designed to work with **SwitchController**.

DisplayTextView A class used for constructing non-editable views containing small titles such as copyright notices. The title information can be displayed either centered or not.

Paragraph A private class used by text window controllers (specifically ParagraphEditor) for maintaining the working text.

ParagraphEditor The controller class that provides the majority of the text editing protocol for text windows; intended as an abstract class to support its various specializations. Paragraph editors maintain the textual information internally in an instance of class Paragraph. The model is distinct from the paragraph.

SelectionInListController The controller class for pluggable menu windows.

SelectionInListView The view class for pluggable menu windows.

StringHolder A class providing the model for string holder windows.

StringHolderController A class providing the controller for string holder windows.

StringHolderView A class providing the view for string holder windows.

TextCollector A class providing the model for text collector windows.

TextCollectorController A class providing the controller for text collector windows.

TextCollectorView A class providing the view for text collector windows.

TextCompositor A class privately used by text window controllers for maintaining the working text. A recent addition that is an efficient substitute for **Paragraph**.

TextController A class of controllers designed to work with **TextView**.

TextList A more efficient specialization of Paragraph that clips individual lines if they are too long rather than using wraparound; used internally by menu windows. Instances of TextList are distinct from the models that are interrogated to obtain the list of menu items.

TextView A class of pluggable text views.

other globals

Transcript A global referencing a text collector; often used for debugging.

Workspace A class variable of **StringHolder** (also an instance of StringHolder) that

contains the contents of the **system workspace**; does not contain boldface or italic information. If additional system workspaces are opened, they all share this one special string holder.

selected terminology

action menus A class of pop-up menus that maintains menu items and menu messages; used by pluggable windows.

caret An insertion point character that indicates where newly typed characters will be inserted.

display-text window A window with a non-editable textual display; uses any object that can be converted to a paragraph as the model; e.g., string, text, or display-text instances.

locked In the context of string holders and string holder controllers, indicates that a working copy is different from the string holder contents. When the controller updates the string holder, the two are unlocked. A user can force the update by choosing **accept** in the yellow pop-up menu. In the context of views, indicates that the display transformation and the display box *have been computed* from the local transformations of the view and its superviews (see the chapter on window overview and basics).

pluggable text window A window that provides access and modification to a textual aspect of an arbitrary model; MVC components include an arbitrary object, **TextView**, and **TextController**.

pluggable view A view that permits application specific behaviors to be added without having to construct specializations. Each pluggable view is designed to interface with a suitably designed model and to react to one **aspect**, or feature, of the model; e.g., its size, color, value, and so on.

pluggable window A **pluggable view** and a special controller that support the parameterization that has been designed into the view. There are currently three classes of pluggable views: for text (**TextView** and **TextController**), for menus (**SelectionInListView** and **SelectionInListController**), and for switches (**BooleanView** and **SwitchController**).

selection The portion of the text that is selected. The selection can be an empty string; it can either be highlighted or not. When highlighted, characters typed or pasted replace the highlighted selection. A caret is visible when the selection is empty.

string holder contents The string kept in the string holder.

string holder window A window providing a scrollable textual workspace that can be edited and modified for arbitrary purposes; also permits selections in the text to be executed as Smalltalk code with the result inserted into the workspace. MVC components include **StringHolder, StringHolderView,** and **StringHolderController.**

standard text window A nonpluggable text window.

system transcript A text collector referenced through global variable **Transcript.**

text window A window that provides the ability to manipulate textual data that may be too voluminous to fit the visible portion of the window; the invisible parts (if any) are made accessible by scrolling.

text collector stream The stream maintained by a text collector for accumulating characters.

text collector window A window that extends string holder windows so they can be used as write streams. MVC components include **TextCollector, TextCollectorView,** and **TextCollectorController.**

unlocked See locked.

working text A copy of the string/text holder contents that is maintained by a string holder controller. The string/text holder contents can be replaced by this working text by choosing **accept** in the yellow button menu — the string part if a string holder and the entire text if a text holder. Alternatively, the working text can be re-initialized to the string/text holder contents by choosing **cancel.** Attempts to close the window when the working text differs from the string/text holder contents result in a confirmer requesting user certification for the close action.

important facts

contents of string holders String holders contain strings and not text; boldface and italic information is maintained only by string holder controllers.

making confirmers work To force a confirmer to appear when a string holder window is closed in the presence of user modifications to the text, the string holder must be made a model of both the top view and the string holder view. See Sect. 3.4.7, *Ensuring That Close Confirmers Work*, for more details.

new system workspaces New system workspaces have no boldface or italic characters since their contents come from class variable **Workspace** (a string holder) in class **StringHolder.**

relaxing MVCs String holder windows and text collector windows are examples of an MVC instance providing a model for the model; i.e., they require a special string

holder or text collector model for keeping what users normally think of as the model, a string.

text collector character limit Unlike string holders, the size of the text collector contents is bounded by a **character limit** that is fixed by the implementation. When this limit is exceeded, the contents of the text collector are replaced by a suffix of itself that is half the size of the character limit.

pluggable text view parameters Pluggable views are provided with three message selectors: an **aspect selector,** a **changed aspect selector,** and a **yellow menu selector.** Depending on the kind of pluggable view, additional parameters might also be required. These specific parameters respectively specify how to get a value for the chosen aspect, how to change its value, and how to get a pop-up menu for the yellow button.

Inside Smalltalk

4

Menu Windows

4.1 INTRODUCTION

Like their text window counterparts, **menu windows** provide the ability to manipulate information that may be too voluminous to fit the visible portion of the window. The invisible parts (if any) are made accessible by scrolling. The difference is that menu windows deal with menu items rather than text. Just as the expression "text windows" was short for "permanently visible scrollable text windows," **menu windows** (see Fig. 4.1) correspon-

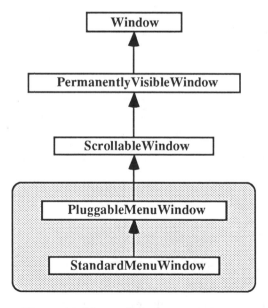

Figure 4.1 Menu windows: A logical view.

dingly is an abbreviation for "permanently visible scrollable menu windows." They, too, are differentiated from their counterpart, **pop-up menu windows**, which are never abbreviated. Because menu windows deal with lists of menu items, they are also interchangeably called **list windows.**

Menu windows are partitioned into two groups: **pluggable menu windows** and **standard menu windows.** Pluggable menu windows are designed for general user applications where the model is arbitrary. Standard menu windows do not have the same generality.

All of the menu windows maintain the collection of menu items internally as an instance of class TextList (see Fig. 4.2). TextList is a specialization of Paragraph that clips individual lines if they are too long rather than using wrap-around. The result is a more efficient implementation. This internal representation is distinct from the models that are interrogated to obtain the list of menu items.

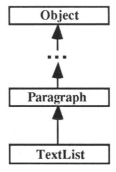

Figure 4.2 Menu windows: Models and support.

The **standard menu** or **list windows** are implemented by text lists, either list controllers or locked-list controllers, and list views (see Figs. 4.3 and 4.4). **Pluggable menu windows** are implemented via selection-in-list controllers and selection-in-list views. They are used extensively in the system browser: one for each of the class category pane, class pane, method category pane, and method pane.

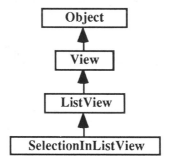

Figure 4.3 Menu windows: The view hierarchy.

The locked-list controllers differ from the list controllers by preventing menu item selection when the model is **locked**; i.e., in a state of partial modification. When the model is no longer locked, selection is again enabled.

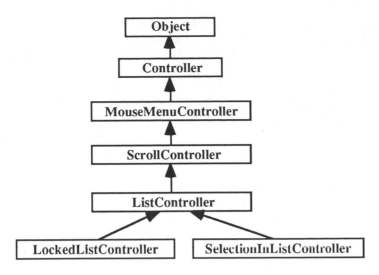

Figure 4.4 Menu windows: The controller hierarchy.

4.2 STANDARD MENU WINDOWS

Standard menu or **list windows** provide access to a list of string items that can be selected one at a time. They are like pop-up menu windows but differ in being permanently visible. Menu windows provide scrolling if there are too many entries to fit vertically in the viewport. They truncate on the right if a string item is too long to fit horizontally. A **standard menu window** is constructed from a list view and either a list controller or a locked-list controller. The controllers make use of text lists instead of paragraphs.

Classes **ListView** and **ListController** (see Fig. 4.5) specialize the protocol inherited from View and ScrollController. The View protocol is marginally extended by the ListView

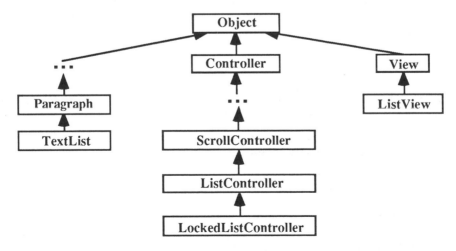

Figure 4.5 The menu (list) hierarchy.

class, but major changes are introduced by the ListController class. These changes have to do with the fact that scroll controllers were designed to manage and display paragraphs. However, paragraphs must manage line wrapping. They must also maintain the manipulated data as a single string with internal carriage returns.

Class **TextList** was designed as an efficient specialization of Paragraph for use by list and locked-list controllers. It gains its efficiency by keeping each selection in a separate string, instead of one long string with carriage returns, and by truncating the string on the right if it is too long, rather than wrapping around to the next line. Since there is no advantage or use in considering its detailed protocol, we will omit it as we have omitted the detailed Paragraph protocol.

Specialization **LockedListController** of ListController was designed to permit scrolling and selecting only when the model is unlocked. When a model is in the process of being changed, it is customary to lock it to prevent the user from accidentally changing the selection.

4.2.1 Creating Standard Menu Windows

To create a menu window, two things must be done: (1) a list view must be created with **new** in the usual way (optionally, top and bottom delimiters may be changed or removed), and (2) the model must be designed to respond to a four-message protocol: **list**, **list:**, **listIndex**, and **toggleListIndex:**. If a list view with a locked-list controller instead of the default list controller is desired, the model must additionally respond to the **isUnlocked** message.

Obtaining a Menu View

Menu views are created via new in the usual way.

- ListView **new**

The resulting view has menu items delimited at the top and bottom by a line of dashes; i.e., '------------'. These delimiters can be removed entirely via the following protocol. If the delimiters are removed, it is important to remove both rather than just one.

- aListView **noTopDelimiter**
- aListView **noBottomDelimiter**

Alternatively, the delimiters can be replaced by any user-specified string. Using **nil** is equivalent to removing the delimiter as above.

- aListView **topDelimiter:** aStringOrNil
- aListView **bottomDelimiter:** aStringOrNil

Designing a Model for the Menu View

To accommodate the view, the model must be designed to respond to a four-message protocol: **list**, **list:**, **listIndex**, and **toggleListIndex:**. If a list view with a locked-list controller instead of the default list controller is used, the model must additionally respond to the **isUnlocked** message. In more detail, these messages must be designed as follows:

selection management

- aListControllerModel **list**

  Returns the model list, a collection of strings for use in the menu entries of the list view.

- aListControllerModel **list**: aList

  Changes the model list, the collection of strings for use in the menu entries of the list view, to aList. Should result in a 'self **changed**: #list' message.

- aListControllerModel **listIndex**

  Returns the currently selected list index; either 0 if no entry is selected or a number between 1 and the size of the model list if one is selected.

- aListControllerModel **toggleListIndex**: aListIndex

  Either deselects the current selection (sets it to 0) if aListIndex is equal to it or records a new selection (sets it to aListIndex) otherwise. Should result in a 'self **changed**: #listIndex' message.

lock management

- aLockedListControllerModel **isUnlocked**

  Returns **true** if no modifications are in progress; otherwise, returns **false**. Can be implemented by asking any dependent that responds to the **isLocked** or **isUnlocked** message whether or not it is locked. A view that is in the process of modifying the model will typically be locked.

Example

As an example, consider the design of a menu window that will display the print strings of the elements of a collection in a menu. We will be permitted to select the entries, but no action is intended (for the moment). We will call it a collection browser, since it allows us to look at the collection entries. Fig. 4.6 illustrates the resulting browser with three entries. Note the truncation of the entries on the right.

Figure 4.6 A Menu window: Note item truncation.

To clarify matters, we create an explicit **menu model** that will respond to the five required messages. The browser is constructed and scheduled by the class operation **openOn:**. Menu items can be selected and deselected; scrolling is also permitted.

Class MenuModel

class name	MenuModel
superclass	Model
instance variable names	list listIndex
comment	A menu model keeps track of a list and the current selection in it.

class methods

instance creation

new
    ↑super **new initialize**

opening

openOn: aCollection
    "Create a standard system view with a menu window for displaying the collection."
    "MenuModel openOn: (Set
        with: (1 to: 100) asArray
        with: 'once upon a time in the land of ooze' asArray
        with: Object subclasses)"

    | topView aMenuModel aMenuView menuItems lastItem |
    topView ← StandardSystemView **new label**: 'Collection Browser'; **borderWidth**: 1.

    "Create an array of the element print strings. Use 'do:' to work on the maximum number of collection classes."
    menuItems ← Array **new**: aCollection **size**. lastItem ← 0.
    aCollection **do**: [:anElement |
        menuItems **at**: (lastItem ← lastItem + 1) **put**: anElement **printString**].

    aMenuModel ← self **new list**: menuItems.
    aMenuView ← ListView **new model**: aMenuModel; **list**: menuItems; **borderWidth**: 1.

    topView **addSubView**: aMenuView.
    topView **controller open**

instance methods

instance initialization

initialize
    list ← #(). listIndex ← 0

selection management

list
    "Returns the list of entries."
    ↑list
list: aList
    "Sets the list of entries."
    list ← aList. listIndex ← 0.
    self **changed**: #list

listIndex
    "Returns the index into the currently selected entry."
    ↑listIndex

toggleListIndex: aListIndex
  "Select the specified entry if it was not already specified; otherwise, deselect it."
  listIndex = aListIndex **ifTrue**: [listIndex ← 0] **ifFalse**: [listIndex ← aListIndex].
  self **changed**: #listIndex

lock management

isUnlocked
  self **dependents do**: [:aDependent |
    ((aDependent **isKindOf**: StringHolderView) **and**: [aDependent **model isLocked**])
        ifTrue: [↑false]].
  ↑true

To illustrate how to make item selection cause external changes, we extend the browser by providing it with an additional text pane below the menu pane. Since the menu pane truncates long lines, we will have the selection display itself in the text pane. The text pane does not truncate; it also permits scrolling if the text is too long. The text pane will be provided with the usual edit facilities. However, changes to the text will have no effect; i.e., the text view is relatively inert.

The main change is to modify **toggleListIndex**: so that it causes something more than toggling the list index. It additionally adds the selected menu item into a string holder that was designed to be the model for the text window. By having the string holder send itself a 'self **changed**' message, the text pane automatically updates itself. Rather than modify the menu model, we create a specialization called a **collection menu model**. The resulting browser appears as shown in Fig. 4.7.

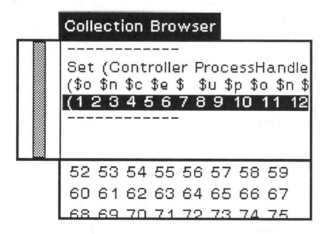

Figure 4.7 A collection browser: Menu and text windows.

Class CollectionMenuModel

class name	CollectionMenuModel
superclass	MenuModel
instance variable names	stringHolder
comment	This model keeps track of a string holder that is used to contain the current selection.

class methods

opening

openOn: aCollection
"Create a standard system view with two subwindows: the top subwindow is a menu window, the bottom subwindow is a text window that displays the selected menu item. The text window is inert."
"CollectionMenuModel openOn: (Set
　　with: (1 to: 100) asArray
　　with: 'once upon a time in the land of ooze' asArray
　　with: Object subclasses)"

| topView aCollectionMenuModel aMenuView aTextView menuItems lastItem |
topView ← StandardSystemView **new label**: 'Collection Browser'; **borderWidth**: 1.

"Create an array of the element print strings. Use 'do:' to work on the maximum number of collection classes."
menuItems ← Array **new**: aCollection **size**. lastItem ← 0.
aCollection **do**: [:anElement |
　　menuItems **at**: (lastItem ← lastItem + 1) **put**: anElement **printString**].

aCollectionMenuModel ← self **new list**: menuItems.
aMenuView ← ListView **new model**: aCollectionMenuModel; **list**: menuItems.
aTextView ← StringHolderView **container**: aCollectionMenuModel **stringHolder**.

topView
　　addSubView: aMenuView **in**: (0@0 **corner**: 1@(2/3)) **borderWidth**: 1;
　　addSubView: aTextView **in**: (0@(2/3) **corner**: 1@1) **borderWidth**: 1.
topView **controller open**

instance methods

instance initialization

initialize
　　super **initialize**.
　　stringHolder ← StringHolder **new**

string holder access

stringHolder
　　↑stringHolder

selection management

toggleListIndex: aListIndex
　　"Override the method to change the contents of the string holder to the selected entry."
　　super **toggleListIndex**: aListIndex.
　　stringHolder **contents**: (listIndex = 0 **ifTrue**: [''] **ifFalse**: [list **at**: listIndex]).
　　stringHolder **changed** "it doesn't do it itself"

So far, our menu window has no yellow button facility. To provide this, we need to specialize the list controller in order to add methods for handling the yellow button messages. To illustrate the approach, we consider providing only one facility: a facility that permits the selected entry to be inspected. Fig. 4.8 illustrates the collection browser with the yellow button **inspect** message being selected.

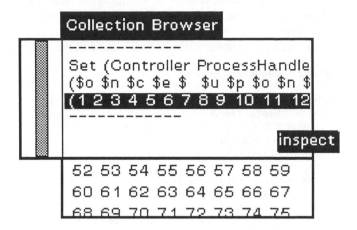

Figure 4.8 A collection browser: Illustrating the yellow button menu.

Class CollectionMenuController

class name	CollectionMenuController
superclass	ListController
instance variable names	"none"
comment	This controller overrides the list controller to provide it with alternative menu messages.

instance methods

instance initialization

initialize
    super **initialize**.
    self **initializeYellowButtonMenu** "supers don't so I will"

initializeYellowButtonMenu
    self
        yellowButtonMenu: (PopUpMenu **labels**: 'inspect')
        yellowButtonMessages: #(inspectMenuItem)

menu messages

inspectMenuItem
    model listIndex = 0
        ifTrue: [view **flash**]
        ifFalse: [(model **list at**: model **listIndex**) **inspect**]

A more complex example is considered after the detailed menu window protocol has been presented.

4.2.2 The ListController Protocol

The ListController class is a specialization of ScrollController designed to manage the scrolling and selection of menu entries in conjunction with a list view. Except for **changeModelSelection:**, most of the protocol consists of a redefinition of the protocol provided in ScrollController; i.e., it redefines the scrolling operations to deal with menu item selection. Internally, it makes use of text lists instead of paragraphs.

control operations redefined specially for this class

- aListController **isControlActive**
- aListController **redButtonActivity**

> When control is initialized, the form underneath the scroll area is saved and the marker is set up at the top. When it is terminated, the saved form is restored. Control is obtained by moving the mouse cursor into the view. It is maintained as long as it remains in the view or the scroll bar area *and the blue button is not depressed* (depressing the blue button causes it to lose control to a higher level controller — typically a standard system controller). Control activity performs scrolling as long as the mouse is in the scroll bar area and performs selection (or deselection) whenever the mouse is depressed on a menu entry.

scrolling and marker operations redefined specially for this class

- aListController **computeMarkerRegion**
- aListController **markerDelta**
- aListController **canScroll**
- aListController **scrollAmount**
- aListController **scrollView**: yDistance
- aListController **viewDelta**

> Refines the templates provided in class ScrollController by making the following substitutions (see *Creating Specializations of ScrollController* in Sect. 2.5.5, *The ScrollController Class*).
>
> > self **visibleRectangle** ⇒ view **list clippingRectangle**
> > self **totalRectangle** ⇒ view **list compositionRectangle**
> > self **canScrollEpsilon** ⇒ view **list lineGrid** // 2
> > self **viewDeltaRoundingAmount** ⇒ view **list lineGrid**
> > self **scrollViewDirectlyBy**: anAmount ⇒
> > > view **deselect**. view **list scrollBy**: anAmount **negated**.
> > > view **isSelectionBoxClipped ifFalse**: [view **displaySelectionBox**].

communication with the model

- aListController **changeModelSelection**: anInteger

> Requests the model to change the current selection (list index) to anInteger via 'model **toggleListIndex**: anInteger'. If the current selection is the same as anInteger, it is deselected; i.e., set to 0; otherwise, it is set to anInteger.

Method **redButtonActivity** (see the following) provides interesting insight into the operation of list controllers. It begins by determining the current selection (an integer specifying the current menu entry by position; 0 if no entry has been selected). Then, as long as the red button is depressed, the entry corresponding to the mouse location is determined and stored in *trialSelection*. If a valid entry is selected, it is highlighted via

moveSelectionBox:. At the same time, whether or not the latest selection differs from the original selection is recorded in *noSelectionMovement*. When the red button is finally released, message **changeModelSelection:** is invoked if a modification has been made. The determination is particularly clever. For instance, no modification is specified if the user moves from a given selection to intermediate selections, and then finally back to the original. On the other hand, a modification is specified if the user selects the original selection without moving off (it is ultimately interpreted as a deselection by **changeModel-Selection:**). Moving to a new selection is always interpreted as a modification.

```
aListController redButtonActivity
    | noSelectionMovement oldSelection trialSelection nextSelection |
    noSelectionMovement ← true. oldSelection ← view selection.
    [sensor redButtonPressed] whileTrue: [
        trialSelection ← view findSelection: sensor cursorPoint.
        trialSelection ~~ nil ifTrue: [
            nextSelection ← trialSelection. view moveSelectionBox: nextSelection.
            nextSelection ~= oldSelection ifTrue: [noSelectionMovement ← false]]].

    "Selection (or deselection) now done."
    nextSelection ~~ nil &
    (nextSelection = oldSelection ifTrue: [noSelectionMovement] ifFalse: [true])
        ifTrue: [self changeModelSelection: nextSelection]
```

4.2.3 The LockedListController Protocol

Specialization **LockedListController** of ListController permits scrolling and selecting only when the model is unlocked. The class is interesting because it is a rare example of a one-method class (although three were actually provided). More specifically, the class redefines method **controlActivity** (the actual code is shown because it is so simple). Note that the two private methods could have been easily absorbed into the **controlActivity** method.

control defaults

- aLockedListController **controlActivity**
    "Executes the standard list controller **controlActivity** if the model is unlocked; otherwise, flashes the view if an attempt is made to make a new menu selection or scroll the menu."
    self **normalResponseTest** ifTrue: [↑super **controlActivity**].
    self **feedbackResponseTest** ifTrue: [↑view **flash**]

operations private to controlActivity

- aLockedListController **normalResponseTest**
    "Returns **true** if the model is unlocked; otherwise, **false**. Hence, a normal response results when the model is unlocked."
    ↑model **isUnlocked**

- aLockedListController **feedbackResponseTest**
    "Returns **true** if the user is attempting to make modifications that are not allowed; otherwise, **false**."
    ↑sensor **anyButtonPressed** | self **scrollBarContainsCursor**

4.2.4 The ListView Protocol

Class **ListView**, a specialization of **View**, provides the protocol for displaying lists of menu items on the screen. By default, the menu items (arbitrary strings, truncated if necessary) are delimited at the top and bottom by a line of dashes; i.e., '------------'. This line can be replaced by any other string or removed entirely if desired.

Recall that the **model list** is a collection of strings denoting the menu items. The list view similarly maintains a **view list** representing the same information. Whereas the model list is a collection, the view list is an instance of TextList (a specialization of Paragraph) that is specially formatted for printing. Note that the two lists need not be exactly the same size. For example, if delimiters are used at the top and bottom, the view list will have two more entries than the model list. Since the model and view protocols refer to their respective lists with the common name **list**, we will have to carefully distinguish the two via comments.

instance initialization

- aListView **initialize**
  Initializes the view list to consist of only the dashed delimiters; i.e., the line of dashes consisting of '------------'.

view list manipulation

- aListView **list**
  Returns the view list.
- aListView **list**: aCollection OfStrings
  Reinitializes the view list to contain the specified collection of strings. Delimiters are included unless they have been explicitly removed. Note that the parameter is usually the model list.
- aListView **positionList**
  Adjusts the view list so that the currently selected entry will be visible when the view is displayed.
- aListView **reset**
  Empties the view list.
- aListView **resetAndDisplayView**
  Empties the view list and redisplays the view if it is changed.

delimiter manipulation

- aListView **topDelimiter**
  Returns the string used to indicate the top of the list.
- aListView **bottomDelimiter**
  Returns the string used to indicate the bottom of the list.
- aListView **topDelimiter**: aStringOrNil
  Sets the top delimiter to aStringOrNil; **nil** means no delimiter. If **nil** is specified for the top delimiter, it must also be specified for the bottom delimiter.
- aListView **bottomDelimiter**: aStringOrNil
  Sets the bottom delimiter to aStringOrNil; **nil** means no delimiter. If **nil** is specified for the bottom delimiter, it must also be specified for the top delimiter.
- aListView **noTopDelimiter**
  Indicates that no top delimiter is to be used. Must also be specified for the bottom delimiter.

- aListView **noBottomDelimiter**

    Indicates that no bottom delimiter is to be used. Must also be specified for the top delimiter.

displaying

- aListView **display**
- aListView **displayView**
- aListView **deEmphasizeView**

    The operations refine the corresponding methods in View. Method **displayView** clears the view, displays the visible portion of the view list, and highlights the selected item (if one is selected). Method **deEmphasizeView** displays the selected item (if one is selected) displaced by 1 pixel to the right and grays it.

- aListView **deselect**
- aListView **displaySelectionBox**

    Both methods essentially reverse the highlighting of the current selection if there is one. Hence two **displaySelectionBox** messages in a row are equivalent to one **displaySelectionBox** message and one **deselect** message. Hence, care must be taken not to accidentally execute the same method twice.

controller access

- aListView **defaultControllerClass**

    Returns class ListController.

box querying

- aListView **selectionBox**

    Returns the rectangle for the current selection.

- aListView **boundingBox**

    Returns the bounding box for the view list.

- aListView **clippingBox**

    Returns the rectangle in which the model can be displayed, the insetDisplayBox inset by the height of a line for one menu item.

selecting

- aListView **selection**

    Returns the current selection.

- aListView **minimumSelection**

    Returns the index of the view list entry that corresponds to the first entry in the model list.

- aListView **maximumSelection**

    Returns the index of the view list entry that corresponds to the last entry in the model list.

- aListView **isSelectionBoxClipped**

    Returns **true** if there is a current selection that is not visible.

- aListView **findSelection**: aPoint

    Determines which displayed selection (if any) contains aPoint. If one does contain aPoint, returns the model list index (as opposed to the view list index) of the selection; otherwise, returns **nil**.

- aListView **moveSelectionBox**: anInteger

    Deselects the previous selection (if there was one), highlights the new one, and records it. Does not notify the model.

• aListView **update**: aSymbol
    Assumes the model has been changed. Updates the view as shown.
    aSymbol == #list **ifTrue**: [self **list**: model **list**. self **displayView**. ↑self].
    aSymbol == #listIndex **ifTrue**: [self **moveSelectionBox**: model **listIndex**. ↑self]

Illustrative Methods

We provide examples of the more illustrative methods. Method **deEmphasizeView** illustrates a simple technique for deemphasis: shifting a section of highlighted text by 1 pixel and graying it. Method **findSelection** shows how a current selection is computed. It illustrates the use of paragraph (text list) specific operations, which we have not discussed.

aListView **deEmphasizeView**
    | aRectangle newForm |
    self **deselect**. "to dehighlight it (does nothing if there was no selection)"
    selection ~= 0 **ifTrue**: [
        aRectangle ← (self **selectionBox intersect**: self **clippingBox**). "the visible part"
        aRectangle ← aRectangle **insetOriginBy**: 0@-1 **cornerBy**: 0@0. "omit top 1
            pixel line. This line does not seem to be needed; removing it has no
            noticeable effect."
        newForm ← Form **fromDisplay**: aRectangle. "get what is there"
        newForm "display it moved right by one pixel"
            displayOn: Display **at**: (aRectangle **topLeft** + (1@0))
            clippingBox: aRectangle **rule**: Form **under mask**: Form **black**.
        Display **fill**: aRectangle **rule**: Form **under mask**: Form **lightGray**] "gray it"

aListView **findSelection**: aPoint
    "Determines which displayed selection (if any) contains aPoint. If one does contain
    aPoint, returns the model list index (as opposed to the view list index) of the
    selection; otherwise, returns **nil**."

    | trialSelection |
    (self **clippingBox containsPoint**: aPoint) **ifFalse**: [↑nil]. "not in menu items area"
    trialSelection ← aPoint **y** - list **compositionRectangle top** // list **lineGrid** + 1.
        "Offset from the top of the total rectangle modulo the width of a menu item
        (line grid). Add 1 since selections are numbered 1... instead of 0.... This
        selection is the view list index (as opposed to the model list index)."
    trialSelection < self **minimumSelection** | (trialSelection > self **maximumSelection**)
        ifTrue: [↑nil] "ignore the top and bottom delimiters"
        ifFalse: [↑trialSelection-self **minimumSelection**+1] "convert to model list index"

4.2.5 Example: An Electronic Phone Book

A **phone book** is a dictionary that maps names to phone numbers. For our purposes, we will consider any dictionary that maps strings to strings to be a phone book. With such generalized phone books, we could map names to addresses or dates to events if we wish. The real goal in this section, however, is to use our knowledge of list views and controllers to develop a simple phone book browser.

The browser we have in mind is shown in Fig. 4.9. It consists of two panes: a locked-list view for the phone book keys and a text view for either the selected entry or a default entry if none was chosen. To use a list view and controller, we need a model that understands messages **list**, **list:**, **listIndex**, and **toggleListIndex:**. We could design phone books to provide this protocol but it is only needed in the context of a browser. A better approach is to create a model for the model. Following the convention used for the system browser, this super model will be called a phone book browser. To use it as a model for a locked-list view, it will also have to be able to understand the **isUnlocked** message.

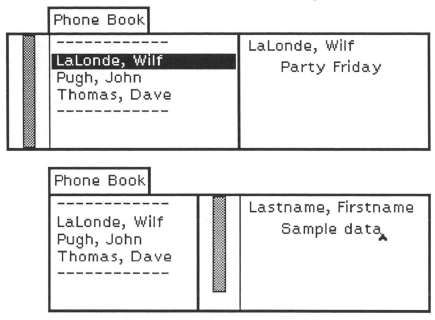

Figure 4.9 Snapshots of the phone book browser.

The browser is expected to provide us with a scrollable list of entries that can be selected with the mouse. Choosing an entry will cause the corresponding phone book value to be displayed in the text view. Conversely, the text in the text view can be edited and either accepted for insertion into the phone book or canceled. When accepted, the list view is also updated to show the new entry as the newly selected entry. When an entry is modified but not accepted, the list view will prohibit a new selection from being made. At the same time, the browser will prevent the user from accidentally closing the browser.

When a new entry is created in the text view, the possibility exists that scrolling may be needed in the corresponding list view to make the new selection visible. Since the list view was designed for interactive use, such automatic scrolling was not built in. Rather, it assumes that no user could have made a selection without properly scrolling beforehand. As it turns out, scrolling can be done explicitly by executing **positionList** after a new selection is made. Rather than modifying the existing implementation, we created a new specialization: a phone book list view (a phone book list controller was not needed since list controllers were suitable). The new view overrides the **moveSelectionBox:** method to perform the additional scrolling when necessary. Additionally, it makes sure via **defaultControllerClass** that the default controller is a locked-list controller.

In order to override the string holder controller **accept** method, we also created a phone book text controller specialization and a corresponding phone book text view that provide a

defaultControllerClass method and an **update:** method for changing the text in response to a selection in the corresponding list pane. The **accept** method is carefully designed to make sure that the text view scroll bars are hidden while the list view updates itself; not hiding the scroll bars causes the list selection highlighting to reverse the portion of the scroll bar that intersects with the selection. Note that the idea is to use **controlTerminate** followed by **controlInitialize**, a technique that is well known to the Smalltalk designers. We also added a **remove** method to permit phone book entries to be discarded.

With respect to dependency maintenance (see Fig. 4.10), changes to the list view require an **update:** method in the text view to handle the changes. Similarly, changes to the text view require an **update:** method in the list view. Since we specially designed the phone book browser (the list view's model in this case) to handle the **list** and **listIndex** protocol (among others), the phone book list view can inherit the **update:** method from the list view. On the other hand, the phone book text view cannot inherit the **update:** method from the text view because it needs to select a new entry from the phone book. However, once a new string is selected and installed in the string holder (the model for the text view), super **update:** can be used to install it in the view.

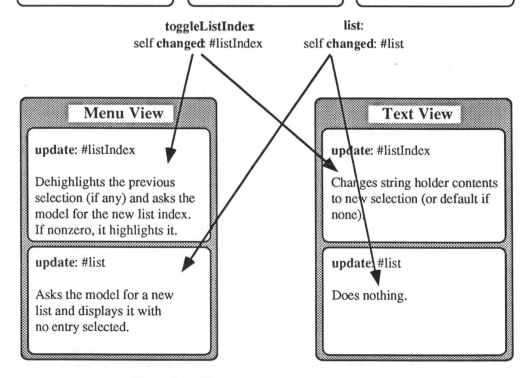

Figure 4.10 The phone book browser dependencies.

Class PhoneBookBrowser

class name	PhoneBookBrowser
superclass	Object
instance variable names	phoneBook list listIndex
comment	A phone book browser keeps track of a phone book and the current selection in it.

class methods

opening

openOn: aPhoneBook
"Creates a standard system view with two windows: a specialization of list view for the phone book keys and a specialization of string holder view for the 'key cr value' associated with the list view. A specialization of string holder controller is used to intercept the accept menu message."
"PhoneBookBrowser openOn: Dictionary new"

| aBrowser topView aListView aStringHolder aTextView |
aBrowser ← self **new phoneBook:** aPhoneBook; **list:** aPhoneBook **keys**.
topView ← StandardSystemView **new**
    label: 'Phone Book';
    model: aBrowser;
    borderWidth: 1.

aListView ← PhoneBookListView **new**
    model: aBrowser;
    list: aBrowser **list**;
    borderWidth: 1.

aStringHolder ← StringHolder **new contents:** PhoneBookBrowser **defaultEntry**.
aTextView ← (PhoneBookTextView **container:** aStringHolder)
    borderWidth: 1.

topView **addSubView:** aListView; **addSubView:** aTextView **toRightOf:** aListView.

aBrowser **addDependent:** aTextView. "The list view is already a dependent"
topView **controller open**

querying

defaultEntry
    ↑'Lastname, Firstname\   Sample data' **withCRs** "there is a tab after the '\'"

instance methods

selection management

list
    "Returns the list of entries."
    ↑list
list: aList
    "Sets the list of entries to aList (internally, keep this list sorted)."
    list ← aList **asSortedCollection asArray**. listItem ← nil.
    self **changed:** #list

listIndex
   "Returns the index into the currently selected entry."
   ↑listItem **isNil ifTrue:** [↑0] **ifFalse:** [↑list **indexOf:** listItem]

listItem
   "Returns the currently selected entry."
   ↑listItem
listItem: aString
   "Changes the currently selected entry."
   listItem ← aString.
   self **changed:** #listIndex

toggleListIndex: aListIndex
   "Selects the specified phone book entry if it was not already specified; otherwise, deselects it."
   self **listIndex** = aListIndex
       ifTrue: [listItem ← nil]
       ifFalse: [listItem ← list **at:** aListIndex.].
   self **changed:** #listIndex

change management

add: aString
   "The string is assumed to be of the form: 'key cr value'."
   | stream key value keyExists |
   stream ← ReadStream **on:** aString.
   key ← stream **upTo:** Character **cr**. value ← stream **upTo:** nil.
   keyExists ← true. phoneBook **at:** key **ifAbsent:** [keyExists ← false].
   phoneBook **at:** key **put:** value.
   keyExists **ifFalse:** [
       self **list:** phoneBook **keys**.
           "Causes 'self **update:** #list', updates the list view's list."
       self **listItem:** key.
           "Causes 'self **update:** #listIndex', updates the list view's selection"]

remove: aString
   "The string is assumed to be of the form: 'key cr value'."
   | key |
   key ← aString **copyUpTo:** Character **cr**.
   phoneBook **removeKey:** key **ifAbsent:** [].
   self **list:** phoneBook **keys**. "Causes 'self **update:** #list' which updates list view's list."

retrieve
   "Returns 'key cr value' if an item was selected; otherwise, the default."
   listItem **isNil**
       ifTrue: [↑PhoneBookBrowser **defaultEntry**]
       ifFalse: [↑listItem, (String **with:** Character **cr**), (phoneBook **at:** listItem)]

lock management

isUnlocked
   self **dependents do:** [:aDependent |
       ((aDependent **isKindOf:** StringHolderView) **and:** [aDependent **model isLocked**])
           ifTrue: [↑false]].
   ↑true

phone book access

phoneBook
    ↑phoneBook

phoneBook: aDictionary
    self **validate**: aDictionary.
    phoneBook ← aDictionary.

phone book validation

validate: aPhoneBook
    "Makes sure the phone book is a dictionary with strings keys and values."

    | errorMessage |
    errorMessage ← 'invalid phone book'.
    (aPhoneBook **isKindOf**: Dictionary) **ifFalse**: [↑self **error**: errorMessage].
    aPhoneBook **associationsDo**: [:anAssociation |
        ((anAssociation **key isKindOf**: String) & (anAssociation **value isKindOf**: String))
            ifFalse: [↑self **error**: errorMessage]]

Class PhoneBookListView

class name	PhoneBookListView
superclass	ListView
instance variable names	"none"
comment	A phone book list view manages updates initiated by a phone book text view.

instance methods

controller access

defaultControllerClass
    ↑LockedListController

displaying

moveSelectionBox: aSelection
    super moveSelectionBox: aSelection. "make the standard move"

    "If it's a deselection or it's visible, do nothing; otherwise, reposition."
    (aSelection = 0 **or**: [self **selectionBox intersects**: self **clippingBox**])
        ifFalse: [self **positionList**. self **displayView**]

Class PhoneBookTextController

class name	PhoneBookTextController
superclass	StringHolderController
instance variable names	"none"
class variable names	PhoneBookTextControllerYellowButtonMenu
	PhoneBookTextControllerYellowButtonMessages
comment	A phone book text controller that handles the accept menu message specially and introduces a remove message.

class methods

class initialization

initialize
    "Initializes the yellow button pop-up menu and corresponding messages."
    "Differs from StringHolderController menu by adding the 'remove' label."

    PhoneBookTextControllerYellowButtonMenu ←
        PopUpMenu
            labels: 'again\undo\copy\cut\paste\doIt\printIt\accept\cancel\remove' **withCRs**
            lines: #(2 5 7).
    PhoneBookTextControllerYellowButtonMessages ←
        #(again undo copySelection cut paste doIt printIt accept cancel remove)

    "PhoneBookTextController initialize"

instance methods

instance initialization

initializeYellowButtonMenu
    self
        yellowButtonMenu: PhoneBookTextControllerYellowButtonMenu
        yellowButtonMessages: PhoneBookTextControllerYellowButtonMessages

menu messages

accept
    "Accepts the text in the view (for insertion)."
    | string aPhoneBookBrowser |
    string ← paragraph **string**. "Note: this is how 'super **accept**' accesses the text. We
        can't say 'model **contents**' because the text has not yet been accepted."
    (string **includes:** Character **cr**)
        ifTrue: [super **accept** "Unlocks the model"]
        ifFalse: [↑3 **timesRepeat:** [view **flash** "illegal"]].

    "Temporarily hide the scroll bars to prevent them from being overwritten by the
    changing list view."
    self **controlTerminate**.

    "Make the change to the browser."
    aPhoneBookBrowser ← view **topView model**. aPhoneBookBrowser **add:** string.

    "Restore the scroll bars."
    self **controlInitialize**

remove
    "Accepts the text in the view (for removal)."
    | string aPhoneBookBrowser |
    string ← paragraph **string**. "Note: this is how 'super **accept**' accesses the text. We
        can't say 'model **contents**' because the text has not yet been accepted."
    (string **includes:** Character **cr**)
        ifTrue: [super **accept** "Unlocks the model"]
        ifFalse: [↑3 **timesRepeat:** [view **flash** "illegal"]].

"Temporarily hide the scroll bars to prevent them from being overwritten by the changing list view."
self **controlTerminate**.

"Make the change to the browser."
aPhoneBookBrowser ← view **topView model**. aPhoneBookBrowser **remove**: string.

"Restore the scroll bars."
self **controlInitialize**

Class PhoneBookTextView

class name	PhoneBookTextView
superclass	StringHolderView
instance variable names	"none"
comment	A phone book text view specially handles update messages from a phone book list view.

instance methods

controller access

defaultControllerClass
    ↑PhoneBookTextController

updating

update: aParameter
    | aPhoneBookBrowser |
    aParameter == #listIndex **ifTrue**: [
        aPhoneBookBrowser ← self **topView model**.
        self **model contents**: aPhoneBookBrowser **retrieve**.
        super **update**: #model "also update the view itself"].

4.3 PLUGGABLE MENU WINDOWS

Specializations **SelectionInListView** and **SelectionInListController** (see Fig. 4.11) of ListView and ListController provide the implementation for **pluggable menus** (also called **pluggable lists**). Pluggable menus permit arbitrary menu items (as opposed to strings) by displaying the first line of the menu item's print string (the entire print string if there are no carriage returns). When a pluggable menu view updates its menu list (at the beginning or in response to a change in the model), it automatically queries the model for a new selection.

4.3.1 Creating Pluggable Menu Windows

Pluggable menu windows are normally created via one of two specialized class messages (although alternatives are used when nondefault delimiters are desired). The class methods are parameterized by a list of five symbols used by the pluggable view and controller as selectors. More details about the basic pluggable windows philosophy is discussed in a special subsection on text windows.

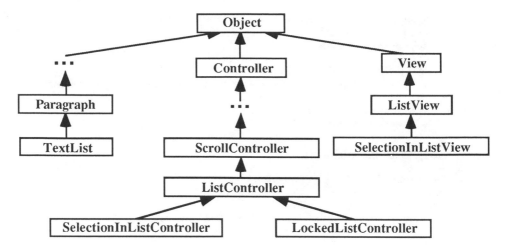

Figure 4.11 The pluggable menu hierarchy.

Obtaining a Pluggable Menu View

Pluggable menu views can be obtained by specifying a model, along with five message selectors that the model must respond to. The first instance creation method is used when the menu items are strings; the second when the items are arbitrary objects (in which case the **printItems** parameter is **true**). If **oneItem** is **true**, the menu list works as a read-only list of one item. This is actually used to provide the root list of subbrowsers spawned from the main browser. It is not likely to be of interest to normal users.

- SelectionInListView
  on: aModel
  aspect: aspectSelector **change**: changeSelector **list**: listSelector
  menu: yellowMenuSelector **initialSelection**: selectionSelector

- SelectionInListView
  on: anObject
  printItems: boolean1 "usually true" **oneItem**: boolean2 "usually false"
  aspect: aspectSelector **change**: changeSelector **list**: listSelector
  menu: yellowMenuSelector **initialSelection**: selectionSelector

If the default delimiters; i.e., the line '------------' of dashes, is to be omitted or replaced, the menu view must instead be obtained in the standard way.

- SelectionInListView **new**

The delimiters are changed or removed with the following protocol inherited from the list view:

- aListView **noTopDelimiter**
- aListView **noBottomDelimiter**
- aListView **topDelimiter**: aStringOrNil
- aListView **bottomDelimiter**: aStringOrNil

The pluggable menu view is then initialized with an instance method that corresponds to the second class method above; i.e.,

- aSelectionInListView
     on: anObject
     printItems: boolean1 "usually true" **oneItem:** boolean2 "usually false"
     aspect: aspectSelector **change:** changeSelector **list:** listSelector
     menu: yellowMenuSelector **initialSelection:** selectionSelector

Designing a Pluggable Menu Model

The model selectors (actually symbols) provided when pluggable menu views are created must be designed to perform the following tasks:

- **aspectSelector** (no parameters) should return the value of the model's aspect; this is part of the general philosophy but is not actually used for pluggable menus. However, this symbol *must* be used as the model's **changed:** parameter for the view to react to the change. Warning: Unlike pluggable text views, pluggable menu views do not have infinite loop protection for the **changed:** message; i.e., the **changed:** message must not result in modifications that cause another **changed:** message on the same aspect.

- **changeSelector** (one parameter) must update the model in response to a new user selection or deselection. The parameter is either a menu item (not a print string of the item but the item itself) if a new selection was made or **nil** if a deselection was made.

- **listSelector** (no parameter) must return an array (not a collection) of the model's menu items. In the situation that the menu items are arbitrary objects, the view must have been created with **printItems** set to **true**.

- **yellowMenuSelector** (no parameter) must return an action menu, a special kind of pop-up menu, that react to yellow button requests.

- **initialSelectionSelector** (no parameters) must return one of the menu items (not its index) or **nil** if no item is to be selected. This selector is not used just once; it is used each time the view reacts to a **changed:** message.

Additionally, the model must be designed to respond to a **changeRequest** message since it is requested by the controller each time a new selection is chosen. This means that the model must have the following method:

- **updateRequest** must return a boolean indicating whether or not the selection should be allowed. If it is disallowed, the view will flash. Note that if omitted, the default **updateRequest** in class Object returns **true**.

The pluggable menu controller, therefore, behaves like a locked-list controller when a suitable **updateRequest** method is provided in the model.

Although standard menu views will work with arbitrary collections (of strings), pluggable menu views require arrays because they search the array to determine the index of the initial selection. It is also possible to set chosen selectors to **nil** to indicate that the corresponding actions are not to be executed. For example, when the change selector is **nil**, new selections are not relayed to the model. When the list selector is **nil**, it assumes an empty list of menu items. When the initial selector is **nil**, it assumes no initial selection. Finally, when the yellow menu selector is **nil**, the standard yellow button menu in the superclass ListView is used.

The pluggable menu views have a much simpler dependency protocol than the nonpluggable variety. The nonpluggable views react to 'model **changed**: #list' or 'model **changed**: #listIndex' messages. The pluggable views react only to 'model **changed**: *aspectSelector*'. When a pluggable menu view reacts, it obtains both a new list and a new list item. As mentioned previously, it also deals with menu items rather than menu item indices.

Example of a Command Executor

For illustration, consider creating a pluggable menu window, as in Fig. 4.12, consisting of commands that can be executed. The menu items play the role of buttons; i.e., selecting an entry causes the associated command to be executed. Note that the menu items are symbols, not strings. Also, the delimiters have been removed.

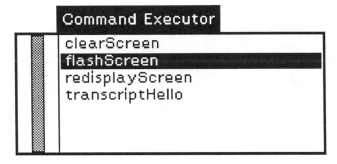

Figure 4.12 A command execution window.

Class CommandExecutor

class name	CommandExecutor
superclass	Object
instance variable names	commands currentCommand
comment	Illustrates a list of commands that can be executed from the menu.

class methods

opening

open
"Create a standard system view with a menu subwindow of commands."
"CommandExecutor open"

| aCommandExecutor topView aMenuView |
aCommandExecutor ← CommandExecutor **new**
    commands: #(clearScreen flashScreen redisplayScreen transcriptHello).

topView ← StandardSystemView **new label**: 'Command Executor'; **borderWidth**: 1.

Inside Smalltalk

```
aMenuView ← (SelectionInListView new)
    noTopDelimiter;
    noBottomDelimiter;
    on: aCommandExecutor printItems: true oneItem: false
        aspect: #newCommands change: #command: list: #commands
        menu: nil initialSelection: #command;
    borderWidth: 1.

topView addSubView: aMenuView.
topView controller open
```

instance methods

commands protocol

command
    ↑currentCommand
command: aCommand
    currentCommand ← aCommand.
    aCommand **isNil ifFalse:** [self **perform:** aCommand]

commands
    ↑commands
commands: aCollectionOfSymbols
    commands ← aCollectionOfSymbols.
    self **changed:** #newCommands

specific commands

clearScreen
    Display **white**

flashScreen
    4 **timesRepeat:** [Display **reverse**]

redisplayScreen
    ScheduledControllers **restore**

transcriptHello
    Transcript **cr; nextPutAll:** 'Hello.'; **cr; endEntry**

4.3.2 The SelectionInListController Protocol

Specialization **SelectionInListController** of ListController simply overrides the red and yellow button activity messages. The code in each case is almost identical to the version higher up in the hierarchy. The **redButtonActivity** method differs by explicitly sending a **changeRequest** message to the model before sending it the changeSelector message. The **yellowButtonActivity** method uses the menu selector associated with the chosen menu item as the message to be sent to the model.

control operations redefined specially for this class

- aSelectionInListController **isControlActive**
- aSelectionInListController **redButtonActivity**
- aSelectionInListController **yellowButtonActivity**
    Minor modifications to ensure that the model is invoked through the proper selector protocols.

4.3.3 The SelectionInListView Protocol

Specialization **SelectionInListView** of ListView provides the majority of the methods for pluggable lists.

instance creation and initialization
- SelectionInListView
    on: anObject
    aspect: aspectSelector **change**: changeSelector **list**: listSelector
    menu: yellowMenuSelector **initialSelection**: selectionSelector
- SelectionInListView
    on: anObject **printItems**: boolean1 **oneItem**: boolean2
    aspect: aspectSelector **change**: changeSelector **list**: listSelector
    menu: yellowMenuSelector **initialSelection**: selectionSelector
- aSelectionInListView
    on: anObject **printItems**: boolean1 **oneItem**: boolean2
    aspect: aspectSelector **change**: changeSelector **list**: listSelector
    menu: yellowMenuSelector **initialSelection**: selectionSelector

list view operations redefined specially for this class
- aSelectionInListView **isEmpty**
- aSelectionInListView **list**: anArray
- aSelectionInListView **displayView**
- aSelectionInListView **update**: aSymbol
- aSelectionInListView **defaultControllerClass**
    The **update**: method obtains a new menu list and selection from the model only if the update parameter is the same as the aspect selector.

operations dealing with the message selectors
- aSelectionInListView **getList**
- aSelectionInListView **initialSelection**
- aSelectionInListView **yellowButtonMenu**
- aSelectionInListView **changeModelSelection**: anInteger
    These messages send corresponding listSelector, selectionSelector, yellowMenuSelector, and changeSelector messages to the model. The **changeModelSelection**: method changes the menu index (anInteger) to an actual menu item or **nil** (if anInteger is zero).

On first glance, it is surprising that so few methods are needed to implement pluggable lists. It is even more surprising when we find that the majority of the methods are small. On second thought, perhaps it is not so surprising. Most of the protocol is actually inherited from list views. Another part of the protocol is left unspecified to be provided as part of the model. For interest's sake, let us consider a few of the methods.

```
aSelectionInListView changeModelSelection: anInteger
    changeMsg ~~ nil ifTrue: [
        model
            perform: changeMsg
            with: (anInteger = 0 ifTrue: [nil] ifFalse: [itemList at: anInteger])]
aSelectionInListView getList
    | item |
    oneItem ifTrue: [
        item ← self initialSelection. item == nil ifTrue: [↑nil]. ↑Array with: item].
    listMsg == nil ifTrue: [↑nil].
    ↑model perform: listMsg
```

```
aSelectionInListView list: anArray
    | item |
    itemList ← anArray. "save it in an instance variable"
    anArray == nil ifTrue: [
        isEmpty ← true. selection ← 0. ↑self changeModelSelection: 0].
    printItems "is it printable"
        ifTrue:[
            super list:
                (anArray collect: [:eachleach printString copyUpTo: Character cr])]
        ifFalse:[super list: anArray].
    item ← self initialSelection.
        "get current selection from the model and convert to an index"
    selection ← item == nil ifTrue: [0] ifFalse: [itemList findFirst: [:x | x = item]].
    selection > 0 ifTrue: [self positionList]. "make it visible"
    self changeModelSelection: selection "superfluous"

aSelectionInListView initialSelection
    initialSelectionMsg == nil ifTrue: [↑nil].
    ↑model perform: initialSelectionMsg

aSelectionInListView yellowButtonMenu
    menuMsg == nil ifTrue: [↑nil].
    ↑model perform: menuMsg

aSelectionInListView update: aSymbol
    aSymbol == partMsg ifTrue: [self list: self getList; displayView]
```

4.3.4 Example: The Electronic Phone Book Revisited

Having previously considered the design of a phone book browser using standard menu and text windows, it is instructive to see the simplification introduced by a pluggable view's implementation. Of course, the design (see Fig. 4.13) looks the same externally. However, it is greatly simplified internally. First of all, the new design consists of only one class: the phone book browser. Second, it profits from a simplified dependency relationship. Also, the text window doesn't have to override the **accept** message; it can use the existing one since it was designed to interface with the pluggable design.

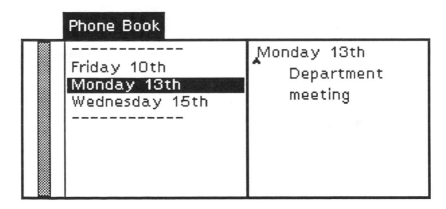

Figure 4.13 Snapshot of the phone book browser implemented with pluggable windows.

We designed the menu view to react only to the #phoneBook aspect and the text view to react only to the #phoneBookEntry aspect. When the menu causes a change that the text view should respond to, we simply make sure that the browser executes 'self **changed**: #phoneBookEntry'. Correspondingly, to make sure that a text view change causes the menu view to respond, we ensure that 'self **changed**: #phoneBook' is executed. This detailed dependency protocol is shown in Fig. 4.14.

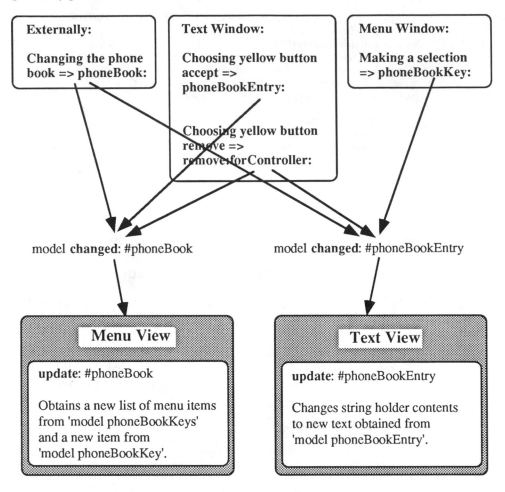

Figure 4.14 The revised phone book browser dependencies.

Class PhoneBookBrowser

class name	PhoneBookBrowser
superclass	Object
instance variable names	phoneBook list listItem
comment	A phone book browser keeps track of a phone book and the current selection in it.

class methods

open: aPhoneBook
"Creates a standard system view with two windows: a pluggable list view for the
phone book keys and a pluggable text view for the value associated with the
selected key in the list view."

"PhoneBookBrowser openPluggableOn: Dictionary new"

| aBrowser topView aMenuView aTextView |
aBrowser ← self **new phoneBook:** aPhoneBook.
topView ← StandardSystemView **new**
    label: 'Phone Book'; **model:** aBrowser; **borderWidth:** 1.

aMenuView ← (SelectionInListView **on:** aBrowser
    aspect: #phoneBook **change:** #phoneBookKey: **list:** #phoneBookKeys
    menu: nil **initialSelection:** #phoneBookKey) **borderWidth:** 1.

aTextView ← (TextView **on:** aBrowser
    aspect: #phoneBookEntry **change:** #phoneBookEntry:
    menu: #yellowButtonMenuForText) **borderWidth:** 1.

topView
    addSubView: aMenuView;
    addSubView: aTextView **toRightOf:** aMenuView.
topView **controller open**

querying

defaultEntry
    ↑'Lastname, Firstname\   Sample data' **withCRs** "there is a tab after the '\'"

instance methods

phone book access

phoneBook
    ↑phoneBook

phoneBook: aDictionary
    self **validate:** aDictionary.
    phoneBook ← aDictionary.
    list ← aDictionary **keys asSortedCollection asArray**. listItem ← nil.
    self **changed:** #phoneBook.
    self **changed:** #phoneBookEntry.

phone book validation

validate: aPhoneBook
    "Makes sure the phone book is a dictionary with strings keys and values."
    | errorMessage |
    errorMessage ← 'invalid phone book'.
    (aPhoneBook **isKindOf:** Dictionary) **ifFalse:** [↑self **error:** errorMessage].
    aPhoneBook **associationsDo:** [:anAssociation |
        ((anAssociation **key isKindOf:** String) & (anAssociation **value isKindOf:** String))
            ifFalse: [↑self **error:** errorMessage]]

phoneBookEntry
"Converts from string to text: The phone book provides a string, the text view requires text."
↑listItem **isNil**
    ifTrue: [PhoneBookBrowser **defaultEntry asText**]
    ifFalse: [(listItem, (String **with**: Character **cr**), (phoneBook **at**: listItem)) **asText**]

phoneBookEntry: aTextValue
    | aStream aStringKey aStringValue |
    "Converts from text to string: The text view provides text, the phone book requires a string."
    (aTextValue **includes**: Character **cr**) **ifFalse**: [↑false "reject the change"].
    aStream ← ReadStream **on**: aTextValue **asString**.
    aStringKey ← aStream **upTo**: Character **cr**. "excluding cr"
    aStringValue ← aStream **upTo**: nil. "the rest of the string"
    phoneBook **at**: aStringKey **put**: aStringValue.
    list ← phoneBook **keys asSortedCollection asArray**. listItem ← aStringKey.
    self **changed**: #phoneBook.
    ↑true "accept the change"

text view support

changeRequestFrom: aTextView
    ↑true "why not"

text view yellow button menu

phoneBookRemove: newText forController: aController
    "Accepts the text in the view."
    | aString aStringKey |
    aString ← newText **asString**.
    (aString **includes**: Character **cr**) **ifFalse**: [↑aController **view flash** "illegal"].
    aStringKey ← aString **copyUpTo**: Character **cr**.
    phoneBook **removeKey**: aStringKey **ifAbsent**: [↑aController **view flash** "illegal"].
    list ← phoneBook **keys asSortedCollection asArray**. listItem ← nil.
    self **changed**: #phoneBook.
    self **changed**: #phoneBookEntry

yellowButtonMenuForText
    ↑ActionMenu
        labels: 'again\undo\copy\cut\paste\do it\print it\accept\cancel\remove' **withCRs**
        lines: #(2 5)
        selectors: #(again undo copySelection cut paste doIt printIt accept cancel
            phoneBookRemove:forController:)

menu view selectors

phoneBookKeys
    "Returns the list of entries."
    ↑list

phoneBookKey
    "Returns the currently selected entry."
    ↑listItem

Inside Smalltalk

phoneBookKey: aString
    "Changes the currently selected entry. We know this comes from the menu window.
    So we do not send a 'self changed: #phoneBook' message. If we did, it would
    deselect and then reselect."
    "Changes the currently selected entry."
    listItem = aString **ifTrue**: [↑self "already done"].
    listItem ← aString.
    self **changed**: #phoneBookEntry

4.4 SUMMARY

This chapter has provided the details of **menu windows** that provide the ability to manipulate scrollable menu items. In particular, we have discussed the following notions:

- The model, view, and controller hierarchies associated with menu windows.

- The standard menu window protocol for classes **ListController**, **LockedList-Controller**, and **ListView**.

- An example that illustrates the use of standard menu windows — an electronic phone book.

- Pluggable menu windows, including the detailed protocol for classes **Selection-InListController** and **SelectionInListView**.

- An example illustrating the use of pluggable menu windows — a simple command executor.

- A more elaborate example that illustrates the use of pluggable menu windows as an alternative to standard menu windows — the electronic phone book revisited.

4.5 EXERCISES

The following exercises are designed to exercise your knowledge of menu windows and their applications.

1. What is the difference between locking for views, string holders, and menu models?

2. Revise **positionList** in ListView so that the current selection is centered (where possible) instead of being at the top of the menu list.

3. Is it true that new selections accepted in the phone book text pane sometimes cause two displays of the list pane? If so, devise a remedy.

4. Use pluggable menu windows to design a facility that permits a user to select one of the messages that a specific object can respond to. Thus '100 **selectMessage**' would provide a list of all messages small integers can respond to. This might be useful in an icon-based environment.

5. Add an Object method, say called **fileRead**, that uses pluggable menus to provide users with a list of files from which to read. The result is the contents of the file as a string.

6. Complete the phone book example so that individual phone books, either in memory or on disk, can be selected by users.

4.6 GLOSSARY AND IMPORTANT FACTS

classes

ListController The basic controller class for standard menu windows.

ListView The view class for standard menu windows.

LockedListController A controller class for standard menu windows that permits scrolling and selecting only when the model is unlocked. When an internal representation of the model differs from the actual model, the actual model is locked.

SelectionInListController The controller class for pluggable menu windows.

SelectionInListView The view class for pluggable menu windows.

TextList A more efficient specialization of Paragraph that clips individual lines if they are too long rather than using wraparound. Used internally by menu windows. This internal representation is distinct from the models that are interrogated to obtain the list of menu items.

selected terminology

delimiter A line of dashes both at the top and bottom of the menu items; can be replaced by any other string or removed entirely if desired.

list controller A controller for list (also called menu) windows.

list window Another term for menu window.

locked The state of a menu window model when it differs from some internal representation of that model. When the two are the same, the model is unlocked.

locked-list controller Differs from a list controller in that menu item selection is prevented when the model is **locked**; i.e., in a state of partial modification. When the model is no longer locked, selection is again enabled.

menu window Provides the ability to manipulate a number of menu items that may not fit in the visible portion of the window; the invisible parts (if any) are made accessible by scrolling.

model list A collection of strings denoting the menu items; differs from the view list maintained internally by the list view.

pluggable list Another term for pluggable menu.

pluggable menu Short for pluggable menu window.

pluggable menu window A menu window designed for user applications where the model is arbitrary; implemented by selection-in-list controllers and selection-in-list views; permits arbitrary menu items (as opposed to strings) by displaying the first line of the menu item's print string (the entire print string if there are no carriage returns).

standard menu window A menu window designed for use in applications where the model is a collection of strings denoting the menu items; scrolls if there are too many menu items; truncates on the right if a menu item is too long to fit; implemented by text lists, either list controllers or locked-list controllers, and list views.

unlocked See locked.

view list An instance of **TextList** (a specialization of **Paragraph**) containing the menu items specially formatted for printing; kept internally by the list view.

list model protocol The list model must respond to messages **list**, **list:**, **listIndex**, and **toggleListIndex:**; if a list view with a locked-list controller instead of the default list controller is desired, the model must additionally respond to the **isUnlocked** message.

pluggable list view parameters Pluggable lists are provided with five message selectors: an **aspect selector**, a **changed aspect selector**, a **list selector**, a **yellow menu selector**, and an **initial menu selection selector**. Additionally, the model must be designed to respond to a **changeRequest** message and an **updateRequest** message. The **aspect selector** returns the **changed:** parameter to be used by the view when reacting to changes to the model (all other parameters result in a no-op). The **changed aspect selector** is used to inform the model of a new selection. The **list selector** is used to obtain the array of menu items. The **yellow menu selector** provides the pop-up menu for the yellow button. Finally, the **initial menu selection selector** provides the menu item to be selected by the view each time a change to the model is made.

5

Switch Windows

5.1 INTRODUCTION

Three varieties of **permanently visible non-scrollable switch windows,** or simply **switch windows** for short, exist (see Fig. 5.1): **pluggable** switch windows, **standard** switch windows, and **switch-menu** windows. The pluggable switch windows permit arbitrary models with model specific yellow button menus and follow the general pluggable windows philosophy. The standard switch windows specialize the pluggable variety by eliminating the ability to create model specific yellow button menus. However, they do permit arbitrary models. Even so, we tend to use pluggable switch windows when dealing with arbitrary models and standard switch windows for switch models. The switch-menu windows permit

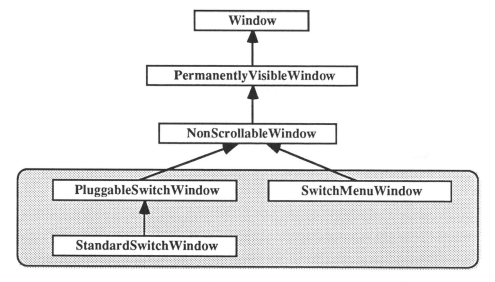

Figure 5.1 Switch windows: A logical view.

menus of pluggable and standard switch windows. They differ from normal windows with associated subwindows only by providing the ability to manipulate the switches through keyboard keys in addition to mouse button activity.

Switches are objects that can be either **on** or **off**. When turned on, an associated block, the **on action**, is executed. Similarly, when turned off, another block, the **off action**, is executed. Two specializations (see Fig. 5.2) exist: buttons and one-on switches. **Buttons** are push-button style switches; i.e., switches that automatically turn off whenever they are turned on. Hence they can't be created in the on position. **One-on switches** are car-radio style switches; i.e., switches connected together in such a manner that only one of them is on at a time. Turning on a one-on switch automatically causes the others connected to it to be turned off. Of course, this also implies that at most one can be on at a time.

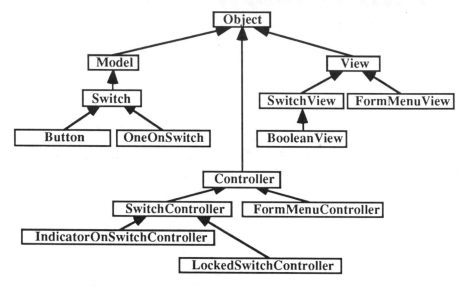

Figure 5.2 The switch model-view-controller hierarchy.

Four kinds of controllers and three kinds of views are provided: (1) **switch controllers, indicator-on switch controllers, locked-switch controllers,** and **form-menu controllers,** along with (2) **switch views, boolean views,** and **form-menu views.**

The switch-menu windows are constructed from form-menu controllers and views. The term form-menu is intended to convey the notion that its subviews are form views; however, this is a clear misnomer since the subviews must actually be switch views. To be correct, we have called them switch-menu windows.

Class **FormMenuController** differs from the standard controller by permitting keyboard characters to switch the subviews; i.e., typing an individual character that has been associated with a specific switch view will cause the switch view's model to switch just as if the mouse button had been depressed on it. The corresponding **FormMenuView** class is essentially the same as class View.

The standard switch windows are obtained by combining any of the remaining model/view/controller possibilities exclusive of boolean views. The pluggable switch windows are obtained by replacing the switch view in a standard switch window by a boolean view. The boolean view is also called a **pluggable switch view**. It is possible to use arbitrary models with standard switch windows, but this is usually relegated to pluggable switch windows by convention.

Class **SwitchController** provides the default controller protocol for switch windows and serves as the basis for its two specializations. Specialization **IndicatorOnSwitchController** provides additional facilities to highlight the view border in gray while switch processing is in progress. This might be used, for example, with a save button that takes a while for the operation to finish. Specialization **LockedSwitchController** provides switch controllers that flash and refuse to take control if the model is locked. This can be used to prevent accidental loss of changes in progress.

Class **SwitchView** provides the standard switch window protocol. Specialization **BooleanView** provides a pluggable facility for displaying switch-like aspects of arbitrary objects. See the section on pluggable windows for more details about their general design and use.

In general, the non-menu views and controllers interface with the models through user-definable **interrogation** and **modification** messages. The default messages are respectively 'model **isOn**' and 'model **switch**'. When these messages are changed, the substitutions enable the windows to treat the models as **switch-like** objects.

5.2 VARIETIES OF SWITCHES

Standard switches, buttons, and one-on switches are often used in switch windows. Nevertheless, they can be used totally independently of such windows.

5.2.1 Creating Switches (a Preview)

All switches except buttons are created with either **newOn** or **newOff**; buttons are created only with **newOff**. Their respective on and off actions are set with **onAction:** and **offAction:**. One-on switches must additionally be associated with a connection object via **connection:**.

Example

- '   switch1 ← Switch **newOn**.
      switch1 **onAction**: [Transcript **show**: 'you turned me on'].
      switch1 **offAction**: [Transcript **show**: 'you turned me off'].

- switch ← (Switch **newOff**) **onAction**: [ScheduledControllers **restore**].
- button← (Button **newOff**) **onAction**: [ScheduledControllers **restore**].

- aSponsor ← Object **new**.
      switchTerse ← OneOnSwitch **newOff**
          connection: aSponsor;
          onAction: [DribbleFile **terse**].
      switchMedium ← OneOnSwitch **newOn**
          connection: aSponsor; **yourself**;
          onAction: [DribbleFile **medium**].
      switchVerbose ← OneOnSwitch **newOff**
          connection: aSponsor;
          onAction: [DribbleFile **verbose**].

Interacting with Switches

In Smalltalk systems prior to version 2.4, when on and off actions are associated with switches, copies are made of the contexts that contain them. To be more specific, a shallow copy of the context is made. The implication is that distinct on and off actions can communicate through local variables in the contexts, but these local variables cannot be changed. For example, consider an example that does not work and one that does.

An Example That Does Not Work

- | counter switchA |
  counter ← 0.
  switchA ← Switch **newOff**.
  switchA **onAction**: [counter ← counter + 1].
  switchA **offAction**: [counter ← counter - 1].

An Example That Does Work

- | counter mailbox switchB |
  counter ← 0. mailbox ← Array **with**: counter.
  switchB ← Switch **newOff**.
  switchB **onAction**: [
      counter←mailbox **at**: 1. counter← counter+1. mailbox **at**: 1 **put**: counter].
  switchB **offAction**: [
      counter←mailbox **at**: 1. counter← counter-1. mailbox **at**: 1 **put**: counter].

When a block is associated with an on or off action, a shallow copy of the block's context is made. Thus, the on action for switchA can be thought of as manipulating counter1; the off action manipulates counter2. Changing counter1 has no effect on counter2. For the second example, the same notion applies; i.e., the on action for switchB can be thought of as manipulating counter1 and mailbox1; the off action manipulates counter2 and mailbox2. Initially, counter1 and counter2 are both zero. More important, mailbox1 and mailbox2 are the same array. Although mailbox2 cannot be rebound to a new value by changing mailbox1, it is nevertheless possible to modify the contents of the shared array.

In Smalltalk version 2.4 or later, blocks are more powerful. Hence, there is no reason for the switches to make copies of the blocks containing contexts. Consequently, both of the previous examples work.

5.2.2 The Switch Protocol

A **switch** is a class of objects that can be either **on** or **off**. Additionally, both an **on action** and an **off action** can be associated with the switch by providing it with corresponding blocks; the default is **nil** (no action). When a switch is turned on (or off), it modifies its local state appropriately, sends itself a *self changed* message, and then executes the corresponding action (if non-**nil**). If the switch is displayed in some view, the view is notified via an *update*: message and appropriately adjusted. The switch protocol is the following:

creating new switch instances

- Switch **newOn**
  Returns a new switch with the on and off actions set to **nil** (no action) and the state set to **on**.
- Switch **newOff**
  Returns a new switch with the on and off actions set to **nil** (no action) and the state set to **off**.
- Switch **new**
  A more traditional alternative to **newOff**.

testing the switch state

- aSwitch **isOn**
  Returns **true** if the switch is on; **false** otherwise.
- aSwitch **isOff**
  Returns **true** if the switch is off; **false** otherwise.

changing the switch state without executing the actions

- aSwitch **set**
  Sets the switch to **on**. If it was previously **off**, *self changed* is sent. The on action is **not** executed.
- aSwitch **clear**
  Sets the switch to **off**. If it was previously **on**, *self changed* is sent. The off action is **not** executed.

changing the switch state with automatic action execution

- aSwitch **turnOn**
  Sets the switch to **on**. If it was previously **off**, *self changed* is sent and the on action is executed.
- aSwitch **turnOff**
  Sets the switch to **off**. If it was previously **on**, *self changed* is sent and the off action is executed.
- aSwitch **switch**
  Performs a **turnOn** if it was originally off; otherwise, a **turnOff**.

setting the actions

- aSwitch **offAction**: anAction
  Sets the off action of the receiver to anAction, either a block or **nil**.
- aSwitch **onAction**: anAction
  Sets the on action of the receiver to anAction, either a block or **nil**.

modifications to the standard dependents processing protocol

- aSwitch **removeDependent**: aDependent
  In addition to the standard dependency processing, sets the on and off actions to **nil** if the last dependent is removed.
- aSwitch **release**
  In addition to the standard dependency processing, sets the on and off actions to **nil**.

It is the on and off actions that provide switches with generality, since these can be tailored to any application. See the **coordinated lights problem** (Sect. 1.4.3) for a detailed example of the use of switches.

5.2.3 The Button Protocol

A **button** is a push-button switch; i.e., a switch that automatically turns itself off when turned on. Since it is a switch, both an **on action** block and an **off action** block can be associated with it; the default is **nil** (no action).

Buttons are assumed to exist only in the off state. Since turning one on immediately causes it to be turned off, there is no need to explicitly record the temporary state change. Since the initial and final states are unchanged, views displaying the button need not be notified. Hence, the two *self changed* messages that would normally result from a turn on followed by an immediate turn off can also be eliminated. This observation leads to an optimization of the **turnOn** and **turnOff** protocol for switches: **turnOn** simply executes the on and off actions; **turnOff** is a no-op.

> *creating new button instances*

- Button **newOn**
  Signals an error. Buttons cannot be created in the on state.
- Switch **newOff**
  When sent to class Button, returns a new button with the on and off actions set to **nil** (no action) and the state set to **off**.
- Switch **new**
  A more traditional alternative to **newOff**.

> *changing the switch state with automatic action execution*

- aButton **turnOn**
  An optimization of 'super **turnOn**' followed by 'super **turnOff**' that eliminates the need to explicitly change the state of the button. It also optimizes out the sending of the two *self changed* messages. The optimized result simply executes the on action followed by the off action.
- aButton **turnOff**
  Effectively a no-op since it assumes the button could not be on. Sets the switch to **off** as a precaution.

Because of the optimizations, the on and off actions should avoid code whose behavior requires testing the status of the button (the status will always be off unless explicitly changed with clear and set — not advisable for buttons).

5.2.4 The OneOnSwitch Protocol

A **one-on switch** is a car-radio type of switch; i.e., when many one-on switches are connected, there is only one on at a time. Turning on a new one automatically causes the others to be turned off. Since it is a switch, both an **on action** block and an **off action** block can be associated with it; the default is **nil** (no action).

To connect a set of one-on switches, an arbitrary object called the **connection** object is created and associated with each one-on switch in the set. This **connection** object is used as a sponsor that keeps track of the one-on switches as dependents. Changing a one-on switch causes a *changed*: self message to be sent to the connection object (for future reference, we'll refer to the self parameter as the turned-on switch). The dependency mechanism causes all connected one-on switches to be sent an *update: turnedOnSwitch* message. The **update**: method turns off the receiver if it is different from the turned-on switch.

instance finalization

- aOneOnSwitch **release**

    Extends the standard switch release protocol by disconnecting itself from the connection.

changing the switch state with automatic action execution

- aOneOnSwitch **turnOn**

    Sets the switch to **on**. If it was previously **off**, *self changed* is sent, all connected one-on switches are turned off, and its on action is executed.

- aSwitch **turnOff**

    Sets the switch to **off**. If it was previously **on**, *self changed* is sent and the off action is executed.

connection manipulation

- aOneOnSwitch **connection**

    Returns this switch's connection object.

- aOneOnSwitch **connection**: anObject

    Associates this switch with the newly specified connection object.

- aOneOnSwitch **isConnectionSet**

    Returns **true** if this switch's connection object is non-**nil**.

- aOneOnSwitch **notifyConnection**

    Turns off all other one-on switches associated with this switch's connection object.

updating

- aOneOnSwitch **update**: triggeringOneOnSwitch

    Does nothing if triggeringOneOnSwitch is this switch; otherwise, turns off this switch. This message is sent (indirectly) by the triggering one-on switch when it is turned on.

Details of the OneOnSwitch Change/Update Protocol

When a one-on switch is turned off, the standard switch protocol is followed; i.e., it sets its state to off, sends itself a '*changed: self*' message, and executes the off action. The protocol changes when such a switch is turned on. In that case, it sets its state to on, sends itself and its connection a '*changed: self*' message, and executes its off action. Sending itself a '*changed: self*' message causes any dependent view, for example, to react and redisplay itself. Sending the connection a '*changed: self*' causes it (and any other switch associated with the same connection) to be sent an '*update: triggeringOneOnSwitch*' message. The triggering switch ignores the message; all others turn off. The details are provided in the following:

- aOneOnSwitch **turnOn**
  "Sets the switch to **on**. If it was previously **off**, *self changed* is sent, all connected one-on switches are turned off, and its on action is executed."
  self **isOff ifTrue**: [
      on ← true. self **changed**. self **notifyConnection**. self **doAction**: onAction]

- aOneOnSwitch **notifyConnection**
  "Turns off all other one-on switches that are connected."
  self **isConnectionSet ifTrue**: [self **connection changed**: self]

- aOneOnSwitch **update**: triggeringOneOnSwitch
  "Does nothing if triggeringOneOnSwitch is identical to this one; otherwise, turns off this switch. This message is sent (indirectly) by the triggering one-on switch when it is turned on."
  self ~~ triggeringOneOnSwitch **ifTrue**: [self **turnOff**]

5.3 STANDARD SWITCH WINDOWS

As we described in a previous section, standard switch windows are normally constructed from standard switch controllers and views (see Fig. 5.3). The standard switch controllers can be replaced by **indicator-on** switch controllers or **locked** switch controllers. The former highlight the view border in gray while switch processing is in progress; the latter flash and refuse to take control if the model is locked.

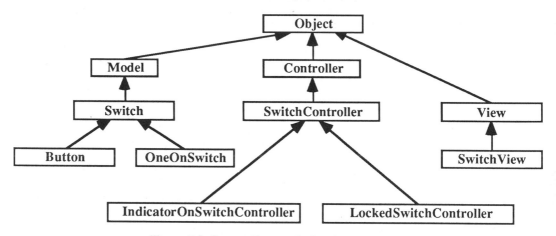

Figure 5.3 Support for standard switch windows.

Indicator-on switch controllers are used to provide visual feedback on switch operations that take a long time to complete; e.g., a file-out operation of some sort. The locked switch controllers are used to prevent accidental loss of changes in progress (see text and menu windows for equivalent controllers). Note that locked switch controllers cannot be used with switches since these to not respond to **isLocked**; they are intended for appropriately designed application models.

5.3.1 Creating Standard Switch Windows (a Preview)

Standard switch windows are obtained by (1) creating a suitable model; e.g., a switch, (2) associating an appropriate on- or off-action for the case where it is a switch, (3) choosing a visual representation for the model; i.e., some display object like a paragraph, form, or path that will serve as the picture for the model (this is called the **label** for the view), (4) optionally choosing a highlight object to be superimposed over the label, (5) instantiating a switch view, and (6) associating the model, label, and highlight object with the view.

When a switch is off, the corresponding view is said to be in **normal mode**; when the switch is on, it is in **complemented mode**. When no label is provided (or **nil** is provided), normal mode is displayed in white and complemented mode in black. If a label is provided (any display object; e.g., display text, paragraphs, forms, paths), it is displayed in the standard way for normal mode and complemented otherwise. If an additional **highlight object** is provided, this object is displayed (over the label) when the view is in complemented mode.

When used by form-menu views (as subviews), it is also possible to associate a **key character** with the switch view. This key character is used for switching the view without having to manipulate the mouse. We will discuss this further in the section dealing with switch-menu windows.

The switch view is also provided with an **interrogation message** in the form of a **selector** and a list of **arguments** that can be sent to the switch to determine its status. The default interrogation message is **isOn** with no arguments; i.e., 'model **isOn**'. Correspondingly, the switch controller is provided with a **modification message** also in the form of **a selector** and a list of **arguments** that can be sent to the switch. The default modification message is **switch** with no arguments; i.e., 'model **switch**'.

Switch views are almost never intended to be scheduled views. They are intended as subviews for other relevant views. All of the examples that follow use standard system views.

Obtaining Simple Switch Windows

The simplest strategy uses labels obtained by converting strings to paragraphs or forms. The former result in unscaled pictures since paragraph text is never size-adjusted when a view is resized. Forms, on the other hand, are adjusted.

For the first example (see Fig. 5.4), we construct a window with three switch views: one for each of three colored buttons. We use the term *pressing the button* to mean depressing the mouse over the corresponding switch view. When a button is pressed (the green button in the figure), the view is temporarily highlighted. If the mouse is released outside the view, the highlighting disappears and nothing happens. If the mouse is released inside the view, the highlighting also disappears but the button is turned on. This causes the corresponding color (as a string) to be sent to the transcript. When the button is on, the view is displayed in reverse video; i.e., black and white interchanged. The view is in complemented mode. However, this is very short lived because buttons can't stay on. The view immediately changes to normal mode.

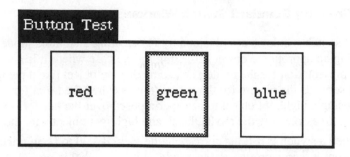

Figure 5.4 Switch windows: Buttons affecting the transcript.

| topView redButton greenButton blueButton redButtonView greenButtonView blueButtonView |

topView ← StandardSystemView **new**
    label: 'Button Test'; **insideColor**: Form **white**; **borderWidth**: 2.

redButton ← Button **newOff onAction**: [Transcript **show**: 'red '].
greenButton ← Button **newOff onAction**: [Transcript **show**: 'green '].
blueButton ← Button **newOff onAction**: [Transcript **show**: 'blue '].

redButtonView ← SwitchView **new label**: 'red' **asParagraph; model**: redButton.
greenButtonView ← SwitchView **new label**: 'green' **asParagraph; model**: greenButton.
blueButtonView ← SwitchView **new label**: 'blue' **asParagraph; model**: blueButton.

topView
    window: Display **boundingBox;** "helps eliminate transformation roundoff errors"
    addSubView: redButtonView **in**: (0.1@0.1 **corner**: 0.3@0.9) **borderWidth**: 1;
    addSubView: greenButtonView **in**: (0.4@0.1 **corner**: 0.6@0.9) **borderWidth**: 1;
    addSubView: blueButtonView **in**: (0.7@0.1 **corner**: 0.9@0.9) **borderWidth**: 1.

topView **controller open**

The next example (Fig. 5.5) demonstrates the button on- and off-actions affecting a locally defined text collector. The standard system view uses a 2-pixel border while the text collector subview uses a 0-pixel border.

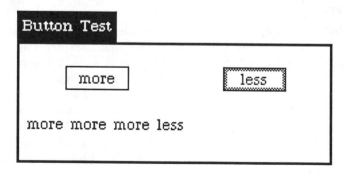

Figure 5.5 Switch windows: Buttons affecting a local text collector window.

```
| topView transcriptView myTextCollector moreButton lessButton moreButtonView
lessButtonView |

topView ← StandardSystemView new
    label: 'Button Test'; insideColor: Form white; borderWidth: 2.
transcriptView ← TextCollectorView container: (myTextCollector ← TextCollector new).

moreButton ← Button newOff onAction: [myTextCollector show: 'more '].
lessButton ← Button newOff onAction: [myTextCollector show: 'less '].

moreButtonView ← SwitchView new label: 'more' asParagraph; model: moreButton.
lessButtonView ← SwitchView new label: 'less' asParagraph; model: lessButton.

topView
    addSubView: transcriptView in: (0@0.6 corner: 1@1) borderWidth: 0;
    addSubView: moreButtonView in: (0.15@0.2 corner: 0.35@0.4) borderWidth: 1;
    addSubView: lessButtonView in: (0.65@0.2 corner: 0.85@0.4) borderWidth: 1.

topView controller open
```

The final example illustrates interacting switches. When the last button change causes both buttons to be off, the output on the local text collector is transparent; when they end up both on, the output is gray; otherwise, either black or white is output. Fig. 5.6 illustrates the two switches while they are on with the white switch about to be turned off.

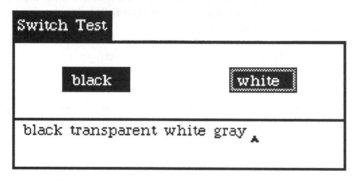

Figure 5.6 Switch windows: Interacting actions.

```
| topView transcriptView myTextCollector aBag color blackButton whiteButton
blackButtonView  whiteButtonView |

topView ← StandardSystemView new
    label: 'Switch Test'; insideColor: Form white; borderWidth: 2.
transcriptView ← TextCollectorView container: (myTextCollector ← TextCollector new).

aBag ← Bag new.
color ← [:bag |
    bag size = 0
        ifTrue: ['transparent ']
        ifFalse: [bag size=2 ifTrue: ['gray '] ifFalse: [bag asOrderedCollection first]]].

blackButton ← Switch newOff
    onAction: [aBag add: 'black '. myTextCollector show: (color value: aBag)];
    offAction: [aBag remove: 'black '. myTextCollector show: (color value: aBag)].
```

```
whiteButton ← Switch newOff
    onAction: [aBag add: 'white '. myTextCollector show: (color value: aBag)];
    offAction: [aBag remove: 'white '. myTextCollector show: (color value: aBag)].

blackButtonView ← SwitchView new
    label: 'black' asDisplayText form; model: blackButton.
whiteButtonView ← SwitchView new
    label: 'white' asDisplayText form; model: whiteButton.

topView
    window: Display boundingBox; "helps eliminate transformation roundoff errors"
    addSubView: blackButtonView in: (0.15@0.2 corner: 0.35@0.4) borderWidth: 1;
    addSubView: whiteButtonView in: (0.65@0.2 corner: 0.85@0.4) borderWidth: 1;
    addSubView: transcriptView in: (0@0.6 corner: 1@1) borderWidth: 0.

transcriptView borderWidthLeft: 0 right: 0 top: 2 bottom: 0. "changed my mind"

topView controller open
```

Obtaining Tailored Switch Windows

Switch windows can be tailored in two ways: (1) by providing a highlight object that is overlaid on top of the label when the switch is on, and (2) by changing the default **interrogation message** 'model **isOn**' and the default **modification message** 'model **switch**' messages. The highlight object is changed via the following. Note that the name is a misnomer; i.e., the object need not be a form.

- aSwitchView **highlightForm**: aDisplayObject

The interrogation message is changed as follows:

- aSwitchView **selector**: aSymbol; **arguments**: anArray

The modification message is changed similarly.

- aSwitchController **selector**: aSymbol; **arguments**: anArray

The view deals with the interrogation message, while the controller deals with the modification message. This can be easy to remember if you notice that "views ask" and "controllers change."

For the first example (see Fig. 5.7), we use a text collector as the model. Both the interrogation and modification messages are changed.

```
| topView transcriptView myTextCollector hotButtonView coldButtonView |

topView ← StandardSystemView new
    label: 'Transcript As Button Test'; insideColor: Form white; borderWidth: 2.
transcriptView ← TextCollectorView container: (myTextCollector ← TextCollector new).

hotButtonView ← SwitchView new label: 'hot' asDisplayText; model: myTextCollector.
coldButtonView ← SwitchView new label: 'cold' asDisplayText; model: myTextCollector.

hotButtonView selector: #isNil; arguments: #(). "anything that returns false => not on"
hotButtonView controller selector: #show:; arguments: #('hot ').
```

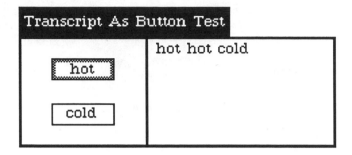

Figure 5.7 Switch windows with text collector models.

coldButtonView **selector**: #isNil; **arguments**: #(). "anything that returns false => not on"
coldButtonView **controller selector**: #show:; **arguments**: #('cold ').

topView
    window: Display **boundingBox**; "helps eliminate transformation roundoff errors"
    addSubView: hotButtonView **in**: (0.1@0.2 **corner**: 0.3@0.4) **borderWidth**: 1;
    addSubView: coldButtonView **in**: (0.1@0.6 **corner**: 0.3@0.8) **borderWidth**: 1;
    addSubView: transcriptView **in**: (0.4@0 **corner**: 1@1) **borderWidth**: 0.

transcriptView **borderWidthLeft**: 2 **right**: 0 **top**: 0 **bottom**: 0. "changed my mind"

topView **controller open**

The second example (see Fig. 5.8) illustrates the use of forms for the first time. The arrow buttons are used to move a box switch in the bottom third of the window. A highlight object (actually a black box) is used with the box switch. When the box switch is off, it is gray; when on, it is black. After it had been moved down and to the right, the box switch, as shown in Fig. 5.8, was about to be turned on.

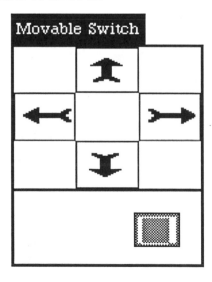

Figure 5.8 Switch windows: A movable switch with a highlight.

| upArrow leftArrow rightArrow downArrow grayBox blackBox upButton leftButton
rightButton downButton topView upButtonView leftButtonView rightButtonView
downButtonView boxSwitchView viewContainingButtons viewContainingBoxSwitch |

leftArrow ← (Form
        extent: 20@20
        fromArray: #(
            2r0000000000000000 2r0000000000000000
            2r0000000000000000 2r0000000000000000
            2r0000000000000000 2r0000000000000000
            2r0000000000000000 2r0000000000000000
            2r0000001000000000 2r0000000000000000
            2r0000011000000000 2r0110000000000000
            2r0000111000000000 2r1110000000000000
            2r0001111000000001 2r1100000000000000
            2r0011111111111111 2r1100000000000000
            2r0111111111111111 2r1000000000000000
            2r0111111111111111 2r1000000000000000
            2r0011111111111111 2r1100000000000000
            2r0001111000000001 2r1100000000000000
            2r0000111000000000 2r1110000000000000
            2r0000011000000000 2r0110000000000000
            2r0000001000000000 2r0000000000000000
            2r0000000000000000 2r0000000000000000
            2r0000000000000000 2r0000000000000000
            2r0000000000000000 2r0000000000000000
            2r0000000000000000 2r0000000000000000)
        offset: 0@0).

rightArrow ← (Form
        extent: 20@20
        fromArray: #(
            2r0000000000000000 2r0000000000000000
            2r0000000000000000 2r0000000000000000
            2r0000000000000000 2r0000000000000000
            2r0000000000000000 2r0000000000000000
            2r0000000000000100 2r0000000000000000
            2r0110000000000110 2r0000000000000000
            2r0111000000000111 2r0000000000000000
            2r0011100000000111 2r1000000000000000
            2r0011111111111111 2r1100000000000000
            2r0001111111111111 2r1110000000000000
            2r0001111111111111 2r1110000000000000
            2r0011111111111111 2r1100000000000000
            2r0011100000000111 2r1000000000000000
            2r0111000000000111 2r0000000000000000
            2r0110000000000110 2r0000000000000000
            2r0000000000000100 2r0000000000000000
            2r0000000000000000 2r0000000000000000
            2r0000000000000000 2r0000000000000000
            2r0000000000000000 2r0000000000000000
            2r0000000000000000 2r0000000000000000)
        offset: 0@0).

```smalltalk
upArrow ← (Form
    extent: 20@20
    fromArray: #( 0 0 96 0 240 0 504 0 1020 0 2046 0 4095 0 240 0 240 0 240 0 240 0
        240 0 240 0 240 0 240 0 504 0 1020 0 1950 0 1542 0 0 0)
    offset: 0@0).

downArrow ← (Form
    extent: 20@20
    fromArray: #( 0 0 1542 0 1950 0 1020 0 504 0 240 0 240 0 240 0 240 0 240 0 240 0
        240 0 240 0 4095 0 2046 0 1020 0 504 0 240 0 96 0 0 0)
    offset: 0@0).


grayBox ← (Form extent: 20@20) gray. blackBox ← (Form extent: 20@20) black.


topView ← StandardSystemView new label: 'Movable Switch'; borderWidth: 1.
boxSwitchView ← SwitchView new
    label: grayBox; highlightForm: blackBox; model: Switch newOff.
viewContainingButtons ← View new insideColor: Form white.
viewContainingBoxSwitch ← View new insideColor: Form white.


upButton ← Button new
    onAction: [boxSwitchView translateBy: 0@-25. viewContainingBoxSwitch display].
leftButton ← Button newOff
    onAction: [boxSwitchView translateBy: -25@0. viewContainingBoxSwitch display].
rightButton ← Button newOff
    onAction: [boxSwitchView translateBy: 25@0. viewContainingBoxSwitch display].
downButton ← Button newOff
    onAction: [boxSwitchView translateBy: 0@25. viewContainingBoxSwitch display].


upButtonView ← SwitchView new label: upArrow; model: upButton.
leftButtonView ← SwitchView new label: leftArrow; model: leftButton.
rightButtonView ← SwitchView new label: rightArrow; model: rightButton.
downButtonView ← SwitchView new label: downArrow; model: downButton.


topView
    window: Display boundingBox; "helps eliminate transformation roundoff errors"
    addSubView: viewContainingButtons in: (0@0 corner: 1@0.66) borderWidth: 1;
    addSubView: viewContainingBoxSwitch in: (0@0.66 corner: 1@1) borderWidth: 1.


viewContainingButtons
    window: Display boundingBox; "helps eliminate transformation roundoff errors"
    addSubView: upButtonView in: (0.33@0 corner: 0.66@0.33) borderWidth: 1;
    addSubView: leftButtonView in: (0.0@0.33 corner: 0.33@0.66) borderWidth: 1;
    addSubView: rightButtonView in: (0.66@0.33 corner: 1@0.66) borderWidth: 1;
    addSubView: downButtonView in: (0.33@0.66 corner: 0.66@1) borderWidth: 1.


viewContainingBoxSwitch
    window: Display boundingBox; "helps eliminate transformation roundoff errors"
    addSubView: boxSwitchView in: (0.4@0.3 corner: 0.6@0.7) borderWidth: 1.


topView controller open
```

5.3.2 Varieties of Switch Controllers

The Switch Controller Protocol

A **switch controller** coordinates the interactions between a switch (the model) and a switch view. The switch controller is also provided with a **modification message** in the form of a **selector** and a list of **arguments** that can be sent to the switch when the mouse button is depressed in the switch view. The default modification message is **switch** with no arguments; i.e., 'model **switch**'.

instance creation

- Controller **new**
    When sent to SwitchController, returns a new initialized switch controller.

instance initialization

- aSwitchController **initialize**
    Initializes the controller by setting the default selector to **switch** and the default arguments to an empty array; i.e., the default modification message to 'model **switch**'.

selector manipulation

- aSwitchController **selector**
    Returns the selector part of the modification message.
- aSwitchController **selector**: aSymbol
    Changes the selector part of the modification message and returns the controller.

argument manipulation

- aSwitchController **arguments**
    Returns the arguments part of the modification message.
- aSwitchController **arguments**: anArray
    Changes the arguments part of the modification message and returns the controller.
- aSwitchController **addArgument**: anObject
    Adds anObject to the arguments part of the modification message (as the last argument) and returns the controller.

cursor manipulation

- aSwitchController **cursor**: aCursor
    Sets up the cursor to be used when the mouse enters the switch view (the default is no change). The cursor is changed even if no button is depressed. No facility is provided to restore the original cursor when the view is left. This feature is used by binary-choice views, for example, to indicate thumbs-up or thumbs-down cursors. Returns the controller.

operations for communicating with the model

- aSwitchController **sendMessage**
    Sends the modification message to the model; i.e., 'model **perform**: selector **withArguments**: arguments'.

basic control sequence

- aSwitchController **isControlWanted**
- aSwitchController **isControlActive**

- aSwitchController **controlActivity**
- aSwitchController **controlInitialize**
- aSwitchController **controlTerminate**

> Provides the basic switch control protocol. See the following section for more details.

The Control Sequence Protocol in More Detail

Control is given (**isControlWanted**) only when the red button is depressed in the view. Additionally, the cursor is changed to the switch controller cursor if the mouse is within the view, independent of whether or not the button is depressed.

When control is granted, the boundary of the view is highlighted (**controlInitialize**) and the controller busy waits (**controlActivity**) as long as the button remains depressed in the view (**isControlActive**). When the button is released or the view is exited, the boundary of the view is again highlighted and the model is sent the modification message if the mouse is in the view (**controlTerminate**).

The default modification message is to switch the polarity of the model. This causes the view to be notified via an **update:** message and redrawn to indicate the new status of the switch. Since the relevant methods are so short, they are provided in detail below.

switch control protocol

- aSwitchController **isControlWanted**
  self **viewHasCursor ifTrue:** [cursor == nil **ifFalse:** [cursor **show**]].
  ↑self **viewHasCursor** & sensor **redButtonPressed**

- aSwitchController **isControlActive**
  ↑sensor **anyButtonPressed** & self **viewHasCursor**

- aSwitchController **controlActivity**
  ↑self

- aSwitchController **controlInitialize**
  view **indicatorReverse** "highlights the boundary"

- aSwitchController **controlTerminate**
  view **indicatorReverse**. "highlights the boundary"
  self **viewHasCursor ifTrue:** [self **sendMessage**]
  "Note: sendMessage invokes the change/update: mechanism."

The IndicatorOnSwitchController Protocol

An **indicator-on switch controller** is a switch controller that grays the border of its view while the model handles the modification messages it is sent. Thus the user can tell that the activity is in progress. An example use for such a controller would be in a save window for a specialized editor like a graphics editor.

extensions to the basic control protocol

- anIndicatorOnSwitchController **sendMessage**
  "Provide the user with a visual indication of activity."
  view **indicatorOnDuring:** [model **perform:** selector **withArguments:** arguments]]

The LockedSwitchController Protocol

A **locked-switch controller** is a switch controller that refuses to take control if the model is locked. As an indication, the view flashes.

extensions to the basic control protocol

- aLockedSwitchController **isControlWanted**
  "Flashes when the model is locked, independent of whether or not control could be given. The remainder of the protocol is inherited from switch controllers."
  model **isLocked ifTrue**: [view **flash**. ↑false].
  ↑super **isControlWanted**

5.3.3 Varieties of Switch Views

The Switch View Protocol

A **switch view** is designed to display a switch either in **normal mode**, when the switch is off, or in **complemented mode**, when the switch is on. The default is to display the view in white for normal mode and in black for complemented mode. If a **label** is provided (any display object; e.g., display text, paragraphs, forms, paths), the label is centered in the view and displayed in the standard way for normal mode and complemented otherwise. If a **highlight object** is provided, it is displayed over the inset display box when the view is in complemented mode. As designed, it is not possible to have distinct forms for each mode. However, it is easy to design a specialization that uses the label in normal mode and the highlight object in complemented mode.

When used in combination with form-menu views (as subviews), it is also possible to associate a **key character** with the switch view. This key character is used for switching the view without having to manipulate the mouse.

The switch view is also provided with an **interrogation message** in the form of a **selector** and a list of **arguments** that can be sent to the switch to determine its status. The default interrogation message is **isOn** with no arguments; i.e., 'model **isOn**'.

Although the feature is not currently used, the label is also permitted to be a view. The protocol is extended to automatically release the label in case it might be a view. It might also be possible to replace the highlight object by a view, but no extension has been provided to automatically release it.

instance creation

- View **new**
  When sent to SwitchView, returns a new initialized switch view.

instance initialization and finalization

- aSwitchView **initialize**
  Initializes the view to normal mode, sets the inside color to white, the label and highlighted form to **nil**, and the default interrogation message to 'model **isOn**'.

Inside Smalltalk

- **aSwitchView release**

  Releases the label in addition to the view. Releasing the label has no effect unless it happens to be a view, a feature that is not currently used.

selector manipulation

- **aSwitchView selector**

  Returns the selector part of the interrogation message.
- **aSwitchView selector**: aSymbol

  Changes the selector part of the interrogation message and returns the view.

argument manipulation

- **aSwitchView arguments**

  Returns the arguments part of the interrogation message.
- **aSwitchView arguments**: anArray

  Changes the arguments part of the interrogation message and returns the view.

label and highlight form manipulation

- **aSwitchView label**

  Returns the label, a display object, that is the switch view's screen image. Example display objects include display text, paragraphs, forms, and paths.
- **aSwitchView label**: aDisplayObject

  Changes the label's screen image to aDisplayObject and returns the view. Automatically releases the original label in case it was a view.
- **aSwitchView centerLabel**

  Centers the label in the view.
- **aSwitchView highlightForm**: aDisplayObject

  Changes the highlight object to aDisplayObject. This object is overlayed on the label's screen image when the view is in complemented mode.

key character manipulation

- **aSwitchView key**: aCharacter

  Changes the switch view's key character to aCharacter. This key character (used by form-menu views when the switch view is a subview) is used for switching the view without having to manipulate the mouse.
- **aSwitchView containsKey**: aCharacter

  Returns **true** if aCharacter is equal to the switch view's key character.

controller access

- **aSwitchView defaultControllerClass**

  Returns class SwitchController.

extensions to the standard window access protocol

- **aSwitchView defaultWindow**

  Returns the usual default window if the label is **nil**, or a slightly enlarged copy of the label's bounding box otherwise. The extra space provides room for highlighting or dehighlighting the boundary of the view in gray (see **indicatorReverse**).
- **aSwitchView window**: aWindow

  Extends the standard protocol by additionally centering the label.

displaying the view

- aSwitchView **display**
- aSwitchView **displaySpecial**
- aSwitchView **displaySpecialComplemented**
- aSwitchView **displayNormal**
- aSwitchView **displayComplemented**
- aSwitchView **displayView**
  Method **display** rather than **displayView** must be used to display the view (see the following section for a more detailed look at the display protocol).

highlighting the boundary of the view

- aSwitchView **indicatorReverse**
  Reverses the boundary highlight; i.e., depending on its current status, either highlights or dehighlights the boundary of the view in gray.
- aSwitchView **indicatorOnDuring**: aBlock
  Executes aBlock while the boundary and view are highlighted. A view is highlighted by complementing it.

deemphasizing the view

- aSwitchView **deEmphasizeView**
  Behaves as a no-op when the view is in normal mode; otherwise, grays the view.

updating

- aSwitchView **update**: aParameter
  Updates the view mode to reflect the on/off status of the model and redisplays the view.

interfacing with the switch model

- aSwitchView **interrogateModel**
  Returns the result of sending the interrogation message to the model (the default is 'model **isOn**').

The Display Protocol in More Detail

The display protocol is partitioned into a number of small methods, presumably to permit specializations in future subclasses.

The complete protocol can be best understood by coalescing the separate methods into one, as shown in the following example. It also contains a minor problem. The display fails if a highlight form is provided without a label, because it attempts to access the nonexistent label bounding box. This problem is fixed by replacing the label bounding box center by the window center. In fact, it should be possible to change all other references to the bounding box center in this same way.

aSwitchView **coalescedDisplay**
"Displays the view taking into account the status of the model, the label, and the highlight form."

self **displayBorder**.
complemented ← self **interrogateModel**. "update the view's mode"
highlightForm == nil
    ifTrue: [
        "If there is no highlight form, clear the inset display box, display the label (if there is one), and additionally highlight it if in complemented mode."
        self **clearInside**.
        label == nil **ifFalse**: [
            label
                displayOn: Display
                transformation: self **displayTransformation**
                clippingBox: self **insetDisplayBox**
                fixedPoint: label **boundingBox** center].
        complemented **ifTrue**: [self **highlight**]]
    ifFalse: [
        "If there is a highlight form, display it if in complemented mode. The label (if non-nil) is displayed under the highlight form."
        complemented
            ifTrue: [
                highlightForm
                    displayOn: Display
                    transformation: self **displayTransformation**
                    clippingBox: self **insetDisplayBox**
                    fixedPoint: *self window center*.
                label == nil **ifFalse**: [
                    label
                        displayOn: Display
                        transformation: self **displayTransformation**
                        clippingBox: self **insetDisplayBox**
                        align: label **boundingBox** center
                        with: label **boundingBox** center
                        rule: Form **under mask**: Form **black**]]

The actual methods provided are detailed below without modification. Note that **displayView** should be taken as a private operation since it always displays the label independent of the view's status.

the display protocol

- aSwitchView **display**
    "Displays the view taking into account the status of the model, the label, and the highlight form."

    self **displayBorder**.
    complemented ← self **interrogateModel**.
    highlightForm == nil
        ifTrue: [self **displayView**. complemented **ifTrue**: [self **highlight**]]
        ifFalse: [self **displaySpecial**]

- aSwitchView **displayView**
  "Displays the view assuming it is in normal mode and there is no highlight form."
  self **clearInside**.
  label == nil **ifFalse**: [
      label
          displayOn: Display
          transformation: self **displayTransformation**
          clippingBox: self **insetDisplayBox**
          fixedPoint: label **boundingBox** center]

- aSwitchView **displaySpecial**
  "Displays the view assuming there is a highlight form."
  complemented **ifTrue**: [self **displaySpecialComplemented**].
  label == nil **ifFalse**: [
      label
          displayOn: Display
          transformation: self displayTransformation
          clippingBox: self **insetDisplayBox**
          align: label **boundingBox** center
          with: label **boundingBox** center
          rule: Form **under mask**: Form **black**]

- aSwitchView **displaySpecialComplemented**
  "Displays the view assuming it is in complemented mode and there is a highlight form."
  highlightForm
      displayOn: Display
      transformation: self **displayTransformation**
      clippingBox: self **insetDisplayBox**
      fixedPoint: label **boundingBox** center

The update method changes the mode of the view to reflect the status of the model and redisplays it. As an optimization, it assumes the view is already visible.

the optimized protocol with side effects for updating

- aSwitchView **displayComplemented**
  "Changes the view to complemented mode and highlights it if it was previously in normal mode."
  complemented **ifFalse**: [complemented ← true. self highlight]

- aSwitchView **displayNormal**
  "Changes the view to normal mode and highlights it if it was previously in complemented mode."
  complemented **ifTrue**: [complemented ← false. self **highlight**]

- aSwitchView **update**: aParameter
  "Updates the view's mode to reflect the status of the model and displays the view."
  highlightForm == nil
      ifTrue: [
          self interrogateModel
              ifTrue: [self **displayComplemented**]
              ifFalse: [self **displayNormal**]]
      ifFalse: [self **display**]

Creating a Specialization with Distinct Label and Highlight Objects

By generalizing the protocol so that labels and highlight objects are not overlayed, switch views with independent on and off pictures can be constructed. Thus, we could have a smiling face for normal mode and a frowning face for complemented mode. Changes to the original are shown below in italics. Of course, it is still possible to get the previous behavior — take the initial highlight object and merge it with the label.

Class NonOverlayingSwitchView

class name	NonOverlayingSwitchView
superclass	SwitchView
instance variable names	"none"
comment	Uses the label in normal mode and the highlight object in complemented mode.

instance methods

the display protocol

displaySpecial
    "Displays the view assuming there is a highlight form."
    complemented
        ifTrue: [self **displaySpecialComplemented**]
        ifFalse: [
            label == nil **ifFalse:** [
                label
                    displayOn: Display
                    transformation: self **displayTransformation**
                    clippingBox: self **insetDisplayBox**
                    align: *self window center*
                    with: *self window center*
                    rule: Form **under mask:** Form **black**]]

displaySpecialComplemented
    "Displays the view assuming it is in complemented mode and there is a highlight form."
    highlightForm
        displayOn: Display
        transformation: self **displayTransformation**
        clippingBox: self **insetDisplayBox**
        fixedPoint: *self window center*

Boundary Highlighting and Deemphasizing in Detail

The **indicatorReverse** method highlights the boundary by reversing the inset display box and then reversing a slightly smaller box (inset by 2 pixels). In effect, this is a no-op for the smaller box. However, the 2-pixel wide border is only reversed once. By using a gray mask instead of a black one, the result is a gray border.

- aSwitchView **indicatorReverse**
  "Reverses the boundary highlight; i.e., either highlights or dehighlights the boundary of the view in gray. Which is done depends on its current status."
  Display **reverse**: self **insetDisplayBox mask**: Form **gray**.
  Display **reverse**: (self **insetDisplayBox insetBy**: 2) **mask**: Form **gray**

The **deEmphasizeView** method is a no-op if the view is in normal mode. Otherwise, the inset display box is shifted right by 1 pixel and filled with a light gray color underneath.

deEmphasizing

- aSwitchView **deEmphasizeView**
  "Shift right and underlay with light gray."
  | newForm |
  complemented **ifTrue**: [
      self **highlight**.
      newForm ← Form **fromDisplay**: self **insetDisplayBox**.
      newForm
          displayOn: Display
          at: (self **insetDisplayBox topLeft** + (1@0))
          clippingBox: self **insetDisplayBox**
          rule: Form **under mask**: Form **black**.
      Display
          fill: self **insetDisplayBox rule**: Form **under mask**: Form **lightGray**]

5.4 PLUGGABLE SWITCH WINDOWS

Pluggable switch windows are obtained from boolean views. These use standard switch controllers as the default (see Fig. 5.9). The standard switch controllers can be replaced by **indicator-on** switch controllers or **locked** switch controllers. As described in a previous section, the former highlight the view border in gray while switch processing is in progress; the latter flash and refuse to take control if the model is locked.

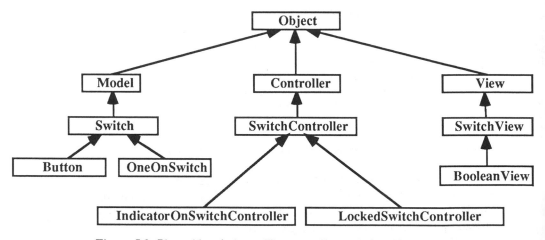

Figure 5.9 Pluggable windows: The controller and view hierarchy.

Specialization **BooleanView** of SwitchView provides **pluggable switch views**; i.e., views that can be tailored to display any two-valued aspect of an arbitrary object (see pluggable windows in Sect. 3.6 for more details). In effect, it permits an arbitrary object to be treated as if it were a switch for display purposes. Of course, switches themselves can be used as a special case.

5.4.1 Creating Pluggable Switch Windows

Pluggable switch views can be created by specifying (1) a model, (2) two message selectors for accessing and changing the model (an **aspect** selector and a **change** selector), (3) a label (any object that can be converted to a paragraph) to serve as the view's screen image, (4) an optional highlight object, and (5) an **on-value**; i.e., an aspect value that should cause the view to be on (in complemented mode) rather than off (in normal mode).

- BooleanView **on:** model
  aspect: aspectSelector **label:** label **change:** changeSelector **value:** onValue

The aspect and change selectors are the interrogation and modification message selectors respectively. They must satisfy the following requirements:

- **aspectSelector** (no parameters) should return the value of the model's aspect. The model is considered to be on (as opposed to off) if this result is equal to the on-value; otherwise, off. Also, the aspect selector *must* be used as the model's **changed:** parameter for the view to react to the change.

- **changeSelector** (one parameter) must update the model in response to a new user selection or deselection. The parameter is the on-value.

Because pluggable switches are a special kind of switch, it is clear that a highlight form can be specified in addition to the label. It is also possible to change the label to an arbitrary displayable object; e.g., a form, after *but not before* the view is constructed. The view's interrogation message and the controller's modification message can also be changed. However, a special restriction must be satisfied by the interrogation message: (1) the selector must be a zero-parameter selector, and (2) the first argument (which is never sent to the model) must contain the on-value.

- aBooleanView **highlightForm:** aDisplayObject
- aBooleanView
  selector: anInterrogationSelectorSymbol; **arguments:** anArray
- aControllerForABooleanView
  selector: aModificationSelectorSymbol; **arguments:** anArray

Example

Consider the third example of the nonpluggable switches section. We simply repeat the example using the revised protocol.

```
| topView transcriptView myTextCollector hotButtonView coldButtonView |

topView ← StandardSystemView new
    label: 'Transcript As Button Test'; insideColor: Form white; borderWidth: 2.
transcriptView ← TextCollectorView container: (myTextCollector ← TextCollector new).
```

```
hotButtonView ← BooleanView on: myTextCollector
    aspect: #isNil label: 'hot' change: #show: value: 'hot '.
coldButtonView ← BooleanView on: myTextCollector
    aspect: #isNil label: 'cold' change: #show: value: 'cold '.

topView
    window: Display boundingBox; "helps eliminate transformation roundoff errors"
    addSubView: hotButtonView in: (0.1@0.2 corner: 0.3@0.4) borderWidth: 1;
    addSubView: coldButtonView in: (0.1@0.6 corner: 0.3@0.8) borderWidth: 1;
    addSubView: transcriptView in: (0.4@0 corner: 1@1) borderWidth: 0.

transcriptView borderWidthLeft: 2 right: 0 top: 0 bottom: 0. "changed my mind"

topView controller open
```

5.4.2 The Boolean View Protocol

The complete boolean view protocol is a small extension to the switch view protocol.

instance creation and initialization

- BooleanView **on:** model
  aspect: aspectSelector **label:** label **change:** changeSelector **value:** onValue
      Returns an initialized pluggable switch view. Assumes the label can be
      converted to a paragraph. A **nil** label can be specified if it is to be changed
      later.

view operations redefined specially for this class

- aBooleanView **interrogateModel**
      Sends the interrogation selector message to the model and returns whether
      or not it is equal to the on-value.
- aBooleanView **update:** aspect
      Executes the standard switch update if the aspect is the same as the
      selector.

The BooleanView Methods

The restrictions on the interrogation (aspect) and modification (change) messages are best understood by looking at the details of the methods.

```
BooleanView on: model
aspect: aspectSelector label: label change: changeSelector value: onValue
    "Returns an initialized pluggable switch view. Assumes the label can be converted
    to a paragraph."

    | view parameters |
    view ← self new.
    view model: model.
    view selector: aspectSelector; arguments: (parameters ← Array with: onValue).
        "the interrogation message (arguments used only to remember the on-value)"
    view controller selector: changeSelector; arguments: parameters.
        "the modification message"
    view label: label asParagraph.
    ↑view
```

aBooleanView **interrogateModel**
"Sends the interrogation selector message to the model and returns whether or not
it is equal to the on-value."
↑(model **perform**: selector) = arguments **first** "compare with the on-value"

aBooleanView **update**: aspect
"Executes the standard switch update if the aspect is the same as the selector."
aspect == selector **ifTrue**: [super **update**: aspect]

Where Boolean Views Are Currently Used

The one example in the system that uses boolean views is the browser. The boolean views
are used for displaying the **instance** and **class** buttons. The browser itself is in one of two
states: either displaying normal (instance) information or meta (class) information. Which
state the browser is in can be determined by sending it a **meta** message; i.e.,

aBrowser **meta** ⇒ **false** (displaying instance information)
aBrowser **meta** ⇒ **true** (displaying class information)

Since the browser itself is playing the role of a switch, there is no need to create special
switches for the instance and class buttons. We only need to create an instance button view
and a class button view that will properly display the information.

Consider the class button view first since it is simplest. We need a view that is **on** (in
complemented mode) when class information is being displayed; i.e., when the meta
message returns **true**. Hence, the aspect message should be **#meta** and the on-value is **true**.
Presumably the state of the browser can be changed by sending it a **meta:** message. Assume
the **meta:** method is implemented as follows:

aBrowser **meta**: aBoolean
   meta ← aBoolean.
   self **changed**: #meta

Hence, we can create a class button view as follows:

aClassButtonView ← BooleanView **on**: aBrowser
   aspect: #meta **label**: 'class' **change**: #meta: **value**: true

Creating an instance button view is similar. However, the instance button view should
appear **on** when the meta message returns **false**. Hence the on-value should be **false**.

anInstanceButtonView ← BooleanView **on**: aBrowser
   aspect: #meta **label**: 'instance' **change**: #meta: **value**: false

If the instance button view is off, clicking on it causes the message 'meta: false' to be
sent to the browser (its model). Since the browser notifies its dependents of the change via
'salf **changed**: #meta', the instance button view is notified. It responds by sending the
message 'meta' to the browser (model); it gets back **false**. Since the result returned
conforms to the value it expects to see (**false**), the instance button view turns on; i.e.,
displays itself in the on state. The class button view is also notified — it turns off because
the returned value did not conform to the value it expected (**true**). Clicking on the instance
button view again does not turn it off. Rather it simply gets turned on a second time — it
sends another "meta: false" message and the same chain of events occurs all over again.

To turn the instance button view off, the class button view must be clicked. This causes the browser to be sent a 'meta: true message. The browser's 'self **changed:** #meta' message causes both views to be sent an **update:** message. Both interrogate the browser by sending it a **meta** message and get the result **true**. The instance button view turns off since the browser's meta state does not match its on-value (**false**); similarly, the class button view turns on since the browser's meta state matches its on-value (**true**). Clicking the instance button view again simply repeats the process but with the opposite effect.

5.4.3 An Example: A Pizza Query Window

Consider a pizza ordering application with its own window for interacting with the customer. A customer might request the menu, make selections, and provide an address for the delivery. When a pizza is ordered, the size of the pizza, the kind, and optional toppings would have to be specified. One way this can be done is to pop-up a window with switches that can be set to indicate the customer's choices. We will not be designing or implementing the pizza ordering application itself — it would be quite a substantial application. However, we would like to illustrate the implementation of the query window for specifying the details for an individual pizza.

To illustrate its design, we will define a simple Pizza class and provide a capability for opening a query window on any instance. The instance of Pizza will serve as the model for the many switches in the query window — permitting direct modification of the instance. We emphasize that this is only to illustrate the principles since such a query window would typically use the pizza ordering application as the model — not the pizza itself.

Sending a 'queryUser' message to a Pizza instance will be very much like sending it an 'inspect' message. To verify that the query window really does modify the instance, we could first inspect an instance, as in Fig. 5.10. Then we could send it the 'queryUser' message from the inspector.

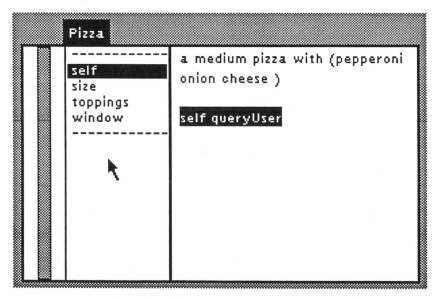

Figure 5.10 Inspecting an instance of Pizza.

The 'queryUser' message will result in the query window shown in Fig. 5.11. This window is interesting for two reasons:

1. The size switches behave like one-on switches; i.e., only one can be on at a time. Selecting size 'large' will automatically cause 'medium' to be deselected. Moreover, it is not possible to deselect the current choice — the customer must select some other choice for his actions to have an effect.

2. The toppings switches can be both selected and deselected. Any number (including none) can be on.

All of this is achieved with only one kind of switch view, and each of these views is on the same model — the Pizza instance. The behavior of the switches is determined by the model and not the switch view or its controller. When the user has made up his mind with respect to all the choices, he either accepts or cancels the window.

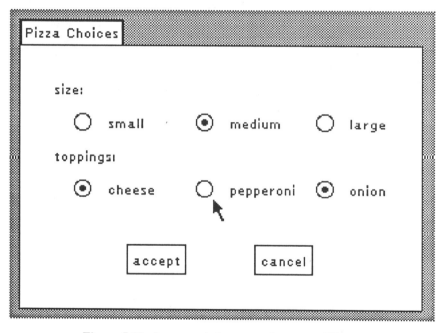

Figure 5.11 A query window on an instance of Pizza.

Class Pizza is deliberately unfinished. But it contains sufficient protocol to illustrate the above. The primary instance variables include 'size' and 'toppings'. The other instance variables provide us with the capability to attach a query window. They would not likely be part of Pizza objects in a finished application; more likely, they would be part of the pizza application's model. Instance variable 'window' is used to keep track of the opened query window. This enables the model to close the window itself and also provides it with the ability to prevent a second window from opening on the same instance. Instance variables 'oldSize' and 'oldToppings' enable the cancel facility to restore the pizza instance's old state. The class variables 'OnForm' and 'OffForm' contain the circular switch pictures. The on-form contains only the filled inner small circle. When the switch is on, the on-form is overlayed on the off-form — actually, the system uses rule **reverse** to display the on-form over the off-form. Both forms were very simply constructed with the bit editor.

Class Pizza

class	Pizza
superclass	Object
instance variables	size toppings window oldSize oldToppings
class variable names	OnForm OffForm

class methods

class initialization

initialize
```
"Pizza initialize"
OffForm ← Form
    extent: 15@15
    fromArray: #( 0 1984 6192 12312 8200 16388 16388 16388 16388 16388 8200
        12296 6192 1984 0)
    offset: 0@0.
OnForm ← Form
    extent: 15@15
    fromArray: #( 0 0 0 0 0 896 1984 1984 1984 896 0 0 0 0 0)
    offset: 0@0
```

instance creation

new
```
↑super new initialize
```

examples

example1
```
"Pizza example1"
Pizza new inspect
"While in the inspector, execute 'self queryUser'. After accepting the changes, see if
the instance has changed. Also see if the cancel works properly."
```

instance methods

instance initialization

initialize
```
size ← #medium.
toppings ← Set new
```

printing

printOn: aStream
```
aStream nextPutAll: 'a '; nextPutAll: size; nextPutAll: ' pizza with '.
toppings asOrderedCollection asArray printOn: aStream
```

When message '**queryUser**' is sent to an instance of Pizza, a window is opened only if none is already open. Additionally, the current size and toppings are saved in case the customer cancels the changes.

The query window (see method **queryWindow**) is constructed from three basic components:

1. a standard system view for the top view,
2. display-text subviews with no controller for the static textual data, and
3. switch views for the switches — three in row 2 using the on- and off-forms, three in row 4 also using the on- and off-forms, and two in the last row using strings 'accept' and 'cancel'.

Each view has an inside color of white. The top view and the accept/cancel switch views have a border width of 1; all others have a border width of 0. For display text views, the textual data to be displayed is stored as a paragraph (a display-text object would also have worked) *in the model*. For the accept/cancel switch views, the textual data is also stored as paragraphs but *in the label* rather than the model. The other six switch views store forms — the off-form *in the label* and the on-form *in the highlight object*. All and only the switch views have the Pizza instance ('self') as the model.

Because forms do not resize well, we take great care to ensure that the query window is fixed-size. In particular, we make sure that the minimum and maximum size for the top view is the same. To ensure that the local transformation for the top view and consequently the display transformation has no scaling, we also set the top view's window to this minimum/maximum size — otherwise, the system uses a default window size that is the entire display.

To position the subviews, each is specified with a window that is exactly the right size to contain the information to be displayed. The viewport is the location in the top view where the subview is to be displayed. It, too, is the same size as the information to be displayed to ensure that the local transformation and consequently the display transformation have no scaling — the display transformation is obtained by composing the local transformation of the subview and its super views. As designed, the display transformation may have a displacement component but no scaling component. In general, the art of creating a nice layout is a trial and error process.

The switch views are provided with the following interrogation and modification messages:

The 3 size switches in row 2:
interrogation messages:
    isSize: #small   **isSize**: #medium   **isSize**: #large
modification messages:
    makeSize: #small   **makeSize**: #medium   **makeSize**: #large
update symbol:
    isSize:

The 3 toppings switches in row 4:
interrogation messages:
    toppingContains: #cheese   **toppingContains**: #pepperoni   **toppingContains**: #onion
modification messages:
    toppingAddOrRemove: #cheese   **toppingAdd**...: #pepperoni   **toppingAdd**...: #onion
update symbol:
    toppingContains:

The 2 accept/cancel switches in row 5:
    interrogation messages:
        isNil   isNil
    modification messages:
        acceptPizzaChoices   cancelPizzaChoices
    update symbol:
        isNil

Note that the update symbol is the same as the selector for the interrogation message. Thus, if the model, the Pizza instance, executes 'self **changed**: #isSize:', only the size switches will update themselves. Similarly, if 'self **changed**: #toppingContains:' is executed, only the topping switches will update themselves. The accept/cancel switches never get the chance to display themselves in the on position since they close the window when depressed. If they did, they would always display themselves in the off position since when interrogated, they always return **false** (the model is never **nil**). We could easily change it so that the accept switch was always on and the cancel switch always off. The interrogation switch could be replaced by something like '**isSwitch**: #accept' versus '**isSwitch**: #cancel' instead of '**isNil**'.

One attribute of switch views that can be a source of problems is the fact that the view physically modifies the label's offset to center it in the window (as opposed to the viewport). In particular, method **centerLabel** is automatically invoked whenever the label or window is changed. By choosing the window so that the origin is 0@0, we are ensuring that the offset needed to center it is also 0@0. In practice, it shouldn't matter where the window is positioned — it's the viewport that specifies where the view is to be displayed. In an earlier version, we used to set the window to the viewport. This made it impossible to use the same off-form because each switch view wanted a different offset to be associated with the label. Each of the six switches had to have its own copy. Even with copies, other problems appeared — the labels still didn't display as they should.

query window

queryUser
    "Asks the user for size and toppings. Flash if an existing window is already open."
    window **isNil ifFalse**: [Display **flash**: Display **boundingBox**. ↑self].
    oldSize ← size. oldToppings ← toppings **deepCopy**. "in case of cancel"
    window ← self **queryWindow**.
    window **controller open**

queryWindow
    "Constructs and returns a standard system view with 3 size switches, 3 topping switches, an accept, and a cancel switch. Only one size is permitted; an arbitrary number of topping switches are permitted."
    | whiteColor noBorder noArguments topViewSize topView picture layout sizeSymbol selectorArguments xStart toppingSymbol acceptPicture cancelPicture pictureExtent |

    "Common information."
    whiteColor ← Form **white**.
    noBorder ← 0.
    noArguments ← #().

```
topViewSize ← 300@200.
topView ← StandardSystemView new
    label: 'Pizza Choices';
    minimumSize: topViewSize; maximumSize: topViewSize;
    insideColor: whiteColor; borderWidth: 1;
    window: (0@0 corner: topViewSize);
    yourself.


"Row 1."
picture ← 'size:' asParagraph.
layout ← 20@25 extent: picture extent.
topView addSubView: (DisplayTextView new
    model: picture;
    controller: NoController new;
    insideColor: whiteColor; borderWidth: noBorder;
    window: layout viewport: layout;
    yourself).


"Row 2."
1 to: 3 do: [:index |
    sizeSymbol ← #(small medium large) at: index.
    selectorArguments ← Array with: sizeSymbol.
    xStart ← (index-1)*90+40.

    layout ← xStart@50 extent: OffForm extent.
    topView addSubView: ((SwitchView new
        model: self;
        label: OffForm;
        selector: #isSize:; arguments: selectorArguments;
        insideColor: whiteColor; borderWidth: noBorder;
        window: OffForm boundingBox viewport: layout;
        highlightForm: OnForm;
        yourself) controller
            selector: #makeSize:; arguments: selectorArguments; view).

    picture ← sizeSymbol asParagraph.
    layout ← xStart+20@50 extent: picture extent.
    topView addSubView: (DisplayTextView new
        model: picture;
        controller: NoController new;
        insideColor: whiteColor; borderWidth: noBorder;
        window: layout viewport: layout;
        yourself)].


"Row 3."
picture ← 'toppings:' asParagraph.
layout ← 20@75 extent: picture extent.
topView addSubView: (DisplayTextView new
    model: picture;
    controller: NoController new;
    insideColor: whiteColor; borderWidth: noBorder;
    window: layout viewport: layout;
    yourself).
```

```
"Row 4."
1 to: 3 do: [:index |
    toppingSymbol ← #(cheese pepperoni onion) at: index.
    selectorArguments ← Array with: toppingSymbol.
    xStart ← (index-1)*90+40.

    layout ← xStart@100 extent: OffForm extent.
    topView addSubView: ((SwitchView new
        model: self; label: OffForm;
        selector: #toppingContains:; arguments: selectorArguments;
        insideColor: whiteColor; borderWidth: noBorder;
        window: OffForm boundingBox viewport: layout;
        highlightForm: OnForm;
        yourself) controller
            selector: #toppingAddOrRemove:; arguments: selectorArguments; view).

    picture ← toppingSymbol asParagraph.
    layout ← xStart+20@100 extent: picture extent.
    topView addSubView: (DisplayTextView new
        model: picture; controller: NoController new;
        insideColor: whiteColor; borderWidth: noBorder;
        window: layout viewport: layout;
        yourself)].

"Eliminate destructive modification to switch labels caused by automatic
centerLabel."
OffForm offset: 0@0.

"Row 5."
acceptPicture ← 'accept' asParagraph.
cancelPicture ← 'cancel' asParagraph.
pictureExtent ← (acceptPicture extent max: cancelPicture extent) + (8@8).

layout ← 80@150 extent: pictureExtent.
topView addSubView: ((SwitchView new
    model: self; label: acceptPicture;
    selector: #isNil; arguments: noArguments;
    insideColor: whiteColor; borderWidth: 1;
    window: layout viewport: layout;
    yourself) controller
        selector: #acceptPizzaChoices; arguments: noArguments; view).

layout ← 175@150 extent: pictureExtent.
topView addSubView: ((SwitchView new
    model: self; label: cancelPicture;
    selector: #isNil; arguments: noArguments;
    insideColor: whiteColor;
    borderWidth: 1;
    window: layout viewport: layout;
    yourself) controller
        selector: #cancelPizzaChoices; arguments: noArguments; view).

"Done."
↑topView
```

Consider method **makeSize:**, which is executed whenever a size switch is pressed. More specifically, if the 'large' switch is depressed, **makeSize:** is executed with aSymbol set to #large. The 'self **changed:** #isSize:' message causes all the size switches to update themselves. The 'small' switch controller will send the '**isSize:** #small' message to the model and get back **false**; similarly for the 'medium' switch controller. On the other hand, the 'large' switch controller will send the '**isSize:** #large' message to the model and get back **true**. Pressing the same switch a second time will have no visual effect because size is unchanged — the 'self **changed:** #isSize:' message in this case causes all the size switches to update themselves to what they used to be.

Methods **toppingContains:** and **toppingAddOrRemove:** respectively play the same role as **isSize:** and **makeSize:** above. However, method **toppingAddOrRemove:** does not behave the same each time a toppings switch is pressed. The first time the 'cheese' switch is pressed, #cheese is added to the instance. The next time it is pressed, #cheese is removed. The third time, #cheese is added, and the fourth, #cheese is removed, and so on. Unlike the size switches that can only be turned on, the toppings switches can be turned on and off.

query window support

isSize: aSymbol
    ↑size == aSymbol

makeSize: aSymbol
    size ← aSymbol.
    self **changed:** #isSize:

toppingContains: aSymbol
    ↑toppings **includes:** aSymbol

toppingAddOrRemove: aSymbol
    (self **toppingContains:** aSymbol)
        ifTrue: [toppings **remove:** aSymbol]
        ifFalse: [toppings **add:** aSymbol].
    self **changed:** #toppingContains:

acceptPizzaChoices
    oldSize ← oldToppings ← nil.
    window **controller closeAndUnschedule**.
    window ← nil

cancelPizzaChoices
    size ← oldSize. toppings ← oldToppings.
    window **controller closeAndUnschedule**.
    window ← nil

5.4.4 Dealing with Switch Sizing

Because switch views automatically translate and rescale when the top view is resized, it can be difficult to create a design that is pleasing for arbitrary window sizes. For example, a bank of vertically stacked switches resized as shown in Fig. 5.12 might not be a problem with textual labels. However, detailed forms can easily be deformed under arbitrary transformations. For such pictorial labels, it might be better to insist that the labels not be scaled.

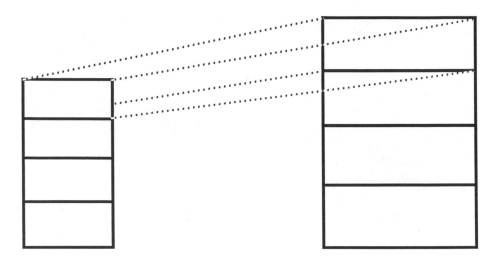

Figure 5.12 A vertical bank of switch windows.

Note that all switch views are transformed in this way, although some labels such as strings, paragraphs, and display text do not get scaled. Independent of whether or not the label is scaled, the display box is, of course, always a scaled version of the window. What we might like to have, on the other hand, is a kind of switch view that prevents both the label and the window from being scaled. We will develop such an **unscaled switch view** in the next section. Such a view, however, does present a problem. If the window is unscaled, it can be positioned anywhere in the original display box. Precisely where it is located is an extra degree of freedom.

One way of specifying this extra degree of freedom is to dictate that one of the window points be a fixed point. A **fixed point** is a window point that transforms exactly where the display transformation dictates. Other points cannot be transformed where the transformation dictates if the window is prevented from being scaled. This is illustrated in Fig. 5.13.

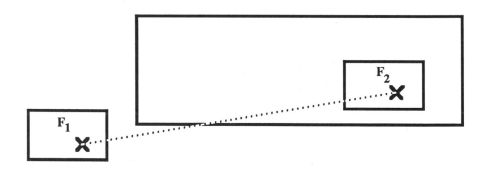

Fixed point F_1 maps to F_2. The rest of the window is translated to accommodate it.

Figure 5.13 Fixed points observe the display transformation.

By specifying the window origin as the fixed point, we end up with the window translated to the top left corner of the original display box. Two other possibilities are shown in Fig. 5.14.

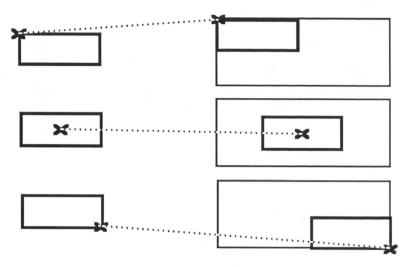

Figure 5.14 Choosing different fixed points.

Note that our design cannot simply translate the window to the new location. It must actually construct a new display transformation that has the required effect. This will ensure that the bounding box will be the same size as the window.

The approach is to use the display transformation that is constructed in the normal way to find out where the fixed point is transformed. Then, assuming the window is to be a fixed size, compute its new origin. This origin becomes the translation for a new display transformation with no scaling. As an aside, we also permit the highlight object to be optionally overlayed over the label.

Class method example1 (see Fig. 5.15) demonstrates how we can use unscaled switch views to construct banks of vertical switches. We show five columns of identical switches. The gridding is provided to show where the display box would have resided had normal switch views been used instead of unscaled switch views. The first three use the top left corner, the center, and the bottom right corner of the respective windows as fixed points. The fourth is discussed specially below. The fifth uses standard switch views to provide a comparison.

The only feature that we have not discussed is a technique to ensure that the resulting switch views touch, as in the fourth bank. The idea is to use the same fixed point for all windows; i.e., a **virtual fixed point**. In our example, the top left corner of the highest switch view is used as the fixed point. For the top window, this point is the origin. For the second window, it is one window's height above its origin. For the third window, it is two windows' height above its own origin, and so on.

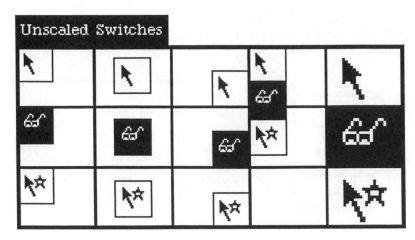

Figure 5.15 Ilustrating banks of switch windows.

Class UnscaledSwitchView

class name	UnscaledSwitchView
superclass	SwitchView
instance variable names	fixedPoint overlayHighlightObject
comment	Permits unscaled switches to be used. Fixed points are window coordinates used to specify which part of the view is to be transformed unaltered. When the fixed point is inside the display object, self relative positioning is obtained. When it is outside, more global positioning permits rows or columns of views to be made adjacent.

class methods

example1

"UnscaledSwitchView example1"

ltopView labels switches switchCount switchHeight switchOffsets banks topWindowOrigin I

topView ← StandardSystemView **new**
    label: 'Unscaled Switches'; **insideColor**: Form **white**; **borderWidth**: 2.
labels ← #(normal read execute) **collect**: [:aSymbol I Cursor **perform**: aSymbol].
switches ← labels **collect**: [:aLabel I Switch **newOff**]. switchCount ← switches **size**.
switchHeight ← (1/switchCount) **asFloat**.
switchOffsets ← 0.0 **to**: 1.0 **by**: switchHeight.
switchOffsets ← switchOffsets
    copyFrom: 1 **to**: switchOffsets **size**-1. "remove last entry"

"Create 5 vertical banks of switches: four unscaled and one scaled. Use the same switches and labels to create five columns differing only in position and scaling."
banks ← (1 **to**: 5) **collect**: [:bankIndex I
    (1 **to**: switchCount) **collect**: [:aSwitchIndex I
        (bankIndex < 5 **ifTrue**: [UnscaledSwitchView] **ifFalse**: [SwitchView]) **new**
            model: (switches **at**: aSwitchIndex);
            label: (labels **at**: aSwitchIndex)]].
topView **window**: Display boundingBox. "helps eliminate roundoff errors"

```
banks with: #(0.0 0.2 0.4 0.6 0.8) do: [:aBank :anXOffset |
    aBank with: switchOffsets do: [:aSwitchView :aYOffset |
        topView
            addSubView: aSwitchView
            in: (anXOffset@aYOffset extent: 0.2@switchHeight)
            borderWidth: 1]].
```

"Now specify the fixed point for the first four banks."
```
(banks at: 1) do: [:aSwitchView | aSwitchView fixTopLeftCorner].
(banks at: 2) do: [:aSwitchView | aSwitchView fixCenter].
(banks at: 3) do: [:aSwitchView | aSwitchView fixBottomRightCorner].
(banks at: 4) with: (0 to: switchCount-1) do: [:aSwitchView :aCount |
    topWindowOrigin ← aSwitchView window origin -
        (0@(aCount * aSwitchView window height)).
    aSwitchView fixPoint: topWindowOrigin].
```

"Add some additional transparent subviews just to provide the grid so we can better see what happened. Note that this will have to be removed since it prevents the switch views from getting control."
```
0.0 to: 0.8 by: 0.2 do: [:anXOffset |
    switchOffsets do: [:aYOffset |
        topView
            addSubView: View new
            in: (anXOffset@aYOffset extent: 0.2@switchHeight)
            borderWidth: 1]].
```

```
topView controller open
```

instance methods

fixed point manipulation

centerLabel
    "Override the inherited version that modifies the label by changing its offset."
    self **fixCenter**
fixTopLeftCorner
    fixedPoint ← self **window origin**. self **unlock**
fixCenter
    fixedPoint ← self **window center**. self **unlock**
fixBottomRightCorner
    fixedPoint ← self **window corner**. self **unlock**
fixPoint: aPoint
    fixedPoint ← aPoint. self **unlock**

highlight object control

doNotOverlayHighlightObject
    overlayHighlightObject ← false
overlayHighlightObject
    overlayHighlightObject ← true

transformation changes

computeDisplayTransformation
    "First computes the standard display transformation and then uses it to determine where the fixed point should display. Then a new display transformation with no scaling is constructed that translates the label origin in such a way that the fixed point is at the position determined above."

    | scaledTransformation sourceFixedPoint destinationFixedPoint sourceOrigin fixedPointOffset destinationOrigin |

```
scaledTransformation ← super computeDisplayTransformation.
sourceFixedPoint ←fixedPoint isNil ifTrue: [self window center] ifFalse: [fixedPoint].
destinationFixedPoint ← scaledTransformation applyTo: sourceFixedPoint.

sourceOrigin ← self window origin.
fixedPointOffset ← sourceFixedPoint - sourceOrigin.
destinationOrigin ← destinationFixedPoint - fixedPointOffset.

↑WindowingTransformation scale: nil translation: destinationOrigin
```

displaying

display

> "Displays the view taking into account the status of the model, the label, and the highlight object."

```
self displayBorder.
complemented ← self interrogateModel. "update the view's mode"
highlightForm isNil
    ifTrue: [
        "If there is no highlight form, clear the inset display box, display the label
        (if there is one), and additionally highlight it if in complemented mode."
        self clearInside.
        label isNil ifFalse: [
            label
                displayOn: Display
                transformation: self displayTransformation
                clippingBox: self insetDisplayBox].
        complemented ifTrue: [self highlight]]
    ifFalse: [
        "If there is a highlight form, display it if in complemented mode either with
        or without the label under it (depending on the state of the view).
        Otherwise, just display the label."
        complemented
            ifTrue: [
                highlightForm
                    displayOn: Display
                    transformation: self displayTransformation
                    clippingBox: self insetDisplayBox].
        ((complemented not) |
         (complemented & (overlayHighlightObject "could be nil" == true))) &
        (label ~= nil) ifTrue: [
            label
                displayOn: Display
                transformation: self displayTransformation
                clippingBox: self insetDisplayBox
                rule: Form under
                mask: Form black]]
```

5.5 SWITCH-MENU WINDOWS

Switch-menu windows provide pallets of switches that can be used as menus. Unlike menu facilities discussed in previous sections, these are not scrollable. For historical reasons, switch-menu windows are implemented with **form-menu views** and **form-menu controllers**. These classes were designed to support the implementation of the bit and form editors. They were not designed to be used publicly for implementing new editors. Nevertheless, they can be used for this purpose.

Class **FormMenuView** (see Fig. 5.16) provides essentially the same functionality as its superclass View. It does, however, provide a different default controller. Class **FormMenuController** is designed to permit switch subviews to be switched by pressing keyboard characters. They can also be switched in the standard way by depressing the mouse button in the appropriate switch view.

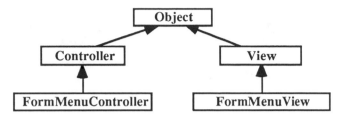

Figure 5.16 Switch-menu windows: The controller and view hierarchy.

5.5.1 Creating Switch-Menu Windows

Switch-menu windows are created by (1) obtaining a form-menu view in the standard way, taking care to have a non-transparent background, (2) obtaining and positioning switch views within the form-menu view, and (3) associating a **key character** with the individual switches to permit character based switching. The key characters are associated via switch view message **key:**.

- aSwitchView **key**: aCharacter

Note that switch-menu windows provide no special facilities for palletizing rows or columns of switch views.

Example

Consider a modification of one of the previous examples dealing with colors. We wish to permit the color switches (red, green, and blue) to be triggered by the corresponding lowercase characters. The modified example is shown below (modifications in italic).

```
| topView menuView redButton greenButton blueButton redButtonView
greenButtonView blueButtonView |

topView ← StandardSystemView new
    label: 'Character Switching Buttons'; insideColor: Form white; borderWidth: 2.
menuView ← FormMenuView new. "use the top view's background"

topView addSubView: menuView.

redButton ← Button newOff onAction: [Transcript show: 'red '].
greenButton ← Button newOff onAction: [Transcript show: 'green '].
blueButton ← Button newOff onAction: [Transcript show: 'blue '].

redButtonView ← SwitchView new label: 'red' asParagraph; model: redButton.
greenButtonView ← SwitchView new label: 'green' asParagraph; model: greenButton.
blueButtonView ← SwitchView new label: 'blue' asParagraph; model: blueButton.

redButtonView key: $r. greenButtonView key: $g. blueButtonView key: $b.
```

menuView
>   window: Display **boundingBox**; "helps eliminate transformation roundoff errors"
>   **addSubView**: redButtonView **in**: (0.1@0.1 **corner**: 0.3@0.9) **borderWidth**: 1;
>   **addSubView**: greenButtonView **in**: (0.4@0.1 **corner**: 0.6@0.9) **borderWidth**: 1;
>   **addSubView**: blueButtonView **in**: (0.7@0.1 **corner**: 0.9@0.9) **borderWidth**: 1.

topView **controller open**

Note that associating a switching key with a switch view would have no effect if the switch view were not imbedded inside a form-menu view. Also, it is not possible to associate more than one key with the switch view. Thus, it is not possible to permit both uppercase and lowercase characters to switch the view.

5.5.2 Switch-Menu Windows: The Implementation

It is important to realize that form-menu views and controllers were designed to support the implementation of bit and form editors. Consequently, they contain a substantial number of private operations that cannot be used publicly, since they access private class variables that must not be modified. These private operations make use of a private class named FormButtonCache, which we will not document. We consider only those public operations that can be used directly.

The FormMenuController Protocol

revised control operations

- aFormMenuController **isControlWanted**
    Obtains control; i.e., returns **true** if the cursor is inside the view or if a keyboard character has been depressed.
- aFormMenuController **isControlActive**
    Retains control; i.e., returns **true** if the cursor is inside the view and the blue mouse button is not depressed.
- aFormMenuController **controlActivity**
    If a keyboard character is typed, overrides the standard control activity by passing control to the subview indicated by the button pressed (if there is one); otherwise discards the character.

private control operation

- aFormMenuController **processMenuKey**
    Extracts the next character from the keyboard and gives control to the subview selected by the character.

Details of the Control Activity

The protocol differs from the standard Controller protocol by processing the keyboard characters and interpreting them as switching characters; i.e., characters to be used to determine which subview to give control to.

revised control operations

- aFormMenuController **isControlActive**
    "Retains control; i.e., returns **true** if the cursor is inside the view and the blue mouse button is not depressed."
    ↑(sensor **keyboardPressed** | (view **containsPoint**: sensor **cursorPoint**)) &
        sensor **blueButtonPressed not**

- aFormMenuController **isControlWanted**
  "Obtains control; i.e., returns **true** if the cursor is inside the view or a keyboard character has been depressed."
  ↑sensor **keyboardPressed** | self **viewHasCursor**

- aFormMenuController **controlActivity**
  "If a keyboard character is typed, overrides the standard control activity by passing control to the subview indicated by the button pressed (if there is one); otherwise discards the character."
  sensor **keyboardPressed**
      ifTrue: [self **processMenuKey**]
      ifFalse: [self **controlToNextLevel**]

private control operation

- aFormMenuController **processMenuKey**
  "Extracts the next character from the keyboard and gives control to the subview selected by the character."
  | aView |
  aView ← view **subViewContainingCharacter**: sensor **keyboard**.
  aView ~~ nil **ifTrue**: [aView **controller sendMessage**]

The FormMenuView Protocol

A form-menu view provides the interface between itself and its subviews, which are switch views. Only one new public operation is provided. A revised method for obtaining the default controller is also provided.

instance creation

- View **new**
  Creates a new initialized view with a transparent background and zero-width border.

communication with subviews

- aFormMenuView **subViewContainingCharacter**: aCharacter
  Returns the subview that will switch on the specified character; **nil** if there is none.

controller access

- aFormMenuView **defaultControllerClass**
  Returns class FormMenuController.

5.6 SUMMARY

This chapter has provided the details of **switch windows**, which provide the ability to turn something on or off. In particular, we have discussed the following notions:

- The model, view, and controller hierarchies associated with switch windows.

- The distinction between switches, buttons, and one-on switches.

- The detailed protocol for classes Switch, Button, and OneOnSwitch.

- Numerous examples showing how switches, buttons, and one-on switches may be created and used.

- The protocol for controller classes SwitchController, IndicatorOnSwitchController, and LockedSwitchController. Class IndicatorOnSwitchController provides additional facilities to highlight the view border in gray while switch processing is in progress. This might be used, for example, with a save button that takes a while for the operation to finish. Class LockedSwitchController provides switch controllers that flash and refuse to take control if the model is locked. This can be used to prevent accidental loss of changes in progress.

- The protocol for class SwitchView — a view that works with each of the above controllers.

- The distinction between a switch view's label and highlight object that can be used to overlay the label.

- An example dealing with the creation of a subclass that permits distinct label and highlight objects, eliminating the requirement that the highlight must overlay the label.

- Pluggable switch windows including the detailed protocol for class BooleanView. Pluggable switch windows use the standard switch controller.

- An example illustrating the use of pluggable switch windows for interrogating a user about pizza parameters.

- A discussion of the problems that arise as switch views are scaled when windows are resized and the creation of a class of switch views that does not scale the labels.

- Switch-menu windows, including the detailed protocol for supporting classes FormMenuView and FormMenuController. Switch-menu windows provide pallets of switches that can be switched using the keyboard in addition to the mouse.

5.7 EXERCISES

The following exercises are intended to provide some experience with switches, switch windows, and related issues.

1. Design a switch window that contains the current time and that additionally updates itself at regular intervals.

2. Design a switch window that counts; i.e., every time the switch is depressed, it increments a counter that is visible as part of the label. Consider adding a yellow button menu that resets it at zero.

3. Create a horizontal (or vertical) row of switches containing all the cursor forms in the system. When one is depressed, change the cursor to match.

4. Create a switch with a frowning face when it is off and a smiling face when it is on.

5. Revise the switch view protocol so that **centerLabel** does not modify the label and so that arbitrary windows may be specified.

6. Revise the tic-tac-toe game to use switch windows for the squares on the game board.

7. Reimplement the solution to the co-ordinated lights problem (page 22) using one-on switches instead of normal switches. Also, use switch windows instead of forms and embed the switches inside a standard system view.

5.8 GLOSSARY AND IMPORTANT FACTS

classes

BooleanView The view class for pluggable switch windows; can be tailored to display any two-valued aspect of an arbitrary object.

FormMenuController A controller class that permits keyboard characters to switch the subviews; i.e., typing an individual character that has been associated with a specific switch view will cause the switch view's model to switch just as if the mouse button had been depressed on it.

FormMenuView The view class associated with FormMenuController; differs from class View by providing a different default controller.

IndicatorOnSwitchController A controller class that provides facilities to highlight the view border in gray while switch processing is in progress; can be used, for example, with a save button that takes a while for the operation to finish.

LockedSwitchController A controller class where instances flash and refuse to take control if the model is locked; can be used to prevent accidental loss of changes in progress.

SwitchController The standard controller class for switch windows; specializations include **IndicatorOnSwitchController** and **LockedSwitchController**.

SwitchView The view class that provides the standard switch window protocol; specializations include **BooleanView**.

selected terminology

button A push-button style switch; i.e., a switch that automatically turns off whenever it is turned on. It can't be created in the on position.

complemented mode The mode the view is in when its switch model is on.

connection object An arbitrary object to which all connected one-on switches must be associated; the association is established via 'aOneOnSwitch **connection:** anObject'.

fixed point A window point that transforms exactly where the display transformation dictates. Other points cannot be transformed where the transformation dictates if the window is prevented from being scaled.

highlight object The display object (paragraph, form, path, and so on) that will be superimposed over the label when the switch is on.

indicator-on switch controller A switch controller that highlights the view border in gray while switch processing is in progress.

interrogation message A message (a **selector** and a list of **arguments**) that can be associated with a switch view; used to determine the status of the model. The default message is 'model **isOn**'.

key character A character that can be associated with a switch view that is a subview of a form-menu view; used for switching the view without having to manipulate the mouse.

label The display object (paragraph, form, path, and so on) that will serve as the picture for the switch window.

locked switch controller A switch controller that flashes and refuses to take control if the model is locked.

modification message A message (a **selector** and a list of **arguments**) that can be associated with a switch controller; used to change the status of the model. The default message is 'model **switch**'.

normal mode The mode the view is in when its switch model is off.

one-on switch A car-radio style switch; i.e., when several such switches are connected together, only one of them is on at a time. Turning on a one-on switch automatically causes the others connected to it to be turned off.

pluggable switch window A window that permits arbitrary models with model specific yellow button menus and follows the general pluggable windows philosophy; can be constructed from boolean views and standard switch controllers (or their specialization **indicator-on** switch controllers or **locked** switch controllers).

standard switch window A window that permits arbitrary models but does not provide the ability to create model specific yellow button menus.

switch An object that can be either **on** or **off**. When turned on, an associated block, the **on action**, is executed. When turned off, another block, the **off action**, is executed. Two specializations exist: buttons and one-on switches.

switch window A window designed to display an icon that represents a switch. This icon can be turned on or off by pressing the mouse button over the icon.

switch-menu window A window that provides pallets of switch windows that can be used as menus; constructed from form-menu controllers and form-menu views.

important facts

communicating on and off actions Distinct on and off actions can communicate through local variables in common contexts but these local variables cannot be changed. The reason is that a shallow copy of each on or off action context is made when it is associated with a switch.

default messages Summarized by "views ask" and "controllers change"; the default **interrogation message** 'model **isOn**' is associated with a switch view; the default **modification message** 'model **switch**' is associated with a switch controller.

pluggable switch view parameters Pluggable switch views are provided with (1) a model, (2) two message selectors for accessing and changing the model (an **aspect** selector and a **change** selector), (3) a label (any object that can be converted to a paragraph) to serve as the view's screen image, (4) an optional highlight object, and (5) an **on-value**; i.e., an aspect value that should cause the view to be on (in complemented mode) rather than off (in normal mode).

6

Form Windows

6.1 INTRODUCTION

There is only one kind of **permanently visible non-scrollable form window**, or simply **form window** for short (see Fig. 6.1). Form windows are designed to display pictorial data. Such windows could be used by paint programs or animation systems, for example. Currently, neither is supplied with the standard Smalltalk image, although developments are in progress. These windows are currently used by the form editor and the screen controller.

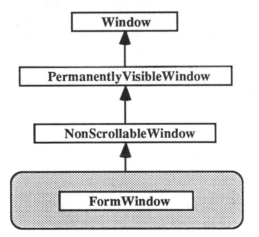

Figure 6.1 Form windows: A logical view.

Form windows are constructed from form views or form holder views (see Fig. 6.2). Any combination of controllers, like mouse menu controllers or instances of NoController, for example, will work. On the other hand, only the FormEditor (this is actually a controller class) will permit interaction with the view. From the user's point of view, form controllers are designed primarily to show pictures, not to provide an interaction facility.

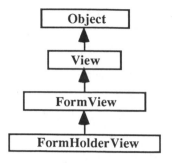

Figure 6.2 The form view hierarchy.

Class **FormView** provides the basic protocol for displaying forms. Specialization **FormHolderView** provides locking on the form so that modifications can be either accepted or canceled.

6.2 CREATING FORM WINDOWS

Form windows are created by instantiating instances of FormView or FormHolderView using **new**. Since this operation is inherited from class View, the default border is zero-width. Of course, we might expect the default transparent inside color to be suitable, since the form itself cannot be transparent. However, forms are often subjected to transformations that are non-integral. For example, a form could be scaled by a factor of 2.37 instead of a nice integer value like 3. The display process must at some point truncate some part of the computation to an integer, since forms must contain an integral number of bits. The consequence is that the forms often don't quite fit the display box. Conclusion: Use a white inside color in case the form is truncated. If the border separates from the containing view, use a zero-width border and increase the border size of the containing view. See paragraph editor views for a more thorough discussion of this same effect. The default controller is class FormEditor; hence, a nonstandard controller is likely to be needed.

Example

Consider a simple inert view containing a portion of the existing screen. Fig. 6.3 illustrates the window with a magnification of some user-chosen portion of the screen.

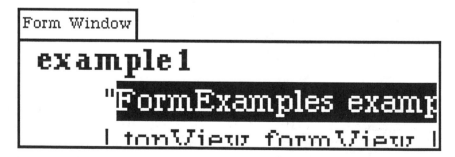

Figure 6.3 An example form window.

```
| topView formView |
topView ← StandardSystemView new
     label: 'Form Window'; insideColor: Form white; borderWidth: 2.
formView ← FormView new model: Form fromUser; controller: NoController new.
topView addSubView: formView.
topView controller open.
```

6.3 THE FORMVIEW PROTOCOL

Class FormView is designed to contain and display form models. For compatibility with its specialization, it provides menu messages **accept** and **cancel** that have no effect. The complete protocol follows.

instance creation

* View **new**
     Creates a new initialized view.

masks and rules

* aFormView **mask**
     Returns the mask used for displaying the model; the default is Form **black**. The mask is a specialized instance of class Form.
* aFormView **mask**: aForm
     Changes the mask used for displaying the model. Returns the view.

* aFormView **rule**
     Returns the rule used for displaying the model; the default is Form **over**. The rule is an integer from 0 to 15 that indicates which of the sixteen display rules to be used when copying the model onto the display screen.
* aFormView **rule**: anInteger
     Changes the rule used for displaying the model. Returns the view.

defaults

* aFormView **defaultControllerClass**
     Returns class FormEditor. This is not likely to be the default needed by users.
* aFormView **defaultWindow**
     Returns a rectangle large enough to contain the form and a border.
* aFormView **defaultMask**
     Returns Form **black**.
* aFormView **defaultRule**
     Returns Form **over**.

model access

* aFormView **changeValueAt**: anIntegerIndex **put**: either0Or1
     The model is a form that can be manipulated as if it were a one-dimensional array of bits. Changes the bit at the given integer index to either 0 or 1 and informs all objects that depend on the value that it has been changed; i.e., executes 'model **changed**: self'. Recall that the number of bits in a form can be determined via 'aForm **size**'; the bits can be accessed and changed via 'aForm **valueAt**: anIntegerIndex' and 'aForm **valueAt**: anIntegerIndex **put**: either0Or1' respectively.

Chapter 6 Form Windows   **301**

displaying

- aFormView **displayView**
  Displays the inside color and the form in the view. Note: the form offset is
  ignored; i.e., it is interpreted as 0@0.

updating

- aFormView **update**: aFormView
  Updates itself only if the parameter is this view.

menu messages

- aFormView **accept**
  Provided for compatibility with form holder views. Has no effect since form
  views have no working copy.
- aFormView **cancel**
  Provided for compatibility with form holder views. Has no effect since form
  views have no working copy.

Where Form Views Are Used

Form-holder views are, of course, used by the bit and form editors. A form view is also used
by the control manager when it creates the scheduled screen controller. Class method
initialize constructs the screen controller as follows:

```
screenView ← FormView new
    model: (InfiniteForm with: Form gray) controller: ScreenController new;
    window: Display boundingBox.
```

6.4 THE FORMHOLDERVIEW PROTOCOL

A **form-holder view** differs from a **form view** by providing a working version of the form
for editing. The message **accept** is used to copy the working version into the model; the
message **cancel** copies the model back to the working version.

revised view releasing operations

- aFormHolderView **release**
  Releases the working form in addition to setting it to **nil**. Since the model is
  usually a form and not a form view, this seems out of place. However,
  releasing a form is a no-op.

revised model referencing operations

- aFormHolderView **changeValueAt**: location put: anInteger
  Overrides the inherited version to cause the working form to be modified
  instead of the original in the model.
- aFormHolderView **model**: aForm
  Sets the model to the form and also makes a deep copy for the working
  form.

revised display operations

- aFormHolderView **displayView**
  Displays the working form. Does not display the inside color.

revised menu message operations

- aFormHolderView **accept**
  Modifies the model by copying the working form into it and informs all objects that depend on the value that it has been changed; i.e., executes 'model **changed**: self'.
- aFormHolderView **cancel**
  Modifies the working form by copying the model into it and informs all objects that depend on the value that it has been changed; i.e., executes 'model **changed**: self'.

new operations

- aFormHolderView **workingForm**
  Returns the working form.

6.5 SUMMARY

This chapter has provided the details of **form windows** that provide the ability to display, but not typically interact with, pictorial data. In particular, we have discussed the following notions:

- The use of form views or form holder views to construct form windows.

- The fact that no corresponding form holder controllers are provided. Nevertheless, mouse menu controllers or instances of NoController can be used to provide non-interactive controllers. The FormEditor (actually a controller class) permits interactions with the view.

- The protocol for classes FormView and FormHolderView.

- Details about the accept/cancel protocol supported by class FormHolderView. It provides a working copy of a form for editing purposes.

6.6 EXERCISES

The following exercises are an introduction to form windows and related concepts.

1. Learn to use the form editor to create pictures; e.g., try **Form fromUser edit**.

2. Learn to use the bit editor; e.g., try **Form fromUser bitEdit**.

3. Determine how to file out forms and also how to file them back in. Your system may also have an interface with a more powerful paint program from which forms can be imported. If so, learn to use it.

4. Create a form that represents a geo- graphical map. Overlay button win- dows on top of cities and use them for displaying the names of cities; i.e., arrange it so that clicking on a city displays its population.

5. Construct a form animator that dis- plays a collection of forms and op- tionally recycles it.

6. Create a form icon, a form window that can be double clicked to reveal a larger form (the background) with ad- ditional form icons overlaid on this background. There should be no limit to depth that such icons could be nested.

7. Devise an adventure-style game based on form icons.

6.7 GLOSSARY

classes

FormEditor A controller class that permits interaction with a form view.

FormHolderView A specialization of **Form- View** that provides locking on the form so that modifications can be either accept- ed or canceled.

FormView A view class that provides the ba- sic protocol for displaying forms.

selected terminology

form window A window designed to dis- play pictorial data; could be used by paint programs or animation systems; currently used by the form editor and the screen con- troller.

7

Pop-up Windows

7.1 INTRODUCTION

Pop-up windows are windows that appear suddenly when an interaction request is required and then immediately disappear after an appropriate reply. They exist in two varieties (see Fig. 7.1): **pop up menu windows** and **pop-up text-query windows**. Pop-up menu windows provide users with a choice of menu entries to select from. It is also possible to make no choice. Pop-up text-query windows are used to request a textual response to some query. **Pop-up binary text-query windows** are a special case in which the response is either **yes** or **no**.

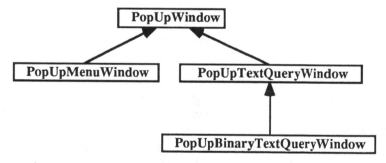

Figure 7.1 Pop-up windows: A logical view.

Pop-up menu windows are provided by classes **PopUpMenu** and **ActionMenu**; pop-up text-query windows by the model-view-controller triple **FillInTheBlank**, **FillInThe-BlankView**, and **CRFillInTheBlankController**; and pop-up binary text-query windows by **BinaryChoice**, **BinaryChoiceView**, and **BinaryChoiceController**. Generalization **FillInTheBlankController** is also used in place of **CRFillInTheBlankController**.

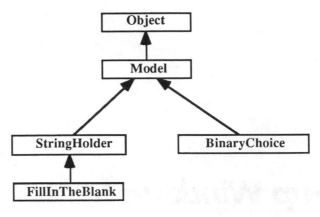

Figure 7.2 The pop-up window model hierarchy.

The model hierarchy (see Fig. 7.2) provides distinct models only for text query windows; i.e., there are no special models for menu windows. In fact, classes PopUpMenu and ActionMenu (see Fig. 7.4) deviate from the standard MVC paradigm. They can be viewed as combining the notion of a model, view, and controller into one object, themselves. Thus, it is not possible to easily change any of these integrated components.

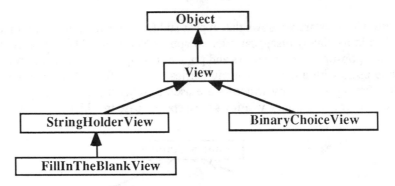

Figure 7.3 The pop-up view hierarchy.

The view class hierarchy (see Fig. 7.3) is relatively shallow. Class FillInTheBlank-View inherits most of its protocol from StringHolderView; class BinaryChoiceView is specially designed.

The corresponding controller classes (see Fig. 7.4) are equally small in number but they form part of a more complex inheritance hierarchy. FillInTheBlankController and CRFillInTheBlankController are string holder controllers with a revised control protocol that forces a user response; e.g., by flashing until its request is satisfied. After typing a response (if different from the sample response), the user can signal acceptance by choosing **accept** in a yellow button pop-up menu. The CRFillInTheBlankController also permits this acceptance to be signaled by typing return (CR is short for carriage return).

Class BinaryChoiceController is much less complex; it is sufficient to have it inherit from the standard Controller class.

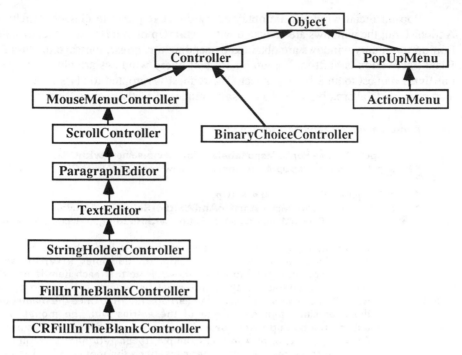

Figure 7.4 The pop-up controller hierarchy.

7.2 CREATING POP-UP WINDOWS

Most of the pop-up window creation protocol has been detailed in Sect. 1.2, *Windows and Window Support for the Novice*. We repeat it here in abbreviated form (see Fig. 7.5 for examples) along with a few additions.

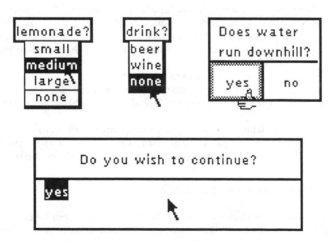

Figure 7.5 Pop-up windows from PopUpMenu, ActionMenu, BinaryChoice, and FillInTheBlank.

Pop-up menu windows are obtained by direct requests to classes PopUpMenu and ActionMenu; the windows are activated with a **startUp** or **startUp:withHeading:** message. Pop-up text-query windows are obtained by sending a **request:** message to class FillInThe-Blank; activation is built-in. Pop-up binary text-query windows are obtained by sending a **confirm:** request to an arbitrary object. The request is rerouted to class BinaryChoice. It is also possible to alternatively send a **message:** request directly to class BinaryChoice.

pop-up menu creation and activation

- aPopUpMenu ← PopUpMenu **labels:** 'pig\cow\horse\hen' **withCRs**.
- aPopUpMenu ← PopUpMenu **labels:** 'pig\cow\horse\hen' **withCRs lines:** #(1 3).

- anInteger ← aPopUpMenu **startUp**.
- anInteger ← aPopUpMenu **startUpAndWaitForSelectionAt:** aPoint.
- anInteger ← aPopUpMenu **startUp:** aButton **withHeading:** 'Which\One?' **withCRs**.

> Constructs a pop-up menu containing the specified labels as menu items. The variation with **lines:** will additionally add lines **after** the specified entries; e.g., after pig and horse above. Note that each item is an arbitrary sequence of characters; the items must be separated by a carriage return (**withCRs** converts backslashes to carriage returns). Once the menu pops up, the user can either select one of the entries with the mouse or select outside the pop-up menu. Selecting an entry will cause the position of the entry; e.g., 1, 2, 3, or 4 in this example, to be returned; selecting outside causes 0 to be returned. In either case, once the mouse button is released, the pop-up menu disappears. The **startUpAndWaitForSelectionAt:** message permits the menu to be positioned at a particular location; e.g., it could be relative to a current active window position. The **startUp:withHeading:** variation permits a multi-line title to be provided; aButton is typically #anyButton but can also be #yellowButton, #redButton, or #blueButton.

action menu creation and activation

- anActionMenu ← ActionMenu **labels:** 'pig\cow\horse\hen' **withCRs**.
- anActionMenu ← ActionMenu **labels:** 'pig\cow\horse\hen' **withCRs lines:** #(1 3).
- anActionMenu ← ActionMenu **labels:** 'yes\no' **withCRs selectors:** #(doYes doNo).
- anActionMenu ← ActionMenu **labels:** 'yes\no' **withCRs lines:** #() **selectors:** #(...).

- anInteger ← anActionMenu **startUp**.
- anInteger ← anActionMenu **startUpAndWaitForSelectionAt:** aPoint.
- anInteger ← anActionMenu **startUp:** aButton **withHeading:** 'Which\One?' **withCRs**.

> Differs from the previous pop-up menu in being able to store selector messages. The sender can explicitly extract these messages via 'anActionMenu **selectorAt:** anIndex' and perform them.

binary choice creation and activation

- aBoolean ← anObject **confirm:** 'Did the chicken come before the egg?\Well!' **withCRs**.
- aBoolean ← BinaryChoice **message:** 'Do you agree?\Well!' **withCRs**.

- aBoolean ← BinaryChoice **message:** aString **displayAt:** aPoint **ifTrue:** aBlock.
- aBoolean ← BinaryChoice **message:** aString **displayAt:** aPoint **ifFalse:** aBlock.

Inside Smalltalk

- aBoolean ← BinaryChoice **message**: aString **displayAt**: aPoint
  ifTrue: aBlock **ifFalse**: aBlock.
- aBoolean ← BinaryChoice **message**: aString **displayAt**: aPoint
  centered: aBoolean **ifTrue**: aBlock **ifFalse**: aBlock.

The **confirm**: message constructs a confirmer; i.e., a window with the above message (multi-lined if carriage returns are contained) with both a **yes** box and a **no** box. The user will be forced to choose one or the other. If **yes** is chosen, **true** is returned; otherwise, **false**. Attempts to ignore the confirmer by trying to activate other windows result in the screen flashing. Once a choice is made, the window disappears. The **confirm**: message can be sent to any object, but the receiver is inconsequential since it is rerouted to BinaryChoice. The BinaryChoice variations are useful if the messages need to be displayed at a specific location. In the last case, either the window center or the window origin is positioned at the point, depending on whether or not the centering parameter is true. The centering default is **true** for **confirm**: and **message**: and **false** for the other variations.

FillInTheBlank creation and activation

- aString ← FillInTheBlank **request**: 'What is your name?'.
- aString ← FillInTheBlank **request**: 'Do you wish to continue?' **initialAnswer**: 'yes'.

- aString ← FillInTheBlank **message**: aString **displayAt**: aPoint **centered**: aBoolean.
  action: aBlock **initialAnswer**: aString.
- aString ← FillInTheBlank **request**: aString **displayAt**: aPoint **centered**: aBoolean
  action: aBlock **initialAnswer**: aString.

Constructs a request window with the above message (multi-lined if carriage returns are contained). The user will be forced to type a response that is terminated either by a carriage return or by choosing **accept** in the yellow button menu. At that point the window disappears. Attempts to ignore the request by trying to make other windows active are signaled by flashing. The typed string is returned to the sender. The initial answer, if provided, is returned by immediately typing a carriage return or accepting the text. It can be edited to provide a different answer. The latter two variations permit explicit control over the positioning of the window. The **message**:... variation requires an explicit **accept** by the user; the **request**:... variation additionally permits acceptance signaled by typing return. Note: if a multi-lined response is desired, the **message**:... variation must be used. The centering default is **true** for both **request**: variations.

7.3 POP-UP MENUS

A **pop-up menu** is an interactive window for selecting an item from a list of menu items. All items in the pop-up menu are displayed one above the other; no scrolling is needed. When the user depresses the mouse button on one of these items, it is highlighted to indicate that it has been selected. Moving the mouse to another item will change the selection. Moving it off all items will result in no selection. When the mouse button is released, the index of the chosen selection is returned; 0 is returned for no selection.

Two varieties of pop-up menus are provided: **standard pop-up menus** and **action menus**. Action menus differ from the former by providing an array of selectors parallel to the menu items. The selectors are usually used to process the selected item; e.g., by using it to send a processing message to some appropriate view's model. Yellow button menus for pluggable windows must be action menus.

7.3.1 The PopUpMenu Protocol

Class **PopUpMenu** is independent of all other windows in the system. As such, it inherits from Object as shown in Fig. 7.6. It is in effect a model, view, and controller all combined into one. Pop-up menus are not scheduled for execution. Rather, they must be started up in the current process. When started, they pop up awaiting a user selection. While it is active, no other window can be activated. After the mouse button is depressed and released, the pop-up menu disappears.

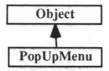

Figure 7.6 The PopUpMenu hierarchy.

A **pop-up menu** is created by specifying **labels**, a string of items separated by carriage returns, and **lines**, an array specifying the item **after which** a line is to be drawn. If no lines are desired, the latter can be omitted.

Menu entries are all the same size. When an entry is selected, a rectangle of the appropriate size, called the **marker**, is moved to the selected entry. Highlighting and dehighlighting are achieved by reversing the portion of the display indicated by the marker.

creating the pop-up menu without start up

- PopUpMenu **labels**: aStringOfItems
- PopUpMenu **labels**: aStringOfItems **lines**: anArrayOfItemPositions
  Returns a pop-up menu whose items are in aStringOfItems. Each item in the string must be separated by a carriage return. When the lines array is specified, causes lines to be drawn after each item specified by anArrayOfItemPositions. Item one is at position 1, item two at position 2, and so on.

starting up the pop-up-menu

- aPopUpMenu **startUp**
- aPopUpMenu **startUpYellowButton**
- aPopUpMenu **startUpRedButton**
- aPopUpMenu **startUpBlueButton**
- aPopUpMenu **startUp**: aSymbol
  Method **startUp** defaults to #anyButton. Displays the pop-up-menu at the current sensor point, waits for the button specified by aSymbol (one of #yellowButton, #redButton, #blueButton, #anyButton) to be depressed, and then continuously highlights and dehighlights the user's selections until the the button is released. Returns the last selection (0 if none was selected).

Inside Smalltalk

- aPopUpMenu **startUp**: aSymbol **withHeading**: aText

    As above, but provides an additional title box with aText displayed in it.

- aPopUpMenu **startUpAndWaitForSelectionAt**: aPoint

    Differs from **startUp** by displaying the pop-up menu at the specified point and by waiting for the button to be depressed inside the pop-up menu display box. Then, it continuously highlights and dehighlights the user's selections until the button is released. Returns the last selection (0 if none was selected).

operations privately used by the start up methods

- aPopUpMenu **buttonPressed**: aSymbol

    Returns whether or not the button specified by aSymbol (one of #yellowButton, #redButton, #blueButton, #anyButton) was depressed.

- aPopUpMenu **displayAt**: aPoint **during**: aBlock

    Displays the pop-up menu centered at aPoint while aBlock is evaluated. If necessary, translates the view so that it is completely on the screen.

- aPopUpMenu **displayAt**: aPoint **withHeading**: aText **during**: aBlock

    As above, but additionally provides title aText for the pop-up-menu.

selection management

- aPopUpMenu **reset**

    Initializes the marker position to the top of the pop-up menu and the current selection to 0 (no selection).

- aPopUpMenu **manageMarker**

    If the cursor is inside the pop-up menu display box, highlights the selected item; otherwise, dehighlights the last selected item (if any).

- aPopUpMenu **markerOn**: aPoint

    The item whose bounding area contains aPoint is selected. Dehighlights the last selected item (if any). Highlights the area and records the index of the selection.

- aPopUpMenu **markerOff**

    Records that no item is selected. Dehighlights the last selected item (if any).

- aPopUpMenu **markerTop**: aPoint

    Returns aPoint gridded to the nearest items in the pop-up menu.

- aPopUpMenu **selection**

    Returns the current selection.

display box accessing

- aPopUpMenu **width**
- aPopUpMenu **height**
- aPopUpMenu **center**
- aPopUpMenu **topLeft**

    Returns sizing information about the pop-up menu display box.

- aPopUpMenu **borderWidth**

    Returns the width of the pop-up menu display box border.

private

- aPopUpMenu **labels**: aStringOfItems **font**: aFont **lines**: anArrayOfItemPositions

    Initializes the pop-up menu in support of the corresponding class methods.

Chapter 7 Pop-up Windows

Example

Suppose we want the user to select an object that is either black or white, large or small. We can create a four-choice pop-up menu (see Fig. 7.7) in two ways.

```
aPopUpMenu ← PopUpMenu
    labels: 'large black\large white\small black\small white'.
aPopUpMenu ← PopUpMenu
    labels: 'large black\large white\small black\small white' lines: #(2)
```

The second approach puts a dividing line after the 'large white' choice; i.e., divides the selections into two equal parts. Normally, the pop-up menu would be activated via

```
aPopUpMenu startUp
```

or

```
aPopUpMenu startUpYellowButton
```

However, occasionally it is useful to add a title to inform the user of what he has to do (see Fig. 7.7). For instance,

```
aPopUpMenu startUp: #anyButton withHeading: 'Please make a choice'.
```

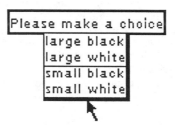

Figure 7.7 A pop-up window (selection not yet made).

The PopUpMenu Creation Protocol

The main protocol is illustrated by public method **labels:lines:** and private method **labels:font:lines:**. No facility is provided for users knowledgeable about fonts to make use of the private facility. The string of items is used to create a paragraph of centered items, which is then converted to a form. Lines are added to the form at the appropriate places by filling small rectangles of height 1. A marker is then created with the same width as the form and the height of one menu entry. The marker is positioned on the first menu entry. It will be moved when new selections are made.

creating the pop-up menu without starting it up

- PopUpMenu **labels:** aStringOfItems **lines:** anArrayOfItemPositions
    "See comment above."
    ↑self **new**
        labels: aStringOfItems
        font: (TextStyle **default fontAt:** 1)
        lines: anArrayOfItemPositions

• aPopUpMenu **labels**: aStringOfItems **font**: aFont **lines**: anArrayOfItemPositions
   "Initializes the pop-up menu in support of the corresponding class methods."
   | style labelParagraph |

   "Save parameters in instance variables."
   labelString ← aStringOfItems. font ← aFont.
   lineArray ← anArrayOfItemPositions.

   "Create a form containing the elements centered one above the other."
   style ← TextStyle **fontArray**: (Array **with**: font).
   style **alignment**: 2 "centered"; **gridForFont**: 1 **withLead**: 0.
   labelParagraph ← Paragraph **withText**: aStringOfItems **asText style**: style.
   form ← labelParagraph **asForm**.

   "Create quadrangle for some extra space around the form and for a border."
   frame ← Quadrangle **new**
       region: (labelParagraph **compositionRectangle expandBy**: 2);
       borderWidth: (1@1 corner: 3@3); yourself.

   "Add separation lines to the form by filling appropriate subrectangles of
   width 1."
   lineArray == nil **ifFalse**: [
       lineArray **do**: [:line |
           form
               fill: (0 @ (line * font **height**) **extent**: (frame **width** @ 1))
               mask: Form **black**]].

   "Create the highlight marker and record that no selection has been taken."
   marker ← frame **inside topLeft**
       extent: frame **inside width** @ labelParagraph **lineGrid**.
   selection ← 0

The PopUpMenu StartUp Protocol

The most complex part is illustrated by methods **startup:withHeading:**, **buttonPressed:**, and **displayAt:withHeading:during:**. The first method sends a block to the display method. When activated, the block busy-waits until the specified button is depressed, flashing if the cursor is outside the pop-up menu. Once the button is depressed, the current selection is highlighted or dehighlighted as appropriate until the button is released. The last selection made is returned once the display message terminates execution.

The **displayAt:withHeading:during:** method creates a title box above the pop-up menu frame and moves both if necessary to place them within the display area. The areas that are to be overwritten by the pop-up window are saved for later restoring. The title and menu frame are subsequently displayed with suitable borders. By sending a value message to the block, selection management is then activated until a selection is finalized. Then the saved forms are restored.

starting up the pop-up-menu

• aPopUpMenu **startUp**
       ↑self **startUp**: #anyButton

- aPopUpMenu **startUp:** aSymbol

  "Displays the pop-up menu at the current sensor point, waits for the button specified by aSymbol to be depressed, and then continuously highlights and dehighlights the user's selections until the the button is released. Returns the last selection (0 if none was selected)."

  self **displayAt:** Sensor **cursorPoint during:** [

      Sensor **cursorPoint:** marker **center.** "Move cursor to top menu item."

      "Busy-wait for button to be depressed."

      [self **buttonPressed:** aSymbol] **whileFalse:** [].

      "While it is depressed, keep highlighting and dehighlighting the selection."

      [self buttonPressed: aSymbol] whileTrue: [self manageMarker]].

  ↑selection

- aPopUpMenu **startUp:** aSymbol **withHeading:** aText

  "Similar to above but with extra title."

  self **displayAt:** Sensor **cursorPoint withHeading:** aText **during:** [

      Sensor **cursorPoint:** marker **center.** "Move cursor to top menu item."

      "Busy-wait for button to be depressed; flash if outside the pop-up menu."

      [self **buttonPressed:** aSymbol] **whileFalse:** [

          (frame **containsPoint:** Sensor **cursorPoint**)

              ifFalse: [Display **flash:** frame]].

      "While it is depressed, keep highlighting and dehighlighting the selection."

      [self **buttonPressed:** aSymbol] **whileTrue:** [self **manageMarker**]].

  ↑selection

operations privately used by the start up methods

- aPopUpMenu **buttonPressed:** aSymbol

  "Returns whether or not the button specified by aSymbol was depressed."

  aSymbol = #redButton **ifTrue:** [↑Sensor **redButtonPressed**].

  aSymbol = #yellowButton **ifTrue:** [↑Sensor **yellowButtonPressed**].

  aSymbol = #blueButton **ifTrue:** [↑Sensor **blueButtonPressed**].

  ↑Sensor **anyButtonPressed**

- aPopUpMenu **displayAt:** aPoint **withHeading:** aText **during:** aBlock

  "Displays the pop-up menu with heading aText centered at aPoint while aBlock is evaluated. If necessary, translates the view so that it is completely on the screen."

  | delta savedArea heading headingBox headingSavedArea |

  "Align the top of the pop-up menu frame with aPoint (the marker is on the top item)."

  frame ← frame **align:** marker **center with:** aPoint.

  "Create title above the pop-up menu frame."

  heading ← aText **asDisplayText.**

  headingBox ← heading **boundingBox expandBy:** 2.

  headingBox ← headingBox

      align: headingBox **bottomCenter**

      with: frame **topCenter** + (0@2).

  "Move the frame, headingBox, and marker if they are outside the display."

  delta ← (frame **merge:** headingBox)

      amountToTranslateWithin: Display **boundingBox.**

  frame **moveBy:** delta.

  headingBox **moveBy:** delta.

  marker ← marker **align:** marker **center with:** aPoint + delta.

Inside Smalltalk

"Save the forms underneath the frame and headingBox rectangles."
savedArea ← Form **fromDisplay**: frame.
headingSavedArea ← Form **fromDisplay**: headingBox.

"Display the title border and the title itself."
Display **border**: (headingBox) **width**: 2 **mask**: Form **black**.
heading **displayAt**: headingBox **origin** + (2@2).

"Display the pop-up menu frame border and the frame itself."
Display **black**: (frame **origin** + (1@1) **corner**: frame **corner**).
Display **black**: (frame **origin corner**: frame **corner** - (1@1)).
"Note: the top right and bottom left corners remain unchanged?"
form **displayOn**: Display **at**: frame **inside topLeft clippingBox**: frame **inside**.
"Handle potential future extension: pre-initialized selection."
selection ~= 0 **ifTrue**: [Display **reverse**: marker].
"Make the actual selection."
aBlock **value**.

"Restore the display to its original state."
savedArea **displayOn**: Display **at**: frame **topLeft**.
headingSavedArea **displayOn**: Display **at**: headingBox **topLeft**

The PopUpMenu Selection Management Protocol

Selection management is relatively simple. As long as the cursor is inside the pop-up menu, the old selection is dehighlighted (if necessary) by reversing the area specified by the marker (a simple rectangle), the marker is moved to the new selection, and it is highlighted by reversing the marker area in the same way. If the cursor is outside the pop-up menu, it is sufficient to dehighlight the old selection (if necessary).

selection management

• aPopUpMenu **manageMarker**
    "If the cursor is inside the pop-up menu display box, highlights the selected item; otherwise, dehighlights the last selected item (if any)."
    | aPoint |
    aPoint ← Sensor **cursorPoint**.
    (frame **inside containsPoint**: aPoint)
            ifTrue: [self **markerOn**: aPoint]
            ifFalse: [self **markerOff**]

• aPopUpMenu **markerOn**: aPoint
    "The item whose bounding area contains aPoint is selected. Dehighlights the last selected item (if any). Highlights the area and records the index of the selection."

    "If the selection is nonzero **and** the marker contains the cursor, do nothing because nothing has changed. Note: (A=B) | C **not ifFalse**: [...] is equivalent to ((A=B) | C **not**) **not ifTrue** : [...] which is (A~=B) & C **ifTrue**: [...]."
    selection = 0 | (marker **containsPoint**: aPoint) **not ifTrue**: [
        selection = 0 & (marker **containsPoint**: aPoint)
                ifTrue: [Display **reverse**: marker] "highlight it"
                ifFalse: [
                    selection ~= 0 **ifTrue**: [Display **reverse**: marker]. "dehighlight it"
                    marker ← marker "move to new selection"
                        align: marker **topLeft**
                        with: marker **left** @ (self **markerTop**: aPoint).
                    Display **reverse**: marker "highlight new selection"]].
    selection ← marker **top** - frame **top** // marker **height** + 1 "record selection"

- aPopUpMenu **markerOff**
  "Records that no item is selected. Dehighlights the last selected item (if any)."
  selection ~= 0 **ifTrue**: [Display **reverse**: marker. selection ← 0]

- aPopUpMenu **markerTop**: aPoint
  "Returns aPoint gridded to the nearest items in the pop-up menu."
  ↑(aPoint **y** - frame **inside top truncateTo**: font **height**) + frame **inside top**

7.3.2 The ActionMenu Protocol

Class **ActionMenu** is a specialization of PopUpMenu (see Fig. 7.8) that provides an additional parallel array of selectors. **Action menus** were designed primarily for use with pluggable views, but they can be used for any newly designed windows. As with pop-up menus, action menus return an index to the menu item selected (0 for no selection) when activated. The index returned is used to select an appropriate selector that is used as a message to send to the view's model. Action menus are documented as pluggable pop-up menus, but this is an error since they do not provide any facility to plug onto an object; i.e., they have no model.

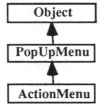

Figure 7.8 The ActionMenu hierarchy.

Action menus can be created with the standard pop-up menu protocol by providing the labels and optionally the lines. It can then be augmented by setting the missing array of selectors. Alternatively, the labels, selectors, and optionally the lines can be provided simultaneously.

instance creation without start up

- PopUpMenu **labels**: aString
- PopUpMenu **labels**: aString **lines**: anArray
- ActionMenu **labels**: aString **lines**: anArray **selectors**: selectorArray
- ActionMenu **labels**: aString **selectors**: selectorArray

instance creation with start up

- ActionMenu **confirm**
  Creates and schedules an action menu with labels 'confirm\abort'. Returns **true** for confirm and **false** otherwise.

selector manipulation

- anActionMenu **selectorAt**: index
- anActionMenu **setSelectors**: selectorArray
  There is no corresponding method for extracting the selector array.

See the sections about pluggable windows, pluggable text windows, pluggable menu windows, and pluggable switch windows for examples using action menus.

7.4 POP-UP TEXT-QUERY WINDOWS

Classes **FillInTheBlank**, **FillInTheBlankView**, and either **FillInTheBlankController** or **CRFillInTheBlankController** form model-view-controller triples that provide pop-up text-query windows. The text editing protocol is inherited from the corresponding string holder classes (see Fig. 7.9). Hence, a **fill-in-the-blank** text window is a special kind of string holder window.

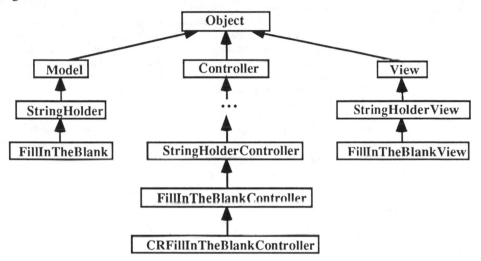

Figure 7.9 Text-Query windows: The FillInTheBlank hierarchy.

Fill-in-the-blank text-query pop-up windows are used for interactively querying users about string information; e.g., descriptive data, a name, a piece of code.

7.4.1 The FillInTheBlank Protocol

Instances of class **FillInTheBlank** are string holders with an associated one-parameter **action block**. They are designed to execute this block when the user accepts the text typed in the corresponding view. The accepted text is passed as a parameter to the action block. For convenience, fill-in-the-blank instances are usually provided with an initial string as a suggestion to the user. This initial string is, of course, the string holder contents.

instance creation without scheduling

- StringHolder **new**
    When sent to FillInTheBlank, returns an initialized instance.
- FillInTheBlank **action:** aBlock **initialAnswer:** aString
    Returns an instance with the specified action block (it should be a one-parameter block) and the specified initial string holder contents.

- FillInTheBlank **request**: queryString
- FillInTheBlank **request**: queryString **initialAnswer**: answerString
  Creates a pop-up window centered at the cursor point with a query message that must be answered interactively by the user. Returns the string accepted by the user; acceptance can be chosen from a menu entry or signaled by typing a carriage return. An empty string is used if the initial answer is not provided.

- FillInTheBlank **message**: queryString **displayAt**: aPoint **centered**: aBoolean **action**: aBlock **initialAnswer**: answerString
- FillInTheBlank **request**: queryString **displayAt**: aPoint **centered**: aBoolean **action**: aBlock **initialAnswer**: answerString
- FillInTheBlank **request**: queryString **displayAt**: aPoint **centered**: aBoolean **action**: aBlock **initialAnswer**: answerString **useCRController**: anotherBoolean
  Creates a pop-up window with a query message that must be answered interactively by the user. Either the window center (if the centering parameter is **true**) or the top left corner (if it is **false** — the default) is positioned at the specified point. When the user accepts the string typed in (or the initial version provided), the action block (if provided) is executed with the accepted string as parameter. The **message**: version requires an explicit accept by the user; the **request**: version additionally accepts automatically when a carriage return is typed; and the **request**:...**useCR-Controller**: version permits the choice of either.

instance initialization

- aFillInTheBlank **initialize**
  Initializes the instance to indicate that there is no action block (**nil**) and that the action block has not yet been executed.

action block manipulation

- aFillInTheBlank **action**: aBlockOrNil
  Records the action block to be used when the user accepts the text in the text window; **nil** indicates that no action block is to be used.
- aFillInTheBlank **selectAction**
  Evaluates the action block with the contents of the instance that is a special kind of string holder.
- aFillInTheBlank **actionTaken**
  Returns **true** if the action block has already been executed; otherwise **false**.
- aFillInTheBlank **setAction**: aBoolean
  Sets whether or not the action block has been executed. Could have been a side effect of **selectAction** but isn't.

Example

Fig. 7.10 illustrates the result of four fill-in-the-blank requests. The two simple request messages are appropriate for most requirements. The two more complicated versions are used primarily when the fill-in-the-blank view can be specially positioned; e.g., relative to some part of the window that is currently in control. The version of the form **message**:... is needed when multiple lines of input are required. The other variation immediately terminates as soon as a carriage return is typed.

aName ← FillInTheBlank **request**: 'Name, please?'.
aClassName ← FillInTheBlank **request**: 'Class name, please' **initialAnswer**: 'Object'.

FillInTheBlank **request**: 'Width, please?' **displayAt**: view **insetDisplayBox center**
    centered: true **action**: [:aString | width ← aString **asNumber**] **initialAnswer**: '100'.
FillInTheBlank **message**: 'Name and address, please' **displayAt**: Sensor **cursorPoint**
    centered: true **action**: [:aString | aMultiLineAddressBookEntry ← aString]
    initialAnswer: 'John Buck\Nowheresland' **withCRs**

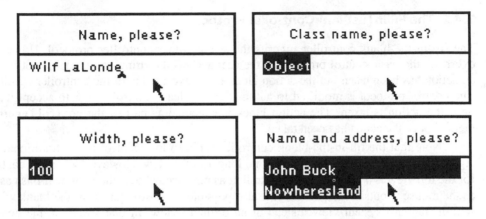

Figure 7.10 Text-query windows.

The ...**useCRController**: version provides the basic implementation for the above by interfacing with a fill-in-the-blank view. Its implementation is the following. Note that it saves the form underneath it before starting up and restores it afterward. Additionally, note that the controller is not scheduled as a separate process. It is started up as part of the current process. This works well because the controller refuses to release control if the user has not accepted a typed string.

instance creation with scheduling

- FillInTheBlank **request**: queryString **displayAt**: aPoint **centered**: centerBoolean
    action: aBlock **initialAnswer**: answerString **useCRController**: useCRControllerBoolean
      "See comment above."
      | newBlank fillInView savedArea |
      newBlank ← self **new**; **action**: aBlock; **contents**: answerString; **yourself**.
      fillInView ←
          FillInTheBlankView **on**: newBlank
              message: queryString
              displayAt: aPoint
              centered: centerBoolean
              useCRController: useCRControllerBoolean.
      savedArea ← Form **fromDisplay**: fillInView **displayBox**.
      fillInView **display**; **controller centerCursorInView**; **controller startUp**; **release**.
      savedArea **displayOn**: Display **at**: fillInView **viewport topLeft**

The top view returned by the fill-in-the-blank **on:message:displayAt:centered:use-CRController:** message is a standard view with two subviews, a display-text view for the query string and a fill-in-the-blank view for the user reply, initialized to the initial answer string. As expected, the fill-in-the-blank view does use a fill-in-the-blank controller. However, the top view does not. It uses a binary-choice controller. The binary-choice controller is unique in that it refuses to relinquish control when no action has been taken on the model. Conversely, it also automatically relinquishes control once the action has been taken. Since it is not a standard system controller, it also prevents the user from explicitly closing or moving the view.

7.4.2 The FillInTheBlankController Protocol

The fill-in-the-blank controller inherits the string holder controller protocol. However, it overrides the basic control protocol. If the user accepts the string, the model is notified that an action has been taken but the action block is not executed until the controller terminates. The control protocol is modified to automatically release control, never to accept it again once the action is taken. The action block is executed as part of the **controlTerminate** method once the action has been taken.

Note that the fill-in-the-blank controller can also lose control in the traditional way; e.g., it loses control when the mouse is no longer in the view. However, when the controller for the top view is a binary-choice controller, as discussed above, the view will flash as long as the mouse is outside its bounds. It is also possible to construct a fill-in-the-blank window with a standard system view instead of an ordinary view. In that situation, the **control-Terminate** method explicitly closes the window (closing it explicitly unschedules it). There is no need to unschedule the controller in the previous situation because it wasn't scheduled; it was given control via **startUp**. The code is explicitly shown to make it more understandable.

overriding the string holder basic control protocol

- aFillInTheBlankController **isControlWanted**
  "Refuses to accept control if the user accepted the string. In other cases, it uses the string holder protocol."
  model **actionTaken ifTrue:** [↑false].
  ↑super **isControlActive**

- aFillInTheBlankController **isControlActive**
  "Refuses to keep control if the user accepted the string. In other cases, it uses the string holder protocol."
  model **actionTaken ifTrue:** [↑false].
  ↑super **isControlActive**

- aFillInTheBlankController **controlTerminate**
  "Extends the string holder protocol if the user accepted the string. In that case, it explicitly unschedules the controller if it was scheduled and then executes the model's action block."
  | topController |
  super **controlTerminate**.
  model **actionTaken ifFalse:** [↑self].
  topController ← view **topView controller**.
  (topController **notNil** & (topController **isKindOf:** StandardSystemController))
       ifTrue: [topController **close**].
  model **selectAction**

- aFillInTheBlankController **accept**
  "Extends the string holder protocol by indicating that the model's action has been taken but it does not execute the model's action block."
  super **accept.**
  model **setAction:** true

special initialization to ensure that the initial string is selected (hightlighted in bold)

- aFillInTheBlankController **resetState**
  "Forces the highlighting of the entire text so that the user can override it simply by typing over it."
  super **resetState.**
  stopBlock ← paragraph **characterBlockForIndex:** paragraph **text size**+1.

7.4.3 The CRFillInTheBlankController Protocol

A **cr-fill-in-the-blank controller** is a special kind of fill-in-the-blank controller that automatically accepts the text when a carriage return is typed. This is done by overriding the paragraph editor **readKeyboard** method.

It also overrides the string holder **controlInitialize** method to eliminate the scroll bars. The method is simply a copy of the version in class ParagraphEditor with the code 'super **controlInitialize**' eliminated; this avoids using the scroll controller's **control-Initialize** method that sets up the scroll bars. For short replies, this works well. For longer replies that wrap around to several lines before a carriage return is typed, it is sometimes necessary to scroll back up in order to review the text already written (or to fix it). Without scroll bars, it is necessary to force the automatic scrolling feature by attempting to select text that extends beyond the visible part.

overriding the standard protocol

- aCRFillInTheBlankController **controlInitialize**
  Deactivates the scroll bars.
- aCRFillInTheBlankController **controlTerminate**
  Unchanged; i.e., executes 'super **controlTerminate**'.
- aCRFillInTheBlankController **readKeyboard**
  Copied from ParagraphEditor to gain access to carriage returns. Invokes the method below when one is found.
- aCRFillInTheBlankController **cr:** aCharacterStream
  "Performs the standard paragraph editor task but additionally accepts the form holder contents."
  sensor **keyboard.** "Remove the carriage return previously peeked at."
  characterStream **isEmpty ifFalse:** [
      "idiosyncratic to the paragraph editor design"
      self **replaceSelectionWith:**
          (Text **string:** aCharacterStream **contents emphasis:** emphasisHere)].
  self **accept** "The important part."

7.4.4 The FillInTheBlankView Protocol

The **fill-in-the-blank view** is primarily concerned with constructing a top view that has two subviews, a display-text view for the query string and a fill-in-the-blank view for the user reply, initialized to the initial answer string. Two of the class methods simply construct such a view and return it. In that case, the top view is a regular view that is not expected to be scheduled; it is expected to be given control via **startUp**. Its associated controller is a binary-choice controller that insists that the user reply be accepted before relinquishing control. A third method constructs and schedules a view. In that case, the top view is a standard system view with a corresponding standard system controller.

creating unscheduled views awaiting start up

- FillInTheBlankView **on**: aFillInTheBlank **message**: queryString **displayAt**: aPoint **centered**: aBoolean
- FillInTheBlankView **on**: aFillInTheBlank **message**: queryString **displayAt**: aPoint **centered**: aBoolean **useCRController**: anotherBoolean

   Creates a regular top view that has two subviews, a display-text view for the query string, and a fill-in-the-blank view for the user reply, initialized to the initial answer string already contained in the fill-in-the-blank instance. The top view's controller is a binary-choice controller. Either the center (if the centering parameter is **true**) or the top left corner (if it is **false**) of the window is positioned at the specified point. The fill-in-the-blank view uses a cr-fill-in-the-blank controller if the use-cr-controller parameter is **true**; otherwise, it uses a fill-in-the-blank controller. The view is returned.

creating scheduled views that are started

- FillInTheBlankView **openOn**: aFillInTheBlank **message**: queryString **displayAt**: aPoint **centered**: aBoolean

   Differs from the above in that the top view/controller is a standard system view/controller and no cr-fill-in-the-blank controller is used. Also schedules and starts the view.

private operations used by the above

- FillInTheBlankView **buildAnswerView**: aFillInTheBlank **frameWidth**: widthInteger
- FillInTheBlankView **buildMessageView**: queryString

controller access

- aFillInTheBlankView **defaultControllerClass**

   Returns class FillInTheBlankController.

The Basic Fill-In-The-Blank Operations

We consider three of the above methods. Hopefully, they are self-explanatory.

creating unscheduled views awaiting start up

- FillInTheBlankView **on**: aFillInTheBlank **message**: queryString **displayAt**: aPoint **centered**: centerBoolean **useCRController**: useCRControllerBoolean
   "See comments above."
   | topView messageView answerView |
   messageView ← self **buildMessageView**: queryString.
   answerView ← self
      buildAnswerView:
         aFillInTheBlank **frameWidth**: messageView **window width**.
   useCRControllerBoolean
      ifTrue: [answerView **controller**: CRFillInTheBlankController **new**].
   topView ← View **new**
      model: aFillInTheBlank;
      controller: BinaryChoiceController **new**;
      addSubView: messageView;
      addSubView: answerView **below**: messageView; **yourself**.

```
topView
    align: (centerBoolean
        ifTrue: [topView viewport center]
        ifFalse: [topView viewport topLeft])
    with: aPoint;
    window: (0 @ 0 extent: messageView window width @
        (messageView window height + answerView window height));
    translateBy: (topView displayBox
        amountToTranslateWithin: Display boundingBox).
    ↑topView
```

private operations used by the above

- FillInTheBlankView **buildAnswerView:** aFillInTheBlank **frameWidth:** widthInteger
```
    | answerView |
    answerView ← self new
        model: aFillInTheBlank;
        window: (0@0 extent: widthInteger @ 40);
        borderWidth: 2.
    ↑answerView
```

- FillInTheBlankView **buildMessageView:** queryString
```
    | messageView |
    messageView ← DisplayTextView new
        model: queryString asDisplayText;
        borderWidthLeft: 2 right: 2 top: 2 bottom: 0;
        insideColor: Form white;
        controller: NoController new.
    messageView
        window: (0@0 extent: (messageView window extent max: 200@30));
        centered.
    ↑messageView
```

7.5 POP-UP BINARY TEXT-QUERY WINDOWS

Pop-up binary text-query windows permit yes/no responses to text queries. The pop-up text-query windows are specialized so that the 'yes/no' text need not be explicitly typed; it is sufficient to click on one of two button windows. Fig. 7.11 illustrates what happens if the user refuses to make a selection. The view flashes (alternates very fast between the two variations shown).

The binary text-query windows are implemented via **binary-choice** model-view-controller triples (see Fig. 7.12). These triples are constructed from instances of **Binary-Choice, BinaryChoiceController**, and **BinaryChoiceView**, which respectively inherit from Model, Controller, and View.

Logically, a binary-choice MVC is also a special kind of a switch MVC that forces the user to choose between two possibilities. The binary-choice controller differs from the switch controller in refusing to relinquish control until a choice has been made. In particular, it is not a standard system controller to ensure that the view cannot be moved. The binary-choice model is designed so that the binary-choice controller can interrogate it to determine if a choice has been made. The binary-choice view displays a user query message along with a yes and no subview that can be clicked on to make a choice. It also switches to thumbs-up and thumbs-down cursors when the mouse enters the yes and no subviews respectively.

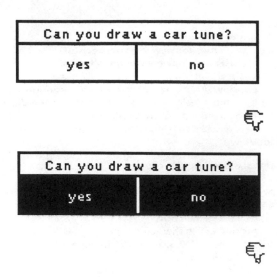

Figure 7.11 Binary text-query windows.

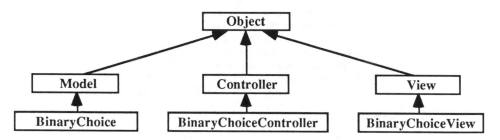

Figure 7.12 Pop-up binary text-query windows: The BinaryChoice hierarchy.

7.5.1 The BinaryChoice Protocol

A **binary-choice** is a special kind of switch designed for interactive querying. The **Binary-Choice** class is typically sent a message that requires a yes/no reply. A special pop-up window is created to request the answer from the user. Binary-choice objects were designed to interact with binary-choice controllers and views. Unlike switches, they were not intended for isolated use. Hence, except for the special class querying messages, most of the protocol is a special case variant of the switch protocol.

binary-choice querying

- BinaryChoice **message:** queryString
  Creates a pop-up window with a query message that must be answered interactively by the user. The window is centered at the cursor point. If the user chooses yes, **true** is returned; otherwise, **false**.
- BinaryChoice **message:** queryString **displayAt:** aPoint **ifTrue:** trueAlternative
- BinaryChoice **message:** queryString **displayAt:** aPoint **ifFalse:** falseAlternative

- BinaryChoice **message**: queryString **displayAt**: aPoint
  ifTrue: trueAlternative **ifFalse**: falseAlternative
- BinaryChoice **message**: queryString **displayAt**: aPoint **centered**: aBoolean
  ifTrue: trueAlternative **ifFalse**: falseAlternative

  Creates a pop-up window with a query message that must be answered
  interactively by the user. Either the center (if centered is **true**) or the top left
  corner (if centered is **false**; the default) of the window is positioned at the
  specified point. If the user chooses yes, the trueAlternative block (if
  provided) is executed; otherwise, the falseAlternative block (if provided) is
  executed.

instance initialization

- aBinaryChoice **initialize**
- aBinaryChoice **trueAction**: aBlock
- aBinaryChoice **falseAction**: aBlock

  Respectively initializes the binary-choice object to indicate that no choice
  has yet been made, records the **true**-alternative block, and records the
  false-alternative block.

executing the block corresponding to the chosen response

- aBinaryChoice **selectTrue**
- aBinaryChoice **selectFalse**

  Records the fact that a choice has been made and executes the
  corresponding **true**- or **false**-alternative block if there is one.

determining if a response has been made

- aBinaryChoice **actionTaken**
  Records **true** if a choice has been made and **false** otherwise.

interfacing with the view

- aBinaryChoice **active**
  Always returns **false**; used in place of the 'model **isOn**' interrogation
  message for the yes and no switch views.

7.5.2 The BinaryChoiceController Protocol

The **binary-choice controller** is a controller that maintains control until the the model
responds **true** to the message actionTaken.

changes to the basic control operations

- aBinaryChoiceController **isControlActive**
  model **actionTaken ifTrue**: [↑false].
  [super **isControlActive**] **whileFalse**: [view **flash**].
  ↑true

- aBinaryChoiceController **startUp**
  Cursor **normal showWhile**: [super **startUp**]

cursor positioning

- aBinaryChoiceController **centerCursorInView**
  Not actually used.

7.5.3 The BinaryChoiceView Protocol

A **binary-choice view** constructs four views: a display-text view for the query message and a standard view to contain two switch views. The two switch views display yes and no respectively. Additionally, when the cursor enters the switch views, the cursor changes to either thumbs-up or thumbs-down respectively.

class initialization

- BinaryChoiceView **initialize**
  Initializes the ThumbsUp and ThumbsDown class variables that are used as the switch cursors.

instance creation and start up

- BinaryChoiceView **openOn**: aBinaryChoice **message**: queryString **displayAt**: aPoint **centered**: aBoolean
  Creates a pop-up window with a query message that must be answered interactively by the user. Depending on the value of centered, either the center or the top left corner of the window is positioned at the specified point. If necessary, the window is adjusted so that all of it is visible. The view is started up rather than being scheduled. If the user chooses yes, the **true** block in aBinaryChoice (if there is one) is executed; otherwise, the **false** block (if there is one) is executed. Does not return anything useful.

used privately to construct switch views

- BinaryChoiceView **buildSwitchesFor**: aBinaryChoice **width**: anInteger
  Constructs a standard view containing a switch view for yes and another one for no.

controller access

- aBinaryChoiceView **defaultControllerClass**
  Returns class BinaryChoiceController.

Consider the open and build-switch methods below (slightly edited to make them more compact). Note that the open method (at the end) saves the form underneath the view prior to starting it up so as to restore it after it relinquishes control. Also, note that the switch views use the binary-choice instance message **active** as the switch interrogation message. Since it always returns **false**, the view will always be displayed in the off state. However, releasing the mouse button will provide a visual indication since the boundary is highlighted. Of course, the binary-choice view is immediately replaced by the saved form as it subsequently relinquishes control.

instance creation and start up

- BinaryChoiceView **openOn**: aBinaryChoice **message**: queryString
  displayAt: aPoint **centered**: aBoolean
      "See comment above"
      | topView messageView switchView alignmentPoint savedArea |
      messageView ← DisplayTextView **new**
          model: messageString **asDisplayText**; **insideColor**: Form **white**.
          controller: NoController **new**; **centered**; **yourself**.
      switchView ← self
          buildSwitchesFor: aBinaryChoice **width**: messageView **window width**.

```
topView ← self new
    model: aBinaryChoice; addSubView: messageView;
    addSubView: switchView below: messageView; yourself.
alignmentPoint ← centered
    ifTrue: [switchView viewport center]
    ifFalse: [topView viewport topLeft].
topView
    align: alignmentPoint with: aPoint; borderWidth: 2;
    translateBy: (topView displayBox
        amountToTranslateWithin: Display boundingBox);
    insideColor: Form white; yourself.
savedArea ← Form fromDisplay: topView displayBox.
    topView display; controller startUp; release.
savedArea displayOn: Display at: topView viewport topLeft
```

used privately to construct switch views

```
• BinaryChoiceView buildSwitchesFor: aBinaryChoice width: anInteger
    | switchView yesSwitchView noSwitchView |
    switchView ← View new
        model: aBinaryChoice; controller: BinaryChoiceController new.

    yesSwitchView ← SwitchView new
        model: aBinaryChoice; label: 'yes' asParagraph;
        borderWidthLeft: 0 right: 2 top: 0 bottom: 0;
        selector: #active.
    (yesSwitchView controller) selector: #selectTrue; cursor: ThumbsUp.
    yesSwitchView window: (0@0 extent:
        anInteger//2 @ yesSwitchView window height).

    noSwitchView ← SwitchView new
        model: aBinaryChoice; label: 'no' asParagraph;
        selector: #active.
    (noSwitchView controller) selector: #selectFalse; cursor: ThumbsDown.
    noSwitchView window: (0@0 extent:
        anInteger//2 @ noSwitchView window height).

    switchView
        addSubView: yesSwitchView;
        addSubView: noSwitchView toRightOf: yesSwitchView;
        borderWidthLeft: 0 right: 0 top: 2 bottom: 0.
    ↑switchView
```

7.6 PIE MENUS[1]

This example was inspired by a paper by Callahan et al.[2] which presented an empirical comparison of pie menus and linear menus. Most menu-based systems use linear menus, where the items in the menu are arranged in a vertical fashion. Smalltalk uses pop-up linear menus where the menu appears or "pops up" at the cursor point. Other systems such as the

---

[1] This example first appeared in the *Journal of Object-Oriented Programming*. This material is republished by kind permission of SIGS Publications, Inc.

[2] Callahan, J., Hopkins, D., Weiser, M., and Shneiderman, B., An Empirical Comparison of Pie vs. Linear Menus, Proceedings of ACM SIGCHI conference, Washington D.C., 1988, pp. 95-100.

Macintosh™ use pull-down linear menus, where the menu drops down from a menu bar at the top of the screen.

Pie menus associate menu items with equal sized slices of a circular pie. As with linear menus, many variations of pie menus are possible. Pop-up (or Smalltalk style) pie menus might appear with their center at the cursor point (see Fig. 7.13), while pull-down (or Macintosh style) pie menus might be semicircular menus that drop down from a menu bar at the top of the screen.

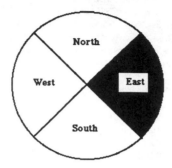

Figure 7.13 A simple pie menu.

Pie menus have an advantage over linear menus in that selection is directional rather than positional. When a pie menu is activated the cursor is at the center of the pie. A user selects an item by moving the cursor in the direction of the item. Only a small movement is required to enter the appropriate slice of the pie and for the system to provide graphical feedback on the item selected. Moreover, as the cursor is moved away from the center, the precision required to select a slice diminishes rapidly.

With a traditional linear menu, selection is achieved by moving the cursor vertically through the list of menu items. The mouse movement required is determined by the initial location of the cursor (usually either the first item or, as in Smalltalk, the item that was selected from the menu the last time it was used) and the position of the required item in the list.

Disadvantages of pie menus include the additional display space they occupy relative to linear menus and the inadequacies (shared with linear menus) when the number of slices in the pie is large. For a full discussion of the relative merits of pie and linear menus, see the paper by Callahan.

7.6.1 Implementing Pie Menus

Recall that classes PopUpMenu and ActionMenu deviate from the standard Smalltalk model-view-controller (MVC) paradigm for constructing window classes. They can be viewed as combining the notion of a model, view, and controller into one object, themselves. They are not scheduled for execution — rather, they must be started up in the current process. When started, they pop up awaiting a user selection. While active, no other window can be activated. After the mouse button is depressed and released, the pop-up menu disappears. We adopt the same approach for pie menus.

Pie menus, as shown in Fig. 7.14, can be added to Smalltalk by defining two classes: **Pie** and **PieMenu**. Pie provides the capability for creating instances with any number of pieces (or slices) numbered 1, 2, 3, and so on and for labeling the slices. It is possible to have fewer labels than slices, although this feature has had little testing. A **laissez-faire** approach is used to initialize pies; e.g., if the radius or number of pieces is unspecified, a default is provided. Also, this design displays the labels outside the pie. Consequently, we distinguish between the pie's **radius** (that excludes the labels) and the pie's **extent** (which includes them). The radius and extent of the pie are determined by the number of slices and the size of the labels. For efficiency, the drawing for the pie, the labels, and the border are placed on a form called the **background**. Because of the laissez-faire approach, the background is computed at the latest possible moment — to permit the user to provide non-defaulted information.

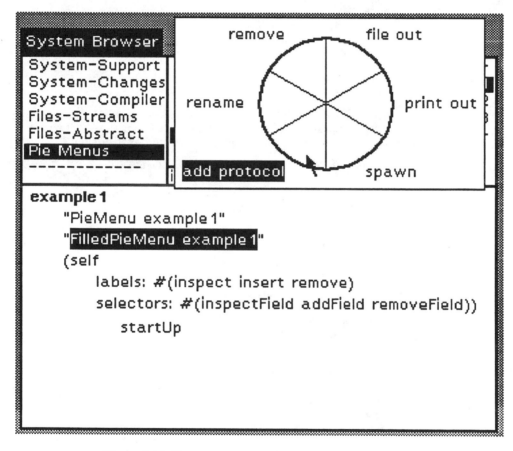

Figure 7.14 The new method category yellow button menu.

Class Pie is shown next. Were it not for the parts concerned with layout, the implementation would be quite small.

Class Pie

class name	Pie
superclass	Object
instance variable names	center radius extent border slices labels background

class methods

examples

example1
```
"Pie example1"
↑Pie new
    radius: 40; pieces: 6; center: Display boundingBox center; display
```

instance methods

initialization

computeLayout
```
self positionParts; drawParts
```

positionParts
```
"Position the labels (assuming the center of the pie is 0@0) and determine the
extent that encompasses both the pie and its labels (if not already provided)."
| textHeight outsideRadius merge angle pen position box halfHeight |

"First, determine the pie radius if not already provided."
radius isNil ifTrue: [
    labels isNil
        ifTrue: [radius ← 60]
        ifFalse: [
            textHeight ← labels first extent y.
            outsideRadius ← (labels size * textHeight) // 4 max: 60. "heuristic"
            radius ← outsideRadius - 10]].

"Second, the label placement."
merge ← radius negated@radius negated corner: radius@radius.
labels isNil ifFalse: [
    angle ← 360 // slices size.
    pen ← Pen new up; turn: (angle // 2) negated.
    labels do: [:displayText |
        position ← (pen
            place: 0@0; turn: angle;
            go: outsideRadius) location rounded.
        box ← displayText boundingBox. halfHeight ← box height // 2.
        position x >= 0
            ifTrue: [box moveTo: position - (0@halfHeight)]
            ifFalse: [box moveTo: position - (box width@halfHeight)].
        displayText offset: box origin.
        merge ← merge merge: box]].

"Third, the extent."
extent isNil ifTrue: [
    extent ← (merge origin abs max: merge corner) * 2. "keep pie in center"
    extent ← extent + (10@10) "extra white space" + (self border@self border)]
```

drawParts
"Construct a background and the slices for later display."
background ← Form **extent**: extent.
self **drawPie**; **drawSlices**; **drawLabels**; **drawBorder**

drawPie
"Draw the pie border and the spokes on the background."
| backgroundCenter pen angle |

"First, the pie border."
backgroundCenter ← extent // 2.
Circle **new**
    form: (Form **extent**: 2@2) **black**; **radius**: radius;
    center: backgroundCenter; **displayOn**: background.

"Second, the spokes."
pen ← Pen **new destForm**: background.
self **pieces** > 1 **ifTrue**: [
    angle ← 360 // self **pieces**.
    self **pieces timesRepeat**: [pen **place**: backgroundCenter; **go**: radius; **turn**: angle]]

drawSlices
"Leave the slices unfilled."
| aForm |
aForm ← Form **extent**: 0@0.
slices ← (1 **to**: self **pieces**) **collect**: [:index | aForm]

drawLabels
"Display the labels."
| backgroundCenter |
labels **isNil ifTrue**: [↑self].
backgroundCenter ← extent // 2.
labels **do**: [:displayText |
    displayText **displayOn**: background **at**: backgroundCenter
        clippingBox: background **boundingBox**
        rule: Form **under mask**: Form **black**]

drawBorder
"Draw the border for the background."
background **border**: background **boundingBox width**: self **border**

access and modification

center
    ↑center
center: aPoint
    center ← aPoint

radius
    background **isNil ifTrue**: [self **computeLayout**].
    ↑radius
radius: anIntegerOrNil
    background ← nil. radius ← anIntegerOrNil

extent
    background **isNil ifTrue**: [self **computeLayout**].
    ↑extent

extent: aPoint
    background ← nil. extent ← aPoint

pieces
    slices **isNil ifTrue**: [↑1] **ifFalse**: [↑slices **size max**: 1]
pieces: anInteger
    background ← nil. slices ← Array **new**: anInteger

labels
    labels **isNil ifTrue**: [↑#()].
    ↑labels **collect**: [:displayText | displayText **string**]
labels: labelArrayOrNil
    "There can be the same or fewer labels than pieces; if more, the extras are ignored."
    background ← nil. labels ← labelArrayOrNil.
    labelArrayOrNil **isNil ifTrue**: [↑self].
    labels ← labels **collect**: [:string | string **asDisplayText**]

border
    border **isNil ifTrue**: [↑1] **ifFalse**: [↑border]
border: anInteger
    border ← anInteger

testing

sliceContainingPoint: aPoint
    "Returns the slice number of the slice containing the point; 0 if none."
    | difference totalAngle sliceAngle |
    difference ← aPoint - center.
    difference **r** > radius **ifTrue**: [↑0].
    totalAngle ← (difference **theta radiansToDegrees** + 90.0) \\ 360. "up is 0"
    sliceAngle ← 360 // self **pieces**.
    ↑totalAngle + sliceAngle - 1 // sliceAngle **min**: self **pieces**

displaying

display
    self **displayBackground**; **displaySlice**: 1

displayBackground
    background **isNil ifTrue**: [self **computeLayout**].
    background **displayAt**: center-(extent // 2)

displaySlice: sliceIndex
    | label |
    label ← labels **at**: sliceIndex.
    Display **reverse**: (center + label **offset extent**: label **extent**)

The implementation of class PieMenu is simpler than class Pie. The standard protocol is sufficient for our needs, but as an experiment, consider changing all menus in the system to pie menus. To achieve this, we must ensure that the pie menu protocol includes the external protocol used by standard pop-up menus and action menus — what we have called the **compatibility protocol**.

The two most important methods are **startUpWithHeading:at:** and **manageFeed-back**. They are concerned with activating the menu (saving and restoring what is underneath and displaying the pie with visual feedback). In this case, when the mouse is in the ith slice, the corresponding label is highlighted using reverse video.

Class PieMenu

class name	PieMenu
superclass	Object
instance variable names	pie selectors selection

class methods

instance creation (standard protocol)

labels: aCollection **selectors**: selectorArray
    "Returns a pie menu with specified labels and selectors."
    | labels aStream |
    (aCollection **isKindOf**: String)
        ifTrue: [
            aStream ← ReadStream **on**: aCollection. labels ← OrderedCollection **new**.
            [aStream **atEnd**] **whileFalse**: [labels **add**: (aStream **upTo**: Character **cr**)]]
        ifFalse: [labels ← aCollection].
    ↑self **new labels**: labels **selectors**: selectorArray

instance creation (compatability protocol)

confirm
    "PieMenu confirm"
    ↑(self **labels**: 'confirm\abort' **withCRs selectors**: nil) **startUp** = 1
labelList: labelArray
    ↑self **labelList**: labelArray **selectors**: #()
labelList: labelArray **selectors**: selectorArray
    ↑self **labels**: labelArray **selectors**: selectorArray
labels: labelArray **lines**: anArray
    ↑self **labels**: labelArray **lines**: anArray **selectors**: #()
labels: labelArray **lines**: anArray **selectors**: selectorArray
    "Ignore lines"
    ↑self **labels**: labelArray **selectors**: selectorArray

installing pie menus

install
    "PieMenu install"
    "FilledPieMenu install"
    | position labels item |
    PopUpMenu **allInstancesDo**: [:menu |
        position ← 1. labels ← OrderedCollection **new**.
        [(item ← menu **labelAt**: position) **isNil**] **whileFalse**: [
            labels **add**: item. position ← position + 1].
        menu **become**: (self **labels**: labels **selectors**: nil)].
    ActionMenu **allInstancesDo**: [:menu |
        position ← 1. labels ← OrderedCollection **new**.
        [(item ← menu **labelAt**: position) **isNil**] **whileFalse**: [
            labels **add**: item. position ← position + 1].
        menu **become**: (self **labels**: labels **selectors**: menu **selectors**)].

example1
    "PieMenu example1"
    "FilledPieMenu example1"
    (self
        labels: #(inspect insert remove)
        selectors: #(inspectField addField removeField)) **startUp**

example2
    "PieMenu example2"
    "FilledPieMenu example2"
    (self
        labels: 'inspect\insert\remove' **withCRs**
        selectors: #(inspectField addField removeField)) **startUp**

example3
    "PieMenu example3"
    "FilledPieMenu example3"
    (self
        labels: #(red green blue white black orange pink purple brown)
        selectors: #(red green blue white black orange pink purple brown)) **startUp**

instance methods

instance initialization

labels: labelArray **selectors**: selectorArray
    pie ← Pie **new pieces**: labelArray **size**; **labels**: labelArray.
    selectors ← selectorArray.
    selection ← 0

accessing

selectorAt: index
    ↑selectors **at**: index

controlling (compatability protocol)

startUp: aSymbol **withHeading**: aText
    "Display the pie menu at the cursor point with title aText (translated if not completely on the screen)."
    ↑self **startUpWithHeading**: aText **at**: Sensor **cursorPoint**

startUpAndWaitForSelectionAt: aPoint
    "Display the pie menu centered at aPoint (translated if not completely on the screen)."
    ↑self **startUpWithHeading**: '' **at**: aPoint

controlling (standard protocol)

startUp
    "Display the pie menu at the cursor point (translated if not completely on the screen)."
    ↑self **startUpWithHeading**: '' **at**: Sensor **cursorPoint**

startUpWithHeading: aString **at**: aPoint
    "Display the pie menu with a heading at the point (translated if not completely on the screen)."

    | title titleBorder pieBox titleBox delta savedArea |
    title ← aString **asDisplayText**.
    titleBorder ← aString **size** > 0
        ifTrue: [Rectangle **left**: 2 **right**: 2 **top**: 2 **bottom**: 1]
        ifFalse: [0].
    pieBox ← aPoint - (pie **extent** // 2) **extent**: pie **extent**.
    titleBox ← title **boundingBox expandBy**: titleBorder.
    titleBox **moveTo**: pieBox **origin** - (0@titleBox **height**).
    delta ← (pieBox **merge**: titleBox) **amountToTranslateWithin**: Display **boundingBox**.
    pieBox **moveBy**: delta. titleBox **moveBy**: delta.
    pie **center**: pieBox **center**.

    savedArea ← Form **fromDisplay**: (pieBox **merge**: titleBox).
        Cursor **normal showWhile**: [
            aString **size** > 0 **ifTrue**: [
                title **displayAt**: titleBox **origin** + (titleBorder@titleBorder).
                Display **border**: titleBox **width**: titleBorder **mask**: Form **black**].
            pie **displayBackground**.
            Sensor **cursorPoint**: pie **center**.
            Sensor **waitButton**.
            [Sensor **anyButtonPressed**] **whileTrue**: [self **manageFeedback**]].
    savedArea **displayOn**: Display **at**: titleBox **origin**.
    ↑selection

manageFeedback
    "If the cursor is inside the pie menu, highlight the selected slice."
    | sliceIndex |
    sliceIndex ← pie **sliceContainingPoint**: Sensor **cursorPoint**.
    sliceIndex = 0 **ifTrue**: [↑self].
    pie **displaySlice**: sliceIndex.
    [(selection ← pie **sliceContainingPoint**: Sensor **cursorPoint**) = sliceIndex] **whileTrue**: [
        Sensor **anyButtonPressed ifFalse**: [↑self]].
    pie **displayBackground**.

7.6.2 Modifying the Existing System to Use Only Pie Menus

To change the existing system so that all pop-up and action menus are pie menus, it is necessary to ensure (1) that all new menus are pie menus, and (2) that all old menus are converted. The first requirement can be satisfied (as an experiment only) by modifying existing methods in the system; or more specifically, by changing the following methods in classes PopUpMenu and ActionMenu.

Changes to Class PopUpMenu

    instance methods

    instance creation

    labelList: labelArray
        ↑PieMenu **labelList**: labelArray

    labels: labelArray **lines**: anArray
        ↑PieMenu **labels**: labelArray **lines**: anArray

Changes to Class ActionMenu

class methods

instance creation

labelList: labelArray **selectors**: selectorArray
   ↑PieMenu **labelList**: labelArray **selectors**: selectorArray

labels: labelArray **lines**: anArray **selectors**: selectorArray
   ↑PieMenu **labels**: labelArray **lines**: anArray **selectors**: selectorArray

instance methods

action symbols

selectors
   ↑selectors

The second requirement can be satisfied by executing the method **install**, which identifies all existing instances of classes PopUpMenu and ActionMenu and mutates them into corresponding pie menus.

7.6.3 Filled Pies

Rather than indicating selections by reversing the appropriate label, it might be nicer to have the pie slice itself turn black. We can add this pie and pie menu variation with the introduction of only three methods. The filled pie menus now appear as shown in Fig. 7.15.

Class FilledPie

class name	FilledPie
superclass	Pie
instance variable names	"none"

instance methods

initialization

drawSlices
   "Draw the slices onto separate forms."
   | backgroundCenter angle pieOrigin offset sliceCenter sliceExtent pen slice
   interiorPoint |

   backgroundCenter ← extent // 2. angle ← 360 // self **pieces**.
   pieOrigin ← backgroundCenter - (radius@radius).
   offset ← pieOrigin **x negated**@pieOrigin **y negated**.
   sliceCenter ← radius@radius. sliceExtent ← sliceCenter*2.

   pen ← Pen **new destForm**: background; **turn**: (angle // 2) **negated**; **up**.

   slices ← (1 **to**: self **pieces**) **collect**: [:index |
      slice ← Form **extent**: sliceExtent.
      background **displayOn**: slice **at**: offset.
      interiorPoint ← (pen **place**: sliceCenter; **turn**: angle; **go**: radius//2; **location**)
         rounded.
      slice **shapeFill**: Form **black interiorPoint**: interiorPoint.
      slice]

displaySlice: sliceIndex
    (slices **at:** sliceIndex) **displayOn**: Display **at:** center-(radius@radius)
        clippingBox: Display **boundingBox**
        rule: Form **under mask**: Form **black**

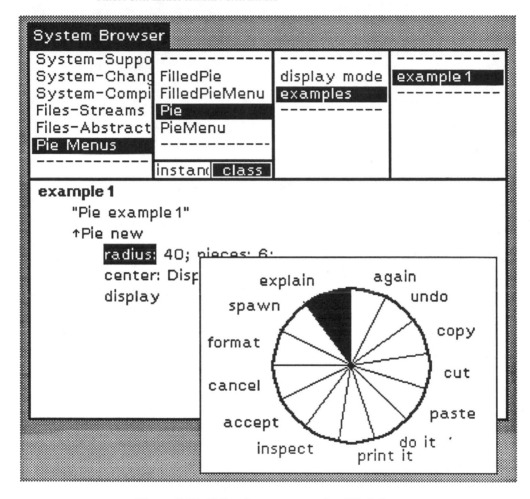

Figure 7.15 Yellow button menu using filled pies.

The problem with the filled pie menus is speed. To fill a slice of the pie, we use the form operation '**shapeFill**: aMask **interiorPoint**: interiorPoint', which fills an enclosed region with a mask given a point lying within the region. This operation is much too slow to dynamically invert pie slices as a user moves the cursor over them in a pie menu.

To mitigate this problem, we precompute forms containing the filled pie slices whenever a filled pie menu is created. The initial creation of the menu is slow, but once initialized in this way, filled pies perform satisfactorily. An interesting artifact of this approach was the discovery that some menus (e.g., the System Menu) are created once when first activated, while other menus (e.g., the Method Category Pane Menu in a class browser) are recreated each time they are used. The former menus appear very quickly on all activations except the first, while the latter suffer an initial delay caused by the recomputation of the slice forms every time they are used.

Class FilledPieMenu

class name	FilledPieMenu
superclass	PieMenu
instance variable names	"none"

class methods

no messages

instance methods

instance initialization

labels: labelArray **selectors:** selectorArray
    pie ← FilledPie **new pieces:** labelArray **size; labels:** labelArray.
    selectors ← selectorArray.
    selection ← 0

Our limited experience using the pie menus suggests that movement within entries in the pie is fast and convenient but that it takes some time to become familiar with the position of commonly used menu items within the pie. Readers may wish to implement other pie menu variations, such as pies where the text lies within the pie slices and the display form itself is circular (see Fig. 7.13), semicircular pull-down pie menus, or even hierarchical pie menus.

7.7 SUMMARY

This chapter has provided the details of **pop-up windows** that appear suddenly when an interaction request is required and then immediately disappear after an appropriate reply. In particular, we have discussed the following notions:

- The model, view, and controller hierarchies associated with pop-up windows.

- The distinction between pop-up menu windows that provide users with a choice of menu entries to select from and pop-up text-query windows that are used to request a textual response to some query. Pop-up binary text-query windows are a special case in which the response is either **yes** or **no**.

- Examples detailing the creation and activation of each variety of pop-up windows.

- The detailed protocol for pop-up menu windows — classes PopUpMenu and ActionMenu.

- The detailed protocol for pop-up text-query windows — the four MVC classes FillInTheBlank, FillInTheBlankView, and CRFillInTheBlankController (and its substitute FillInTheBlankController).

- The detailed protocol for pop-up binary text-query windows — the three MVC classes BinaryChoice, BinaryChoiceView, and BinaryChoiceController.

- A detailed example dealing with the design and implementation of pie menus.

7.8 EXERCISES

The following exercises may require some original thought, rereading some of the material, and/or browsing through the system.

1. Create a pop-up menu to choose between 'mean/vegetables/fruits' and for each selection, create a new pop-up menu with specific entries.

2. Design a multi-level pop-up menu that returns a collection of integer choices (one per level). The previous example could be done with one multi-level pop-up menu.

3. Design a class of pop-up menus that is supplied with an array of blocks to be executed when a selection is made. Consider whether the block should be provided with the selection index and/or a rectangle denoting the selected menu entry. With the latter information, for instance, secondary pop-up menus could be made to appear at the selection point. This would work well only if the associated menu block were executed before closing the pop-up menu.

4. Design a multi-response pop-up menu that permits a user to select many entries at once (perhaps only when the shift key is down, for example). The result would be a collection of selection indices.

5. Use a text-query window to obtain a point from the user. You will have to convert the string that is returned from the text request.

6. How do you ask for a multi-line response to a question?

7. Create an aggravation window that continually pops up until the user answers **yes**. To be more interesting, the window could traverse the screen alternately from left to right and right to left. A suitable question might be "Are you angry yet?"

8. Implement variations on the pie menus introduced in this chapter, such as pies where the text lies within the pie slices and the display form itself is circular (see Fig. 7.13), semicircular pull-down pie menus, or even hierarchical pie menus.

7.9 GLOSSARY

classes

ActionMenu A class of pop-up menu windows that combines the notion of a model, view, and controller into one; differs from PopUpMenu by providing an array of selectors parallel to the menu items. The selectors are usually used to process the selected item; e.g., by using it to send a processing message to some appropriate view's model. Yellow button menus for pluggable windows must be action menus.

BinaryChoice The model class for pop-up binary text-query windows.

BinaryChoiceController The controller class for pop-up binary text-query windows.

BinaryChoiceView The view class for pop-up binary text-query windows.

CRFillInTheBlankController A controller class for pop-up text-query windows; similar to a **FillInTheBlankController** but also permits acceptance to be signaled by typing return (CR is short for carriage return).

FillInTheBlank The model class for pop-up text-query windows.

FillInTheBlankController A controller class for pop-up text-query windows; a special kind of string holder controller that forces a user response; e.g., by flashing until its request is satisfied. After typing a response (if different from the sample response), the user can signal acceptance by choosing **accept** in a yellow button pop-up menu.

FillInTheBlankView The view class for pop-up text-query windows.

PopUpMenu A class of pop-up menu windows that combines the notion of a model, view, and controller into one; maintains a user-specifiable string of menu items separated by carriage returns and an array specifying the item **after which** a line is to be drawn. If no lines are desired, the latter can be omitted.

class variables

ThumbsDown A class variable in **BinaryChoiceView** containing the form that indicates **no**.

ThumbsUp A class variable in **BinaryChoiceView** containing the form that indicates **yes**.

selected terminology

pop-up binary text-query windows A confirmer window.

pop-up menu Short for **pop-up menu window**.

pop-up menu window An interactive window for selecting between a number of menu items. All items in the pop-up menu are displayed one above the other; no scrolling is needed.

pop-up text-query window A pop-up window used to request a textual response to some query; **pop-up binary text-query windows** are a special case in which the response is either **yes** or **no**.

pop-up window A window that appears suddenly when an interaction request is required and then immediately disappears after an appropriate reply. They exist in two varieties: **pop-up menu windows** and **pop-up text-query windows**.

8

A Window Application

8.1 INTRODUCTION

Application specific windows are difficult to create. The task becomes simpler with more experience but it never becomes easy. Designing windows is primarily an interactive process because the visual effect is all-important. Even an experienced designer will find designing window-based applications to be an error-prone and time-consuming process.

Our goal here is twofold: (1) to provide more experience with windows, and (2) to provide a tool, a **window maker**, that will simplify this task. The window maker is designed to be used by relatively experienced programmers who understand the notion of pluggable views. It is not intended to completely eliminate the programming process; i.e., it will still be necessary to write the methods that provide the interface between the window (and subwindows) and the application model.

We will begin with an application that actually uses the window maker — a **librarian** for creating and storing libraries of forms. This will provide us with an opportunity to use the window maker before we get into specifics of its design and implementation. Next, we consider extensions to pluggable views that will support the window maker. A goal was to avoid modifications to existing system classes. Unfortunately, two modifications had to be made. The window maker is considered last.

8.2 A FORM LIBRARIAN

The **form librarian** permits a user to create, edit, and store forms. It also provides a new class of forms that has two display images — one when it is off and another when it is on. We call them **forms with highlight** — the form itself provides the off image; its **highlight** provides the on image. We needed a form librarian so that we could provide users with useful switches. Only three kinds of switches have been provided so far. An example of the form librarian editor is shown in Fig. 8.1.

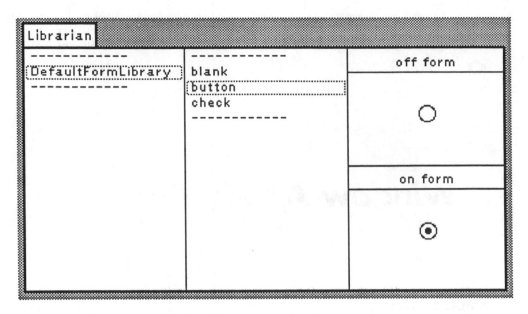

Figure 8.1 The form librarian editor.

Although the form librarian permits us to make and delete libraries, as shown in Fig. 8.2, we only used it to create the default library with the **blank**, **button**, and **check** forms. We use the latter two extensively in the window maker.

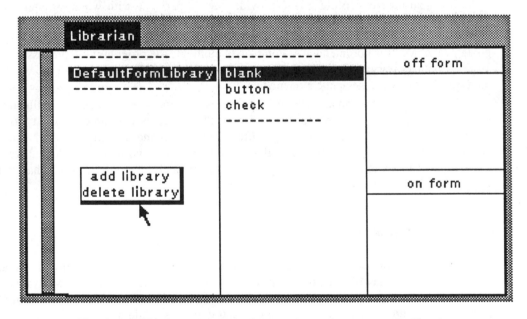

Figure 8.2 The form librarian editor can be used to create new libraries.

Once a library is created, we can add forms to it or modify existing forms. The check highlight form in Fig. 8.3, for example, was created by copying the button form and then editing it. Choosing 'edit off-form' or 'edit on-form' pops up a bit editor that can be used to edit the form.

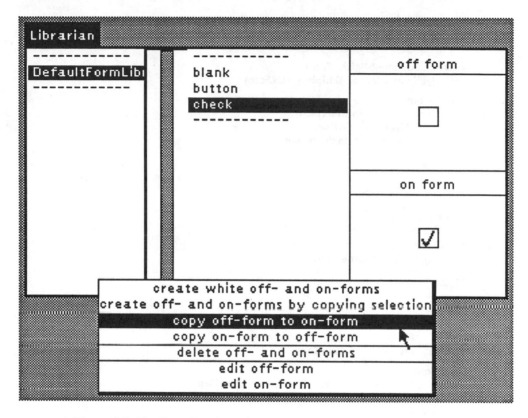

Figure 8.3 The form librarian editor can be used to edit the library forms.

The form librarian editor consists of six subwindows: (1) a menu window to select libraries, (2) a menu window to select forms in that library, (3) two picture forms that display the text 'off form' and 'on form' respectively, and (4) two more dynamic picture forms that actually display the form image and its highlight.

8.2.1 Forms with Highlight

We began by creating the FormWithHighlight class and providing it with the following very simple protocol. Basically, a form with highlight is a form that carries an additional form — its highlight. It is up to the user to explicitly use the highlight. The reader might wish to consider a more advanced design that keeps track of a state to determine whether or not to display itself on or off.

Class FormWithHighlight

class	FormWithHighlight
superclass	Form
instance variables	highlight

class methods

instance creation

extent: aPoint **highlight:** aForm
    ↑(self **extent:** aPoint) **highlight:** aForm

from: aForm
    ↑(self **extent:** aForm **extent**)
        offset: aForm **offset**;
        bits: aForm **bits deepCopy**

instance methods

access and modification

highlight
    ↑highlight
highlight: anotherForm
    highlight ← anotherForm

copying

asForm
    ↑(Form **extent:** self **extent**)
        offset: self **offset**;
        bits: self **bits deepCopy**

deepCopy
    ↑super **deepCopy highlight:** highlight **deepCopy**

printing

storeOn: aStream
    "Re-creates the receiver assuming there is no circularity."
    aStream **nextPut:** $(.
    super **storeOn:** aStream.
    aStream **nextPutAll:** ' highlight: '.
    highlight **storeOn:** aStream.
    aStream **nextPut:** $).

8.2.2 Form Libraries

A **form library** was then provided. It is essentially a dictionary with a name. We considered having it inherit from dictionary (indeed this was our original design). However, we found that the code was not portable. Some Smalltalk systems could not properly handle a subclass that added named instance variables to one that already had indexed instance variables. Note that the initialization code for the default library was actually obtained by inspecting it after we constructed it with the library editor. It was then easy to obtain store strings for the forms it contained.

Class FormLibrary

class	FormLibrary
superclass	Object
instance variables	name dictionary
class variables	DefaultFormLibrary

class methods

class initialization

initialize
    "FormLibrary initialize"

    DefaultFormLibrary **isNil ifTrue:** [
        DefaultFormLibrary ← FormLibrary **new name:** #DefaultFormLibrary.
        DefaultFormLibrary
            at: #blank
            put: ((FormWithHighlight **extent:** 15@15) **highlight:** (Form **extent:** 15@15)).
        DefaultFormLibrary
            at: #button
            put: ((FormWithHighlight
                extent: 15@15
                fromArray: #(0 1984 6192 12312 8200 16388 16388 16388 16388
                    16388 8200 12296 6192 1984 0)
                offset: 0@0)
                    highlight: (Form
                        extent: 15@15
                        fromArray: #(0 1984 6192 12312 8200 17284 18372 18372
                          18372 17284 8200 12312 6192 1984 0)
                        offset: 0@0)).
        DefaultFormLibrary
            at: #check
            put: ((FormWithHighlight
                 extent: 15@15
                 fromArray: #(65534 32770 32770 32770 32770 32770 32770 32770
                    32770 32770 32770 32770 32770 32770 65534)
                 offset: 0@0)
                    highlight: (Form
                        extent: 15@15
                        fromArray: #(65534 32770 32818 32818 32866 32866 32962
                          32962 45442 45442 39682 40706 36354 33794 65534)
                        offset: 0@0))].

reInitialize
    "FormLibrary reInitialize"

    DefaultFormLibrary ← nil.
    self **initialize**

instance creation

new
    ↑super **new initialize**

instance methods

instance initialization

initialize
    dictionary ← IdentityDictionary **new**

naming

name
  ↑name
name: aString
  name ← aString **asSymbol**

access and modification

at: key
  ↑dictionary **at:** key **asSymbol**
at: key **ifAbsent:** aBlock
  ↑dictionary **at:** key **asSymbol ifAbsent:** aBlock
at: key **put:** aForm
  ↑dictionary **at:** key **asSymbol put:** aForm

printing

printOn: aStream
  aStream **nextPutAll:** 'FormLibrary '; **nextPutAll:** name; **space**.
  dictionary **printOn:** aStream

operations normally inherited

includesKey: aKey
  ↑dictionary **includesKey:** aKey
keys
  ↑dictionary **keys**
removeKey: aKey
  ↑dictionary **removeKey:** aKey

8.2.3 Form Librarians

The **form librarian** is a model for an editor that permits form libraries to be constructed, changed, and extended. By using the window maker to construct the window that displays it, it must subscribe to the pluggable views philosophy. Consequently, the fact that two menu subwindows are used (see Figs. 8.1, 8.2, and 8.3) implies that the model must be able to keep track of (1) the libraries and the library name selected (the leftmost menu subwindow), in addition to (2) the library itself and the form in it that is selected. A preliminary design might include the following:

Class FormLibrarian

class	FormLibrarian
superclass	Model
instance variables	libraries librariesSelection library librarySelection
class variables	KnownLibraries

class methods

class initialization

initialize
  "FormLibrarian initialize"

  KnownLibraries **isNil ifTrue:** [KnownLibraries ← IdentityDictionary **new**]

reInitialize
    "FormLibrarian reInitialize"

    KnownLibraries ← IdentityDictionary **new**

instance creation

new
    ↑super **new initialize**

querying

allLibraries
    "FormLibrarian allLibraries inspect"
    | result |
    result ← IdentityDictionary **new**.
    FormLibrary **allInstances do:** [:aLibrary | result **at:** aLibrary **name put:** aLibrary].
    ↑result

formForLibraryName: libraryName **formName**: formName
    ↑(self **libraryForName:** libraryName)
        at: formName **asSymbol**
        ifAbsent: [
            self **error:** 'library ', libraryName, ' does not contain form name ', formName]

formForPathName: path
    ↑self **formForLibraryName:** (path **at:** 1) **formName:** (path **at:** 2)

libraryForName: libraryName
    | librarySymbol |
    librarySymbol ← libraryName **asSymbol**.
    FormLibrary **allInstances do:** [:aLibrary |
        aLibrary **name** == librarySymbol **ifTrue:** [↑aLibrary]].
    self **error:** 'library ', librarySymbol, ' does not exist'

pathNameForForm: aForm
    FormLibrary **allInstances do:** [:aLibrary |
        aLibrary **keys do:** [:key |
            (aLibrary **at:** key) == aForm
                ifTrue: [↑Array **with:** aLibrary **name with:** key **asSymbol**]]].
    ↑nil

instance methods

instance initialization

initialize
    libraries ← FormLibrarian **allLibraries**.
    librariesSelection ← nil.
    library ← nil.
    librarySelection ← nil

external queries

selectedForm
    librarySelection **isNil**
        ifTrue: [↑nil]
        ifFalse: [↑library **at:** librarySelection]

selectedFormName
    ↑librarySelection

selectedLibrary
    ↑library
selectedLibraryName
    ↑librariesSelection

selectedPathName
    "Returns nil or a pair denoting #(libraryName formName)."
    librarySelection **isNil**
        ifTrue: [↑nil]
        ifFalse: [↑Array **with:** library **name with:** librarySelection]

external modification

library: libraryName **form:** formName
    librariesSelection ← libraryName **asSymbol**.
    library ← librariesSelection **isNil ifTrue:** [nil] **ifFalse:** [libraries **at:** librariesSelection].
    librarySelection ← formName **asSymbol**

selectedPathName: path
    "Changes the current path so that views on the librarian displays these as the
    current selections."
    librariesSelection ← (path **at:** 1) **asSymbol**.
    library ← libraries **at:** librariesSelection.
    librarySelection ← (path **at:** 2) **asSymbol**

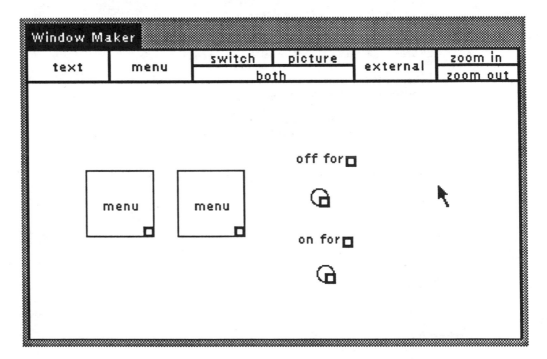

Figure 8.4 The preliminary icons for the librarian editor.

So far, the librarian protocol has not considered the window interface. We begin (as a novice might) by using the window maker to create the desired subwindows and thereby determine what that additional protocol should be. An initial session with the window maker might result in the icons shown in Fig. 8.4.

After suitably resizing the icons, aligning them, and providing them with borders and relevant backgrounds, the window might appear as in Fig. 8.5. Note that we have resized the window maker to encapsulate the icons exactly.

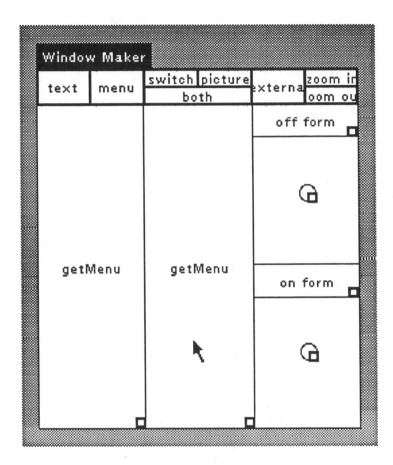

Figure 8.5 The finalized icons for the librarian editor.

At any point (before the window is output), it is necessary to have specified the external interface for each of the subwindows. A sample external interface pop-up menu for the leftmost menu window is shown in Fig. 8.6. In this case, the designer is about to change the name of the message to be used by the window for getting the menu entries.

Chapter 8 A Window Application   **349**

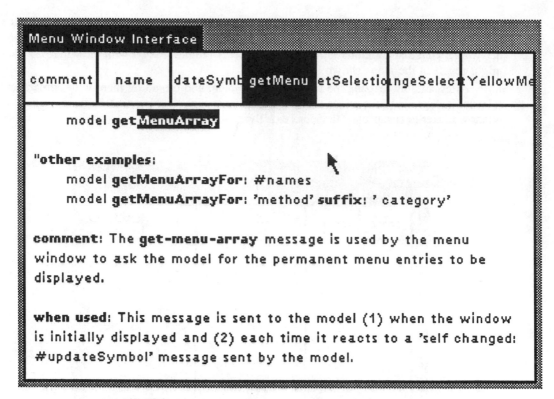

Figure 8.6 Setting up the external interface for a menu window.

To produce the form librarian editor window of Fig. 8.3 which is partially constructed in Fig. 8.5, the designer had to provide the following interface information interactively. In general, the details differ for each kind of subwindow.

For the left menu subwindow:

update symbol:	#libraries
getMenu:	model **getLibrariesList**
getSelection:	model **getLibrariesSelection**
changeSelection:	model **changeLibrariesSelection**: #selection
getYellowMenu:	model **getLibrariesYellowMenu**

For the right menu subwindow:

update symbol:	#library
getMenu:	model **getLibraryList**
getSelection:	model **getLibrarySelection**
changeSelection:	model **changeLibrarySelection**: #selection
getYellowMenu:	model **getLibraryYellowMenu**

For the top dynamic picture subwindow (below text 'off form'):

update symbol:	#pictures
getLabel:	model **getOffForm**

For the bottom dynamic picture subwindow (below text 'on form'):

update symbol:	#pictures
getLabel:	model **getOnForm**

To consider one example, suppose the user selects a new library in the left menu subwindow of the librarian editor. As a result, the menu subwindow will send message **changeLibrariesSelection:** to the model (a librarian). The parameter #selection specified above is replaced by the actual selection when the message is sent. As a result, the model must change its current librariesSelection (the name) and consequently librarySelection (the library with that name). To ensure that the second menu window removes the entries for the old library, the model need only send a 'self **changed:** #library' message. The second menu subwindow will use its own protocol for getting up-to-date entries and a new selection (in this case, no selection). Additionally, the on and off dynamic pictures must also change. This is done by the model sending itself a 'self **changed:** #pictures' message. The librarian protocol for doing all of this is provided next:

libraries window messages

getLibrariesList
    ↑libraries **keys asSortedCollection asArray**

getLibrariesSelection
    ↑librariesSelection

changeLibrariesSelection: aStringOrNil
    librariesSelection = aStringOrNil **ifTrue:** [↑self].
    librariesSelection ← aStringOrNil.
    library ← librariesSelection **isNil**
        ifTrue: [nil]
        ifFalse: [libraries **at:** librariesSelection **asSymbol**].
    librarySelection ← nil.
    self **changed:** #library.
    self **changed:** #pictures

getLibrariesYellowMenu
    ↑ActionMenu
        labels: 'add library\delete library' **withCRs**
        lines: #()
        selectors: #(addLibrary deleteLibrary)

library window messages

getLibraryList
    librariesSelection **isNil**
        ifTrue: [↑Array **new**]
        ifFalse: [↑library **keys asSortedCollection asArray**]

getLibrarySelection
    ↑librarySelection

changeLibrarySelection: aStringOrNil
    librarySelection = aStringOrNil **ifTrue:** [↑self].
    librarySelection ← aStringOrNil.
    self **changed:** #pictures

```
getLibraryYellowMenu
    ↑ActionMenu
        labels: ('create white off- and on-forms\',
                 'create off- and on-forms by copying selection\',
                 'copy off-form to on-form\copy on-form to off-form\',
                 'delete off- and on-forms\',
                 'edit off-form\edit on-form') withCRs
        lines: #(2 4 5)
        selectors: #(createWhiteOffAndOnForms createOffAndOnFormsFromSelection
            copyOffFormToOnForm copyOnFormToOffForm deleteOffAndOnForms
            editOffForm editOnForm)
```

picture windows messages

```
getOffForm
    librarySelection isNil
        ifTrue: [↑Form extent: 0@0]
        ifFalse: [↑library at: librarySelection]

getOnForm
    | offForm |
    librarySelection isNil
        ifTrue: [↑Form extent: 0@0]
        ifFalse: [
            offForm ← library at: librarySelection.
            (offForm respondsTo: #highlight)
                ifTrue: [↑offForm highlight]
                ifFalse: [↑Form extent: 0@0]]
```

By far, the greater amount of code is required to support the yellow button menu selections, since there are so many of them.

libraries window menu messages

```
addLibrary
    | newName |
    newName ← self newLibraryNameAndIfNone: [↑nil].
    libraries at: newName put: (library ← FormLibrary new name: newName).
    KnownLibraries at: newName put: library.
    librariesSelection ← newName. librarySelection ← nil.
    self changed: #libraries.
    self changed: #library.
    self changed: #pictures

deleteLibrary
    | newName |
    self verifyLibrarySelectionAndIfNone: [↑nil].
    KnownLibraries
        removeKey: librariesSelection
        ifAbsent: [
            self confirm: 'cannot delete since not owned by librarian. Proceed to cancel'.
            ↑nil].
    libraries removeKey: librariesSelection ifAbsent: [].
    librariesSelection ← nil. library ← nil. librarySelection ← nil.
    self changed: #libraries.
    self changed: #library.
    self changed: #pictures
```

newLibraryNameAndIfNone: aBlock
"Returns a name for a new library; an empty string indicates cancelation. If this name is already in use, reports the problem and repeats the process unless the user elects to quit (in this case, returns the result of executing the block)."
| request newName |

request ← [FillInTheBlank
    request: 'Specify a name for the new library'
    initialAnswer: 'unusedName'].
request **size** = 0 **ifTrue**: [↑aBlock **value** "cancel requested"].

[libraries **includesKey**: (newName ← request **value asSymbol**)] **whileTrue**: [
    (self **confirm**: 'Name already exists. Try again?') **ifFalse**: [↑aBlock **value**]].

↑newName

verifyLibrarySelectionAndIfNone: aBlock
"If no library has been selected, complains and executes the block."

librariesSelection **isNil ifTrue**: [
    self **confirm**: 'You must first select a library\Try again?'.
    aBlock **value**]

library window menu messages

createWhiteOffAndOnForms
| newName size |

(self **confirm**: 'You will be prompted with the form name\',
    'and then for the size of the form to be used.\Continue?' **withCRs**) **ifFalse**: [↑nil].

newName ← self **newFormNameAndIfNone**: [↑nil].

(self **confirm**: 'The form size can be specified as a point or interactively.\',
    'The interactive approach is less accurate.\',
    'Do you wish to specify it as a point?' **withCRs**)
    ifTrue: [
        size ← Compiler
            evaluate: (FillInTheBlank **request**: 'Form size?' **initialAnswer**: '16@16')]
    ifFalse: [size ← Rectangle **fromUser extent**].

library
    at: newName
    put: (FormWithHighlight **extent**: size **highlight**: (Form **extent**: size)).
self **changed**: #library.
self **changed**: #pictures

createOffAndOnFormsFromSelection
| newName |
self **verifyFormSelectionAndIfNone**: [↑nil].
newName ← self **newFormNameAndIfNone**: [↑nil].

library **at**: newName **put**: (library **at**: librarySelection) **deepCopy**.
librarySelection ← newName.
self **changed**: #library

```
copyOffFormToOnForm
    | offForm |
    self verifyFormSelectionAndIfNone: [↑nil].
    offForm ← self selectedForm.
    (offForm isKindOf: FormWithHighlight)
        ifTrue: [offForm highlight: offForm asForm]
        ifFalse: [
            offForm become:
                ((FormWithHighlight from: offForm) highlight: offForm deepCopy)].
    self changed: #pictures

copyOnFormToOffForm
    | offForm |
    self verifyFormSelectionAndIfNone: [↑nil].
    offForm ← self selectedForm.
    (offForm isKindOf: FormWithHighlight)
        ifTrue: [
            offForm extent: offForm highlight extent.
            offForm offset: offForm highlight offset.
            offForm bits: offForm highlight bits deepCopy]
        ifFalse: [offForm white "there isn't any on form"].
    self changed: #pictures

deleteOffAndOnForms
    self verifyFormSelectionAndIfNone: [↑nil].
    library removeKey: librarySelection.
    librarySelection ← nil.
    self changed: #library.
    self changed: #pictures

editOffForm
    self verifyFormSelectionAndIfNone: [↑nil].
    (library at: librarySelection) bitEdit.
    self changed: #pictures

editOnForm
    | offForm |
    self verifyFormSelectionAndIfNone: [↑nil].
    offForm ← self selectedForm.
    (offForm isKindOf: FormWithHighlight)
        ifFalse: [
            offForm become:
                ((FormWithHighlight from: offForm)
                        highlight: (offForm deepCopy white))].
    offForm highlight bitEdit.
    self changed: #pictures
```

library window menu messages support

verifyFormSelectionAndIfNone: aBlock
    "If no form has been selected, complains and executes the block."

```
    librarySelection isNil ifTrue: [
        self confirm: 'You must first select a form\Try again?'.
        aBlock value]
```

newFormNameAndIfNone: aBlock
"Returns a name for a new form; an empty string indicates cancelation. If this name is already in use, reports the problem and repeats the process unless the user elects to quit (in this case, returns the result of executing the block)."
| request newName |

request ← [FillInTheBlank
    request: 'Specify a name for the new form'
    initialAnswer: 'unusedName'].
request **size** = 0 **ifTrue:** [↑aBlock **value** "cancel requested"].

[library **includesKey:** (newName ← request **value asSymbol**)] **whileTrue:** [
    (self **confirm:** 'Name already exists. Try again?') **ifFalse:** [↑aBlock **value**]].

↑newName

The methods supporting the protocol required by the subwindows can be implemented at any time; i.e., either before, during, or after the session with the window maker. In any case, the window maker session is ended by generating a method that creates a window whose subwindows follow the specified protocol. This method could be generated either in encoded form or as standard code (the former being substantially more compact). Additionally, it can be generated either as a top view or a subview.

Since we want to be able to use the library editor as a component of the window maker, we generated it as a subview (see method **subview** that follows; it's not encoded). So that the librarian editor can be used independently of the window maker, we also constructed a top view that uses the subview as a subwindow (see method **topView** that follows; it's

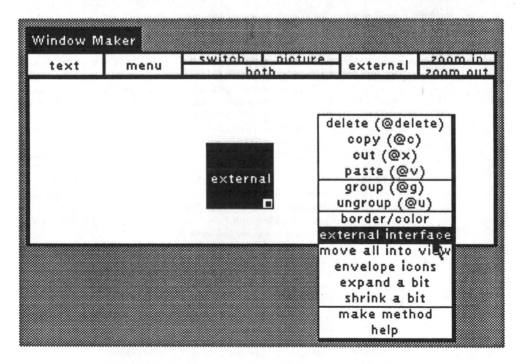

Figure 8.7 Creating a top view with an external subwindow.

Chapter 8 A Window Application

355

encoded). The window maker permits an externally constructed subview to be used via an **external** icon (see Fig. 8.7) that externally references the method for constructing the subview.

To compress (or decompress) the view, it is sufficient to execute 'WindowMaker **edit:** FormLibrarian **topView**', for example, and choose a different option when the method is generated.

class methods

editing

edit
    "FormLibrarian edit"
    WindowMaker **open:** self **topView on:** FormLibrarian **new**

view

topView
    "Returns an initialized view."
    | anArray |

    anArray ← "WindowMaker edit:" #(Master nil (-286 -201 286 201) white 2
        (1.11518 1.12944 320.0 227.599) true 'Librarian' (nil) (nil) (0 0) (1000
        1000) (classMethod notEncoded FormLibrarian view topView 'view overflow')
        ((External nil (-284.0 -199.0 284.0 199.0) nil 0 (FormLibrarian subView)))).
    ↑anArray

subView
    "Returns an initialized view."
    | anArray aView |

    anArray ← "WindowMaker edit:" #(Master librarian (-222 -179 222 180) white
        0 (1.43652 1.2647 320.0 227.039) false nil (nil) (nil) (250 100) (1000 1000)
        (classMethod notEncoded FormLibrarian view subView 'view overflow')
        ((Menu nil (-222.0 -179.0 -74.0 180.0) white (0 0 1 0) (libraries (getLibrariesList)
        (getLibrariesSelection) (changeLibrariesSelection: aSelectionObject)
        (getLibrariesYellowMenu))) (Menu nil (-74.0 -179.0 78.0 180.0) white
        (0 0 1 0) (library (getLibraryList) (getLibrarySelection) (changeLibrarySelection:
        aSelectionObject) (getLibraryYellowMenu))) (Picture nil (143.0 87.0 158.0 102.0)
        white 0 (form DefaultFormLibrary button) (lockedConstant fixCenter 0)
        (pictures (getOnForm))) (Picture nil (143.0 -88.0 158.0 -73.0) white 0
        (form DefaultFormLibrary button) (lockedConstant fixCenter 0) (pictures
        (getOffForm))) (Picture nil (78.0 -179.0 222.0 -142.0) white (0 0 0 1)
        (text 'off form') (varying) (nil (nil))) (Picture nil (78.0 -3.0 222.0 34.0) white
        (0 1 0 1) (text 'on form') (varying) (nil (nil))))).

    aView ← (ExtendedView **new**
        name: #librarian;
        encoding: anArray;
        insideColor: Form **white;**
        borderWidth: 0;
        window: (-222@-179 **corner:** 222@180);
        transformation: (WindowingTransformation
            scale: 1.43652@1.2647 **translation:** 320.0@227.039);
        yourself).

```
aView addSubView: ((ExtendedMenuView on: nil
    printItems: true oneItem: false
    aspect: #libraries
    change: (ExtendedMessage
        selector: #changeLibrariesSelection: arguments: #(aSelectionObject))
    list: #getLibrariesList
    menu: #getLibrariesYellowMenu
    initialSelection: #getLibrariesSelection)
    name: nil;
    insideColor: Form white;
    borderWidthLeft: 0 right: 1 top: 0 bottom: 0;
    window: (-222.0@-179.0 corner: -74.0@180.0);
    transformation: (WindowingTransformation scale: nil translation: 0@0);
    yourself).

aView addSubView: ((ExtendedMenuView on: nil
    printItems: true oneItem: false
    aspect: #library
    change: (ExtendedMessage
        selector: #changeLibrarySelection: arguments: #(aSelectionObject))
    list: #getLibraryList
    menu: #getLibraryYellowMenu
    initialSelection: #getLibrarySelection)
    name: nil;
    insideColor: Form white;
    borderWidthLeft: 0 right: 1 top: 0 bottom: 0;
    window: (-74.0@-179.0 corner: 78.0@180.0);
    transformation: (WindowingTransformation scale: nil translation: 0@0);
    yourself).

aView addSubView: ((ExtendedPictureView on: nil
    aspect: #pictures
    label: #(DefaultFormLibrary button)
    getLabel: #getOnForm)
    name: nil;
    insideColor: Form white;
    borderWidth: 0;
    window: (143.0@87.0 corner: 158.0@102.0);
    transformation: (WindowingTransformation scale: nil translation: 0@0);
    mode: #constant;
    fixCenter;
    yourself).

aView addSubView: ((ExtendedPictureView on: nil
    aspect: #pictures
    label: #(DefaultFormLibrary button)
    getLabel: #getOffForm)
    name: nil;
    insideColor: Form white;
    borderWidth: 0;
    window: (143.0@-88.0 corner: 158.0@-73.0);
    transformation: (WindowingTransformation scale: nil translation: 0@0);
    mode: #constant;
    fixCenter;
    yourself).
```

```
aView addSubView: ((ExtendedPictureView on: nil
    aspect: nil
    label: 'off form' asParagraph
    getLabel: nil)
    name: nil;
    insideColor: Form white;
    borderWidthLeft: 0 right: 0 top: 0 bottom: 1;
    window: (78.0@-179.0 corner: 222.0@-142.0);
    transformation: (WindowingTransformation scale: nil translation: 0@0);
    mode: #varying;
    fixMiddleLeft;
    yourself).
aView addSubView: ((ExtendedPictureView on: nil
    aspect: nil
    label: 'on form' asParagraph
    getLabel: nil)
    name: nil;
    insideColor: Form white;
    borderWidthLeft: 0 right: 0 top: 1 bottom: 1;
    window: (78.0@-3.0 corner: 222.0@34.0);
    transformation: (WindowingTransformation scale: nil translation: 0@0);
    mode: #varying;
    fixMiddleLeft;
    yourself).
↑aView
```

8.3 EXTENDED VIEWS

Originally, an attempt was made to construct windows that used the existing system window classes. As the window maker evolved, it became increasingly difficult to reconcile the existing classes with the design goals. By the time the design was finished, these included

1. A facility for referencing subwindows by name.

2. A facility that permits preprocessing when a window is opened and postprocessing when it is closed.

3. An extension that permits all view messages to be provided with an arbitrary number of constant parameters. Switch views, for example, already permit this, but none of the other classes of windows did.

4. Special windows that permit capabilities totally missing from the existing system; e.g., switches with constant-size forms, dynamic pictures (unlike switches, depressing a mouse over a picture has no effect), external reference windows.

5. Changes to the standard method for computing the display transformation that eliminates the built-in imprecision (see Fig. 3.7 in Sect. 3.3.1 or Sect. 8.3.2). Without this, consecutive side-by-side subwindows would unpredictably overlap borders (when they shouldn't).

6. Infinite loop protection for the change/update protocol for all application windows.

Inside Smalltalk

In the end, it was easiest to provide a new class of windows for each of the existing ones, including one new one. Figs. 8.8 and 8.9 provide a summary. Except for ExtendedExternalView, every other view is an extension of a corresponding view already in the system; i.e., all (and only) new classes are prefixed by '*Extended*'. In most cases, the corresponding controller was used without modification. The two exceptions are ExtendedMenuController and ExtendedSwitchController.

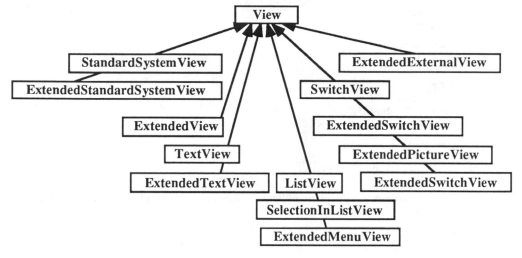

Figure 8.8 The extended views.

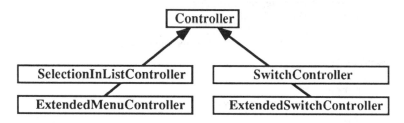

Figure 8.9 The extended controllers.

8.3.1 Common Extensions

Three extensions are common to the extended views:

1. A **naming** facility.
2. A **model initialization** facility.
3. A **modified** algorithm for computing display transformations.

Since few of the extended classes inherit from a common extended class, adding a special class containing the extensions and then using multiple-inheritance to share them with all extended classes seemed attractive. As we will see, this new class introduced seven new methods to be shared. In our case, multiple-inheritance is something we considered after the fact since the extensions evolved piece-meal; i.e., first two methods, then four, then five, and finally seven. Using multiple-inheritance, however, causes four inheritance conflicts. To eliminate these, four distinct methods had to be physically added to each extended class. On the one hand, we wanted to use multiple-inheritance to avoid duplicating seven methods; on the other, we had to duplicate four others. Clearly, the win was marginal. In the end, we decided not to use multiple-inheritance.

Class Extended...View

class	Extended...View
superclass	...
instance variables	name ...

instance methods

name

name
    ↑name
name: aSymbolOrNil
    name ← aSymbolOrNil

viewNamed: aSymbol
    | answer |
    name == aSymbol **ifTrue**: [↑self].
    subViews **do**: [:aView |
        answer ← aView **viewNamed**: aSymbol. answer **isNil ifFalse**: [↑answer]].
    ↑nil

model

models: anObject
    "If this view's model is nil, changes it to anObject and repeats the process for all subviews; otherwise, does nothing."
    model **isNil ifFalse**: [↑self].
    self **model**: anObject.
    subViews **do**: [:aView | aView **models**: anObject]

resetModels
    "Sets this view's model to nil and repeats for all subviews."
    self **model**: nil.
    subViews **do**: [:aView | aView **resetModels**]

displaying

computeDisplayTransformation
    "Since the borders in the containing view do not actually scale, this view (if left unchanged) will be positioned at a point that assumes the borders did scale. This can be eliminated by transforming into the inset display box rather than the display box. See View | computeDisplayTransformation for the difference."

    self **isTopView**
        ifTrue: [↑transformation]
        ifFalse: [↑superView **insetDisplayTransformation compose**: transformation]

insetDisplayTransformation
    "Ignores the borders."
    ↑WindowingTransformation
        window: self **insetWindow**
        viewport: self **insetDisplayBox**

The naming facility provides advanced designers with the ability to reference and manipulate specific windows associated with their application models. We use it, for example, to (1) reactivate the window maker window after an options window is closed, and to (2) reference a librarian subview to enable the model to interact directly with it.

The model initialization facility permits a whole collection of windows to be initialized to the same model. Moreover, those that are already initialized are unmodified. In most cases, this is used invisibly by extended standard system views when an application window is opened. However, it could be used explicitly for special preopening processing.

8.3.2 The Revised Display Transformation Algorithm

The existing algorithm for computing display transformations works most of the time but it is unreliable. Typically, a window designer has three tasks to perform: (1) choosing appropriate subwindows, (2) specifying and implementing the interface for the subwindows, and (3) specifying a layout. For illustrative purposes (see Fig. 8.10), suppose our task is to position the subwindow w exactly inside the superwindow sw so that the superwindow's borders touch it exactly. This layout is most easily specified interactively by placing the subwindow into its container superwindow.

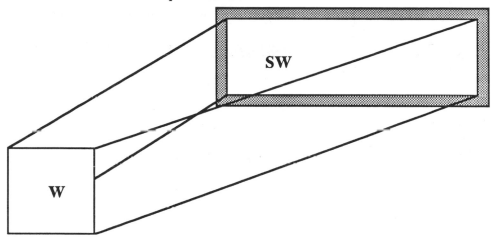

Figure 8.10 Mapping the window into the superview's window.

This layout process is entirely equivalent to providing the system with the local transformation for the subwindow; i.e.

localTransformation$_w$ is the mapping from w into sw.

Generally, the superwindow is resized and positioned when it is opened. Suppose the superwindow was made five times bigger on the screen, as in Fig. 8.11. The system maintains a transformation from the existing superwindow to its new position and size called the display transformation; i.e.,

displayTransformation$_{sw}$ is the mapping from the original sw to the resized sw.

A display transformation is also needed to determine where w resides on the screen. The subwindow's display transformation is computed as follows:

displayTransformation$_w$ is displayTransformation$_{sw}$ **compose**: localTransformation$_w$.

Because the resized superwindow sw is so large (five times bigger), it should be clear that the border is five times bigger. Hence, the resized window (resized w) is placed directly inside the larger border. The system, however, refuses to draw larger borders; they end up being drawn in the original size. So what the user sees is his original subwindow w resized in such a way that it **does not touch the borders** of the resized superwindow sw.

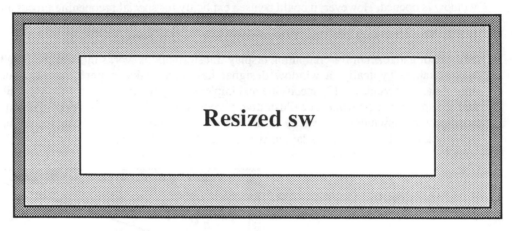

Figure 8.11 When the superview is enlarged (exaggerated).

Why isn't this more evident in the system? The answer is simple. The superwindow is generally large to begin with. Resizing rarely results in a magnification larger than 1.4. When this magnified border width is rounded to integer coordinates, it usually works out to be the original size. However, if the magnification were 1.6, a noticeable 1-pixel gap would result. Of course, if the window is made smaller by a factor of five, the converse occurs. The border shrinks by a factor of five but actually gets drawn in the original size. Hence, part of the resized subwindow w gets covered. Generally, the only way to get the subwindow exactly right with the existing algorithm is to overcompensate. If you expect the superwindow to be magnified, have the subwindow encroach into the superwindow's border. Conversely, if you expect it to be shrunk, inset the subwindow away from the superwindow's border. It is impossible to make it work for both possibilities, and it is quite error prone.

A solution that eliminates these problems is quite simple — simply change the meaning of the local transformation so that borders are not part of the transformation. Instead of having the local transformation map from the window to the superwindow, have the *local transformation map from the window to the inset superwindow* (the part without the borders). Now, however, there is a mismatch when composing transformations. To couple properly, we need to instead compose this modified transformation with one that maps inset superwindows to inset resized superwindows; i.e.,

insetDisplayTransformation$_{sw}$ is

> the mapping from the original inset sw to the resized inset sw.

displayTransformation$_w$ is

> insetDisplayTransformation$_{sw}$ **compose:** localTransformation$_w$.

Now, w via localTransformation$_w$ maps exactly inside the borders of sw; the inset window for sw maps exactly, via insetDisplayTransformation$_{sw}$, to the resized inset window. Since the normal display transformation for w is supposed to map w into the resized inset window, the composition of these two mappings is what is needed. In each case, the mappings are exact and overcompensation is no longer required.

8.3.3 Similar Operations

There are also a number of conversion and copy methods different for each class but with the same basic structure. For reference purposes, we have gathered them together in Appendix B.1. We don't consider method **storeOn:** that follows to be a good candidate for multiple-inheritance, for example, because it generates a conflict in each class. Conse-quently, it must be explicitly added in each class anyway to eliminate the conflict. An example taken from extended menu views is shown.

```
copying

deepCopy
    ↑self shallowCopy
        superView: nil; resetSubViews;
        model: model deepCopy controller: nil;
        transformation: transformation "stores a copy";
        window: window "stores a copy";
        yourself

printing

storeOn: aStream
    self storeOn: aStream indent: 2

storeOn: aStream indent: indentation
    "Store this instance of an ExtendedMenuView with indentation for readability."
    | return continue |
    return ← (WriteStream on: (String new: 16)) crtab: indentation; contents.
    continue ← ';', return.
    aStream
        nextPutAll: '((ExtendedMenuView on: nil'; nextPutAll: return;
        nextPutAll: 'printItems: true oneItem: false'; nextPutAll: return;
        nextPutAll: 'aspect: '; store: partMsg; nextPutAll: return;
        nextPutAll: 'change: '; store: changeMsg; nextPutAll: return;
        nextPutAll: 'list: '; store: listMsg; nextPutAll: return;
        nextPutAll: 'menu: '; store: menuMsg; nextPutAll: return;
        nextPutAll: 'initialSelection: '; store: initialSelectionMsg; nextPut: $);
            nextPutAll: return;
        nextPutAll: 'name: '; store: name; nextPutAll: continue;
        nextPutAll: 'insideColor: '.
            ExtendedStandardSystemView storeInsideColor: insideColor on: aStream.
            aStream nextPutAll: continue.
        ExtendedStandardSystemView
            storeBorderWidth: borderWidth messageOn: aStream.
            aStream nextPutAll: continue;
        nextPutAll: 'window: '; store: window; nextPutAll: continue;
        nextPutAll: 'transformation: ('; print: transformation; nextPut: $);
            nextPutAll: continue;
        nextPutAll: 'yourself)'
```

8.3.4 System Modifications

Recall that our goal was to design the window maker via extensions to the systems; i.e., by providing additions but not modifications. Unfortunately, two different kinds of modifications were required:

1. The **storeOn:** method for literal arrays incorrectly prints subarrays if these subarrays are large. More specifically, elements of these large subarrays are truncated using a dot-dot-dot notation; e.g., they might store as #(1 2 3 (4 5 6 ...etc...) 2000 2001) where "...etc..." is explicitly part of the store string.

2. The compiler has an extremely useful feature whereby users can provide a **requestor** for handling error messages. When an error is detected, the compiler sends the requestor a **notify:** message with the error message string as a parameter (or it sends variants of this **notify:** message with additional parameters). This is used by the browser, for example, to obtain and display the error message in the code pane. Unfortunately, the compiler doesn't follow this protocol for all error messages. Four cases have been inadvertently omitted.

The source of the first problem can be seen by considering the actual Array instance methods that follow. If an array to be stored is a literal (see **storeOn:** below), a subarray element is stored using **printOn:**. In the situation that the subarray contains more than **maxPrint** elements, it is truncated. It turns out that this actually occurs for some encodings (actually arrays) of the windows used by our window maker.

printing

isLiteral
>"Answer whether all the elements of the array are literal."
>
>self **detect:** [:element | element **isLiteral not**] **ifNone:** [↑true].
>↑false

printOn: aStream
>"Append to the argument, aStream, the elements of the Array enclosed by parentheses."
>
>| tooMany |
>tooMany ← aStream **position** + self **maxPrint**.
>aStream **nextPut:** $(.
>self **do:** [:element |
>   aStream **position** > tooMany **ifTrue:** [aStream **nextPutAll:** '...etc...)'. ↑self].
>   element **printOn:** aStream.
>   aStream **space**].
>aStream **nextPut:** $)

storeOn: aStream
>"Append to the argument aStream a sequence of characters that is an expression whose evaluation creates an object similar to the receiver. Use the literal form if possible."
>
>self **isLiteral**
>   **ifTrue:** [
>   aStream **nextPut:** $#; **nextPut:** $(.
>   self **do:** [:element | element **printOn:** aStream. aStream **space**].
>   aStream **nextPut:** $)]
>   **ifFalse:** [super **storeOn:** aStream]

Inside Smalltalk

One solution is to eliminate the problem temporarily by making the value returned by method **maxPrint** in class Collection larger; e.g., by changing the existing value from 1000 to 10000 as shown next.

private

maxPrint
"Answer the maximum number of characters to print with printOn:."

↑10000

A better solution is to replace **printOn:** in the **storeOn:** method by **storeOn:**. However, it does introduce superfluous '#' symbols.

The second problem needs to be fixed to permit an application window generated as a method by the window maker to be split into several pieces when it is too large to compile as one method. Two critical pieces of information are stored in an instance of class Parser prior to parsing the source code: (1) the **requestor**, and (2) a block called the **fail block** that also gets executed after error notification has occurred. If an error is encountered during parsing (and scanning), the requestor is notified. Once parsing is complete, the requestor and fail blocks are destroyed. Unfortunately, four potential error situations are possible after that point. Since the requestor is no longer available, they are reported as follows:

self **error:** 'Too many temporary variables'
self **error:** 'Too many literals referenced'
self **error:** 'Compiler stack discrepancy'
self **error:** 'Compiler code size discrepancy'

Our solution is to prevent the destruction of the requestor and fail block by commenting out two assignments in the following Parser instance method.

public access

parse: sourceStream **class**: class **noPattern**: noPattern **context**: ctxt
notifying: req **ifFail**: aBlock
"MODIFIED not to destroy the requestor or fail block."

... only the modified part is shown ...

encoder ← "failBlock ← requestor ←" parseNode ← nil.
"break cycles & mitigate refct overflow"

... more code follows ...

If this is done, we need only find a way to notify the requestor instead of generating a standard error message. The error messages are generated in an instance method of class MethodNode. As it turns out, the instance of Parser previously mentioned is kept in a MessageNode instance variable called *encoder*. The encoder relays **notify:** messages to the requestor in the Parser instance.

The short of it is that it is sufficient to replace the four occurrences of 'self **error:** aString' by 'encoder **notify:** aString' in the following MethodNode instance method.

code generation

generateAt: aRemoteString
  "MODIFIED by replacing 4 occurrences of 'self **error:** ...' by 'encoder **notify:** ...'."
  "I am the root of a parse tree; answer with an instance of CompiledMethod."

  ... only the modified parts are shown ...

  ... encoder **notify:** 'Too many temporary variables' ...
  ... encoder **notify:** 'Too many literals referenced' ...
  ... encoder **notify:** 'Compiler stack discrepancy' ...
  ... encoder **notify:** 'Compiler code size discrepancy'

  ... more code follows ...

8.3.5 The ExtendedMessage Class

One of our goals is to permit interface messages to have any number of constant parameters. This could be done with the existing Message class. However, we wanted a few additional methods to simplify its use. Class ExtendedMessage was added to avoid modifying the system.

Class ExtendedMessage

class   ExtendedMessage
superclass   Message
instance variables "none"

instance methods

sending

sendTo: receiver
  ↑receiver **perform:** selector **withArguments:** args

sendTo: receiver **replacingParameter:** anInteger **by:** anObject
  ↑receiver
      perform: selector
      withArguments: (args **copyReplaceFrom:** anInteger **to:** anInteger
          with: (Array **with:** anObject))

printing

storeOn: aStream
  "Same as Message storeOn: but with the class name changed."

  aStream
      nextPut: $(;
      nextPutAll: self **class name;**
      nextPutAll: ' selector: '; **store:** selector;
      nextPutAll: ' arguments: '; **store:** args;
      nextPut: $)

8.3.6 The ExtendedStandardSystemView Class

The ExtendedStandardSystemView class incorporates the common extensions along with a few others. These include the following:

1. Extensions for preprocessing by the model before the view (window) is opened (handled via a special **open** method) and postprocessing after it is closed (handled by overidding method **release**).

2. Printing support (class methods) for the other extended views.

3. Compilation support (plus class methods) also used by class ExtendedView.

4. Support to maintain and extract a window encoding.

Generally, the window maker allows designers to create windows with large numbers of subwindows. In some cases, the generated methods may be too large for successful compilation. In that case, the method is automatically partitioned into several pieces and compiled separately. For this to work, it is necessary to be able to attempt compilation and to get feedback from the compiler when unsuccessful. Error messages to the user must be avoided. The solution is to provide an error notifier as a parameter to the compiler. This notifier gets control when an error is encountered. To support this easily, we introduced a class called ErrorHandler. Class method **tryCompiling:class:classified:** in Extended-StandardSystemView uses it. Finally, the size of each of the pieces is a function of the capability of the existing compiler. Our goal is to have the fewest number of pieces as possible; hence the largest possible number of subwindow initialization in each method. We introduce a class variable CompilationHeuristic that keeps track of the size (number of pieces) of the last successfully compiled method and adjusts it dynamically. Because of their length, most of the compilation methods have been placed in Appendix B.2.

Class ErrorHandler

class	ErrorHandler
superclass	Object
instance variables	errorBlock

instance methods

instance initialization

errorBlock: aBlock
    errorBlock ← aBlock

error handling

notify: aString **at**: anInteger **in**: aStream
    errorBlock **value**: aString **value**: anInteger
select
    "Ignore"
deselect
    "Ignore"
selectFrom: start **to**: end
    "Ignore"
selectInvisiblyFrom: start **to**: end
    "Ignore"
selectionInterval
    ↑1 **to**: 0

Class ExtendedStandardSystemView

class	ExtendedStandardSystemView
superclass	StandardSystemView
instance variables	name preOpeningSelector postClosingSelector encoding
class variables	CompilationHeuristic

class methods

compiling support

compile: view **intoClass**: class **method**: methodName **category**: categoryName
    "Compile the receiver into the specified class."
    ↑self **compile**: view **intoClass**: class **method**: methodName **category**: categoryName
        overFlowCategory: categoryName, ' overflow'

compile: view **intoClass**: class **method**: methodName **category**: categoryName
overFlowCategory: overflowCategoryName
    "Compile the receiver into the specified class."
    ↑self **compileOneOrMoreMethods**: view **intoClass**: class **method**: methodName
        category: categoryName **overFlowCategory**: overflowCategoryName

private compiling support

tryCompiling: aMethodString **class**: class **classified**: aCategoryString
    "Returns true if compilation is successful; false otherwise. Note: this method is
    invoked rather than executing the code inline to force compiler data structures to
    disappear (it only happens when a return from compile:classified:notifying: occurs
    or the error block is executed)."
    | notifier |
    notifier ← ErrorHandler **new errorBlock**: [:message :position | ↑false].
    class **compile**: aMethodString **classified**: aCategoryString **notifying**: notifier.
    ↑true

... see Appendix B.2 for additional operations ...

private printing support

storeInsideColor: insideColor **on**: aStream
    insideColor **isNil ifTrue**: [↑aStream **nextPutAll**: 'nil'].
    #(black darkGray gray lightGray veryLightGray white) **do**: [:candidate |
        (insideColor == (Form **perform**: candidate))
            ifTrue: [↑aStream **nextPutAll**: 'Form '; **print**: candidate]].
    self **error**: 'unknown insideColor'

storeBorderWidth: borderWidth **messageOn**: aStream
    borderWidth = ((0@0 **extent**: 0@0) **translateBy**: borderWidth **left**)
        ifTrue: [
            aStream **nextPutAll**: 'borderWidth: '; **store**: borderWidth **left**]
        ifFalse: [
            aStream
                nextPutAll: 'borderWidthLeft: '; **store**: borderWidth **left**;
                nextPutAll: ' right: '; **store**: borderWidth **right**;
                nextPutAll: ' top: '; **store**: borderWidth **top**;
                nextPutAll: ' bottom: '; **store**: borderWidth **bottom**]

storeEncoding: encoding **on**: aStream **indent**: indentation
"Store the windowMakerEncoding with indented line continuations (assuming lines
of approximately 80 characters)."

| return internalStream leaderSize size character start end |
return ← (WriteStream **on**: (String **new**: 16)) **crtab**: indentation; **contents**.
internalStream ← ReadWriteStream **on**: (String **new**: 10000).
internalStream **nextPutAll**: '"WindowMaker edit:" '; **store**: encoding; **reset**.

leaderSize ← return **asDisplayText width** // ' ' **asDisplayText width**.
size ← leaderSize + 'encoding: ' **size**.
[internalStream **atEnd**] **whileFalse**: [
    character ← internalStream **next**.
    character = $'
      ifTrue: [
        size > 80 **ifTrue**: [aStream **nextPutAll**: return. size ← leaderSize].
        internalStream **skip**: -1. start ← aStream **position**.
        [internalStream **peek** == $'] **whileTrue**: [
          aStream
            nextPut: internalStream **next**;
            nextPutAll: (internalStream **upTo**: $');
            nextPut: $'].
        end ← aStream **position**. size ← size + (end - start)]
      ifFalse: [
        character = $
          ifTrue: [
            internalStream **peek** == $) "eliminate space in ')'"
              ifTrue: [
                aStream **nextPut**: internalStream **next**.
                size ← size + 11]
              ifFalse: [
                size > 80
                  ifTrue: [
                    aStream **nextPutAll**: return.
                    size ← leaderSize]
                  ifFalse: [
                    aStream **nextPut**: character.
                    size ← size + 1]]]
          ifFalse: [aStream **nextPut**: character. size ← size + 1]]]

instance methods

name
model
displaying
    ... *see common extensions ...*

copying
printing
    ... see Appendix B.1 ...

encoding

encoding
    ↑encoding
encoding: anArray
    encoding ← anArray

preopening/postclosing selectors

preOpeningSelector
    ↑preOpeningSelector

preOpeningSelector: aSymbolOrNil
    preOpeningSelector ← aSymbolOrNil

postClosingSelector
    ↑postClosingSelector

postClosingSelector: aSymbolOrNil
    postClosingSelector ← aSymbolOrNil

opening and preopening

open
    preOpeningSelector **isNil ifFalse**: [
        (preOpeningSelector **isKindOf**: Message)
            ifTrue: [preOpeningSelector **sendTo**: model **replacingParameter**: 1 **by**: self]
            ifFalse: [model **perform**: preOpeningSelector **with**: self]].
    self **controller open**

openOn: aModel
    preOpeningSelector **isNil**
        ifTrue: [self **models**: aModel]
        ifFalse: [
            (preOpeningSelector **isKindOf**: Message)
                ifTrue: [
                    preOpeningSelector **sendTo**: model **replacingParameter**: 1 **by**: self]
                ifFalse: [model **perform**: preOpeningSelector **with**: self]].
    self **controller open**

postclosing

release
    postClosingSelector **isNil ifFalse**: [
        (postClosingSelector **isKindOf**: Message)
            ifTrue: [postClosingSelector **sendTo**: model **replacingParameter**: 1 **by**: self]
            ifFalse: [model **perform**: postClosingSelector **with**: self]].
    super **release**

compiling

compileIntoClass: class **method**: methodName **category**: categoryName
    "Compile the receiver into the specified class."

    ExtendedStandardSystemView
        compile: self **intoClass**: class **method**: methodName **category**: categoryName

compileIntoClass: class **method**: methodName **category**: categoryName
overflow: overflowName
    "Compile the receiver into the specified class."

    ExtendedStandardSystemView
        compile: self **intoClass**: class **method**: methodName
        category: categoryName **overFlowCategory**: overflowName

8.3.7 The ExtendedView Class

The ExtendedView class is similar to the ExtendedStandardSystemView class but lacks the preopening and postclosing facility.

Class ExtendedView

class	ExtendedView
superclass	View
instance variables	name encoding

instance methods

name
model
displaying
    ... see common extensions ...

encoding

encoding
    ↑encoding
encoding: anArray
    encoding ← anArray

copying
printing
    ... see Appendix B.1 ...

compiling

compileIntoClass: class **method:** methodName **category:** categoryName
    "Compile the receiver into the specified class."
    ExtendedStandardSystemView
        compile: self **intoClass:** class **method:** methodName **category:** categoryName

compileIntoClass: class **method:** methodName **category:** categoryName
overflow: overflowName
    "Compile the receiver into the specified class."
    ExtendedStandardSystemView
        compile: self **intoClass:** class **method:** methodName
        category: categoryName **overFlowCategory:** overflowName

8.3.8 The ExtendedMenuView Class

The ExtendedMenuView class extends SelectionInListView (a pluggable view) in three ways:

1. The interface selectors (categories updating and adaptor) are augmented to permit extended messages instead of simple selector symbols. The extension is upward compatible.

2. An infinite loop tolerance mechanism is added to ensure that messages 'self **changed**: #updateSymbol' by the model will not result in an infinite loop when an update is already in progress.

3. A corresponding controller was also added because the existing one did not permit control for menus that were empty. Hence the yellow button pop-up menu could never get activated. Aside from additions to the menu by the model, this pop-up menu is the most obvious way of permitting a user to interactively add entries (see the 'add libraries' entry in the librarian editor for an example).

Some small additional perturbations were introduced. These can be determined from the methods.

Class **ExtendedMenuView**

class	ExtendedMenuView
superclass	SelectionInListView
instance variables	name updateInProgress ignoreChangeMessage

instance methods

initialization

on: anObject **printItems**: flag1 **oneItem**: flag2 **aspect**: m1 **change**: m2 **list**: m3 **menu**: m4
initialSelection: m5
    "Override SelectionInListView to avoid getting and changing the initial list until after the view is opened."
    self **model**: anObject.
    printItems ← flag1. oneItem ← flag2.
    partMsg ← m1. changeMsg ← m2. listMsg ← m3. menuMsg ← m4.
    initialSelectionMsg ← m5.
    oneItem **ifTrue**: [
        self **noTopDelimiter noBottomDelimiter**.
        initialSelectionMsg == nil **ifTrue**: [
            self **error**: 'initialSelection must be specified for oneItem mode']].
    "Commented out the following:
    self **list**: self **getList** "

name
model
displaying
    see common extensions (see below for an addition to displaying)

copying
printing
    ... see Appendix B.1 ...
controller

defaultControllerClass
    ↑ExtendedMenuController

list access

list: anArray
    "Eliminate built-in update in progress loop; more specifically, avoid changing the list selection to what it is."
    ignoreChangeMessage ← true. super **list**: anArray. ignoreChangeMessage ← nil

updating

aspect: aSymbol
   partMsg ← aSymbol

update: aSymbol
   "Upward compatible with selectionInList views."

   updateInProgress **isNil ifFalse**: [↑self]. updateInProgress ← true.
   super **update**: aSymbol. updateInProgress ← nil

adaptor

getList
   (listMsg **isKindOf**: Message) **ifTrue**: [↑listMsg **sendTo**: model].
   ↑super **getList**

initialSelection
   (initialSelectionMsg **isKindOf**: Message)
      ifTrue: [↑initialSelectionMsg **sendTo**: model].
   ↑super **initialSelection**

changeModelSelection: anInteger
   "Get the new menu list's selection unless requested not to do so."
   | newSelection |
   ignoreChangeMessage **isNil ifFalse**: [↑self].
   self **controller controlTerminate**.
      (changeMsg **isKindOf**: Message)
         ifTrue: [
            newSelection ← anInteger = 0
               ifTrue: [nil]
               ifFalse: [itemList **at**: anInteger].
            changeMsg **sendTo**: model **replacingParameter**: 1 **by**: newSelection]
         ifFalse: [↑super **changeModelSelection**: anInteger].
   self **controller controlInitialize**

yellowButtonMenu
   (menuMsg **isKindOf**: Message) **ifTrue**: [↑menuMsg **sendTo**: model].
   ↑super **yellowButtonMenu**

displaying

displayView
   "Ensure that the item list is set up when the view is first displayed."
   itemList **size** = 0 **ifTrue**: [self **list**: self **getList**].
   super **displayView**

Class ExtendedMenuController

class   ExtendedMenuController
superclass   SelectionInListController
instance variables   "none"

class methods

no messages

instance methods

control defaults

isControlWanted
   ↑self **viewHasCursor**

8.3.9 The ExtendedTextView Class

Like the ExtendedMenuView class, class ExtendedTextView extends the TextView class (a pluggable view) in three ways. The first two are similar but the third is unique to this class.

1. The interface selectors (categories updating and adaptor) are augmented to permit extended messages instead of simple selector symbols. The extension is upward compatible.

2. An infinite loop tolerance mechanism is added to ensure that messages 'self **changed**: #updateSymbol' by the model will not result in an infinite loop when an update is already in progress.

3. An explicit instance variable (aspect) for keeping track of the update symbol is added. The system class insists that this be the same as the getText (instance variable getMsg) message. There is no need for the two names to be correlated.

Class ExtendedTextView

```
class                   ExtendedTextView
superclass              TextView
instance variables      name aspect updateInProgress
```

class methods

instance creation

on: anObject **aspect**: aSymbol **get**: getMsg **change**: changeMsg **menu**: menuMsg
    ↑(super **on**: anObject **aspect**: getMsg **change**: changeMsg **menu**: menuMsg)
        aspect: aSymbol

instance methods

name
model
displaying
    ... see common extensions ...

copying
printing
    ... see Appendix B.1 ...

updating

aspect: aSymbol
    aspect ← aSymbol

update: aSymbol
    "Upward compatible with text views; i.e. missing aspect results in using the partMsg selector instead."
    | actualAspect |
    updateInProgress **isNil ifFalse**: [↑self].
    updateInProgress ← true.
        actualAspect ← aspect **isNil**
            ifTrue: [
                (partMsg **isKindOf**: Message)
                    ifTrue: [partMsg **selector**] **ifFalse**: [partMsg]]
            ifFalse: [aspect].
        actualAspect == aSymbol **ifTrue**: [super **update**: partMsg].
    updateInProgress ← nil

adaptor

accept: aText **from**: aController
    (acceptMsg **isKindOf**: Message)
        ifTrue: [↑acceptMsg **sendTo**: model **replacingParameter**: 1 **by**: aText].
    ↑super **accept**: aText **from**: aController

getText
    (partMsg **isKindOf**: Message) **ifTrue**: [↑partMsg **sendTo**: model].
    ↑super **getText**

yellowButtonMenu
    (menuMsg **isKindOf**: Message) **ifTrue**: [↑menuMsg **sendTo**: model].
    ↑super **yellowButtonMenu**

8.3.10 The ExtendedExternalView Class

The ExtendedExternalView class provides an indirect reference to an extended view. It is provided mainly to support external windows constructed by the window maker. With small extensions to the window maker, they could be eliminated.

Class ExtendedExternalView

class	ExtendedExternalView
superclass	View
instance variables	name className newMessage

class methods

no messages
instance methods

instance initialization

external: anArray
    "Initializes the external view by obtaining the subview denoted by the parameter: anArray having the form #(className selectorOrMessage). The external view's inset window and the subview's viewport must be made to correspond. Two solutions are possible: (1) make the external view's inset window the same as the subview's viewport, or (2) make the subview's viewport the same as the external view's inset window. Solution (1) is used here. This leaves the subview unaffected."
    | class subview |
    className ← anArray **at**: 1. newMessage ← anArray **at**: 2.
    class ← Smalltalk **at**: className.
    subview ← WindowMaker **asView**: ((newMessage **isKindOf**: Message)
        ifTrue: [newMessage **sendTo**: class]
        ifFalse: [class **perform**: newMessage]).
    self **addSubView**: subview.
    self
        window: (subview **getViewport expandBy**: self **borderWidth**)
        viewport: self **getViewport**.

name
model
displaying
    see common extensions
copying
printing
    ... see Appendix B.1 ...

8.3.11 The ExtendedSwitchView Class

The ExtendedSwitchView class provides a major extension to the SwitchView class. These include the following. All but the first and last are also provided by extended text and menu views.

1. A facility to handle fixed- and varying-size labels.
2. The interface selectors (categories updating and adaptor) are augmented to permit extended messages instead of simple selector symbols. The extension is upward compatible.
3. An infinite loop tolerance mechanism is added so that 'self **changed**: #update-Symbol' messages by the model will not result in an infinite loop when an update is in progress.
4. An explicit instance variable (aspect) for keeping track of the update symbol is added. The system class insists that this be the same as the isOn (instance variable selector) message. There is no need for the two names to be correlated.
5. Knowledge about highlight forms and the librarian, so that switches may be specified via library path names; i.e., library name and form name pairs.
6. The ability to have on and off representations that are different (**replacement** style) versus those that are meant to be merged (**overlay** style).

In more detail, extended switch views provide two **modes** for displaying the switch labels: **constant-size** mode and **varying-size** mode. The first is meant for labels that don't scale; the second for labels that do. The second also permits a switch label that doesn't scale to be displayed in a varying-size area. An example of an object that scales is a form; an example of one that doesn't is a string converted to a paragraph or a display text. Constant-size views have display boxes that are the same size as the window. There is no such correlation for varying-size views. Portions of extended switch views have been previously discussed in Sect. 3.4.4 under the title *Unscaled Switch Views*.

To better explain the two varieties, suppose an extended switch view's label size is 10 by 10. Also, suppose the view's window of size 50@50 would under normal circumstances transform to a display box of size 100@100. Let's call this display box — the expected display box. Three cases are possible:

1. **constant-size view:** The actual display box ends up being 50 by 50. Where the display box is actually positioned will depend on a specified fixed point (discussed below).
2. **varying-size view and a label that doesn't scale:** The actual display box is the expected display box of size 100@100 and the label (unscaled) is positioned in the center.
3. **varying-size view and a label that scales:** The actual display box is the expected display box of size 100@100 and the label is scaled to fit exactly.

Fixed points are used to specify which part of the view's window is to be transformed unaltered. When the fixed point is inside the window, self relative positioning is obtained. When it is outside, more global positioning permits rows or columns of views to be made adjacent. For example, methods **fixTopLeftCorner**, **fixCenter**, and **fixBottom-RightCorner** cause the 50 by 50 window previously mentioned to be positioned at the top left, center, and bottom right respectively of the expected display box (inside positioning). Correspondingly, methods **fixInHorizontalBankAtPosition:** and **fixInVerticalBankAt-Position:** cause the 50 by 50 window to be positioned in a row or column respectively (the row or column index is a parameter).

Users can also provide a **highlight object** and specify whether or not it is to be **overlaid** over the label as opposed to **replacing** it when the switch is depressed (the default is to replace). If no highlight object is provided, highlighting is performed in the standard way (using reverse video).

Additionally, the view permits an arbitrary change/update symbol called the aspect symbol to be specified. By contrast, switch views use the selector as the aspect symbol. It also provides infinite loop protection, as does the extended menu and text views.

The controller class is listed first because it is so simple; the corresponding view class follows immediately.

Class ExtendedSwitchController

class	ExtendedSwitchController
superclass	SwitchController
instance variables	"none"

class methods

no messages

instance methods

model querying

sendMessage
　　(selector **isKindOf:** Message) **ifTrue:** [↑selector **sendTo:** model].
　　↑super **sendMessage**

Class ExtendedSwitchView

class	ExtendedSwitchView
superclass	SwitchView
instance variables	name labelSource labelSourceForm highlightSource aspect fixedPoint fixedPointCode mode highlightOverlay updateInProgress

class methods

instance creation

on: anObject **aspect:** aSymbol **label:** aDisplayObject
isOn: isOnMessage **switch:** switchMessage
　　"Both the isOn and switch messages may be ExtendedMessage instances."
　　↑((self **new**
　　　　model: anObject; **aspect:** aSymbol; **label:** aDisplayObject;
　　　　selector: isOnMessage; **arguments:** #();
　　　　mode: #constant; **fixCenter) controller**
　　　　　　selector: switchMessage; **arguments:** #()) **view**

```
on: anObject aspect: aSymbol label: aDisplayObject
isOnSelector: isOnSelector isOnParameters: isOnParms
switchSelector: switchSelector switchParameters: switchParms
    ↑((self new
        model: anObject; aspect: aSymbol; label: aDisplayObject;
        selector: isOnSelector; arguments: isOnParms;
        mode: #constant; fixCenter) controller
            selector: switchSelector; arguments: switchParms) view
```

private printing support

```
storeLabel: label on: aStream
    "Attempt to store the most compact representation possible."
    | path |
    label isNil ifTrue: [↑aStream nextPutAll: 'nil'].
    (label isKindOf: Paragraph)
        ifTrue: [↑aStream store: label asString; nextPutAll: ' asParagraph'].
    (label isKindOf: Form) ifTrue: [
        path ← FormLibrarian pathNameForForm: label.
        path isNil ifFalse: [
            ↑aStream
                nextPutAll: '(FormLibrarian formForPathName: ';
                store: path; nextPut: $)]].
    label storeOn: aStream
```

```
storeHighlight: highlight givenLabel: label on: aStream
    "Attempt to store the most compact representation possible."
    | path |
    (label isKindOf: FormWithHighlight) ifTrue: [
        (path ← FormLibrarian pathNameForForm: label) isNil ifFalse: [
            (FormLibrarian formForPathName: path) highlight == highlight ifTrue: [
                ↑aStream
                    nextPutAll: '(FormLibrarian formForPathName: ';
                    store: path; nextPutAll: ') highlight']]].
    ↑self storeLabel: highlight on: aStream
```

examples

example1
```
    "ExtendedSwitchView example1"
```

    "Mixes forms and paragraphs. Since they are no longer identical in size, some
    differences will be apparent. Also, note that the fixed points have no effect in
    varying mode."

```
    | topView labels switches switchCount switchHeight switchOffsets banks
    switchWidth |

    topView ← StandardSystemView new
        label: 'Unscaled/Unscaled Switches (Forms and Paragraphs)';
        insideColor: Form white; borderWidth: 2.
    labels ←
        (#(normal read execute) collect: [:aSymbol | Cursor perform: aSymbol]),
        (#('aa' 'bb' 'cc') collect: [:aString | aString asParagraph]).
    switches ← labels collect: [:aLabel | Switch newOff].
    switchCount ← switches size.
    switchHeight ← (1/switchCount) asFloat.
    switchOffsets ← 0.0 to: 1.0-(switchHeight/10.0) by: switchHeight.
```

"Create 8 vertical banks of switches: the first four unscaled, the last four scaled.
Use the same switches and labels to create eight columns differing only in position
and scaling."
switchWidth ← (1/8) **asFloat**.
banks ← (1 **to**: 8) **collect**: [:bankIndex |
    (1 **to**: switchCount) **collect**: [:aSwitchIndex |
        ExtendedSwitchView **new**
            model: (switches **at**: aSwitchIndex);
            label: (labels **at**: aSwitchIndex);
            mode: (bankIndex < 5 **ifTrue**: [#constant] **ifFalse**: [#varying])]].

topView **window**: Display **boundingBox**.
    "helps eliminate transformation roundoff errors"
banks **with**: (0.0 **to**: 1.0-switchWidth **by**: switchWidth) **do**: [:aBank :anXOffset |
    aBank **with**: switchOffsets **do**: [:aSwitchView :aYOffset |
        topView
            addSubView: aSwitchView
            in: (anXOffset@aYOffset **extent**: switchWidth@switchHeight)
            borderWidth: 1]].

"Now specify the fixed point for the first four banks."
(banks **at**: 1) **do**: [:aSwitchView | aSwitchView **fixTopLeft**].
(banks **at**: 2) **do**: [:aSwitchView | aSwitchView **fixCenter**].
(banks **at**: 3) **do**: [:aSwitchView | aSwitchView **fixBottomRight**].
(banks **at**: 4) **with**: (1 **to**: switchCount) **do**: [:aSwitchView :aCount |
    aSwitchView **fixColumn**: aCount].

"Ditto for the next four banks."
(banks **at**: 5) **do**: [:aSwitchView | aSwitchView **fixTopLeft**].
(banks **at**: 6) **do**: [:aSwitchView | aSwitchView **fixCenter**].
(banks **at**: 7) **do**: [:aSwitchView | aSwitchView **fixBottomRight**].
(banks **at**: 8) **with**: (1 **to**: switchCount) **do**: [:aSwitchView :aCount |
    aSwitchView **fixColumn**: aCount].

"Add some unnecessary transparent subviews just to provide the grid so we can
better see what happened."
(0.0 **to**: 1.0-switchWidth **by**: switchWidth) **do**: [:anXOffset |
    switchOffsets **do**: [:aYOffset |
        topView
            addSubView: View **new**
            in: (anXOffset@aYOffset **extent**: switchWidth@switchHeight)
            borderWidth: 1]].

"Turn on the 2nd switch."
(switches **at**: 2) **turnOn**. "Note: causes spurious switches to be displayed since the
top controller is not yet opened."

topView **controller open**

instance methods

instance initialization

defaultWindow
    "If the label exists, returns a rectangle large enough (but not much more) to contain
the label and its border. Otherwise, returns a small rectangle."
    label == nil
        ifTrue: [↑0@0 **corner**: 25@25]
        ifFalse: [↑(label **boundingBox expandBy**: borderWidth) **expandBy**: 5]

initialize
> super **initialize**.
> "aspect, fixedPoint, updateInProgress are nil"
> fixedPointCode ← #center.
> mode ← #constant.
> highlightOverlay ← false.
> "Until user initialized, ensure the selector test returns false."
> self **selector**: #==; **arguments**: (Array **with**: Object **new**)

name
model
displaying
> *... see common extensions (see below for additions to displaying) ...*

copying
printing
> *... see Appendix B.1 ...*

mode and highlighting

mode
> ↑mode
mode: aSymbol
> "Checks for erroneous settings."
> (#(constant varying) **indexOf**: aSymbol) = 0
> > **ifTrue**: [self **error**: 'allowable modes are #constant or #varying'].
> mode ← aSymbol. self **unlock**

overlayHighlight
> ↑highlightOverlay
overlayHighlight: aBoolean
> highlightOverlay ← aBoolean

fixed point querying

fixedPoint
> | aPoint xIndex yIndex topWindowOrigin oldWindow |
> fixedPoint **isNil ifTrue**: [
> > fixedPointCode **isNil**
> > > **ifTrue**: [↑fixedPoint ← self **getWindow center**].
> > (fixedPointCode **isKindOf**: Symbol)
> > > **ifTrue**: [↑fixedPoint ← self **getWindow perform**: fixedPointCode].
> > (fixedPointCode **isKindOf**: Point)
> > > **ifTrue**: [↑fixedPoint ← fixedPointCode]
> > > **ifFalse**: ["must be a row, column, or matrix"
> > > > "Assumes all switches are the same size"
> > > > "The vertical bank is numbered 1, 2, 3, ... from the top."
> > > > "The horizontal bank is numbered 1, 2, 3, ... from the left"
> > > > aPoint ← fixedPointCode **at**: 1. xIndex ← aPoint **x**. yIndex ← aPoint **y**.
> > > > oldWindow ← self **getWindow**.
> > > > topWindowOrigin ← oldWindow **origin** -
> > > > > (((xIndex-1) * oldWindow **width**)@((yIndex-1) *
> > > > > oldWindow **height**)).
> > > > ↑fixedPoint ← topWindowOrigin]].
> ↑fixedPoint

fixedPointEncoding
    fixedPoint **isNil ifTrue:** ["force the code to be computed" self **fixedPoint**].
    fixedPointCode **isNil ifTrue:** [↑#fixCenter].
    (fixedPointCode **isKindOf:** Symbol) **ifTrue:** [
        ↑#(fixBottomLeft fixBottomRight fixCenter fixMiddleLeft
            fixMiddleRight fixTopLeft fixTopRight)
                at: (#(bottomLeft corner center leftCenter
                      rightCenter origin topRight) **indexOf:** fixedPointCode)].
    (fixedPointCode **isKindOf:** Point)
        ifTrue: [↑'fixPoint: ', fixedPointCode **printString**]
        ifFalse: [↑'fixMatrix: ', (fixedPointCode **at:** 1) **printString**]

fixed point manipulation

fixBottomLeft
    fixedPointCode ← #bottomLeft. self **unlock**
fixBottomRight
    fixedPointCode ← #corner. self **unlock**
fixMiddleLeft
    fixedPointCode ← #leftCenter. self **unlock**
fixMiddleRight
    fixedPointCode ← #rightCenter. self **unlock**
fixTopLeft
    fixedPointCode ← #origin. self **unlock**
fixTopRight
    fixedPointCode ← #topRight. self **unlock**
fixCenter
    fixedPointCode ← #center. self **unlock**

fixRow: anInteger
    "Assumes all switches in the row are the same size and numbered 1, 2, 3, ... from
    the left."
    fixedPointCode ← Array **with:** anInteger@0. self **unlock**
fixColumn: anInteger
    "Assumes all switches in the column are the same size and numbered 1, 2, 3, ...
    from the top."
    fixedPointCode ← Array **with:** 0@anInteger. self **unlock**
fixMatrix: aPoint
    "Assumes all switches are the same size with x rows and y columns."
    "The rows are numbered 1, 2, 3, ... from the top."
    "The columns are numbered 1, 2, 3, ... from the left"
    fixedPointCode ← Array **with:** aPoint. self **unlock**

fixPoint: aPoint
    fixedPointCode ← aPoint. self **unlock**

label/highlight modification

label: displayObjectOrLibraryPathName
    (displayObjectOrLibraryPathName **isKindOf:** Array)
        ifTrue: [
            labelSource ← displayObjectOrLibraryPathName.
            labelSourceForm ← FormLibrarian **formForPathName:** labelSource.
            super **label:** labelSourceForm]
        ifFalse: [
            labelSource ← labelSourceForm ← nil.
            super **label:** displayObjectOrLibraryPathName]

highlight: aDisplayObjectOrSymbolOrNil
    highlightSource ← aDisplayObjectOrSymbolOrNil.
    highlightSource == #fromLabel
        ifTrue: [
            (labelSourceForm **respondsTo:** #highlight)
                ifTrue: [super **highlightForm:** labelSourceForm **highlight**]
                ifFalse: [super **highlightForm:** nil]]
        ifFalse: [super **highlightForm:** highlightSource]

centerLabel
    "Deactivated because too many inherited methods attempt to center the label by destructively modifying it."

controller access

defaultControllerClass
    ↑ExtendedSwitchController

emphasizing

deEmphasizeView
    "Deactivated. See View|deEmphasizeView."
    ↑self
emphasizeView
    "Deactivated. See View|deEmphasizeView."
    ↑self

adaptor

interrogateModel
    (selector **isKindOf:** Message) **ifTrue:** [↑selector **sendTo:** model].
    ↑super **interrogateModel**

displaying

display
    "Displays the view taking into account the status of the model, the label, and the highlight object. To present an instantaneous picture, the view is first internally displayed on a form."

    | aForm displayBox |
    "Take the inside color into account when obtaining the form."
    aForm ← insideColor **isNil**
        ifTrue: [Form **fromDisplay:** (displayBox ← self **displayBox**)]
        ifFalse: [Form **extent:** (displayBox ← self **displayBox**) **extent**].
    self **displayOn:** aForm **at:** 0@0 **clippingBox:** aForm **boundingBox**
        rule: Form **under mask:** Form **black**.
    "Display the form."
    aForm **displayOn:** Display **at:** displayBox **origin**

displayOn: aForm **at:** aPoint **clippingBox:** aRectangle **rule:** ruleInteger **mask:** maskForm
    "Displays the view taking into account the status of the model, the label, and the highlight object."

    | outside displayBox inside newTransformation |
    outside ← aPoint **extent:** (displayBox ← self **displayBox**) **extent**.
    inside ← outside **insetBy:** borderWidth.
    newTransformation ← self **transformationToDisplayIn:** inside.
    complemented ← self **interrogateModel**. "update the view's status"

"The border."
(outside **areasOutside**: inside) **do**: [:area |
    aForm **fill**: (area **intersect**: aRectangle) **rule**: ruleInteger **mask**: borderColor].
outside ← outside **intersect**: aRectangle.
inside ← inside **intersect**: aRectangle.

"The inside."
insideColor **isNil**
    ifFalse: [aForm **fill**: inside **rule**: ruleInteger **mask**: insideColor].

"The label."
label **notNil** & (complemented & highlightForm **notNil** & highlightOverlay) **not**
    ifTrue: [
        "Avoid displaying label if highlight is to be overlaid (can't erase label with
        rule under)."
        label
            displayOn: aForm **transformation**: newTransformation
            clippingBox: inside **rule**: ruleInteger **mask**: maskForm].

"The highlight."
complemented **ifTrue**: [
    highlightForm **isNil**
        ifTrue: [aForm **reverse**: inside]
        ifFalse: [
            highlightForm
                displayOn: aForm **transformation**: newTransformation
                clippingBox: inside
                rule: (highlightOverlay **ifTrue**: [Form **under**] **ifFalse**: [ruleInteger])
                mask: maskForm]]

indicatorReverse
    "Show that the switch has been pressed."
    | inside outside newTransformation |

    inside ← self **insetDisplayBox**.
    highlightForm **isNil**
        ifTrue: [Display **reverse**: inside **mask**: Form **gray**]
        ifFalse: [
            newTransformation ← self **transformationToDisplayIn**: inside.
            (self **interrogateModel** **ifTrue**: [label] **ifFalse**: [highlightForm])
                displayOn: Display **transformation**: newTransformation
                clippingBox: inside **rule**: Form **reverse** **mask**: Form **gray**]

transformationToDisplayIn: aRectangle
    "The given display transformation is designed to transform the window (which may
    be located anywhere) to the display box. Returns the transformation needed to
    transform the label into the center of the same display box."
    | center |
    (mode == #varying **and**: [(label **isKindOf**: Path) | (label **isKindOf**: Form)])
        ifTrue: ["Object can resize - begs for canResize method."
            "Start displaying at inside origin rather than outside origin."
            ↑WindowingTransformation
                window: label **boundingBox** **viewport**: aRectangle]
        ifFalse: ["Object should not resize - center in inset display box."
            center ← (label **isNil**
                ifTrue: [aRectangle]
                ifFalse: [label **boundingBox**]) **center**.
            ↑WindowingTransformation
                scale: nil **translation**: aRectangle **center** - center].

computeDisplayTransformation

"For varying-size switches, the default computeDisplayTransformation is used. For constant-size switches, additional computation is required. First, the default display transformation is computed and then used to determine where the fixed point should be displayed. Then a new display transformation with no scaling is constructed which translates the label origin in such a way that the fixed point is at the position determined above. Note that the resulting display box is consequently the same size as the window (not necessarily the same size as the label)."

| scaledTransformation sourceFixedPoint destinationFixedPoint |
fixedPoint ← nil.
scaledTransformation ← self **superComputeDisplayTransformation**.
mode == #constant **ifFalse**: [↑scaledTransformation].

sourceFixedPoint ← self **fixedPoint**.
destinationFixedPoint ← scaledTransformation **applyTo**: sourceFixedPoint.
↑WindowingTransformation
    scale: nil **translation**: destinationFixedPoint - sourceFixedPoint

superComputeDisplayTransformation

"Since the borders in the containing view do not actually scale, this view (if left unchanged) will be positioned at a point that assumes the borders did scale. This can be eliminated by transforming into the inset display box rather than the display box. See View | computeDisplayTransformation for the difference."

self **isTopView**
    ifTrue: [↑transformation]
    ifFalse: [↑superView **insetDisplayTransformation compose**: transformation]

insetDisplayTransformation

"Ignores the borders."
↑WindowingTransformation
    window: self **insetWindow**
    viewport: self **insetDisplayBox**

updating

aspect: aSymbol
    aspect ← aSymbol

update: aSymbol
"Upward compatible with switch views; i.e. missing aspect results in using the selector instead."
| actualAspect |
updateInProgress **isNil ifFalse**: [↑self].
actualAspect ← aspect **isNil**
    ifTrue: [
        (selector **isKindOf**: Message) **ifTrue**: [selector **selector**] **ifFalse**: [selector]]
    ifFalse: [aspect].
actualAspect == aSymbol
    ifTrue: [updateInProgress ← true. self **display**. updateInProgress ← nil]

8.3.12 The ExtendedPictureView Class

To support pictures with the power and flexibility that extended switch views provided, it is convenient to think of pictures as switches without controllers. Unlike display text views, that assume the picture will be forever unchanged, extended pictures provide for **dynamic** pictures; i.e., pictures that can be changed any time the model decides. When the model wants a new picture displayed, it simply sends a 'self **changed**: #updateSymbol' message, where #updateSymbol is the aspect for the extended picture view.

Class ExtendedPictureView

class	ExtendedPictureView
superclass	ExtendedSwitchView
instance variables	labelMessage

class methods

instance creation

on: anObject **aspect**: aSymbol **label**: aDisplayObjectOrNil
getLabel: getLabelMessageOrNil
    "If the 'get label' message is nil, the supplied label is displayed (nil results in a picture with the view's inside color and border color). Otherwise, the 'get label' message is sent to the model to obtain the current label."
    ↑(self **new**
        model: anObject; **aspect**: aSymbol; **label**: aDisplayObjectOrNil;
        selector: #isNil; **arguments**: #();
        mode: #constant; **fixCenter**)
          labelMessage: getLabelMessageOrNil

instance methods

controller access

defaultControllerClass
    ↑NoController

updating

labelMessage
    ↑labelMessage
labelMessage: aSymbolOrNil
    labelMessage ← aSymbolOrNil

update: aSymbol
    aspect == aSymbol **ifTrue**: [self **display**]

displaying

display
    labelMessage **isNil ifFalse**: [
        self **label**: ((labelMessage **isKindOf**: Message)
            ifTrue: [labelMessage **sendTo**: model]
            ifFalse: [model **perform**: labelMessage])].
    super **display**

name
model
displaying
copying
    inherited from ExtendedSwitchView

printing
    ... see Appendix B.1 ...

8.3.13 The ExtendedSwitchAndPictureView Class

Since switches, as in Fig. 8.12, are normally to the left of text that explains the switch (a picture), it is convenient to provide a class of views that combines the two — an extended switch and picture view. One advantage of the combination is the ability to specify the **separation** between the two exactly .

Figure 8.12 A switch (left), a picture (middle), and a switch/picture.

Class ExtendedSwitchAndPictureView

class	ExtendedSwitchAndPictureView
superclass	ExtendedSwitchView
instance variables	labelSwitchPathName labelSeparation labelPictureString

instance methods

label/highlight modification

label: anArray
"Label is constructed from anArray of form #(switchPathName separation pictureString)."

| savedForm |
labelSource ← anArray.
labelSwitchPathName ← anArray **at:** 1.
labelSeparation ← anArray **at:** 2.
labelPictureString ← anArray **at:** 3.
labelSourceForm ← FormLibrarian **formForPathName:** labelSwitchPathName.
savedForm ← labelSourceForm.
super **label:** self **getLabel.** "label: destroys labelSource and labelSourceForm"
labelSource ← anArray.
labelSourceForm ← savedForm

highlight: aDisplayObjectOrSymbol
"The highlight must be made the same size as the label to properly overlap (they are centered in their display boxes)."
super **highlight:** aDisplayObjectOrSymbol. "sets the user supplied highlight"
highlightForm ← self **getHighlight** "recomputes it to properly overlap the label"

printing

storeLabelOn: aStream
"Stores the label in the form #(switchPathName separation pictureString)."
labelSource **isNil**
    ifTrue: [super **storeLabelOn:** aStream]
    ifFalse: [labelSource **storeOn:** aStream]

getLabel
"Constructs a form from the switch path name, separation, and picture string."

| switchForm pictureForm width height combinedForm |
switchForm ← labelSourceForm **isNil**
    ifTrue: [Form **extent**: 0@0]
    ifFalse: [labelSourceForm].
pictureForm ← labelPictureString **asParagraph asForm**.

width ← switchForm **width** + labelSeparation + pictureForm **width**.
height ← switchForm **height max**: pictureForm **height**.
combinedForm ← Form **extent**: width@height.

switchForm **displayOn**: combinedForm
    at: 0@((height - switchForm **height**) // 2).
pictureForm **displayOn**: combinedForm
    at: (switchForm **width** + labelSeparation)@((height - pictureForm **height**) // 2).

↑combinedForm

getHighlight
"Constructs a highlight that parallels the label in size."

| combinedForm |
highlightForm **isNil ifTrue**: [↑nil].
combinedForm ← Form **extent**: label **extent**.
highlightForm **displayOn**: combinedForm
    at: 0@((combinedForm **height** - highlightForm **height**) // 2).
↑combinedForm

8.4 THE WINDOW MAKER

The **window maker** (see Fig. 8.13) provides the designer with the capability to (1) create text, menu, switch, picture, and external windows, (2) specify their interfaces, and (3) provide a suitable layout (resizing, bordering, coloring, moving, and aligning).

The top row consists of switches. The bottom pane, the **icon container pane**, is the repository for newly created subwindows — **window maker icons**. A new icon is created by depressing one of the switches at the top. It will pop up out of the switch and follow the mouse until deposited in the icon container pane. Failure to deposit the icon in the container pane results in the icon sliding back into the switch and vaporizing. Unlike the other switches, the **zoom switches** at the top right corner cause the window to magnify or shrink the container pane, providing the designer with the specified change in perspective.

The window maker is invoked by executing 'WindowMaker **edit**'. A standard system view is constructed with switch views for the switches at the top (see Fig. 8.14) and a special view, an instance of WindowMakerMasterIcon, for the container pane. When a switch is depressed, message '**makeIcon**: #WindowMaker???Icon' is sent to the associated window maker model, an instance of WindowMaker. This message is routed to the master icon, which creates an instance of the specified icon, provides the visual feedback mentioned previously, and adds it (if the icon is deposited in the container pane) to the existing collection

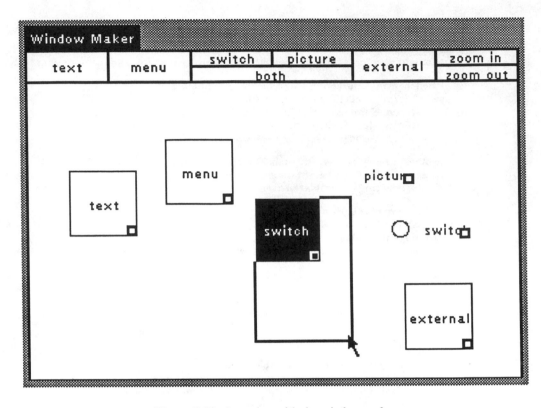

Figure 8.13 A session with the window maker.

of icons in the master icon (as a subview). The zooming switch views are similar but send their messages directly to the master icon. Unlike the nonzooming switches that use default controllers, the zooming switches make use of a special controller that provides for continuous zooming; i.e., the designer need not provide a separate push-down action to obtain the zooming — it is sufficient to keep the button depressed on the switch. The reader might note that the window maker model (aWindowMaker in Fig. 8.14) is not playing an essential role. It could be bypassed as it is by the zooming switches. We leave this simplification as an exercise to the reader.

We first consider the **continuous switch controller**. Unlike switch controllers that send their message only when they lose control (see **controlTerminate**), the continuous switch controller keeps sending the message associated with the switch as long as it maintains control; i.e., as long as the mouse is depressed in the switch view.

Class ContinuousSwitchController

class	ContinuousSwitchController
superclass	SwitchController
instance variables	"none"

instance methods

controlling

controlActivity
"Continuously sends the message as long as the button is depressed."
self **sendMessage**

controlTerminate
"Restores the button without doing anything more."
view **indicatorReverse**

The window maker's major role is to provide an interface with a designer who wishes to construct an application specific window (class method **edit**) or who wishes to modify an existing window (class method **edit:**). In general, an application window can be generated as an extended standard system view (with all the requisite subviews) or as an encoding of this view. The window maker **open** method permits either of these representations to be opened in a transparent manner. If it is an encoding, for example, it is first converted to an extended standard system view. Other class methods are used primarily by the master icon, which provides the editing functions. A secondary role is to serve as a model for the editor (as described previously). Only two instance methods are provided for this purpose: **iconView:** and **makeIcon:**.

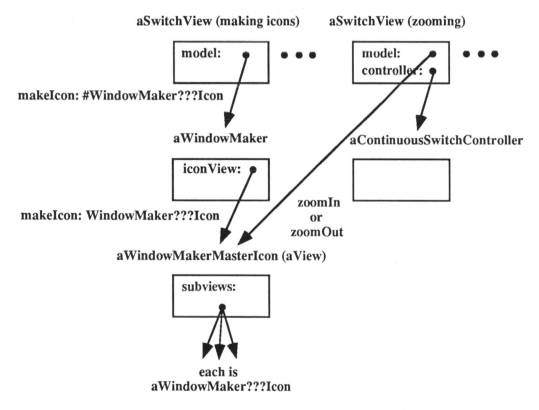

Figure 8.14 WindowMaker model/view/controller details.

The most interesting and complicated method to study is the method **privateEditorOn:**, which creates the top view with the relationships described in Fig. 8.13. The reader will note that it does not make use of the extended views discussed in prior sections. This is due mainly to historical development — we could have used them or we could have used the window maker itself to create a bootstrapped version. This would be analogous to producing a compiler for a language that did not exist and having the compiler written in this new language. A consequence of not bootstrapping or not using extended views is that bordering inaccuracies, as discussed in *The Revised Display Transformation Algorithm* of Sect. 8.3.2, are occasionally evident. None of our figures demonstrates this because we were careful to avoid such pictures. The designer, however, will notice it. Sometimes, the border between two random switches will be 1 pixel wide rather than 2. Resizing the window maker to a different size will often eliminate it. In some cases, however, it will simply cause some other border to deviate. The same problem occurs with the border for the bottom view — the top border is 3 pixels high rather than two; the bottom border may sometimes be 1 pixel high rather than 2.

Class WindowMaker

class	WindowMaker
superclass	Model
instance variables	iconView

class methods

class initialization

initialize
    "WindowMaker initialize"
    (self **confirm:** 'initialize WindowMaker? Reply no if filing in classes; yes otherwise')
        ifFalse: [↑self].
    FormLibrary **initialize**.
    FormLibrarian **initialize**.
    FormLibrarian **decompress**.
    WindowMakerMasterIconController **decompress**

converting

asIcon: encodingOrView
    "Convert the window maker encoding or extended view (an extended standard system view or an extended view) to an icon."
    (encodingOrView **respondsTo:** #encoding)
        ifTrue: [↑self **decode:** encodingOrView **encoding**]
        ifFalse: [↑self **decode:** encodingOrView]

asView: encodingOrView
    "Convert the window maker encoding or extended view (any kind of extended view) to an extended view."
    (encodingOrView **isKindOf:** View)
        ifTrue: [↑encodingOrView]
        ifFalse: [↑(self **decode:** encodingOrView) **asView**]

opening

edit
    "Open a new window maker editor."
    (self **privateEditorOn:** WindowMakerMasterIcon **new**) **controller open**
    "WindowMaker edit"

edit: iconItemsOrAView
    "Open a new editor on the parameter."
    (self **privateEditorOn:** (self **asIcon:** iconItemsOrAView)) **controller open**

open: iconItemsOrAView
    "Open the parameter."
    ↑self **open:** iconItemsOrAView **on:** nil

open: encodedWindowOrView **on:** aModel
    "Open the parameter (an encoded window or a view) on the model."
    (self **asView:** encodedWindowOrView) **openOn:** aModel

encoding/decoding

decode: encoding
    "Convert the encoding to an icon"
    | aStream |
    aStream ← ReadStream **on:** encoding.
    ↑(Smalltalk **at:** ('WindowMaker', aStream **next,** 'Icon') **asSymbol) new**
        decodeFrom: aStream

encode: anIcon
    "Convert the icon to an encoding"
    | aStream |
    aStream ← WriteStream **on:** (String **new:** 10000).
    self **encode:** anIcon **on:** aStream.
    ↑aStream **contents**

encode: anIcon **on:** aStream
    "Convert the icon to an encoding"
    aStream **nextPutAll:** '#('.
    anIcon **encodeOn:** aStream.
    aStream **nextPut:** $)

private

privateEditorOn: anIcon
    "Create and return an editor on the given window maker but does not open or start
    it up."
    | aWindowMaker topView iconView switchesView isOnSelector
    isOnSelectorArguments switchSelector subviews textView menuView switchView
    pictureView switchAndPictureView externalView zoomInView zoomOutView
    subRectangles iconContainerView |

    aWindowMaker ← WindowMaker **new.**
    topView ← StandardSystemView **new**
        label: 'Window Maker'; **minimumSize:** 200@100.
    iconView ← anIcon **model:** aWindowMaker.
    iconContainerView ← View **new.**
    switchesView ← View **new.**

    topView
        label: 'Window Maker'; **borderWidth:** 1; **insideColor:** Form **white;**
        addSubView: switchesView **in:** (0@0 **corner:** 1@0.1) **borderWidth:** 0;
        addSubView: iconContainerView **in:** (0@0.1 "0.09" **corner:** 1@1) **borderWidth:** 1.

    iconContainerView
        addSubView: iconView **viewport:** iconContainerView **insetWindow.**

```
isOnSelector ← #isNil. isOnSelectorArguments ← #(). "anything returning false"
switchSelector ← #makeIcon:.

subviews ← OrderedCollection new
    add: ((textView ← SwitchView new
        label: 'text' asParagraph; model: aWindowMaker;
        selector: isOnSelector; arguments: isOnSelectorArguments) controller
            selector: switchSelector; arguments: #(WindowMakerTextIcon); view);
    add: ((menuView ← SwitchView new
        label: 'menu' asParagraph; model: aWindowMaker;
        selector: isOnSelector; arguments: isOnSelectorArguments) controller
            selector: switchSelector; arguments: #(WindowMakerMenuIcon); view);
    add: ((switchView ← SwitchView new
        label: 'switch' asParagraph; model: aWindowMaker;
        selector: isOnSelector; arguments: isOnSelectorArguments) controller
            selector: switchSelector; arguments: #(WindowMakerSwitchIcon); view);
    add: ((pictureView ← SwitchView new
        label: 'picture' asParagraph; model: aWindowMaker;
        selector: isOnSelector; arguments: isOnSelectorArguments) controller
            selector: switchSelector; arguments: #(WindowMakerPictureIcon); view);
    add: ((switchAndPictureView ← SwitchView new
        label: 'both' asParagraph; model: aWindowMaker;
        selector: isOnSelector; arguments: isOnSelectorArguments) controller
            selector:switchSelector;
            arguments:#(WindowMakerSwitchAndPictureIcon); view);
    add: ((externalView ← SwitchView new
        label: 'external' asParagraph; model: aWindowMaker;
        selector: isOnSelector; arguments: isOnSelectorArguments) controller
            selector: switchSelector; arguments: #(WindowMakerExternalIcon); view);
    add: ((zoomInView ← SwitchView new
        label: 'zoom in' asParagraph; model: iconView;
        controller: ContinuousSwitchController new;
        selector: isOnSelector; arguments: isOnSelectorArguments) controller
            selector: #zoomIn; arguments: #(); view);
    add: ((zoomOutView ← SwitchView new
        label: 'zoom out' asParagraph; model: iconView;
        controller: ContinuousSwitchController new;
        selector: isOnSelector; arguments: isOnSelectorArguments) controller
            selector: #zoomOut; arguments: #(); view);
    yourself.

subRectangles ← OrderedCollection new
    addAll: ((1 to: 2) collect: [:i | ((i-1)/6)@0 corner: (i/6)@1]); "text, menu"
    addAll: ((3 to: 4) collect: [:i | ((i-1)/6)@0 corner: (i/6)@(1/2)]); "switch, picture"
    add: ([:i :j | ((i-1)/6)@(1/2) corner: (j/6)@1] value: 3 value: 4); "switchAndPicture"
    addAll: ((5 to: 5) collect: [:i | ((i-1)/6)@0 corner: (i/6)@1]); "external"
    addAll: ((6 to: 6) collect: [:i | ((i-1)/6)@0 corner: (i/6)@(1/2)]); "zoom in"
    addAll: ((6 to: 6) collect: [:i | ((i-1)/6)@(1/2) corner: (i/6)@1]); "zoom out"
    yourself.

1 to: subviews size do: [:i |
    switchesView
        addSubView: (subviews at: i) in: (subRectangles at: i) borderWidth: 1].

aWindowMaker iconView: iconView.

↑topView
```

instance methods

instance initialization

iconView: aView
   iconView ← aView

menu messages

makeIcon: anIconClassName
   iconView **makeIcon**: (Smalltalk **at**: anIconClassName)

8.4.1 The Icon Classes

The **window maker master icon** is the heart of the window maker editor. It is the container for all newly created icons. One icon class exists for each window category, in addition to a special **group icon** that permits sets of icons to be manipulated as individual icons. Like the master icon, it is a container for the same class of icons; this includes other group icons. Fig. 8.15 summarizes the master icon part hierarchy.

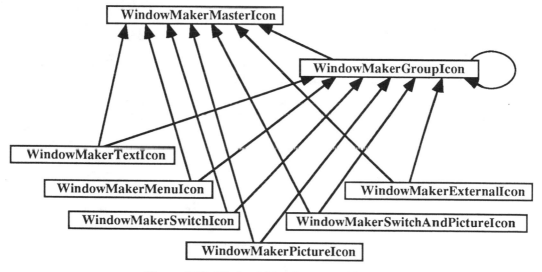

Figure 8.15 WindowMaker icon parts hierarchy.

Each icon is in fact a view (see Fig. 8.16). Since the switch and picture icons can be either fixed- or varying-size, it is most convenient to implement all icons by inheriting the functionality from extended switch views (even if it isn't needed for some of them). Because there is a great deal of common functionality, it is also useful to make use of an abstract class — WindowMakerIcon.

In general, the master icon is the controlling view. Hence, it needs a special controller (see Fig. 8.17) — an instance of WindowMakerMasterIconController. The associated yellow button pop-up menu contains a number of menu items that result in special options windows popping up. These are scheduled extended standard system views — hence, they may be left temporarily unattended, for example, to browse the application class or create an interface method. These options windows are removed with the standard close mechanism. However, some of them have a cancel facility. To provide this cancel facility, an alternative to the standard system controller is provided via class WindowMakerControllerWithCancel.

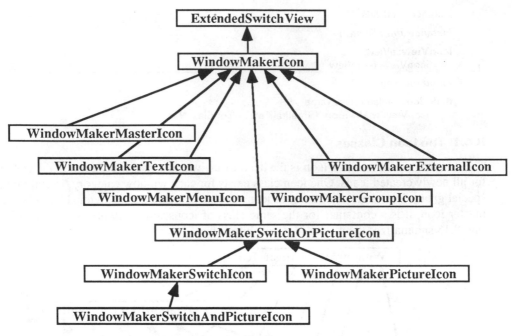

Figure 8.16 WindowMaker icon (view) hierarchy.

One way of investigating the design is to consider the hierarchy along with the instance variables provided by the individual classes. A summary is provided next. Unfortunately, this approach is relatively unproductive.

```
ExtendedSwitchView
   WindowMakerIcon
                  message messageView messageInitializers messageSources
                  messageCodings messageParsers sizeLocked defaultLabelSelector
   WindowMakerMasterIcon
                  selections minimumSize maximumSize outputOption
   WindowMakerGroupIcon
                  librarianForBackground width height leftRightAlignment
                  upDownAlignment horizontalAbutment verticalAbutment
   WindowMakerTextIcon
                  "none"
   WindowMakerMenuIcon
                  "none"
   WindowMakerSwitchOrPictureIcon
                  pictureVariety pictureString pictureFormPathName
                  lockedSizeExpansion
      WindowMakerSwitchIcon
                  "none"
         WindowMakerSwitchAndPictureIcon
                  separation
      WindowMakerPictureIcon
                  "none"
   WindowMakerExternalIcon
                  "none"
```

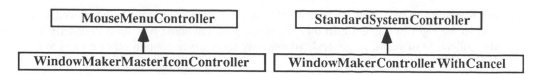

Figure 8.17 WindowMaker icon controller hierarchy.

A more standard approach to presenting the design is to consider the classes one by one, starting from the top of the hierarchy and proceeding downward — a **vertical presentation**. Another way is to focus on general aspects or properties of the design that are supported by each of the classes — a **horizontal presentation**. For example, every class has an operation to convert an icon into an extended view. By gathering and discussing this conversion operation in one section, we decrease the detail that has to be considered later in a vertical presentation. On the other hand, there are some aspects that fit neither presentation mode either because they represent a major feature of a class among a number of minor aspects or because they represent a feature that is distributed in a more ad hoc manner among a number of relatively independent classes.

In practice, it is difficult to partition the design into horizontal and vertical presentation modes because of the interrelationships between the parts. No matter what order is chosen to describe the design, there will always be some aspects that cannot be adequately presented without forward references. Our approach will be to provide some of the basic features of the design horizontally and to follow this up with a vertical presentation that is interspersed with a discussion of aspects that are relatively distributed. More specifically, the design is presented by describing the major functional components. These include

1. group sequencing
2. displaying, moving, sizing
3. labeling the icons
4. the master icon controller
5. the master icon view
6. options windows
7. encoding/decoding, conversion to extended views, and copying
8. the remaining icons (everything that wasn't discussed above)

In general, the greatest amount of code and also the least interesting is devoted to processing options. The most interesting has to do with the interaction interface provided by the master icon controller and its view.

8.4.2 Group Sequencing

One feature of the window maker is its ability to group icons into individual units. This can simplify positioning or size adjustments, since the modification will apply to all icons in the unit. Sometimes the grouping is explicitly requested by the designer — in this situation, the icons in the grouping remain together until explicitly ungrouped; e.g., see the leftmost three icons in Fig. 8.18. At other times, the grouping is implicit; e.g., when several icons are selected and moved as a whole — consider the three bold icons being moved downward and to the right in Fig. 8.18. In this situation, selecting some new icon implicitly ungroups the collection of icons. In general, groups may themselves contain other groups to arbitrary levels.

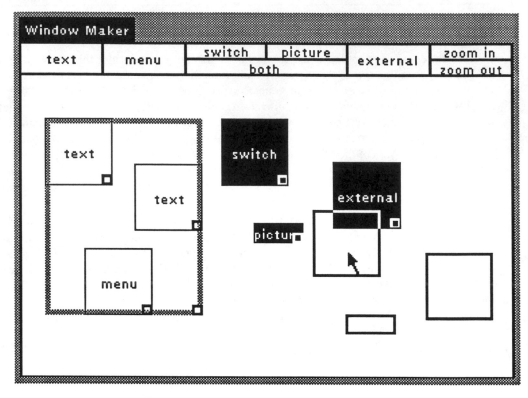

Figure 8.18 A session with the window maker.

In this section, we are not concerned with the mechanism for grouping or ungrouping or how control is managed to provide the above visual effects. Rather, we are concerned with a much simpler protocol — one that enables icons to be manipulated independent of whether or not they are grouped. We call this the **group sequencing facility**. It provides us with the ability to process an icon independent of whether or not it is a group and to sequence through nongroup icons in a group independent of how deeply nested the icons are in a group.

For example, if our aim was to change the border width of all nongroup icons associated with *candidate*, our solution would look something like

    candidate **groupDo:** [:icon | icon **borderWidth:** 1]

In this case, groups are effectively transparent to the **borderWidth:** message. Another goal might be to retrieve the border width of all nongroup icons. Typically, this would be successful only if the border width were the same for all nongroup icons. Our group sequencing facility would permit the following:

    candidate **groupGet:** [:icon | icon **borderWidth**] **ifUnequal:** [nil]

This facility is really a horizontal facility, since all icons respond to the group sequencing operations. However, it is sufficient to implement the operations in two places: in abstract class WindowMakerIcon and in the group management class WindowMakerGroupIcon. To understand the latter implementation, it is sufficient to know that the group icon maintains the icons in its group as subviews.

Class WindowMakerIcon

class	WindowMakerIcon
superclass	ExtendedSwitchView
instance variables	...

group sequencing

groupDo: aBlock
    aBlock **value**: self

groupGet: aBlock **ifUnequal**: anotherBlock
    ↑aBlock **value**: self

Class WindowMakerGroupIcon

class	WindowMakerGroupIcon
superclass	WindowMakerIcon
instance variables	...

group sequencing

groupDo: aBlock
    subViews **do**: [:icon | icon **groupDo**: aBlock]

groupGet: aBlock **ifUnequal**: unequalBlock
    | firstTime result |
    firstTime ← true. result ← nil.
    self **groupDo**: [:icon |
        firstTime
            ifTrue: [result ← aBlock **value**: icon. firstTime ← false]
            ifFalse: [result = (aBlock **value**: icon) **ifFalse**: [↑unequalBlock **value**]]].
    ↑result

If a group element is itself a group, method **groupDo**: in WindowMakerGroupIcon is applied recursively, but it must terminate since circular structures are never created for subviews (or groups). When it does terminate, it will terminate on a nongroup at which point method **groupDo**: in WindowMakerIcon will execute the block with the nongroup icon parameter. Hence, the block is executed only for nongroup icons.

The facility is used in the WindowMakerMasterIcon, for example, to provide access to nongroup selections. This is illustrated in the following:

Class WindowMakerMasterIcon

class	WindowMakerMasterIcon
superclass	WindowMakerIcon
instance variables	selections ...

selections

selections
    ↑selections

ungroupedSelections
    | ungroupedSelections |
    ungroupedSelections ← OrderedCollection **new**.
    selections **do**:
        [:selection | selection **groupDo**: [:icon | ungroupedSelections **add**: icon]].
    ↑ungroupedSelections

Note that *selections* is just an ordered collection — hence, it is incorrect to attempt to execute "selections **groupDo**: ..." in method **ungroupedSelections**.

8.4.3 Displaying, Moving, and Sizing

Several icons are displayed in Fig. 8.19 — each has an 8@8 **grow box** at the bottom right corner of the icon. To resize the icon, it is a simple matter of moving the grow box. To move the icon, it is a matter of moving any other part of the icon. When an icon is selected, it is **highlighted**; when deselected, it is **dehighlighted**. Both highlighting and dehighlighting are accomplished by **reversing** the inside of the icon — everything excluding the border.

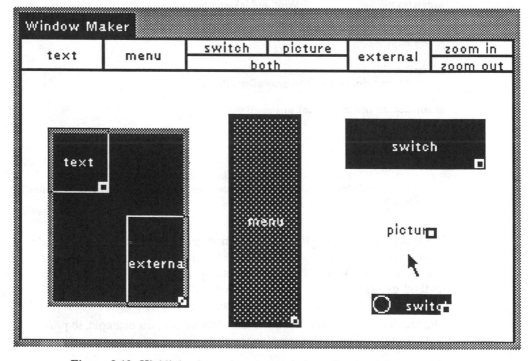

Figure 8.19 Highlighted group, menu, switch, and switch/picture icons.

The basic display facility is inherited from class ExtendedSwitchView and is extended with a grow box. For switches, pictures, and switch/pictures (the combination), designers have the ability to specify whether or not the icons are to be fixed-size or varying-size. Generally, when it is to be fixed-size, this size is a function of the icon's **background** — either a textual name or a form; i.e., just big enough to contain the name or the form, possibly with some additional white space around it. Nevertheless, it is still possible to resize the icon by dragging on the grow box. To prevent this, we also permit fixed-size icons to be **locked**.

Class WindowMakerIcon

class	WindowMakerIcon
superclass	ExtendedSwitchView
instance variables	... sizeLocked ...

instance methods

instance initialization

initializeMessages
> *... see Sect. 8.4.7, Initializing a New Icon's Interface Data ...*

initialize
> "Initializes all components of the icon."
> | box |
> super **initialize**.
> self **mode:** #varying.
> box ← 0@0 **extent:** 50@50.
> self **window:** box **viewport:** box. "=> transformation is identity"
> sizeLocked ← false.
> self **borderWidth:** 1; **insideColor:** Form **white**.
> defaultLabelSelector ← #subclassResponsibility.
> self **initializeMessages**

size locking

sizeLocked
> ↑sizeLocked

sizeLocked: aBoolean
> sizeLocked ← aBoolean

displaying

displayOn: aForm **at:** aPoint **clippingBox:** aRectangle **rule:** ruleInteger **mask:** maskForm
> "Display the icon and its grow box."
> "The border, inside color, and background."
> super **displayOn:** aForm **at:** aPoint **clippingBox:** aRectangle
>   **rule:** ruleInteger **mask:** maskForm.
> "The grow box."
> ↑self **displayGrowBoxOn:** aForm **at:** aPoint **clippingBox:** aRectangle

displayGrowBoxOn: aForm **at:** aPoint **clippingBox:** aRectangle
> | growBox |
> growBox ← (aPoint + self **displayBox extent** - (8@8)) **extent:** 8@8.
> (aRectangle **contains:** growBox) **ifTrue:** [
>   aForm **black:** growBox.
>   aForm **white:** (growBox **insetBy:** 2)].

highlight
    self **reverse**

highlightOn: aForm **at:** aPoint **clippingBox:** aRectangle
    self **reverseOn:** aForm **at:** aPoint **clippingBox:** aRectangle

dehighlight
    self **reverse**

dehighlightOn: aForm **at:** aPoint **clippingBox:** aRectangle
    self **reverseOn:** aForm **at:** aPoint **clippingBox:** aRectangle

reverse
    self **reverseOn:** Display **at:** self **displayBox origin**
        clippingBox: superView **insetDisplayBox**

reverseOn: aForm **at:** aPoint **clippingBox:** aRectangle
    aForm **reverse:** (((aPoint **extent:** self **displayBox extent**) **insetBy:** borderWidth)
        intersect: aRectangle)

reverseBoundary
    Display
        border: (self **displayBox intersect:** superView **insetDisplayBox**)
        width: 2 **rule:** Form **reverse mask:** Form **black.**

computeInsetDisplayBox
    "Overrides the default method to avoid intersecting the result with the superview's
    display box."
    ↑(self **displayTransform:** self **getWindow**) **insetBy:** borderWidth

growBoxContainsPoint: aPoint
    ↑(self **displayBox corner** - (8@8) **extent:** 8@8) **containsPoint:** aPoint

Note that **highlight** and **dehighlight** are synonymous with **reverse**. However, they are semantically more meaningful. We always use the paired terms rather than the implementation level **reverse** when it makes sense. Method **reverseBoundary** is used to produce an outline of an icon as it is moved by a designer; e.g., as shown in Fig. 8.18.

Early in the design stage, we decided that growing or shrinking an icon *would not be done by adjusting the icon's local transformation*. In fact, we decided to maintain the constraint that the local transformation would always be the identity transformation. On the other hand, when the window maker itself is repositioned or resized, we don't want the icons to move relative to the window they are displayed in. Since the icons are contained and managed by an instance of WindowMakerMasterIcon, this can be achieved by permitting the master icon to introduce an offset into its local transformation. The resulting display transformation for an icon then has a translation associated with it but no scaling. There are several consequences of this design decision:

1. The local transformation need not be saved with an icon's encoding because it is the identity transformation.

2. The size of an icons's **window**, **viewport**, and **display box** are the same; i.e., they have identical extents.

3. The origin of an icon's **window** may be different from the origin of its **display box**.

Icon movement is specified via methods **moveTo:** and **moveBy:**, resizing via methods **growTo:** and **growBy:**, and rescaling via **scaleBy:**. To simplify the implementation, **moveTo:** and **growBy:** are implemented in terms of the others. Two benefits result: (1) it was easier to get it right, and (2) subclasses such as WindowMaker-GroupIcon only had to reimplement the three primitives (**moveBy:**, **growTo:**, and **scaleBy:**) to get them all. Recall that **unlock** causes a view's display transformation and inset display box to be discarded; **lock** causes them to be recomputed.

moving/growing primitives

moveBy: aPoint
　　"Parameter aPoint is in display coordinates."
　　aPoint = (0@0) **ifFalse:** [window **moveBy:** aPoint. self **unlock; lock**]

growTo: aPoint
　　"Parameter aPoint is in display coordinates."
　　sizeLocked **ifTrue:** [↑self].
　　window **extent** = aPoint **ifFalse:** [window **extent:** aPoint. self **unlock; lock**]

scaleBy: scale
　　"Scales in the normal way but ensures that the window is the same size as the display box."

　　| oldExtent |
　　oldExtent ← window **extent**.
　　super **scaleBy:** scale. "this will change the local transformation"
　　self **lock**.
　　　　window ← superView **inverseDisplayTransform:** self **displayBox**.
　　　　transformation ← WindowingTransformation **identity**.
　　　　sizeLocked **ifTrue:** [window **extent:** oldExtent].
　　self **unlock; lock**

moving/growing nonprimitives

moveTo: aPoint
　　"Parameter aPoint is in display coordinates."
　　self **moveBy:** (aPoint - self **displayBox origin**)

growBy: aPoint
　　"Parameter aPoint is in display coordinates."
　　self **growTo:** (aPoint + self **displayBox extent**)

inverseDisplayScale: aPoint
　　"Applies the inverse of the scale of the receiver's display transformation. Used to convert a width in display coordinates to window coordinates."

　　↑aPoint **scaleBy:** (1.0@1.0) / self **displayTransformation scale**

A group icon can be displayed, moved, and resized like any other icon by redefining two display methods and the three primitives discussed previously.

Class WindowMakerGroupIcon

class	WindowMakerGroupIcon
superclass	WindowMakerIcon
instance variables	...

instance methods

displaying

displayBox
```
    | box |
    box ← nil.
    self groupDo: [:icon |
            box ← box isNil ifTrue: [icon displayBox] ifFalse: [box merge: icon displayBox]].
    ↑box
```

displayOn: aForm **at**: aPoint **clippingBox**: aRectangle **rule**: ruleInteger **mask**: maskForm
```
    | offset |
    offset ← self displayBox origin.
    subViews do: [:icon |
            icon displayOn: aForm at: icon displayBox origin - offset + aPoint
                    clippingBox: aRectangle rule: ruleInteger mask: maskForm].
    super displayOn: aForm at: aPoint clippingBox: aRectangle
            rule: ruleInteger mask: maskForm
```

moving/growing primitives

growTo: aPoint
```
        "Parameter aPoint is in display coordinates."
        | oldBox scale newBox delta |
        oldBox ← self displayBox. scale ← aPoint / oldBox extent.
        subViews do: [:icon | icon scaleBy: scale].
        newBox ← self displayBox.
        delta ← oldBox origin - newBox origin. "bring back to old origin"
        delta = (0@0) ifFalse: [subViews do: [:icon | icon moveBy: delta]]
```

moveBy: aPoint
```
        "Parameter aPoint is in display coordinates."
        self groupDo: [:icon | icon moveBy: aPoint]
```

scaleBy: scale
```
        subViews do: [:icon | icon scaleBy: scale]
```

Note that no caching is provided by method **displayBox**. It could be speeded up by performing the above computation only when the inset display box is **nil** and caching the inset display box. However, we haven't noticed any slowdown due to the above, even on slow machines.

8.4.4 Labeling the Icons

When a designer creates an application specific window, the subwindows (icons) in that application window are provided with names associated with the class of icon they represent. In Fig. 8.20, for example, icons are shown with labels *text, menu, switch, picture*, and *external*. These labels are provided only for aesthetic reasons — they do not exist in the final application window. Nevertheless, there should be some correspondence between the icon labels seen in the editor and the subwindows in the application window. How else could we distinguish two text subwindows or two picture windows representing different pictures?

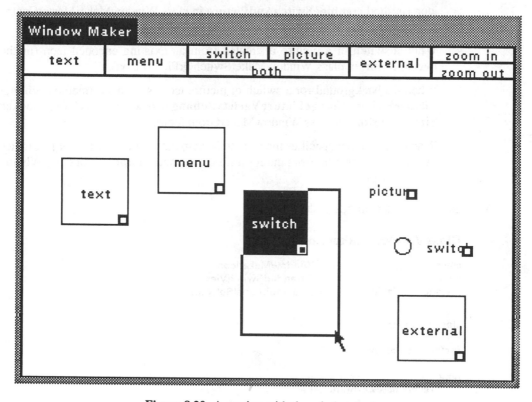

Figure 8.20 A session with the window maker.

An approach we used in the early implementation stages was to manufacture numeric suffixes — the result was labels like *text1, text2,* and so on when more than one text subwindow was created. Ultimately, this proved inadequate, as it became increasingly difficult, as designers, to remember which text subwindow was which. Our latest solution is to use some aspect of the subwindow interface that has to be provided by the designer. In the case of a text subwindow, it is the *getText* message. For a menu subwindow, it is the *getMenuArray* message. For subwindows like switches and pictures, we use the actual display form.

In general, we provide each icon with a **computeLabel** method whose task it is to set the icon's label. The default method makes use of the string associated with a default interface message. More sophisticated icons actually redefine the **computeLabel** method. The more interesting question is "when must the label be recomputed?" The answer is generally "whenever something is done that might result in a change to the label." A summary of such locations includes the following:

1. When a new icon is constructed (method **new** in class WindowMakerIcon).

2. When changes are made to the external interface (methods **messageSource:** and **changeMessage:coding:** in class WindowMakerGroupIcon).

3. When a switch icon and a picture icon are combined into a separate switch/picture icon (method **combineSwitchAndPicture** in class WindowMakerMasterController).

4. When a switch or a picture is created from an existing encoded icon (method **decodeFrom:** in class WindowMakerSwitchOrPictureIcon).

5. When the background for a switch or picture icon is changed (methods **changePictureString:**, **changePictureVariety:**, **changeLocking:**, and **changeLockedSizeExpansion:** in class WindowMakerGroupIcon).

6. When the designer specifies the form to be associated with a switch or picture icon by making a selection from the form librarian (method **update:** in class WindowMakerGroupIcon).

A sampling of these methods is shown below:

Class WindowMakerIcon

```
class                   WindowMakerIcon
superclass              ExtendedSwitchView
instance variables      ... defaultLabelSelector
```

class methods

instance creation

new
        ↑super **new computeLabel**

instance methods

instance initialization

initialize
        ... not all of the method shown ...
        defaultLabelSelector ← #subclassResponsibility.

displaying

computeLabel
        "If the user has changed the more important message selector for the icon (which it
        is depends on the icon), then use the new selector as the label; otherwise, do
        nothing."
        | theSelector |
        theSelector ← self **selectorFor:** defaultLabelSelector.
        self **label:** (theSelector == defaultLabelSelector
            ifTrue: [self **classNamePicture**]
            ifFalse: [theSelector **asParagraph**])

Class WindowMakerTextIcon

class	WindowMakerTextIcon
superclass	WindowMakerIcon
instance variables	...

instance methods

instance initialization

initialize
    super **initialize**.
    defaultLabelSelector ← #getText

Class WindowMakerMenuIcon

class	WindowMakerMenuIcon
superclass	WindowMakerIcon
instance variables	...

instance methods

instance initialization

initialize
    super **initialize**.
    defaultLabelSelector ← #getMenuArray

Class WindowMakerExternalIcon

class	WindowMakerExternalIcon
superclass	WindowMakerIcon
instance variables	...

instance methods

instance initialization

initialize
    super **initialize**.
    defaultLabelSelector ← #getView

Class WindowMakerMasterIcon

class	WindowMakerMasterIcon
superclass	WindowMakerIcon
instance variables	...

instance methods

background

computeLabel
    "There is no label for the master icon."
    self **label:** nil

Class WindowMakerGroupIcon

class	WindowMakerGroupIcon
superclass	WindowMakerIcon
instance variables	...
instance methods	

background window messages

changePictureString: aText
    | aString |
    aString ← aText **asString**.
    self **groupDo**: [:icon | icon **pictureString**: aString; **computeLabel**].
    ↑true

changePictureVariety: aSymbol
    self **groupDo**: [:icon | icon **pictureVariety**: aSymbol; **computeLabel**].
    self **changed**: #pictureVariety
    ↑true

changeLocking: aBoolean
    aBoolean
        ifTrue: [
            self **groupDo**: [:icon |
                icon **sizeLocked**: true; **mode**: #constant; **computeLabel**].
            self **changed**: #mode; **changed**: #locking]
        ifFalse: [
            self **groupDo**: [:icon | icon **sizeLocked**: false].
            self **changed**: #locking]

changeLockedSizeExpansion: aText
    | integer |
    integer ← Number **readFrom**: aText **asString**.
    self **groupDo**: [:icon | icon **lockedSizeExpansion**: integer; **computeLabel**].
    ↑true

background window support

computeLabel
    "There is no label for a group icon."
    self **label**: nil

update: aSymbol
    "Provide the connection from switches and pictures to the librarian view. See
    method preOpenBackground: in WindowMakerGroupIcon."
    | path |
    aSymbol == #pictures
        ifTrue: [
            (path ← librarianForBackground **selectedPathName**) isNil ifFalse: [
                subViews **do**: [:icon |
                    icon **pictureFormPathName**: path; **computeLabel**]]]
        ifFalse: [super **update**: aSymbol]

For switches or pictures, the label could be either a paragraph or a form, depending on the options specified. Switch/pictures are a combination of the two. A special method **getLabel** is provided to compute the resulting label.

Class WindowMakerSwitchOrPictureIcon

class	WindowMakerSwitchOrPictureIcon
superclass	WindowMakerIcon
instance variables	pictureVariety pictureString pictureFormPathName
	lockedSizeExpansion

instance methods

background

computeLabel

"Construct a new label from the current settings; i.e., from the switch path name or picture string. The icon display box may change if the label changes size."

| newLabel |
newLabel ← self **getLabel**.

sizeLocked **ifTrue:** [
    sizeLocked ← false.
    "Avoid the following method since it computes the display box (works only if this icon has a superview; e.g., after initialization)."
    "self growTo: (newLabel extent max: 10@10)."
    window **extent:** (newLabel **extent** + (lockedSizeExpansion*2) **max:** 10@10).
    self **unlock; lock.**
    sizeLocked ← true].

self **label:** newLabel

getLabel

"Construct a new label from the current settings; one that permits the extent to be computed."

↑pictureVariety == #text
    ifTrue: [pictureString **asParagraph**]
    ifFalse: [FormLibrarian **formForPathName:** pictureFormPathName]

Class WindowMakerSwitchAndPictureIcon

class	WindowMakerSwitchAndPictureIcon
superclass	WindowMakerSwitchIcon
instance variables	separation

instance methods

background

getLabel

"Constructs a form from the switch path name, separation, and the picture string."

| switchForm pictureForm width height combinedForm |
switchForm ← FormLibrarian **formForPathName:** pictureFormPathName.
switchForm **isNil ifTrue:** [switchForm ← Form **extent:** 0@0].
pictureForm ← pictureString **asParagraph asForm.**

width ← switchForm **width** + separation + pictureForm **width.**
height ← switchForm **height max:** pictureForm **height.**
combinedForm ← Form **extent:** width@height.

switchForm **displayOn:** combinedForm
    at: 0@((height - switchForm **height**) // 2).
pictureForm **displayOn:** combinedForm
    at: (switchForm **width** + separation)@((height - pictureForm **height**) // 2).

↑combinedForm

Chapter 8 A Window Application

Generally, the label form, paragraph, or display text used by method **computeLabel** is manufactured by **getLabel** in class WindowMakerSwitchOrPictureIcon. This method works for switches or pictures but must be redefined in subclass WindowMakerSwitchAndPicture-Icon for switch/picture combinations.

When a switch or picture icon is converted to the corresponding extended view, the label's form, paragraph, or display text could be passed directly to the view as a parameter to message **label:**. When and if a store string is required of the extended view, a corresponding store string for the label must also be constructed. If the label is a paragraph, it is easy to retrieve the corresponding string and generate a store string such as 'aString **asParagraph**'. However, there is no simple equivalent for forms — the entire form must be re-created. On the other hand, extended switches and pictures do have the capability to accept labels that are library path names such as #(libraryName formName). In that situation, the label's store string can be generated quite compactly as the path name. Because this information is available to the switch and picture icons, we provide another method, **generateLabel**, that can be used by the conversion operation.

Class WindowMakerSwitchOrPictureIcon

class	WindowMakerSwitchOrPictureIcon
superclass	WindowMakerIcon
instance variables	pictureVariety pictureString pictureFormPathName ...

instance methods

background

generateLabel
> "Construct a new label from the current settings; one that can be used to specify a label for a new view."
> ↑pictureVariety == #text
>   **ifTrue:** [pictureString **asParagraph**]
>   **ifFalse:** [pictureFormPathName]

Class WindowMakerSwitchAndPictureIcon

class	WindowMakerSwitchAndPictureIcon
superclass	WindowMakerSwitchIcon
instance variables	separation

instance methods

background

generateLabel
> "Label must be of the form #(pictureFormPathName separation pictureString)."
> ↑Array **with:** pictureFormPathName **with:** separation **with:** pictureString

Finally, switches and switch/pictures can have both on- and off-forms. This is called the highlight object in an extended view. Just as a label can be specified by a path name, so can its highlight indirectly reference this path name by providing #fromLabel as the highlight object instead of a paragraph, form, or display text.

Class WindowMakerSwitchIcon

```
class                  WindowMakerSwitchIcon
superclass             WindowMakerSwitchOrPictureIcon
instance variables     "none"
```

instance methods

background

generateHighlight
```
    | offForm |
    pictureVariety == #form
        ifTrue: [
            offForm ← FormLibrarian formForPathName: pictureFormPathName.
            (offForm respondsTo: #highlight)
                ifTrue: [↑#fromLabel]
                ifFalse: [↑nil]]
        ifFalse: [↑nil]
```

8.4.5 The MasterIconController Class

Class MasterIconController is a subclass of MouseMenuController with extensions to provide facilities such as the following:

1. A copy buffer to permit icons (rather than characters) to be copied, cut, pasted, and deleted.

2. Both menu and keyboard processing for the above, in addition to a facility to permit grouping and ungrouping of icons.

3. A facility to keep track of the current pop-up options window (at most one is permitted at any time).

4. A rather complex yellow button menu that is constructed dynamically to take into account the currently selected icons; e.g., some entries are permitted only for a subset of the selected icons.

5. Mouse controlled icon selection, deselection, moving, and size adjusting.

6. A repository for the pop-up options windows — the window maker is boot-strapped.

In general, the methods needed for options processing are distributed, since each different kind of icon has its own special options. The methods that construct the views for the options windows could likewise be distributed, but it is more convenient to gather them together in one place. They are kept as class methods in the master icon controller. We will consider this repository first, but we will not go into the details of the pluggable methods used by the options windows until we discuss class WindowMakerGroupIcon. Class WindowMakerGroupIcon is the repository for the pluggable methods as distinct from this class, which is the repository for the options window view construction methods. Next we will consider the primary control aspects (facilities 1 through 5 above). As we discuss yellow button menu processing, we will also consider a special support class, WindowMakerControllerWithCancel, that provides the special controllers used by options windows.

The Repository for Option Windows

Because the options windows were bootstrapped using the window maker, they can be either encoded or unencoded. The unencoded form is required for fast interactive performance, but the encoded form is dramatically more compact. Reversible conversion from one form to the other is possible via methods **compress** and **decompress**.

Class WindowMakerMasterIconController

class	WindowMakerMasterIconController
superclass	MouseMenuController
instance variables	previousPopUpWindow
class variables	IconCopyBuffer

class methods

class initialization

compress
```
"WindowMakerMasterIconController compress"
| time |
Transcript cr; show: 'Compressing'.
time ← WindowMakerMasterIconController timeFor: [
    #(alignment background borderingAndColoring makeMethod
        switchAndPictureBackground) do: [:part |
        Transcript show: ' ', part, '.... '.
        ExtendedStandardSystemView
            compileEncoding: (WindowMakerMasterIconController windowFor: part)
            intoClass: WindowMakerMasterIconController class
            method: part, 'Window' category: 'generic windows'].
    #(external master masterSizing menu picture switch text) do: [:part |
        Transcript show: ' ', part, '.... '.
        ExtendedStandardSystemView
            compileEncoding: (WindowMakerMasterIconController windowFor: part)
            intoClass: WindowMakerMasterIconController class
            method: part, 'Window' category: 'specific windows']].
Transcript cr; show: 'Total time ', time, '.'; cr
```

decompress
```
"WindowMakerMasterIconController decompress"
| time |
Transcript cr.
time ← WindowMakerMasterIconController timeFor: [
    #(alignment background borderingAndColoring makeMethod
        switchAndPictureBackground) do: [:part |
        WindowMakerMasterIconController
            decodeAndCompile: part
            method: part, 'Window' category: 'generic windows'].
    #(external master masterSizing menu picture switch text) do: [:part |
        WindowMakerMasterIconController
            decodeAndCompile: part
            method: part, 'Window' category: 'specific windows']].
Transcript show: 'Total time ', time, '.'; cr
```

class initialization support

decodeAndCompile: aSymbol **method**: methodName **category**: categoryName
"Explicitly re-encodes the view in case modifications to the encoding was done by
hand."

```
| time view |
Transcript show: 'Decoding ', aSymbol, ' ....'.
time ← self timeFor: [
     view ← WindowMaker asView: (self windowFor: aSymbol) encoding].
Transcript show: ' done in ', time, '.'; cr.

Transcript tab; show: 'Compiling ', aSymbol, ' ....'.
time ← self timeFor: [
     view
          compileIntoClass: WindowMakerMasterIconController class
          method: methodName category: categoryName].
Transcript show: ' done in ', time, '.'; cr.
↑view
```

timeFor: aBlock

```
| time1 time2 difference minutes seconds |
time1 ← Time now asSeconds.
aBlock value.
time2 ← Time now asSeconds.
difference ← time2 - time1.
minutes ← difference // 60. seconds ← difference \\ 60.
↑(minutes > 1
     ifTrue: [minutes printString, ' minutes ']
     ifFalse: [minutes = 1
          ifTrue: ['1 minute ']
          ifFalse: ['']]),
(seconds > 1
     ifTrue: [seconds printString, ' seconds']
     ifFalse: [seconds = 1
          ifTrue: ['1 second']
          ifFalse: ['']])
```

In general, conversion is slow. Hence, it is appropriate to report on its progress in the transcript. The **timeFor:** method provides slightly nicer print results than the millisecond facility associated with class **Time**. Also, note that both the **compress** and **decompress** methods reference their class explicitly rather than using *self* — this was useful during development because extensions were often added by hand modifying the encoded version and then decompressing it. In this case, it was sufficient to modify the body of the method by eliminating the cases that were unaffected; e.g., by keeping only #alignment, and then selecting and executing the modified code. The method itself was never recompiled.

As can be deduced from the **compress** and **decompress** methods, twelve options windows are provided:

1. alignment window
2. borderingAndColoring window
3. background window

4.   switchAndPictureBackground window

5.   masterSizing window

6.   makeMethod window

7.   master window

8.   text window

9.   menu window   (7 through 12 are individual interface windows)

10.   switch window

11.   picture window

12.   external window

For space reasons, the detailed encoded forms have been relegated to Appendix B.3. For illustrative purposes, the encoding for the last window, the **external window** (the simplest and shortest), has been shown (see method **externalWindow**). When an options window is needed, a request such as

WindowMakerMasterIconController **windowFor:** #alignment

is made. If the window, in this case the alignment window, is encoded, it is first decoded and converted into an extended view. If it is not encoded, it is already an extended view and no conversion is required.

windows

windowFor: aSymbol
    ↑WindowMaker **asView:** (self **perform:** (aSymbol, 'Window') **asSymbol**)

generic windows

alignmentWindow
borderingAndColoringWindow
backgroundWindow
switchAndPictureBackgroundWindow
masterSizingWindow
makeMethodWindow
    ... see Appendix B.3 ...

generic windows overflow
    Methods could be added to this category by decompressing the windows

specific windows

switchandpictureWindow
    ↑self **switchWindow**

masterWindow
textWindow
menuWindow
switchWindow
pictureWindow
    ... see Appendix B.3 ...

externalWindow
> "Returns an initialized view."
> | anArray |
> anArray ← "WindowMaker edit:" #(Master nil (-137 -89 138 89) white 1 (3.73091
>   2.43963 510.135 263.873) true 'External Window Interface' (preOpenInterface:
>   anExtendedStandardSystemView) (nil) (350 180) (1000 1000) (classMethod
>   notEncoded WindowMakerMasterIconController 'specific windows'
>   externalWindow 'specific windows overflow') ((Text messageSource
>   (-136.0 -63.0 137.0 88.0) white 1 (messageSource (messageSource)
>   (messageSource: aText) (messageMenu))) (Switch nil (-136.0 -88.0 -45.0 -63.0)
>   white 1 (text 'comment') (varying) (message (isMessage: comment) (message:
>   comment))) (Switch nil (-45.0 -88.0 46.0 -63.0) white 1 (text 'name') (varying)
>   (message (isMessage: name) (message: name))) (Switch nil (46.0 -88.0 137.0
>   -63.0) white 1 (text 'getView') (varying) (message (isMessage: getView)
>   (message: getView)))))).
> ↑anArray

specific windows overflow
> *Methods could be added to this category by decompressing the windows*

The Basic Controller Facility

The controller's main concern is to determine what kind of user interaction is occurring and to process it in coordination with the view. The view keeps track of all icons in the window, including those that are currently selected.

> instance methods
>
> *controlling*
>
> **controlInitialize**
> > ↑view **displayView**
>
> **controlActivity**
> > super **controlActivity**.
> > self **processKeyboard**
>
> **redButtonActivity**
> > [sensor **redButtonPressed**] **whileTrue**: [self **processSelections**]
>
> **yellowButtonActivity**
> > "Determine which menu items are permitted in this context and provide only those to the user via a pop-up menu."
> >
> > ... details considered in a later section ...
> >
> > index ← (PopUpMenu **labels**: labels **lines**: lines) **startUp**.
> > index ~= 0 **ifTrue**: [self **perform**: (selectors **at**: index)]
>
> **processKeyboard**
> > "Determine whether the user pressed the keyboard. If so, read the keys."
> > [sensor **keyboardPressed**] **whileTrue**: [self **dispatchOnCharacter**: sensor **keyboard**]

The mouse menu controller's main task (method **controlActivity**) is to determine whether or not a button has been depressed and if it has, to send a corresponding message (message **yellowButtonActivity**, **redButtonActivity**, or **blueButtonActivity**) to itself for further processing. However, it ignores keyboard characters. Our version of **control-Activity** inherits this behavior but also processes keyboard requests. Blue button activity is defaulted while red and yellow button activities are handled specially. In order of complexity, keyboard activity is the simplest to process, next is red button, and last is yellow button.

A Standard System Controller with a Cancel Facility

Before we get into the details of the master icon controller, we present a variation of the standard system controller with a cancel facility. This controller is used by pop-up windows that appear as a result of yellow button menu choices. It actually provides two facilities:

1. A close facility that causes the master controller to regain control no matter what window had previous control.
2. A cancel facility that records the fact that it was canceled and closes as above.

The initiator, the master icon controller in our case, can query the controller after the fact to determine whether a close or cancel caused termination. In our case, we will actually use a postclosing operation to perform the querying. These details, however, are premature to the discussion — they may be safely ignored for the time being.

Class WindowMakerControllerWithCancel

class	WindowMakerControllerWithCancel
superclass	StandardSystemController
instance variables	canceled initiator

class methods

instance creation

withCancelFor: aController
    ↑self **new initiator**: aController; **initializeBlueButtonMenuWithCancel**

withoutCancelFor: aController
    ↑self **new initiator**: aController

instance methods

instance initialization

initialize
    super **initialize**.
    canceled ← false

initializeBlueButtonMenuWithCancel
    "Initialize the blue button pop-up menu and corresponding array of messages for the receiver. Refer to class method initialize in StandardSystemController for up-to-date menu items."
    self
        blueButtonMenu: (PopUpMenu
            labels: 'new label\under\move\frame\collapse\close\cancel' **withCRs**
            lines: #(1 5))
        blueButtonMessages: #(newLabel under move frame collapse close cancel)

initiator: aController
    initiator ← aController

querying

canceled
    ↑canceled

menu messages

cancel
>   canceled ← true. "for postclosing interrogation"
>   self **close**

close
>   "Signal the initiating controller."
>   initiator **forgetPopUpWindow**. view **erase; release**.
>   ScheduledControllers
>   **unschedule**: self;
>   **activeController**: initiator **view topView controller**.
>   Processor **terminateActive**

As we will see, the yellow button menu choices will result in a pop-up window. These windows will make use of the above controller (see yellow button activity below).

Keyboard Activity (Copy, Cut, Paste, Delete, Group, Ungroup)

Our approach is to process only the characters corresponding to the copy, cut, paste, delete, group, and ungroup operations and to ignore the rest. Since our window maker was developed on a Mac II, we used standard Macintosh characters to denote copy, cut, and paste; i.e., c, x, and v respectively. Additionally, we introduced two new characters, g and u, for **group** and **ungroup** respectively. These characters were determined interactively by uncommenting the code at the end of the **dispatchOnCharacter:** method and physically typing the characters desired. Their equivalents were then integrated explicitly into the method.

character processing

dispatchOnCharacter: aCharacter
>   "Carry out the action associated with this character."
>
>   "ParcPlace Smalltalk equivalents."
>   aCharacter = Character **backspace ifTrue**: [↑self **processCharacterDelete**].
>   aCharacter = (Character **value**: 3) "ctl c" **ifTrue**: [↑self **processCharacterCopy**].
>   aCharacter = (Character **value**: 24) "ctl x" **ifTrue**: [↑self **processCharacterCut**].
>   aCharacter = (Character **value**: 22) "ctl v" **ifTrue**: [↑self **processCharacterPaste**].
>   aCharacter = (Character **value**: 7) "ctl g" **ifTrue**: [↑self **processCharacterGroup**].
>   aCharacter = (Character **value**: 21) "ctl u" **ifTrue**: [↑self **processCharacterUngroup**].
>
>   "Apple Smalltalk equivalents.
>   aCharacter = Character **backspace ifTrue**: [↑self **processCharacterDelete**].
>   aCharacter = (Character **value**: 3) ?ctl c? **ifTrue**: [↑self **processCharacterCopy**].
>   aCharacter = (Character **value**: 151) ?ctl x? **ifTrue**: [↑self **processCharacterCut**].
>   aCharacter = (Character **value**: 134) ?ctl v? **ifTrue**: [↑self **processCharacterPaste**].
>   aCharacter = (Character **value**: 231) ?ctl g? **ifTrue**: [↑self **processCharacterGroup**].
>   aCharacter = (Character **value**: 21) ?ctl u? **ifTrue**: [↑self **processCharacterUngroup**]."
>
>   "Ignore anything else"
>
>   "To determine what character some control character is, uncomment the following
>   code, open a WindowMaker editor, and type it."
>   "Transcript **cr; show**: 'Ignored character ', aCharacter **storeString**,
>   ' <', aCharacter **asInteger printString**, '>'; **cr**"

Note that the copy buffer used (IconCopyBuffer) is a class variable. Consequently, it is possible to cut from one window maker editor to another. Additionally, when selected icons are copied and later pasted, two copies are made rather than one — one copy at the source (the copy operation) and another at the destination (the paste operation). Clearly, we need to copy at the destination, because the same icons can be pasted more than once to produce duplicates. Originally, we didn't copy at the source. However, the following sequence of events occurred and caused us to change our strategy. First, we made a copy of an icon. Then we forgot about it and made changes to it; e.g., changing its size and background color. Next we pasted the icon and found not the icon that we had copied but the icon as it currently existed. It is clearly important to copy at both the source and the destination.

Recall that the view for the master controller keeps track of the icons and which ones are selected. The icons themselves can resize and change their locations. Correspondingly, there are several view and icon methods used by the controller that we haven't discussed yet; e.g., **selections**, **clearSelections**, and **moveBy**:. In each case, the intent should be evident. Additionally, grouping and ungrouping make use of the special WindowMaker-GroupIcon class, which we will discuss in more detail in a later section.

character processing

processCharacterCopy
    IconCopyBuffer ← view **selections collect**: [:icon | icon **shallowCopy**]

processCharacterCut
    self **processCharacterCopy**; **processCharacterDelete**

processCharacterPaste
    | newIcon selections |
    IconCopyBuffer **isNil ifTrue**: [↑self].
    view **clearSelections**. selections ← view **selections**.
    IconCopyBuffer **do**: [:icon |
        newIcon ← icon **shallowCopy**. view **addSubView**: newIcon.
        selections **add**: newIcon. newIcon **moveBy**: 10@10].
    view **displayView**

processCharacterDelete
    view **selections do**: [:icon | view **removeSubView**: icon].
    view **clearSelections**; **displayView**

processCharacterGroup
    | group newIcon selections |
    selections ← view **selections**.
    selections **size** < 2 **ifTrue**: [↑self]. "avoid grouping unnecessarily"
    selections **do**: [:icon | view **removeSubView**: icon].
    newIcon ← WindowMakerGroupIcon **new group**: selections.
    view **clearSelections**. view **selections add**: newIcon.
    view **addSubView**: newIcon; **displayView**

processCharacterUngroup
    | newSelections oldSelections |
    oldSelections ← view **selections**.
    view **clearSelections**.
    newSelections ← view **selections**.
    oldSelections **do**: [:icon |
        (icon **isKindOf**: WindowMakerGroupIcon)
            ifTrue: [
                view **removeSubView**: icon.
                icon **subViews shallowCopy do**: [:groupIcon |
                    view **addSubView**: groupIcon.
                    newSelections **add**: groupIcon]]
            ifFalse: [newSelections **add**: icon]].
    view **displayView**

Red Button Activity (Selection Processing)

Red button activity is concerned with processing mouse interactions that control selecting, deselecting, moving, and resizing icons. More specifically, it provides the following capabilities:

1. The ability to select an icon by pressing the (red) mouse button over it.

2. The **shift-clicking** facility that permits additional icons to be selected or deselected by pressing the mouse button over them while the shift key is down. Shift-clicking over a previously selected icon deselects it.

3. The rectangular **lasso-selection** facility (see Fig. 8.21) that provides an alternative approach to selecting a set of icons. Depressing the mouse over an open area and moving it causes a rectangle to appear and track the mouse (the lasso). When the button is released, all icons touching the rectangle are selected. The shift-clicking facility can then be used to add or remove specific icons.

4. The ability to move a set of selections (see Fig. 8.22) by depressing the mouse over one of them and moving it without releasing the button. An abstracted picture of the selected icons track the mouse until the button is released.

5. The ability to change the size of an icon (see Fig. 8.23) by depressing the mouse inside the grow box (at the bottom right corner) and either moving toward the center of the icon (shrinking it) or moving away from the icon (growing it).

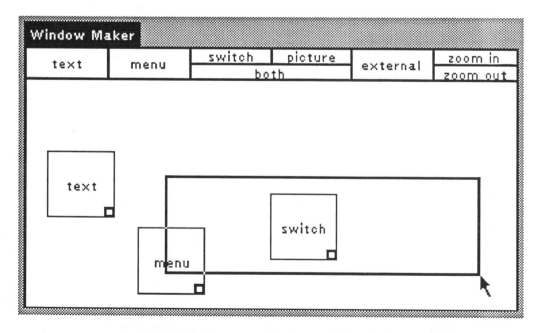

Figure 8.21 The rectangular lasso-selection facility.

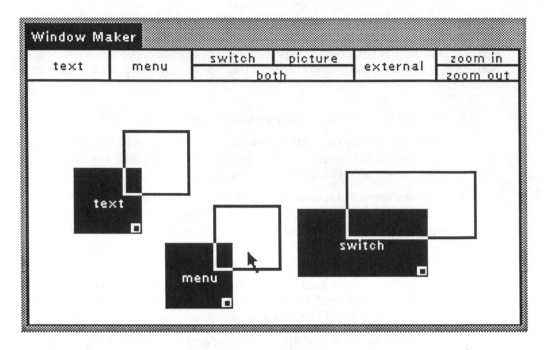

Figure 8.22 Moving a set of icons.

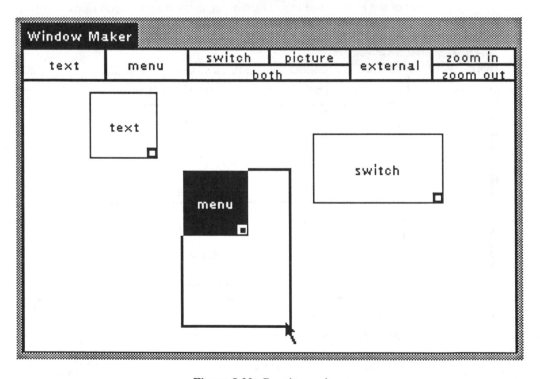

Figure 8.23 Growing an icon.

Inside Smalltalk

In cases where a boundary rectangle is drawn, the basic strategy is the same. A rectangle is drawn with rule 'Form **reverse**' twice in succession — the first rectangle ends up being erased by the second. In some cases, explicit rectangles are drawn by the controller, as in method **processNoSelection**; in others, the icons explicitly reverse their own boundary.

selection processing

processSelections
>"If the shift key is down, a new selection is added and an old selection is removed. If the shift key is up, new selections replace existing selections; old selections are moved. If nothing is selected, all old selections are removed."
>| selectionPoint |
>
>selectionPoint ← Sensor **cursorPoint**.
>view **subViews do**: [:icon |
>   (icon **containsPoint**: selectionPoint) **ifTrue**: [
>   Sensor **leftShiftDown**
>   **ifTrue**: [
>   (view **selections includes**: icon)
>   **ifTrue**: [view **deselect**: icon]
>   **ifFalse**: [view **select**: icon].
>   Sensor **waitNoButton**]
>   **ifFalse**: [
>   (view **selections includes**: icon)
>   **ifFalse**: [view **deselectAll**; **select**: icon].
>   self
>   **moveOrAdjustSelections**: icon
>   **initialMousePoint**: selectionPoint].
>   ↑self]].
>self **processNoSelection**

processNoSelection
>"For choosing multiple selections, draw a rectangle that tracks the mouse. Draws by repeatedly erasing the previous rectangle and redrawing the new. By using rule reverse for all drawing, we guarantee that all lines drawn can be undone."
>
>| startPosition endPosition draw borderRectangle newEndPosition |
>view **deselectAll**.
>
>startPosition ← Sensor **cursorPoint**. endPosition ← startPosition.
>draw ← [
>   borderRectangle ← (startPosition **min**: endPosition)
>   **corner**: (startPosition **max**: endPosition).
>   Display
>   **border**: borderRectangle
>   **width**: 2 **rule**: Form **reverse mask**: Form **black**].
>
>"The first time a border is drawn, a no-op results; the borderRectangle is empty."
>[Sensor **redButtonPressed**] **whileTrue**: [
>   newEndPosition ← Sensor **cursorPoint**.
>   newEndPosition = endPosition **ifFalse**: [
>   draw **value**. "Erase the old."
>   endPosition ← newEndPosition.
>   draw **value** "Draw the new."]].
>draw **value**. "Erase the last borderRectangle"
>
>view **subViews do**: [:icon |
>   (icon **displayBox intersects**: borderRectangle) **ifTrue**: [
>   view **select**: icon]]

When start and end points are provided (the top left and bottom right corners respectively), it is easy to draw a rectangle using method **border:width:rule:mask:** (see method **processNoSelection**). However, the rectangle is drawn only if the origin is to the left and above the corner. If it isn't, nothing is drawn at all. Consequently, if borderRectangle were set to the obvious 'startPosition **corner:** endPosition', the visual effect provided the designer would change dramatically. In particular, dragging the mouse down and/or to the right would produce a rectangle as shown in Fig. 8.21. However, dragging it up and/or to the left would have no visual effect — no rectangle would display; it would be a no-op.

moveOrAdjustSelections: icon **initialMousePoint**: start
    "If the mouse is on the grow box, deselect all other windows and adjust the size of this one; otherwise, move the selections."

(icon **growBoxContainsPoint:** start)
    ifTrue: [self **adjustSelections:** icon **initialMousePoint:** start]
    ifFalse: [self **moveSelectionsInitialMousePoint:** start]

adjustSelections: icon **initialMousePoint**: start
    "Deselect all other windows and adjust the size of this one."
    | startPoint draw endPoint |
    startPoint ← start.
    view **deselectAll**; **select:** icon.
    draw ← [icon **reverseBoundary**].

    draw **value**. "Draw initial selection boundaries."
    [Sensor **redButtonPressed**] **whileTrue:** [
        endPoint ← Sensor **mousePoint**.
        startPoint = endPoint **ifFalse:** [
            draw **value**. "Erase selection boundaries."
            icon **growBy:** endPoint - startPoint.
            draw **value**. "Redraw selection boundaries."
            startPoint ← endPoint]].
    draw **value**. "Erase final selection boundaries."
    view **displayView**

moveSelectionsInitialMousePoint: start
    "Have the selections track the mouse as long as it is depressed."
    | startPoint draw endPoint displacement |
    startPoint ← start.
    draw ← [view **selections do:** [:icon | icon **reverseBoundary**]].

    draw **value**. "Draw initial selection boundaries."
    [Sensor **redButtonPressed**] **whileTrue:** [
        endPoint ← Sensor **mousePoint**.
        startPoint = endPoint **ifFalse:** [
            displacement ← endPoint - startPoint.
            draw **value**. "Erase selection boundaries."
            view **selections do:** [:icon | icon **moveBy:** displacement].
            draw **value**. "Redraw selection boundaries."
            startPoint ← endPoint]].
    draw **value**. "Erase final selection boundaries."
    view **displayView**

In each case above, the start point is passed along as a parameter for accuracy. If the start point were recomputed locally, it would be noticeably different in situations where the mouse was moving reasonably fast.

Yellow Button Activity (Pop-up Option Menus)

Normally, yellow button activity is a simple process that includes (1) constructing a list of possibilities, (2) using it as data to create an instance of PopUpMenu or ActionMenu, (3) starting it up, and (4) executing the method corresponding to the selection (if any). The difficulty here is that the list is not fixed. It depends on the icons selected, their number, and in some cases, their class. It also depends on the prior state of the controller; i.e., whether or not an options window is currently open as a consequence of a prior yellow button menu choice.

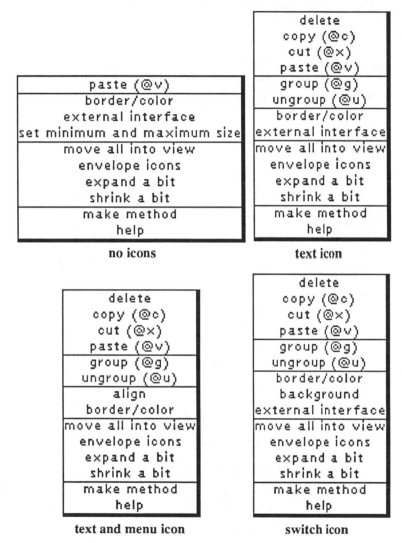

Figure 8.24 Examples of yellow button menus.

Some yellow button menu examples are shown in Fig. 8.24. When no icons are selected, the master icon is implicitly chosen. The minimum and maximum size, for example, only applies to the master icon. When a single icon is selected, the external interface for that icon can be specified. When several icons are selected, common features like bordering/coloring and alignment can be specified. The switch icon, among others, permits more detailed specification of the background — either textual or pictorial. Of course, some entries (the bottom entries, for example) are provided in all cases.

yellowButtonActivity

"Determine which menu items are permitted in this context and provide only those to the user via a pop-up menu."

| selections ungroupedSelections labels lines selectors atLeastOneSwitchAndPictures selectionsAllSwitchesOrPictures index |

"Refuse to permit two pop-up windows."
previousPopUpWindow **isNil ifFalse:** [
    (PopUpMenu
        labels: 'cancel previously active pop-up window'
        lines: #()) **startUp** ~= 0 **ifTrue:** [self **cancelPopUpWindow**]].

selections ← view **selections**. ungroupedSelections ← view **ungroupedSelections**.
labels ← OrderedCollection **new**. lines ← OrderedCollection **new**.
selectors ← OrderedCollection **new**.

"The <delete, copy, cut, paste> entries."
selections **size** > 0
    ifTrue: [
        labels **addAll:** #('delete' 'copy (@c)' 'cut (@x)').
        selectors **addAll:** #(processCharacterDelete processCharacterCopy
            processCharacterCut)].
labels
    add: 'paste (@v)'. selectors **add:** #processCharacterPaste. lines **add:** labels **size**.

"The <group, ungroup> entries."
selections **size** > 0
    ifTrue: [
        labels **addAll:** #('group (@g)' 'ungroup (@u)').
        selectors **addAll:** #(processCharacterGroup processCharacterUngroup).
        lines **add:** labels **size**].

"The <icon visual adjustment> entries."
selections **size** > 1
    ifTrue: [labels **add:** 'align'. selectors **add:** #align].

labels **add:** 'border/color'. selectors **add:** #borderAndColor.

selectionsAllSwitchesOrPictures ← (ungroupedSelections
    detect: [:anIcon | (anIcon **isKindOf:** WindowMakerSwitchOrPictureIcon) **not**]
    ifNone: [nil]) **isNil**.
(selections **size** > 0) & selectionsAllSwitchesOrPictures
    ifTrue: [
        labels **add:** 'background'.
        atLeastOneSwitchAndPicture ← (ungroupedSelections
            detect: [:anIcon |
                anIcon **isKindOf:** WindowMakerSwitchAndPictureIcon]
            ifNone: [nil]) **notNil**.
        atLeastOneSwitchAndPicture
            ifTrue: [selectors **add:** #switchAndPictureBackground]
            ifFalse: [selectors **add:** #background]].
selections **size** <= 1
    ifTrue: [labels **add:** 'external interface'. selectors **add:** #interface].

selections **size** = 0
    ifTrue: [labels **add:** 'set minimum and maximum size'. selectors **add:** #setSize].

```
self combinableSwitchAndPicture
    ifTrue: [
            labels add: 'combine switch and picture'.
            selectors add: #combineSwitchAndPicture].

lines add: labels size.

"The <editor adjustment> entries."

labels addAll: #('move all into view' 'envelope icons' 'expand a bit' 'shrink a bit').
selectors addAll: #(show envelope grow shrink).
lines add: selectors size.

"The <window output and help> entries."

labels addAll: #('make method' 'help'). selectors addAll: #(makeMethod help).

"Ask the user for a selection."
labels ← labels inject: '' into: [:result :selector |
        result isEmpty
            ifTrue: [selector]
            ifFalse: [result, (String with: Character cr), selector]].
index ← (PopUpMenu labels: labels lines: lines) startUp.
index ~= 0 ifTrue: [self perform: (selectors at: index)]
```

Note that delete, copy, cut, paste, group, and ungroup are handled by the existing character processing methods; e.g., delete can be specified via either a keyboard character or a menu choice.

Before we consider the methods for handling the actual menu messages, it is worth recalling that the master controller has an instance variable *previousPopUpWindow*. When a window pops up in response to a menu selection, the view for that window is saved in *previousPopUpWindow*. If an attempt is made to open a second window, it is possible to inform the designer or cancel the first window. Twelve different windows can pop up, each corresponding to a different menu selection. The views for these windows are obtained from the class method **windowFor:**. The controller is an instance of WindowMakerController-WithCancel. The model could be either one of the icons selected or a group of such icons encapsulated in an instance of class WindowMakerGroupIcon. Several methods are provided to set up this MVC triad.

menu messages support

```
popUpWithCancel: windowName onGroup: selections
    self
        popUp: (WindowMakerIconController windowFor: windowName)
        controller: (WindowMakerControllerWithCancel withCancelFor: self)
        on: (WindowMakerGroupIcon new temporaryGroup: selections)

popUpWithCancel: windowName onIndividual: selection
    self
        popUp: (WindowMakerIconController windowFor: windowName)
        controller: (WindowMakerControllerWithCancel withCancelFor: self)
        on: selection

popUpWithoutCancel: windowName onGroup: selections
    self
        popUp: (WindowMakerIconController windowFor: windowName)
        controller: (WindowMakerControllerWithCancel withoutCancelFor: self)
        on: (WindowMakerGroupIcon new temporaryGroup: selections)
```

popUpWithoutCancel: windowName **onIndividual**: selection
    self
        popUp: (WindowMakerIconController **windowFor**: windowName)
        controller: (WindowMakerControllerWithCancel **withoutCancelFor**: self)
        on: selection

popUp: aView **controller**: aController **on**: aModel
    ((previousPopUpWindow ← aView) **controller**: aController; **models**: aModel) **open**

forgetPopUpWindow
    previousPopUpWindow ← nil

The following menu messages that result in the appearance of option windows typi-cally rely on the fact that method **yellowButtonActivity** has prescreened the icon or icons to which they apply. For example, some apply to individual icons only, some require a set of two or more icons, some apply only to switch icons. Additionally, since icons can be grouped, some menu messages treat these as individual icons. Others want the grouping to be essentially transparent so that the icons in the group are individually affected. This is actually recursive, since a group can contain other groups. This is the case for the menu messages that set the border width or the inside color. A group doesn't have a border width or inside color. These respective icons can be obtained from the view via messages **selections** and **ungroupedSelections** respectively.

Note that only seven messages are explicitly provided in the following, rather than the twelve discussed previously. However, method **interface** actually retrieves master, text, menu, switch, picture, and external windows. Also, note that variation **popUp...onIndivi-dual**: is not actually used. Earlier versions used it in methods **interface**, **setSize**, and **makeMethod**. In the current design, all models are group icons. Consequently, all pluggable messages are centralized in the WindowMakerGroupIcon class.

menu messages (options windows)

align
    self **popUpWithCancel**: #alignment **onGroup**: view **selections**

borderAndColor
    | selections |
    (selections ← view **ungroupedSelections**) isEmpty
        ifTrue: [selections ← Array **with**: view].
    self **popUpWithoutCancel**: #borderingAndColoring **onGroup**: selections

background
    self **popUpWithoutCancel**: #background **onGroup**: view **ungroupedSelections**

switchAndPictureBackground
    self **popUpWithoutCancel**: #switchAndPictureBackground
        onGroup: view **ungroupedSelections**

interface
    "Warning: only individual icons are handled."
    | selections name selection |
    (selections ← view **selections**) isEmpty ifTrue: [selections ← Array **with**: view].
    selections **size** > 1 **ifTrue**: [self **error**: 'Implementation oversight'].
    selection ← selections **first**.
    name ← selection **shortClassName asLowercase**. "??? in WindowMaker???Icon"
    self **popUpWithoutCancel**: name **onGroup**: selections

setSize
> self **popUpWithoutCancel**: #masterSizing **onGroup**: (OrderedCollection **with**: view)

makeMethod
> self **popUpWithCancel**: #makeMethod **onGroup**: (OrderedCollection **with**: view)

The **short class name** used by the **interface** method is provided by the Window-MakerIcon abstract class.

Class WindowMakerIcon

class	WindowMakerIcon
superclass	ExtendedSwitchView
instance variables	...

default naming

classNamePicture
> ↑self **shortClassName asLowercase asParagraph**

shortClassName
> | className |
> className ← self **class name**. "WindowMaker...Icon"
> ↑className **copyFrom**: 12 **to**: className **size** - 4 "the ... portion"

Not all menu messages result in options windows popping up. In particular, the following menu messages are processed directly. Additionally, the **help** menu message results in a confirmer with instructions. The designer's response to the confirmation is simply ignored.

1. **cancelPopUpWindow** — eliminates the previously opened options window.

2. **combineSwitchAndPicture** — permits two separate icons (a switch and a picture, as shown in Fig. 8.12) to be combined into one. Originally, this message was used to convert our own windows after we added combined switch/picture icons; this conversion operation was intended to be temporary. However, we ended up using the facility at isolated times every now and then. In the end, we decided to keep it as a useful facility. Note, however, that no converse operation is provided.

3. **show** — forces all icons in the window to be moved so as to be visible. Because of zooming, it is possible to focus in a small area and lose track of icons that are not directly visible. This is another example of a menu message that was provided to aid development but that proved useful enough to be retained.

4. **envelope** — causes the window to adjust itself in order to exactly surround the icons it contains. This is typically the last operation done before generating a method for an application window. Alternatively, it is sometimes followed by a grow operation to provide a little extra white space around the icons. Fig. 8.25 provides an illustration of the facility.

5. **grow** — enlarges the window by a small fixed amount. The icons remain unchanged.

6. **shrink** — shrinks the window by the same small fixed amount. The icons remain unchanged.

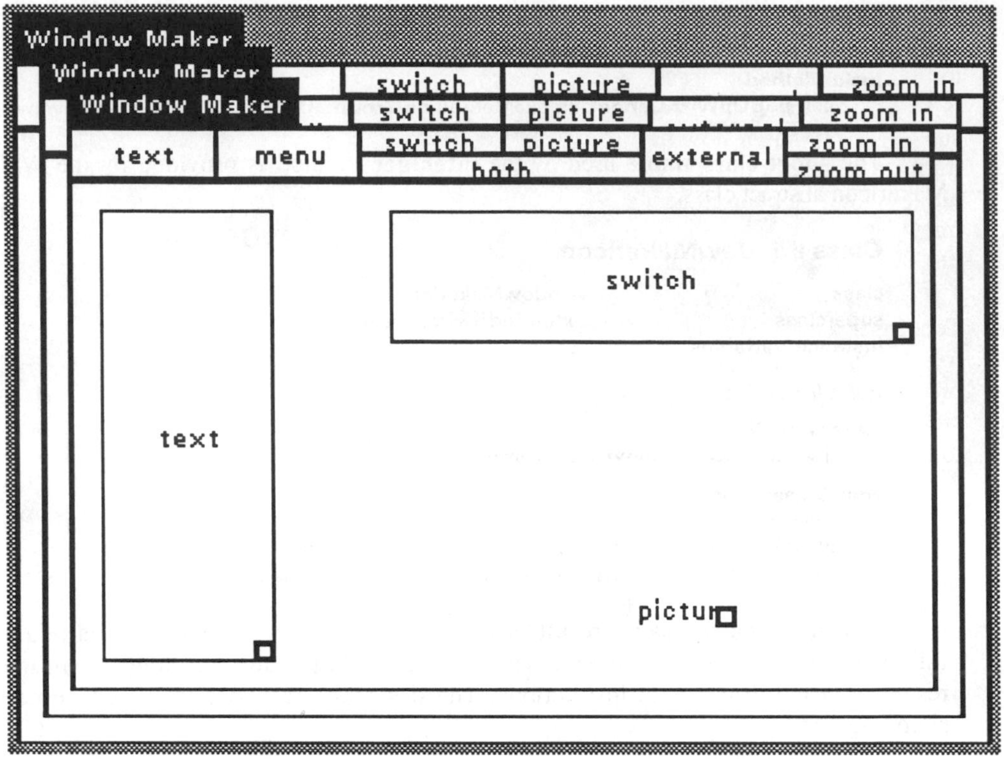

Figure 8.25 Adjusting the window—envelope, 3 grows, 2 shrinks.

When a window is adjusted via **envelope, grow,** or **shrink,** the old image is retained. This is inconsequential when growing, since the larger image obliterates the smaller one underneath. However, the older image is still perceived when shrinking. Redrawing the screen will eliminate these superfluous images. Nevertheless, it can provide a useful history of the changes. To obtain Fig. 8.25, an arbitrarily sized window maker editor was opened and then three icons were constructed, sized, and arbitrarily placed in the icon window. Then we enveloped the icons and performed three grow operations in a row. No history of these three grow operations is evident. However, the two subsequent shrink operations can be clearly seen. One more shrink operation (had we done it) would have resulted in the window exactly surrounding the three icons.

Changing the size of a top view is relatively simple — execute 'topView **window:** existingWindow **viewport:** desiredDisplayBox'. This will change the local transformation and unlock all subviews. Attempts to display a subview will cause its display transformation and consequently the new display box that corresponds with the above to be recomputed.

The difficulty in our case is that the icons are not in the top view but in a subview. Even though we may be able to determine what the display box should be for the subview, there is no direct way to determine how that affects the display box for the top view. Auxiliary method '**resize:** aView **displayBoxTo:** aViewDisplayBox' is provided to solve this problem. Given the desired display box for a subview, it is possible to compute the required display box for its superview. By iteratively performing this computation until the top view is reached, we will have solved the initial problem.

Let us now concentrate on the simpler problem. It can be paraphrased as "given that subview w is to have display box d, determine the display box D for superview W." The key to a solution is the observation that the only local transformation modified when a top view is resized is the local transformation of the top view. The local transformations of all subviews, no matter how deeply nested, are unchanged. Of course, this causes the display transformation for the top view to change, and consequently the display transformations of all subviews to change because they are computed in terms of their superview's display transformations. What this means intuitively is that we don't need to change anything — we just need to use existing information judiciously.

Note that w is mapped into some portion w' of W by the local transformation. Technically, w' is w's viewport. If d is the display box associated with w' (since it is related to w), and D is the display box for W, it should be clear (see Fig. 8.26) that d and D are proportional to each other in the same way that w' and W are proportional to each other. If we can determine the transformation that maps w' to d, the same transformation will map W to D. If t is this transformation, then

```
w' ← w viewport
t ← WindowingTransformation window: w' viewport: d
D ← t applyTo: W
```

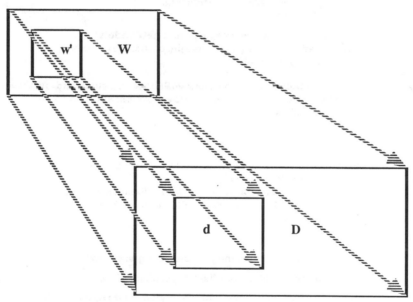

Figure 8.26 Adjusting the window —envelope, 3 grows, 2 shrinks.

menu messages (no options windows)

cancelPopUpWindow
    "In case it cannot be closed, pretend it did."
    | save |
    save ← previousPopUpWindow.
    self **forgetPopUpWindow**.
    ScheduledControllers **unschedule**: save **controller**.
    save **release**.
    ScheduledControllers **restore**

combineSwitchAndPicture
    | switch picture combined border box |
    switch ← view **selections detect**: [:icon | icon **isMemberOf**: WindowMakerSwitchIcon].
    picture ← view **selections detect**: [:icon | icon **isMemberOf**: WindowMakerPictureIcon].

    combined ← WindowMakerSwitchAndPictureIcon **new**
        name: switch **name**;
        transformation: switch **transformation**;
        window: switch **window**;
        insideColor: switch **insideColor**;
        borderWidthLeft: (border ← switch **borderWidth**) **left**
            right: border **right top**: border **top bottom**: border **bottom**;

        pictureFormPathName: (switch **encodedPictureData copyFrom**: 2 **to**: 3);
        lockedSizeExpansion: switch **lockedSizeExpansion**;
        "The following 3 messages are explained in the next section."
        changeMessage: #updateSymbol
            receiver: (switch **receiverFor**: #updateSymbol);
        changeMessage: #isOn
            selectorArguments: (switch **codingWithoutReceiverFor**: #isOn);
        changeMessage: #switch
            selectorArguments: (switch **codingWithoutReceiverFor**: #switch);
        pictureString: picture **pictureString**;
        fixMiddleLeft.

    box ← switch **getWindow merge**: picture **getWindow**.
    combined **getWindow origin**: box **origin**; **corner**: box **corner**.
    combined **computeLabel**.

    view **removeSubView**: switch; **removeSubView**: picture; **addSubView**: combined.
    view **selections remove**: switch; **remove**: picture; **add**: combined.
    combined **unlock**; **lock**.
    view **displayView**

show
    "Move all icons into the view to ensure their visibility."
    view **subViews do**: [:anIcon |
        anIcon **displayBox extent** > (10@10) **ifFalse**: [anIcon **growTo**: 10@10].
        anIcon **moveBy**: (anIcon **displayBox amountToTranslateWithin**: view **displayBox**)].
    view **displayView**

envelope
    "Make the view exactly contain the existing subviews."

    | subViews newDisplayBox offset superDisplayBox |

    subViews ← view **subViews**. subViews **size** = 0 **ifTrue**: [view **flash**. ↑self].

    "The new display box must contain all subviews and the border."
    newDisplayBox ← (subViews **inject**: subViews **first displayBox into**: [:box :aView |
        box **merge**: aView **displayBox**]) **expandBy**: view **borderWidth**.

    "Moreover, the center of the new display box must be at the center of the view.
    This can be achieved only if the subviews are offset by the same amount."
    offset ← view **displayBox center** - newDisplayBox **center**.
    newDisplayBox **moveBy**: offset. "Move its center to the old one."
    subViews **do**: [:aView | aView **moveBy**: offset].

    "Change the display box for the top view."
    self **resize**: view **displayBoxTo**: newDisplayBox

Inside Smalltalk

grow

"Enlarge this view's display box by 10@10."
self **resize**: view **displayBoxTo**: (view **displayBox expandBy**: 10)

shrink

"Shrink this view's display box by 10@10."
self **resize**: view **displayBoxTo**: (view **displayBox insetBy**: 10)

help

self **confirm**: (
    'A detailed description of master windows can be obtained \',
    'by ensuring that nothing is selected and choosing the   \',
    'external interface entry in the yellow button pop-up   \',
    'menu. Similar descriptions for the other classes of windows\',
    'can be obtained by selecting one of these windows and   \',
    'choosing the same external interface entry.   \',
    '\',
    'If no such window exists, one can be created by pressing \',
    'one of the switches at the top. The new window that   \',
    'appears can be placed anywhere in the pane below   \',
    'the switches.   ') **withCRs**

menu messages support

combinableSwitchAndPicture

    | switch picture |
    ↑view **selections size** = 2 **and**: [
    (switch ← view **selections**
        detect: [:icon | icon **isMemberOf**· WindowMakerSwitchIcon]
        ifNone: [nil]) **notNil and**: [
    (picture ← view **selections**
        detect: [:icon | icon **isMemberOf**: WindowMakerPictureIcon]
        ifNone: [nil]) **notNil and**: [
    switch **pictureVariety** == #form]]]

resize: aView **displayBoxTo**: aViewDisplayBox

"This is achieved by recursively computing the display boxes of all super views. It is physically changed for the top view."
| currentView newDisplayBox |

"Determine the successive superview display boxes (remember the last)."
currentView ← aView. newDisplayBox ← aViewDisplayBox.
[currentView **isTopView**] **whileFalse**: [
    newDisplayBox ← self **superViewDisplayBoxFrom**: currentView
        and: newDisplayBox.
    currentView ← currentView **superView**].

currentView **window**: currentView **getWindow viewport**: newDisplayBox.

"Make the close box visible?"
((Display **boundingBox insetBy**: (Rectangle **left**: 0 **right**: 1 **top**: 1 **bottom**: 0))
    containsPoint: newDisplayBox **origin**) **ifFalse**: [
        currentView
            align: currentView **displayBox topLeft**
            with: 0@currentView **labelDisplayBox height**].

currentView **lock**; **displayEmphasized**

superViewDisplayBoxFrom: aView **and**: aViewDisplayBox
"Determines the superview's display box from a new (arbitrary) display box for the
view. Note: if t maps this view's viewport to aViewDisplayBox, then t will also map
the superview's window to its new display box."
↑(WindowingTransformation
    window: aView **getViewport**
    viewport: aViewDisplayBox) "t"
      applyTo: aView **superView getWindow**

8.4.6 The WindowMakerMasterIcon Class

The **window maker master icon** supports the **window maker master icon controller** by
keeping track of the currently selected icons, the minimum and maximum sizes for the
application window, and a set of output options that specifies how the application window is
to be generated; e.g., in the transcript, as a class method, or as an instance method. In the
last two cases, additional information must also be provided; i.e., the class name, method
name, category name, and overflow category name (in case more than one method is needed
to generate the application window).

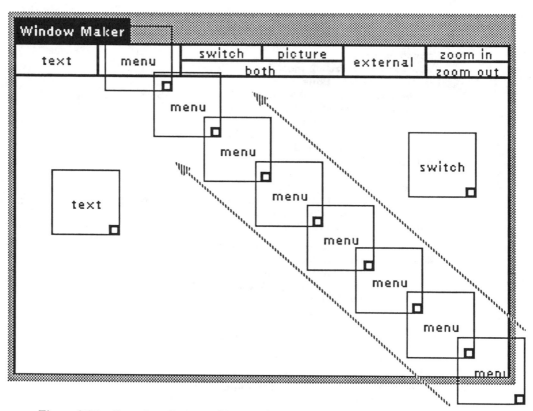

Figure 8.27   Dropping the menu icon outside the icon container pane causes it to
slide back into the menu switch.

The WindowMakerIcon class also supports the WindowMaker class by providing method **makeIcon**: for instantiating icons. An icon is created when a designer depresses one of the top switches. It is added to the icon container pane if the user deposits it inside the bottom pane. Otherwise, it slides back (as shown in Fig. 8.27) to the menu switch from which it appeared.

Those methods discussed in special sections are referenced but omitted to eliminate unnecessary duplication.

Class WindowMakerMasterIcon

class	WindowMakerMasterIcon
superclass	WindowMakerIcon
instance variables	selections minimumSize maximumSize outputOption

class methods

no messages

instance methods

instance initialization

initializeMessages
    ... see Sect. 8.4.2, Initializing a New Icon's Interface Data ...

initialize
    super **initialize**.
    window ← Display **boundingBox**. "minimize transformation roundoff errors."
    selections ← OrderedCollection **new**.

    minimumSize ← 50@50.
    maximumSize ← Display **boundingBox extent**.

    outputOption ← #(transcript "versus instanceMethod versus classMethod"
        encoded "versus notEncoded"
        aClassName aCategoryString aMethodName anOverFlowCategoryString) **copy**

makeIcon: anIconClass
    "Creates a new icon and keeps it if the user positions it inside the view."
    | center icon aForm offset position aRectangle |

    "Deselect all icons and make an icon at the current cursor point; set up initial information."
    center ← Sensor **cursorPoint**. self **deselectAll**.
    self **addSubView**: (icon ← anIconClass **new**).

    "First draw the icon onto a form."
    aForm ← Form **extent**: icon **displayBox extent**.
    icon
        displayOn: aForm **at**: 0@0 **clippingBox**: aForm **boundingBox rule**: Form **over**
        mask: Form **black**.

    "Next, make it follow the cursor until it is depressed."
    offset ← aForm **extent** // 2.
    aForm
        follow: [position ← Sensor **cursorPoint** - offset]
        while: [Sensor **redButtonPressed** not].

"Make the new icon permanent only if it is inside the window maker view."
aRectangle ← position **extent:** aForm **extent.**
(self **insetDisplayBox contains:** aRectangle)
    ifTrue: ["Make it permanent."
        icon **moveTo:** position.
        aForm **displayAt:** position.
        self **select:** icon]
    ifFalse: ["Make it go back into the switch."
        self **removeSubView:** icon.
        aForm **slideFrom:** position **to:** center-offset **nSteps:** 20]

encoding/decoding
    ... see Sect. 8.4.8, Encoding/Decoding ... (also see Appendix B.5) ...

generating views
    ... see Sect. 8.4.8, ... Converting to Extended Views, ... (also see Appendix B.6) ...

Recall (see Sect. 8.4.3, *Displaying, Moving, and Sizing*) that each icon was designed to ensure that its window, viewport, and display box would all have the same extent. However, the window origin was permitted to be different from the display box origin.

To maintain this constraint, scaling the master icon must not result in a rescaling of its local transformation. If it did, the display boxes for the contained icons (the subviews) would change without the windows changing. Consequently, the default **scaleBy:** method must be superseded by one that specifically rescales the icons. An icon rescales itself by changing its window rather than its local transformation, which is always the identity transformation.

zooming

zoomIn
    self **scaleBy:** 1.1@1.1.
    self **displayView**

zoomOut
    self **scaleBy:** 0.9@0.9.
    self **displayView**

scaleBy: scale
    "Since this view does not scale, scale the subviews."
    subViews **do:** [:anIcon | anIcon **scaleBy:** scale]

If the window maker is moved or resized, the icons at the center of the icon container pane should remain at the center of the newly positioned pane. Moreover, resizing the window maker should result in seeing more or less of the icons, not in the icons changing size. To achieve this, it would be nice if we didn't have to do anything special to the icons in the container pane.

One approach is to have all the icon windows positioned in a master window whose center is always a constant; e.g., 0@0 for simplicity. If this window (with center 0@0) is the same size as the display box, providing a local transformation that maps it to the display box will result in a display transformation without scaling.

computeDisplayTransformation
"Ensure that (1) this view does not scale, and (2) the window center maps to the display box center. One solution is to ensure that the window center is 0@0 and the same as the display box; a side benefit is that the subicons need never be moved since they are always positioned in a window that appears to be fixed."
| box |
"First, compute the normal way (need the display box) and then change it."
displayTransformation ← superView **displayTransformation**
    compose: transformation.
box ← self **displayBox**.
window ← box **copy moveTo**: 0@0 - (box **extent** // 2).
viewport ← superView **inverseDisplayTransform**: box.
transformation ← WindowingTransformation
    window: window **viewport**: viewport.
displayTransformation ← WindowingTransformation
    scale: nil **translation**: (box **origin** - window **origin**).
↑displayTransformation

Windows (consider the system browser) are generally displayed by painting local information, such as the border and inside color, and then recursively displaying the contained views. The result is a noticeable sequence of painting activities as the successive subwindows are displayed. A better approach is to paint the entire window on an internal form and then display the form in one step.

displaying

display
    self **displayView**

displayView
"Creates a form with the existing icons and then displays the form. This prevents the user from seeing the icons individually displayed one after the other."
| displayArea extent canvas offset canvasDisplayArea labelDisplayBox |

self **isUnlocked ifTrue**: [self **lock**].
displayArea ← self **displayBox**.
offset ← displayArea **origin**. extent ← displayArea **extent**.
canvas ← Form **extent**: extent.
canvasDisplayArea ← (0@0 **extent**: extent) **insetBy**: self **borderWidth**.

Cursor **normal showWhile**: [
    canvas **black**; **fill**: canvasDisplayArea **mask**: insideColor.
    subViews **do**: [:icon |
        icon **displayOn**: canvas
            at: icon **displayBox origin** - offset **clippingBox**: canvasDisplayArea
            rule: Form **under mask**: Form **black**].
    selections **do**: [:icon |
        icon **highlightOn**: canvas
            at: icon **displayBox origin** - offset **clippingBox**: canvasDisplayArea]].

canvas **displayOn**: Display **at**: offset.

When a user selects an icon, the master icon controller manages the mouse interactions and asks the master icon to either select or deselect a new candidate. The candidate is immediately highlighted or dehighlighted. Hence, there is no need to redisplay the entire view. This permits fast interactive feedback.

selections

select: icon
    selections **add:** icon. icon **highlight.**

deselect: icon
    selections **remove:** icon. icon **dehighlight.**

deselectAll
    [selections **size** = 0] **whileFalse:** [selections **removeFirst dehighlight**].

clearSelections
    selections ← OrderedCollection **new**

selections
    ↑selections

ungroupedSelections
    | ungroupedSelections |
    ungroupedSelections ← OrderedCollection **new**.
    selections **do:** [:selection |
        selection **groupDo:** [:icon | ungroupedSelections **add:** icon]].
    ↑ungroupedSelections

The master icon controller associated with the master icon is specified via the standard method **defaultControllerClass**. The controller, however, never permits an individual icon to get control because it handles all the mouse and keyboard interactions itself.

controller

defaultControllerClass
    ↑WindowMakerMasterIconController

subViewWantingControl
    "This is handled by redButtonActivity."
    ↑nil

background

computeLabel
    "There is no label for the master icon."
    self **label:** nil

interface window defaults

defaultComment
defaultPreOpeningSelector
defaultPostClosingSelector
defaultTitle
defaultTopView
    ... *see Sect. 8.4.7, Interface Window Defaults (also see Appendix B.4)* ...

The following methods provide access to the master icon's instance variables. They are used by two option windows: the master sizing window and the method creation window (see Sect. 8.4.7, *Options Processing*).

master sizing window support

minimumSize
 ↑minimumSize
minimumSize: aPoint
 minimumSize ← aPoint

maximumSize
 ↑maximumSize
maximumSize: aPoint
 maximumSize ← aPoint

method window support

outputOption
 ↑outputOption
outputOption: anArray
 outputOption ← anArray

outputOptionAt: aSymbol
 ↑outputOption
   at: (#(destination encoding methodClass methodCategory
     methodName overflowCategory) **indexOf**: aSymbol)

outputOptionAt: aSymbol **put**: anObject
  outputOption
   at: (#(destination encoding methodClass methodCategory
     methodName overflowCategory) **indexOf**: aSymbol)
   put: anObject

8.4.7 Options Processing

Options processing is simpler than mouse and keyboard processing but support for it is pervasive and substantial in terms of the sheer volume of code. A three-stage process is involved:

1. The designer selects a menu item in the yellow button pop-up menu associated with the window maker icon container pane (see Fig. 8.28). The yellow button activity is processed by the master icon controller. See Sect. 8.4.5 for a review of the details.

2. Assuming that an item associated with an options window has been selected, e.g., *align*, the view associated with this window is retrieved from the master icon controller, a model is constructed that consists of a group icon containing the selected icons, and the view, for the alignment window in this case, is opened.

3. The options window, in this case the alignment window, interacts with the group icon (its model), which in turn relays all interrogations and modifications to the group members.

Clearly, information is distributed throughout the entire system. However, some effort has been made to centralize as much of the information as possible. To summarize:

1. All option window methods for generating views are centralized as class methods in class WindowMakerMasterIconController.

2. All option window models are instances of WindowMakerGroupIcon.

3. All pluggable messages for option windows are centralized as instance methods in class WindowMakerGroupIcon.

4. Support for the pluggable messages is distributed in the appropriate icons. When they are generic messages, they are kept in the abstract class WindowMakerIcon.

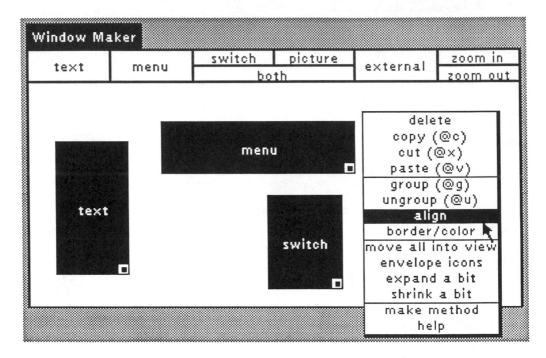

Figure 8.28 Invoking the yellow button alignment options.

We begin by considering the group icons in detail. Then we consider the individual option windows one by one. In each case, we will provide the following information:

1. The yellow button selector that created the window (in class WindowMakerIcon-Controller).

2. A summary of the pluggable messages and update symbols used by the subwindows.

3. The methods for the pluggable messages (in class WindowMakerGroupIcon).

4. The support methods for the pluggable messages (in the classes associated with the group icon's members).

The WindowMakerGroupIcon

The window maker group icon provides the ability to group icons on either a **temporary** basis or a **permanent** basis. The keyboard commands g and u, for example, create permanent group icons. On the other hand, group icons for options processing are always temporary. They may be discarded after processing without fear of side effects.

Group icons contain instance variables for processing background and alignment windows. These instance variables are unused for permanent group icons. An additional group sequencing method is provided for handling groups known to consist of exactly one member (method **isolatedGroupMember**). This is used, for example, for processing the sizing and method creation options windows.

Class WindowMakerGroupIcon

class	WindowMakerGroupIcon
superclass	WindowMakerIcon
instance variables	librarianForBackground width height leftRightAlignment upDownAlignment horizontalAbutment verticalAbutment

instance methods

group sequencing

groupDo: aBlock
groupGet: aBlock **ifUnequal**: unequalBlock
    ... see Sect. 8.4.2, Group Sequencing ...

isolatedGroupMember
    | count answer |
    count ← 0.
    self **groupDo**: [:icon | count ← count+1. answer ← icon].
    count = 1 **ifFalse**: [self **error**: 'expected isolated icon'].
    ↑answer

Several options windows provide text subwindows for one reason or another. In each case, it is sufficient to provide a simple yellow button pop-up menu with menu items **accept** and **cancel**. Additionally, we deactivated the prompt that asks "*Are you sure you want to close?*" when some of the text subwindows have been changed but not accepted. This was done by redefining the default **changeRequestFrom:** method.

generic window messages

acceptCancelYellowButtonMenu
    ↑ActionMenu
        labels: 'accept\cancel' **withCRs**
        lines: #()
        selectors: #(accept cancel)

generic window support (general)

changeRequestFrom: aView
    ↑true

generic window support (preopening/postclosing)
... see alignment, background, make method, and interface windows ...

alignment window messages
alignment window support
        ... see alignment windows ...

border window messages
color window messages
        ... see bordering/coloring windows ...

background window messages
background window support
        ... see background windows ...

master sizing window messages
        ... see master sizing windows ...

method window messages
        ... see make method windows ...

interface window messages
        ... see interface windows ...

The Alignment Window

Alignment is invoked by the *align* entry in the master controller's yellow button pop-up menu (the associated selector is repeated below for ease of reference). It is a facility that works on groups of two or more icons (see Fig. 8.29). Hence the primary facility is centered in class WindowMakerGroupIcon. On the other hand, the icons being aligned must be individually modified — hence, all icons must have a relevant modification protocol. This secondary protocol is provided in abstract class WindowMakerIcon.

Class WindowMakerMasterIconController

class	WindowMakerMasterIconController
superclass	MouseMenuController
instance variables	....

menu messages (options windows)

align
        self **popUpWithCancel**: #alignment **onGroup**: view **selections**

Operationally, the designer selects one switch from each of the six rows in the alignment window and then either **closes** or **cancels** the window. A normal close causes the grouped icons to be operated upon by the designer's last selections. The method that actually performs the work is a postclosing operation called **postCloseAlignment**. A cancel is effectively a no-op.

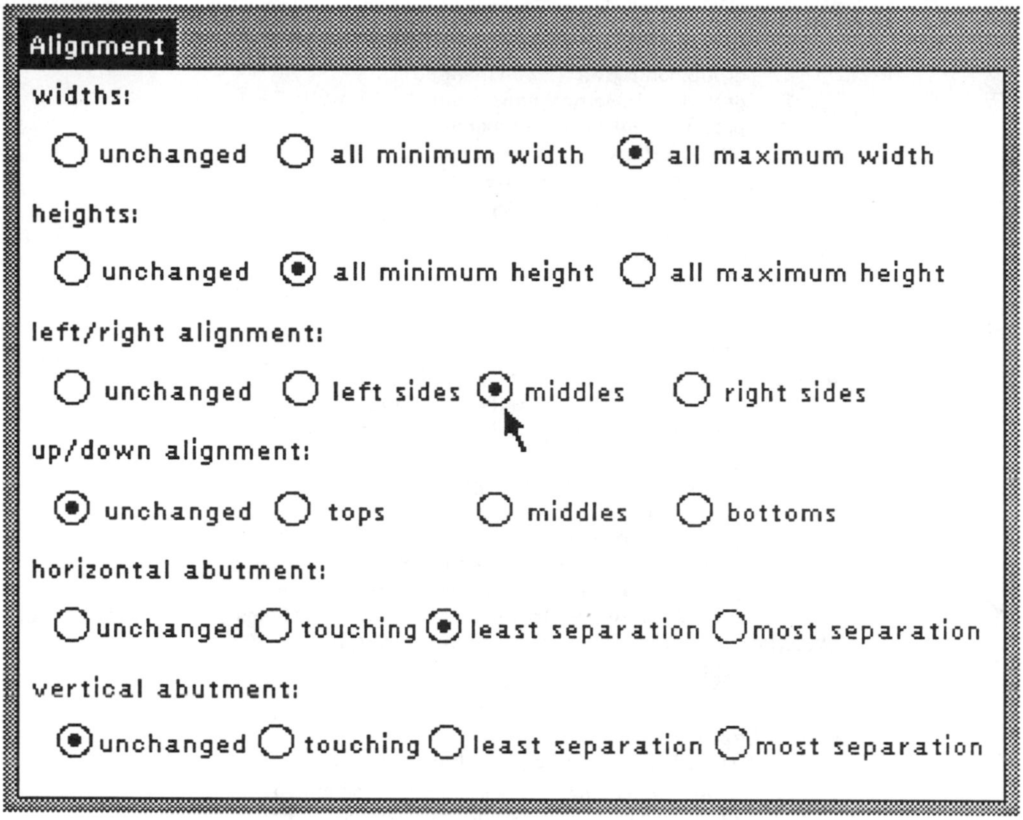

Figure 8.29 The alignment window.

With so many switches, it is clear that a large number of distinct messages will have to be processed. For the alignment window of Fig. 8.29, the protocol is as follows:

widths:
    how the switch determines if it should be on:
      1.   groupIcon **isWidth**: #unchanged
      2.   groupIcon **isWidth**: #minimum
      3.   groupIcon **isWidth**: #maximum
    what the switch does if it is pressed:
      1.   groupIcon **makeWidth**: #unchanged
      2.   groupIcon **makeWidth**: #minimum
      3.   groupIcon **makeWidth**: #maximum
    the update symbol to make the switch react:
      #width

heights:
   how the switch determines if it should be on:
   1.   groupIcon **isHeight**: #unchanged
   2.   groupIcon **isHeight**: #minimum
   3.   groupIcon **isHeight**: #maximum
   what the switch does if it is pressed:
   1.   groupIcon **makeHeight**: #unchanged
   2.   groupIcon **makeHeight**: #minimum
   3.   groupIcon **makeHeight**: #maximum
   the update symbol to make the switch react:
   #height

left/right alignment:
   how the switch determines if it should be on:
   1.   groupIcon **isLeftRightAlignment**: #unchanged
   2.   groupIcon **isLeftRightAlignment**: #leftSides
   3.   groupIcon **isLeftRightAlignment**: #middles
   4.   groupIcon **isLeftRightAlignment**: #rightSides
   what the switch does if it is pressed:
   1.   groupIcon **makeLeftRightAlignment**: #unchanged
   2.   groupIcon **makeLeftRightAlignment**: #leftSides
   3.   groupIcon **makeLeftRightAlignment**: #middles
   4.   groupIcon **makeLeftRightAlignment**: #rightSides
   the update symbol to make the switch react:
   #leftRightAlignment

up/down alignment:
   how the switch determines if it should be on:
   1.   groupIcon **isUpDownAlignment**: #unchanged
   2.   groupIcon **isUpDownAlignment**: #tops
   3.   groupIcon **isUpDownAlignment**: #middles
   4.   groupIcon **isUpDownAlignment**: #bottoms
   what the switch does if it is pressed:
   1.   groupIcon **makeUpDownAlignment**: #unchanged
   2.   groupIcon **makeUpDownAlignment**: #tops
   3.   groupIcon **makeUpDownAlignment**: #middles
   4.   groupIcon **makeUpDownAlignment**: #bottoms
   the update symbol to make the switch react:
   #upDownAlignment

horizontal abutment
   how the switch determines if it should be on:
   1.   groupIcon **isHorizontalAbutment**: #unchanged
   2.   groupIcon **isHorizontalAbutment**: #touching
   3.   groupIcon **isHorizontalAbutment**: #leastSeparation
   4.   groupIcon **isHorizontalAbutment**: #mostSeparation
   what the switch does if it is pressed:
   1.   groupIcon **makeHorizontalAbutment**: #unchanged
   2.   groupIcon **makeHorizontalAbutment**: #touching
   3.   groupIcon **makeHorizontalAbutment**: #leastSeparation
   4.   groupIcon **makeHorizontalAbutment**: #mostSeparation
   the update symbol to make the switch react:
   #horizontalAbutment

vertical abutment
   how the switch determines if it should be on:
      1.   groupIcon **isVerticalAbutment**: #unchanged
      2.   groupIcon **isVerticalAbutment**: #touching
      3.   groupIcon **isVerticalAbutment**: #leastSeparation
      4.   groupIcon **isVerticalAbutment**: #mostSeparation
   what the switch does if it is pressed:
      1.   groupIcon **makeVerticalAbutment**: #unchanged
      2.   groupIcon **makeVerticalAbutment**: #touching
      3.   groupIcon **makeVerticalAbutment**: #leastSeparation
      4.   groupIcon **makeVerticalAbutment**: #mostSeparation
   the update symbol to make the switch react:
         #verticalAbutment

When a designer modifies switches in the alignment window, the mutually exclusive choices (one per row of switches) are recorded in corresponding instance variables in the group icon. These instance variables are used by the postclosing alignment operation to effect the final changes.

Class WindowMakerGroupIcon

class	WindowMakerGroupIcon
superclass	WindowMakerIcon
instance variables	... width height leftRightAlignment upDownAlignment horizontalAbutment verticalAbutment

instance methods

generic window support (preopening/postclosing)

postCloseAlignment: anExtendedStandardSystemView
   "Make the alignment specification permanent if not canceled. USED by Group."
   anExtendedStandardSystemView **controller canceled ifFalse**: [
      self **adjustWidths; adjustHeights**.
      self **adjustLeftRightAlignment; adjustUpDownAlignment**.
      self **adjustHorizontalAbutment; adjustVerticalAbutment**]

alignment window messages

isWidth: aSymbol
   ↑width == aSymbol

makeWidth: aSymbol
   width ← aSymbol.
   self **changed**: #width

isHeight: aSymbol
   ↑height == aSymbol

makeHeight: aSymbol
   height ← aSymbol.
   self **changed**: #height

isLeftRightAlignment: aSymbol
   ↑leftRightAlignment == aSymbol

makeLeftRightAlignment: aSymbol
    leftRightAlignment ← aSymbol.
    self **changed**: #leftRightAlignment

isUpDownAlignment: aSymbol
    ↑upDownAlignment == aSymbol

makeUpDownAlignment: aSymbol
    upDownAlignment ← aSymbol.
    self **changed**: #upDownAlignment

isHorizontalAbutment: aSymbol
    ↑horizontalAbutment == aSymbol

makeHorizontalAbutment: aSymbol
    horizontalAbutment ← aSymbol.
    self **changed**: #horizontalAbutment

isVerticalAbutment: aSymbol
    ↑verticalAbutment == aSymbol

makeVerticalAbutment: aSymbol
    verticalAbutment ← aSymbol.
    self **changed**: #verticalAbutment

Adjustment to the icons being aligned is performed sequentially in the order *width*, *height*, *left/right alignment*, *up/down alignment*, *horizontal abutment*, and *vertical abutment*.

alignment window support

adjustWidths
    "Adjust the widths of all icons in the group - width options: unchanged, minimum, maximum."
    | operation newWidth |
    width == #unchanged **ifTrue**: [↑self].

    operation ← #(min: max:) **at**: (#(minimum maximum) **indexOf**: width).

    newWidth ← subViews **first displayBox width**.
    subViews **do**: [:icon |
        newWidth ← newWidth **perform**: operation **with**: icon **displayBox width**].

    subViews **do**: [:icon | icon **changeWidth**: newWidth]

adjustHeights
    "Adjust the heights of all icons in the group - height options: unchanged, minimum, maximum."
    | operation newHeight |
    height == #unchanged **ifTrue**: [↑self].

    operation ← #(min: max:) **at**: (#(minimum maximum) **indexOf**: height).

    newHeight ← subViews **first displayBox height**.
    subViews **do**: [:icon |
        newHeight ← newHeight **perform**: operation **with**: icon **displayBox height**].

    subViews **do**: [:icon | icon **changeHeight**: newHeight].

adjustLeftRightAlignment
"Adjust the left/right alignment of all icons in the group - makeLeftRightAlignment
options: unchanged, leftSides, middles, rightSides."
| index operation newX maxMin |
leftRightAlignment == #unchanged **ifTrue**: [↑self].

index ← #(leftSides middles rightSides) **indexOf**: leftRightAlignment.
operation ← #(origin center corner) **at**: index.
maxMin ← #(min: min: max:) **at**: index.

newX ← (subViews **first displayBox perform**: operation) **x**.
subViews **do**: [:icon |
    newX ← newX **perform**: maxMin **with**: (icon **displayBox perform**: operation) **x**].

operation ← #(changeLeftSide: changeMiddleHorizontally: changeRightSide:) **at**: index.
subViews **do**: [:icon | icon **perform**: operation **with**: newX]

adjustUpDownAlignment
"Adjust the up/down alignment of all icons in the group - makeUpDownAlignment
options: unchanged, tops, middles, bottoms."
| index operation newY maxMin |
upDownAlignment == #unchanged **ifTrue**: [↑self].

index ← #(tops middles bottoms) **indexOf**: upDownAlignment.
operation ← #(origin center corner) **at**: index.
maxMin ← #(min: min: max:) **at**: index.

newY ← (subViews **first displayBox perform**: operation) **y**.
subViews **do**: [:icon |
    newY ← newY **perform**: maxMin **with**: (icon **displayBox perform**: operation) **y**].

operation ← #(changeTop: changeMiddleVertically: changeBottom:) **at**: index.
subViews **do**: [:icon | icon **perform**: operation **with**: newY]

adjustHorizontalAbutment
"Adjust the horizontal abutment of all icons in the group - horizontalAbutment
options: unchanged, touching, leastSeparation, mostSeparation."
| newGroup firstIcon firstRightSide secondIcon secondLeftSide minimumSeparation
maximumSeparation newLeftSide newSeparation separation |
horizontalAbutment == #unchanged **ifTrue**: [↑self].

"First, sort horizontally."
newGroup ← (subViews **asSortedCollection**: [:a :b |
    (a **displayBox origin x** < b **displayBox origin x**) **or**: [
    (a **displayBox origin x** = b **displayBox origin x**) **and**: [
    (a **displayBox corner x** <= b **displayBox corner x**)]]]) **asArray**.

"Second, determine the minimum and maximum separations between icons."
firstIcon ← newGroup **at**: 1. firstRightSide ← firstIcon **displayBox corner x**.
secondIcon ← newGroup **at**: 2. secondLeftSide ← secondIcon **displayBox origin x**.
minimumSeparation ← maximumSeparation ← secondLeftSide - firstRightSide.

(newGroup **copyFrom**: 3 **to**: newGroup **size**)
    inject: secondIcon **displayBox corner x into**: [:lastRightSide :icon |
        newLeftSide ← icon **displayBox origin x**.
        newSeparation ← newLeftSide - lastRightSide.
        minimumSeparation ← minimumSeparation **min**: newSeparation.
        maximumSeparation ← maximumSeparation **max**: newSeparation.
        icon **displayBox corner x**].

"Watch out for overlapping icons."
minimumSeparation ← minimumSeparation **max**: 0.
maximumSeparation ← maximumSeparation **max**: 0.

"Third, determine the separation to use."
separation ← (Array **with**: 0 **with**: minimumSeparation **with**: maximumSeparation)
    at: (#(touching leastSeparation mostSeparation) **indexOf**: horizontalAbutment).

"Fourth, make the changes."
(newGroup **copyFrom**: 2 **to**: newGroup **size**)
    inject: firstRightSide **into**: [:lastRightSide :icon |
        icon **moveTo**: (lastRightSide+separation)@(icon **displayBox origin y**).
        icon **displayBox corner x**]

adjustVerticalAbutment

"Adjust the vertical abutment of all icons in the group - verticalAbutment options:
unchanged, touching, leastSeparation, mostSeparation."
| newGroup firstIcon firstBottom secondIcon secondTop minimumSeparation
maximumSeparation newTop newSeparation separation |
verticalAbutment == #unchanged **ifTrue**: [↑self].

"First, sort vertically."
newGroup ← (subViews **asSortedCollection**: [:a :b |
    (a **displayBox origin y** < b **displayBox origin y**) **or**: [
    (a **displayBox origin y** = b **displayBox origin y**) **and**: [
    (a **displayBox corner y** <= b **displayBox corner y**)]]]) **asArray**.

"Second, determine the minimum and maximum separations between icons."
firstIcon ← newGroup **at**: 1. firstBottom ← firstIcon **displayBox corner y**.
secondIcon ← newGroup **at**: 2. secondTop ← secondIcon **displayBox origin y**.
minimumSeparation ← maximumSeparation ← secondTop - firstBottom.

(newGroup **copyFrom**: 3 **to**: newGroup **size**)
    inject: secondIcon **displayBox corner y into**: [:lastBottom :icon |
        newTop ← icon **displayBox origin y**.
        newSeparation ← newTop - lastBottom.
        minimumSeparation ← minimumSeparation **min**: newSeparation.
        maximumSeparation ← maximumSeparation **max**: newSeparation.
        icon **displayBox corner y**].

"Watch out for overlapping icons."
minimumSeparation ← minimumSeparation **max**: 0.
maximumSeparation ← maximumSeparation **max**: 0.

"Third, determine the separation to use."
separation ← (Array **with**: 0 **with**: minimumSeparation **with**: maximumSeparation)
    at: (#(touching leastSeparation mostSeparation) **indexOf**: verticalAbutment).

"Fourth, make the changes."
(newGroup **copyFrom**: 2 **to**: newGroup **size**)
    inject: firstBottom **into**: [:lastBottom :icon |
        icon **moveTo**: (icon **displayBox origin x**)@(lastBottom+separation).
        icon **displayBox corner y**]

The secondary alignment protocol provided in abstract class **WindowMakerIcon** includes the following operations in addition to the operations for moving and resizing discussed in Sect. 8.4.3.

Class WindowMakerIcon

class	WindowMakerIcon
superclass	ExtendedSwitchView
instance variables	...

alignment window support

changeWidth: aDisplayCoordinateInteger
    self **growTo**: aDisplayCoordinateInteger @ self **displayBox height**

changeHeight: aDisplayCoordinateInteger
    self **growTo**: self **displayBox extent x** @ aDisplayCoordinateInteger

changeTop: aDisplayCoordinateInteger
    self **moveBy**: 0 @ (aDisplayCoordinateInteger - self **displayBox origin y**)

changeBottom: aDisplayCoordinateInteger
    self **moveBy**: 0 @ (aDisplayCoordinateInteger - self **displayBox corner y**)

changeLeftSide: aDisplayCoordinateInteger
    self **moveBy**: (aDisplayCoordinateInteger - self **displayBox origin x**) @ 0

changeRightSide: aDisplayCoordinateInteger
    self **moveBy**: (aDisplayCoordinateInteger - self **displayBox corner x**) @ 0

changeMiddleHorizontally: aDisplayCoordinateInteger
    self **moveBy**: (aDisplayCoordinateInteger - self **displayBox center x**) @ 0

changeMiddleVertically: aDisplayCoordinateInteger
    self **moveBy**: 0 @ (aDisplayCoordinateInteger - self **displayBox center y**)

The Bordering and Coloring Window

When a designer chooses the *border/color* entry in the master controller's yellow button pop-up menu (the associated selector is shown next for ease of reference), the intent is to be operating on the currently selected icons where group icons are viewed transparently. If no icon is selected, this is interpreted to mean the master icon. We don't provide a designer with the capability to change the border width or inside color of an individual group icon.

Class WindowMakerMasterIconController

class	WindowMakerMasterIconController
superclass	MouseMenuController
instance variables	...

menu messages (options windows)

borderAndColor
    | selections |
    (selections ← view **ungroupedSelections**) **isEmpty**
        ifTrue: [selections ← Array **with**: view].
    self **popUpWithoutCancel**: #borderingAndColoring **onGroup**: selections

The bordering and coloring window subscribes to an **immediate action philosophy** and to a **display what is known philosophy.** The immediate action philosophy implies that window changes apply immediately. Currently, there is no facility for canceling the changes. The display what is known facility must resolve what is to be done if, for example, the icons affected do not all have the same color. Our choice in such a situation is to display no choice at all. The window shown in Fig. 8.30 indicates that all affected icons have a gray color. If that were not the case, no color choice would be indicated. The philosophy also extends to modifications. For example, if we decide to change the width of the top border by changing the 1 to the right of *top* to 2 (and accepting the change), then the '1 point' selection in the menu subwindow would be automatically deselected — no selection would be indicated since the menu subwindow indicates a border width that applies all around the icon (the top, left and right sides, and bottom). Likewise, selecting '2 point' in the menu subwindow would cause all four text entries to the left to change automatically to 2. Finally, coloring can be achieved by selecting either one of the switches to the left of the color column or by selecting one of the color column members itself; i.e., there are actually two columns of switches — one for a check mark and another to display the actual color.

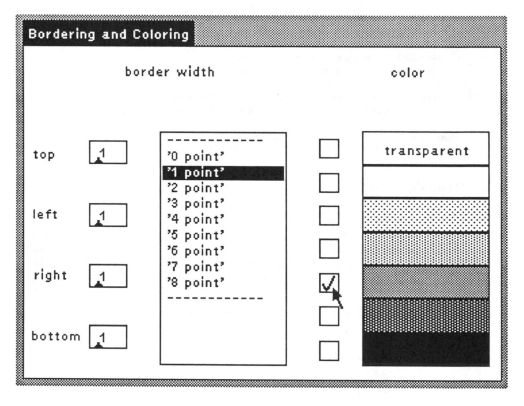

Figure 8.30 The bordering and coloring window.

With so many text subwindows and switches, it is clear that a large number of distinct messages will have to be processed. For the bordering/coloring window of Fig. 8.30, the protocol is as follows:

Inside Smalltalk

the top, left, right, and bottom text subwindows
    how the text window determines what to display:
      1.   groupIcon **getTopThickness**
      2.   groupIcon **getLeftThickness**
      3.   groupIcon **getRightThickness**
      4.   groupIcon **getBottomThickness**
    what happens if the designer accepts a modification in the text subwindow:
      1.   groupIcon **changeTopThickness**: aText
      2.   groupIcon **changeLeftThickness**: aText
      3.   groupIcon **changeRightThickness**: aText
      4.   groupIcon **changeBottomThickness**: aText
    what yellow button pop-up menu is associated with the text subwindow:
      1.   groupIcon **acceptCancelYellowButtonMenu**
    the update symbol to make the text subwindow react:
        #border

the middle all-around border width menu subwindow:
    how the menu subwindow determines the initial menu entries:
      1.   groupIcon **getBordersMenuList**
    how the menu subwindow determines which menu entry to select:
      1.   groupIcon **getBordersMenuSelection**
    what happens if the designer makes a menu entry selection:
      1.   groupIcon **changeBordersMenuSelection**: aStringOrNil
    the update symbol to make the menu subwindow react:
        #color

the check mark and color columns
    how the check mark switch determines if it should be on:
      1.   groupIcon **isInsideColor**: nil "transparent"
      2.   groupIcon **isInsideColor**: #white
      3.   groupIcon **isInsideColor**: #veryLightGray
      4.   groupIcon **isInsideColor**: #lightGray
      5.   groupIcon **isInsideColor**: #gray
      6.   groupIcon **isInsideColor**: #darkGray
      7.   groupIcon **isInsideColor**: #black
    how the color column switch determines if it should be on:
      1.   groupIcon **isNil** "always off"
    what the check mark and color column switch does if it is pressed:
      1.   groupIcon **makeInsideColor**: nil "transparent"
      2.   groupIcon **makeInsideColor**: #white
      3.   groupIcon **makeInsideColor**: #veryLightGray
      4.   groupIcon **makeInsideColor**: #lightGray
      5.   groupIcon **makeInsideColor**: #gray
      6.   groupIcon **makeInsideColor**: #darkGray
      7.   groupIcon **makeInsideColor**: #black
    the update symbol to make the check mark and color column switch react:
        #color

Because this window subscribes to the immediate action philosophy and no cancel facility is provided, there is no need to provide special instance variables in the group icon class. By using the group sequencing facility, it is possible to directly modify all affected icons via messages that already exist in abstract class WindowMakerIcon or its superclasses.

Class WindowMakerGroupIcon

class	WindowMakerGroupIcon
superclass	WindowMakerIcon
instance variables	....

border window messages

getTopThickness
    ↑self **privateGetThickness:** #top
changeTopThickness: aText
    ↑self **privateChangeThickness:** #top: **from:** aText

getLeftThickness
    ↑self **privateGetThickness:** #left
changeLeftThickness: aText
    ↑self **privateChangeThickness:** #left: **from:** aText

getRightThickness
    ↑self **privateGetThickness:** #right
changeRightThickness: aText
    ↑self **privateChangeThickness:** #right: **from:** aText

getBottomThickness
    ↑self **privateGetThickness:** #bottom
changeBottomThickness: aText
    ↑self **privateChangeThickness:** #bottom: **from:** aText

privateGetThickness: sideSymbol
    ↑(self **groupGet:** [:icon | icon **borderWidth perform:** sideSymbol] **ifUnequal:** [↑Text **new**])
        printString asText

privateChangeThickness: sideSymbol **from:** aText
    | result |
    result ← Compiler **evaluate:** aText.
    (result **isKindOf:** Integer) **ifFalse:** [↑false].
    self **groupDo:** [:icon | icon **borderWidth perform:** sideSymbol **with:** result].
    self **changed:** #border.
    ↑true

border window messages

getBordersMenuList
    ↑(0 **to:** 8) **collect:** [:index | index **printString**, ' point']

getBordersMenuSelection
    | border |
    border ← self **groupGet:** [:icon | icon **borderWidth**] **ifUnequal:** [↑nil].
    border = ((0@0 **extent:** 0@0) **translateBy:** border **left**) **ifFalse:** [↑nil].
    ↑border **left printString**, ' point'

changeBordersMenuSelection: aStringOrNil
    | border |
    aStringOrNil **isNil ifTrue:** [↑self].
    border ← (aStringOrNil **at:** 1) **digitValue**.
    self **groupDo:** [:icon | icon **borderWidth:** border].
    self **changed:** #border

color window messages

isInsideColor: aColorSymbol
    ⌐ actualColor ⌐
    actualColor ← aColorSymbol **isNil ifTrue:** [nil] **ifFalse:** [self **decodeColor:** aColorSymbol].
    self **groupDo:** [:icon ⌐ (icon **insideColor** == actualColor) **ifFalse:** [↑false]].
    ↑true

makeInsideColor: aColorSymbol
    ⌐ actualColor ⌐
    actualColor ← aColorSymbol **isNil ifTrue:** [nil] **ifFalse:** [self **decodeColor:** aColorSymbol].
    self **groupDo:** [:icon ⌐ icon **insideColor:** actualColor].
    self **changed:** #color

Class WindowMakerIcon

class	WindowMakerIcon
superclass	ExtendedSwitchView
instance variables	...

encoding/decoding

decodeColor: aColorSymbol
    aColorSymbol == #nil
        ifTrue: [↑nil]
        ifFalse: [↑Form **perform:** aColorSymbol]

The Size Options Window

To avoid the default, a designer has to specify the minimum and maximum window sizes for his application window. This is done by choosing the *set minimum and maximum size* option in the master controller's yellow button pop-up menu (the associated selector is repeated next for ease of reference).

Class WindowMakerMasterIconController

class	WindowMakerMasterIconController
superclass	MouseMenuController
instance variables	...

menu messages (options windows)

setSize
    "The view below is the master icon."
    self **popUpWithoutCancel:** #masterSizing **onGroup:** (OrderedCollection **with:** view)

As can be seen in Fig. 8.31, the sizes can be set by providing explicit point sizes in corresponding text subwindows or by clicking on a switch that causes a framing rectangle to appear — only the extent (not the actual position) of the rectangle is recorded.

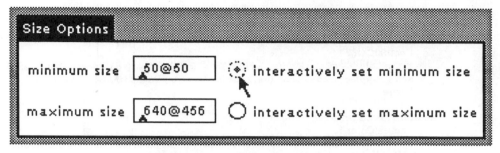

Figure 8.31 The size options window.

In this case, the size options window protocol in class WindowMakerGroupIcon assumes that only one icon is in the group.

the text subwindows:
   how the text subwindow determines what to display:
      1.   masterIcon **getMinimumSize**
      2.   masterIcon **getMaximumSize**
   what happens if the designer accepts a modification in the text subwindow:
      1.   masterIcon **changeMinimumSize:** aText
      2.   masterIcon **changeMaximumSize:** aText
   what yellow button pop-up menu is associated with the text subwindow:
      1.   masterIcon **acceptCancelYellowButtonMenu**
   the update symbol to make the text subwindow react:
      #sizing

the switches:
   how the switch determines if it should be on:
      1.   masterIcon **isNil** "always off"
   what the switch does if it is pressed:
      1.   masterIcon **setSize:** #minimum
      2.   masterIcon **setSize:** #maximum
   the update symbol to make the switch react:
      nil "never reacts"

The protocol for changing the minimum and maximum size of the application window is provided in class WindowMakerGroupIcon and relayed to the contained icon, the master icon. The code shown next uses the standard group sequencing protocol for modifying the contained icon. However, unlike previous options windows, it makes the explicit assumption that only one icon is contained by the group. Thus, **getMinimumSize**, for example, returns the first (and therefore only) value encountered.

Class WindowMakerGroupIcon

class   WindowMakerGroupIcon
superclass   WindowMakerIcon
instance variables   ...

instance methods

master sizing window messages

getMinimumSize
   self **groupDo:** [:icon | ↑icon **minimumSize printString asText**]

changeMinimumSize: aText
    | result |
    result ← Compiler **evaluate:** aText.
    (result **isKindOf:** Point) **ifFalse:** [↑false].
    self **groupDo:** [:icon | icon **minimumSize:** result].
    ↑true

getMaximumSize
    self **groupDo:** [:icon | ↑icon **maximumSize printString asText**]

changeMaximumSize: aText
    | result |
    result ← Compiler **evaluate:** aText.
    (result **isKindOf:** Point) **ifFalse:** [↑false].
    self **groupDo:** [:icon | icon **maximumSize:** result].
    ↑true

setSize: aSymbol
    "aSymbol is either #minimum or #maximum."
    self **groupDo:** [:icon |
        icon **perform:** (aSymbol, 'Size:') **asSymbol with:** Rectangle **fromUser extent**].
    self **changed:** #sizing

The master icon class (see Sect. 8.4.6, *The WindowMakerMasterIcon Class*) provides the access and modification methods **minimumSize**, **minimumSize:**, **maximumSize**, and **maximumSize:** used above. The minimum and maximum size defaults are '50@50' and 'Display **boundingBox extent**' respectively.

The Background Windows

If all selected icons are switches or pictures, the background for the icons can be specified by selecting the *background* entry in the master controller's yellow button pop-up menu. One of two windows will appear — either a general window, such as shown in Fig. 8.32, or a more restrictive window, such as shown in Fig. 8.33, if at least one of the icons is a combined switch/picture icon. The corresponding yellow button selectors, respectively **background** and **switchAndPictureBackground**, are repeated next for ease of reference. Both windows use models that are temporary group icons containing the nongroup members of the selected icons.

Class WindowMakerMasterIconController

class	WindowMakerMasterIconController
superclass	MouseMenuController
instance variables	....

menu messages (options windows)

background
    self **popUpWithoutCancel:** #background **onGroup:** view **ungroupedSelections**

switchAndPictureBackground
    self **popUpWithoutCancel:** #switchAndPictureBackground
        onGroup: view **ungroupedSelections**

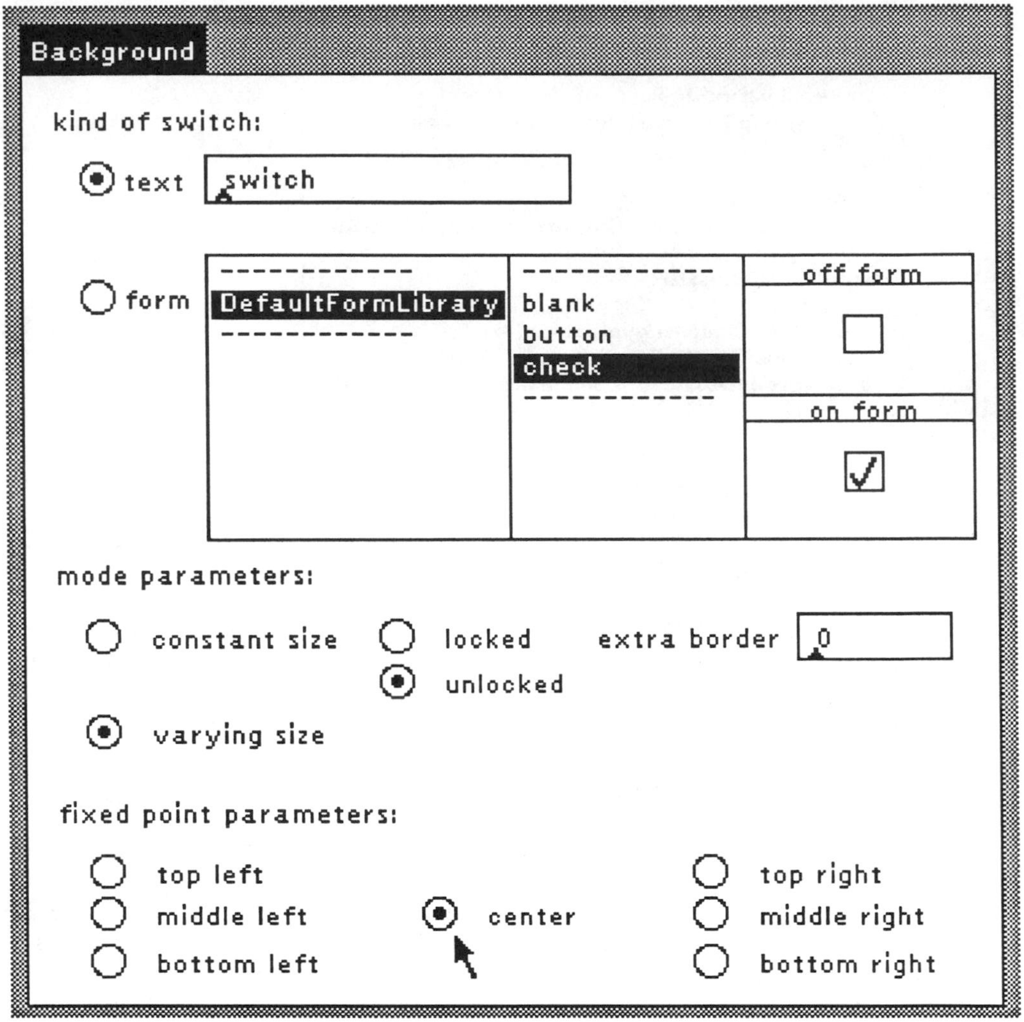

Figure 8.32 The background window for switches and pictures with no combined switch/pictures.

The specialized background window in Fig. 8.33 uses a subset of the pluggable protocol provided by the more general window in Fig. 8.32. We can see that Fig. 8.33 consists of the top portion of Fig. 8.32, reorganized to provide the switch information first and the picture information second (the icons being affected are switch/pictures).

A variety of distinct messages has to be processed to provide the functionality of Fig. 8.32. A summary is provided next.

kind of switch:
    the text and form switches
        how the text and form switches determine if they should be on:
            1.   groupIcon **isPictureVariety**: #text
            2.   groupIcon **isPictureVariety**: #form
        what the text and form switches do if they are pressed:
            1.   groupIcon **changePictureVariety**: #text
            2.   groupIcon **changePictureVariety**: #form
        the update symbol to make the text and form switches react:
            #pictureVariety
    the text subwindow associated with the text switch
        how the text subwindow determines what to display:
            1.   groupIcon **getPictureString**
        what happens if the designer accepts a change in the text subwindow:
            1.   groupIcon **changePictureString**: aText
        what yellow button pop-up menu is associated with the text subwindow:
            1.   groupIcon **acceptCancelYellowButtonMenu**
    the update symbol to make the text and form switches react:
            nil "never reacts"
    the form library subwindow associated with the form switch
        how the form library determines what to display:
            It is an external window referencing an extended view on a librarian.
            This view is autonomous (see method **subView** in Sect. 8.2.3, *Form Librarians*)
        what happens if the designer changes the pictures in the library subwindow:
            The subwindow asks all dependents to update their #pictures. The groupIcon is a dependent. It reacts with its own special **update**: method.
        the update symbol to make the library subwindow react:
            External windows have no update symbols.

mode parameters:
    the constant size and varying size switches
        how the switches determine if they should be on:
            1.   groupIcon **isMode**: #constant
            2.   groupIcon **isMode**: #varying
        what the switches do if they are pressed:
            1.   groupIcon **changeMode**: #constant
            2.   groupIcon **changeMode**: #varying
        the update symbol to make the constant size and varying size switches react:
            #mode
    the locked and unlocked switches
        how the switches determine if they should be on:
            1.   groupIcon **isLocking**: true
            2.   groupIcon **isLocking**: false
        what the switches do if they are pressed:
            1.   groupIcon **changeLocking**: true
            2.   groupIcon **changeLocking**: false
        the update symbol to make the locked and unlocked switches react:
            #locking

the extra border text subwindow:
   how the text subwindow determines what to display:
      1.   groupIcon **getLockedSizeExpansion**
   what happens if the designer accepts a change in the text subwindow:
      1.   groupIcon **changeLockedSizeExpansion**: aText
   what yellow button pop-up menu is associated with the text subwindow:
      1.   groupIcon **acceptCancelYellowButtonMenu**
   the update symbol to make the extra border subwindow react:
         nil "never reacts"

fixed point parameters:
   how the switches determine if they should be on:
      1.   groupIcon **isFixedPointEncoding**: #fixTopLeft
      2.   groupIcon **isFixedPointEncoding**: #fixMiddleLeft
      3.   groupIcon **isFixedPointEncoding**: #fixBottomLeft
      4.   groupIcon **isFixedPointEncoding**: #fixCenter
      5.   groupIcon **isFixedPointEncoding**: #fixTopRight
      6.   groupIcon **isFixedPointEncoding**: #fixMiddleRight
      7.   groupIcon **isFixedPointEncoding**: #fixBottomRight
   what the switches do if they are pressed:
      1.   groupIcon **changeFixedPointEncoding**: #fixTopLeft
      2.   groupIcon **changeFixedPointEncoding**: #fixMiddleLeft
      3.   groupIcon **changeFixedPointEncoding**: #fixBottomLeft
      4.   groupIcon **changeFixedPointEncoding**: #fixCenter
      5.   groupIcon **changeFixedPointEncoding**: #fixTopRight
      6.   groupIcon **changeFixedPointEncoding**: #fixMiddleRight
      7.   groupIcon **changeFixedPointEncoding**: #fixBottomRight
   the update symbol to make the switches react:
         #fixedPoint

Because the background window deals with switches and pictures, it is clear that the capability to access and modify switch and picture attributes is crucial to background windows.

Class WindowMakerSwitchOrPictureIcon

class   WindowMakerSwitchOrPictureIcon
superclass   WindowMakerIcon
instance variables   pictureVariety pictureString pictureFormPathName lockedSizeExp

instance methods

instance initialization

initialize
    super **initialize**.
    pictureVariety ← #text. "or #form"
    pictureString ← 'picture'.
    pictureFormPathName ← #(DefaultFormLibrary button).
    lockedSizeExpansion ← 0

access/modification

pictureVariety
    ↑pictureVariety
pictureVariety: aSymbol
    pictureVariety ← aSymbol

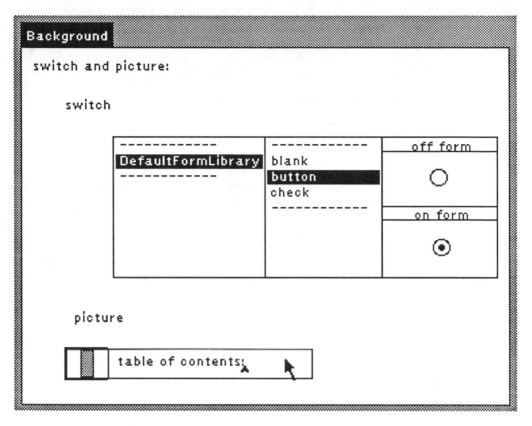

Figure 8.33 The background window if at least one of the icons is a combined switch/picture icon.

access/modification (continued)

pictureString
    ↑pictureString
pictureString: aString
    pictureString ← aString

pictureFormPathName
    ↑pictureFormPathName
pictureFormPathName: anArray
    pictureFormPathName ← anArray

lockedSizeExpansion
    ↑lockedSizeExpansion
lockedSizeExpansion: anInteger
    lockedSizeExpansion ← anInteger

The protocol for background windows is provided by class **WindowMakerGroup-Icon.** Because of the sheer number of subwindows, this protocol is substantial.

Class WindowMakerGroupIcon

class	WindowMakerGroupIcon
superclass	WindowMakerIcon
instance variables	librarianForBackground ...

background window messages

isPictureVariety: aSymbol
    self **groupDo**: [:icon | icon **pictureVariety** == aSymbol **ifFalse**: [↑false]].
    ↑true

changePictureVariety: aSymbol
    self **groupDo**: [:icon | icon **pictureVariety**: aSymbol; **computeLabel**].
    self **changed**: #pictureVariety

Like the bordering and coloring window, the background window also subscribes to the **display what is known philosophy**. If, for example, distinct icons have different picture strings, an empty text string is displayed. Recall also that all text windows use the generic yellow button pop-up menu provided by method **acceptCancelYellowButtonMenu** (see *The WindowMakerGroupIcon* subsection).

background window messages

getPictureString
    ↑(self **groupGet**: [:icon | icon **pictureString**] **ifUnequal**: [↑Text **new**]) **asText**

changePictureString: aText
    | aString |
    aString ← aText **asString**.
    self **groupDo**: [:icon | icon **pictureString**: aString; **computeLabel**].
    ↑true

The form library subwindow is an example of an **external** window. When the form librarian subwindow is integrated (automatically) with the background window, the model associated with it (if we didn't do anything special) would be the same group icon that is the model for all the other components of the background window. To provide it with a more relevant model, a form librarian, we associate a preopening method with the background window that (1) extracts the librarian view from the background window and (2) explicitly associates a new form librarian as its model. When we designed this librarian view, we designed it to be an extended view (as opposed to an extended standard system view) by specifying that it not be a top view in the master icon interface window and we provided it with the name #librarian so that we could reference it in the preopening method.

When the designer makes selections in the form library subwindow, it is clear that pluggable messages will be sent to the corresponding model — in this case, the form librarian. How can this result in changes to the members of the group icon? Clearly, some mechanism is needed to correlate the two. Our goal is the following: When the on and off pictures in the form library change, we want the path name for the new pictures; e.g., #(DefaultFormLibrary button), to be associated with the group icon members. But new pictures in the form library are displayed as a consequence (either directly or indirectly) of the message 'self **changed**: #pictures' sent by some part of the form library window. To get the group icon to react, we make the group icon a dependent of the form librarian. Since the 'self **changed**: #pictures' message causes all dependents, including the group icon to be sent an '**update**: #pictures' message, it is sufficient to provide an **update**: method in the group icon that will retrieve the path name from the librarian.

To review this scenario, the preopening method creates a new librarian, extracts the librarian view, and sets the librarian as the model for the librarian view. Additionally, it makes the group icon a dependent of the librarian. When the designer makes a form selection in the library subwindow's middle menu pane, a 'self **changed**: #pictures' message is sent by the librarian as a result of the selection. This causes (1) new off- and on-forms to be displayed, and (2) all dependents to react to an '**update**: #pictures' message — this includes the group icon. The group icon explicitly asks the librarian for the path name of the selected pictures. If there is a selection (the path name is non-nil), the path name is associated with all members (subviews) of the group. This path name is used by member icons only when the form switch (as opposed to the text switch) is depressed. Finally, the dependent link is undone in the postclosing method.

generic window support (preopening/postclosing)

```
preOpenBackground: anExtendedStandardSystemView
    "USED by Switch, Picture, and SwitchAndPicture."
    | librarian path librarianView |
    librarian ← FormLibrarian new. self librarianForBackground: librarian.
    librarianView ← anExtendedStandardSystemView viewNamed: #librarian.
    librarianView resetModels; models: librarian.
    librarian addDependent: self.
        "handled by special update: method in WindowMakerGroup"
    path ← subViews first pictureFormPathName.
    (subViews detect: [:icon | icon pictureFormPathName ~= path] ifNone: [nil]) isNil
        ifTrue: [librarian selectedPathName: path]

postCloseBackground: anExtendedStandardSystemView
    "USED by Switch, Picture, and SwitchAndPicture."
    self librarianForBackground removeDependent: self
```

background window support

```
librarianForBackground
    ↑librarianForBackground

librarianForBackground: aLibrarian
    librarianForBackground ← aLibrarian

update: aSymbol
    "Provide the connection from switches and pictures to the librarian view. See
    method preOpenBackground: in WindowMakerGroupIcon."
    | path |
    aSymbol == #pictures
        ifTrue: [
            (path ← librarianForBackground selectedPathName) isNil ifFalse: [
                subViews do: [:icon |
                    icon pictureFormPathName: path; computeLabel]]]
        ifFalse: [super update: aSymbol]
```

The mode switches provide the designer with the capability to determine and specify whether or not the switch or picture is to be fixed-size or varying-size. This capability is inherited from the WindowMakerIcon's superclass — ExtendedSwitchView.

background window messages

isMode: aSymbol
    self **groupDo**: [:icon | icon **mode** == aSymbol **ifFalse**: [↑false]].
    ↑true

changeMode: aSymbol
    aSymbol == #varying
        ifTrue: [
            self **groupDo**: [:icon | icon **sizeLocked**: false; **mode**: #varying].
            self **changed**: #mode; **changed**: #locking]
        ifFalse: [
            self **groupDo**: [:icon | icon **mode**: #constant].
            self **changed**: #mode]

As might be deduced from the layout of Fig. 8.32, locking/unlocking applies only to constant-size icons. Consequently, clicking on the mode switch to change to a varying-size icon automatically unlocks the icon (if it was locked). Additionally, locking an icon automatically changes it to a constant-size icon. Recall (see Sect. 8.4.3, *Displaying, Moving, and Sizing*) that query and modification messages **sizeLocked** and **sizeLocked:** are provided in abstract class WindowMakerIcon.

background window messages

isLocking: aBoolean
    self **groupDo**: [:icon | icon **sizeLocked** == aBoolean **ifFalse**: [↑false]].
    ↑true

changeLocking: aBoolean
    aBoolean
        ifTrue: [
            self **groupDo**: [:icon |
                icon **sizeLocked**: true; **mode**: #constant; **computeLabel**].
            self **changed**: #mode; **changed**: #locking]
        ifFalse: [
            self **groupDo**: [:icon | icon **sizeLocked**: false].
            self **changed**: #locking]

When a constant-size icon is specified by depressing the constant-size mode switch, the change of mode triggers a computation to determine the actual size of the icon. This size is computed as a function of the icon's background; i.e., the specified string or form (the kind of switch information). Generally, the size is computed to contain the background information exactly; i.e., there is no padding. However, it is possible to provide additional white space around the icon by specifying an amount to be used for **extra border**. This extra border information is maintained in instance variable *lockedSizeExpansion* of class **WindowMakerSwitchOrPicture** (as presented previously).

getLockedSizeExpansion
    ↑(self **groupGet**: [:icon | icon **lockedSizeExpansion**] **ifUnequal**: [↑Text **new**])
        printString asText

changeLockedSizeExpansion: aText
    | integer |
    integer ← Number **readFrom**: aText **asString**.
    self **groupDo**: [:icon | icon **lockedSizeExpansion**: integer; **computeLabel**].
    ↑true

As discussed in the extended switch view class of Sect. 8.3.11, constant-size windows need a fixed point to specify which portion of the window is to serve as the anchor when the containing window is resized. If the fixed point is the center of an icon, for example, then this anchor point will move when the container window is resized. However, the icon will be positioned in such a way that its center is at that anchor point. Generally, the two most useful fixed points are the middle left and center.

background window messages

isFixedPointEncoding: aSymbol
    self **groupDo**: [:icon | icon **fixedPointEncoding** == aSymbol **ifFalse**: [↑false]].
    ↑true

changeFixedPointEncoding: aSymbol
    self **groupDo**: [:icon | icon **perform**: aSymbol].
    self **changed**: #fixedPoint

The Output (Make Method) Window

Once the designer has finalized his application window, he can select the *make method* entry in the icon window pane's yellow button pop-up menu to output the application window. An output window, as shown in Fig. 8.34, will appear. The designer can specify where to output the method (in the transcript, as a class method, or an instance method), how to output it (as an array — an encoding or a view — the encoding is incorporated to permit later editing). As expected, the class name, method category, and method name must be provided if the method is to be output either as a class or instance method. Additionally, an overflow category (which could be the same as the method category) must be provided in case the output doesn't fit in one method. None of this information is needed if only the encoding is to be output in the transcript.

Once all the information is provided, the designer closes the window using the standard blue button pop-up menu. A cancel menu item is also provided if the designer has changed his mind. Note that changes made in the output options window are permanent. If the designer decides to output the application window a second time (perhaps because modifications were made), the previously provided output window information will be in the window when it pops up a second time.

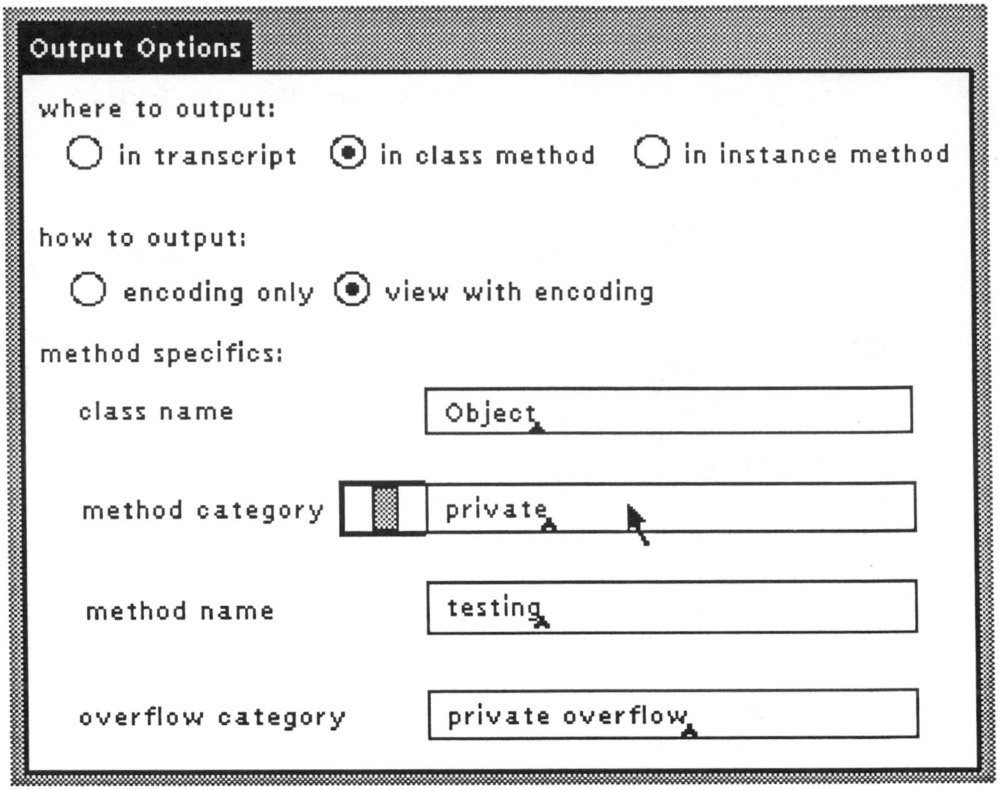

Figure 8.34 The output (make method) window.

With only switch and text subwindows, the number of pluggable messages is relatively small. For the output window in Fig. 8.34, the protocol is as follows:

where to output:
    how the switch determines if it should be on:
        1.   groupIcon **outputOptionAt**: #destination **is**: #transcript
        2.   groupIcon **outputOptionAt**: #destination **is**: #classMethod
        3.   groupIcon **outputOptionAt**: #destination **is**: #instanceMethod
    what the switch does if it is pressed:
        1.   groupIcon **outputOptionPutText**: #transcript **at**: #destination
        2.   groupIcon **outputOptionPutText**: #classMethod **at**: #destination
        3.   groupIcon **outputOptionPutText**: #instanceMethod **at**: #destination
    the update symbol to make the switch react:
        #outputOption

how to output:
    how the switch determines if it should be on:
        1.   groupIcon **outputOptionAt**: #encoding **is**: #encoded
        2.   groupIcon **outputOptionAt**: #encoding **is**: #notEncoded
    what the switch does if it is pressed:
        1.   groupIcon **outputOptionPutText**: #encoded **at**: #encoding
        2.   groupIcon **outputOptionPutText**: #notEncoded **at**: #encoding
    the update symbol to make the switch react:
        #outputOption

method specifics:
 how the text subwindow determines what to display:
  1. groupIcon **outputOptionTextAt**: #methodClass
  2. groupIcon **outputOptionTextAt**: #methodCategory
  3. groupIcon **outputOptionTextAt**: #methodName
  4. groupIcon **outputOptionTextAt**: #overflowCategory
 what happens if the designer accepts a change in the text subwindow:
  1. groupIcon **outputOptionPutText**: aText **at**: #methodClass
  2. groupIcon **outputOptionPutText**: aText **at**: #methodCategory
  3. groupIcon **outputOptionPutText**: aText **at**: #methodName
  4. groupIcon **outputOptionPutText**: aText **at**: #overflowCategory
 what yellow button pop-up menu is associated with the text subwindow:
  1. groupIcon **acceptCancelYellowButtonMenu**
 the update symbol to make the text and form switches react:
   nil "never reacts"

The pluggable messages are provided in class **WindowMakerGroupIcon**. Unlike previous options windows, we avoid the group sequencing operations and instead make use of the more restrictive **isolatedGroupMember** method for retrieving the one instance of the group icon — the master icon.

Support methods **outputOption**, **outputOption:**, **outputOptionAt:**, and **output-OptionAt:put:** are provided by class **WindowMakerMasterIcon** (see Sect. 8.4.6, *The WindowMakerMasterIcon Class*).

Class WindowMakerGroupIcon

class   WindowMakerGroupIcon
superclass   WindowMakerIcon
instance variables ...

method window messages

outputOptionAt: index **is**: aSymbol
 | icon |
 icon ← self **isolatedGroupMember**.
 ↑(icon **outputOptionAt**: index) == aSymbol

outputOptionPutText: aText **at**: index
 | data icon |
 data ← (index == #methodCategory) | (index == #overflowCategory)
  ifTrue: [aText **asString**]
  ifFalse: [aText **asString asSymbol**].
 icon ← self **isolatedGroupMember**.
 icon **outputOptionAt**: index **put**: data.
 self **changed**: #outputOption.
 ↑true

outputOptionTextAt: index
 | icon |
 icon ← self **isolatedGroupMember**.
 ↑(icon **outputOptionAt**: index) **asText**

generic window support (preopening/postclosing)

postCloseMakeMethod: anExtendedStandardSystemView
    "Make the method if not canceled. USED by Master."

    | masterIcon className category methodName class time overflowCategory |

    "Is it canceled?"
    anExtendedStandardSystemView **controller canceled ifTrue**: [↑self].

    "No, output it."
    masterIcon ← self **isolatedGroupMember**.
    (masterIcon **outputOptionAt**: #destination) == #transcript
        ifTrue: [
            Transcript
                cr; nextPutAll: (
                      (masterIcon **outputOptionAt**: #encoding) == #encoded
                          ifTrue: [WindowMaker **encode**: masterIcon]
                          ifFalse: [masterIcon **asView storeString**]);
                show: ' '. ↑self].

    className ← (masterIcon **outputOptionAt**: #methodClass) **asSymbol**.
    category ← masterIcon **outputOptionAt**: #methodCategory.
    methodName ← (masterIcon **outputOptionAt**: #methodName) **asSymbol**.
    overflowCategory ← masterIcon **outputOptionAt**: #overflowCategory.
    class ← Smalltalk **at**: className
        ifAbsent: [↑self **error**: 'class ', className, ' does not exist. Proceed to cancel'].
    (masterIcon **outputOptionAt**: #destination) == #classMethod
        ifTrue: [class ← class **class**].

    Transcript **tab; show**: 'Compiling Window ', methodName, ' ....'.
    time ← WindowMakerMasterIconController **timeFor**: [
        (masterIcon **outputOptionAt**: #encoding) == #encoded
            ifTrue: [
                ExtendedStandardSystemView **compileEncoding**: masterIcon **asView**
                    intoClass: class **method**: methodName **category**: category]
            ifFalse: [
                masterIcon **asView**
                    compileIntoClass: class **method**: methodName
                    category: category **overflow**: overflowCategory]].
    Transcript **show**:' done in ', time, '.'; **cr**

The Interface Window

To specify the interface for an application subwindow, the designer selects exactly one subwindow (or none if the master window is to be specified) and chooses the *external interface* menu entry associated with the yellow button pop-up menu in the icon container pane. The external interface entry will not appear if two or more icons are selected. Because only one icon is being specified, the interface window that pops up is unique to the class of icon selected. In general, the interface window permits interfacing information to be associated with the icon so that it will function properly when the application window is opened. Although the information is unique to the icon selected, the facility that provides the different interface window variations is placed centrally in the WindowMakerIcon abstract class. However, following our convention for all option windows, the pluggable messages are provided in the WindowMakerGroupIcon class. Example information needed for interfacing a subwindow with the application model might include

1. A **name** for the subwindow if it is to be referenced while preopening or postclosing the window.
2. An **update** symbol that enables the application model to cause the subwindow to update itself by having the application send itself a 'self **changed:** *updateSymbol*' message.

In general, the interfacing protocol will depend on the kind of subwindow provided. For example, for text windows (see Fig. 8.35), three specific interface messages must be specified.

1. The **getText** message; e.g., 'model **getTextFor:** #address'.
2. The **changeText** message; e.g., 'model **changeText:** #someText **for:** #address'.
3. The **getMenu** message; e.g., 'model **getYellowButtonMenu**'.

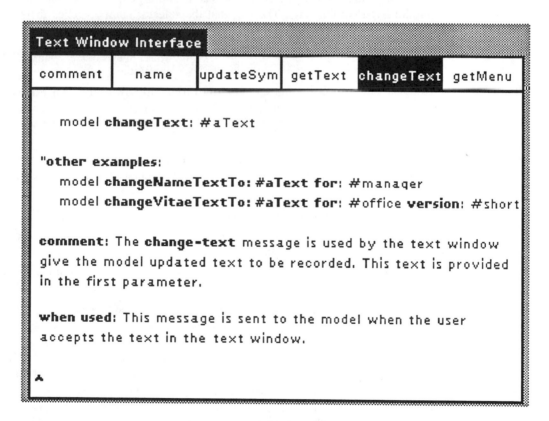

Figure 8.35 The interface for text windows.

Similarly, for switch windows (see Fig. 8.36), two specific interface messages are needed.

1. The **isOn** message; e.g., 'model **isSex**: #male'.
2. The **switch** message; e.g., 'model **changeSex**: #male'.

There are actually six distinct options windows for interface specification: one for master, text, menu, switch, picture, and external subwindows. In each case, the number of switches at the top is a function of the kind of subwindow. Consequently, it is useful to additionally provide each such interface window with a general description.

1. A **comment** (as shown in Fig. 8.35) that explains the special requirements for that kind of subwindow and provides a unifying description for the individual interface messages.

When the **isOn** switch in the interface window of Fig. 8.36, for example, is depressed, switch specific information appears in the bottom pane. Typically, this information consists of two parts:

1. A complete message with receiver, selector, and arguments; e.g., the message 'model **isOn**' in this case. The fact that the selector name matches the switch name is a coincidence.
2. A comment immediately below the message that explains the purpose of the message and special restrictions on the message (if any).

The designer can substitute this message by one of his own choosing and select *accept* in the yellow button pop-up menu. The substitute will replace the existing message if all specified restrictions are satisfied and if it is syntactically legal. Otherwise, an appropriate error message is generated.

Because there are more similarities than differences between the different kinds of interface windows, it is best to provide a common facility in an abstract class. The facility should satisfy several properties.

1. It should permit an unlimited number of entries.
2. It should permit each entry to be supplied with associated text that can be displayed. It would be nice if parts of the text could be in bold.
3. It should provide a compilation capability that can take into account individual restrictions.

The facility is imbedded in class **WindowMakerIcon** and intended for use as follows. When the interface to a switch icon, for example, is to be specified, the designer selects the switch icon and chooses the *external interface* entry in the yellow button pop-up menu (this was discussed in detail in Sect. 8.4.5, subsection *Yellow Button Activity (Pop-Up Option Menus)*). An interface window, as shown in Fig. 8.36, is constructed (method **interface** in Sect. 8.4.5) with the switch icon as the model for each part of the window. In addition, the view for the text pane at the bottom is explicitly retrieved and stored in the model as the *messageView*. All parts of the window consequently communicate with the switch icon using the protocol provided below. Of course, this protocol is available to all

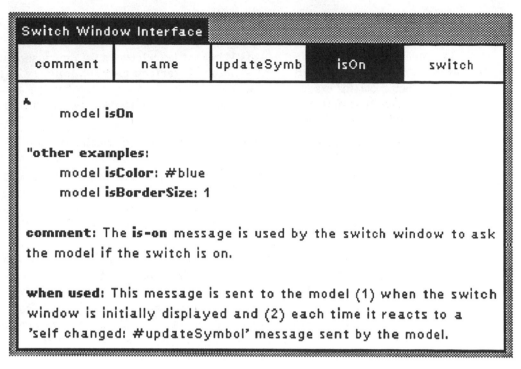

Figure 8.36 The interface for switch windows.

icons since it is provided in the abstract class **WindowMakerIcon**. For the particular window of Fig. 8.36, the protocol is as follows:

initialization:
1. message is set to #comment (the default).
2. messageView is set to the text view for the bottom pane.

how the switches at the top determine whether or not they are on:
1. switchIcon **isMessage:** #comment
2. switchIcon **isMessage:** #name
3. switchIcon **isMessage:** #updateSymbol
4. switchIcon **isMessage:** #isOn
5. switchIcon **isMessage:** #switch

what happens when a switch at the top is depressed:
1. switchIcon **message:** #comment
2. switchIcon **message:** #name
3. switchIcon **message:** #updateSymbol
4. switchIcon **message:** #isOn
5. switchIcon **message:** #switch

how the text pane at the bottom determines what to display:
1. switchIcon **messageSource**

what happens if we change and accept modified text in the bottom text pane:
1. switchIcon **messageSource:** aText

what happens if we reset the bottom text pane:
1. switchIcon **resetSource**

what happens if we accept modified text permanently in the bottom text pane:
1.   switchIcon **acceptPermanently**

The generic facility is provided in class **WindowMakerIcon**. In the presentation that follows, we consider only that part of the **WindowMakerIcon** protocol dealing with the external interface. Note, for example, that additional instance variables for the class are not divulged since they have nothing to do with the generic interface facility. In general, all icons are provided with the following instance variables:

1.   *message* — a symbol representing the currently selected switch in the top row of the interface window.

2.   *messageView* — the view at the bottom of the interface window, used to physically display the text selected by one of the switches.

3.   *messageInitializers* — a dictionary indexed by message symbols; the associated values are symbols for selectors that can be performed to obtain the initial source to be displayed in the message view.

4.   *messageSources* — a dictionary indexed by message symbols; the associated values consist of text. Initially, this is the text provided by the message initializers. If modified by the designer, it consists of the modified text.

5.   *messageCodings* — a dictionary indexed by message symbols; the associated values consist of an array of objects denoting the parsed source. For example, if the message source for key #isOn were 'model **isSex:** #male', the corresponding message coding would be #(model isSex: male).

6.   *messageParsers* — a dictionary indexed by message symbols; the associated values are symbols for selectors that can be used to parse the corresponding message source.

Initializing a New Icon's Interface Data

When a new icon is constructed, all instance variables except for *messageView* must be initialized; *messageView* is initialized when the interface window is constructed. This initialization is performed by message **initializeMessages** (see *instance initialization* below). In particular, four of the instance variables are initialized as dictionaries. Each of these dictionaries must be provided with one key-value association for each interface switch. The following method is used for this purpose:

interface window support

```
addMessage: nameSymbol default: defaultSymbol
parser: parseSymbol coding: anArrayOrNil
    messageInitializers at: nameSymbol put: defaultSymbol.
    messageSources at: nameSymbol put: (self perform: defaultSymbol).
    messageParsers at: nameSymbol put: parseSymbol.
    messageCodings at: nameSymbol put: anArrayOrNil
```

The name symbol is the key for all four dictionaries — one per interface switch. The default symbol is stored as a message initializer, and the text obtained by performing the selector is stored as a message source. The parse symbol is stored as a message parser. If this message parser were performed with the message source as its data, the result would be a coded version of the stored source. The coding parameter eliminates the need to actually parse the source at initialization time. However, it is used later when and if the designer modifies the text in the message view and accepts it.

Class WindowMakerIcon

class	WindowMakerIcon
superclass	ExtendedSwitchView
instance variables	message messageView messageInitializers messageSources messageCodings messageParsers ...

instance initialization

initializeMessages
    message ← #comment.
    messageInitializers ← IdentityDictionary **new**.
    messageSources ← IdentityDictionary **new**.
    messageCodings ← IdentityDictionary **new**.
    messageParsers ← IdentityDictionary **new**.
    self **addMessage:** #name **default:** #defaultName
        parser: #parseNilOrSymbol: **coding:** #(nil)

interface window direct support

message
    ↑message
message: aSymbol
    message ← aSymbol

messageCodings
    ↑messageCodings
messageInitializers
    ↑messageInitializers
messageSources
    ↑messageSources

messageView
    ↑messageView
messageView: aView
    messageView ← aView

Class WindowMakerMasterIcon

class	WindowMakerMasterIcon
superclass	WindowMakerIcon
instance variables	...

instance initialization

initializeMessages
    super **initializeMessages**.
    self
        addMessage: #comment **default:** #defaultComment
            parser: #parseComment: **coding:** nil;
        addMessage: #topView **default:** #defaultTopView
            parser: #parseBoolean: **coding:** #(true);
        addMessage: #title **default:** #defaultTitle
            parser: #parseNilOrString: **coding:** #(nil);
        addMessage: #preOpeningSelector **default:** #defaultPreOpeningSelector
            parser: #parseNilOrZeroOrMoreParameterMessage: **coding:** #(nil);
        addMessage: #postClosingSelector **default:** #defaultPostClosingSelector
            parser: #parseNilOrZeroOrMoreParameterMessage: **coding:** #(nil)

Class WindowMakerTextIcon

class	WindowMakerTextIcon
superclass	WindowMakerIcon
instance variables	...

instance initialization

initializeMessages
    super **initializeMessages**.
    self
        addMessage: #comment **default**: #defaultComment
           parser: #parseComment: **coding**: nil;
        addMessage: #updateSymbol **default**: #defaultUpdateSymbol
           parser: #parseNilOrSymbol: **coding**: #(nil);
        addMessage: #getText **default**: #defaultGetText
           parser: #parseZeroOrMoreParametersMessage:
           coding: #(model getText);
        addMessage: #changeText **default**: #defaultChangeText
           parser: #parseOneOrMoreParametersMessage:
           coding: #(model changeText: aText);
        addMessage: #getMenu **default**: #defaultGetYellowMenu
           parser: #parseNilOrZeroOrMoreParameterMessage:
           coding: #(model getMenu)

Class WindowMakerMenuIcon

class	WindowMakerMenuIcon
superclass	WindowMakerIcon
instance variables	...

instance initialization

initializeMessages
    super **initializeMessages**.
    self
        addMessage: #comment **default**: #defaultComment
           parser: #parseComment: **coding**: nil;
        addMessage: #updateSymbol **default**: #defaultUpdateSymbol
           parser: #parseNilOrSymbol: **coding**: #(nil);
        addMessage: #getMenuArray **default**: #defaultGetMenuArray
           parser: #parseZeroOrMoreParametersMessage:
           coding: #(model getMenuArray);
        addMessage: #getMenuSelection **default**: #defaultGetMenuSelection
           parser: #parseZeroOrMoreParametersMessage:
           coding: #(model getMenuSelection);
        addMessage: #changeMenuSelection **default**: #defaultChangeMenuSelection
           parser: #parseOneOrMoreParametersMessage:
           coding: #(model changeMenuSelection: entryObject);
        addMessage: #getYellowMenu **default**: #defaultGetYellowMenu
           parser: #parseNilOrZeroOrMoreParameterMessage:
           coding: #(model getYellowMenu)

Class WindowMakerSwitchIcon

class	WindowMakerSwitchIcon
superclass	WindowMakerSwitchOrPictureIcon
instance variables	...

instance initialization

initializeMessages
    super **initializeMessages**.
    self
        addMessage: #comment **default**: #defaultComment
            parser: #parseComment: **coding**: nil;
        addMessage: #updateSymbol **default**: #defaultUpdateSymbol
            parser: #parseNilOrSymbol: **coding**: #(nil);
        addMessage: #isOn **default**: #defaultIsOn
            parser: #parseZeroOrMoreParametersMessage: **coding**: #(model isOn);
        addMessage: #switch **default**: #defaultSwitch
            parser: #parseZeroOrMoreParametersMessage: **coding**: #(model switch)

Class WindowMakerPictureIcon

class	WindowMakerPictureIcon
superclass	WindowMakerSwitchOrPictureIcon
instance variables	...

instance initialization

initializeMessages
    super **initializeMessages**.
    self
        addMessage: #comment **default**: #defaultComment
            parser: #parseComment: **coding**: nil;
        addMessage: #updateSymbol **default**: #defaultUpdateSymbol
            parser: #parseNilOrSymbol: **coding**: #(nil);
        addMessage: #getLabel **default**: #defaultGetLabel
            parser: #parseNilOrZeroOrMoreParameterMessage: **coding**: #(nil)

Class WindowMakerExternalIcon

class	WindowMakerExternalIcon
superclass	WindowMakerIcon
instance variables	...

instance initialization

initializeMessages
    super **initializeMessages**.
    self
        addMessage: #comment **default**: #defaultComment
            parser: #parseComment: **coding**: nil;
        addMessage: #getView **default**: #defaultGetView
            parser: #parseClassMessage: **coding**: #(ExtendedView getView)

A few observations are noteworthy. The #comment message is treated specially — the coding supplied is not actually used. The #updateSymbol message permits either a symbol or nil — this is reflected in the name of the corresponding parser. Other variations are possible; e.g., see #topView and #title in the master icon. Some messages like #getText and #changeText in text icons require receiver/selector/argument messages with respectively (a) zero or more parameters, or (b) one or more parameters. Others, like #getYellowMenu, are similar to #getText but additionally permit nil.

The Interface Window Messages

Since the bottom pane is a text view, a yellow button pop-up menu can be supplied that contains all the standard text editing menu items. Fig. 8.37 illustrates the existing yellow button menu. Note that it contains two nonstandard entries: reset and accept permanently. The former permits the original window contents to be retrieved even after substantial changes have been accepted. The latter permits the designer to refine the contents of the window in a permanent way — it results in the recompilation of the message initializer that returns the associated text object (with boldfacing included).

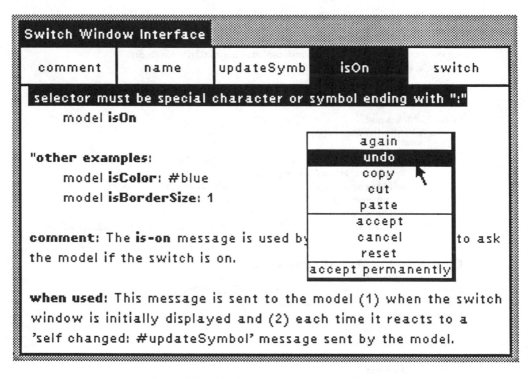

Figure 8.37 The interface for switch windows.

Fig. 8.37 also illustrates the result of attempting to accept an illegal message. For example, 'model **isOn** 3' is illegal; a legal possibility would have been 'model **isOn**' or 'model **isOn:** 3'.

By the time the interface window is opened, all interface properties of the icon (except for the message view) can be accessed and modified via WindowMakerIcon methods such as **message, message:, messageCodings, messageInitializers, messageSources, messageView,** and **messageView:**. The message view is provided by the preopening method **preOpenInterface:** just before the interface window is opened. The message view is needed for generating error messages. Note that the icon for which the interface is being specified is extracted with message **isolatedGroupMember.**

Class WindowMakerGroupIcon

class   WindowMakerGroupIcon
superclass   WindowMakerIcon
instance variables   ...

generic window support (preopening/postclosing)

preOpenInterface: anExtendedStandardSystemView
    "USED by External, Menu, Picture, Switch, Text, and Master."
    | icon |
    icon ← self **isolatedGroupMember**.
    icon **messageView**:
        (anExtendedStandardSystemView **viewNamed**: #messageSource)

interface window messages

messageMenu
    ↑ActionMenu
        labels: ('again\undo\copy\cut\paste\',
            'accept\cancel\reset\accept permanently') **withCRs**
        lines: #(2 5 8)
        selectors: #(again undo copySelection cut paste
            accept cancel resetSource acceptPermanently)

isMessage: aSymbol
    | icon |
    icon ← self **isolatedGroupMember**.
    ↑icon **message** == aSymbol

message: aSymbol
    "Changes the message to aSymbol if possible; otherwise, flashes."
    | icon view |
    icon ← self **isolatedGroupMember**.
    icon **message** == aSymbol **ifTrue**: [↑self "already as requested"].
    (view ← icon **messageView**) controller **textHasChanged**
        ifTrue: [view **flash**. ↑self "can't do it"]
        ifFalse: [
            icon **message**: aSymbol.
            self **changed**: #message; **changed**: #messageSource]

messageSource
    | icon |
    icon ← self **isolatedGroupMember**.
    ↑(icon **messageSources at**: icon **message**) **copy**

messageSource: aText
    "Parses the given text (if possible) and creates the corresponding coded version."
    | icon iconMessage coding |
    icon ← self **isolatedGroupMember**. iconMessage ← icon **message**.
    coding ← icon **parseText**: aText **forMessage**: iconMessage.
    coding **isEmpty ifTrue**: [↑false].
    icon **messageCodings at**: iconMessage **put**: coding.
    icon **messageSources at**: iconMessage **put**: aText **copy**.
    iconMessage == defaultLabelSelector **ifTrue**: [icon **computeLabel**].
    ↑true

resetSource
    | icon iconMessage aText |
    icon ← self **isolatedGroupMember**. iconMessage ← icon **message**.
    aText ← icon **perform**: (icon **messageInitializers at**: iconMessage).
    icon **messageSources at**: message **put**: aText.
    icon **messageCodings at**: message **put**: (icon **parseText**: aText **forMessage**: iconMessage).
    self **changed**: #messageSource

acceptPermanently
    "Replace the appropriate messageInitializer method with revised text."
    | icon iconMessage handler newText methodName containerClass methodCategory
    code |

    "First, accept the changes."
    icon ← self **isolatedGroupMember**. iconMessage ← icon **message**.
    (handler ← icon **messageView controller**) **textHasChanged ifTrue**: [
        handler **accept**.
        handler **textHasChanged ifTrue**: [↑self "not accepted; an error was detected"]].

    "Next, create a method with the changes."
    newText ← icon **messageSources at**: iconMessage.
    methodName ← icon **messageInitializers at**: iconMessage.
    containerClass ← icon **class whichClassIncludesSelector**: methodName.
    containerClass **isNil ifTrue**: [↑self **error**: 'where is method ', methodName].
    methodCategory ← containerClass **whichCategoryIncludesSelector**: methodName.

    "Format the text construction part of the code better than the standard storeString."
    code ← WriteStream **on**: (String **new**: 1000).
    code
        nextPutAll: methodName; **crtab**;
        nextPutAll: '↑Text'; **crtab**: 2;
            nextPutAll: 'string: '; **store**: newText **string**; **crtab**: 2;
            nextPutAll: 'runs: (RunArray'; **crtab**: 3;
                nextPutAll: 'runs: '; **store**: newText **runs runs**; **crtab**: 3;
                nextPutAll: 'values: '; **store**: newText **runs values**; **nextPut**: $).

    containerClass **compile**: code **contents classified**: methodCategory

The standard yellow button message selectors in **messageMenu** are handled by the text window itself. It is only the two nonstandard selectors **resetSource** and **acceptPermanently** that are handled by the model — this icon. The latter permits the designer to change the information in the message view permanently; e.g., to correct, simplify, or extend the information it provides. It causes the edited text to be compiled into the method that was originally used to retrieve the text.

472   Inside Smalltalk

Extracting and Modifying Interface Coding

When a message such as 'model **isColor:** #black **andWidth:** 2' is accepted in the interface window, it is parsed and stored as an array #(model **isColor:** #black **andWidth:** 2) that we call its **coding**. The receiver in this case is 'model', the selector is '**isColor:andWidth:**', and the arguments are #(black 2). As far as the encoding for the icon is concerned, the receiver is seldom retained since it is usually the literal symbol 'model'.

The protocol that follows permits different parts of this coding to be retrieved and also permits the defaults to be modified. This will occur, for example, when an existing application window is edited — to replace the default coding for the individual icons by new values.

Class WindowMakerIcon

class	WindowMakerIcon
superclass	ExtendedSwitchView
instance variables	message messageView messageInitializers messageSources messageCodings messageParsers ...

interface window support

codingFor: nameSymbol
    "Entire coding is returned."
    ↑messageCodings **at**: nameSymbol

codingWithoutReceiverFor: nameSymbol
    "Treats situation with missing selector; i.e., #(nil), specially by returning #(nil)."
    | coding |
    (coding ← messageCodings **at**: nameSymbol) = #(nil) **ifTrue**: [↑coding].
    ↑coding **copyFrom**: 2 **to**: coding **size** "eliminate receiver"

receiverFor: nameSymbol
    "Translates constants."
    | receiver |
    receiver ← (messageCodings **at**: nameSymbol) **first**.
    ↑(self **translateConstants**: (Array **with**: receiver)) **first**

selectorFor: nameSymbol
    "Treats situation with missing selector; i.e., #(nil) specially by returning nil."
    | coding result |
    (coding ← messageCodings **at**: nameSymbol) = #(nil) **ifTrue**: [↑nil].
    result ← ''.
    2 **to**: coding **size by**: 2 **do**: [:index | result ← result, (coding **at**: index)].
    ↑result **asSymbol**

argumentsFor: nameSymbol
    "Assumes the coding is not #(nil)."
    | coding result |
    coding ← messageCodings **at**: nameSymbol. result ← OrderedCollection **new**.
    3 **to**: coding **size by**: 2 **do**: [:index | result **add**: (coding **at**: index)].
    ↑self **translateConstants**: result **asArray**

selectorArgumentsFor: nameSymbol
    "Treats situation with missing selector; i.e., #(nil) specially by returning nil."
    | theSelector theArguments |
    (messageCodings **at**: nameSymbol) = #(nil) **ifTrue**: [↑nil].
    theSelector ← self **selectorFor**: nameSymbol.
    theArguments ← self **argumentsFor**: nameSymbol.
    theArguments **isEmpty**
        ifTrue: [↑theSelector]
        ifFalse: [↑ExtendedMessage **selector**: theSelector **arguments**: theArguments]

receiverSelectorArgumentsFor: nameSymbol
    "Treats situation with missing selector; i.e., #(nil) specially by returning nil."
    | theReceiver theSelector theArguments |
    (messageCodings **at**: nameSymbol) = #(nil) **ifTrue**: [↑nil].
    theReceiver ← self **receiverFor**: nameSymbol.
    theSelector ← self **selectorFor**: nameSymbol.
    theArguments ← self **argumentsFor**: nameSymbol.
    ↑Array **with**: theReceiver **with**: (theArguments **isEmpty**
        ifTrue: [theSelector]
        ifFalse: [ExtendedMessage **selector**: theSelector **arguments**: theArguments])

addMessage: nameSymbol **default**: defaultSymbol **parser**: parseSymbol **coding**: anArrayOrNil
    messageInitializers **at**: nameSymbol **put**: defaultSymbol.
    messageSources **at**: nameSymbol **put**: (self **perform**: defaultSymbol).
    messageParsers **at**: nameSymbol **put**: parseSymbol.
    messageCodings **at**: nameSymbol **put**: anArrayOrNil

changeMessage: nameSymbol **receiver**: aSymbol
    "Places the symbol into an array as required for the coding."
    ↑self **changeMessage**: nameSymbol **coding**: (Array **with**: aSymbol)

changeMessage: nameSymbol **selectorArguments**: anArray
    "Adds 'model' in front of arrays other than #(nil)."
    | coding |
    coding ← anArray = #(nil) **ifTrue**: [#(nil)] **ifFalse**: [(Array **with**: #model), anArray].
    ↑self **changeMessage**: nameSymbol **coding**: coding

changeMessage: nameSymbol **receiverSelectorArguments**: anArray
    "Passes it on as a private message."
    ↑self **changeMessage**: nameSymbol **coding**: anArray

Parsing Interface Window Messages

When a message is accepted by the designer in an interface window, '**messageSource:** aText' is sent by the text pane to the model — the icon whose interface is being specified. An attempt is then made via message **parseText:forMessage:** to parse the text. Generally, the parsing process is achieved very simply by surrounding the text with '#(' and ')' and evaluating it. In the case of arguments, the constants **nil**, **true**, and **false** replace the symbols of the same name; e.g., #true is replaced by **true**. If the parse is successful, a nonempty array is returned. Otherwise, an error message is generated in the text pane of the interface window, as shown in Fig. 8.37. The compiler-generated error message is trapped by providing it with our own error notifier — an instance of class ErrorHandler discussed in Sect. 8.3.6.

message parsing

parseText: aText **forMessage**: aSymbol
    ↑self **perform**: (messageParsers **at**: aSymbol) **with**: aText

parseComment: aText
    ↑#(nil)

parseBoolean: aText
    | anArray receiver object |
    anArray ← self **parseText**: aText. anArray **isEmpty ifTrue**: [↑#()].
    (anArray = #(true)) | (anArray = #(false)) **ifTrue**: [↑anArray].
    self **reportError**: 'expected "true" or "false"'.
    ↑#()

parseNilOrString: aText
    ↑self **parseNilOrString**: aText **symbolNeeded**: false

parseNilOrSymbol: aText
    ↑self **parseNilOrString**: aText **symbolNeeded**: true

parseClassMessage: aText
    | anArray receiver object |
    anArray ← self **parseText**: aText. anArray **isEmpty ifTrue**: [↑#()].
    receiver ← anArray **at**: 1.
    (self **messageSizeOk**: anArray size: -2) **ifFalse**: [↑#()].
    object ← Smalltalk **at**: receiver **ifAbsent**: [#()].
    (object **respondsTo**: #superclass) **ifFalse**: [
        self **reportError**: 'expected "', receiver **printString**, '" to be a class'.
        ↑#()].
    (self **messageSelectorsOk**: anArray) **ifFalse**: [↑#()].
    ↑anArray

parseNilOrZeroOrMoreParameterMessage: aText
    ↑self **parseMessage**: aText **nilOk**: true **size**: -2

parseZeroOrMoreParametersMessage: aText
    ↑self **parseMessage**: aText **nilOk**: false **size**: -2

parseOneOrMoreParametersMessage: aText
    ↑self **parseMessage**: aText **nilOk**: false **size**: -3

unparseMessage: aSymbol
    "Converse of the parseMessage methods. Must be generalized if additional cases
    need to be handled."
    | parser coding element string |
    parser ← messageParsers **at**: aSymbol. coding ← messageCodings **at**: aSymbol.
    parser == #parseComment **ifTrue**: [↑self **perform**: (messageInitializers **at**: aSymbol)].
    parser == #parseNilOrSymbol: **ifTrue**: [↑(coding **at**: 1) **storeString asText**].
    1 **to**: coding **size do**: [:index |
        element ← coding **at**: index.
        index = 1
            ifTrue: [string ← element **printString**]
            ifFalse: [
                index **even**
                    ifTrue: [string ← string, ' ', element **printString**]
                    ifFalse: [string ← string, ' ', element **storeString**]]].
    ↑string **asText**

parseNilOrString: aText **symbolNeeded:** symbolNeeded
"Returns an array containing the text; either a symbol (name), a string, or nil for legal text (the former only if symbolNeeded is true); #() is returned if an error is reported."
| anArray legal string |
anArray ← self **parseText:** aText. anArray **isEmpty ifTrue:** [↑#()].
anArray = #(nil) **ifTrue:** [↑anArray].
legal ← (anArray **size** = 1) **and:**
    [symbolNeeded
        ifTrue: [
            ((string ← anArray **first**) **isKindOf:** Symbol) **and:** [string **first isLetter**]]
        ifFalse: [anArray **first isKindOf:** String]].
legal **ifTrue:** [↑anArray].
self **reportError:** (symbolNeeded
    ifTrue: ['expected "symbol"']
    ifFalse: ['expected "string"']).
↑#()

parseMessage: aText **nilOk:** nilLegal **size:** legalSize
"Returns an array containing the text; either the elements of a message or nil for legal text (the latter only if nilLegal is true); #() is returned if an error is reported. The message elements have the form <receiver selector> or <receiver keyword1: constant1 keyword2: constant2 ...>."
| anArray |
anArray ← self **parseText:** aText. anArray **isEmpty ifTrue:** [↑#()].
(nilLegal **and:** [anArray = #(nil)]) **ifTrue:** [↑anArray].
(self **messageSizeOk:** anArray **size:** legalSize) **ifFalse:** [↑#()].
(self **messageReceiverOk:** anArray) **ifFalse:** [↑#()].
(self **messageSelectorsOk:** anArray) **ifFalse:** [↑#()].
↑anArray

parseText: aText
"Returns an array containing the text objects with symbols #nil, #true, and #false translated to the corresponding constants. If an error is detected, a message is generated and an empty array is returned. Note that later processing is unable to differentiate between symbols like '#hello' and variables like 'hello' because the evaluation step has eliminated the distinction."
| coding |
coding ← self **evaluate:** aText.
coding **isNil ifTrue:** [↑#()] **ifFalse:** [↑coding "an Array"]

evaluate: aText
| notifier |
notifier ← ErrorHandler **new errorBlock:** [:string :position |
    "Eliminate '#(' part of '#(....)'."
    self **reportError:** string **at:** position-2.
    ↑nil].
↑Compiler **evaluate:** '#(', aText, ')' **notifying:** notifier **logged:** false

reportError: aString
self **reportError:** aString **at:** 1

reportError: aString **at:** position
messageView **isNil ifTrue:** [↑self "can't report it"].
messageView **controller insertAndSelect:** aString **at:** position

```
messageReceiverOk: anArray
    (anArray at: 1) == #model
        ifTrue: [↑true]
        ifFalse: [self reportError: 'expected "model"'. ↑false]

messageSelectorsOk: anArray
    | even element |

    "Special case: <receiver selector>."
    anArray size = 2 ifTrue: [
        (((element ← anArray at: 2) isKindOf: Symbol) and:
        [element first isLetter])
            ifTrue: [↑true]
            ifFalse: [self reportError: 'selector must be a symbol'. ↑false]].

    "Special case: <receiver selector operand>."
    anArray size = 3 ifTrue: [
        (((element ← anArray at: 2) isKindOf: Symbol) and:
        [element first isLetter ifTrue: [element last == $:] ifFalse: [true]])
            ifTrue: [↑true]
            ifFalse: [
                self reportError: 'selector must be special character',
                    ' or symbol ending with ":"'.
                ↑false]].

    "General case: <receiver keyword: operand keyword: operand ...>."
    even ← false.
    anArray do: [:element |
        even ifTrue: [
            ((element isKindOf: Symbol) and: [element first isLetter])
                ifFalse: [self reportError: 'selector must be a symbol'. ↑false].
            (element last = $:)
                ifFalse: [self reportError: 'selector must end with ":"'. ↑false]].
        even ← even not].
    ↑true

messageSizeOk: anArray size: legalSize
    "If legalSize is positive, exactly that size is required; if negative, any size >=
    legalSize abs is permitted."
    legalSize negative
        ifTrue: [
            anArray size >= legalSize abs
                ifTrue: [↑true]
                ifFalse: [self reportError: 'expected more parameters'. ↑false]]
        ifFalse: [
            anArray size = legalSize
                ifTrue: [↑true]
                ifFalse: [
                    anArray isEmpty
                        ifTrue: [self reportError: 'expected something'. ↑false].
                    legalSize = 2
                        ifTrue: [self reportError: 'expected "model selector"'. ↑false].
                    self reportError: 'expected "model keyword1: constant1',
                        ' keyword2: constant2 ..."'.
                    ↑false]]
```

```
translateConstants: anArray
    | map |
    map ← Dictionary new
        at: #nil put: nil;
        at: #true put: true;
        at: #false put: false;
        yourself.
    ↑anArray collect: [:element | map at: element ifAbsent: [element]]

changeMessage: nameSymbol coding: coding
    messageCodings at: nameSymbol put: coding.
    messageSources at: nameSymbol put: (self unparseMessage: nameSymbol).
    nameSymbol == defaultLabelSelector ifTrue: [self computeLabel].
```

Interface Window Defaults

Interface window text defaults are summarized in Appendix B.4. We provide one example from abstract class WindowMakerIcon to illustrate the basic format of the method. Note that carriage returns and spaces are significant. Also, recall that the methods are not hand-constructed. Rather, they are obtained by editing an existing definition and compiled by selecting yellow button menu entry **acceptPermanently**. The original version of a method, for example, with name **defaultName** might have been defined as

```
defaultName
    ↑" asText
```

By editing it appropriately, it evolved into the following:

```
interface window defaults

defaultName
    ↑Text
            string:'
    nil

"other examples:
    workWindow
    top

comment: A view name can be used to access the view when preopening or postclosing
an extended standard system view.

restrictions: A view name must either be nil or a symbol.

additional information: For a more detailed explanation, see comment in the external
interface for the master window; i.e., get the yellow button pop-up menu when no icons
are selected and choose the external interface entry."
        runs: (RunArray
            runs: #(8 14 20 7 9 4 37 11 4 12 36 12 47 22 204)
            values: #(1 2 1 2 1 2 1 2 1 2 1 2 1 2 1))

defaultUpdateSymbol
    ... see Appendix B.4 ...

defaultGetYellowMenu
    ... see Appendix B.4 ...
```

8.4.8 Encoding/Decoding, Converting to Extended Views, and Copying

Each window maker icon can be **encoded** for ease of storage and manipulation. The encoding for a container icon such as a master icon or a group icon also contains the encoding for the contained icons. Hence, a master icon encoding is a compact representation for an entire application window. An encoding can of course be **decoded** into the corresponding icon. The icon itself can then be converted into a corresponding extended view. In general, the encoding contains more information than the corresponding extended view. Hence it is not possible to go back the other way. For this reason, the encoding is maintained with extended standard system views and extended views (although not with other views). Once a method is generated to produce an application window from extended views, it is possible to discard the encoding. However, it is needed if the window is to be edited for changes in the future.

An **encoding** is an appropriately initialized array of constants. It cannot, for example, contain store strings or objects such as rectangles or points. A point like 10@20 has to be encoded in the array either as a subarray (10 20) or as two consecutive integers 10 and 20. Decoding in this case is a matter of extracting this information and reconstructing the point. There is nothing particularly illuminating about the encoding/decoding process. Although the gist of the encoding/decoding methods for abstract class WindowmakerIcon is provided next, the details of the code for this class and the subclasses have been gathered in Appendix B.5. The encoding/decoding facility is an example of a horizontal facility since every class in the WindowMakerIcon hierarchy is affected.

Class WindowMakerIcon

class	WindowMakerIcon
superclass	ExtendedSwitchView
instance variables	...

instance methods

encoding/decoding

encodeOn: aStream
    "iconClass iconName window insideColor borderWidth"
    aStream
        nextPutAll: self **shortClassName; space;**
        store: (self **receiverFor**: #name); **space**. self
        encodeWindowOn: aStream. aStream **space**. self
        encodeColor: insideColor **on**: aStream. aStream **space**. self
        encodeBorderWidthOn: aStream

decodeFrom: aStream
    "iconClass iconName window insideColor borderWidth"
    | border |
    self
        changeMessage: #name **receiver**: aStream **next;**
        window: (self **decodeWindow**: aStream **next**);
        insideColor: (self **decodeColor**: aStream **next**);
        borderWidthLeft: (border ← self **decodeBorderWidth**: aStream **next**) **left**
            right: border **right top**: border **top bottom**: border **bottom**

encodeWindowOn: aStream
 aStream **print**: (Array
   with: window **origin x with**: window **origin y**
   with: window **corner x with**: window **corner y**).

encodeColor: aPoint **on**: aStream
encodeBorderWidthOn: aStream
 ... see Appendix B.5 ...

decodeWindow: anArray
 "decode #(<origin x> <origin y> <corner x> <corner y>)"
 ↑(anArray **at**: 1)@(anArray **at**: 2) **corner**: (anArray **at**: 3)@(anArray **at**: 4)

decodeColor: aColorSymbol
decodeBorderWidth: data
 ... see Appendix B.5 ...

Another horizontal facility permits icons to be copied and converted to extended views. A shallow copy is needed to support the copy/paste facility in the window maker. The conversion operation provides an approach to generating an application window; e.g., by converting all icons to extended views and then obtaining the corresponding store strings. As for the encoding/decoding facility, the copying and conversion methods have been gathered in Appendix B.6.

We provide two examples from the abstract class WindowMakerIcon and its subclass WindowMakerExternalIcon. The shallow copy operation makes a temporary destructive modification to the receiver. Such destructive changes could be avoided by providing additional supporting methods.

Class WindowMakerIcon

class	WindowMakerIcon
superclass	ExtendedSwitchView
instance variables	... messageInitializers messageSources messageCodings messageParsers ...

generating views

asView
 self **subclassResponsibility**

copying

shallowCopy
 | copy oldMessageInitializers oldMessageSources oldMessageCodings oldMessageParsers |

 "Modify temporarily"
 oldMessageInitializers ← messageInitializers.
 messageInitializers ← messageInitializers **copy**.
 oldMessageSources ← messageSources.
 messageSources ← messageSources **copy**.
 oldMessageCodings ← messageCodings.
 messageCodings ← messageCodings **copy**.
 oldMessageParsers ← messageParsers.
 messageParsers ← messageParsers **copy**.

```
"Make the copy."
copy ← super shallowCopy
        superView: nil; resetSubViews;
        borderWidthLeft: borderWidth left right: borderWidth right
            top: borderWidth top bottom: borderWidth bottom;
        transformation: transformation; "stores a copy"
        window: window; "stores a copy"
        yourself.
subViews do: [:icon | copy addSubView: icon shallowCopy].

"Restore."
messageInitializers ← oldMessageInitializers.
messageSources ← oldMessageSources.
messageCodings ← oldMessageCodings.
messageParsers ← oldMessageParsers.

↑copy
```

Class WindowMakerExternalIcon

class	WindowMakerExternalIcon
superclass	WindowMakerIcon
instance variables	"none"

generating views

asView
```
    ↑ExtendedExternalView new
        model: nil; name: (self receiverFor: #name);
        insideColor: insideColor;
        borderWidthLeft: borderWidth left right: borderWidth right
            top: borderWidth top bottom: borderWidth bottom;
        window: window; transformation: transformation;
        external: (self receiverSelectorArgumentsFor: #getView);
        yourself
```

8.4.9 The Remaining Icons

Since we have provided bits and pieces of most icon classes while describing the important functions of the window maker, the parts of the classes that have yet to be discussed are relatively short. In this section, we present the remaining classes with appropriate references to the parts that were presented elsewhere.

Class WindowMakerIcon (An Abstract Class)

class	WindowMakerIcon
superclass	ExtendedSwitchView
instance variables	message messageView messageInitializers messageSources messageCodings messageParsers sizeLocked defaultLabelSelector

class methods

instance creation

new
```
    ↑super new computeLabel
```

instance methods

instance initialization

initializeMessages
    ... see Sect. 8.4.7, Initializing a New Icon's Interface Data ...

initialize
    "Initializes all components of the icon."
    | box |
    super **initialize**.
    self **mode**: #varying.
    box ← 0@0 **extent**: 50@50.
    self **window**: box **viewport**: box. "=> transformation is identity"
    sizeLocked ← false.
    self **borderWidth**: 1; **insideColor**: Form **white**.
    defaultLabelSelector ← #subclassResponsibility.
    self **initializeMessages**

encoding/decoding
    ... see Sect. 8.4.8, Encoding/Decoding ... (also see Appendix B.5) ...

generating views

asView
    self **subclassResponsibility**

group sequencing
    ... see Sect. 8.4.2 , Group Sequencing ...

copying
    ... see Sect. 8.4.8, ... Converting ..., and Copying (also see Appendix B.6) ...

size locking
    ... see Sect. 8.4.3, Displaying, Moving, and Sizing ...

default naming

classNamePicture
    ↑self **shortClassName asLowercase asParagraph**

shortClassName
    | className |
    className ← self **class name**. "WindowMaker...Icon"
    ↑className **copyFrom**: 12 **to**: className **size** - 4 "the ... portion"

moving/growing primitives
moving/growing nonprimitives
displaying
    ... see Sect. 8.4.3, Displaying, Moving, and Sizing ...

alignment window support
    ... see Sect. 8.4.7, The Alignment Window ...

interface window direct support
interface window general support
    ... see Sect. 8.4.7, The Interface Window ...

interface window defaults
    ... see Sect. 8.4.7, Interface Window Defaults (also see Appendix B.4) ...

message parsing
private message parsing support
    ... see Sect. 8.4.7, The Interface Window ...

Class WindowMakerTextIcon

class	WindowMakerTextIcon
superclass	WindowMakerIcon
instance variables	"none"

class methods

no messages

instance methods

instance initialization

initializeMessages
    ... see Sect. 8.4.7, Initializing a New Icon's Interface Data ...

initialize
    super **initialize**.
    defaultLabelSelector ← #getText

encoding/decoding
    ... see Sect. 8.4.8, Encoding/Decoding ... (also see Appendix B.5) ...

generating views
    ... see Sect. 8.4.8, ... Converting to Extended Views, and ... (also see Appendix B.6) ...

interface window defaults

defaultComment
defaultGetText
defaultChangeText
    ... see Sect. 8.4.7, Interface Window Defaults (also see Appendix B.4) ...

Class WindowMakerMenuIcon

class	WindowMakerMenuIcon
superclass	WindowMakerIcon
instance variables	"none"

class methods

no messages

instance methods

instance initialization

initializeMessages
    ... see Sect. 8.4.7, Initializing a New Icon's Interface Data ...

initialize
    super **initialize**.
    defaultLabelSelector ← #getMenuArray

encoding/decoding
    ... see Sect. 8.4.8, Encoding/Decoding ... (also see Appendix B.5) ...

generating views
    ... see Sect. 8.4.8, ... Converting to Extended Views, ... (also see Appendix B.6) ...

interface window defaults

defaultComment
defaultGetMenuArray
defaultGetMenuSelection
defaultChangeMenuSelection
    ... *see Sect. 8.4.7, Interface Window Defaults* (also see Appendix B.4) ...

Class WindowMakerSwitchOrPictureIcon

class	WindowMakerSwitchOrPictureIcon
superclass	WindowMakerIcon
instance variables	pictureVariety pictureString pictureFormPathName
	lockedSizeExpansion

class methods

no messages

instance methods

instance initialization

initialize
    super **initialize**.
    pictureVariety ← #text.
    pictureString ← 'picture'.
    pictureFormPathName ← #(DefaultFormLibrary button).
    lockedSizeExpansion ← 0

access/modification
    ... *see Sect. 8.4.7, The Background Windows* ...

encoding/decoding
    ... *see Sect. 8.4.8, Encoding/Decoding* ... (also see Appendix B.5) ...

background
    ... *see Sect. 8.4.4, Labeling the Icons* ...

Class WindowMakerSwitchIcon

class	WindowMakerSwitchIcon
superclass	WindowMakerSwitchOrPictureIcon
instance variables	"none"

class methods

no messages

instance methods

instance initialization

initializeMessages
    ... *see Sect. 8.4.7, Initializing a New Icon's Interface Data* ...

initialize
>   super **initialize**.
>   pictureString ← 'switch'. "override default"

encoding/decoding
>   *... see Sect. 8.4.8, Encoding/Decoding ... (also see Appendix B.5) ...*

generating views
>   *... see Sect. 8.4.8, ... Converting to Extended Views, ... (also see Appendix B.6) ...*

interface window defaults

defaultComment
defaultIsOn
defaultSwitch
>   *... see Sect. 8.4.7, Interface Window Defaults* (also see Appendix B.4) *...*

background
>   *... see Sect. 8.4.4, Labeling the Icons ...*

Class WindowMakerPictureIcon

class   WindowMakerPictureIcon
superclass   WindowMakerSwitchOrPictureIcon
instance variables   "none"

class methods

no messages

instance methods

instance initialization

initializeMessages
>   *... see Sect. 8.4.7, Initializing a New Icon's Interface Data ...*

initialize
>   super **initialize**.
>   self **sizeLocked**: true; **mode**: #constant; **fixMiddleLeft**; **lockedSizeExpansion**: 0.
>   self **borderWidth**: 0. "override"

encoding/decoding
>   *... see Sect. 8.4.8, Encoding/Decoding ... (also see Appendix B.5) ...*

generating views
>   *... see Sect. 8.4.8, ... Converting to Extended Views, ... (also see Appendix B.6) ...*

interface window defaults

defaultComment
defaultGetLabel
>   *... see Sect. 8.4.7, Interface Window Defaults* (also see Appendix B.4) *...*

Class WindowMakerSwitchAndPictureIcon

class	WindowMakerSwitchAndPictureIcon
superclass	WindowMakerSwitchIcon
instance variables	separation

class methods

no messages

instance methods

instance initialization

initialize
> super **initialize**.
> self **borderWidth**: 0. "override"
> separation ← 10.
> self **sizeLocked**: true; **mode**: #constant; **fixMiddleLeft**; **lockedSizeExpansion**: 0.
> pictureVariety ← #form

encoding/decoding
> *... see Sect. 8.4.8, Encoding/Decoding ... (also see Appendix B.5) ...*

generating views
> *... see Sect. 8.4.8, ... Converting to Extended Views, ... (also see Appendix B.6) ...*

background
> *... see Sect. 8.4.4, Labeling the Icons ...*

Class WindowMakerExternalIcon

class	WindowMakerExternalIcon
superclass	WindowMakerIcon
instance variables	"none"

class methods

no messages

instance methods

instance initialization

initializeMessages
> *... see Sect. 8.4.7, Initializing a New Icon's Interface Data ...*

initialize
> super **initialize**.
> defaultLabelSelector ← #getView

encoding/decoding
> *... see Sect. 8.4.8, Encoding/Decoding ... (also see Appendix B.5) ...*

generating views
> *... see Sect. 8.4.8, ... Converting to Extended Views, ... (also see Appendix B.6) ...*

interface window defaults

defaultComment
defaultGetView
    ... *see Sect. 8.4.7, Interface Window Defaults* (also see Appendix B.4) ...

8.5 CONCLUSIONS

Generally, the window maker was substantially more complex than we had expected it to be. The browser was a good vehicle to study it in a relatively effortless way. However, it was virtually impossible to obtain a linear listing that could easily be followed. In fact, we found it as difficult to describe our design as it was to produce it.

Two areas that warrant further work have to do with form libraries and the canceling protocol. In particular, our form library design was sufficient to manage switch forms. As it is, each form library consists of small forms that are all the same size. We haven't considered what would happen if the forms were to be different sizes. Additionally, it is not clear how more general forms for pictures should be handled. For example, how should we display a large form in the window maker's background window or a library editor? With respect to the canceling protocol, it is unsatisfying to terminate options processing by closing the window. In an earlier design, we had introduced two switches in alignment windows: an OK switch and a CANCEL switch. This worked well for alignment processing. However, we have not provided a cancel facility for all options windows — perhaps we should. More important, we had great difficulty in finding a suitable layout that could incorporate these two switches. Although it was fine for the alignment window, we could find no nice place to put it in an interface window.

8.6 SUMMARY

This chapter has provided the design and implementation of an extensive **window application** — the **window maker** for constructing application windows. In particular, we have discussed the following notions:

- A simple extension of forms called **forms with highlight** that carry a secondary form to replace it when it is considered *on*. The original is the *off* version.

- The design of form libraries for the storage of small forms.

- The design and implementation of a form librarian to permit users to create, edit, and store small forms. It also serves as an extensive example of the use of the window maker.

- The design of extended views that permit (1) referencing by name, (2) preprocessing when a window is opened and postprocessing when it is closed, (3) an arbitrary number of constant parameters, (4) special capabilities such as switches with constant-size forms, dynamic pictures, and external reference windows, (5) a method for computing the display transformation that eliminates the imprecision built in to standard windows, and (6) infinite loop protection for the change/update protocol.

- The detailed protocol for classes ExtendedStandardSystemView, ExtendedView, ExtendedMenuView, ExtendedTextView, ExtendedSwitchView, ExtendedPictureView, ExtendedSwitchAndPictureView, and ExtendedExternalView.

- The design of the window maker including the parts hierarchy, the view hierarchy, and the controller hierarchy.

- Details about the window maker; specifically, (1) group sequencing, (2) view displaying, moving, and sizing, (3) labeling the icons, (4) the master icon controller, (5) the master icon view, (6) compressing and decompressing views, (7) options windows, (8) encoding/decoding, conversion to extended views, and copying, and (9) the remaining icons (everything that wasn't discussed previously).

- Details about specific options windows including the alignment, borderingAndColoring, background, switchAndPictureBackground, masterSizing, makeMethod, master, text, menu, switch, picture, and external options window.

8.7 EXERCISES

The following exercises are designed to test your knowledge of windows, models, views, and controllers by suggesting possible extensions to the window maker application.

1. Change the design for a highlight form so that it keeps track of a state that determines whether or not to display itself on or off.

2. Change the form library implementation so that it inherits from dictionary.

3. Add a **storeOn**: method to form libraries so that they can better store themselves.

4. Extend the editing facilities of the form librarian so that a form editor appears instead of a bit editor if the form is too large.

5. Change the model-view-controller relationships for the window maker window by eliminating the window maker model (aWindowMaker in Fig. 8.4). Hint: See how it is bypassed by the zooming switches.

6. Eliminate the existing window maker bordering inaccuracies by changing method **privateEditorOn**: in class WindowMaker to use extended views. Note: To gain the benefits of extended views, subviews may have to be positioned more exactly using **window:viewport**: instead of **addSubView:in:borderWidth**:.

7. Gain experience with the window maker (if you've managed to file in the code) by bootstrapping the editor window.

8. Extend the option windows so that they can all be canceled. Make sure that canceling has the same effect as **undo**.

9. Design a better alternative to finalizing options processing. Currently, it is finalized by closing the window.

10. Add another yellow button pop-up menu entry to the icon container pane that permits stubs to be generated for the pluggable interface messages.

11. Design an alternative interface window that permits the interfacing information to be displayed together for all icons at once. This would provide a better overview of the pluggable protocol.

8.8 GLOSSARY AND IMPORTANT FACTS

classes

ContinuousSwitchController An extension of class **SwitchController** that keeps sending the message associated with the switch as long as it maintains control; i.e., as long as the mouse is depressed in the switch view.

ErrorHandler An error notifier serving as a parameter to the compiler. It gets control when an error is encountered. Can be used to support an editor that needs to display the error message in one of its panes.

ExtendedExternalView A class that provides an indirect reference to an extended view. It is provided mainly to support external windows constructed by the window maker.

ExtendedMenuView An extension of pluggable class **SelectionInListView** providing (1) extended messages as pluggable selectors, (2) infinite loop protection so that 'self **changed**: #updateSymbol' messages by the model will not result in an infinite loop when an update is in progress, and (3) a controller that permits empty menus to gain control (this is not permitted by class **SelectionInList-View**).

ExtendedMessage An extension of class **Message** with a few additional methods to simplify its use.

ExtendedPictureView An extension of class **ExtendedSwitchView** that provides (1) both **static** pictures (the usual kind), and (2) **dynamic** pictures; i.e., pictures that can be changed any time the model decides. When the model wants a new picture displayed, it simply sends a 'self **changed**: #updateSymbol' message; #updateSymbol is the update symbol for the extended picture view.

ExtendedStandardSystemView An extension of class **StandardSystemView** providing (1) preprocessing by the model before the view (window) is opened and postprocessing after it is closed, (2) printing support for the other extended views, (3) compilation support for class ExtendedView, and (4) support to maintain and extract a window encoding.

ExtendedSwitchAndPictureView An extension of class **ExtendedSwitchView** that simultaneously provides both an extended switch view and a picture view with a specifiable **separation** between the two.

ExtendedSwitchView An extension of class **SwitchView** that provides (1) fixed- and varying-size labels, (2) extended messages as pluggable selectors, (3) infinite loop protection so that 'self **changed**: #updateSymbol' messages by the model will not result in an infinite loop when an update is in progress, (4) an explicit instance variable (aspect) for keeping track of the update symbol, permitting it to be different from the **isOn** message, (5) knowledge about highlight forms and the librarian so that switches may be specified via library path names; i.e., library name and form name pairs, and (6) the ability to have on and off representations that are different (**replacement** style) as opposed to merged (**overlay** style).

ExtendedTextView An extension of pluggable class **TextView** providing (1) extended messages as pluggable selectors, (2) infinite loop protection so that 'self **changed**: #updateSymbol' messages by the model will not result in an infinite loop when an update is in progress, and (3) an explicit instance variable (aspect) for keeping track of the update symbol permitting it to be different from the **getText** message.

ExtendedView An extension of class **View** that is similar to class **ExtendedStandardSystemView** but lacking the pre-opening and postclosing facility.

FormLibrarian A model for an editor that permits form libraries to be constructed, changed, and extended.

FormLibrary A named dictionary of forms. Permits the retrieval and storage of forms (and/or forms with highlight) by name; i.e., the key-value pairs are name-form pairs. One instance, **DefaultFormLibrary**, contains three forms with highlight indexed by the symbols #blank, #button, #check.

FormWithHighlight   A class of forms that has two display images — one when it is off and another when it is on. The form itself provides the off image; its **highlight** provides the on image.

WindowMaker   An extension of class **Object** that provides (1) an interface for a designer who wishes to construct or edit an application specific window, and (2) a model for this editor.

WindowMakerControllerWithCancel   An extension of class **StandardSystemController** for use by window maker options windows. It provides two facilities: (1) a close facility that causes the window maker's master controller to regain control no matter what window had previous control and (2) a cancel facility that works like the close facility but additionally records the fact that it was canceled so that it can be interrogated by a postclosing operation.

WindowMakerExternalIcon   An extension of class **WindowMakerIcon** that provides the external icon protocol.

WindowMakerGroupIcon   An extension of class **WindowMakerIcon** that provides the grouping protocol. It permits collections of icons to be grouped either temporarily or permanently. Once grouped, such collections can be manipulated as individual icons.

WindowMakerIcon   An abstract class for all window maker icons. An extension of class **ExtendedSwitchView** that provides the common functionality for all icons.

WindowMakerMasterIcon   An extension of class **WindowMakerIcon** for keeping track of the currently selected icons, the minimum and maximum sizes for the application window, and a set of output options that specifies how the application window is to be generated; e.g., in the transcript, as a class method, or as an instance method. In the last two cases, additional information must also be provided; i.e., the class name, method name, category name, and overflow category name (in case more than one method is needed to generate the application window).

WindowMakerMasterIconController   An extension of class **MouseMenuController** that provides (1) a copy buffer to permit icons (rather than characters) to be copied, cut, pasted, and deleted, (2) both menu and keyboard processing for the above in addition to a facility to permit grouping and ungrouping of icons, (3) a facility to keep track of the currently active pop-up options window, (4) a rather complex yellow button menu that is constructed dynamically to take into account the currently selected icons, (5) mouse controlled icon selection, deselection, moving, and size adjusting, and (6) a repository for the pop-up options windows — the window maker is bootstrapped.

WindowMakerMenuIcon   An extension of class **WindowMakerIcon** that provides the menu icon protocol.

WindowMakerPictureIcon   An extension of class **WindowMakerSwitchOrPictureIcon** that provides the picture icon protocol.

WindowMakerSwitchAndIconIcon   An extension of class **WindowMakerSwitchIcon** that provides the protocol for the combined switch and picture icons.

WindowMakerSwitchIcon   An extension of class **WindowMakerSwitchOrPictureIcon** that provides the switch icon protocol.

WindowMakerSwitchOrPictureIcon   An extension of class **WindowMakerIcon** that provides common access/modification, encoding/decoding, and background protocol for the switch and picture subclasses.

WindowMakerTextIcon   An extension of class **WindowMakerIcon** that provides the text icon protocol.

blank One of the three switch forms in the default form library (also see **button** and **check**).

button One of the three switch forms in the default form library (also see **blank** and **check**).

check One of the three switch forms in the default form library (also see **blank** and **button**).

compressed The status of a window maker's option window when the construction method generates an encoding (as opposed to a view).

constant-size An extended switch views mode where the switch labels don't scale. Such views stay the same size when a containing view is resized. An example of an object that scales is a form; an example of one that doesn't is a string converted to a paragraph or a display text.

decompressed The status of a window maker's option window when the construction method generates a view (as opposed to an encoding).

encoding An appropriately initialized array of constants that is a compact representation for an icon. The encoding for a container icon such as a master icon or a group icon also contains the encoding for the contained icons. Hence, a master icon encoding is a compact representation for an entire application window. In general, an encoding contains more information than a corresponding extended view. For this reason, the encoding is maintained with extended standard system views and extended views (though not with other views). Once a method is generated to produce an application window from extended views, it is possible to discard the encoding. However, it is needed if the window is to be edited for changes in the future.

extended view An extension of pluggable windows that provides (1) a name, (2) a preprocessing and postprocessing facility, (3) view messages with an arbitrary number of constant parameters, (4) a method for computing the display transformation that eliminates the built-in imprecision (see Fig. 3.7 in Sect. 3.3.1 or Sect.

8.3.2), and (5) infinite loop protection for the change/update protocol. It also provides switch views with constant-size forms, dynamic picture views, and external reference views.

fixed point Constant-size windows need a fixed point to specify which portion of the window is to serve as the anchor when the containing window is resized. If the fixed point is the center of an icon, for example, then this anchor point will move when the container window is resized. However, the icon will be positioned in such a way that its center is at that anchor point. Generally, the two most useful fixed points are the middle left and center. Seven different fixed point specifications are permitted; namely, top left, middle left, bottom left, center, top right, middle right, and bottom right.

form librarian A tool for creating, editing, and storing libraries of forms.

form library A dictionary of forms with a name.

forms with highlight A class of forms that has two display images — one when it is off and another when it is on. The form itself provides the off image; its **highlight** provides the on image.

group icon A window maker icon that permits sets of icons to be manipulated as individual icons either on a temporary or permanent basis.

group sequencing facility A protocol that permits nongroup icons to be processed transparently independent of how deeply nested the icons are in a group.

grow box An 8@8 rectangle at the bottom right corner of a window maker icon.

highlight The on image (as opposed to off image) for a form with highlight.

icon background The textual name or form that is displayed in the icon's display box.

icon container pane The bottom pane of the window maker editor that serves as the repository for newly created subwindows — **window maker icons**.

icon dehighlighting Reversing the bits of an icon's inset display box a second time.

icon highlighting Reversing the bits of an icon's inset display box.

icon locking Ensures that the icon's size remains constant; i.e., deactivates the grow box. This is permitted only on constant-size switch icons.

interface window An option window that permits interfacing information (pluggable messages) to be associated with the icon (subwindow) so that it will function properly when the application window is opened.

interface window defaults Text strings provided by default methods for display in the interface option window. These default strings are specific to each class of icon provided by the window maker.

lasso-selection facility A facility that provides an alternative approach to selecting a set of icons. Depressing the mouse over an open area and moving it cause a rectangle to appear and track the mouse (the lasso). When the button is released, all icons touching the rectangle are selected. The shift-clicking facility can then be used to add or remove specific icons.

master icon The container for all newly created icons in the window maker editor.

mode One of two possibilities provided by extended switch views; i.e., **constant-size** mode and **varying-size** mode.

option window The scheduled window that pops up as a result of a yellow button pop-up menu selection in the window maker's icon container pane. There are twelve option windows: an alignment window, a borderingAndColoring window, a background window, a switchAndPicture-Background window, a masterSizing window, a makeMethod window, a master interface window, a text interface window, a menu interface window, a switch interface window, a picture interface window, and an external interface window.

overlay option An extended switch view option that specifies whether or not the highlight object (when provided) is to be displayed **over** the label as opposed to **replacing** it when the switch is depressed (the default is to replace).

replace option An extended switch view option that specifies whether or not the highlight object (when provided) is to **replace** the label as opposed to being displayed **over** the label when the switch is depressed (the default is to replace).

shift-clicking facility A facility that permits icons to be added or removed from the set of selected icons by pressing the mouse button over it while the shift key is down. Shift-clicking over a previously unselected icon selects it; shift-clicking over a selected icon deselects it.

varying-size An extended switch view mode where the switch labels can scale or where they can't scale and yet must be displayed in a varying-size area. Such views change size when a containing view is resized — the label changes size only if it can. An example of an object that scales is a form; an example of one that doesn't is a string converted to a paragraph or a display text.

window maker A tool for use by relatively experienced programmers who understand the notion of pluggable views to simplify the task of designing application specific windows. It provides the designer with the capability to (1) create text, menu, switch, picture, and external subwindows, (2) specify their interfaces, and (3) provide a suitable layout (resizing, bordering, coloring, moving, and aligning).

window maker icon A subwindow in the **icon container pane.**

zoom switches Switches at the top right corner of the window maker editor that cause the window to magnify or shrink the contents of the container pane.

important facts

revised transformation display algorithm An accurate algorithm for computing a window's display transformation. It eliminates the inaccuracy that results because borders do not scale.

Appendix A

Source Code Revisions

A.1 REVISIONS TO DISPLAY TRANSFORMATIONS

In order to display graphical objects (windows included), one of a large number of display operations must be selected. The simpler ones are of the form

- aGraphicalObject **display**
- aGraphicalObject **displayAt:** aPoint
- aGraphicalObject **displayOn:** aDisplayMedium **at:** aPoint

For more complex control, especially in the context of windows that can be resized and repositioned, it is necessary to specify a display transformation. The operations are of the form

- aGraphicalObject ...
- aGraphicalObject ... **rule:** aRuleNumber **mask:** aForm
- aGraphicalObject ... **align:** destinationPoint1 **with:** destinationPoint2
- aGraphicalObject ... **align:** ..Point1 **with:** ..Point2 **rule:** aRuleNumber **mask:** aForm
- aGraphicalObject ... **fixedPoint:** sourcePoint

where "..." denotes

displayOn: aDisplayMedium **transformation:** aTransformation
      clippingBox: aRectangle

The **align:with:** variety permits the transformed graphical object to be further offset in such a manner that destinationPoint1 is on top of destinationPoint2 when it is displayed. The **fixedPoint:** variety permits a specific source point to display at its intended transformed location even if the graphical object does not know how to scale itself. To be clear, these two notions need pictures and further elaboration.

What Alignment Means

Alignment is an operation that is used extensively during window creation for positioning a window's viewport in the superview window. This kind of positioning is never specified in terms of source coordinates; i.e., window coordinations. Rather it is specified in destination or viewport coordinates. Figure A.1 illustrates how a viewport can be positioned in the superview's window by aligning point1 in the viewport with point2 in the superview window.

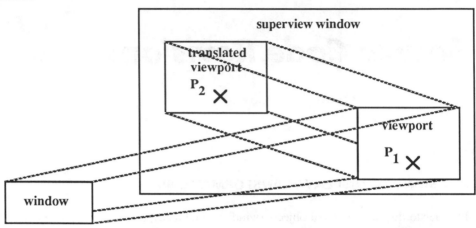

By aligning P_1 with P_2, the viewport is translated to that P_1 is on top of P_2.

Figure A.1 What alignment means.

The alignment mechanism simply offsets the transformed window by P_1-P_2. If P_1 = P_2, no offsetting is performed. The same idea applies to an arbitrary object like a form. For example, if the goal is to display a form in the top left corner of a window and this form is to be transformed using the window's display transformation, we will need to move its transformed origin to the desired display box origin. The display would be achieved by executing

```
aForm
    displayOn: Display
    transformation: aDisplayTransformation
    clippingBox: aDisplayBox
    align: (aDisplayTransformation applyTo: aForm origin) with: aDisplayBox origin
```

Note that the alignment points need not be inside the graphical object to be displayed. Specifying '... **align:** point1 **with:** point2' simply indicates that *if point1 were to be displayed, it should be displayed at point2*.

What Fixed Points Are All About

A **fixed point** is a point that transforms exactly where the display transformation dictates. The notion is interesting only when objects to be displayed cannot be scaled because otherwise, all points are fixed points. For example, if a paragraph is displayed, no scaling is performed even if the transformation indicates that the paragraph should be magnified by a factor of two, say. In that situation, it is always possible to ensure that at least one point

494   Inside Smalltalk maps to the location specified by the display transformation. Other points, however, will not. Figure A.2 illustrates how a paragraph would be displayed if a fixed point were specified along with a transformation that magnifies it.

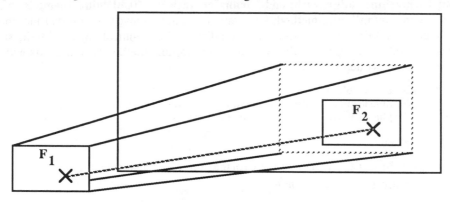

Fixed point F$_1$ maps to F$_2$.

If the graphical object is prevented from scaling to its intended size, only one of the points in the object will actually transform to its intended location; namely, the fixed point.

Figure A.2 What a fixed point means.

By making different choices for the fixed point, the graphical object ends up being displayed at slightly different locations. The results from three different choices are shown in Figure A.3.

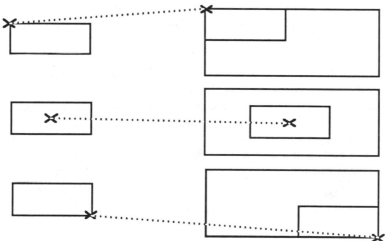

Figure A.3 Choosing different choices for the fixed point.

Note that specifying a fixed point for objects that are able to scale is superfluous because any point specified will map to its intended destination. Additionally, note that the fixed point is specified in source coordinates.

How Alignment and Fixed Points Are Handled

The easiest way to understand how these two notions are handled is to rewrite the **...transformation:...align:with:** and **...transformation:...fixedPoint:** methods in terms of the **...transformation:...** method; i.e., construct a new transformation that incorporates the alignment and fixed point information and display the graphical object with the simpler display method. More specifically, we would like to take the last two methods and show how they can be written in terms of the first.

- aGraphicalObject ...
- aGraphicalObject ... **align**: destinationPoint1 **with**: destinationPoint2
- aGraphicalObject ... **fixedPoint**: sourcePoint

where "..." denotes

> **displayOn**: aDisplayMedium **transformation**: oldTransformation
> **clippingBox**: aRectangle

To do this, it is sufficient to provide the new transformation to be used.

Handling Alignment

```
newTransformation ← WindowingTransformation
    scale: oldTransformation scale
    translation: oldTransformation translation +
        (destinationPoint2 - destinationPoint1).
```

Handling a Fixed Point (Objects That Scale)

```
newTransformation ← oldTransformation.
```

Handling a Fixed Point (Objects That Do Not Scale)

```
newTransformation ← WindowingTransformation
    scale: nil
    translation: (oldTransformation applyTo: sourcePoint) - sourcePoint.
```

To justify why this works, consider each case separately. For alignment, the only difference between the old transformation and the new is that an extra offset is supplied. Since transformations always apply scaling before translation, all points mapped with the new transformation must differ from the corresponding points obtained with the old transformation by the constant offset 'destinationPoint2 - destinationPoint1'. So, let's consider just one point that is used to map to destinationPoint1; i.e., consider aPoint such that (oldTransformation **applyTo**: aPoint) = destinationPoint1. Now,

```
newTransformation applyTo: aPoint
    = destinationPoint1 + "contant offset"
    = destinationPoint1 + (destinationPoint2 - destinationPoint1)
    = destinationPoint2
```

The second case is trivial. If an object can scale, all points are fixed points and no special adjustment is needed.

The third case is more complex but the idea is simple: If an object cannot scale, the distance between the origin and the fixed point must be the same both in source coordinates and in destination coordination. In source coordinates, this distance is 'sourcePoint - 0@0', or simply sourcePoint. The transformed origin is determined by subtracting this distance from the transformed fixed point. An equivalent explanation could be provided by expanding on the simplified code as follows:

```
fixedPoint ← sourcePoint.
distanceBetweenOriginAndFixedPoint ← sourcePoint.
transformedFixedPoint ← displayTransformation applyTo: sourcePoint.
transformedOrigin ← transformedFixedPoint -
    distanceBetweenOriginAndFixedPoint.
newTransformation ← WindowingTransformation
    scale: nil
    translation: transformedOrigin.
```

What Is Wrong with the Existing Implementation

The existing implementation attempts to use "two wrongs to make a right" and partly succeeds. More specifically, the current approach is the following:

Handling Alignment

```
newTransformation ← WindowingTransformation
    scale: oldTransformation scale
    translation: (oldTransformation applyTo: destinationPoint2) -
        destinationPoint1.
```

Handling a Fixed Point

```
uses ... align: sourcePoint with: sourcePoint.
```

The fixed point display methods were incorrectly written in terms of alignment, which of course should simply not work. This error was fixed by changing the alignment code so that it would do the fixed point computation. Of course, this means that alignment doesn't work.

It is easy to check that neither works properly. For example, try executing

```
Form fromUser
    displayOn: Display
    transformation: (WindowingTransformation scale: 2@2 translation: 0@0)
    clippingBox: Display boundingBox
    align: 0@0 with: Display boundingBox center
    rule: Form over mask: Form black
```

This, of course, should magnify the form by a factor of two and display it so that its origin is at the center of the screen. Instead, the form is entirely off the screen. Alternatively, try executing

```
Form fromUser
    displayOn: Display
    transformation: (WindowingTransformation
        scale: 2@2
        translation: Display boundingBox center)
    clippingBox: Display boundingBox
    fixedPoint: Display boundingBox corner
```

In this case, you expect the same result because the form is to be scaled and translated to the center. The fixed point here is a red herring because all points are fixed points. Again, the form is off the screen.

What is amazing is that most things work in spite of these errors. The explanation is simple. Little use is made of the ...align:with:... methods. The major user is the ...fixedPoint: method, and this method was designed exclusively for use in switch windows. Currently, switch windows use only paragraphs as labels; these are fixed-size. It's not surprising that the method works for such labels but not for forms as labels.

How to Fix the Display Methods

To fix the display methods, three things must be done:

1. The **applyTo:** operation must be eliminated from all **...align:with:...** methods. You can find them all by asking for all users of **applyTo:**.
2. The **...fixedPoint:** methods must be revised as previously indicated.
3. Methods **boundingBox** and **computeBoundingBox** in class Form must be revised to use the offset as the origin rather than 0@0. The old versions must be added to class Cursor.

To ensure that the changes are properly made, the actual code is shown next.

displaying-generic

```
aDisplayObject
    displayOn: aDisplayMedium transformation: displayTransformation
    clippingBox: clipRectangle align: destinationPoint1 with: destinationPoint2
    rule: ruleInteger mask: aForm
        "Display the receiver where a DisplayTransformation is provided as an
        argument, rule is ruleInteger and mask is aForm. Translate by destinationPoint2
        - destinationPoint1. Assumes the display object is fixed-size. Must be
        overridden if otherwise. Information to be displayed must be confined to the
        area that intersects with clipRectangle."

        | newOffset |
        newOffset ← displayTransformation translation +
            (destinationPoint2 - destinationPoint1).
        self displayOn: aDisplayMedium
            at: newOffset x truncated @ newOffset y truncated
            clippingBox: clipRectangle
            rule: ruleInteger
            mask: aForm

aDisplayObject
    displayOn: aDisplayMedium transformation: displayTransformation
    clippingBox: clipRectangle fixedPoint: aPoint
        "Display the receiver where a DisplayTransformation is provided as an
        argument, rule is Form over and mask is Form black. Assumes the display
        object is fixed-size. Must be overridden if otherwise. Information to be
        displayed must be confined to the area that intersects with clipRectangle."

        self displayOn: aDisplayMedium
            transformation: (WindowingTransformation
                scale: nil
                translation: (displayTransformation applyTo: aPoint) - aPoint)
            clippingBox: clipRectangle
            align: aPoint with: aPoint
            rule: Form over mask: Form black
```

displaying

aDisplayText
> **displayOn**: aDisplayMedium **transformation**: displayTransformation
> **clippingBox**: clipRectangle **align**: destinationPoint1 **with**: destinationPoint2
> **rule**: ruleInteger **mask**: aForm
>> "Assumes the display object is fixed-size. Must be overridden if otherwise. Refer to the comment in DisplayObjectldisplayOn:transformation:clippingBox:align:with:rule:mask:."
>
>> | newOffset |
>> newOffset ← displayTransformation **translation** +
>>> (destinationPoint2 - destinationPoint1).
>> self **displayOn**: aDisplayMedium
>>> **at**: newOffset **x truncated** @ newOffset **y truncated**
>>> **clippingBox**: clipRectangle
>>> **rule**: ruleInteger **mask**: aForm

displaying

aForm
> **displayOn**: aDisplayMedium **transformation**: displayTransformation
> **clippingBox**: clipRectangle **align**: destinationPoint1 **with**: destinationPoint2
> **rule**: ruleInteger **mask**: aForm
>> "Graphically, it means nothing to scale a Form by floating point values. Because scales and other display parameters are kept in floating point to minimize round off errors, we are forced in this routine to round off to the nearest integer."
>
>> | scale magnifiedForm newOffset |
>> displayTransformation **noScale**
>>> **ifTrue**: [magnifiedForm ← self]
>>> **ifFalse**: [
>>>> scale ← displayTransformation **scale**.
>>>> scale ← scale **x rounded** @ scale **y rounded**.
>>>> (1@1 = scale)
>>>>> **ifTrue**: [scale ← **nil**. magnifiedForm ← self]
>>>>> **ifFalse**: [
>>>>>> magnifiedForm ← self **magnify**: self **boundingBox by**: scale]].
>> newOffset ← displayTransformation **translation** +
>>> (destinationPoint2 - destinationPoint1).
>> magnifiedForm
>>> **displayOn**: aDisplayMedium
>>> **at**: newOffset **x truncated** @ newOffset **y truncated**
>>> **clippingBox**: clipRectangle
>>> **rule**: ruleInteger **mask**: aForm

aForm
> **displayOn**: aDisplayMedium **transformation**: displayTransformation
> **clippingBox**: clipRectangle **fixedPoint**: aPoint
>> "Display the receiver where a DisplayTransformation is provided as an argument, rule is Form over and mask is Form black. No translation. Information to be displayed must be confined to the area that intersects with clipRectangle. Since forms can scale, all points are fixed points."
>
>> self **displayOn**: aDisplayMedium
>>> **transformation**: displayTransformation **clippingBox**: clipRectangle
>>> **align**: 0@0 **with**: 0@0
>>> **rule**: Form **over mask**: Form **black**

display box access

aForm **boundingBox**
      ↑Rectangle **origin**: offset **extent**: width@height

aForm **computeBoundingBox**
      ↑Rectangle **origin**: offset **extent**: width@height

aCursor **boundingBox**
      ↑Rectangle **origin**: 0@0 **extent**: width@height

aCursor **computeBoundingBox**
      ↑Rectangle **origin**: 0@0 **extent**: width@height

displaying

aParagraph
      displayOn: aDisplayMedium **transformation**: displayTransformation
      clippingBox: clipRectangle **align**: destinationPoint1 **with**: destinationPoint2
      rule: ruleInteger **mask**: aForm

            | newOffset |
            newOffset ← offset + displayTransformation **translation** +
                  (destinationPoint2 - destinationPoint1).
            self
                  displayOn: aDisplayMedium **at**: newOffset **rounded**
                  clippingBox: clipRectangle **rule**: ruleInteger **mask**: aForm

A.2 Revisions to Paths

Class Path and its subclasses Arc, Line, Circle, and so on, have four minor problems that should be fixed. We consider them one by one.

Modification 1: General Display Fixes

Class Path and its specializations Arc, Circle, Line, Curve, LinearFit, and Spline each have method **displayOn:transformation:clippingBox:rule:mask**: specially implemented to properly handle the transformation. On the other hand, **displayOn:transformation:clippingBox:align:with:** was not redefined and is therefore inherited from DisplayObject. This method does not work with paths because the scaling information is ignored; i.e., the method assumes the graphical object is fixed-size. For example, if a line from 0@0 to 10@10 were to be displayed using a transformation of the form '**scale**: 10 **translation**: 5@5', the latter method simply offsets the display by 5@5 so that the line actually displayed begins at 5@5 and ends at 15@15. The correct version requires more than a simple offset; the entire line must be transformed and, in this case, magnified. It should display the line from 5@5 (0@0 transformed) to 105@105 (10@10 transformed).

A correct version of **displayOn:transformation:clippingBox:align:with:rule:mask:** can be created by adding the additional parameters '**align**: destinationPoint1 **with**: destinationPoint2' to the existing **displayOn:transformation:clippingBox:rule:mask:** method in Path and each of its subclasses (seven classes in all).

For all classes except **Circle**, 'at: 0@0' in the code body is replaced by the difference of the alignment points. More specifically, if the method is of the following form, '0@0' is replaced by '(destinationPoint2 - destinationPoint1)'.

```
aPathOrArcOrCurveOrSplineOr...
        displayOn: aDisplayMedium transformation: displayTransformation
        clippingBox: clipRectangle align: destinationPoint1 with: destinationPoint2
        rule: ruleInteger mask: aForm
            ...
            aTransformedCopy
                    displayOn: aDisplayMedium
                    at: 0 @ 0
                    clippingBox: aClippingRectangle
                    rule: aRuleInteger
                    mask: aMaskForm
        ...
```

For class **Circle**, 'super **displayOn**:...**transformation**:...**clippingBox**:...**rule**:...-**mask**:...' in the code body is replaced by 'super **displayOn**:...**transformation**:...**clippingBox**:...**align**: destinationPoint1 **with**: destinationPoint2 **rule**:...**mask**:...'.

Note that method **displayOn:transformation:clippingBox:rule:mask:** can be removed from each of the subclasses since the version inherited from DisplayObject makes use of the new corrected methods.

Modification 2: Path Display Fix

The generic **displayOn:transformation:clippingBox:** method inherited from DisplayObject fails for **Path** and its subclasses. A copy of the DisplayObject version can be added to **Path** (all subclasses can inherit from this one) and modified as follows: "change the **align:?with:?** portion of the **displayOn:transformation:clippingBox:align:with:rule:mask:** message to contain any point constants that are identical; e.g., **align:0@0with:0@0**".

Modification 3: Missing 'do:' Operation in Path

Path is missing a **do:** operation required and used by its subclass **LinearFit**. It can easily be added by modifying method **collect:**.

Modification 4: Spline Display Fix

The **Spline displayOn:transformation:**... method constructs a new transformed spline prior to displaying it. However, it fails to compute the curve using **computeCurve**. Simply add 'newSpline **computeCurve**' after the code that constructs it.

Example

The following can serve as a test of the above modifications. The intent is to draw six special paths in two rows of three squares. The squares should be adjacent to each other without overlapping.

| aDot aLine aCircle aCurve aPath aLinearFit aSpline aTransformation aBox d t |
aDot ← (Form **extent**: 4@4) **black**.

"Create display objects intended for display on a 10 by 10 area."
aLine ← Line **from**: 2@2 **to**: 8@8 **withForm**: aDot.
aCircle ← Circle **new**
      form: aDot; **radius**: 4; **center**: 5@5; **yourself**.
aCurve ← Curve **new**
      form: aDot; **firstPoint**: 2@8; **secondPoint**: 5@2; **thirdPoint**: 8@8; **yourself**.
aPath ← Path **new**
      form: aDot; **add**: 2@8; **add**: 2@2; **add**: 5@8; **add**: 8@2; **add**: 8@8; **yourself**.
aLinearFit ← LinearFit **new**
      form: aDot; **add**: 2@8; **add**: 2@2; **add**: 5@8; **add**: 8@2; **add**: 8@8; **yourself**.
aSpline ← Spline **new**
      form: aDot; add: 2@8; **add**: 2@2; **add**: 5@8; **add**: 8@2; **add**: 8@8; **yourself**.
aSpline **computeCurve**. "Otherwise, the spline cannot be displayed"

"Display in two rows of three squares each 113 by 113 units (just to pick an odd size)."
aTransformation ← WindowingTransformation
      window: (0@0 **corner**: 10@10) viewport: (0@0 **corner**: 113@113).
aBox ← Display **boundingBox**. "The rectangle for the entire display"

Display **white**. "Start with a nice display"

d ← Display. t ← aTransformation. "Just to fit subsequent statements into one line."
aLine **displayOn**: d **transformation**: t **clippingBox**: aBox **align**: 0@0 **with**: 100@100.
aCircle **displayOn**: d **transformation**: t **clippingBox**: aBox **align**: 0@0 **with**: 213@100.
aCurve **displayOn**: d **transformation**: t **clippingBox**: aBox **align**: 0@0 **with**: 326@100.
aPath **displayOn**: d **transformation**: t **clippingBox**: aBox **align**: 0@0 **with**: 100@213.
aLinearFit **displayOn**: d **transformation**: t **clippingBox**: aBox **align**: 0@0 **with**: 213@213.
aSpline **displayOn**: d **transformation**: t **clippingBox**: aBox **align**: 0@0 **with**: 326@213.

"By aligning 0@0 with 213@100, for example, we are causing the display to shift right by 213 pixels. Clearly, 213 must be in destination coordinates. If it were in source coordinates, the actual amount shifted would be "t **applyTo**: 213"; to get exactly 213, we would have to actually supply "t **applyInverseTo**: 213" (the display method would then transform it to cancel out the inverse operation; i.e., "t **applyTo**: (t **applyInverseTo**: 213)" is 213."

ScheduledControllers **restore**. "To place the display into its previous state"

Appendix B

Window Maker Extras

B.1 COPY AND STORE OPERATIONS FOR EXTENDED VIEWS

B.1.1 ExtendedStandardSystemView Operations

copying

deepCopy
    | copy |
    copy ← self **shallowCopy**
        superView: nil; **resetSubViews**;
        model: model **deepCopy controller**: nil;
        transformation: transformation "stores a copy";
        window: window "stores a copy";
        labelFrame: labelFrame **deepCopy**;
        label: (labelText **isNil ifTrue**: [nil] **ifFalse**: [self **label**]);
        minimumSize: minimumSize **copy**;
        maximumSize: maximumSize **copy**;
        yourself.
    subViews **do**: [:aView | copy **addSubView**: aView **deepCopy**].
    ↑copy

printing

storeOn: aStream
    self **storeOn**: aStream **indent**: 2

storeOn: aStream **indent**: indentation
    "Store this instance of an ExtendedStandardSystemView with indentation for readability."
    self **storeOn**: aStream **encoding**: nil **subViews**: true **indent**: indentation

storeOn: aStream **encoding:** aStringOrNil **subViews:** aBoolean **indent:** indentation
"Store this ExtendedStandardSystemView using indentation for readability. Either
generates the encoding or uses the one provided if aStringOrNil is non-nil. Only
generates the subviews if aBoolean is true."

| return continue |
return ← (WriteStream **on:** (String **new:** 16)) **crtab:** indentation; **contents**.
continue ← ';', return.

aStream
    nextPutAll: '(ExtendedStandardSystemView new'; **nextPutAll:** return;
    nextPutAll: 'name: '; **store:** name; **nextPutAll:** continue;
    nextPutAll: 'preOpeningSelector: '; **store:** preOpeningSelector;
        nextPutAll: continue;
    nextPutAll: 'postClosingSelector: '; **store:** postClosingSelector;
        nextPutAll: continue;
    nextPutAll: 'encoding: '.

aStringOrNil **isNil**
    ifTrue: [ExtendedStandardSystemView **storeEncoding:** encoding **on:** aStream
        indent: indentation+1]
    ifFalse: [aStream **nextPutAll:** aStringOrNil].
aStream **nextPutAll:** continue.

aStream
    nextPutAll: 'label: '; **store:** self **label; nextPutAll:** continue;
    nextPutAll: 'minimumSize: '; **store:** minimumSize; **nextPutAll:** continue;
    nextPutAll: 'maximumSize: '; **store:** maximumSize; **nextPutAll:** continue;
    nextPutAll: 'insideColor: '.
        ExtendedStandardSystemView **storeInsideColor:** insideColor **on:** aStream.
        aStream **nextPutAll:** continue.
    ExtendedStandardSystemView **storeBorderWidth:** borderWidth
        messageOn: aStream. aStream **nextPutAll:** continue;
    nextPutAll: 'window: '; **store:** window; **nextPutAll:** continue;
    nextPutAll: 'transformation: ('; **print:** transformation; **nextPut:** $);
        nextPutAll: continue.

aBoolean **ifTrue:** [
    subViews **do:** [:subView |
        aStream **nextPutAll:** 'addSubView: '.
        subView **storeOn:** aStream **indent:** indentation+1.
        aStream **nextPutAll:** continue]].

aStream **nextPutAll:** 'yourself)'

B.1.2 ExtendedView Operations

copying

deepCopy
    | copy |
    copy ← self **shallowCopy**
        superView: nil; **resetSubViews;**
        model: model **deepCopy controller:** nil;
        transformation: transformation "stores a copy";
        window: window "stores a copy";
        yourself.
    subViews **do:** [:aView | copy **addSubView:** aView **deepCopy**].
    ↑copy
printing

storeOn: aStream
    self **storeOn:** aStream **indent:** 2

storeOn: aStream **indent:** indentation
    "Store this instance of an ExtendedView with indentation for readability."
    self **storeOn:** aStream **encoding:** nil **subViews:** true **indent:** indentation

storeOn: aStream **encoding:** aStringOrNil **subViews:** aBoolean **indent:** indentation
    "Store this ExtendedStandardSystemView using indentation for readability. Either
    generates the encoding or uses the one provided if aStringOrNil is non-nil. Only
    generates the subviews if aBoolean is true."

    | return continue |
    return ← (WriteStream **on:** (String **new:** 16)) **crtab:** indentation; **contents.**
    continue ← ';', return.

    aStream
        nextPutAll: '(ExtendedView new'; **nextPutAll:** return;
        nextPutAll: 'name: '; **store:** name; **nextPutAll:** continue;
        nextPutAll: 'encoding: '.
    aStringOrNil **isNil**
        ifTrue: [ExtendedStandardSystemView **storeEncoding:** encoding **on:** aStream
            indent: indentation+1]
        ifFalse: [aStream **nextPutAll:** aStringOrNil].
    aStream **nextPutAll:** continue.

    aStream
        nextPutAll: 'insideColor: '.
            ExtendedStandardSystemView **storeInsideColor:** insideColor **on:** aStream.
            aStream **nextPutAll:** continue.
        ExtendedStandardSystemView **storeBorderWidth:** borderWidth
            messageOn: aStream. aStream **nextPutAll:** continue;
        nextPutAll: 'window: '; **store:** window; **nextPutAll:** continue;
        nextPutAll: 'transformation: ('; **print:** transformation; **nextPut:** $);
            nextPutAll: continue.

    aBoolean **ifTrue:** [
        subViews **do:** [:subView |
            aStream **nextPutAll:** 'addSubView: '.
            subView **storeOn:** aStream **indent:** indentation+1.
            aStream **nextPutAll:** continue]].

    aStream **nextPutAll:** 'yourself)'

B.1.3 ExtendedMenuView Operations

copying

deepCopy
    ↑self **shallowCopy**
        superView: nil; **resetSubViews;**
        model: model **deepCopy controller:** nil;
        transformation: transformation "stores a copy";
        window: window "stores a copy";
        yourself

printing

storeOn: aStream
    self **storeOn:** aStream **indent:** 2

storeOn: aStream **indent:** indentation
"Store this instance of an ExtendedMenuView with indentation for readability."
| return continue |
return ← (WriteStream **on:** (String **new:** 16)) **crtab:** indentation; **contents**.
continue ← ';', return.
aStream
    nextPutAll: '((ExtendedMenuView on: nil'; **nextPutAll:** return;
    nextPutAll: 'printItems: true oneItem: false'; **nextPutAll:** return;
    nextPutAll: 'aspect: '; **store:** partMsg; **nextPutAll:** return;
    nextPutAll: 'change: '; **store:** changeMsg; **nextPutAll:** return;
    nextPutAll: 'list: '; **store:** listMsg; **nextPutAll:** return;
    nextPutAll: 'menu: '; **store:** menuMsg; **nextPutAll:** return;
    nextPutAll: 'initialSelection: '; **store:** initialSelectionMsg; **nextPut:** $);
        nextPutAll: return;
    nextPutAll: 'name: '; **store:** name; **nextPutAll:** continue;
    nextPutAll: 'insideColor: '.
        ExtendedStandardSystemView **storeInsideColor:** insideColor **on:** aStream.
        aStream **nextPutAll:** continue.
    ExtendedStandardSystemView **storeBorderWidth:** borderWidth
        messageOn: aStream. aStream **nextPutAll:** continue;
    nextPutAll: 'window: '; **store:** window; **nextPutAll:** continue;
    nextPutAll: 'transformation: ('; **print:** transformation; **nextPut:** $); **nextPutAll:** continue;
    nextPutAll: 'yourself)'

B.1.4 ExtendedTextView Operations

copying

deepCopy
    ↑self **shallowCopy**
        superView: nil; **resetSubViews;**
        model: model **deepCopy controller:** nil;
        transformation: transformation "stores a copy";
        window: window "stores a copy";
        yourself

printing

storeOn: aStream
    self **storeOn:** aStream **indent:** 2

storeOn: aStream **indent:** indentation
    "Store this instance of an ExtendedTextView with indentation for readability."
    | return continue |
    return ← (WriteStream **on:** (String **new:** 16)) **crtab:** indentation; **contents**.
    continue ← ';', return.
    aStream
        nextPutAll: '((ExtendedTextView on: nil'; **nextPutAll:** return;
        nextPutAll: 'aspect: '; **store:** aspect; **nextPutAll:** return;
        nextPutAll: 'get: '; **store:** partMsg; **nextPutAll:** return;
        nextPutAll: 'change: '; **store:** acceptMsg; **nextPutAll:** return;
        nextPutAll: 'menu: '; **store:** menuMsg; **nextPut:** $); **nextPutAll:** return;
        nextPutAll: 'name: '; **store:** name; **nextPutAll:** continue;
        nextPutAll: 'insideColor: '.
            ExtendedStandardSystemView **storeInsideColor:** insideColor **on:** aStream.
            aStream **nextPutAll:** continue.
        ExtendedStandardSystemView **storeBorderWidth:** borderWidth
            messageOn: aStream. aStream **nextPutAll:** continue;

```
        nextPutAll: 'window: '; store: window; nextPutAll: continue;
        nextPutAll: 'transformation: ('; print: transformation; nextPut: $);
            nextPutAll: continue;
        nextPutAll: 'yourself)'
```

B.1.5 ExtendedExternalView Operations

copying

deepCopy
```
    | copy |
    copy ← self shallowCopy
        superView: nil; resetSubViews;
        model: model deepCopy controller: nil;
        transformation: transformation "stores a copy";
        window: window "stores a copy";
        yourself.
    subViews do: [:aView | copy addSubView: aView deepCopy].
    ↑copy
```

printing

storeOn: aStream
```
    self storeOn: aStream indent: 2
```

storeOn: aStream **indent:** indentation
```
    "Store this instance of an ExtendedView with indentation for readability."
    | return continue |
    return ← (WriteStream on: (String new: 16)) crtab: indentation; contents.
    continue ← ';', return.
    aStream
        nextPutAll: '(ExtendedExternalView new'; nextPutAll: return;
        nextPutAll: 'name: '; store: name; nextPutAll: continue;
        nextPutAll: 'insideColor: '.
            ExtendedStandardSystemView storeInsideColor: insideColor on: aStream.
            aStream nextPutAll: continue.
        ExtendedStandardSystemView storeBorderWidth: borderWidth
            messageOn: aStream. aStream nextPutAll: continue;
        nextPutAll: 'window: '; store: window; nextPutAll: continue;
        nextPutAll: 'transformation: ('; print: transformation; nextPut: $);
            nextPutAll: continue;
        nextPutAll: 'external: '; store: (Array with: className with: newMessage);
            nextPutAll: continue;
        nextPutAll: 'yourself)'
```

B.1.6 ExtendedSwitchView Operations

copying

deepCopy
```
    ↑self shallowCopy
        superView: nil; resetSubViews;
        model: model deepCopy controller: nil;
        transformation: transformation "stores a copy";
        window: window "stores a copy";
        yourself
```

printing

storeOn: aStream
```
    self storeOn: aStream indent: 2
```

storeOn: aStream **indent:** indentation
"Store this instance of an ExtendedSwitchView with indentation for readability."
| return continue |
return ← (WriteStream **on:** (String **new:** 16)) **crtab:** indentation; **contents**.
continue ← ';', return.
aStream
nextPutAll: '(('; **nextPutAll:** self **class name**; **nextPutAll:** ' on: nil';
nextPutAll: return;
nextPutAll: 'aspect: '; **store:** aspect; **nextPutAll:** return;
nextPutAll: 'label: '. self **storeLabelOn:** aStream. aStream **nextPutAll:** return;
nextPutAll: 'isOnSelector: '; **store:** selector;
nextPutAll: ' isOnParameters: '; **store:** arguments; **nextPutAll:** return;
nextPutAll: 'switchSelector: '; **store:** self **controller selector**;
nextPutAll: ' switchParameters: '; **store:** self **controller arguments**;
nextPut: $); **nextPutAll:** return;
nextPutAll: 'name: '; **store:** name; **nextPutAll:** continue;
nextPutAll: 'insideColor: '.
ExtendedStandardSystemView **storeInsideColor:** insideColor **on:** aStream.
aStream **nextPutAll:** continue.
ExtendedStandardSystemView **storeBorderWidth:** borderWidth
messageOn: aStream. aStream **nextPutAll:** continue;
nextPutAll: 'window: '; **store:** window; **nextPutAll:** continue;
nextPutAll: 'transformation: ('; **print:** transformation; **nextPut:** $);
nextPutAll: continue;
nextPutAll: 'highlight: '. self **storeHighlightOn:** aStream. aStream
nextPutAll: continue;
nextPutAll: 'mode: '; **store:** self **mode**; **nextPutAll:** continue;
nextPutAll: self **fixedPointEncoding**; **nextPutAll:** continue;
nextPutAll: 'yourself)'

storeLabelOn: aStream
"Attempt to store the most compact representation possible."
labelSource **isNil**
ifTrue: [↑self **storeDisplayObject:** label **on:** aStream]
ifFalse: [↑aStream **store:** labelSource]

storeHighlightOn: aStream
"Attempt to store the most compact representation possible."
self **storeDisplayObject:** highlightSource **on:** aStream

storeDisplayObject: anObject **on:** aStream
"Attempt to store the most compact representation possible."
(anObject **isKindOf:** DisplayText)
ifTrue: [aStream **store:** anObject **string**; **nextPutAll:** ' asParagraph']
ifFalse: [anObject **storeOn:** aStream]

B.1.7 ExtendedPictureView Operations

printing

storeOn: aStream **indent:** indentation
"Store this instance of an ExtendedPictureView with indentation for readability."
| return continue |
return ← (WriteStream **on:** (String **new:** 16)) **crtab:** indentation; **contents**.
continue ← ';', return.
aStream
nextPutAll: '((ExtendedPictureView on: nil'; **nextPutAll:** return;
nextPutAll: 'aspect: '; **store:** aspect; **nextPutAll:** return;
nextPutAll: 'label: '. self **storeLabelOn:** aStream. aStream **nextPutAll:** return;
nextPutAll: 'getLabel: '; **store:** labelMessage; **nextPut:** $); **nextPutAll:** return;

nextPutAll: 'name: '; **store**: name; **nextPutAll**: continue;
nextPutAll: 'insideColor: '.
    ExtendedStandardSystemView **storeInsideColor**: insideColor **on**: aStream.
    aStream **nextPutAll**: continue.
ExtendedStandardSystemView **storeBorderWidth**: borderWidth
    messageOn: aStream. aStream **nextPutAll**: continue;
nextPutAll: 'window: '; **store**: window; **nextPutAll**: continue;
nextPutAll: 'transformation: ('; **print**: transformation; **nextPut**: $);
    nextPutAll: continue;
nextPutAll: 'mode: '; **store**: self **mode**; **nextPutAll**: continue;
nextPutAll: self **fixedPointEncoding**; **nextPutAll**: continue;
nextPutAll: 'yourself)'

B.2 COMPILATION OPERATIONS FOR EXTENDED STANDARD SYSTEM VIEWS

class methods

private compiling support

compileOneOrMoreMethods: view **intoClass**: class **method**: methodName
category: categoryName **overFlowCategory**: overflowCategoryName
    "Attempts to compile one method in the specified class that re-creates the view. If
    it is too large to compile, breaks it up by creating additional overflow methods with
    suffixes 'Continue1:', 'Continue2:', ... that add the subviews. These overflow
    methods are placed in category overflowCategoryName."
    | aStream source |

    "Create the method."
    Transcript **show**: ' method 1'.
    aStream ← WriteStream **on**: (String **new**: 10000).
    aStream
        nextPutAll: methodName; **crtab**;
        nextPutAll: '"Returns an initialized view."'; **crtab**;
        nextPut: $↑; **store**: view.

    "Compile it."
    source ← aStream **contents**. aStream ← nil.
    (self **tryCompiling**: source **class**: class **classified**: categoryName)
        ifTrue: [
            Transcript **show**: '+'.
            self **removeContinuationsStartingAt**: 1 **for**: methodName **class**: class]
        ifFalse: [
            Transcript **show**: '-'. source ← nil.
            ↑self **compileTwoOrMoreMethods**: view **intoClass**: class
                method: methodName **category**: categoryName
                overFlowCategory: overflowCategoryName]

compileTwoOrMoreMethods: view **intoClass**: class **method**: methodName
category: categoryName **overFlowCategory**: overflowCategoryName
    "Compile the view in pieces where the encoding is considered one piece (piece -1),
    the top view is considered another piece (piece 0), and the individual subviews are
    pieces (1, 2, 3, ...). Attempt to put at many pieces into each method as the compiler
    will permit. The first method with name methodName is place in category
    categoryName. The overflow methods have suffixes 'Continue1:', 'Continue2:', ...
    appended to the method name. They are placed in category overflowCategory-
    Name."
    | lastPiece limit continuation mostPieces fewestPieces pieces next |

    "Iterate to create the maximal sized compiled method."

```smalltalk
    Transcript nextPutAll: ' method 1 <'.
    lastPiece ← -2. limit ← view subViews size.
    continuation ← 0. mostPieces ← nil. fewestPieces ← nil. pieces ← 0.

    [lastPiece <= limit] whileTrue: [
        next ← self whatToDoNextGiven: view and: lastPiece + pieces
            and: mostPieces and: fewestPieces.
        next == #done ifTrue: [
            Transcript nextPutAll: '>'.
            self removeContinuationsStartingAt: continuation+1 for: methodName
                class: class.
            ↑self].
        next == #doneEnough ifTrue: [
            lastPiece ← lastPiece + mostPieces.
            CompilationHeuristic ← mostPieces.
            continuation ← continuation + 1.
            Transcript nextPutAll: '>, '; print: continuation+1; nextPutAll: ' <'.
            mostPieces ← nil. fewestPieces ← nil. pieces ← 0].
        next == #tryAgain ifTrue: [
            pieces ← self piecesToTryGiven: mostPieces and: fewestPieces.
            pieces < 1 ifTrue: [
                Transcript show: '>-'.
                ↑self error: 'method too large -- cannot be compiled. Continue to give up'].
            Transcript show: pieces printString.
            (self tryCompilingContinuation: continuation view: view intoClass: class
                method: methodName category: categoryName
                overFlowCategory: overflowCategoryName
                lastPiece: lastPiece pieces: pieces)
                ifTrue: [Transcript show: '+'. mostPieces ← pieces]
                ifFalse: [Transcript show: '-'. fewestPieces ← pieces. pieces ← 0]]]
```

compileEncoding: view intoClass: class method: methodName category: categoryName
    "Attempts to compile just the encoding as a method."

```smalltalk
    Transcript show: ' method 1'.
    (self tryCompilingContinuation: 0 view: view intoClass: class method: methodName
    category: categoryName overFlowCategory: nil lastPiece: -2 pieces: 1)
        ifTrue: [
            Transcript show: '+'.
            self removeContinuationsStartingAt: 1 for: methodName class: class]
        ifFalse: [
            Transcript show: '-'.
            ↑self error: 'method too large -- cannot be compiled. Continue to give up']
```

tryCompilingContinuation: continuationIndex view: view intoClass: class
method: methodName category: categoryName
overFlowCategory: overflowCategoryName
lastPiece: lastPiece pieces: pieces
    "Compiles a method with with name methodName (for continuationIndex 0) and
    suffixes 'Continue1:', 'Continue2:', ... for (continuationIndex > 0). Piece -1 is
    interpreted as the encoding, piece 0 is the top view, and pieces 1, 2, 3, ... are the
    subviews. No additional overflow methods are generated if overflowCategoryName
    is nil."
    | views start end aStream source |

    "Determine the output range for the pieces."
    views ← view subViews.
    start ← lastPiece + 1. end ← lastPiece + pieces min: views size.

```
"Create the method."
"First, the method header."
aStream ← WriteStream on: (String new: 10000).
start = -1
    ifTrue: [
        aStream
            nextPutAll: methodName; crtab;
            nextPutAll: '"Returns an initialized view."'; crtab;
            nextPutAll: (end > -1 ifTrue: ['| anArray aView |'] ifFalse: ['| anArray |']);
            cr; crtab]
    ifFalse: [
        aStream
            nextPutAll: (self continuationName: continuationIndex
                for: methodName);
            nextPutAll: (start = 0 ifTrue: [' anArray'] ifFalse: [' aView']); crtab;
            nextPutAll: '"Continues initializing view."'; cr.
        start = 0 ifTrue: [aStream tab; nextPutAll: '| aView |'; cr].
        aStream crtab].

"Second, the actual code."
start to: end do: [:index |
    index = -1
        ifTrue: [
            aStream nextPutAll: 'anArray ← '.
            ExtendedStandardSystemView storeEncoding: view encoding
                on: aStream indent: 2]
        ifFalse: [
            index = 0
                ifTrue: [
                    aStream nextPutAll: 'aView ← '.
                    view storeOn: aStream encoding: 'anArray'
                        subViews: false indent: 2]
                ifFalse: [
                    aStream nextPutAll: 'aView addSubView: '.
                    (views at: index) storeOn: aStream indent: 2]].
    aStream nextPut: $.; crtab].

"Third, the end of the method."
end = views size
    ifTrue: [aStream nextPutAll: '↑aView']
    ifFalse: [
        overflowCategoryName isNil
            ifTrue: [
                aStream
                    nextPut: $↑;
                    nextPutAll: (end = -1 ifTrue: ['anArray'] ifFalse: ['aView'])]
            ifFalse: [
                aStream
                    nextPutAll: '↑self ';
                    nextPutAll: (self continuationName: continuationIndex+1
                        for: methodName);
                    nextPutAll: (end = -1 ifTrue: [' anArray'] ifFalse: [' aView'])]].

"Compile it."
source ← aStream contents. aStream ← nil.
↑self tryCompiling: source class: class classified:
    (continuationIndex = 0
        ifTrue: [categoryName]
        ifFalse: [overflowCategoryName])
```

tryCompiling: aMethodString **class:** class **classified:** aCategoryString
"Returns true if compilation is successful; false otherwise. Note: This method is invoked rather than executing the code inline to force compiler data structures to disappear (it only happens when a return from compile:classified:notifying: occurs or the error block is executed)."
| notifier |
notifier ← ErrorHandler **new errorBlock:** [:message :position | ↑false].
class **compile:** aMethodString **classified:** aCategoryString **notifying:** notifier.
↑true

whatToDoNextGiven: view **and:** totalSoFar **and:** mostSuccessful **and:** leastUnsuccessful
totalSoFar >= view **subViews size ifTrue:** [↑#done].
mostSuccessful **isNil ifTrue:** [↑#tryAgain].
leastUnsuccessful **isNil ifTrue:** [↑#tryAgain].
mostSuccessful + 1 = leastUnsuccessful
    ifTrue: [↑#doneEnough]
    ifFalse: [↑#tryAgain]

piecesToTryGiven: mostSuccessful **and:** leastUnsuccessful
mostSuccessful **isNil** & leastUnsuccessful **isNil**
    ifTrue: [CompilationHeuristic **isNil ifTrue:** [5] **ifFalse:** [↑CompilationHeuristic]]
    ifFalse: [
        mostSuccessful **isNil**
            ifTrue: [↑leastUnsuccessful - 1]
            ifFalse: [↑mostSuccessful + 1]].

continuationName: index **for:** methodName
↑(methodName, 'Continue', index **printString**, ':') **asSymbol**

removeContinuationsStartingAt: start **for:** methodName **class:** class
| index selector |
index ← start. selector ← self **continuationName:** index **for:** methodName.
[class **includesSelector:** selector] **whileTrue:** [
    class **removeSelector:** selector.
    index ← index + 1.
    selector ← self **continuationName:** index **for:** methodName]

B.3 OPTIONS WINDOWS FOR THE MASTER ICON CONTROLLER

class methods

generic windows

alignmentWindow
"Returns an initialized view."
| anArray |

anArray ← "WindowMaker edit:" #(Master nil (-239 -167 239 167) white 1 (2.14644 1.29816 512.0 264.208) true 'Alignment' (nil) (postCloseAlignment: anExtendedStandardSystemView) (350 180) (1000 1000) (classMethod notEncoded WindowMakerMasterIconController 'generic windows' alignmentWindow 'generic windows overflow') ((Picture nil (-228.0 -156.0 -187.0 -141.0) white 0 (text 'widths:') (lockedConstant fixMiddleLeft 0) (nil (nil))) (Picture nil (-228.0 -102.0 -183.0 -87.0) white 0 (text 'heights:') (lockedConstant fixMiddleLeft 0) (nil (nil))) (Picture nil (-228.0 6.0 -111.0 21.0) white 0 (text 'up/down alignment:') (lockedConstant fixMiddleLeft 0) (nil (nil))) (Picture nil (-228.0 -48.0 -110.0 -33.0) white 0 (text 'left/right alignment:') (lockedConstant fixMiddleLeft 0) (nil (nil))) (Picture nil (-228.0 60.0

-109.0 75.0) white 0 (text 'horizontal abutment:') (lockedConstant fixMiddleLeft
0) (nil (nil))) (Picture nil (-228.0 114.0 -124.0 129.0) white 0 (text
'vertical abutment:') (lockedConstant fixMiddleLeft 0) (nil (nil))) (Group nil (-205
-114 203 -91) nil 4 ((SwitchAndPicture nil (-209.0 -129.0 -120.0 -114.0) white 0
(form DefaultFormLibrary button separation 10 text 'unchanged')
(lockedConstant fixMiddleLeft 0) (width (isWidth: unchanged) (makeWidth:
unchanged))) (SwitchAndPicture nil (-103.0 -129.0 33.0 -114.0) white 0 (form
DefaultFormLibrary button separation 10 text 'all minimum width')
(lockedConstant fixMiddleLeft 0) (width (isWidth: minimum) (makeWidth:
minimum))) (SwitchAndPicture nil (55.0 -129.0 191.0 -114.0) white 0 (form
DefaultFormLibrary button separation 10 text 'all maximum width')
(lockedConstant fixMiddleLeft 0) (width (isWidth: maximum) (makeWidth:
maximum))))) (Group nil (-205 -68 207 -45) nil 4 ((SwitchAndPicture nil
(-209.0 -75.0 -120.0 -60.0) white 0 (form DefaultFormLibrary button separation
10 text 'unchanged') (lockedConstant fixMiddleLeft 0) (height (isHeight:
unchanged) (makeHeight: unchanged))) (SwitchAndPicture nil (-103.0 -75.0 37.0
-60.0) white 0 (form DefaultFormLibrary button separation 10 text 'all minimum
height') (lockedConstant fixMiddleLeft 0) (height (isHeight: minimum)
(makeHeight: minimum))) (SwitchAndPicture nil (55.0 -75.0 195.0 -60.0) white 0
(form DefaultFormLibrary button separation 10 text 'all maximum height')
(lockedConstant fixMiddleLeft 0) (height (isHeight: maximum) (makeHeight:
maximum))))) (Group nil (-205 -23 167 0) nil 4 ((SwitchAndPicture nil (-209.0
-21.0 -120.0 -6.0) white 0 (form DefaultFormLibrary button separation 10 text
'unchanged') (lockedConstant fixMiddleLeft 0) (leftRightAlignment
(isLeftRightAlignment: unchanged) (makeLeftRightAlignment: unchanged)))
(SwitchAndPicture nil (-103.0 -21.0 -27.0 -6.0) white 0 (form
DefaultFormLibrary button separation 10 text 'left sides') (lockedConstant
fixMiddleLeft 0) (leftRightAlignment (isLeftRightAlignment: leftSides)
(makeLeftRightAlignment: leftSides))) (SwitchAndPicture nil (-16.0 -21.0 52.0
-6.0) white 0 (form DefaultFormLibrary button separation 10 text 'middles')
(lockedConstant fixMiddleLeft 0) (leftRightAlignment (isLeftRightAlignment:
middles) (makeLeftRightAlignment: middles))) (SwitchAndPicture nil (70.0 -21.0
155.0 -6.0) white 0 (form DefaultFormLibrary button separation 10 text 'right
sides') (lockedConstant fixMiddleLeft 0) (leftRightAlignment
(isLeftRightAlignment: rightSides) (makeLeftRightAlignment: rightSides)))))
(Group nil (-205 20 149 43) nil 4 ((SwitchAndPicture nil (-209.0 33.0 -120.0 48.0)
white 0 (form DefaultFormLibrary button separation 10 text 'unchanged')
(lockedConstant fixMiddleLeft 0) (upDownAlignment (isUpDownAlignment:
unchanged) (makeUpDownAlignment: unchanged))) (SwitchAndPicture nil
(-103.0 33.0 -56.0 48.0) white 0 (form DefaultFormLibrary button separation 10
text 'tops') (lockedConstant fixMiddleLeft 0) (upDownAlignment
(isUpDownAlignment: tops) (makeUpDownAlignment: tops)))
(SwitchAndPicture nil (-16.0 33.0 52.0 48.0) white 0 (form DefaultFormLibrary
button separation 10 text 'middles') (lockedConstant fixMiddleLeft 0)
(upDownAlignment (isUpDownAlignment: middles) (makeUpDownAlignment:
middles))) (SwitchAndPicture nil (70.0 33.0 137.0 48.0) white 0 (form
DefaultFormLibrary button separation 10 text 'bottoms') (lockedConstant
fixMiddleLeft 0) (upDownAlignment (isUpDownAlignment: bottoms)
(makeUpDownAlignment: bottoms))))) (Group nil (-205 66 240 89) nil 4
((SwitchAndPicture nil (-209.0 87.0 -120.0 102.0) white 0 (form
DefaultFormLibrary button separation 10 text 'unchanged') (lockedConstant
fixMiddleLeft 0) (horizontalAbutment (isHorizontalAbutment: unchanged)
(makeHorizontalAbutment: unchanged))) (SwitchAndPicture nil (-103.0 87.0
-27.0 102.0) white 0 (form DefaultFormLibrary button separation 10 text
'touching') (lockedConstant fixMiddleLeft 0) (horizontalAbutment
(isHorizontalAbutment: touching) (makeHorizontalAbutment: touching)))
(SwitchAndPicture nil (-7.0 87.0 105.0 102.0) white 0 (form DefaultFormLibrary

button separation 10 text 'least separation') (lockedConstant fixMiddleLeft 0)
(horizontalAbutment (isHorizontalAbutment: leastSeparation)
(makeHorizontalAbutment: leastSeparation))) (SwitchAndPicture nil
(116.0 87.0 228.0 102.0) white 0 (form DefaultFormLibrary button separation
10 text 'most separation') (lockedConstant fixMiddleLeft 0)
(horizontalAbutment (isHorizontalAbutment: mostSeparation)
(makeHorizontalAbutment: mostSeparation))))) (Group nil (-204 111 240 134) nil
4 ((SwitchAndPicture nil (-208.0 141.0 -119.0 156.0) white 0 (form
DefaultFormLibrary button separation 10 text 'unchanged') (lockedConstant
fixMiddleLeft 0) (verticalAbutment (isVerticalAbutment: unchanged)
(makeVerticalAbutment: unchanged))) (SwitchAndPicture nil (-103.0 141.0 -27.0
156.0) white 0 (form DefaultFormLibrary button separation 10 text 'touching')
(lockedConstant fixMiddleLeft 0) (verticalAbutment (isVerticalAbutment:
touching) (makeVerticalAbutment: touching))) (SwitchAndPicture nil (-7.0 141.0
105.0 156.0) white 0 (form DefaultFormLibrary button separation 10 text
'least separation') (lockedConstant fixMiddleLeft 0) (verticalAbutment
(isVerticalAbutment: leastSeparation) (makeVerticalAbutment:
leastSeparation))) (SwitchAndPicture nil (116.0 141.0 228.0 156.0) white 0
(form DefaultFormLibrary button separation 10 text 'most separation')
(lockedConstant fixMiddleLeft 0) (verticalAbutment (isVerticalAbutment:
mostSeparation) (makeVerticalAbutment: mostSeparation))))))))).
↑anArray

backgroundWindow

"Returns an initialized view."
| anArray |

anArray ← "WindowMaker edit:" #(Master nil (-235 -192 236 192) white 1
(1.35381 1.18038 319.323 228.065) true 'Background' (preOpenBackground:
anExtendedStandardSystemView) (postCloseBackground:
anExtendedStandardSystemView) (500 350) (1000 1000) (classMethod
notEncoded WindowMakerMasterIconController 'generic windows'
backgroundWindow 'generic windows overflow' ((Picture nil (-224.0 -181.0
-147.0 -166.0) white 0 (text 'kind of switch:') (lockedConstant fixMiddleLeft
0) (nil (nil))) (Picture nil (-224.0 6.0 -129.0 21.0) white 0 (text 'mode parameters:')
(lockedConstant fixMiddleLeft 0) (nil (nil))) (Picture nil (-224.0 104.0
-99.0 119.0) white 0 (text 'fixed point parameters:') (lockedConstant
fixMiddleLeft 0) (nil (nil))) (SwitchAndPicture nil (-204.0 -107.0 -154.0
-92.0) white 0 (form DefaultFormLibrary button separation 10 text 'form')
(lockedConstant fixMiddleLeft 0) (pictureVariety (isPictureVariety: form)
(changePictureVariety: form))) (SwitchAndPicture nil (-204.0 71 -115.0
86) white 0 (form DefaultFormLibrary button separation 10 text 'varying size')
(lockedConstant fixMiddleLeft 0) (mode (isMode: varying) (changeMode:
varying))) (SwitchAndPicture nil (-48.0 50 22.0 65) white 0 (form
DefaultFormLibrary button separation 10 text 'unlocked') (lockedConstant
fixMiddleLeft 0) (locking (isLocking: false) (changeLocking: false))) (Group nil
(-218 121 137 144) nil 4 ((SwitchAndPicture nil (-204.0 128.0 -139.0 143.0)
white 0 (form DefaultFormLibrary button separation 10 text 'top left')
(lockedConstant fixMiddleLeft 0) (fixedPoint (isFixedPointEncoding: fixTopLeft)
(changeFixedPointEncoding: fixTopLeft))) (SwitchAndPicture nil (68.0 128.0
139.0 143.0) white 0 (form DefaultFormLibrary button separation 10 text
'top right') (lockedConstant fixMiddleLeft 0) (fixedPoint (isFixedPointEncoding:
fixTopRight) (changeFixedPointEncoding: fixTopRight))))) (Group nil (-218
139 158 162) nil 4 ((SwitchAndPicture nil (-204.0 146.0 -123.0 161.0)
white 0 (form DefaultFormLibrary button separation 10 text 'middle left')
(lockedConstant fixMiddleLeft 0) (fixedPoint (isFixedPointEncoding:
fixMiddleLeft) (changeFixedPointEncoding: fixMiddleLeft))) (SwitchAndPicture
nil (-48.0 146.0 11.0 161.0) white 0 (form DefaultFormLibrary button separation

10 text 'center') (lockedConstant fixMiddleLeft 0) (fixedPoint
(isFixedPointEncoding: fixCenter) (changeFixedPointEncoding: fixCenter)))
(SwitchAndPicture nil (68.0 146.0 155.0 161.0) white 0 (form
DefaultFormLibrary button separation 10 text 'middle right') (lockedConstant
fixMiddleLeft 0) (fixedPoint (isFixedPointEncoding: fixMiddleRight)
(changeFixedPointEncoding: fixMiddleRight))))) (Group nil (-218 159 157 182) nil
4 ((SwitchAndPicture nil (-204.0 166.0 -119.0 181.0) white 0 (form
DefaultFormLibrary button separation 10 text 'bottom left') (lockedConstant
fixMiddleLeft 0) (fixedPoint (isFixedPointEncoding: fixBottomLeft)
(changeFixedPointEncoding: fixBottomLeft))) (SwitchAndPicture nil (68.0
166.0 159.0 181.0) white 0 (form DefaultFormLibrary button separation
10 text 'bottom right') (lockedConstant fixMiddleLeft 0) (fixedPoint
(isFixedPointEncoding: fixBottomRight) (changeFixedPointEncoding:
fixBottomRight))))) (Group nil (-218 23 198 50) nil 4 ((Picture nil (68 32 136 47)
white 0 (text 'extra border') (lockedConstant fixMiddleLeft 0) (nil (nil))) (Text nil
(149.0 30.0 204.0 49.0) white 1 (nil (getLockedSizeExpansion)
(changeLockedSizeExpansion: aText) (acceptCancelYellowButtonMenu)))
(SwitchAndPicture nil (-204.0 32.0 -110.0 47.0) white 0 (form
DefaultFormLibrary button separation 10 text 'constant size') (lockedConstant
fixMiddleLeft 0) (mode (isMode: constant) (changeMode: constant)))
(SwitchAndPicture nil (-48.0 32.0 10.0 47.0) white 0 (form DefaultFormLibrary
button separation 10 text 'locked') (lockedConstant fixMiddleLeft 0) (locking
(isLocking: true) (changeLocking: true))))) (SwitchAndPicture nil (-204.0 -156.0
-156.0 -141.0) white 0 (form DefaultFormLibrary button separation 10 text
'text') (lockedConstant fixMiddleLeft 0) (pictureVariety (isPictureVariety: text)
(changePictureVariety: text))) (Group nil (-136 -162 229 5) nil 4 ((External nil
(-132.0 -117.0 225.0 1.0) nil 1 (FormLibrarian subView)) (Text nil (-132.0 -158.0
-4.0 -138.0) white 1 (nil (getPictureString) (changePictureString: aText)
(acceptCancelYellowButtonMenu)))))))).
↑anArray

borderingAndColoringWindow
"Returns an initialized view."
| anArray |

anArray ← "WindowMaker edit:" #(Master nil (-254 -129 255 130) white 1
(2.01572 1.6749 510.992 263.263) true 'Bordering and Coloring' (nil) (nil) (350
180) (1000 1000) (classMethod notEncoded WindowMakerMasterIconController
'generic windows' borderingAndColoringWindow 'generic windows overflow')
((Group nil (-318 -121 -27 124) nil 4 ((Picture nil (-139.0 -118.0 -65.0 -103.0)
white 0 (text 'border width') (constant fixMiddleLeft) (nil (nil))) (Group nil
(-318 -65 -27 124) nil 4 ((Menu nil (-77.0 -62.0 40.0 119.0) white 1 (border
(getBordersMenuList) (getBordersMenuSelection) (changeBordersMenuSelection:
aSelectionObject) (nil))) (Group nil (-318 -58 -193 111) nil 4 ((Text
nil (-161.0 -55.0 -126.0 -37.0) white 1 (border (getTopThickness)
(changeTopThickness: aText) (acceptCancelYellowButtonMenu))) (Picture nil
(-243.0 -53.0 -226.0 -38.0) white 0 (text 'top') (constant fixCenter) (nil (nil)))
(Picture nil (-243.0 88.0 -206.0 103.0) white 0 (text 'bottom') (constant
fixCenter) (nil (nil))) (Picture nil (-243.0 41.0 -215.0 56.0) white 0 (text 'right')
(constant fixCenter) (nil (nil))) (Picture nil (-243.0 -6.0 -224.0 9.0)
white 0 (text 'left') (constant fixCenter) (nil (nil))) (Text nil (-161.0
-6.0 -126.0 12.0) white 1 (border (getLeftThickness) (changeLeftThickness:
aText) (acceptCancelYellowButtonMenu))) (Text nil (-161.0 41.0 -126.0
59.0) white 1 (border (getRightThickness) (changeRightThickness: aText)
(acceptCancelYellowButtonMenu))) (Text nil (-161.0 88.0 -126.0 106.0)
white 1 (border (getBottomThickness) (changeBottomThickness: aText)
(acceptCancelYellowButtonMenu)))))))))) (Group nil (14 -121 177 124) nil 4
((Picture nil (153.0 -118.0 180.0 -103.0) white 0 (text 'color') (constant

fixMiddleLeft) (nil (nil))) (Group nil (85 -66 248 124) nil 4 ((Switch nil (127.0 -37.0 244.0 -11.0) white 1 (text '') (varying) (color (isNil) (makeInsideColor: white))) (Switch nil (127.0 -11.0 244.0 15.0) veryLightGray 1 (text '') (varying) (color (isNil) (makeInsideColor: veryLightGray))) (Switch nil (127.0 15.0 244.0 41.0) lightGray 1 (text '') (varying) (color (isNil) (makeInsideColor: lightGray))) (Switch nil (127.0 93.0 244.0 119.0) black 1 (text '') (varying) (color (isNil) (makeInsideColor: black))) (Switch nil (127.0 67.0 244.0 93.0) darkGray 1 (text '') (varying) (color (isNil) (makeInsideColor: darkGray))) (Switch nil (127.0 41.0 244.0 67.0) gray 1 (text '') (varying) (color (isNil) (makeInsideColor: gray))) (Switch nil (127.0 -63.0 244.0 -37.0) white 1 (text 'transparent') (varying) (color (isNil) (makeInsideColor: nil))) (Switch nil (89 -57 104 -42) white 1 (form DefaultFormLibrary check) (lockedConstant fixCenter 0) (color (isInsideColor: nil) (makeInsideColor: nil))) (Switch nil (89 -31 104 -16) white 1 (form DefaultFormLibrary check) (lockedConstant fixCenter 0) (color (isInsideColor: white) (makeInsideColor: white))) (Switch nil (89 -5 104 10) white 1 (form DefaultFormLibrary check) (lockedConstant fixCenter 0) (color (isInsideColor: veryLightGray) (makeInsideColor: veryLightGray))) (Switch nil (89 21 104 36) white 1 (form DefaultFormLibrary check) (lockedConstant fixCenter 0) (color (isInsideColor: lightGray) (makeInsideColor: lightGray))) (Switch nil (89 47 104 62) white 1 (form DefaultFormLibrary check) (lockedConstant fixCenter 0) (color (isInsideColor: gray) (makeInsideColor: gray))) (Switch nil (89 73 104 88) white 1 (form DefaultFormLibrary check) (lockedConstant fixCenter 0) (color (isInsideColor: darkGray) (makeInsideColor: darkGray))) (Switch nil (89 99 104 114) white 1 (form DefaultFormLibrary check) (lockedConstant fixCenter 0) (color (isInsideColor: black) (makeInsideColor: black))))))))).
↑anArray

makeMethodWindow

"Returns an initialized view."
| anArray |

anArray ← "WindowMaker edit:" #(Master nil (-204 -165 205 165) white 2 (1.56968 1.26297 319.215 248.61) true 'Output Options' (nil) (postCloseMakeMethod: anExtendedStandardSystemView) (350 180) (1000 1000) (classMethod notEncoded WindowMakerMasterIconController 'generic windows' makeMethodWindow 'generic windows overflow') ((Picture nil (-168.0 -10.0 -107.0 5.0) white 0 (text 'class name') (constant fixMiddleLeft) (nil (nil))) (Text nil (-29.0 -12.0 192.0 11.0) white 1 (nil (outputOptionTextAt: methodClass) (outputOptionPutText: aText at: methodClass) (acceptCancelYellowButtonMenu))) (Picture nil (-168.0 36.0 -74.0 51.0) white 0 (text 'method category') (constant fixMiddleLeft) (nil (nil))) (Text nil (-29.0 33.0 193.0 57.0) white 1 (nil (outputOptionTextAt: methodCategory) (outputOptionPutText: aText at: methodCategory) (acceptCancelYellowButtonMenu))) (Picture nil (-168.0 83.0 -92.0 98.0) white 0 (text 'method name') (constant fixMiddleLeft) (nil (nil))) (Text nil (-29.0 79.0 193.0 103.0) white 1 (nil (outputOptionTextAt: methodName) (outputOptionPutText: aText at: methodName) (acceptCancelYellowButtonMenu))) (Picture nil (-192 -153 -104 -138) white 0 (text 'where to output:') (lockedConstant fixMiddleLeft 0) (nil (nil))) (Picture nil (-192 -92 -115 -77) white 0 (text 'how to output:') (lockedConstant fixMiddleLeft 0) (nil (nil))) (Picture nil (-192 -37 -102 -22) white 0 (text 'method specifics:') (lockedConstant fixMiddleLeft 0) (nil (nil))) (Picture nil (-168.0 132.0 -69.0 147.0) white 0 (text 'overflow category') (lockedConstant fixMiddleLeft 0) (nil (nil))) (Text nil (-29.0 129.0 193.0 153.0) white 1 (nil (outputOptionTextAt: overflowCategory) (outputOptionPutText: aText at: overflowCategory) (acceptCancelYellowButtonMenu))) (Group nil (-201 -126 166 -103) nil 4

((SwitchAndPicture nil (-168 -130 -77 -115) white 0 (form DefaultFormLibrary
button separation 10 text 'in transcript') (lockedConstant fixMiddleLeft 0)
(outputOption (outputOptionAt: destination is: transcript)
(outputOptionPutText: transcript at: destination))) (SwitchAndPicture nil
(-57 -130 49 -115) white 0 (form DefaultFormLibrary button separation 10 text
'in class method') (lockedConstant fixMiddleLeft 0) (outputOption
(outputOptionAt: destination is: classMethod) (outputOptionPutText:
classMethod at: destination))) (SwitchAndPicture nil (67 -130 191 -115)
white 0 (form DefaultFormLibrary button separation 10 text 'in instance
method') (lockedConstant fixMiddleLeft 0) (outputOption (outputOptionAt:
destination is: instanceMethod) (outputOptionPutText: instanceMethod at:
destination))))) (Group nil (-199 -62 68 -39) nil 4 ((SwitchAndPicture nil (-168 -66
-72 -51) white 0 (form DefaultFormLibrary button separation 10 text 'encoding
only') (lockedConstant fixMiddleLeft 0) (outputOption (outputOptionAt:
encoding is: encoded) (outputOptionPutText: encoded at: encoding)))
(SwitchAndPicture nil (-35 -66 91 -51) white 0 (form DefaultFormLibrary button
separation 10 text 'view with encoding') (lockedConstant fixMiddleLeft 0)
(outputOption (outputOptionAt: encoding is: notEncoded) (outputOptionPutText:
notEncoded at: encoding))))))))).
        ↑anArray

switchAndPictureBackgroundWindow
"Returns an initialized view."
| anArray |

anArray ← "WindowMaker edit:" #(Master nil (-210 -128 210 129) white 1
        (1.51809 1.7661 320.0 226.853) true 'Background' (preOpenBackground:
        anExtendedStandardSystemView) (postCloseBackground:
        anExtendedStandardSystemView) (500 300) (1000 1000) (classMethod
        notEncoded WindowMakerMasterIconController 'generic windows'
        switchAndPictureBackgroundWindow 'generic windows overflow') ((Picture nil
        (-199.0 -117.0 -98.0 -102.0) white 0 (text 'switch and picture:') (lockedConstant
        fixMiddleLeft 0) (nil (nil))) (Picture nil (-179.0 -91.0 -145.0 -76.0) white 0 (text
        'switch') (lockedConstant fixMiddleLeft 0) (nil (nil))) (Picture nil (-179.0 70.0
        -142.0 85.0) white 0 (text 'picture') (lockedConstant fixMiddleLeft 0)
        (nil (nil))) (External nil (-158.0 -66.0 199.0 52.0) nil 1 (FormLibrarian
        subView)) (Text nil (-158.0 98.0 -30.0 118.0) white 1 (nil (getPictureString)
        (changePictureString: aText) (acceptCancelYellowButtonMenu)))))).
        ↑anArray

specific windows

externalWindow
"Returns an initialized view."
| anArray |

anArray ← "WindowMaker edit:" #(Master nil (-137 -89 138 89) white 1 (3.73091
        2.43963 510.135 263.873) true 'External Window Interface' (preOpenInterface:
        anExtendedStandardSystemView) (nil) (350 180) (1000 1000) (classMethod
        notEncoded WindowMakerMasterIconController 'specific windows'
        externalWindow 'specific windows overflow') ((Text messageSource (-136.0 -
        63.0 137.0 88.0) white 1 (messageSource (messageSource) (messageSource:
        aText) (messageMenu))) (Switch nil (-136.0 -88.0 -45.0 -63.0) white 1 (text
        'comment') (varying) (message (isMessage: comment) (message: comment)))
        (Switch nil (-45.0 -88.0 46.0 -63.0) white 1 (text 'name') (varying) (message
        (isMessage: name) (message: name))) (Switch nil (46.0 -88.0 137.0 -63.0) white
        1 (text 'getView') (varying) (message (isMessage: getView) (message:
        getView)))))).
        ↑anArray

masterSizingWindow
"Returns an initialized view."
| anArray |

anArray ← "WindowMaker edit:" #(Master nil (-221 -37 222 37) white 2 (1.44921
5.63832 319.275 248.382) true 'Size Options' (nil) (nil) (440 72) (572
76) (classMethod notEncoded WindowMakerMasterIconController
'specific windows' masterSizingWindow 'specific windows overflow') ((Picture
nil (-209 -23 -125 -8) white 0 (text 'minimum size') (constant fixMiddleLeft) (nil
(nil))) (Text nil (-83.0 -25.0 -22.0 -7.0) white 1 (sizing (getMinimumSize)
(changeMinimumSize: aText) (acceptCancelYellowButtonMenu)))
(SwitchAndPicture nil (19 -23 205 -8) white 0 (form DefaultFormLibrary button
separation 10 text 'interactively set minimum size') (lockedConstant
fixMiddleLeft 0) (nil (isNil) (setSize: minimum))) (Picture nil (-209 9 -125 24)
white 0 (text 'maximum size') (constant fixMiddleLeft) (nil (nil))) (Text nil (-83.0
7.0 -22.0 25.0) white 1 (sizing (getMaximumSize) (changeMaximumSize: aText)
(acceptCancelYellowButtonMenu))) (SwitchAndPicture nil (19 9 210 24) white 0
(form DefaultFormLibrary button separation 10 text
'interactively set maximum size') (lockedConstant fixMiddleLeft 0)
(nil (isNil) (setSize: maximum)))))).
↑anArray

masterWindow
"Returns an initialized view."
| anArray |

anArray ← "WindowMaker edit:" #(Master nil (-274 -114 274 115) white 1
(1.87226 1.8919 512.0 263.431) true 'Master Window Interface'
(preOpenInterface: anExtendedStandardSystemView) (nil) (350 180) (1000
1000) (classMethod notEncoded WindowMakerMasterIconController
'specific windows' topWindow 'specific windows overflow') ((Text
messageSource (-273.0 -88.0 273.0 114.0) white 1 (messageSource
(messageSource) (messageSource: aText) (messageMenu))) (Group nil
(-277 -117 277 -84) nil 4 ((Switch nil (-273.0 -113.0 -182.0 -88.0) white 1
(text 'comment') (varying) (message (isMessage: comment) (message:
comment))) (Switch nil (-182.0 -113.0 -91.0 -88.0) white 1 (text 'name') (varying)
(message (isMessage: name) (message: name))) (Switch nil (-91.0 -113.0
0.0 -88.0) white 1 (text 'topView') (varying) (message (isMessage: topView)
(message: topView))) (Switch nil (0.0 -113.0 91.0 -88.0) white 1 (text
'title') (varying) (message (isMessage: title) (message: title))) (Switch
nil (91.0 -113.0 182.0 -88.0) white 1 (text 'preOpen') (varying) (message
(isMessage: preOpeningSelector) (message: preOpeningSelector))) (Switch
nil (182.0 -113.0 273.0 -88.0) white 1 (text 'postClose') (varying) (message
(isMessage: postClosingSelector) (message: postClosingSelector)))))))).
↑anArray

menuWindow
"Returns an initialized view."
| anArray |

anArray ← "WindowMaker edit:" #(Master nil (-256 -89 257 89) white 1 (2.0
2.43465 511.0 264.316) true 'Menu Window Interface' (preOpenInterface:
anExtendedStandardSystemView) (nil) (350 180) (1000 1000) (classMethod
notEncoded WindowMakerMasterIconController 'specific windows'
menuWindow 'specific windows overflow') ((Text messageSource (-255.0 -63.0
256.0 88.0) white 1 (messageSource (messageSource) (messageSource: aText)
(messageMenu))) (Group nil (-370 -93 141 -68) nil 4 ((Switch nil (-255.0
-88.0 -182.0 -63.0) white 1 (text 'comment') (varying) (message (isMessage:
comment) (message: comment))) (Switch nil (-182.0 -88.0 -109.0 -63.0) white 1

(text 'name') (varying) (message (isMessage: name) (message: name))) (Switch nil (-109.0 -88.0 -36.0 -63.0) white 1 (text 'updateSymbol') (varying) (message (isMessage: updateSymbol) (message: updateSymbol))) (Switch nil (-36.0 -88.0 37.0 -63.0) white 1 (text 'getMenu') (varying) (message (isMessage: getMenuArray) (message: getMenuArray))) (Switch nil (37.0 -88.0 110.0 -63.0) white 1 (text 'getSelection') (varying) (message (isMessage: getMenuSelection) (message: getMenuSelection))) (Switch nil (110.0 -88.0 183.0 -63.0) white 1 (text 'changeSelection') (varying) (message (isMessage: changeMenuSelection) (message: changeMenuSelection))) (Switch nil (183.0 -88.0 256.0 -63.0) white 1 (text 'getYellowMenu') (varying) (message (isMessage: getYellowMenu) (message: getYellowMenu))))))).
↑anArray

pictureWindow

"Returns an initialized view."
| anArray |

anArray ← "WindowMaker edit:" #(Master nil (-183 -85 183 86) white 1 (2.80328 2.53821 512.0 262.714) true 'Picture Window Interface' (preOpenInterface: anExtendedStandardSystemView) (nil) (350 180) (1000 1000) (classMethod notEncoded WindowMakerMasterIconController 'specific windows' pictureWindow 'specific windows overflow') ((Text messageSource (-182.0 -59.0 182.0 85.0) white 1 (messageSource (messageSource) (messageSource: aText) (messageMenu))) (Group nil (-272 -89 92 -64) nil 4 ((Switch nil (-91.0 -84.0 0.0 -59.0) white 1 (text 'name') (varying) (message (isMessage: name) (message: name))) (Switch nil (-182.0 -84.0 -91.0 -59.0) white 1 (text 'comment') (varying) (message (isMessage: comment) (message: comment))) (Switch nil (0.0 -84.0 91.0 -59.0) white 1 (text 'updateSymbol') (varying) (message (isMessage: updateSymbol) (message: updateSymbol))) (Switch nil (91.0 -84.0 182.0 -59.0) white 1 (text 'getLabel') (varying) (message (isMessage: getLabel) (message: getLabel)))))))).
↑anArray

switchWindow

"Returns an initialized view."
| anArray |

anArray ← "WindowMaker edit:" #(Master nil (-228 -100 229 101) white 1 (2.24508 2.16009 510.877 262.831) true 'Switch Window Interface' (preOpenInterface: anExtendedStandardSystemView) (nil) (350 180) (1000 1000) (classMethod notEncoded WindowMakerMasterIconController 'specific windows' switchWindow 'specific windows overflow') ((Text messageSource (-227.0 -74.0 228.0 100.0) white 1 (messageSource (messageSource) (messageSource: aText) (messageMenu))) (Group nil (-283 -91 172 -66) nil 4 ((Switch nil (-227.0 -99.0 -136.0 -74.0) white 1 (text 'comment') (varying) (message (isMessage: comment) (message: comment))) (Switch nil (-136.0 -99.0 -45.0 -74.0) white 1 (text 'name') (varying) (message (isMessage: name) (message: name))) (Switch nil (-45.0 -99.0 46.0 -74.0) white 1 (text 'updateSymbol') (varying) (message (isMessage: updateSymbol) (message: updateSymbol))) (Switch nil (46.0 -99.0 137.0 -74.0) white 1 (text 'isOn') (varying) (message (isMessage: isOn) (message: isOn))) (Switch nil (137.0 -99.0 228.0 -74.0) white 1 (text 'switch') (varying) (message (isMessage: switch) (message: switch)))))))).
↑anArray

textWindow
   "Returns an initialized view."
   | anArray |

   anArray ← "WindowMaker edit:" #(Master nil (-274 -114 274 115) white 1
      (1.87226 1.89432 512.0 263.153) true 'Text Window Interface'
      (preOpenInterface: anExtendedStandardSystemView) (nil) (350 180) (1000
      1000) (classMethod notEncoded WindowMakerMasterIconController
      'specific windows' textWindow 'specific windows overflow') ((Text
      messageSource (-273.0 -88.0 273.0 114.0) white 1 (messageSource
      (messageSource) (messageSource: aText) (messageMenu))) (Group nil
      (-344 -134 202 -109) nil 4 ((Switch nil (-273.0 -113.0 -182.0 -88.0) white 1
      (text 'comment') (varying) (message (isMessage: comment) (message:
      comment))) (Switch nil (-182.0 -113.0 -91.0 -88.0) white 1 (text 'name') (varying)
      (message (isMessage: name) (message: name))) (Switch nil (-91.0 -113.0
      0.0 -88.0) white 1 (text 'updateSymbol') (varying) (message (isMessage:
      updateSymbol) (message: updateSymbol))) (Switch nil (0.0 -113.0 91.0 -88.0)
      white 1 (text 'getText') (varying) (message (isMessage: getText) (message:
      getText))) (Switch nil (91.0 -113.0 182.0 -88.0) white 1 (text 'changeText')
      (varying) (message (isMessage: changeText) (message: changeText))) (Switch
      nil (182.0 -113.0 273.0 -88.0) white 1 (text 'getMenu') (varying) (message
      (isMessage: getMenu) (message: getMenu)))))))).
   ↑anArray

B.4 TEXT DEFAULTS FOR INTERFACE WINDOWS

In general, the text provided in the default methods is left justified. Paragraphs wrap around without explicit carriage returns. Superfluous tabs or blanks must not be introduced since they will change the position of the boldfaced sections. As can be seen, the run values alternate between normal (1) and boldface (2). Should there be an inadvertent mismatch, the easiest solution may be to add additional blank characters at the end, edit the text while in the window maker editor to correct obvious deficiencies, and save it permanently via the yellow button menu.

B.4.1 WindowMakerIcon Defaults

interface window defaults

defaultName
   ↑Text
      string:'
   nil

"other examples:
   workWindow
   top

comment: A view name can be used to access the view when pre-opening or post-closing an extended standard system view.

restrictions: A view name must either be nil or a symbol.

additional information: For a more detailed explanation, see comment in the external interface for the master window; i.e., get the yellow-button pop-up menu when no icons are selected and choose the external interface entry."'
      runs: (RunArray
         runs: #(8 14 20 7 9 4 37 11 4 12 36 12 47 22 204)
         values: #(1 2 1 2 1 2 1 2 1 2 1 2 1 2 1))

defaultUpdateSymbol
　　↑Text
　　　　string:'
　　nil

"other examples:
　　color
　　shade

comment: An update symbol can be used by the model to cause all (and only) windows with the corresponding update symbol to update themselves. To do this, the model sends the message "self changed: #updateSymbol".

restrictions: An update symbol must either be nil or a symbol.

how windows update: The exact manner depends on the kind of window; e.g., a text window obtains new text from the model, a menu window obtains a new permanent menu and a new selection from the model, a switch window asks the model if it is on, and a picture window with dynamic pictures asks the model for a new picture.

illustration: Suppose a number of switches select shades (white, gray, black) by sending appropriate "switchColor: aSymbol" messages to the model. Moreover, suppose a text window is intended to display the current shade and a menu window is intended to display all three entries with the appropriate one selected. Communication between the switches and the text and menu window can be achieved by providing the following methods in the model.

```
switchColor: aSymbol
    ""This is a switch window method""
    currentColor ← aSymbol.
    self changed: #color

getText
    ""This is a text window method""
    ↑currentColor asText

getMenu
    ""This is a menu window method""
    ↑#(white gray black)

getMenuSelection
    ""This is a menu window method""
    ↑currentColor
```

The "self changed: #shade" message will cause all windows with update symbol "shade" to update themselves. In this case, the text window uses its getText message while the menu window uses its getMenu and getMenuSelection messages. Alternate names for getText, getMenu, and getMenuSelection can be specified by the window designer."'
　　runs: (RunArray
　　　　runs: #(8 14 17 7 5 13 189 12 52 18 304 12 433 12 79 8 10 7 61 7 61 16 385)
　　　　values: #(1 2 1 2 1 2 1 2 1 2 1 2 1 2 1 2 1 2 1 2 1 2 1))

defaultGetYellowMenu
　　↑Text
　　　　string:'
　　model getYellowMenu

"other examples:
　　nil
　　model getYellowMenu: #leftPane
　　model getYellowMenu: "method" suffix: " categories"

comment: The get-menu message (if not nil) is used by the window to ask the model for the yellow-button pop-up menu to be used.

when used: This message is sent to the model each time the user presses the yellow button while in this window. The entries in the menu may be different each time.

restrictions: For non-nil messages, the receiver must be "model". Any number of constant parameters can be specified; nil, true, and false are permitted. The result returned must be either an action menu or nil.

action menus: For text windows (only), the action menu normally includes the standard text editing selectors "again, undo, copySelection, cut, paste, accept, cancel" in addition to user selectors. The user selectors can either have no parameters or two parameters (the current text and the controller). When selected, the editing selectors are handled automatically by the text window; the user selectors are sent as messages to the model.

action menu example:

    ActionMenu
        labels: "again\undo\copy\cut\paste\accept\cancel\mine1\mine2" withCRs
        lines: #(2 5 7)
        selectors: #(again undo copySelection cut paste accept cancel mine1 mine2:and:)

warning: The text object passed in the first of two parameter selectors (e.g., mine2:and: above) is the actual text used by the text window. This text could be stored in the model. However, subsequent destructive changes by the window will cause it to change. If the stored version is to be left intact, care should be taken to store a copy."'

        runs: (RunArray
            runs: #(8 13 3 14 14 13 19 13 11 6 17 7 5 9 17 3 89 9 156 12 106 3 2 4 6 5
                54 11 4 3 4 12 98 5 2 4 2 13 2 3 2 5 2 6 2 6 37 14 17 13 4 14 178 19 17
                6 66 5 13 9 72 7 72 5 1 3 240 12 2)
            values: #(1 2 1 2 1 2 1 2 1 2 1 2 1 2 1 2 1 2 1 2 1 2 1 2 1 2 1 2 1 2 1 2 1 2
                1 2 1 2 1 2 1 2 1 2 1 2 1 2 1 2 1 2 1 2 1 2 1 2 1 2 1 2 1 2 1 2 1 2 1))

B.4.2 WindowMakerMasterIcon Defaults

interface window defaults

defaultComment
    ↑Text
        string: '
A master window is a window that contains all the subwindows obtained from the window maker. A method can be generated that produces the corresponding view. Two varieties exist:

(1) an extended standard system view (a standalone top view).
(2) an extended view (a subview).

Either one of these can incorporate a separately generated subview by constructing an external window that references it. At open time, such external windows are replaced by the corresponding extended view. See external windows for more details.

options: The topView option specifies whether a top view or subview is desired. The title, preOpen, and postOpen options apply only to top views. The title provides the tab at the top of the window (e.g., "Master Window Interface" for this window); a nil title implies no tab at all. The preOpen and postClose options (when not nil) are messages sent to the model immediately before the window is opened and immediately after it is closed respectively.

opening windows: A top window is opened by providing either an encoding of the window which is compact or an extended standard system view which is lengthy but much faster. The method construction option gives you a choice of the two. In either case, the window maker uses this view or creates one if necessary and distributes the model to all subviews. A preOpen message (if it exists) is then sent to the model.

   WindowMaker open: encodedWindowOrView on: aModel

preOpen and postClose messages: These messages permit the model to find and store (by name) subviews useful for the application and to redistribute (or change) the models associated with them. The preOpen and postClose messages include the extended systandard system view as a parameter. A preOpen message might be used (1) to record, for example, an error message subwindow called "error" for later use (assuming such a window was part of the master window) or (2) to initialize some of the subwindows with models other than itself; this might be needed for setting up the model for an external window. A postClose message might be used to perform final post-processing; e.g., if a window provides alignment options, closing the window might be the signal to actually perform the alignment. An example preOpen method is

   preOpen: anExtendedStandardSystemView
      | librarian librarianView |
      librarian ← FormLibrarian new.
      librarianView ← anExtendedStandardSystemView viewNamed: #librarianView.
      librarianView resetModels; models: librarian.

Method viewNamed: retrieves the subview with the specified name. Method models: recursively replaces nil models by the parameter for all subviews; non-nil models are unmodified and stop the recursion. Method resetModels recursively sets all non-nil models to nil in the same way.'
   runs: (RunArray
         runs: #(3 13 172 29 34 13 101 8 153 7 6 7 130 5 133 7 5 10 144 15 413 4 22
            2 10 30 557 8 225 40 59 3 49 9 34 11 2 6 21 9 56 6 130 11 60)
         values: #(1 2 1 2 1 2 1 2 1 2 1 2 1 2 1 2 1 2 1 2 1 2 1 2 1 2 1 2 1 2 1 2
            1 2 1 2 1 2 1 2 1))

defaultPreOpeningSelector
   ↑Text
      string:'
   model preOpen: #anExtendedStandardSystemView

"other examples:
   nil
   model preInitialize: #anExtendedStandardSystemView
   model setup: #anExtendedStandardSystemView forPane: 2

comment: The pre-open message (if not nil) is sent to the model immediately before the window (view) is opened. The view replaces the first parameter.

restrictions: For non-nil messages, the receiver must be "model". One or more constant parameters can be specified; nil, true, and false are permitted. The result returned is not used."'
   runs: (RunArray
         runs: #(8 7 34 14 14 13 39 5 32 7 5 7 5 9 17 3 111 12 104 3 2 4 6 5 49)
         values: #(1 2 1 2 1 2 1 2 1 2 1 2 1 2 1 2 1 2 1 2 1 2 1 2 1))

defaultPostClosingSelector
   ↑Text
      string:'
   model postClose: #anExtendedStandardSystemView

"other examples:
   nil
   model finalize: #anExtendedStandardSystemView

model closeup: #anExtendedStandardSystemView forPane: 2

comment: The post-close message (if not nil) is sent to the model immediately after the window (view) is closed. The view replaces the first parameter.

restrictions: For non-nil messages, the receiver must be "model". One or more constant parameters can be specified; nil, true, and false are permitted. The result returned is not used."'

   runs: (RunArray
    runs: #(8 9 34 14 14 8 39 7 32 7 5 7 5 11 17 3 110 12 104 3 2 4 6 5 49)
    values: #(1 2 1 2 1 2 1 2 1 2 1 2 1 2 1 2 1 2 1 2 1 2 1 2 1))

defaultTitle
 ↑Text
   string: '
 "Application Window"

"other examples:
 nil
 "Top Window Interface Options"

comment: The title provides the tab at the top of the window; a nil title implies no tab at all.

restrictrions: Only a string or nil is permitted."'

   runs: (RunArray
    runs: #(25 14 40 7 6 5 80 13 37)
    values: #(1 2 1 2 1 2 1 2 1))

defaultTopView
 ↑Text
   string: '
 true

"other examples:
 false

comment: Specifies whether or not this master window is a top view.

 (1) true => an extended standard system view (it can be used as a top view).
 (2) false => an extended view (it can be used as a subview via an external window)."'
   runs: (RunArray
    runs: #(9 14 10 7 78 29 50 13 37 8 10)
    values: #(1 2 1 2 1 2 1 2 1 2 1))

B.4.3 WindowMakerTextIcon Defaults

interface window defaults

defaultComment
 ↑Text
   string: '
A text window communicates with its model via messages

 (1) getText to obtain the text to be displayed from the model.
 (2) changeText to provide the model with modified text.
 (3) getMenu to obtain the yellow pop-up menu from the model.

updateSymbol comments: If the model changes its copy of the text and the window should reflect the model's version, the model should send a "self changed:

#updateSymbol" message. This could be done anywhere including in the above three methods.

text comments: The getText and changeText messages respectively obtain and provide a text object; a string is not allowed. Moreover, the text object is destructively modified by the view. If the model''s version of the text is to be separate from the view''s version, a copy should be saved or provided respectively.'

> **runs**: (RunArray
>   **runs**: #(3 11 48 7 57 10 47 7 51 21 225 13 301)
>   **values**: #(1 2 1 2 1 2 1 2 1 2 1 2 1))

defaultGetText
> ↑Text
>   **string**: '
> model getText

"other examples:
> model getNameTextFor: #manager
> model getVitaeTextFor: #personnel version: #short

comment: The get-text message is used by the text window to ask the model for the text to be displayed.

when used: This message is sent to the model (1) when the window is initially displayed and (2) each time it reacts to a "self changed: #updateSymbol" message sent by the model.

restrictions: The receiver must be "model". Any number of constant parameters can be specified; nil, true, and false are permitted. The result returned must be a text object; a string will not suffice.

warning: The text object given to the text window is physically modified. To ensure that the version maintained by the model is left intact, the getText method should return a copy."

> **runs**: (RunArray
>   **runs**: #(8 7 3 14 9 14 18 15 13 7 10 7 5 9 84 9 171 12 84 3 2 4 6 5 87 7
>   134 39 2)
>   **values**: #(1 2 1 2 1 2 1 2 1 2 1 2 1 2 1 2 1 2 1 2 1 2 1 2 1 2 1))

defaultChangeText
> ↑Text
>   **string**: '
> model changeText: #aText

"other examples:
> model changeNameTextTo: #aText for: #manager
> model changeVitaeTextTo: #aText for: #personnel version: #short

comment: The change-text message is used by the text window give the model updated text to be recorded. This text is provided in the first parameter.

when used: This message is sent to the model when the user accepts the text in the text window.

restrictions: The receiver must be "model". One or more constant parameters can be specified; nil, true, and false are permitted. The first parameter (#aText above) is replaced by the actual text before the message is sent. The result returned must be a boolean with the following interpretation: true - the text has been recorded, false - the text has not been recorded (it has been rejected). Typically, true is returned.

warning: The text object given to the model is the actual text used by the text window. Hence, the window may subsequently physically modify it. To ensure that the version maintained by the model is left intact, the changeText method should store a copy.

optional: Prior to sending a changeText message, the window always asks the model for permission by sending it a "changeRequestFrom: aView" message. The default inherited by all objects is to reply true if no other windows contain unaccepted modified text (interactive prompting occurs). If this default is not acceptable, the model will need to incorporate its own special version such as the following:

```
changeRequestFrom: aView
    ↑true"
    runs: (RunArray
        runs: #(8 10 11 14 9 28 18 29 13 7 10 7 5 12 127 9 89 12 82 3 2 4 6 5
            183 4 31 5 88 7 205 41 1 10 106 24 270 17 16)
        values: #(1 2 1 2 1 2 1 2 1 2 1 2 1 2 1 2 1 2 1 2 1 2 1 2 1 2 1 2 1 2 1 2
            1 2 1 2 1))
```

B.4.4 WindowMakerMenuIcon Defaults

interface window defaults

defaultComment
    ↑Text
        string: '
A menu window communicates with its model via messages

(1)   getMenu to obtain the permanent menu from the model
        (an array of objects with distinct print strings).
(2)   getSelection to obtain the menu selection to be displayed from the model
        (one of the objects in the above array or nil).
(3)   changeSelection to tell the model of a menu selection change
        (one of the objects in the above array or nil).
(4)   getYellowMenu to obtain the yellow button pop-up menu from the model
        (an action menu).

updateSymbol comments: If the model changes its version of the permanent menu or the menu selection and the window should reflect the model''s version, the model should send a "self changed: #updateSymbol" message. This could be done anywhere including in the above four methods.'
        runs: (RunArray
            runs: #(3 11 48 8 104 13 117 16 102 14 78 21 257)
            values: #(1 2 1 2 1 2 1 2 1 2 1 2 1))

defaultGetMenuArray
    ↑Text
        string: '
model getMenuArray

"other examples:
    model getMenuArrayFor: #names
    model getMenuArrayFor: "method" suffix: " category"

comment: The get-menu-array message is used by the menu window to ask the model for the permanent menu entries to be displayed.

when used: This message is sent to the model (1) when the window is initially displayed and (2) each time it reacts to a "self changed: #updateSymbol" message sent by the model.

restrictions: The receiver must be "model". Any number of constant parameters can be specified; nil, true, and false are permitted. The result returned must be an array of arbitrary objects with distinct print strings; an ordered collection instead of an array, for example, is not permitted."'

    runs: (RunArray
        runs: #(8 12 3 14 9 15 16 15 11 6 15 7 5 15 103 9 171 12 84 3 2 4 6 5 177)
        values: #(1 2 1 2 1 2 1 2 1 2 1 2 1 2 1 2 1 2 1 2 1 2 1))

defaultGetMenuSelection
    ↑Text
        string: '
    model getMenuSelection

"other examples:
    model getMenuSelectionFor: #names
    model getMenuSelectionFor: ''method'' suffix: '' category"

comment: The get-selection message is used by the menu window to ask the model for the current selection. If a selection has been made, the corresponding getMenu array element is returned; otherwise, nil.

when used: This message is sent to the model (1) when the window is initially displayed and (2) each time it reacts to a "self changed: #updateSymbol" message sent by the model.

restrictions: The receiver must be "model". Any number of constant parameters can be specified; nil, true, and false are permitted. The result returned must be one of the objects in the permanent menu array (the one selected) or nil (for no selection)."'

    runs: (RunArray
        runs: #(8 16 3 14 9 19 16 19 11 6 15 7 5 14 180 9 170 12 84 3 2 4 6 5 137)
        values: #(1 2 1 2 1 2 1 2 1 2 1 2 1 2 1 2 1 2 1 2 1 2 1))

defaultChangeMenuSelection
    ↑Text
        string: '
    model changeMenuSelection: #aSelection

"other examples:
    model changeMenuSelection: #aSelection forPane: 1
    model changeMenuSelection: #aSelection for: ''method'' suffix: '' category"

comment: The change-menu-selection message is used by the menu window to inform the model that a new selection has been made. This selection is provided in the first parameter; either a getMenu array entry if a selection has been made or nil if a deselection has occurred.

when used: This message is sent to the model whenever the user interactively modifies the window.

restrictions: The receiver must be "model". One or more constant parameters can be specified; nil, true, and false are permitted. The first parameter (#aSelection above) is replaced by the actual selection object (if an actual selection was made) or nil (if a deselection was made) before the message is sent. The result returned is ignored."'

    runs: (RunArray
        runs: #(8 19 16 14 9 19 13 8 11 19 13 4 11 6 15 7 5 22 240 9 91 12 82 3
          2 4 6 5 75 23 38 3 89)
        values: #(1 2 1 2 1 2 1 2 1 2 1 2 1 2 1 2 1 2 1 2 1 2 1 2 1 2 1 2 1))

B.4.5 WindowMakerSwitchIcon Defaults

interface window defaults

defaultComment
↑Text
string: '
A switch window communicates with its model via 2 messages

(1) isOn to ask the model if the switch is on (the switch status).
(2) switch to tell the model that the switch has been pressed.

updateSymbol comments: If the model changes the switch status and the window should reflect the model''s version, the model should send a ''self changed: #updateSymbol'' message. This could be done anywhere including in the above two methods.'
runs: (RunArray
runs: #(3 13 50 4 43 13 8 6 54 21 218)
values: #(1 2 1 2 1 2 1 2 1 2 1))

defaultIsOn
↑Text
string: '
model isOn

"other examples:
model isColor: #blue
model isBorderSize: 1

comment: The is-on message is used by the switch window to ask the model if the switch is on.

when used: This message is sent to the model (1) when the switch window is initially displayed and (2) each time it reacts to a ''self changed: #updateSymbol'' message sent by the model.

restrictions: The receiver must be ''model''. Any number of constant parameters can be specified; nil, true, and false are permitted. The result returned must be a boolean: true to indicate the switch is down (depressed), false to indicate the switch is up (not depressed)."'
runs: (RunArray
runs: #(8 4 3 14 9 7 15 12 5 7 5 6 78 9 178 12 84 3 2 4 6 5 55 4 45 5 47)
values: #(1 2 1 2 1 2 1 2 1 2 1 2 1 2 1 2 1 2 1 2 1 2 1 2 1))

defaultSwitch
↑Text
string: '
model switch

"other examples:
model turnOn
model turnOff
model makeColor: #blue
model makeBorderSize: 1

comment: The switch message is used by the switch window to tell the model that the switch has been pressed. The model will appropriately change its state; e.g., by setting one of its instance variables. The switch window subsequently asks the model (using the isOn message) to find out whether this caused the switch to turn on (the isOn message replies true) or off (the isOn message replies false).

when used: when the user interactively pushes the mouse button while in the switch window.

restrictions: The receiver must be "model". Any number of constant parameters can be specified; nil, true, and false are permitted. The result returned is ignored.

sample methods: If the methods for the above messages are implemented as follows, then the switch, turnOn, and turnOff methods will work as expected.

```
turnOn
    internalState ← true
turnOff
    internalState ← false
switch
    internalState ← internalState not
isOn
    ↑internalState"'
```

runs: (RunArray
    runs: #(8 6 3 14 9 6 8 7 8 9 15 14 5 7 5 7 242 4 69 4 17 4 14 4 17 5 4 9 83
        12 84 3 2 4 6 5 49 14 138 6 25 7 26 6 38 4 18)
    values: #(1 2 1 2 1 2 1 2 1 2 1 2 1 2 1 2 1 2 1 2 1 2 1 2 1 2 1 2 1 2 1 2
        1 2 1 2 1 2 1 2 1 2 1))

B.4.6 WindowMakerPictureIcon Defaults

interface window defaults

defaultComment
    ↑Text
        string: '

Normally, a picture window contains a label (picture) that remains unchanged throughout its existence. However, there may be situations where this label may have to vary dynamically. For an example, see the form librarian editor. In that case, 2 additional pieces of information must be provided:

  (1) #updateSymbol that identifies the window for changes,
  (2) getLabel message to obtain a new display object; e.g., a form or a paragraph.

If the model changes in such a way that this picture window must be updated, it is sufficient for the model to execute "self changed: #updateSymbol".'
        runs: (RunArray
            runs: #(13 14 12 5 2 7 538)
            values: #(1 2 1 2 1 2 1))

defaultGetLabel
    ↑Text
        string: '
    nil

"other examples:
    model getLabel
    model getLabelFor: #firstName

comment: The get-label message (when not nil) is used by the window to ask the model for a new label (picture) to be displayed. This label must be nil or a display object such as a display text, a paragraph, or a form.

when used: This message is sent to the model (1) each time the window is displayed and (2) each time it reacts to a "self changed: #updateSymbol" message sent by the model.

aside: A non-nil get-label message is useful only if the window picture must change dynamically.

restrictions: The receiver for a non-nil get-label message must be "model". Any number of constant parameters can be specified; nil, true, and false are permitted. The result returned must be nil or a display object; e.g., a paragraph, display text, or form."'

 runs: (RunArray
   runs: #(8 14 9 8 8 12 13 7 5 10 198 9 166 5 93 12 116 3 2 4 6 5 111)
   values: #(1 2 1 2 1 2 1 2 1 2 1 2 1 2 1 2 1 2 1 2 1))

B.4.7 WindowMakerExternalIcon Defaults

interface window defaults

defaultComment
 ↑Text
  string: '

An external window is used to reference and obtain a previously constructed extended view. This extended view replaces the external window at open time. An external window references its extended view via one message:

 (1) getView to obtain an extended view.

An extended view may constructed in the WindowMaker by specifying that it be a subview (as opposed to a top view) in the external interface for the master window.'

 runs: (RunArray
   runs: #(4 15 405)
   values: #(1 2 1))

defaultGetView
 ↑Text
  string: '
 Object getView

"other examples:
 FormLibrarian subView
 Object getView: #blueButton version: 2

comment: Permits an externally constructed extended view to be integrated with the current view. The extended view replaces this external view at open time.

restrictions: The receiver must be a class name. Any number of constant parameters can be specified; nil, true, and false are permitted. An extended view must be returned.

constructing extended views: An extended view can be constructed by the window maker by specifying a subview (as opposed to top view) in the interface at the top level (master window); i.e., by not selecting any icons, choosing the external interface entry in the yellow pop-up menu, and setting the topView option to false."'

 runs: (RunArray
   runs: #(19 14 66 7 151 12 25 10 54 3 2 4 6 5 19 13 21 27 298)
   values: #(1 2 1 2 1 2 1 2 1 2 1 2 1 2 1 2 1 2 1))

B.5 WINDOW MAKER ENCODING/DECODING

Each window maker icon can be **encoded** for ease of storage and manipulation. An encoding is an appropriately initialized array of constants. It cannot, for example, contain store strings or objects as rectangles or points. A point such as 10@20 has to be encoded in the array either as a subarray (10 20) or as two consecutive integers 10 and 20. The encoding for a container icon such as a master icon or a group icon also contains the encoding for the contained icons. Hence, a master icon encoding is a compact representation for an entire application window. An encoding can, of course, be **decoded** into the corresponding icon. Decoding a point in this case is a matter of extracting the previously encoded information and reconstructing the point. The icon that results can, if desired, be converted into a corresponding extended view. In general, the encoding contains more information than the corresponding extended view. Hence, it is not possible to go back the other way. For this reason, the encoding is maintained with extended standard system views and extended views (although not with other views). Once a method is generated to produce an application window from extended views, it is possible to discard the encoding. However, it is needed if the window is to be edited for changes in the future. The encoding/decoding facility is an example of a horizontal facility, since every single class in the WindowMakerIcon hierarchy is affected.

Class WindowMakerIcon

class	WindowMakerIcon
superclass	ExtendedSwitchView
instance variables	...

instance methods

encoding/decoding

encodeOn: aStream
    "iconClass iconName window insideColor borderWidth"
    aStream
        nextPutAll: self **shortClassName**; **space**;
        store: (self **receiverFor**: #name); **space**. self
        encodeWindowOn: aStream. aStream **space**. self
        encodeColor: insideColor **on**: aStream. aStream **space**. self
        encodeBorderWidthOn: aStream

decodeFrom: aStream
    "iconClass iconName window insideColor borderWidth"
    | border |
    self
        changeMessage: #name **receiver**: aStream **next**;
        window: (self **decodeWindow**: aStream **next**);
        insideColor: (self **decodeColor**: aStream **next**);
        borderWidthLeft: (border ← self **decodeBorderWidth**: aStream **next**) **left**
            right: border **right top**: border **top bottom**: border **bottom**

encodeWindowOn: aStream
    aStream **print**: (Array
        with: window **origin x with**: window **origin y**
        with: window **corner x with**: window **corner y**).

encodeColor: aPoint **on**: aStream
    insideColor **isNil ifTrue**: [↑aStream **print**: #nil].
    #(black darkGray gray lightGray veryLightGray white) **do**: [:candidate |
        (insideColor == (Form **perform**: candidate)) **ifTrue**: [↑aStream **print**: candidate]].
    self **error**: 'unknown insideColor'

encodeBorderWidthOn: aStream
    borderWidth = ((0@0 **extent**: 0@0) **translateBy**: borderWidth **left**)
        ifTrue: [aStream **print**: borderWidth **left**]
        ifFalse: [aStream **print**: (Array **with**: borderWidth **left with**: borderWidth **top**
            with: borderWidth **right with**: borderWidth **bottom**)]

encodePoint: aPoint **on**: aStream
    aStream **print**: (Array **with**: aPoint **x with**: aPoint **y**).

decodeWindow: anArray
    "decode #(<origin x> <origin y> <corner x> <corner y>)"
    ↑(anArray **at**: 1)@(anArray **at**: 2) **corner**: (anArray **at**: 3)@(anArray **at**: 4)

decodeColor: aColorSymbol
    aColorSymbol == #nil
        ifTrue: [↑nil]
        ifFalse: [↑Form **perform**: aColorSymbol]

decodeBorderWidth: data
    "decode integer or #(<left> <top> <right> <bottom>)"
    (data **isKindOf**: Integer)
        ifTrue: [↑data@data **corner**: data@data]
        ifFalse: [↑(data **at**: 1)@(data **at**: 2) **corner**: (data **at**: 3)@(data **at**: 4)]

decodePoint: anArray
    "decode #(<x> <y>)"
    ↑(anArray **at**: 1)@(anArray **at**: 2)

decodeSymbolOrNil: aSymbolOrNil
    "decode #symbol or #nil"
    aSymbolOrNil == #nil **ifTrue**: [↑nil] **ifFalse**: [↑aSymbolOrNil]

Class WindowMakerMasterIcon

class	WindowMakerMasterIcon
superclass	WindowMakerIcon
instance variables	... minimumSize maximumSize outputOption
instance methods	

encoding/decoding

encodeOn: aStream
    "iconClass iconName window insideColor borderWidth transformation topView title
    preOpeningSelector postClosingSelector minimumSize maximumSize outputOption
    (encodedIcon1 encodedIcon2 ...)"

    super **encodeOn**: aStream.
    aStream
        space. self **encodeTransformationOn**: aStream. aStream
        nextPutAll: ' "topView" '; **store**: (self **receiverFor**: #topView);
        nextPutAll: ' "title" '; **store**: (self **receiverFor**: #title);
        nextPutAll: ' "preOpening" ';
            store: (self **codingWithoutReceiverFor**: #preOpeningSelector);
        nextPutAll: ' "postClosing" ';
            store: (self **codingWithoutReceiverFor**: #postClosingSelector);
        space. self **encodePoint**: minimumSize **on**: aStream. aStream
        space. self **encodePoint**: maximumSize **on**: aStream. aStream
        space; **store**: outputOption;
        nextPutAll: ' ('.
            subViews **do**: [:icon |
                WindowMaker **encode**: icon **on**: aStream. aStream **space**].
            subViews **isEmpty ifFalse**: [aStream **skip**: -1]. aStream
        nextPut: $)

decodeFrom: aStream
"iconClass iconName window insideColor borderWidth transformation topView title preOpeningSelector postClosingSelector minimumSize maximumSize outputOption (encodedIcon1 encodedIcon2 ...)"

super **decodeFrom:** aStream.
self
    transformation: (self **decodeTransformation:** aStream **next**);
    changeMessage: #topView **receiver:** aStream **next**;
    changeMessage: #title **receiver:** aStream **next**;
    changeMessage: #preOpeningSelector **selectorArguments:** aStream **next**;
    changeMessage: #postClosingSelector **selectorArguments:** aStream **next**.

minimumSize ← self **decodePoint:** aStream **next**.
maximumSize ← self **decodePoint:** aStream **next**.
outputOption ← aStream **next**.
aStream **next do:** [:anItem | self **addSubView:** (WindowMaker **decode:** anItem)]

encodeTransformationOn: aStream
"encode as #(<scale x> <scale y> <translation x> <translation y>)"
aStream **print:** (Array
    with: transformation **scale x with:** transformation **scale y**
    with: transformation **translation x with:** transformation **translation y**).

decodeTransformation: anArray
"decode #(<scale x> <scale y> <translation x> <translation y>)"
↑WindowingTransformation
    scale: (anArray **at:** 1)@(anArray **at:** 2)
    translation: (anArray **at:** 3)@(anArray **at:** 4)

Class WindowMakerGroupIcon

class	WindowMakerGroupIcon
superclass	WindowMakerIcon
instance variables	...

encoding/decoding

encodeOn: aStream
"iconClass iconName window insideColor borderWidth (encodedIcon1 encodedIcon2 ...)"

super **encodeOn:** aStream.
aStream
    nextPutAll: ' ('.
        subViews **do:** [:icon |
            WindowMaker **encode:** icon **on:** aStream. aStream **space**].
        subViews **isEmpty ifFalse:** [aStream **skip:** -1]. aStream
    nextPut: $)

decodeFrom: aStream
"iconClass iconName window insideColor borderWidth (encodedIcon1 encodedIcon2 ...)"

super **decodeFrom:** aStream.
aStream **next do:** [:anItem | self **addSubView:** (WindowMaker **decode:** anItem)]

Class WindowMakerTextIcon

class	WindowMakerTextIcon
superclass	WindowMakerIcon
instance variables	...

instance methods

encoding/decoding

encodeOn: aStream
    "iconClass iconName window insideColor borderWidth (updateSymbol getTextMessage
    changeTextMessage getMenuMessage)"

    super **encodeOn**: aStream.
    aStream
        space; **nextPut**: $(; **store**: (self **receiverFor**: #updateSymbol);
        space; **store**: (self **codingWithoutReceiverFor**: #getText);
        space; **store**: (self **codingWithoutReceiverFor**: #changeText);
        space; **store**: (self **codingWithoutReceiverFor**: #getMenu);
        nextPut: $)

decodeFrom: aStream
    "iconClass iconName window insideColor borderWidth (updateSymbol getTextMessage
    changeTextMessage getMenuMessage)"

    | newStream |
    super **decodeFrom**: aStream.
    newStream ← ReadStream **on**: aStream **next**.
    self
        changeMessage: #updateSymbol **receiver**: newStream **next**;
        changeMessage: #getText **selectorArguments**: newStream **next**;
        changeMessage: #changeText **selectorArguments**: newStream **next**;
        changeMessage: #getMenu **selectorArguments**: newStream **next**

Class WindowMakerMenuIcon

class	WindowMakerMenuIcon
superclass	WindowMakerIcon
instance variables	...

instance methods

encoding/decoding

encodeOn: aStream
    "iconClass iconName window insideColor borderWidth (updateSymbol
    getMenuArrayMessage getMenuSelectionMessage changeMenuSelectionMessage
    getYellowMenuMessage)"

    super **encodeOn**: aStream.
    aStream
        space; **nextPut**: $(; **store**: (self **receiverFor**: #updateSymbol);
        space; **store**: (self **codingWithoutReceiverFor**: #getMenuArray);
        space; **store**: (self **codingWithoutReceiverFor**: #getMenuSelection);
        space; **store**: (self **codingWithoutReceiverFor**: #changeMenuSelection);
        space; **store**: (self **codingWithoutReceiverFor**: #getYellowMenu);
        nextPut: $)

decodeFrom: aStream

"iconClass iconName window insideColor borderWidth (updateSymbol
getMenuArrayMessage getMenuSelectionMessage changeMenuSelectionMessage
getYellowMenuMessage)"

| newStream |
super **decodeFrom:** aStream.
newStream ← ReadStream **on:** aStream **next**.
self
    changeMessage: #updateSymbol **receiver:** newStream **next;**
    changeMessage: #getMenuArray **selectorArguments:** newStream **next;**
    changeMessage: #getMenuSelection **selectorArguments:** newStream **next;**
    changeMessage: #changeMenuSelection **selectorArguments:** newStream **next;**
    changeMessage: #getYellowMenu **selectorArguments:** newStream **next**

Class WindowMakerSwitchOrPictureIcon

class   WindowMakerSwitchOrPictureIcon
superclass   WindowMakerIcon
instance variables   pictureVariety pictureString pictureFormPathName
instance methods

encoding/decoding

encodeOn: aStream

"iconClass iconName window insideColor borderWidth pictureData modeData"

super **encodeOn:** aStream.
aStream
    space; store: self **encodedPictureData;**
    space; store: self **encodedModeData**

decodeFrom: aStream

"iconClass iconName window insideColor borderWidth pictureData modeData"

super **decodeFrom:** aStream.
self **decodePictureData:** aStream **next**.
self **decodeModeData:** aStream **next**.
self **computeLabel**

encodedPictureData

"The picture data is either of the form
    #text 'string' or
    #form libraryName switchName"

pictureVariety == #text
    ifTrue: [↑Array **with:** #text **with:** pictureString]
    ifFalse: [↑(Array **with:** #form), pictureFormPathName]

encodedModeData

"The mode data is of the form
    #varying
    #constant fixedPoint or
    #lockedConstant fixedPoint lockedSizeExpansion where
        fixedPoint is one of
            #fixCenter, #fixTopLeft, #fixBottomRight, ...
        lockedSizeExpansion is an integer"

mode == #varying **ifTrue:** [↑Array **with:** #varying].
sizeLocked **ifFalse:** [↑Array **with:** #constant **with:** self **fixedPointEncoding**].
↑Array
    with: #lockedConstant **with:** self **fixedPointEncoding with:** lockedSizeExpansion

decodePictureData: data
"The picture data is either of the form
#text 'string' or
#form libraryName switchName"

pictureVariety ← data **at**: 1.
pictureVariety == #text
    ifTrue: [
        pictureString ← data **at**: 2.
        pictureFormPathName ← #(DefaultFormLibrary button)]
    ifFalse: [
        pictureString ← ''.
        pictureFormPathName ← data **copyFrom**: 2 **to**: 3]

decodeModeData: data
"The mode data is of the form
    #varying
    #constant fixedPoint or
    #lockedConstant fixedPoint lockedSizeExpansion where
        fixedPoint is one of
            #fixCenter, #fixTopLeft, #fixBottomRight, ...
        lockedSizeExpansion is an integer"

| newMode |
self **fixMiddleLeft**; **lockedSizeExpansion**: 0. sizeLocked ← false.
(newMode ← data **at**: 1) == #varying **ifFalse**: [
    self **perform**: (data **at**: 2). "#fixCenter, #fixTopLeft, #fixBottomRight, ..."
    newMode == #lockedConstant **ifTrue**: [
        sizeLocked ← true. newMode ← #constant.
        self **lockedSizeExpansion**: (data **at**: 3)]].
self **mode**: newMode

Class WindowMakerPictureIcon

class	WindowMakerPictureIcon
superclass	WindowMakerSwitchOrPictureIcon
instance variables	...

instance methods

encoding/decoding

encodeOn: aStream
"iconClass iconName window insideColor borderWidth pictureData modeData
(updateSymbol getLabelMessage)"

super **encodeOn**: aStream.
aStream
    space; **nextPut**: $(; **store**: (self **receiverFor**: #updateSymbol);
    space; **store**: (self **codingWithoutReceiverFor**: #getLabel);
    nextPut: $)

decodeFrom: aStream
"iconClass iconName window insideColor borderWidth pictureData modeData
(updateSymbol getLabelMessage)"

| newStream |
super **decodeFrom**: aStream.
newStream ← ReadStream **on**: aStream **next**.
self
    changeMessage: #updateSymbol **receiver**: newStream **next**;
    changeMessage: #getLabel **selectorArguments**: newStream **next**

Class WindowMakerSwitchIcon

class	WindowMakerSwitchIcon
superclass	WindowMakerSwitchOrPictureIcon
instance variables	...

instance methods

encoding/decoding

encodeOn: aStream
"iconClass iconName window insideColor borderWidth pictureData modeData
(updateSymbol isOnMessage switchMessage)"

super **encodeOn**: aStream.
aStream
    space; **nextPut**: $(; **store**: (self **receiverFor**: #updateSymbol);
    space; **store**: (self **codingWithoutReceiverFor**: #isOn);
    space; **store**: (self **codingWithoutReceiverFor**: #switch);
    nextPut: $)

decodeFrom: aStream
"iconClass iconName window insideColor borderWidth pictureData modeData
(updateSymbol isOnMessage switchMessage)"

| newStream |
super **decodeFrom**: aStream.
newStream ← ReadStream **on**: aStream **next**.
self
    changeMessage: #updateSymbol **receiver**: newStream **next**;
    changeMessage: #isOn **selectorArguments**: newStream **next**;
    changeMessage: #switch **selectorArguments**: newStream **next**

Class WindowMakerSwitchAndPictureIcon

class	WindowMakerSwitchAndPictureIcon
superclass	WindowMakerSwitchIcon
instance variables	separation

instance methods

encoding/decoding

decodePictureData: data
"The picture data is of the form
    #form libraryName switchName #separation separation #text 'string'"

pictureFormPathName ← data **copyFrom**: 2 **to**: 3.
separation ← data **at**: 5.
pictureString ← data **at**: 7

decodeModeData: data
"The mode data is of the form
    #lockedConstant fixedPoint lockedSizeExpansion where
        fixedPoint is one of
            #fixCenter, #fixTopLeft, #fixBottomRight, ...
        lockedSizeExpansion is an integer"

self
    mode: #constant;
    perform: (data **at**: 2); "#fixCenter, #fixTopLeft, #fixBottomRight, ..."
    lockedSizeExpansion: (data **at**: 3)

encodedPictureData
    "The picture data is of the form
            #form libraryName switchName #separation separation #text 'string' "

    ↑OrderedCollection **new**
        add: #form;
        addAll: pictureFormPathName;
        add: #separation;
        add: separation;
        add: #text;
        add: pictureString;
        asArray

encodedModeData
    "The mode data is of the form
        #lockedConstant fixedPoint lockedSizeExpansion where
            fixedPoint is one of
                #fixCenter, #fixTopLeft, #fixBottomRight, ...
            lockedSizeExpansion is an integer"

    ↑Array
        with: #lockedConstant **with:** self **fixedPointEncoding with:** lockedSizeExpansion

Class WindowMakerExternalIcon

class   WindowMakerExternalIcon
superclass   WindowMakerIcon
instance variables   ...

instance methods

encoding/decoding

encodeOn: aStream
    "iconClass iconName window insideColor borderWidth getViewMessage"

    super **encodeOn:** aStream.
    aStream **space; store:** (self **codingFor:** #getView)

decodeFrom: aStream
    "iconClass iconName window insideColor borderWidth getViewMessage"

    super **decodeFrom:** aStream.
    self **changeMessage:** #getView **receiverSelectorArguments:** aStream **next**

B.6 WINDOW MAKER COPYING AND CONVERTING TO EXTENDED VIEWS

These methods permit icons to be converted to views to obtain corresponding store strings when an application window is to be generated and also permit them to be duplicated via a shallow copy to support the copy/paste facility in the window maker. The main copy facility is provided in abstract class WindowMakerIcon. It will work for all subclasses except WindowMakerMasterIcon.

Class WindowMakerIcon

class	WindowMakerIcon
superclass	ExtendedSwitchView
instance variables	... messageInitializers messageSources messageCodings messageParsers ...

generating views

asView
    self **subclassResponsibility**

copying

shallowCopy
    | copy oldMessageInitializers oldMessageSources oldMessageCodings oldMessageParsers |

    "Modify temporarily"
    oldMessageInitializers ← messageInitializers.
    messageInitializers ← messageInitializers **copy**.
    oldMessageSources ← messageSources.
    messageSources ← messageSources **copy**.
    oldMessageCodings ← messageCodings.
    messageCodings ← messageCodings **copy**.
    oldMessageParsers ← messageParsers.
    messageParsers ← messageParsers **copy**.

    "Make the copy."
    copy ← super **shallowCopy**
        superView: nil; **resetSubViews**;
        borderWidthLeft: borderWidth **left right**: borderWidth **right**
            top: borderWidth **top bottom**: borderWidth **bottom**;
        transformation: transformation; "stores a copy"
        window: window; "stores a copy"
        yourself.
    subViews **do**: [:icon | copy **addSubView**: icon **shallowCopy**].

    "Restore"
    messageInitializers ← oldMessageInitializers.
    messageSources ← oldMessageSources.
    messageCodings ← oldMessageCodings.
    messageParsers ← oldMessageParsers.

    ↑copy

Class WindowMakerGroupIcon

class	WindowMakerGroupIcon
superclass	WindowMakerIcon
instance variables	...

generating views

asView
    self **error**: 'sender should have used groupDo:'

Class WindowMakerMasterIcon

class	WindowMakerMasterIcon
superclass	WindowMakerIcon
instance variables	... minimumSize maximumSize outputOption

generating views

asView
```
| aView |
aView ← (self receiverFor: #topView)
    ifFalse: [ExtendedView new]
    ifTrue: [ExtendedStandardSystemView new
        preOpeningSelector: (self selectorArgumentsFor: #preOpeningSelector);
        postClosingSelector: (self selectorArgumentsFor: #postClosingSelector);
        label: (self receiverFor: #title);
        minimumSize: minimumSize;
        maximumSize: maximumSize;
        yourself].
aView encoding: (Compiler evaluate: (WindowMaker encode: self)).
aView
    model: nil;
    name: (self receiverFor: #name);
    insideColor: insideColor;
    borderWidthLeft: borderWidth left right: borderWidth right
        top: borderWidth top bottom: borderWidth bottom;
    window: window;
    transformation: transformation;
    yourself.
"Eliminate all groups."
subViews do: [:subView |
    subView groupDo: [:icon | aView addSubView: icon asView]].
↑aView
```

copying

shallowCopy
```
↑super shallowCopy outputOption: self outputOption deepCopy
```

Class WindowMakerTextIcon

class	WindowMakerTextIcon
superclass	WindowMakerIcon
instance variables	"none"

generating views

asView
```
↑(ExtendedTextView on: nil
    aspect: (self receiverFor: #updateSymbol)
    get: (self selectorArgumentsFor: #getText)
    change: (self selectorArgumentsFor: #changeText)
    menu: (self selectorArgumentsFor: #getMenu))
    name: (self receiverFor: #name);
    insideColor: insideColor;
```

borderWidthLeft: borderWidth **left right**: borderWidth **right**
    top: borderWidth **top bottom**: borderWidth **bottom**;
window: window;
transformation: transformation;
yourself

Class WindowMakerMenuIcon

class   WindowMakerMenuIcon
superclass   WindowMakerIcon
instance variables   "none"

generating views

asView
    | aView |
    aView ← ExtendedMenuView **on**: nil
        printItems: true **oneItem**: false
        aspect: (self **receiverFor**: #updateSymbol)
        change: (self **selectorArgumentsFor**: #changeMenuSelection)
        list: (self **selectorArgumentsFor**: #getMenuArray)
        menu: (self **selectorArgumentsFor**: #getYellowMenu)
        initialSelection: (self **selectorArgumentsFor**: #getMenuSelection).
    aView
        name: (self **receiverFor**: #name);
        insideColor: insideColor;
        borderWidthLeft: borderWidth **left right**: borderWidth **right**
            top: borderWidth **top bottom**: borderWidth **bottom**;
        window: window;
        transformation: transformation.
    ↑aView

Class WindowMakerSwitchOrPictureIcon

class   WindowMakerSwitchOrPictureIcon
superclass   WindowMakerIcon
instance variables   pictureVariety pictureString pictureFormPathName ...

background

generateLabel
    "Construct a new label from the current settings; one that can be used to specify a
    label for a new view."

    ↑pictureVariety == #text
        ifTrue: [pictureString **asParagraph**]
        ifFalse: [pictureFormPathName]

Class WindowMakerPictureIcon

class	WindowMakerPictureIcon
superclass	WindowMakerSwitchOrPictureIcon
instance variables	...

generating views

asView
    ↑(ExtendedPictureView **on**: nil
        aspect: (self **receiverFor**: #updateSymbol)
        label: self **generateLabel**
        getLabel: (self **selectorArgumentsFor**: #getLabel))
        name: (self **receiverFor**: #name);
        insideColor: insideColor;
        borderWidthLeft: borderWidth **left right**: borderWidth **right**
            top: borderWidth **top bottom**: borderWidth **bottom**;
        window: window;
        transformation: transformation;
        mode: self **mode**;
        perform: self **fixedPointEncoding**;
        yourself

Class WindowMakerSwitchIcon

class	WindowMakerSwitchIcon
superclass	WindowMakerSwitchOrPictureIcon
instance variables	...

generating views

asView
    ↑(self **viewClass on**: nil
        aspect: (self **receiverFor**: #updateSymbol)
        label: self **generateLabel**
        isOn: (self **selectorArgumentsFor**: #isOn)
        switch: (self **selectorArgumentsFor**: #switch))
        name: (self **receiverFor**: #name);
        insideColor: insideColor;
        borderWidthLeft: borderWidth **left right**: borderWidth **right**
            top: borderWidth **top bottom**: borderWidth **bottom**;
        window: self **window**;
        transformation: self **transformation**;
        highlight: self **generateHighlight**;
        mode: self **mode**;
        perform: self **fixedPointEncoding**;
        yourself

viewClass
    ↑ExtendedSwitchView

background

generateHighlight
    | offForm |
    pictureVariety == #form
        ifTrue: [
                offForm ← FormLibrarian **formForPathName:** pictureFormPathName.
                (offForm **respondsTo:** #highlight)
                    ifTrue: [↑#fromLabel]
                    ifFalse: [↑nil]]
        ifFalse: [↑nil]

Class WindowMakerSwitchAndPictureIcon

class   WindowMakerSwitchAndPictureIcon
superclass   WindowMakerSwitchIcon
instance variables   separation

generating views

viewClass
    ↑ExtendedSwitchAndPictureView

background

generateLabel
    "label must be of the form #(pictureFormPathName separation pictureString)."
    ↑Array **with:** pictureFormPathName **with:** separation **with:** pictureString

Class WindowMakerExternalIcon

class   WindowMakerExternalIcon
superclass   WindowMakerIcon
instance variables   "none"

generating views

asView
    ↑ExtendedExternalView **new**
        model: nil;
        name: (self **receiverFor:** #name);
        insideColor: insideColor;
        borderWidthLeft: borderWidth **left right:** borderWidth **right**
            top: borderWidth **top bottom:** borderWidth **bottom;**
        window: window;
        transformation: transformation;
        external: (self **receiverSelectorArgumentsFor:** #getView);
        yourself

Class Index

SYSTEM CLASSES

DEMONSTRATION CLASSES

GLOBAL VARIABLES

Index